PATHWAYS IN PHILOSOPHY

I came to my truth
by diverse paths
and diverse ways;
it wasn   le
ladd   dto
the   es
cou
distances

PATHWAYS IN PHILOSOPHY

An Introductory Guide with Readings

DALE JACQUETTE

The Pennsylvania State University

NEW YORK OXFORD
OXFORD UNIVERSITY PRESS
2004

Oxford University Press

Oxford   New York
Auckland   Bangkok   Buenos Aires   Cape Town   Chennai
Dar es Salaam   Delhi   Hong Kong   Istanbul   Karachi   Kolkata
Kuala Lumpur   Madrid   Melbourne   Mexico City   Mumbai
Nairobi   São Paulo   Shanghai   Taipei   Tokyo   Toronto

Published by Oxford University Press, Inc.
198 Madison Avenue, New York, New York, 10016
http://www.oup-usa.org

Library of Congress Cataloging-in-Publication Data
Jacquette, Dale.
      Pathways in philosophy : an introductory guide with readings /
      Dale Jacquette.
         p. cm.
      Includes bibliographical references and index.
      ISBN 0-19-513131-2 (pbk. : alk. paper)
         1. Philosophy—Introductions. I. Title.
   BD21.J327 2003
   100—dc21   2003048628

Printing number: 9 8 7 6 5 4 3 2 1

Printed in the United States of America
on acid-free paper

FOR TINA, COMPANION IN ALL MY WANDERINGS

I came to my truth by diverse paths and in diverse ways:
it was not upon a single ladder that I climbed to the height
where my eyes survey the distances.

— Friedrich Nietzsche, *Also Sprach Zarathustra*

CONTENTS

Preface **ix**
Acknowledgments **xi**
Introduction **xiii**

PART ONE
METAPHYSICS AND EPISTEMOLOGY

1 THE SOUL AND ITS WISDOM
Plato's *Meno* 3

2 SUBSTANCE AND THE CHANGING WORLD
Aristotle's *Metaphysics* **56**

3 UNIVERSALS, PARTICULARS, AND THE CONCEPT OF TRUTH
Ockham's *Summa Logicae I* **107**

4 REASON, KNOWLEDGE, AND CERTAINTY
Descartes's *Meditations on First Philosophy* **151**

5 EXISTENCE AND NATURE OF GOD
Berkeley's *Three Dialogues Between Hylas and Philonous* **203**

PART TWO
ETHICS AND POLITICAL PHILOSOPHY

6 MORAL RIGHTS, OBLIGATIONS, AND
RESPONSIBILITY
Kant's *Grounding for the Metaphysics of Morals* **265**

7 CONSEQUENCES OF ACTIONS IN
ETHICAL CONDUCT
Mill's *Utilitarianism* **318**

8 INDIVIDUAL VALUES AND THE WILL TO POWER
Nietzsche's *On the Genealogy of Morality* **370**

9 PHILOSOPHICAL ANALYSIS OF THE
CONCEPT OF GOOD
Moore's *Principia Ethica* **419**

10 JUSTICE AND THE SOCIAL GOOD IN POLITICAL
DECISION MAKING
Rawls's *A Theory of Justice* **463**

Glossary **514**
Index **541**

PREFACE

This book, *Pathways in Philosophy*, offers both a historical and topical introduction to some of the most important problems of philosophy. We will take
a close critical look at a selection of ten primary sources written by ten different
philosophers. The chapters are organized into two main parts: (1) Metaphysics and
Epistemology and (2) Ethics and Political Philosophy.

Taking this cross-section from the history and problems of philosophy offers
unique opportunities to learn about philosophical problems and methods from points
of interest chosen from every major period in philosophy's history. The book offers
a natural but not inevitable way to divide up the subject matter of a historical introduction to philosophy. We must begin somewhere, end somewhere, and make good
choices along the way about what to include and what to ignore as we try to tell a
unified story about the development of Western philosophy. We shall explore some
of the most prominent peaks and valleys, proceeding chronologically from the origins of ancient Greek thought to contemporary philosophy.

In discussing each philosopher, we are not merely reporting on their ideas in historical context. We are actively engaging in philosophical dispute with the authors
we have chosen to study on the topics for which they are especially well known. We
shall read and criticize extensive passages from classic writings of Plato, Aristotle,
William of Ockham, René Descartes, George Berkeley, Immanuel Kant, John Stuart
Mill, Friedrich Nietzsche, G. E. Moore, and John Rawls. By the time we are done, we
will have a vivid picture of revolutionary ideas throughout the history of philosophy,
of the problems that have interested philosophers, and the methods they have developed to address them. The interpretation of historical philosophical writings is an art
and a pleasure, but not necessarily an end in itself. We may become fascinated with
the questions posed or suggested by the thinkers we will study and decide that we
want to work out a new and different philosophy, carrying their traditions in a new
direction.

Pathways in Philosophy, accordingly, has two main goals: (1) to understand accurately and in good detail the philosophical positions adopted by each thinker on
particular topics and (2) to evaluate critically each thinker as we try to decide whether
what he says is true or philosophically insightful. We not only want to know what
Plato, Aristotle, Descartes, and other philosophers believed and why they believed it,
but more important, whether their ideas are right or wrong and whether or not they

are on the right track with good reasoning leading to philosophical positions that we can accept and make our own. We want to learn how to evaluate the philosophical ideas of these thinkers by clarifying concepts and identifying, criticizing, and constructing good arguments. We want to know why philosophers think the way they do, why they are right if they are right, and why they are wrong if they are wrong. We learn philosophy and not just history in the process of studying philosophy's history.

To immerse ourselves in philosophy, to understand the point of it and appreciate what it can offer, we need to become philosophically minded. We must read philosophical works, not as we would read a novel or newspaper, but with a sense for the ideas and arguments that have shaped the history of thought. We should not only think about what each philosopher says, but about whether or not we agree, and why. Entering deeply into a choice of philosophical texts and making the authors' problems our own is the best way to enjoy and profit from an introduction to philosophy. We must read and re-read philosophical writings carefully, wonder why philosophers would want to say the things they do, and be prepared to offer objections and arguments of our own to test their conclusions. We become philosophers when we read and think about the problems of philosophy, grappling with the difficult concepts and inferences that lead from one philosophical stepping stone to another. This, after all, is how great philosophers of the past became philosophers. By thinking about these problems in depth, reflecting on philosophical dilemmas, puzzles, paradoxes, and thought experiments, we discover a remarkable world of absorbing intellectually challenging ideas. We will learn to combine accurate historical exposition of a thinker's ideas in a sound interpretation of their writings with a full engagement of critical attention to their philosophical arguments. Reading, thinking about, and evaluating the ideas presented in these commentaries on passages from the history of philosophy help us to define our own philosophical views—which is an excellent reason for studying great moments in the history of philosophy.

ACKNOWLEDGMENTS

I am grateful to Robert Miller, philosophy editor at Oxford University Press, for encouraging me to write this historical introduction to philosophy. I am indebted to the students in my introductory philosophy courses at The Pennsylvania State University. Throughout the last two decades, they have been the primary audience for my approach to the history of philosophy. Emily Voigt oversaw the project in its final stages, and Brian Kinsey and his production team did a superb job of designing and preparing the book for publication. Scott K. Templeton, obs and graphics consultant, located the cover photograph. Finally, but most of all, I thank my wife, Tina, for editorial assistance in preparing references and citations, and for absolutely everything else she does.

The following texts and translations are the sources of quotations:

CHAPTER ONE: The Soul and Its Wisdom
Plato, *Meno*, translated by G. M. A. Grube. Indianapolis: Hackett Publishing Company, 1981 (second edition). Reprinted by permission of Hackett Publishing Company. All rights reserved.

CHAPTER TWO: Substance and the Changing World
Aristotle, *Metaphysics*, translated by W. D. Ross. Oxford: Clarendon Press, 1924.

CHAPTER THREE: Universals, Particulars, and the Concept of Truth
William of Ockham, *Ockham's Theory of Terms, Part I of the Summa Logicae*, translated by Michael J. Loux. Notre Dame: University of Notre Dame Press, 1974. Reprinted by permission of the publisher.

CHAPTER FOUR: Reason, Knowledge, and Certainty
René Descartes, *Meditations on First Philosophy in Which the Existence of God and the Distinction of the Soul from the Body are Demonstrated*, translated from the Latin by Donald A. Cress. Indianapolis: Hackett Publishing Company, 1979. Reprinted by permission of Hackett Publishing Company. All rights reserved.

CHAPTER FIVE: Existence and Nature of God
George Berkeley, *Three Dialogues Between Hylas and Philonous (The Design of Which is Plainly to Demonstrate the Reality and Perfection of Human Knowledge, the Incorporeal Nature of the Soul, and the Immediate Providence of a Deity in Opposition to Sceptics and Atheists. Also to Open a Method for Rendering*

the Sciences More Easy, Useful, and Compendious), in *The Works of George Berkeley*, collected and edited with prefaces and annotations by Alexander Campbell Fraser. Oxford: Clarendon Press, 1871.

CHAPTER SIX: Moral Rights, Obligations, and Responsibility
Immanuel Kant, *Grounding for the Metaphysics of Morals*, translated by James W. Ellington. Indianapolis: Hackett Publishing Company, 1993 (third edition). Reprinted by permission of Hackett Publishing Company. All rights reserved.

CHAPTER SEVEN: Consequences of Actions in Ethical Conduct
John Stuart Mill, *Utilitarianism*. London: Longmans, Green, and Co., 1907 (fifteenth edition).

CHAPTER EIGHT: Individual Values and the Will to Power
Friedrich Nietzsche, *On the Genealogy of Morality*, translated with an introduction and notes by Maudemarie Clark and Alan J. Swensen. Indianapolis: Hackett Publishing Company, 1998. Reprinted by permission of Hackett Publishing Company. All rights reserved.

CHAPTER NINE: Philosophical Analysis of the Concept of Good
G. E. Moore, *Principia Ethica*. Cambridge: Cambridge University Press, 1903; 1922.

CHAPTER TEN: Justice and the Social Good in Political Decision Making
John Rawls, *A Theory of Justice*. Cambridge, Mass.: Belknap Press of Harvard University Press, Copyright © 1971, 1999 (second edition) by the President and Fellows of Harvard College. Reprinted by permission of the publisher.

INTRODUCTION

A Compass and Map

In *Pathways in Philosophy,* we study philosophy by analyzing the work of ten philosophers on ten philosophical topics. Each thinker introduces a different philosophical problem in a different way, and each offers philosophical insights into an aspect of existence, knowledge, moral or political value. We shall combine historical background with critical engagement in philosophical problems to begin exploring the world of philosophy.

The writings considered here represent major thinkers from a variety of philosophical perspectives on a variety of philosophical problems. Selections of passages from primary texts are integrated with extensive commentary and philosophical questions that lead us to what are widely regarded as some of the most important conclusions in philosophy. We consider the writings of famous philosophers not only in order to know from a historical standpoint what they believed and why, but as a source of ideas to stimulate our own philosophical reflections. From the philosophy of antiquity to today, the point of each chapter is to identify the ideas and methods that philosophers have explored—that are at once a vital part of our cultural and intellectual heritage and an inducement to think philosophically about problems that have interested philosophers from ancient Greece to the present day.

Thus, in each chapter we will learn:

- To interpret and critically analyze philosophical texts.
- To recognize and critically analyze philosophical concepts, ideas, and arguments, beginning with characteristic selections from every major period in philosophy's history; to engage in philosophical dialogue with some of the most important great philosophers of the past.
- To construct, criticize, and refine philosophical definitions and arguments in the course of developing a philosophical perspective; to identify defensible philosophical positions and philosophically defend them; to carry forward in new ways the work of great philosophical traditions.

Along the way, we will learn many facts about philosophers and the history of philosophical movements. We will get to know all ten philosophers personally as we examine their ideas and begin to fit them together into a picture of philosophy's history that will help us to understand other thinkers and provide essential background to contemporary philosophical disputes.

Philosophy is unlike other disciplines. It is at once a forward-looking search for understanding, enlightenment, and truth that remains constantly in dialogue with its own history. We can think of philosophy as a network of branching pathways, like hiking paths in the woods. Philosophy presents endlessly interconnecting linkages of ideas that sometimes diverge and sometimes come together again in unexpected ways. We can follow along some of these routes at least for a while to see where they lead, or we can go forward in search of our own principles, extending the walk in new directions. We can stroll casually through the history of philosophy, just as we can in other subjects, sniffing at things to see if they interest us without bothering to learn much about them. With a definite purpose in mind, however, a specific set of questions to address, we can better find our way about the major landmarks in the history of philosophy or blaze our own trail. There are some paths we may choose not to follow, but if we give them a chance and try to see where they are going, we will at least be in a position to make informed choices, and we might surprise ourselves by discovering new things we had not expected to enjoy.

When you first set foot on a hiking path, you generally do so with a purpose. You are in search of something, even if it is only a bit of fresh air and exercise or an interesting landscape to enjoy in the course of the walk. Perhaps the point is to be able to talk at length with a friend. There is always a reason why we embark upon a particular pathway, especially in philosophy. The reason usually involves our natural curiosity and a desire to understand something remarkable about the world. The history of philosophy takes us along routes that have been laid down by others who came before us. It is the meaning of their work in understanding philosophical problems that we are challenged to interpret and apply. Each of us passes through the scenery in a different way and sees and thinks about things from a different perspective. No two individuals wandering the same course will notice precisely the same features or think precisely the same thoughts. They will interpret what they encounter by their own lights, so that the pathway accordingly has an individual meaning for everyone who makes the journey. The questions and problems that interest you when you pick up any of the classics in the history of philosophy will direct your attention in particular ways and color and influence your understanding.

We need a compass and map to find our way into unknown territory. If you have ever gone hiking in the woods or mountains, the chances are you made your way into the country by following a preexisting trail. This makes it appropriate to begin by considering more philosophically what is meant by the idea of a path. To enter onto a path means among other things that someone has been there before. The path is trodden or marked by another walker, someone who has sought out a way to get from one place to another just like you and has left a track for others to follow if they choose. Much the same is true in the history of philosophy. If we study philosophy by way of its history, we follow in the footsteps of major thinkers who have come before us and have partly shown the way that they found best in trying to understand philosophical concepts and answer philosophical problems. The pathways that we shall traverse have been visited by some of the most widely discussed thinkers in the history of philosophy. They have chosen directions for thought by beginning with one set of assumptions rather than another, with one choice of methods as opposed to others, which somehow seemed to them to be the right starting places, the right trailheads. We must eventually choose paths that are right for us, and thereby make them our own, even when the trails have been cut in the past by major thinkers in the history of philosophy. Nor should our respect for previous philosophers inhibit us from giving close critical evaluations of their ideas. The signposts are there for us to use in the great works of philosophy, but we must decide whether to use them and how, for we are each moving step-by-step through our own personally meaningful philosophical journey.

By following established guides, seeing where paths lead, and understanding many of the alternatives in established philosophical traditions, we come to appreciate the diversity of philosophical perspectives that have earned them a prominent place in history. The joy of philosophy is not merely to find a predetermined path that we think is right for us, but to achieve a higher level of understanding by learning about the multiplicity of choices, the many different pathways available to thought. If we want to improve our understanding of philosophy, then we need to see how many different directions it can take. We need to sympathize at least to a certain extent with the reasons why other philosophers have chosen to follow one path rather than another, even if that trail is very different from any we may choose to follow ourselves. In this way, we broaden our philosophical horizons beyond the limits of our own unassisted wayfaring. This in itself can become an important source of philosophical understanding as we develop a sense of the many directions the mind can follow in its efforts to bring clarity to ideas as it struggles to solve philosophical problems.

What, then, should be our orientation as we enter on these historical pathways in philosophy and begin to think about going forward toward new destinations of our own? What is our compass and what is our map? If we think of ourselves as groundbreaking explorers, then part of our task will be to create a map of the philosophical topography as we proceed. We have already remarked that in this historical introduction to the problems and methods of philosophy we are starting out by retracing the pathways that great thinkers in philosophy's history have staked out. We shall, at least at the outset, go where these philosophers have gone before. Thus, a map of sorts exists that we can use to our advantage without having to discover absolutely everything for ourselves, as though there had never been any philosophical predecessors who also thought about the same problems.

We learn above all in the process how to think philosophically. This book is not only engaged in historical inquiry, but points us toward a philosophical goal. We hope by following this route to arrive at good answers to interesting philosophical questions, most of which have a direct or indirect effect on the way we live and the science, art, religion, and political realities in the cultural milieu in which we find ourselves. The quest for philosophical insight in the history of philosophy requires careful reading and critical interaction with the ideas each philosopher has contributed to philosophical discussion, not only for its own sake but as a preparation for self-guided philosophical excursions. An introduction to philosophy, after all, regardless of its orientation and selection of thinkers and topics, is also an invitation for every reader to learn more about philosophy and its history. Whatever your reasons for setting forth on these philosophical pathways, you can expect to discover something valuable that other travelers have overlooked.

PATHWAYS IN PHILOSOPHY

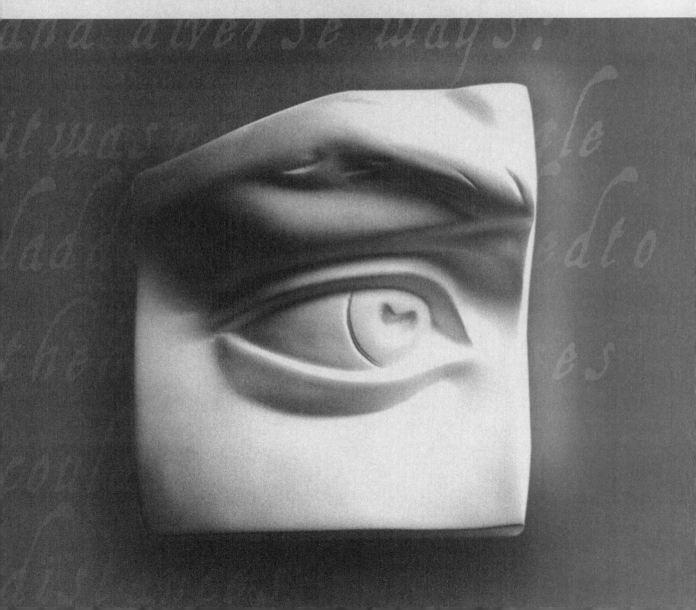

PART 1

METAPHYSICS AND EPISTEMOLOGY

CHAPTER 1

THE SOUL AND ITS WISDOM

Plato's *Meno*

In this chapter we enter the world of ancient Greek philosophy. We learn about Socrates and Plato as we work through one of Plato's most interesting early dialogues. We study the Socratic method as Socrates investigates the concept of virtue, the nature of knowledge, and an argument for the immortality of the soul. In Plato's writings we witness the birth of philosophy in the Western tradition.

SOCRATES AND PLATO

Plato's dialogues provide an excellent introduction to philosophy. The *Meno*, one of Plato's early dialogues, is in many ways the perfect place to start in understanding his thought. Plato (427–347 B.C.E.) was one of many young persons in ancient Greece who admired the philosopher Socrates (469–399 B.C.E.).

During his lifetime, Socrates attracted a circle of followers who were interested in philosophy. They enjoyed hearing Socrates discuss philosophical problems, during the course of which he would often refute the ideas of persons who were supposed to be authorities on a variety of topics. The established rulers in the city, politicians, religious leaders, and others, presented themselves as experts in specialized areas of knowledge. As such, these persons, Socrates assumes, must understand the concepts required by their trades. If they are judges, they must understand the concept of justice; if they are priests, they must understand the concept of piety; if they are artists, they must understand the concept of beauty.

As the promising young son of a wealthy aristocratic family, Plato was expected to undertake a career in politics. Plato, however, at first wanted to become a playwright and to write tragedies for national dramatic competitions. Later, especially after Socrates' trial and execution by the city-state of Athens on trumped-up charges of corrupting the youth of the city and failing to respect the city's gods, Plato turned increasingly to philosophy and eventually started his own philosophical school. Plato's Academy was a model for modern universities that existed for about seven hundred years, longer than any other institution of higher learning in history. At the Academy, Plato taught many famous students, including Aristotle, and wrote dialogues that are somewhat like philosophical plays in which Socrates appears as the main character who is also a moral and intellectual hero.

Socrates never wrote books or essays in philosophy, at least none that have survived to modern times. Socrates is primarily interested in the idea of virtue, and of what he refers to in Plato's dialogues as "the care of the soul." We are fortunate in that, while we have lost many classical writings of other ancient philosophers, such as the voluminous manuscripts of the Presocratic materialist thinker Democritus of Abdera and even some of Aristotle's works, all of Plato's known dialogues and many of his interesting letters have survived to the present day. The result is that we have in Plato's dialogues not only an enormously valuable resource on Plato's thought, offering a picture of life and ideas in the world of ancient Athens, but also indirectly of Socrates' philosophy. Plato's portrait of Socrates is largely confirmed by the writings of other contemporaries such as Xenophon, who also knew Socrates personally. Together, Plato's and Xenophon's dialogues and other authors in antiquity provide the only account of the life and work of Socrates as a brilliant and morally dedicated thinker whom many commentators continue to regard as the founder of Western philosophy.

Typically, in Plato's dialogues, Socrates confronts a fellow Athenian citizen somewhere in the city, in the *agora* or marketplace, for example, or on the steps of the law court, and begins to engage the person in conversation that quickly leads to the painstaking examination of a philosophical concept. Socrates buttonholes these unsuspecting individuals and after a series of questions, and a particular style of criticizing his interlocutors' replies, convinces them to reject or at least rethink their views. Eventually, Socrates was brought before the law because of his practice of philosophy. We learn a great deal about him from Plato's description of these events. When Socrates was put on trial for his life, he remarks that his practice of engaging in dispute was inspired by respect for the gods. He was indirectly told by the divine oracle of Apollo at Delphi that he was the wisest person in Athens. With typical Socratic irony, Socrates accepts this pronouncement, but only if it is interpreted as meaning that he knows that he does not know, while others claim to know things that they really do not know. Socrates explains that in order to prove that what the oracle said was true, he proceeded to question others to see whether or not he was wiser than anyone else.

Socrates' day in court is portrayed in almost identical terms in Plato's and Xenophon's dialogues both titled the *Apology*, meaning "defense," from the Greek word *apologia*, rather than an expression of remorse or request for forgiveness or pardon. Socrates, we soon learn, is completely unrepentant about his philosophical challenges to the pretensions of established thinking. When he demonstrates that persons do not always know what they claim to know or are supposed to know, Socrates admits that he may have inadvertently encouraged idle young men in the city to associate with him for the sheer sport of seeing their elders refuted, which is probably one but not the only thing that eventually got Socrates into legal hot water. Raising philosophical doubts about what other people claim to know evidently contributed to a climate of hostility and dislike for him personally among some of the most powerful people in the city. By maintaining that he has practiced his confrontational method of dialectic in order to verify the pronouncement of the god Apollo, Socrates seeks to avoid direct responsibility for corrupting the youth of Athens and to show that far from failing to respect the gods, his life of philosophical inquiry has been devoted to their service.

An interesting subtext to Socrates' trial and execution is the fact that Socrates was an avowed opponent of democracy on philosophical grounds. We see Socrates' critique of democracy explored in detail in Plato's most famous dialogue, the *Republic*. Socrates, as Plato represents his position, argues that democracy as rule by the many is one of the worst forms of government. The many can never have the specialized native ability and training to qualify them for the most important offices in ruling the ideal city-state. The comparison Socrates is fond of making is that we would never choose the opinion of the many who merely have untutored opinions versus the one who knows if we were in need of serious medical attention. Would we prefer the judgment of a large body of persons from every walk of life, and ask them to vote about whether or not we should have an operation, over that of a professional qualified physician? Socrates assumes that any reasonable person would base such an important decision on the wisdom of the one who knows versus the many who have many different inadequately supported opinions. The many are also more generally influenced by emotion and fleeting impressions, which should not be allowed to determine decision making in a matter as important as our physical health.

Should we not, then, apply the same principle in deciding who should rule the city-state and have responsibility for the political health of all its citizens? Athens, which had just gone through a period of upheavals in which its democratic institutions had been threatened, overturned, and only recently restored, saw in Socrates' teachings a real and present danger to its love of democracy. In this regard, some scholars have speculated that the main charge made against Socrates of corrupting the youth of Athens may not have had so much to do with publicly arguing down any of the city's respected citizens, but more specifically because of his well-reasoned criticisms of democracy and his advocacy of government by the aristocracy. Similarly with regard to the indictment that Socrates fails to honor the city gods, one of which is believed to have been a goddess personifying Democracy. Whatever the historical reasons for Socrates' tragic end, his decision not to flee Athens but accept the death sentence reported in Plato's dialogues the *Crito* and *Phaedo* was as much a defense of the life of philosophy as of his own circumstances. As a believer in the immortality of the soul, as we find also in Plato's dialogue the *Meno*, Socrates regards his death as a freeing of his soul from its imprisonment in the human body; he expresses no regrets about the court's decision and offers the jury no opportunity to avoid the consequences of issuing his death sentence.

Plato's dialogues are standardly divided into three categories, early, middle, and late. Although the principle of division is somewhat controversial, and there remains disagreement about which particular dialogues belong to which period, many scholars accept this framework and the historical analysis behind it. The early dialogues are thought to be Plato's first efforts to transcribe conversations in which Socrates actually engaged. These include Plato's *Euthyphro, Apology, Crito, Phaedo, Symposium,* and others. The middle dialogues continue to feature Socrates as the main protagonist, but begin increasingly to involve more and more of Plato's own ideas, for which Socrates eventually becomes more of a spokesperson and literary foil. Writings from the middle period prominently include the *Republic,* probably Plato's most famous and arguably most important dialogue. The later period of Plato's work is distinguished by dialogues in which Plato's ideas predominate and Socrates as a participant in discussion is limited to a minimum. Characteristic examples of Plato's later philosophy are seen in his dialogues the *Laws* and possibly the *Timaeus.* One clue to the placement of any particular dialogue in Plato's œuvre is the extent to which topics involving mathematics and science, in which Socrates himself as opposed to Plato seems to have had little interest, begin to take precedence over topics in which Socrates is believed to have been more deeply concerned, notably virtue, ethics, morality, political ideals, the nature of beauty and the good, and the "care of the soul."

SOCRATIC ELENCHUS

Socrates makes use of a distinctive form of argument, known as the Socratic *elenchus.* The *Meno* offers a classic example of its application. Socratic *elenchus* involves a chain of reasoning and a distinctive mode of inquiry in which there is an exchange of questions and answers between two speakers. The *elenchus* can be divided structurally into six stages, although not all instances include all six ingredients in precisely the same order. The following are the basic components of Socratic *elenchus,* the movements of the dialectic and exchange between the speakers:

Six Step Method of Socrates' Elenchus

1. A question is posed about the meaning of a general philosophical concept.

   The *elenchus* begins with a problem about what is meant by the concept of virtue, justice, beauty, piety, or the like.

2. Socrates' interlocutor tries to define the concept by advancing a number of instances or examples that are believed to fall under the concept.

   Efforts to provide this type of definition can be seen in a proposal to define the concept of beauty by listing out, for example, beauty in art, beauty in nature, beauty in a mathematical proof, and the like; or even more specific cases, such as this or that beautiful person or this or that beautiful artwork.

3. Socrates then rejects this type of definition as having the wrong form, objecting to its effort to explain a general concept by means of particular examples.

   Standardly, the problem with a definition of this type is that it does not provide an analysis of the underlying concept. Trying to define a general concept by means of specific cases reverses the priority of conceptual analysis. We have no reason in that case to agree that any of the examples provided are actually instances of the concept unless or until we know what the concept means in its most general terms. Thus, we have no justification to agree, for example, that this or that style of art or particular artwork is beautiful.

4. Next, Socrates' interlocutor comes to understand what is required in a correct definition of a general concept and attempts to provide a definition of the form

that Socrates would approve, offering to explain the general concept in appropriately general terms.

At this stage of the *elenchus*, if the discussion were about the concept of beauty, Socrates' interlocutor might try to define the general concept of beauty, for example, as whatever delights the eye in art.

5. Socrates' then proceeds to refute the interlocutor's general definition by means of counterexamples.

Counterexamples are cases that satisfy the concept to be defined but not the conditions of the proposed definition, or that satisfy the conditions of the proposed definition but not are not instances of the concept to be defined. If the concept is satisfied but not the conditions of the proposed definition, then the definition is said to provide at most *necessary* but not *sufficient* conditions for the concept. If the conditions of the definition are satisfied but are not instances of the concept to be defined, then the definition may specify sufficient but not necessary conditions for the concept. In either case, the proposed definition is inadequate, as the counterexample is meant to prove. A counterexample to the above definition of beauty as whatever delights the eye in art is that it fails to take into account the beauty in nature or the beauty in music, or for that matter beauty that is not necessarily a source of aesthetic delight. A definition of that sort would be said to provide neither necessary nor sufficient conditions for beauty. The definition's conditions are not necessary because there is beauty that does not involve visual delight, and are not sufficient because there are instances of visual delight that are not beautiful.

6. The classical *elenchus* ends in a recognition on the part of Socrates and his interlocutor that after all they do not fully understand the concept they have been trying to define. The chain of question and answer in Socrates' method of argument thus terminates in puzzlement or *aporia*.

Socrates ironically describes his wisdom as consisting in the recognition that by contrast with others who claim to be experts in their fields he at least knows that he does not know. The *aporia* in which the Socratic *elenchus* culminates is supposed in turn to be the first step toward Socratic *maieutic*, a program of moral self-improvement that can only begin with an acknowledgment of ignorance and the need for personal reform. *Maieusis* is the Greek word for midwifery, and Socrates, whose mother was a midwife, sometimes describes himself as a midwife of the soul, whose purpose is to help others to give rebirth to new and morally enlightened selves. This is part of what Socrates means by characterizing his mission in philosophy as concerned with the care of the soul.

Socratic *elenchus* is the heart of many of Plato's dialogues. If we want to understand Plato's philosophy, we must be alert to the separate stages of the *elenchus*, which in some dialogues are abbreviated or modified. The *Meno*, among all of Plato's dialogues, is one of the most pure and complete examples of Socratic *elenchus*. We can learn much about Socrates' and Plato's thought by considering the course of Socrates' chain of questions and answers in the *Meno*.

The *elenchus* is Socrates' dialectical method of arriving at philosophical truths in conversation with other persons whose backgrounds suggest that they are supposed to have specialized knowledge of general concepts. By challenging their understanding of these ideas, Socrates hopes to improve his own grasp of the concepts of virtue, to help his fellow citizens realize the extent of their own misunderstandings, and thereby to lead them toward a path of moral self-improvement, benefiting the city-state directly by contributing to the philosophical enlightenment of its citizens. In the process, unfortunately, Socrates also manages to make a number of powerful enemies who do not appreciate having their ignorance of things they are supposed to know publicly exposed.

Meno's Query: Can Virtue Be Taught?

The *Meno*, which we shall now begin to examine in detail, is usually thought to be a dialogue from the latter part of Plato's early period or a relatively early dialogue from Plato's middle period. Unlike most of Plato's dialogues, in which Socrates questions someone about the meaning of a general concept, in the *Meno*, the dialogue's title character begins by posing Socrates a difficult question:

> MENO: Can you tell me, Socrates, can virtue be taught? Or is it not teachable but the result of practice, or is it neither of these, but men possess it by nature or in some other way? (3)

The question is important, not only for purely theoretical or abstract reasons, but in deciding as a practical matter for example how to raise children and how to administer the law and other aspects of social policy. If virtue is not teachable, then there is no hope of reforming or trying to rehabilitate criminals, at least not as an effort aimed at making them become virtuous; nor does it make sense in that case to try to educate children to be virtuous. If virtue is unteachable in principle, then no matter what teaching method is applied, virtuous citizens cannot be made out of persons who would otherwise be unvirtuous.

Some people nowadays refer to the issue Meno raises as a problem of nature versus nurture. To put the question in modern terms which Socrates would not immediately recognize, we might ask whether being good and acting with a sense of moral responsibility is genetic (in the DNA of each individual) or part of learned behavior. If virtue is genetic or acquired exclusively through heredity (Meno says "possessed by nature"), then it may be a waste of time trying to teach people to be good; they will either be virtuous or not, just as they will either have blue eyes or not, freckles or no freckles. If, on the other hand, virtue is something for which persons can be taught or trained, then we open up the possibility of discovering how this might be done and the kind of training that might enable a person to improve their moral behavior.

Meno, we should note, is not a fictional character, but a real historical figure known to the Athenians of his time as a scoundrel who betrayed the city during its war with the Persians. There is therefore more than a touch of irony in the fact that in Plato's dialogue Meno of all persons should approach Socrates with a riddle about the nature of virtue. Socrates does not simply try to answer Meno's question yes or no, but claims that he cannot even begin to address the problem. Far from knowing whether or not virtue can be taught or is acquired in a different manner, Socrates insists that he does not know even what is meant by the concept of virtue, and hence cannot intelligibly decide how it is that some persons rather than others become virtuous. To know whether virtue can be taught, what properties virtue has, Socrates claims that he would first need to know what virtue is, something he freely admits he does not know.

For Socrates, to understand the concept of virtue would require an ability to define the idea of virtue exactly. It would be necessary to specify the necessary and sufficient conditions for virtue, the general requirements that must be satisfied in order for something to qualify as virtue. Socrates holds Meno at bay with characteristic irony, indicating that the question is presumptuous, a sign of Meno's audaciousness as a Thessalian, demanding a "bold and grand answer" to any question posed. He credits the Thessalians with a reputation for great horsemanship, and maintains that now, given the kind of question Meno has raised, they will also earn an equal reputation for wisdom. Of course, Socrates is being ironic and not speaking literally; he intends the opposite of what he has said. For he thinks that to put forward a question of this sort, without first determining the meaning of the concept of virtue, is a sign of folly. Socrates emphasizes the point when he offers this cautious reply:

> SOCRATES: If then you want to ask one of us that sort of question, everyone will laugh and say: "Good stranger, you must think me happy indeed if you think I know whether virtue can taught or how it comes to be; I am so far from knowing whether virtue can be taught or not that I do not even have any knowledge of what virtue itself is." (3)

When Meno expresses surprise at Socrates' reluctance to answer his question, and at Socrates' assertion that the citizens of Athens are equally too lacking in wisdom to help solve the problem, Socrates indicates that he is also in precisely the same situation, unable to explain whether virtue can be taught because he does not fully understand what virtue is, and so is in no position to say what special properties virtue has or does not have. He adds:

> SOCRATES: I myself, Meno, am as poor as my fellow citizens in this matter, and I blame myself for my complete ignorance about virtue. If I do not know what something is, how could I know what qualities it possesses? Or do you think that someone who does not know at all who Meno is could know whether he is good-looking or rich or well-born, or the opposite of these? Do you think that is possible? (4)

Socrates' final question is rhetorical, one for which he expects no answer. He claims not only that he personally does not know what virtue is, but that he has never met anyone who does. He states that he can no more know whether virtue can be taught unless or until he knows what virtue is than someone could know whether Meno was handsome without first knowing who Meno is, without being able to recognize him and distinguish him from others. It is only after we know what something is, Socrates maintains, that we can ask what properties it has or does not have. The Socratic *elenchus* is engaged in order to uncover the meanings of these kinds of concepts, but the dialectic of questions and answers almost always ends in a recognition of what we do not know.

Among the persons whom Socrates criticizes as claiming to know but not actually knowing, he singles out the *sophists* who taught rhetoric for a fee in Athens and the ancient Greek colonies. In particular, Socrates mentions Gorgias, an itinerant rhetorician with whom Meno had studied, as someone who does not understand the concept of virtue. The sophists are criticized in many of Plato's dialogues, ostensibly because they charged money for their lessons, although there appears to be another philosophically more interesting reason. Socrates had inherited a modest sum after the death of his father, on which he was able to live within his limited means by simplifying his needs and working occasionally as a stone cutter. Socrates had a wife and several children, some of which he sired late in life, and one of whom was still a child when Socrates was brought to trial at the age of seventy. He might also have been able to teach students for a fee like the sophists, but disdained doing so. Plato was part of a wealthy family, and had no need to work for a living.

The fact that sophists, including Gorgias as one of the most famous of their profession, charged tuition for their lessons, was not the only reason why Socrates and Plato found the sophists objectionable. The ancient Greek world was democratic in political structure, and its citizens could distinguish themselves and earn respect, power, position in society, and wealth by skillful public speaking in government assemblies. The sophists promised to teach these abilities to aspiring orators, concentrating on methods of persuading an audience and moving them by argument, emotional appeal, and clever rhetorical tricks. The deeper reason why Socrates and Plato objected to the sophists was that they used methods of philosophical argument, not as a mode of *inquiry* for discovering the truth, letting the best argument prevail, and following its conclusions wherever they led, but instead proliferated the use of dialectical techniques as a method of *advocacy*, of supporting any position regardless of its truth or falsehood.

One of the most revealing lessons of the sophists was to encourage students to defend either side of a contradictory dispute. A good sophist was able to hold up either side of an argument with equal effectiveness, suggesting that there was no more to the truth of any matter than the persuasiveness with which a case could be presented. The sophists often relied on polemical devices in the service of spurious argument to support conclusions that the orator did not personally believe. This aspect of sophism was highly objectionable to Socrates and Plato, who thought of philosophy and its methods of argument instead as a way of discovering truth.

PHILOSOPHICAL ANALYSIS OF CONCEPTS

Meno, astonished at Socrates' declaration that he does not know what virtue is and that he has never met anyone else who knew, asks Socrates whether he has not heard Gorgias speak. Socrates replies that he had seen Gorgias when the orator was in Athens, but could not remember whether or not he thought at the time that Gorgias understood the concept of virtue. He taunts Gorgias gently by reversing the question, asking Meno to recall what Gorgias had said. The sophists were renowned for their expertise in the art of memory, teaching orators to memorize long speeches for delivery on public occasions. Socrates invites Meno, as a student of Gorgias, to remember what Gorgias had to say about the concept of virtue, and, as it turns out, Meno is unable to recall. Socrates accordingly asks Meno to speak for himself:

SOCRATES: Let us leave Gorgias out of it, since he is not here. But Meno, by the gods, what do you yourself say that virtue is? Speak and do not begrudge us, so that I may have spoken a most unfortunate untruth when I said that I had never met anyone who knew, if you and Gorgias are shown to know. (4)

Meno proceeds as boldly in answering Socrates' question as he was in asking Socrates whether virtue can be taught. He divides the concept up into distinct meanings and distinct applications, specifying a different concept of virtue for each of the kinds of individuals who might be said to be virtuous. He declares:

MENO: It is not hard to tell you, Socrates. First, if you want the virtue of a man, it is easy to say that a man's virtue consists of being able to manage public affairs and in so doing to benefit his friends and harm his enemies and to be careful that no harm comes to himself; if you want the virtue of a woman, it is not difficult to describe: she must manage the home well, preserve its possessions, and be submissive to her husband; the virtue of a child, whether male or female, is different again, and so is that of an elderly man, if you want that, or if you want that of a free man or a slave. And there are very many other virtues, so that one is not at a loss to say what virtue is. There is virtue for every action and every age, for every task of ours and every one of us—and Socrates, the same is true for wickedness. (4)

We notice immediately that Meno has not defined the general concept of virtue, but distinguishes between different kinds of virtues that different persons in different stations of life might have attributed to them. There is the virtue of a man, the virtue of a woman, the virtue of a free person, the virtue of a slave, and the like. It is worth noticing that whereas Meno argues that men and women have different virtues, Socrates in Plato's *Republic* holds that men and women alike, if appropriately gifted by nature and properly educated, can equally serve as soldiers and rulers in the guardian class, regardless of gender, and are to be treated as equals capable of the same virtues. Meno advances the contrary point of view, that, proper to each gender, men and women have inherently different virtues and hence, presumably, inherently different functions in society. Socrates objects to Meno's definition, but only on the grounds that it conflicts with Socrates' preconception of the basic equality of women and men. Rather, Socrates criticizes Meno's attempt to define the concept of virtue because it fails to have the necessary generality for the definition of a concept. Socrates continues, again with characteristic irony:

SOCRATES: I seem to be in great luck, Meno; while I am looking for one virtue, I have found you to have a whole swarm of them. But, Meno, to follow up the image of swarms, if I were asking you what is the nature of bees, and you said that they are many and of all kinds, what would you answer if I asked you: "Do you mean that they are many and varied and different from one another in so far as they are bees? Or are they no different in that regard, but in some other respect, in their beauty, for example, or their size or in some other such way?" Tell me, what would you answer if thus questioned?

MENO: I would say that they do not differ from one another in being bees. (4)

Socrates reasons by analogy. He points out the limitations of Meno's definition as inadequate in form by comparing it to a swarm of bees. Socrates had requested one thing, a single definition of the general concept of virtue. Meno, on the contrary, tries at first to answer by advancing a large indefinite number of multiple definitions of distinct kinds of virtue, one for each of the many different categories of persons who might be virtuous in different ways. It is, Socrates contends, like offering a swarm of bees when what was requested was to know what it means for any of the particular items in the swarm to be a bee.

There are many kinds of bees, including, among others, bumblebees, honey bees, and African killer bees. Socrates does not want and will not accept a catalog of the many different kinds of bees or the many different kinds of virtues; he requires a definition of what it means for any of these things to be a bee or to be a virtue. This is what Meno fails to provide, reflecting his misunderstanding of how philosophy should approach the problem of analyzing a difficult concept, and his preoccupation with the concrete world of particular perceivable things rather than general concepts. The opposition between the one and the many, as in the choice between an aristocracy or democracy as a preferred form of government, is implied in Socrates' objection to Meno's first effort to define the concept. Socrates is focused on trying to identify the one concept of virtue that is instantiated in many different examples, such as the one concept of bee by which bumblebees, honey bees, African killer bees, and other species are all rightly classified as particular types of bees. Meno, in keeping with his philosophically less developed understanding, naturally splinters his attention up into many different instances, each of which might or might not properly be designated as an example of virtue.

The problem is that we cannot even decide whether Meno is right to consider the applications of the concept of virtue he offers as a way of defining the concept as a whole, unless or until we are in possession of a correct analysis of the concept. It is clear that in this part of their discussion Socrates and Meno are at the second stage of the Socratic *elenchus.* Socrates would no doubt want to object that this is why Meno goes astray in assuming without being in a sound position to prove that the virtue of men is different from the virtue of women, and that the virtue of free individuals is different again from the virtue of slaves. Meno reverses the order of inquiry and puts the horse before the cart, by beginning with the claim that these are different virtues belonging to different persons in different walks of life. Whereas, for Socrates, in order to judge the matter properly, we would first need to correctly understand the concept of virtue in its most general terms, and then go on to ask whether or not it is true that men and women, slaves and free individuals are or are not capable of the same kinds of virtues, and whether or not they can be virtuous in precisely the same sense of the word, or only in different and potentially incompatible ways.

The difficulty Meno gets himself into by dividing up the concept of virtue into multiple categories is thus another manifestation of the problem with which the dialogue begins. Socrates and Meno have not made the least progress in their inquiry. Socrates argues that he cannot answer Meno's question whether or not virtue can be taught unless or until he first knows what virtue is and can provide a correct analysis of the concept. The same is true of Meno's claim that there are different virtues for men and women, children and adults, free persons and slaves, in which Meno claims in effect to discern particular properties belonging to the nature of virtue without first explaining the nature of virtue in general. Socrates draws the moral from the bees analogy to the problem of defining the general concept of virtue:

> SOCRATES: The same is true in the case of the virtues. Even if they are many and various, all of them have one and the same form which makes them virtues, and it is right to look to this when one is asked to make clear what virtue is. Or do you not understand what I mean?
>
> MENO: I think I understand, but I certainly do not grasp the meaning of the question as fully as I want to. (5)

In the *theory of Forms* or *Ideas*, developed most completely in Plato's *Republic*, there is supposed to be a single Form (*eidos*, in Greek) in a realm of abstract ideal entities, sometimes referred to as Platonic heaven. This is described by Plato as the *world of Being*, in which many different instances participate, or whose one Form multiple instances are said imperfectly to imitate in the spatiotemporal *world of Becoming* that we experience in sensation.

From the standpoint of Plato's theory of Forms, the objection Socrates raises to Meno's first attempt to define the concept of virtue by a strategy of divide and conquer can be described as Meno's fixation on the transient ephemeral world of Becoming. For it is only in the perceivable world of Becoming that many individual instances of virtues superficially appear to casual inspection, instead of identifying the one Form or Idea of virtue belonging to the real changeless world of Being. The difference between the *one and the many* with its political ramifications in Socrates' thought is thus grounded in a more fundamental metaphysical distinction between one Form and its many instances. Meno is mired in his thinking to the changing world of the many, the world of Becoming, while Socrates suggests that he must raise his sights from the many to the one, from the world of appearances to the world of reality, or from the world of Becoming to the world of Being. It is not an easy shift of perspective for Meno. Socrates makes another analogy, comparing the concepts of health, size, and strength and their many instances in the health, size, and strength of men and women to the concept of virtue as it might be exemplified in the special cases of women and men. As Socrates says:

> SOCRATES: I am asking whether you think it is only in the case of virtue that there is one for man, another for woman, and so on, or is the same true in the case of health and size and strength? Do you think that there is one health for man and another for woman? Or, if it is health, does it have the same form everywhere, whether in man or in anything else whatever?
>
> MENO: The health of a man seems to me the same as that of a woman.
>
> SOCRATES: And so with size and strength? If a woman is strong, that strength will be the same and have the same form, for by "the same" I mean that strength is no different as far as being strength, whether in a man or a woman. Or do you think there is a difference?
>
> MENO: I do not think so. (5)

Meno admits that in these cases there is no difference between the health, size, or strength of a man or woman. The implication is that the same general applicability should hold true for the general concept of virtue, which ought to be the same in principle, however differently the concept is instantiated in men or women, free persons or slaves. It is necessary to see beyond the superficial appearances of virtues as they are manifested in individuals in order to grasp the one underlying Form of virtue, which Socrates demands of an adequate definition. The choice of analogy, especially the example of health, is significant for Socrates, because in Plato's *Republic* Socrates compares the general concept of justice with the health or harmony of the soul or city-state, the very same Form of which is manifested in different ways in an individual and in a political body.

Socrates and Meno then engage in the following exchange:

SOCRATES: And will there be any difference in the case of virtue, as far as being virtue is concerned, whether it be in a child or an old man, in a woman or in a man?

MENO: I think, Socrates, that somehow this is no longer like those other cases.

SOCRATES: How so? Did you not say that the virtue of a man consists of managing the city well, and that of a woman managing the household?

MENO: I did.

SOCRATES: Is it possible to manage a city well, or a household, or anything else, while not managing it moderately and justly?

MENO: Certainly not.

SOCRATES: Then if they manage justly and moderately, they must do so with justice and moderation.

MENO: Necessarily.

SOCRATES: So both the man and the woman, if they are to be good, need the same things, justice and moderation.

MENO: So it seems.

SOCRATES: What about a child and an old man? Can they possibly be good if they are intemperate and unjust?

MENO: Certainly not.

SOCRATES: But if they are moderate and just?

MENO: Yes.

SOCRATES: So all human beings are good in the same way, for they become good by acquiring the same qualities.

MENO: It seems so.

SOCRATES: And they would not be good in the same way if they did not have the same virtue.

MENO: They certainly would not be. (5–6)

Here Socrates slowly begins to convince Meno of his error in trying to define the concept of virtue in the manner of a swarm of bees. Socrates does not argue in completely general terms about the requirements for an adequate definition, nor does he mention the Platonic theory of Forms or the opposition between the one and the many. Instead, he deals very concretely with the details of Meno's distinct definitions of the distinct types of virtue, which Meno had urged must be different in the case of women and men, young people and old, free persons and slaves.

Socrates considers each part of Meno's divisions and asks whether Meno truly finds it reasonable to suppose that, for example, a man can manage a city well and a woman can manage a household well, and fulfill their respective obligations which Meno identifies with their distinctive virtues, if they do not share alike in the same general properties of justice and moderation, which are themselves sometimes said to be particular virtues. Meno does not stubbornly cling to his original definition, but is reasonable and flexible enough in his thinking to appreciate the force of Socrates' argument.

Socrates then lifts the discussion to a higher level of abstraction. He begins to guide Meno toward a clearer understanding of the generality of the concept of virtue. In effect, Socrates has in mind the general concept as a Platonic Form, although he does not use this terminology. Socrates does not refer to particular virtues such as justice and moderation observed in common by men and women, and persons in other categories, but ascends to a more abstract consideration of the metaphysics of particular virtues as individual or general kinds of entities. The inquiry is shaped by Socrates through an examination of the appropriate grammatical categories in terms of which we think about virtue and the virtues. Thus, Socrates states:

SOCRATES: Consider this further point: you say that virtue is to be able to rule. Shall we not add to this justly and not unjustly?

MENO: I think so, Socrates, for justice is virtue.

SOCRATES: Is it virtue, Meno, or a virtue?

MENO: What do you mean?

SOCRATES: As with anything else. For example, if you wish, take roundness, about which I would say that it is a shape, but not simply that it is shape. I would not so speak of it because there are other shapes.

MENO: You are quite right. So I too say that not only justice is a virtue but there are many other virtues. (6)

Socrates and Meno are now more explicitly engaged in the topic of the one and the many. Virtue is like shape; it is not any particular virtue, say, courage, or temperance or moderation, all of which are specific virtues, just as shape is not any particular shape, such as being round, triangular, or rectangular, or color any particular color such as blue or red or green. Although Socrates does not address the further implication, it is obvious in connection with what has gone before that for Socrates on the same general grammatical grounds we can no more correctly conclude that the virtue of men as opposed to the virtue of women, in Meno's original formulation, is virtue rather than at most a particular virtue or collection of particular virtues. Socrates has not admitted that there are different virtues for women and men; on the contrary, he has already indicated his disagreement with Meno in this regard. Rather, by a succession of inferences, Socrates tries to enlighten Meno about the utmost generality of a concept such as that of virtue, that it must be a one rather than a many, as Plato in his theory of Forms would also insist.

The moral should be plain. As in the attempt to define the general concept of shape or color, an acceptable definition of the concept of virtue must not try to make do with a list of many specific virtues, regardless of their level of detail. To do so would confuse the concept of a particular shape, a particular color, or a particular virtue with the general concept of shape, color, or virtue. The grammatical differences between these concepts are revealing, and Socrates exploits their distinctions in language to help Meno understand what is required of a correct definition of the general concept of virtue. Meno finally seems to get the point, but his conceptual analytic resources are overextended, and he admits that he cannot provide a definition of the kind that would satisfy Socrates. Socrates in turn tries to illustrate what is needed by sketching a theory of color with the requisite form and at the requisite level of generality. The hope is that, if he leads by example by defining the concept of color as opposed to that of any particular color, Socrates will suggest to Meno how he might proceed in satisfying the requirements of an adequate definition of the general concept of virtue.

MENO: I cannot yet find, Socrates, what you are looking for, one virtue for them all, as in the other cases.

SOCRATES: That is likely, but I am eager, if I can, that we should make progress, for you understand that the same applies to everything. If someone asked you what I mentioned just now: "What is shape, Meno?" and you told him that it was roundness, and if then he said to you what I did: "Is roundness shape or a shape? you would surely tell him that it is a shape?

MENO: I certainly would.

SOCRATES: That would be because there are other shapes?

MENO: Yes.

SOCRATES: And if he asked you further what they were, you would tell him?

MENO: I would.

SOCRATES: So too, if he asked you what colour is, and you said it is white, and your questioner interrupted you, "Is white colour or a colour?" you would say that it is a colour, because there are also other colours?

MENO: I would.

SOCRATES: And if he bade you mention other colours, you would mention others that are no less colours than white is?

MENO: Yes.

SOCRATES: Then if he pursued the argument as I did and said: "We always arrive at the many; do not talk to me in that way, but since you call all these many by one name, and say that no one of them is not a shape even though they are opposites, tell me what this is which applies as much to the round as to the straight and which you call shape, as you say the round is as much a shape as the straight." Do you not say that?

MENO: I do. (7)

Meno admits that it would not do to answer a question about the general concept of shape by saying that shape is triangle, since that is only *a* particular shape, one among many. Nor, for the same reason, can we understand the general concept of color by the proposition that blue is color or white is color. The reason in both cases is that there are shapes other than that of a triangle, and colors other than blue or white. We can only say that blue is *a* color and that white is *a* color. Meno nevertheless makes precisely this mistake when he says that justice is virtue, in answer to Socrates' question whether the virtue of men as opposed to women is to rule. Socrates, ignoring Meno's gender bias for the moment, asks whether it is virtue simply to rule or to rule justly. Would it be virtuous for men (or women) to rule unjustly? Meno, reluctantly perhaps, admits that the answer is "no." He acknowledges the problem in his original definition, and maintains that it can only be virtuous for men to rule justly or with justice, because, as he crudely puts it, conflating the two concepts, justice *is* virtue. Socrates accordingly wages a grammatical critique of Meno's way of characterizing justice, distinguishing between justice as virtue or as a virtue, which is to say, only one among many virtues—*a* virtue rather than virtue as such.

MENO'S GENERAL DEFINITION AND SOCRATES' COUNTEREXAMPLES

Meno finally grasps the kind of definition Socrates requires and tries to follow Socrates' example by providing a general analysis of the concept of virtue, modeled on Socrates' definition of color. The definition Socrates provides is meant to appeal to Meno by providing the sort of "theatrical" explanation that the sophists were expected to give. The definition nevertheless has the right sort of form for an analysis of a general concept. Meno takes the hint and tries to satisfy Socrates by giving up the particular examples of virtues he has thus far mentioned and trying to characterize the general concept of virtue as he sees it. Socrates first admonishes Meno to fulfill his promise by providing the right sort of definition:

SOCRATES: . . . Come now, you too try to fulfill your promise to me and tell me the nature of virtue as a whole and stop making many out of one, as jokers say whenever someone breaks something; but allow virtue to remain whole and sound, and tell me what it is, for I have given you examples. (10)

Meno responds:

MENO: I think, Socrates, that virtue is, as the poet says, "to find joy in beautiful things and have power." So I say that virtue is to desire beautiful things and have the power to acquire them. (10)

Here, at last, is an effort to define the general concept of virtue in general terms. Meno does not rely on specific particular examples of virtues or kinds of virtues, those of a man or woman, or the virtues of courage and moderation, but seeks to articulate what must hold true of any kind of virtue in any context. The definition Meno offers remains connected with the style of the sophists, making fine speeches by relying on the authority of poets, who are often believed to be divinely inspired in their pronouncements.

The definition invokes a certain image of the virtuous person, as one who has cultivated tastes for beautiful things and the ability to possess them. The definition should not be entirely unexpected coming from Meno, who is a prime example of a type of individual the ancient Greeks referred to as an *erotic man*. An erotic man is not necessarily a person preoccupied with sex, although this is also usually an aspect of their character. Instead, an erotic man in the Greek conception is someone who is driven by desires of various kinds, motivated in their actions by the wish to enhance their material status, to gain things for their use and for the sake of the social prestige that often accompanies successful endeavors to gather not only the necessities of life but luxuries as well. The two key elements of the erotic man are present in Meno's definition of virtue: desire and power. The Greek word for virtue is *aretē*, but it is significant that the English word derives from the Latin *virtus*, which is etymologically related to the Latin root specifically for a man, *vir*, as we also see in the modern English word *virile*. It is the mark of the erotic man considered as virtuous in this sense to desire things and to seek to acquire them through the exercise of power. By defining the concept of virtue as he does in accordance with Socrates' insistence on a general definition, Meno proclaims himself an erotic man, as any classical Greek reader of Plato's dialogue would immediately recognize.

Meno's attempt at definition now has the right sort of form to satisfy Socrates. But is Meno's new definition correct in its content, in the conditions it specifies as necessary and sufficient for virtue? Socrates thinks it is not, and tries to refute the definition by offering counterexamples. The question for Socrates is whether or not Meno's proposal is adequate, whether it is true that to be virtuous is to desire and have the ability to acquire beautiful things. We might anticipate Socrates' response by considering whether it is true that it is always virtuous to desire and be able to acquire what is beautiful, or whether it makes a difference what we desire and how we exercise power in trying to acquire such things. Socrates first asks Meno to clarify his meaning, whether he intends to refer to the person who desires beautiful things as one who thereby necessarily desires things that are also good. He asks, and Meno replies:

> SOCRATES: Do you mean that the man who desires beautiful things desires good things?
>
> MENO: Most certainly. (10)

This is an interesting but by no means obvious identification. Why should Meno assume that to be beautiful is automatically to be morally good? Many things that are beautiful in the first place seem to be morally neutral. The sun is good, and a sunset can be beautiful, but why should anyone agree that a beautiful sunset is good, let alone morally good? What could be the connection between beauty and virtue that Meno's definition presupposes?

Moreover, we might expect that some beautiful things might not be morally good or virtuous, not merely in the sense that, like the sunset, they are morally neutral, but positively immoral or evil. A destructive virus might have a very beautiful appearance under the microscope, while constituting a terrible danger to health. The burning of a valuable library from a distance might make an extraordinarily beautiful appearance, in terms of its colors and movement, and the sound of a bone breaking might be as beautiful as any delightful strain of music. Where persons as moral agents are concerned, there again seems to be no obvious link between someone's being physically attractive in appearance and being morally upright. A physically beautiful person might be morally corrupt, even evil. Beauty alone, in any case, which people say is only skin-deep, does not seem to be a sufficient condition for virtue. Nor does beauty seem to be necessary for virtue or moral goodness. There are many aesthetically neutral or even ugly things that are good, and persons who are not particularly physically attractive but are consistently virtuous in all their moral conduct. Thus, it already appears that there may be difficulties in Meno's general definition of the concept of virtue that may make it vulnerable to counterexamples in the further progress of the Socratic *elenchus*. Finally, we should remark that beauty is often if not usually or even always a matter of subjective judgment. What appears beautiful to some may appear aesthetically neutral or even unbeautiful or ugly to others. As well as being only skin-deep, beauty is further said to reside in the eye of the beholder. If virtue is supposed to be a more objective ground of moral judgment and guide to moral decision making, then it seems misguided once again to try as Meno does to connect virtue with beauty or the desire for and power to acquire beautiful things.

Socrates nevertheless approaches the evaluation of Meno's definition from a somewhat different direction. As Plato describes Socrates' interaction with Meno at this juncture in the dialogue, Socrates sounds a theme that occurs in many places in Plato's writings, concerning the view that no one ever knowingly acts wrongly, but does so only through ignorance, failing to recognize that immoral behavior is personally harmful in unexpected ways. The conversation takes shape in this way:

SOCRATES: Do you assume that there are people who desire bad things, and others who desire good things? Do you not think, my good man, that all men desire good things?

MENO: I do not.

SOCRATES: But some desire bad things?

MENO: Yes.

SOCRATES: Do you mean that they believe the bad things to be good, or that they know they are bad and nevertheless desire them?

MENO: I certainly do. (10)

Socrates attacks, not the beauty part of Meno's definition, but Meno's reference to the desire for beautiful things. Socrates asks in effect whether anyone ever desires things that are not good. Meno claims that sometimes they do, which he must say if his definition is to be sustained. If Socrates' contrary thesis that no one ever desires what is bad knowing beforehand that it is bad is true, then it would be mistaken for Meno to define virtue as the desire for beautiful things, given Meno's problematic admission to Socrates' first question that what is beautiful is also good.

The definition would be trivial in that case. If no one ever desires what is bad, then everyone desires only what is good; hence, by Meno's equation of beauty with good, everyone desires what is beautiful. That would imply that Meno's attempt to define the concept of virtue as desiring beauty would not say enough to distinguish between the virtuous and the nonvirtuous. The definition would also be mistaken in another way, because it would implausibly imply that everyone is virtuous, which Meno would presumably deny. Meno must therefore maintain, at least in the absence of counterargument by Socrates, that some persons sometimes desire what is bad rather than good, and thereby what is unbeautiful rather than beautiful. Socrates now proceeds to criticize Meno's assumption, in a pointed series of questions:

SOCRATES: What do you mean by desiring? Is it to secure for oneself?

MENO: What else?

SOCRATES: Does he think that the bad things benefit him who possesses them, or does he know they harm him?

MENO: There are some who believe that the bad things benefit them, others who know that the bad things harm them.

SOCRATES: And do you think that those who believe that bad things benefit them know that they are bad?

MENO: No, that I cannot altogether believe.

SOCRATES: It is clear then that those who do not know things to be bad do not desire what is bad, but they desire those things that they believe to be good but that are in fact bad. It follows that those who have no knowledge of these things and believe them to be good clearly desire good things. Is that not so?

MENO: It is likely. (10)

Socrates has no special difficulty convincing Meno that reasonable persons do not knowingly or deliberately choose what is bad, provided that they understand that they are thereby harming themselves. The thesis is nevertheless controversial. Most people realize that smoking cigarettes is harmful to their health, and would not deliberately choose the harm that is likely to come about from prolonged use of tobacco. Yet many persons choose to smoke despite recognizing the harm, possibly in psychological denial that they will actually be harmed, for the sake of the enjoyment they experience. We must therefore wonder whether Socrates is right to argue and whether Meno is right to agree that no one ever voluntarily chooses to do that which is personally harmful. It may be irrational for them to do so, but it does not follow that no one actually knowingly and deliberately chooses what is personally bad or harmful; for it does not follow that reasonable people are never imprudent in their choices of individual actions or lifestyles that can adversely affect their good.

The issue of whether Socrates is right to conclude that no one ever knowingly does anything personally harmful has wider implications in his philosophy. It is the centerpiece of his solution to the problem of why anyone ought to be moral or to follow the ethical precepts they know to be correct. It is one thing, we might say, to know in the abstract what it is morally right for us to do, and another actually to do it. Just because I know it is wrong to steal, does not necessarily give me a strong enough motivation to resist the temptation to steal, especially if I am desperately in need and I believe that I can escape discovery and punishment for my wrongful act. Why should I do what I know I should do? Socrates in Plato's *Republic* answers this question in a particularly colorful argument context, in which he is called upon to explain why someone would prefer to be virtuous in reality while having a reputation for being unvirtuous, rather than being unvirtuous in reality but enjoying the reputation for being virtuous. Socrates considers a thought experiment in which someone is in possession of a magic ring, which, when the stone is twisted, makes the wearer invisible, so that he can perpetrate all sorts of wrongdoing without ever being detected, brought to law, or tarnishing his public reputation for moral virtue. Why should someone having use of a such a ring refrain from acting immorally?

Socrates tries to solve the problem by arguing that, whether they know it or not, such persons are harming the health of their immortal souls. They do so, first, in the present life, where it is essential to maintain the proper harmony between the several parts of the soul, the rational, spirited, and appetitive, the preservation of which is essential to the soul's good health, and, second, in the afterlife. Socrates again maintains that no one would voluntarily bring ruin upon themselves by deliberately choosing to harm what is most important to them. The health and harmony of their immortal souls is the most precious thing persons possess, Socrates believes, and as such it is not to be lightly exchanged for the sake of temporal values, including whatever pleasures might be afforded by misdeeds performed under cover of a magic ring. Again, we must ask whether Socrates is correct to maintain that no one freely knowingly chooses to harm themselves. For some people, however imprudently but still perhaps rationally, do indeed seem to prefer harm that will only occur later on for the sake of passing enjoyments, and may even be self-destructive in their inclination toward what is bad rather than good.

Socrates, however, persuades Meno of the truth of his thesis. They continue their exchange and Meno finally consents:

SOCRATES: Well then, those who you say desire bad things, believing that bad things harm their possessor, know that they will be harmed by them?

MENO: Necessarily.

SOCRATES: And do they not think that those who are harmed are miserable to the extent that they are harmed?

MENO: That too is inevitable.

SOCRATES: And that those who are miserable are unhappy?

MENO: I think so.

SOCRATES: Does anyone want to be miserable and unhappy?

MENO: I do not think so, Socrates.

SOCRATES: No one then wants what is bad, Meno, unless he wants to be such. For what else is being miserable but to desire bad things and secure them?

MENO: You are probably right, Socrates, and no one wants what is bad. (10–11)

The difficulty with Socrates' argument appears to be its oversimplification. If we ask in stark terms whether anyone would knowingly choose to be unhappy and miserable, then it is probably true that few if any persons would strike such a bargain. On the other hand, looking more realistically at the way in which these kinds of choices actually arise, it is seldom that we are presented with the options for happiness or unhappiness and misery in quite this way. What happens as a rule is that, even when we know the likely outcome of a given set of choices, the situation is complicated by a trade-off between the unhappiness or even misery that will probably occur and the happiness that might be purchased by exchanging later unhappiness for immediate happiness.

This undoubtedly enters into the reasoning of persons who choose to smoke cigarettes knowing the risks to their long-term health. Interestingly, the same kind of reasoning is also involved in the thinking of persons who knowingly choose short-term unhappiness for the sake of what is expected to be long-term happiness. There are many ways in which people suffer misfortune, and we cannot perfectly predict what will happen to any of us in the long run. If I enjoy cigarettes, why should I forego the pleasure, since I might after all be killed or experience ill health from other causes before the bad effects of cigarette smoking ever have a chance over time to take effect? Maybe I will be killed in a car accident before I can be afflicted with any of the diseases associated with cigarette smoking, in which case it might not be in my interest to avoid cigarettes if they truly give me pleasure. Similarly, why should I experience the displeasure of studying mathematics late into the night when I could be enjoying my time more frivolously, given that the chances of a better career and more interesting life that might obtain as a result of improving my mathematical skills might never actually be realized? If it is painful work to try to master mathematics, then why would I knowingly choose that bad experience for the sake of what might or might not ever benefit me in the unforeseen future?

Socrates builds on Meno's concessions to the previous line of argument. He refocuses attention on the definition's condition involving the desire for good things and the power to acquire them on the part of the virtuous. Socrates now points out that Men's definition of virtue as the desire for and power to acquire beautiful things is trivial if, as Meno now admits, no one knowingly chooses what is bad or harmful, and if the good is simply equated with the beautiful. Socrates, at this stage of their discussion, slips back and forth between speaking of Meno's definition as involving desire for the beautiful and desire for the good. There are unvirtuous as well as virtuous persons. If this were not true, then there would be no point to Meno's opening question as to whether virtue is learned or acquired in some other way, for it would then be the common possession of everyone. Since Meno has acknowledged that no one knowingly chooses what is harmful and in that sense bad, it follows that no one desires what is bad.

Meno's definition is trivialized by Socrates' objection, because there can be no basis for distinguishing the virtuous from the unvirtuous if we try to define the virtuous merely as *desiring* what is good. Everyone, in that case, the virtuous and unvirtuous alike, according to Socrates and in agreement with Meno, desires what is good. If beauty is what is good and all persons regardless of whether or not they are virtuous desire only the good, then virtuous and nonvirtuous persons all desire beautiful things. Then the only part of Meno's definition that could distinguish between virtuous and unvirtuous persons concerns the power to acquire rather than mere desire for beautiful things. This feature of Meno's definition now comes under Socrates' scrutiny. Socrates asks:

> SOCRATES: Were you not saying just now that virtue is to desire good things and have the power to secure them?
>
> MENO: Yes, I was.
>
> SOCRATES: The desiring part of this statement is common to everybody, and one man is no better than another in this?
>
> MENO: So it appears.
>
> SOCRATES: Clearly then, if one man is better than another, he must be better at securing them.
>
> MENO: Quite so.
>
> SOCRATES: This then is virtue according to your argument, the power of securing good things. (11)

The possession and exercise of power is the second main component in the classical character of the erotic man. The erotic man desires many things and has the power and ability to obtain them. It is part and parcel of the erotic man's life to want to surround himself with worldly possessions.

The erotic man, as the ancient Greeks understood this category of personality (and presumably the same might be said of an erotic woman with these same traits), is someone who exemplifies these characteristics to an extreme and exaggerated degree, who subordinates other values for the sake of desire and power. It is the overemphasis on these pursuits in life that makes for the particular nature of the erotic man, which Meno explicitly reveals in his attempt to define the general concept of virtue.

After further requests for clarification, Meno admits that the things for which the virtuous person strives are health and wealth, gold and silver, honors and offices in the city. Socrates does not argue against the value of such worldly pursuits, although it is easy to imagine that he regards them as ultimately unworthy. Instead, he directs his criticism to the inadequacy of the definition on its own terms. He argues that regardless of the kinds of things for which the virtuous person on Meno's definition acts to achieve, we cannot accurately define the concept of virtue simply in terms of its objects, but we must consider the way in which the virtuous person attempts to obtain these things, whether by morally acceptable or unacceptable means.

We would not call someone virtuous who desires good things, possibly as in Meno's original formulation in the form of beautiful things, but is able to obtain them only through theft and deceit. I might admire a beautiful painting, or the good and beautiful things that can be mine through health and wealth, gold and silver and offices in the city, but I will assuredly not be a virtuous person if my manner of acquiring them is by exercising my proficient skill as a swindler, con artist, or cat burglar. Socrates challenges the adequacy of this part of Meno's definition in this way:

> SOCRATES: Very well. According to Meno, the hereditary guest friend of the Great King, virtue is the acquisition of gold and silver. Do you add to this acquiring,

Meno, the words justly and piously, or does it make no difference to you but even if one secures these things unjustly, you call it virtue none the less?

MENO: Certainly not, Socrates.

SOCRATES: You would then call it wickedness?

MENO: Indeed I would.

SOCRATES: It seems then that the acquisition must be accompanied by justice or moderation or piety or some other part of virtue; if it is not, it will not be virtue, even though it provides good things.

MENO: How could there be virtue without these? (11)

At this stage of the *elenchus*, Socrates has thoroughly defeated Meno's definition. The definition is eventually presented as a definition of the sort that Socrates requires, formulated as a general definition of the general concept of virtue in general terms, like a Platonic Form. Despite having the right style, the content of Meno's definition of virtue as the desire for and power to acquire beautiful or good things in other respects gets things disastrously wrong. Socrates points out the defects of the definition by means of counterexamples, which Meno is intellectually honest enough to recognize as refuting his definition.

The upshot is that Meno has been routed in his efforts to explain the concept of virtue. Socrates had claimed at the outset of their inquiry that he could not begin to answer the question of whether virtue can be taught or is acquired in another way, because he did not even know what virtue is or how to define the concept. Meno, brash young fellow that he is, bolstered by the overconfident teachings of the sophist Gorgias into thinking he can deliver excellent sounding speeches on any topic, believes that he knows perfectly well what is meant by the concept of virtue. Socrates puts Meno to the test, and the two, after lengthy discussion, demonstrate the philosophical inadequacy of Meno's understanding. Meno unhesitatingly thought he knew what was meant by the concept of virtue, whereas Socrates had admitted his ignorance right from the start. Now, at last, Meno is in the same boat as Socrates. This is precisely the outcome that the *elenchus* is supposed to have, the final result it is meant to produce. Socrates and Meno alike are now reduced to the state of *aporia* or puzzlement, in this case about the meaning of the concept of virtue.

SOCRATES AS TORPEDO FISH

Where can the two philosophical inquirers go from here? Meno, unsurprisingly, as an erotic man and student of the sophists, attempts a rhetorical diversion. Previously in the dialogue, Socrates chastises Meno for taking unfair advantage of his youth and beauty to pressure him into answering questions that the older and by all accounts physically unattractive Socrates is unwilling to address.

Socrates, even before this point, had emphasized the difficulty in trying to say whether virtue can be taught without first knowing what virtue is, just as no one could informedly answer whether Meno was good-looking, rich and well-born, without first knowing who Meno is, by being able to identify him as an individual and distinguish him from other persons. Meno's handsome appearance is integral to the

complete portrait of the erotic man, and fits well into the discussion of whether superficial beauty as Meno thinks of it is necessarily identical with good in the sense
of moral virtue. Socrates complains:

> SOCRATES: You are outrageous, Meno. You bother an old man to answer ques-
> tions, but you yourself are not willing to recall and to tell me what Gorgias
> says that virtue is.
>
> MENO: After you have answered this, Socrates, I will tell you.
>
> SOCRATES: Even someone who was blindfolded would know from your con-
> versation that you are handsome and still have lovers.
>
> MENO: Why so?
>
> SOCRATES: Because you are forever giving orders in a discussion, as spoiled peo-
> ple do, who behave like tyrants as long as they are young. And perhaps you
> have recognized that I am at a disadvantage with handsome people, so I will
> do you the favour of an answer. (8–9)

Socrates might be concerned that Meno's beauty could become an impediment to
his discovery of philosophical truth and his setting forth on the road to moral self-
improvement. If so, he wants to put Meno on notice that he must be allowed no special privilege in their inquiry. Once Socrates has refuted Meno's best attempt to define the concept of virtue, Meno does not simply admit defeat and acknowledge with
Socrates that the true nature of virtue is more elusive than he had previously thought.
Instead, Meno attempts to derail their discussion, making it seem that there can be
no progress in efforts to discover philosophical truths. Meno tries to distract Socrates
from the question at issue by referring indirectly to the philosopher's physical appearance in one of the most famous metaphors in all of Plato's writings. He compares
Socrates to a *torpedo fish* or electric ray that stuns its prey into silence, just as Socrates
through skillful deployment of the *elenchus* has left Meno speechless concerning the
concept of virtue, which he otherwise thought he understood. Meno now portrays
himself as a victim of Socrates' dialectical prowess:

> MENO: Socrates, before I even met you I used to hear that you are always in a
> state of perplexity and that you bring others to the same state, and now I think
> you are bewitching and beguiling me, simply putting me under a spell, so that
> I am quite perplexed. Indeed, if a joke is in order, you seem, in appearance and
> in every other way, to be like the broad torpedo fish, for it too makes anyone
> who comes close and touches it feel numb, and you now seem to have had that
> kind of effect on me, for both my mind and my tongue are numb, and I have
> no answer to give you. Yet I have made many speeches about virtue before large
> audiences on a thousand occasions, very good speeches as I thought, but now I
> cannot even say what it is. I think you are wise not to sail away from Athens
> to go and stay elsewhere, for if you were to behave like this as a stranger in an-
> other city, you would be driven away for practising sorcery. (12–13)

The final sentence in Meno's remark prefigures the hostility that Socrates' practice of philosophy aroused among the people of Athens. By questioning the citizens
and exposing their false pretensions to knowledge, Meno asserts that Socrates is en-

gaged in a kind of sorcery, the consequences of which Meno indicates Socrates would do well to avoid, if necessary, by leaving the city. More importantly, Meno draws an image of Socrates as able like the torpedo fish to shock and silence his dialectical opponents. Socrates responds as follows:

> SOCRATES: You are a rascal, Meno, and you nearly deceived me.
>
> MENO: Why so particularly, Socrates?
>
> SOCRATES: I know why you drew this image of me.
>
> MENO: Why do you think I did?
>
> SOCRATES: So that I should draw an image of you in return. I know that all handsome men rejoice in images of themselves; it is to their advantage, for I think that the images of beautiful people are also beautiful, but I will draw no image of you in turn. Now if the torpedo fish is itself numb and so makes others numb, then I resemble it, but not otherwise, for I myself do not have the answer when I perplex others, but I am more perplexed than anyone I cause perplexity in others. So now I do not know what virtue is; perhaps you knew before you contacted me, but now you are certainly like one who does not know. Nevertheless, I want to examine and seek together with you what it may be. (13)

Socrates claims that he will not offer an image of Meno in return for Meno's image of him as a torpedo fish. Socrates accepts Meno's caricature of himself as a torpedo fish, but only on the condition that, unlike a real torpedo fish, he is able to stun his prey into silence because he is also unable to speak, having been numbed into silence by his own perplexity about the meaning of concepts.

Socrates believes he has uncovered Meno's ulterior motive in proposing the image of the torpedo fish, and declares that he will not do the same for Meno, which would be favorable to the handsome young Thessalian. It is not entirely clear that Socrates sticks to his resolve of not offering an image of Meno, although the image he finally presents is arguably even less flattering than the one Meno offers of Socrates.

Meno makes a purely physical comparison that emphasizes Socrates' unhandsome appearance. The image by which Socrates ironically depicts Meno in contrast is not a superficial representation of Meno's external appearance, but of Meno's soul, as that with which Socrates is generally concerned, as something deeper and more important from Socrates' perspective. The state of Meno's soul, if the interpretation is correct, is by no means in agreement with his handsome physical appearance, but suggests a perceptive diagnosis by Socrates of Meno's underlying character defects. To consider this reading of the text, we must first see how the rest of Plato's dialogue plays out, in order to understand the hidden image of Meno about which Socrates offers only implicit hints.

SOLUTION TO THE SOPHIST'S DILEMMA

After drawing an image of Socrates as a torpedo fish, Meno attempts another trick. He proposes a *sophist's dilemma*, typical of the sophists' rhetorical devices, undermining the use of dialectic as a method of searching for truth, while raising skeptical doubts about the possibility of knowledge. Meno's dilemma posits two choices, both of which lead to the conclusion that acquiring knowledge is impossible. Meno presents the dilemma in the following terms, when he says to Socrates, concerning the correct definition of virtue:

> MENO: How will you look for it, Socrates, when you do not know at all what it is? How will you aim to search for something you do not know at all? If you should meet with it, how will you know that this is the thing that you did not know? (13)

The structure of Meno's argument is this. Either we already know or we do not already know that which we seek to know. If we already know that which we seek to know, then we cannot acquire knowledge of it, because, as a logical or conceptual thesis, we cannot acquire what we already have. This certainly seems correct. If Meno already owns a particular tunic, then he cannot acquire it, since he can only acquire something he does not already possess. If, on the other hand, we do not already know that which we seek to know, then once again we cannot acquire it, Meno claims, because in that case we will not know what to look for, and we will not be able to recognize it even if we should happen to encounter it by accident.

Socrates is by no means intimidated by Meno's ploy. Meno tries to undermine further inquiry, to which Socrates offers a complex reply consisting of several parts. Socrates refers to Meno's dilemma as a debater's argument, thereby referring to the sophists' penchant for trying to make the weaker position appear stronger and the stronger position appear weaker. Socrates sees through Meno's strategy:

> SOCRATES: I know what you want to say, Meno. Do you realize what a debater's argument you are bringing up, that a man cannot search either for what he knows or for what he does not know? He cannot search for what he knows—since he know it, there is no need to search—nor for what he does not know, for he does not know what to look for.
>
> MENO: Does that argument not seem sound to you, Socrates?
>
> SOCRATES: Not to me.
>
> MENO: Can you tell me why? (13)

When confronted with a *dilemma*, we have three choices. We can either: (1) accept the dilemma's conclusion; (2) grasp one of the *horns* of the dilemma, by arguing that although the two choices presented by the dilemma seem to lead to the same undesirable conclusion, they do not actually do so or we can somehow live with at least one of the possibilities; or (3) we can go between the horns of the dilemma, by arguing that the dilemma actually constitutes a false set of alternatives, that there is a third way to go in addition to the two possibilities misleadingly indicated as the only available choices.

Considering Meno's sophist's dilemma or debater's argument, for Socrates to adopt response (1) would amount to his agreeing with Meno that it is impossible under any circumstances to acquire knowledge. Socrates' reply above already indicates that he does not accept this alternative, but proposes instead to overturn the dilemma. Socrates does not attempt to go between the horns of Meno's dilemma by suggesting a third alternative as in response (3). It seems in any case that Socrates would be hard-pressed to accept this manner of dealing with the dilemma, because the dilemma seems to be based on what logicians sometimes refer to as an *excluded middle* of logically mutually exclusive and logically mutually exhaustive alternatives. The dilemma depends on the logical truth that either we already know or we do not already know that which we seek to know. What third choice could there be, and what possibility for going between the horns of such a logically tight dilemma?

Socrates argues instead in line with response type (2) that we can grasp one of the horns in order to solve the sophist's dilemma. But which one? Socrates invokes the authority of priests and priestesses, religious practitioners, and poets, in overcoming Meno's skeptical argument. He continues:

> SOCRATES: The speakers were among the priests and priestesses whose care it
> is to be able to give an account of their practices. Pindar too says it, and many
> other of the divine among our poets. What they say is this; see whether you
> think they speak the truth: They say that the human soul is immortal; at times
> it comes to an end, which they call dying, at times it is reborn, but it is never
> destroyed, and one must therefore live one's life as piously as possible:

> *Persephone will return to the sun above in the ninth year*
> *the souls of those from whom*
> *she will exact punishment for old miseries,*
> *and from these come noble kings,*
> *mighty in strength and greatest in wisdom,*
> *and for the rest of time men will call them sacred heroes.*

> As the soul is immortal, has been born often and has seen all things here and
> in the underworld, there is nothing which it has not learned; so it is in no way
> surprising that it can recollect the things it knew before, both about virtue and
> other things. As the whole of nature is akin, and the soul has learned every-
> thing, nothing prevents a man, after recalling one thing only—a process men
> call learning—discovering everything else for himself, if he is brave and does
> not tire of the search, for searching and learning are, as a whole, recollection.
> We must, therefore, not believe that debater's argument, for it would make
> us idle, and fainthearted men like to hear it, whereas my argument makes
> them energetic and keen on the search. I trust that this is true, and I want to
> inquire along with you into the nature of virtue. (13–14)

Socrates' solution has two parts. He grasps the horn of Meno's dilemma according to which we already know that which we seek to know. Socrates in effect admits that when we inquire into the general concepts we want to investigate we do in fact already know the meaning of the concept. The soul, Socrates maintains, has prior perfect knowledge of the Platonic Forms or Ideas, the general concepts, including the concept of virtue.

By grasping this horn of the dilemma, Socrates argues that to accept the alternative is in some sense and for some reason unobjectionable. He maintains that, although we already know that which we seek to know, our knowledge is locked away as a permanent possession of our immortal souls, and therefore, although knowledge cannot be acquired, it does not need to be because we already have it.

The soul, Socrates believes, goes through numerous reincarnations, births, deaths, and rebirths, and through it all retains its knowledge of the Forms. What we call searching for knowledge of a Form such as the general concept of virtue for Socrates is therefore a matter of memory or recollection. We already know what virtue is, in a sense, because the knowledge is hidden away in our souls; we only need to be reminded of what the concept means. Such recollection can be accomplished, perhaps among other methods, through a process of dialectical inquiry in which we are stimulated to recall the right answer by the questions of an enlightened teacher. This is how Socrates understands the purpose of philosophical inquiry. It is not a matter of acquiring something we do not already have, but of rediscovering something we already have and recalling it from the depths of our faulty memories into present awareness. Socrates as a result is often described as accepting an *anamnesis* or recollection theory of knowledge.

Additionally, Socrates offers what is sometimes called a *pragmatic* or action-related reason for resisting the sophist's dilemma. He argues that if we agree to the inference, then we will become lazy instead of searching energetically for the truth. Socrates interprets this effort as an attempt to recall or recollect our hidden knowledge of the meaning of general concepts, such as the concept of virtue, the understanding of which Socrates and Meno had first set out to discover. This is a curious reason for Socrates to endorse, because it seems to imply that there is a reason for us to believe that knowledge about general concepts can be recovered from memory even if were not true that we could. It is almost as though Socrates is saying that we should pretend that we can recall knowledge of the Forms because of the benefits conferred by maintaining that belief, keeping us from being "idle" and "fainthearted." But why should we not be idle and fainthearted with respect to philosophical inquiry, if Meno is right to conclude as the result of his sophist's dilemma that inquiry into the meanings of general concepts is ultimately futile? Why should we try to fool ourselves about such an important matter, and why should we waste our energy if there is no real prospect of succeeding? Why, moreover, should we accept the myths and legends about the immortality of the soul on which Socrates bases his recollection theory of knowledge? Can Socrates hope to answer Meno's logic on such a shaky foundation as religious belief in the immortality of the soul, as reported by priests and priestesses and poets? How can such an article of faith possibly provide an adequate philosophical foundation for something as vital to Socrates' philosophy as the pursuit of knowledge?

The answer is that Socrates does not rely on religious belief as an article of faith in the immortality of the soul in order to answer the sophist's dilemma. He merely introduces the *anamnesis* theory of knowledge by referring to poetically expressed religious doctrines. True to his philosophical methods, Socrates offers an argument for this conclusion that he is pleased to note agrees with religious traditions about the soul's immortality. Socrates' next move in his exchange with Meno is to argue that the soul is immortal and that it contains unchanging permanent knowledge of Platonic Forms.

Meno's Slave and Socrates' Geometry Lesson

Socrates' attempt to prove that the soul is immortal is one of the most exciting but also controversial parts of Plato's dialogue. The possibility of demonstrating that the soul is immortal is a remarkable proposition, and therefore one that must be examined with the greatest care. If Socrates is right, then he will have established one of the most important conclusions that could ever be imagined as part of any philosophical system. If, on the other hand, Socrates' effort to prove the immortality of the soul on philosophical grounds fails, then so does his solution to Meno's sophist's dilemma. At stake is the possibility of knowledge versus skepticism, if there is no better way of answering Meno's dilemma.

Socrates adopts a curious method. He proposes to prove that the soul is immortal by conducting an interview about a geometry problem with one of Meno's slaves. The slave, Meno testifies, was raised in his household and knows Greek, but has never studied mathematics. Socrates questions the boy about a theorem of geometry, helping him to discover the length of a line by which the area of a square is doubled. Socrates instructs Meno to pay attention to whether the slave boy seems to be recalling the truth of the theorem, or is being taught the theorem by Socrates in the course of their discussion. Socrates' geometry lesson is supposed to prove that Meno's slave has geometrical knowledge prior to any experience, since according to Meno the boy has never been taught mathematics. Socrates supposedly does not instruct the boy, but elicits the right answers from him by asking pertinent questions and correcting his mistaken replies until the boy grasps the solution. It seems, if Socrates is right, that the slave boy knew geometry all along, but did not know that he knew it; in a way, the knowledge is buried and forgotten deep inside him, awakened by Socrates' questions, just as Socrates' *anamnesis* theory of knowledge implies. Socrates begins his conversation with Meno's slave:

> SOCRATES: Tell me now, boy, you know that a square figure is like this?
>
> SLAVE: I do.
>
> SOCRATES: A square then is a figure in which all these four sides are equal?
>
> SLAVE: Yes indeed.
>
> SOCRATES: And it also has these lines through the middle equal?
>
> SLAVE: Yes.
>
> SOCRATES: And such a figure could be larger or smaller?
>
> SLAVE: Certainly. (14–15)

If we imagine Socrates drawing figures in the sand with a stick, he is asking Meno's slave about the observable properties of the diagram of a square shown in Figure 1.1.

After Socrates familiarizes the slave boy with some of the terminology for describing the basic properties of a square, he invites the boy to consider how to construct a square of twice the area as the original square. Meno, in the meantime, is supposed to be observing what transpires between Socrates and the slave, judging for himself whether Socrates is teaching the boy geometrical truths or merely soliciting opinions from him and checking his answers for truth or falsehood, and guiding him to the right solution. Socrates next asks Meno's slave:

> SOCRATES: Now we could have another figure twice the size of this one, with the four sides equal like this one.

SLAVE: Yes.

SOCRATES: How many feet will that be?

SLAVE: Eight.

SOCRATES: Come now, try to tell me how long each side of this will be. The side of this is two feet. What about each side of the one which is its double?

SLAVE: Obviously, Socrates, it will be twice the length. (15)

Meno's slave guesses incorrectly. Socrates asks the boy what the length of a square must be in order to double the area of a given square. The boy thinks, reasonably enough, despite arriving at the wrong answer, that to double the area of a square one simply doubles the length of its side. This method, doubling the length of the sides of a square, produces a square that is too large for a square that is supposed to have only twice the area. Socrates turns from the boy with this remark to Meno:

SOCRATES: You see, Meno, that I am not teaching the boy anything, but all I do is question him. And now he thinks he knows the length of the line on which an eight-foot figure is based. Do you agree?

MENO: I do.

SOCRATES: And does he know?

MENO: Certainly not.

SOCRATES: He thinks it is a line twice the length?

MENO: Yes. (15–16)

This passage does not immediately seem particularly important, but it is central in understanding Socrates' method and answering an objection that is often raised against Socrates' conclusions in this part of the dialogue. Socrates is sometimes said not to elicit any knowledge already present in the slave's soul, but to give away the answers, asking leading questions and more or less putting the answers in the boy's mouth. It is nevertheless clear from the exchange at this point that Socrates cannot be doing this, because otherwise the slave boy would not have produced a false solution. Socrates knows the right answer, so if he had simply been teaching the boy geometry, presumably the boy would not have erred. The boy's mistake indicates that

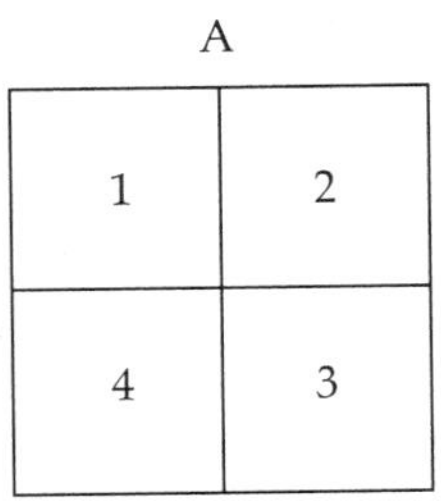

Side of Square A = 2
Area of Square A = $2^2 = 4$

FIGURE 1.1 Socrates' Square A

he is proceeding in response to Socrates' questions by his own light and using his own judgment.

The geometry lesson concludes when Socrates' further questions the slave about these answers. First, Socrates shows that it is incorrect to double the length of the side of a square in order to obtain a square with twice the area, since in the case of an original square with side length 2, doubling its length to 4 produces a square with an area of $4 \times 4 = 16$, whereas the area of a square twice as large as the original square should only have an area of 8. Since doubling the length of the square's side produces a square that is too large in area, the boy infers that the length is between 2 and 4, and guesses that it must be 3. Socrates reminds the boy that this is also wrong, because it produces a square with area of $3 \times 3 = 9$. 9 is closer to 8 than 16, but still not the right answer. Finally, Socrates draws the diagonals of the inside square of the figure with sides of length 2, and by questioning the boy permits him to see for himself that the way to double the area of the square is to take its diagonal as the side length for the enlarged figure. Socrates continues, dividing his attention between Meno and the boy:

> SOCRATES: Watch him now recollecting things in order, as one must recollect. Tell me, boy, do you say that a figure double the size is based on a line double the length? Now I mean such a figure as this, not long on one side and short on the other, but equal in every direction like this one, and double the size, that is, eight feet. See whether you still believe that it will be based on a line double the length.
>
> SLAVE: I do.
>
> SOCRATES: Now the line becomes double its length if we add another of the same length here?
>
> SLAVE: Yes indeed.
>
> SOCRATES: And the eight-foot square will be based on it, if there are four lines of that length?
>
> SLAVE: Yes.
>
> SOCRATES: Well, let us draw from it four equal lines, and surely that is what you say is the eight-foot square?
>
> SLAVE: Certainly.
>
> SOCRATES: How big is it then? Is it not four times as big?
>
> SLAVE: Of course.
>
> SOCRATES: Is this square then, which is four times as big, its double?
>
> SLAVE: No, by Zeus. (16)

The boy suggests the way of doubling the area of Square A shown in Figure 1.2, which, of course, makes the resulting square much too big. Socrates verifies to his own satisfaction yet again that the boy is answering from the standpoint of his own understanding of the concepts about which he is being questioned. He wants to make

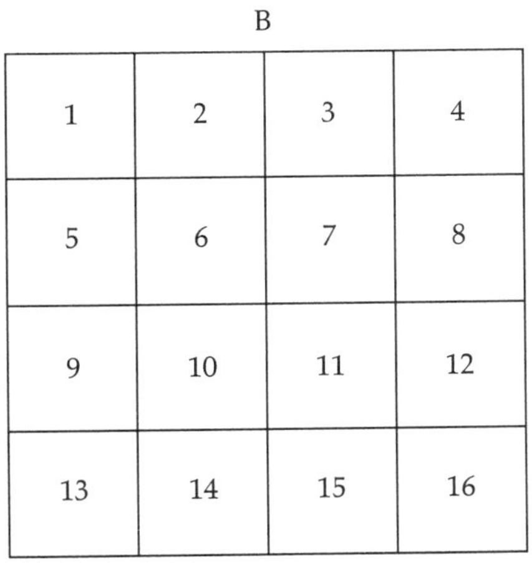

B

1	2	3	4
5	6	7	8
9	10	11	12
13	14	15	16

Side of Square B = $2 \times 2 = 4$
Area of Square B = $4^2 = 16$

FIGURE 1.2 Slave boy's first guess about how to double the area of Square A

sure that the boy is not simply repeating things he has told him, using short-term memory to indicate a grasp of the information about which he has just been instructed. The important point for Socrates' purposes is not whether or how soon Meno's slave gets the right answer, but that he answers the questions he is posed at each stage entirely according to his own opinions, searching his thoughts for what he believes to be true.

Having wrongly guessed that the answer must be to double the length of the square, Meno's slave, realizing that he has suggested a way of making too large a square, now assumes that the answer should be 3, as shown in Figure 1.3. Socrates and the boy try again:

SOCRATES: Good, you answer what you think. And tell me, was this one not two feet long, and that one four feet?

SLAVE: Yes.

SOCRATES: Try to tell me then how long a line you say it is.

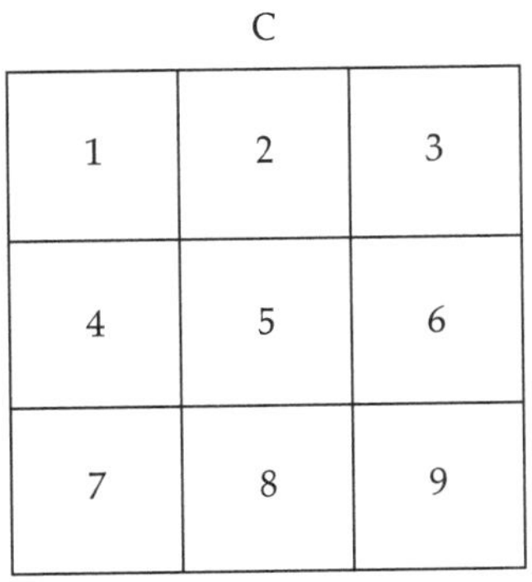

C

1	2	3
4	5	6
7	8	9

Side of Square C = 3
Area of Square C = $3^2 = 9$

FIGURE 1.3 Slave boy's second guess about how to double the area of Square A

SLAVE: Three feet.

SOCRATES: Then if it is three feet, let us add the half of this one, and it will be three feet? For these are two feet, and the other is one. And here, similarly, comes to be?

SLAVE: Yes.

SOCRATES: Now if it is three feet this way and three feet that way, will the whole figure be three times three feet?

SLAVE: So it seems.

SOCRATES: How much is three times three feet?

SLAVE: Nine feet.

SOCRATES: And the double square was to be how many feet?

SLAVE: Eight.

SOCRATES: So the eight-foot figure cannot be based on the three-foot line?

SLAVE: Clearly not. (16–17)

It does not appear that the slave boy is not just trying to please Socrates by answering what he believes Socrates wants to hear. The reason is that he provides intuitively correct answers and has good reasons for rejecting his previous opinions. The boy knows that the answer cannot be to double the length of the side of the square, because that would produce too big a square. Similarly when he guesses that the length of side needed to double the area of the original square should be the next smallest whole number, 3. The boy easily sees, once Socrates calls attention to the implications of his proposal, that the answer also cannot be 3. The boy can see from his own understanding that 9 is still too big, still greater than the required area of 8, so he knows without simply being taught the answer that the right length has yet to be found.

Socrates asks Meno to take stock of the exchange he has had with the slave boy. Meno, from his vantage point, has been observing things carefully and should be able to judge what happened. Socrates remarks that the boy does not yet have the right answer, but that he has made some progress in having clarified the problem and set aside the incorrect possibilities that had first occurred to him. Socrates summarizes their discussion in the following terms:

SOCRATES: You realize, Meno, what point he has reached in his recollection. At first he did not know what the basic line of the eight-foot square was; even now he does not yet know, but then he thought he knew, and answered confidently as if he did know, and he did not think himself at a loss, but now he does think himself a loss, and he does not know, neither does he think he knows.

MENO: That is true.

SOCRATES: So he is now in a better position with regard to the matter he does not know?

MENO: I agree with that too. (17)

Socrates makes it clear that he regards his conversation with Meno's slave boy as a small-scale application of the same exchange he has previously had with Meno, in undertaking the method of *elenchus*. The clue is explicit when Socrates refers in the same terms Meno had previously used in his image of Socrates as a torpedo fish.

Socrates now reminds Meno that in refuting the slave boy's attempts to answer the mathematical problem, leaving him with nothing to say, he has been silenced in much the same way that Meno has already complained of when Socrates numbed Meno by refuting Meno's misguided efforts to define the general concept of virtue. Socrates' geometry lesson with Meno's slave is thus a miniature version of his *elenchus* examination of the idea of virtue with Meno. Interestingly, Meno, who seems a bit thick in this regard, does not see the parallel, and draws no direct conclusions about his previous discussion with Socrates. Could it be that Socrates, despite his disclaimer, is offering an image of Meno after all in return for Meno's image of Socrates as a torpedo fish? Is Socrates hinting that Meno himself is also a kind of slave? Socrates asks, concerning Meno's slave:

SOCRATES: Have we done him any harm by making him perplexed and numb as the torpedo fish does?

MENO: I do not think so. (17)

The path of Socratic *maieutic* or moral self-improvement is indicated by Socrates in this passage. Again, Meno does not seem to grasp the parallels between Socrates' discussion with the slave boy and his own case. Socrates has worn down the slave boy's *hubris* or inflated self-confidence, and the boy now realizes that he does not know what he thought he knew. Thus, unlike Meno in some ways, he is ready to learn. Meno agrees that this is true of the boy, but does not remember that only a few minutes before he had been put in precisely the same situation. By contrast, at this stage of his discussion with Socrates, instead of being receptive to the truth, Meno tries instead to block Socrates' inquiry by likening Socrates to a torpedo fish and raising the sophist's dilemma. Socrates stays focused on resolving the dilemma and persuading Meno that it is worthwhile to continue investigating the concept of virtue. Now Socrates says with biting irony to which Meno seems oblivious:

SOCRATES: Indeed, we have probably achieved something relevant to finding out how matters stand, for now, as he does not know, he would be glad to find out, whereas before he thought he could easily make many fine speeches to large audiences about the square of double size and said that it must have a base twice as long.

MENO: So it seems.

SOCRATES: Do you think that before he would have tried to find out that which he thought he knew though he did not, before he fell into perplexity and realized he did not know and longed to know?

MENO: I do not think so, Socrates.

SOCRATES: Has he then benefitted from being numbed?

MENO: I think so. (17)

Socrates promises to help lead Meno's slave out of his perplexity about the geometry problem. He declares again his intention not to teach the boy, but only to ask him what he thinks in considering how to double the area of a square:

> SOCRATES: Look then how he will come out of his perplexity while searching along with me. I shall do nothing more than ask questions and not teach him. Watch whether you find me teaching and explaining things to him instead of asking for his opinion. (17)

During the course of their discussion, Socrates, in the same manner we have already seen him follow in philosophical conversation with the boy up to this point and with Meno in his earlier use of the *elenchus*, eventually suggests to Meno's slave that the diagonal of the square if taken as the side of another square will exactly double the area of the original square. The idea is presented in this form, when Socrates remarks:

> SOCRATES: That is, on the line that stretches from corner to corner of the four-foot figure?
>
> SLAVE: Yes.
>
> SOCRATES: Clever men call this the diagonal, so that if diagonal is its name, you say that the double figure would be that based on the diagonal?
>
> SLAVE: Most certainly, Socrates. (19)

The final diagram that Socrates and Meno's slave consider might look something like Figure 1.4. The original Square A is represented in bold lines, and its diagonal is taken as the length of the side of a new square, D, constructed with the diagonal of A as the length of its four sides. We can easily determine visually that two of the smaller internal triangles put together will equal in area the area of one of the component four squares of the original Square A. When we add them all together in the new Square D, we see that there are 8, which is precisely double the area of original

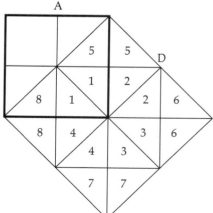

Side of Square D $= 2\sqrt{2}$

Area of Square D $= (2\sqrt{2})^2 = 2^2 \times \sqrt{2}^2 = 4 \times 2 = 8$

FIGURE 1.4 Diagonal method of doubling the area of Square A

Square A. Thus, the diagonal of a square is the correct answer to the length of side needed to construct another triangle with twice its area. This is one way to represent the new square and number its component internal triangles in order to demonstrate that Square D is twice the size of Square A.

It is worth remarking that the diagonal of a unit square is an irrational length. Without special knowledge of this fact of mathematics, it is not surprising that Meno's slave does not know of the right number for doubling the area of a square, for he has no reason to expect the existence of such a peculiar length between 3 and 2. He might, if he were very clever, begin to make guesses about rational fractions between those values, but irrational numbers reportedly came as a shock to even the most mathematically sophisticated among the ancient Greeks. Pythagoras or his school is said to have discovered irrationals as a consequence of the famous Pythagorean theorem for determining the length of the hypotenuse of a right-angled triangle. If the sides of such a triangle are labeled "a" and "b," and the hypotenuse is labeled "c," then the Pythagorean theorem states that $a^2 + b^2 = c^2$. Where the sides of Square A are all 2, the theorem implies for the length of the diagonal of A that $2^2 + 2^2 = c^2$, so that $c^2 = 8$, from which it follows algebraically that $c = \sqrt{8} = \sqrt{4 \times 2} = 2\sqrt{2}$, which we know is an irrational number.

At this stage, Socrates is finally positioned to answer Meno's dilemma about the impossibility of acquiring knowledge. Knowledge in the true sense of the word concerns eternal truths about the Forms of things, as opposed to their particular many appearances in the world of sensation. They are like the truths of mathematics, which do not become true, nor change from being true to false or false to true at any given time as a result of changes in the physical world. The soul has knowledge of such things as a permanent possession from the time before its embodiment in a particular human body, and therefore has no need to acquire it. Socrates returns to the problem he had earlier been discussing with Meno:

> SOCRATES: What do you think, Meno? Has he [the slave boy], in his answers, expressed any opinion that was not his own?
>
> MENO: No, they were all his own.
>
> SOCRATES: And yet, as we said a short time ago, he did not know?
>
> MENO: That is true. (19)

Thus ends Socrates' geometry lesson. There is nevertheless more to say about the full implications of what transpires in his exchange with Meno's slave. We have yet to see what conclusions can be drawn from the boy's slow-going recognition of the mathematical principle that Socrates has patiently tried to help him understand.

Again, what is crucial for Socrates, and Meno apparently agrees, is that, although Socrates in the end must finally show the boy what is meant by a diagonal and walk him step-by-step through the explanation that enables him to see that taking the diagonal of a square as the side of a new square produces a square with double the original square's area, the boy recognizes the truth of the conclusion and somehow intuits that the answer is correct. Socrates does not simply give the boy a formula to memorize as the right answer and then test him to see if he later remembers it correctly. What happens instead, if Socrates and Meno have understood the situation properly, is that Meno's slave with his own insight comes to the conclusion that Socrates' explanation concerning the diagonal of a square solves the problem of how to double its area must be right. There is, so to speak, a kind of fit between the solution Socrates suggests and something in the boy's soul, a satisfying feeling like a piece of a puzzle snapping exactly into place that indicates the boy's recognition of truth.

KNOWLEDGE AND CORRECT OPINION

The beauty of this part of the dialogue is that now that Socrates has finished questioning Meno's slave boy, eliciting a correct geometrical intuition from him, he applies the same method to Meno. Socrates and Meno are not directly interested in geometry, but in the problems they were previously discussing, concerning the concept of virtue and the question of whether virtue can be taught.

Socrates distinguishes between genuine knowledge and correct opinion. For him, knowledge concerns eternal truths, like the abstract truths of mathematics. So-called "knowledge" about matters of fact, as we ordinarily think of it, for example, that Elizabeth II is the queen of England, do not constitute genuine knowledge for Socrates, because they are changeable. Elizabeth II was not always the queen of England, and eventually she will no longer be the queen. Knowledge in the true sense of the word for Socrates can only be about what is unchanging, fixed, and certain. It concerns only the Forms, the ideal essences of things, the kinds of ideas common to particular instances of a general category that he wants Meno to identify in the search for a philosophically satisfactory definition of such concepts as virtue. Socrates believes that the immortal soul, before it is embodied in human shape, has perfect knowledge of eternal Forms by direct acquaintance with them. In Plato's *Republic*, Socrates indicates that the soul before it is born may drink from Lethe, the river of forgetfulness in ancient Greek mythology, causing its perfect knowledge to be obscured by a dimmed memory.

Socrates also invokes a popular myth about the statues of Daedalus. Daedalus was an artisan and military engineer in antiquity who designed siege vehicles for the Greek army, and, according to later legend, constructed wings to fly with feathers attached by wax. He and his son Icarus were supposed to have flown from a high cliffside, but Icarus flew too near the sun, the wax melted, and he fell into the sea and perished. Daedalus was a distant relative of Socrates', and his statues were said to be so lifelike that they would run away if they were not chained in place. Socrates claims that knowledge is like one of Daedalus's statues, valuable only if chained down or anchored by reason or justification.

To see the difference between correct opinion and what Socrates means by knowledge, consider that if we go to a fortune teller, we might learn that we will meet a tall stranger. If we believe that the fortune teller knows the future, then we might as a result acquire the belief that we will meet a tall stranger. Now suppose that we actually do meet a tall stranger. In that case, our belief is also true. Most people would urge that a true belief under the circumstances still does not constitute knowledge, because we had no reason or justification for it, on the grounds that fortune tellers do not really know the future, and their predictions are just sideshow hocus-pocus. Correct opinion that falls short of knowledge is like an unchained statue of Daedalus, fleeting, lacking in solid reasons, warrant, or justification for true belief. We can believe what happens to be true, but without good reasons to support the belief, we do not yet know.

Socrates disposes of the sophist's dilemma by convincing Meno that genuine knowledge in the sense of unchanging truths about the eternal forms is not and does not need to be acquired, but is a permanent possession of the immortal soul. Meno's slave boy's answers to Socrates' questions in the geometry lesson do not yet constitute knowledge, but only right opinion. Socrates maintains that if the boy's correct opinions were sufficiently reinforced over time they would amount to genuine knowledge. For eventually the boy would arrive at the point of having warrant or justification for his correct opinion, in effect tying down the statues of Daedalus with good reasons for accepting the geometrical beliefs that Socrates' questions and corrections of mistaken answers have helped him to intuit. The boy's correct opinion can be transformed into knowledge, if he can later provide his own justification for them.

The immediate point of interest for Socrates and Meno, looking back to the point of their discussion when they became sidetracked by Meno's attempt to interpose the sophist's dilemma, is that the slave boy's correct opinions about the geometry theorem were already "in" him, called up from the depths of his soul's innate memory by Socrates' prodding questions. Socrates and Meno pick up the thread of their discussion in this way:

SOCRATES: So these opinions were in him, were they not?

MENO: Yes.

SOCRATES: So the man who does not know has within himself true opinions about the things that he does not know?

MENO: So it appears.

SOCRATES: These opinions have now just been stirred up like a dream, but if he were repeatedly asked these same questions in various ways, you know that in the end his knowledge about these things would be as accurate as anyone's.

MENO: It is likely.

SOCRATES: And is not finding knowledge within oneself recollection?

MENO: Certainly.

SOCRATES: Must he not either have at some time acquired the knowledge he now possesses, or else have always possessed it?

MENO: Yes.

SOCRATES: If he always had it, he would always have known. If he acquired it, he cannot have done so in his present life. Or has someone taught him geometry? For he will perform in the same way about all geometry, and all other knowledge. Has someone taught him everything? You should know, especially as he has been born and brought up in your house.

MENO: But I know that no one has taught him.

SOCRATES: Yet he has these opinions, or doesn't he? (19)

Socrates draws what he seems to believe is the only possible explanation of the fact that Meno's slave has correct opinions that he has not been taught. If he did not acquire the information through instruction, then, Socrates reasons and Meno agrees, the boy must have imbibed an understanding of geometry in a previous life, at a time when his immortal soul was not yet embodied in human form. It is a startling conclusion, which Socrates suddenly but confidently presents as an unavoidable implication of his conversation with Meno's slave:

MENO: That seems indisputable, Socrates.

SOCRATES: If he has not acquired them in his present life, is it not clear that he had them and had learned them at some other time?

MENO: It seems so.

SOCRATES: Then that was the time he exists and is not a human being?

MENO: Yes.

SOCRATES: If then, during the time he exists and is not a human being he will have true opinions which, when stirred by questioning, become knowledge, will not his soul have learned during all time? For it is clear that during all time he exists, either as a man or not.

MENO: So it seems. (19–20)

If Socrates and Meno correctly interpret the moral of Socrates' geometry lesson with Meno's slave, then Socrates has established several remarkable conclusions. He proves the immortality of the soul and he answers the sophist's dilemma by grasping the horn of the dilemma according to which we already know that which we seek to know.

Socrates avoids skepticism by claiming that we do not need to acquire new knowledge about general concepts such as virtue. As the interview with Meno's slave boy is supposed to prove, we already have the only kind of knowledge it is possible to have, which is knowledge of the Forms, including mathematical principles and general concepts such as virtue, justice, beauty, truth, and the like, as a permanent possession of our immortal souls. All that is required is to have the memory of the sought-for knowledge "stirred" by the right sort of questions, in order to bring the knowledge into conscious awareness.

This awakening of knowledge is evidently a rather difficult matter, as judged by the fact that even Socrates, who is at least by his own testimony embarked on the right course of inquiry for discovering the meaning of general concepts, in trying to get in touch with the necessary and jointly sufficient conditions required for understanding and correctly defining the Forms, cannot explain what virtue means. Socrates' ironic sense of wisdom consists in knowing at least that he does not know, which is to say that he is unable to articulate the relevant definitions, despite his belief that the knowledge also resides deep within his soul, as a part of his hidden memory that is only waiting to be recollected to consciousness. Socrates concludes:

SOCRATES: Then if the truth about reality is always in our soul, the soul would be immortal so that you should always confidently try to seek out and recollect what you do not know at present—that is, what you do not recollect? (20)

Socrates finally answers Meno's dilemma. He provides a good reason to continue the inquiry into the concept of virtue that he and Meno had previously undertaken, but which Meno thought might be pointless if for logical reasons it turned out to be impossible to acquire knowledge. Socrates admits that we cannot acquire knowledge, but only because, as the first horn of the dilemma states, we do not need to do so because we already have knowledge as a permanent possession.

What is needed, then, is what Socrates describes as a diligent effort, not to acquire knowledge that we lack, but to recollect or remember or recall the knowledge that is already warehoused in our souls, in our deeply hidden memories. There is a definite purpose to the inquiry into general concepts such as those Socrates investigates in the *elenchus*, including the general concept of virtue which he and Meno had begun to explore. They can meaningfully return to the investigation at this point, with a clearer understanding of the nature of their task. Socrates, however, has already admitted that he does not know what virtue is, presumably, as we now see, in the sense of not being able readily to recall to immediate awareness the definition or necessary and sufficient conditions for virtue. If Socrates' immortal soul knows what virtue is, Socrates the man nevertheless cannot put it into words.

Hypothetical Inquiry and the Geometer's Method

What, then, are Socrates and Meno to do? Socrates maintains that he cannot directly answer Meno's question whether virtue can be taught unless he first knows what virtue is, which, in the appropriate sense, he admits he does not know. Further, Socrates removes the possibility of evading the difficult work of trying to understand the concept of virtue which the sophist's dilemma might have afforded. Surprisingly, at least in the present context in which he is discussing the problem in company with Meno, Socrates does not propose to dig deeper into his memory and try to dredge up an adequate definition of the concept of virtue. Instead, he recommends a different approach, which he refers to as the geometer's method. Socrates' proposal appears in the following lengthy discussion with Meno:

> SOCRATES: If I were directing you, Meno, and not only myself, we would not have investigated whether virtue is teachable or not before we had investigated what virtue itself is. But because you do not even attempt to rule yourself, in order that you may be free, but you try to rule me and do so, I will agree with you—for what can I do? So we must, it appears, inquire into the qualities of something the nature of which we do not yet know. However, please relax your rule a little bit for me and agree to investigate whether it is teachable or not by means of a hypothesis. I mean the way geometers often carry on their investigations. For example, if they are asked whether a specific area can be inscribed in the form of a triangle within a given circle, one of them might say: "I do not yet know whether that area has that property, but I think I have, as it were, a hypothesis that is of use for the problem, namely this: If that area is such that when one has applied it as a rectangle to the given straight line in the circle it is deficient by a figure similar to the very figure which is applied, then I think one alternative results, whereas another results if it is impossible for this to happen. So, by using this hypothesis, I am will-

ing to tell you what results with regard to inscribing it in the circle—that is, whether it is impossible or not." So let us speak about virtue also, since we do not know either what it is or what qualities it possesses, and let us investigate whether it is teachable or not by means of a hypothesis, and say this: Among the things existing in the soul, of what sort is virtue, that it should be teachable or not? First, if it is another sort than knowledge, is it teachable or not, as we were just saying, recollectable? Or is it plain to anyone that men cannot be taught anything but knowledge?

MENO: I think so. (20–21)

The *geometer's method* that Socrates proposes to follow in trying to answer Meno's question whether virtue can be taught has the following structure. In mathematics when we do not know whether a certain mathematical entity has a certain property, we can entertain the hypothesis that it does in order to see what follows from the assumption. If the assumption entails consequences that we can determine are not satisfied, then we can at least know that the hypothesis or assumption is false, which is significant progress in understanding the entity's properties. Socrates gives a good example in the passage above, which we need not repeat. The application of the hypothetical method to the problem of whether virtue can be taught is similar. Socrates offers a hypothesis concerning the nature of virtue and the conditions under which it might turn out to be teachable. He begins in this way:

SOCRATES: But, if virtue is a kind of knowledge, it is clear that it could be taught.

MENO: Of course.

SOCRATES: We have dealt with that question quickly, that if it is of one kind it can be taught, if it is of a different kind, it cannot.

MENO: We have indeed.

SOCRATES: The next point to consider seems to be whether virtue is knowledge or something else.

MENO: That does seem to be the next point to consider.

SOCRATES: Well now, do we say that virtue is itself something good, and will this hypothesis stand firm for us, that it is something good?

MENO: Of course. (21)

The hypothesis by which Socrates hopes to gain leverage on Meno's question whether virtue can be taught or is acquired in some other way, is to say that *if* virtue is a kind of knowledge, *then* it can be taught. This seems reasonable enough, especially if we take into consideration Socrates' assumption that the type of knowledge under which virtue is considered is, in Greek, a *techné*, which is to say a skill that can be reduced to a formulaic recipe or step-by-step method that, if we follow its prescriptions, will result in proficiency. It is in this sense, for example, that knowing how to bake a soufflé, play the guitar, or perform a certain judo or karate move is something that can be known, a skill to be mastered by virtually anyone who puts the requisite principles into practice and makes the necessary effort. If virtue is a *techné*, then, as Socrates hypothesizes, it is something that can be taught. Meno agrees, and from this common basis, the two move forward toward a more elaborate sequence of inferences that is meant to shed light on the nature of virtue as teachable or unteachable.

We shall not try to track every fine point in Socrates' and Meno's consideration of the hypothetical method. They apply the hypothesis to the question of whether virtue can be taught, whether virtue is in whole or in part wisdom, and whether or not it is something beneficial. Socrates in any case is quick to eliminate the alternative possibility that virtue might be a quality had by certain persons by nature. We might say in contemporary terms that some people are virtuous because of genetics, possessing the right sort of chromosomes to be virtuous rather than unvirtuous. This possibility Socrates discounts by means of an interesting but not especially convincing proof. Socrates reasons that if virtue is wisdom, then it cannot be possessed by nature. He maintains that:

SOCRATES: Then, if that is so, the good are not so by nature?

MENO: I do not think they are.

SOCRATES: For if they were, this would follow: if the good were so by nature, we would take those whom they had pointed out and guard them in the Acropolis, sealing them up there much more carefully than gold so that no one could corrupt them, and when they reached maturity they would be useful to their cities.

MENO: Reasonable enough, Socrates. (22)

The idea is that if virtue were naturally possessed by some persons, then there would be other persons in the city who would be able to judge by observing little children that they have been blessed by nature as virtuous. Since this furthermore would be of great benefit to the city-state, such virtue-detectors would somehow be able to see the signs of virtue in persons at a very early age and would protect them from corruption and evil influences so that their virtue could be preserved for the sake of the public good. If, as seems correct, we do not believe that anyone can make such judgments from observing children, then, Socrates concludes, virtue is not a product of nature. Whether this is a good argument or not is open to dispute. It might be objected that there are many properties of persons that are not manifested until adulthood that cannot be judged by casual observation of children before they have matured. Who could determine by careful but superficial inspection, for example, without looking into the human genome and knowing all the environmental factors that will affect gene expression in each case, whether a particular child will grow up to be bald or not? Who can judge in this way whether a child will eventually turn out to have diabetes or not, or to need eyeglasses or corrective lenses or not? Yet presumably all of these eventualities are largely if not entirely a matter of nature, or, in modern terms, of each individual's genetic endowment.

Rightly or wrongly setting aside the idea that virtue might be possessed by nature, Socrates next considers a second hypothesis to supplement the first assumption that if virtue is knowledge, then it can be taught. Socrates now argues that if virtue can be taught, then there must be teachers and students of virtue. The argument takes this direction:

SOCRATES: I will tell you, Meno. I am not saying that it is wrong to say that virtue is teachable if it is knowledge, but look whether it is reasonable of me to doubt whether it is knowledge. Tell me this: if not only virtue but anything whatever can be taught, should there not be of necessity people who teach it and people who learn it?

MENO: I think so.

SOCRATES: Then again, if on the contrary there are no teachers or learners of something, we should be right to assume that the subject cannot be taught?

MENO: Quite so, but do you think that there are no teachers of virtue? (23)

Socrates argues in the sequel that there are no teachers of virtue. His reasoning on this score is interesting because it seems to depend on empirical evidence, or rather on the lack of empirical evidence, of the existence of any teachers of virtue. Socrates' argument has been subject to criticism because he claims in effect that he personally does not know of any teachers of virtue, although his justification for this important conclusion in his inference appears far from conclusive. First, we find Socrates arguing as follows:

SOCRATES: I have often tried to find out whether there were any teachers of it, but in spite of all my efforts I cannot find any. And yet I have searched for them with the help of many people, especially those whom I believed to be most experienced in this matter. And now, Meno, Anytus here has opportunely come to sit down by us. Let us share our search with him. It would be reasonable for us to do so, for Anytus, in the first place, is the son of Anthemion, a man of wealth and wisdom, who did not become rich automatically or as the result of a gift like Ismenias the Theban, who recently acquired the possessions of Polycrates, but through his own wisdom and efforts. Further, he did not seem to be an arrogant or puffed up or offensive citizen in other ways, but he was a well-mannered and well-behaved man. Also he gave our friend here a good upbringing and education, as the majority of Athenians believe, for they are electing him to the highest offices. It is right then to look for the teachers of virtue with the help of men such as he, whether there are any and if so who they are. Therefore, Anytus, please join me and your guest friend Meno here, in our inquiry as to who are the teachers of virtue. Look at it in this way: if we wanted Meno to become a good physician, to what teachers would we send him? Would we not send him to the physicians?

ANYTUS: Certainly. (23)

Socrates claims not to know of any teachers of virtue. Even if we take Socrates at his word, it surely does not follow that therefore there are no teachers of virtue. Perhaps there are, but Socrates simply does not know of them. Socrates mentions the case of Themistocles, who apparently was a virtuous man, who wanted very much but was apparently unable to find teachers to help his son Cleophantus also to become a virtuous man.

Themistocles was wealthy enough to afford special teachers to instruct Cleophantus in many highly specialized skills. For example, according to Socrates, the boy was taught to ride horseback standing up in the saddle and throwing a javelin with great accuracy. This skill is the sort of *techné* that presumably can be taught and for which teachers are available. If Themistocles was willing to spare no expense in order to help his son perfect all the qualities that would be useful to him in adult life, and also wanted his son in particular to be virtuous, then one would think that someone with his advantages in life would be able to find a teacher of virtue if there were any to be found. Socrates, however, relies on Meno's admission of the fact that Cleophantus, unlike his father Themistocles, was anything but a virtuous person. From this fact we are left to draw the obvious inference that therefore Themistocles, despite all his efforts, was ultimately unsuccessful in finding a teacher of virtue for his son. Socrates seems to regard this as adequate proof that there simply are no teachers of virtue.

In fairness to Socrates, the question of whether there are or are not teachers of virtue is ultimately an empirical matter. It can only be settled by investigating the world as best as one can to determine whether or not any teachers of virtue anywhere happen to exist. Socrates, like other thinkers addressing this kind of issue, can only make the best use of available evidence to decide whether or not there are teachers of virtue. To the best of his knowledge, Socrates reports, he does not know of any such teachers, to which he adds the anecdote about Themistocles and Cleophantus as further proof that there do not seem to be any such teachers. We cannot in any case object that there might exist teachers of virtue who choose to hold back their knowledge and refuse to teach others, because if anyone were truly a teacher of virtue, she or he would have to be virtuous, and as such, as a truly virtuous person, could not refrain from helping others to become virtuous in any way they could. Socrates asks:

> SOCRATES: But have you ever heard anyone, young or old, say that Cleophantus, the son of Themistocles, was a good and wise man at the same pursuits as his father?
>
> MENO: Never. (26)

Socrates additionally mentions Aristides and his son Lysimachus, Pericles and his sons Paralus and Xanthippus, and Thucydides and his sons Melesias and Stephanus. All of these young men were taught to be excellent athletes, but from this we are supposed to infer they were by no means as virtuous as their fathers. Their fathers were virtuous and wanted their sons to be virtuous, and they were able to provide other teachers of valuable teachable skills for them. The sons excelled in these skills, indicating that they could be apt pupils for whatever could be taught. Socrates then reasons that if the sons are known nevertheless to have been unvirtuous, the only reasonable conclusion seems to be that there simply were no teachers of virtue available for their fathers to hire who could have instructed them in virtue as a *techné*. Hence, virtue is not a skill or *techné*. As Socrates concludes:

> SOCRATES: Can you mention any other subject of which those who claim to be teachers not only are not recognized to be teachers of others but are not recognized to have knowledge of it themselves, and are thought to be poor in the very matter which they profess to teach? Or any other subject of which those who are recognized as worthy teachers at one time say it can be taught and at other times that it cannot? Would you say that people who are so confused about a subject can be effective teachers of it?
>
> MENO: No, by Zeus, I would not. (28)

The point is well taken. In no other area would we agree that there were teachers of a subject if persons who are supposed to have been instructed in the art are not improved in their abilities. Nor does it seem reasonable to persist in the belief that there must somewhere be teachers of virtue or of any other teachable subject if definite procedures or definite skills cannot be imparted by any program of instruction. If we put together all of Socrates' considerations, we might agree that he makes a good case for the conclusion that there are no teachers of virtue. Still, we might wonder whether Socrates does not need to defend a stronger thesis, not only that there are no known teachers of virtue, but that there cannot be any. This is a proposition that Socrates does not try to uphold, nor is it clear what kind of argument could be offered to support a result as powerful and general as this.

If we grant Socrates' conclusion, as Meno does at last, then we arrive at a compact formulation of the essential inference in Socrates' application of the geometer's hypothetical mode of reasoning about the question whether virtue can be taught. Socrates argues as follows:

> SOCRATES: If there are no teachers, neither are there pupils?
>
> MENO: As you say.
>
> SOCRATES: And we agreed that a subject that has neither teachers nor pupils is not teachable?
>
> MENO: We have so agreed.
>
> SOCRATES: Now there seem to be no teachers of virtue anywhere?
>
> MENO: That seems so.
>
> SOCRATES: Then virtue cannot be taught?
>
> MENO: Apparently not, if we have investigated this correctly. I certainly wonder, Socrates, whether there are no good men either, or in what way good men come to be. (28)

In this brief exchange, the main part of Socrates' hypothetical geometer's method is explained. The inference goes something like this, distinguishing the assumptions from the conclusions in the conventional way by a horizontal line:

Socrates' Argument That Virtue Is Not Teachable
1. If virtue is a kind of knowledge, then it can be taught.
2. If virtue can be taught, then there are students and teachers of virtue.
3. As experience shows, however, there are no teachers of virtue.
4. If there are no teachers of virtue, then neither are there any students of virtue.

---

5. There are no teachers or students of virtue. (3,4)
6. Virtue cannot be taught. (2,5)
7. Virtue is not a kind of knowledge. (1,6)

Socrates has already discounted the possibility that virtue might be possessed by nature, and now he believes he has shown that virtue cannot be taught and is therefore not a kind of knowledge. These results leave two unanswered questions to which

Plato devotes the remainder of the dialogue. The first question is, if virtue is not a kind of knowledge, but it is something valuable, beneficial to the city-state and as such a kind of wisdom, what exactly is its philosophical status? The second question is, if virtue cannot be taught, then how is it acquired, and how is it that some persons are virtuous while others are not? These topics are considered in the following section.

RIGHT OPINION AND VIRTUE AS A GIFT OF THE GODS

We have already observed that Socrates distinguishes between knowledge and right opinion or correct opinion. Right opinion is similar to knowledge, but lacking in warrant or justification for the beliefs a person holds. Meno's slave boy has right opinion but not yet knowledge about the length of side needed to double the area of a square, as a result of Socrates' geometry lesson. Right opinion, moreover, in many instances is good enough, even if it does not qualify as knowledge, for many practical applications. It would be sufficient, for example, for Meno's slave to arrive at all the same conclusions about how the area of a square can be doubled in planning a garden or building a box. Socrates, as we now see, draws much the same inference about the adequacy of right opinion in moral and political conduct, in all areas where virtue is required of ethical agents and participants in political events, in the absence of genuine knowledge. Socrates states:

> SOCRATES: What if someone had had a correct opinion as to which was the way but had not gone there nor indeed had knowledge of it, would he not also lead correctly?
>
> MENO: Certainly.
>
> SOCRATES: And as long as he has the right opinion about that of which the other has knowledge, he will not be a worse guide than the one who knows, as he has a true opinion, though not knowledge.
>
> MENO: In no way worse.
>
> SOCRATES: So true opinion is in no way a worse guide to correct action than knowledge. It is this that we omitted in our investigation of the nature of virtue, when we said that only knowledge can lead to correct action, for true opinion can do so also.
>
> MENO: So it seems. (29)

Socrates puts together all the separate elements of the argument in one extended series of questions and answers in the following rapid-fire exchange with Meno:

> SOCRATES: We thought it could be taught, if it was knowledge?
>
> MENO: Yes.
>
> SOCRATES: And that it was knowledge if it could be taught?
>
> MENO: Quite so.
>
> SOCRATES: And that if there were teachers of it, it could be taught, but if there were not, it was not teachable?

MENO: That is so.

SOCRATES: And then we agreed that there were no teachers of it?

MENO: We did.

SOCRATES: So we agreed that it was neither teachable nor knowledge?

MENO: Quite so.

SOCRATES: Now because it cannot be taught, virtue no longer seems to be knowledge?

MENO: It seems not.

SOCRATES: So one of the two good and useful things has been excluded, and knowledge is not the guide in public affairs.

MENO: I do not think that is so.

SOCRATES: So it is not by some kind of wisdom, or by being wise, that such men lead their cities, those such as Themistocles and those mentioned by Anytus just now? That is the reason why they cannot make others be like themselves, because it is not knowledge which makes them what they are.

MENO: It is likely to be as you say, Socrates.

SOCRATES: Therefore, if it is not through knowledge, the only alternative is that it is through right opinion that statesmen follow the right course for their cities. As regards knowledge, they are no different from soothsayers and prophets. They too say many true things when inspired, but they have no knowledge of what they are saying.

MENO: That is probably so. (30–31)

By eliminating the alternatives, Socrates believes he has finally narrowed down the answer to Meno's original question. The two have already agreed that virtue cannot be taught, but it remains to say how virtue is acquired. Virtue has been shown to be unteachable as a *techné* and also not something that is had by nature, genetically, so to speak, like height or eye color. The only remaining choice, which Socrates at last proposes, is that virtue is a gift of the gods. This is an interesting answer for Socrates to have given, assuming that Plato accurately reports Socrates' belief. It seems to solve Meno's problem, and at the same time it supports the claim, contrary to Socrates' accusers later at his trial, that he does after all believe in the existence of the gods and is not an atheist. If Socrates did not think that the gods exist, then he could hardly have concluded that virtue is the gift of the gods, given to some and not to others, as a matter of divine grace and dispensation. Socrates states in the final sentences of the dialogue:

SOCRATES: It follows from this reasoning, Meno, that virtue appears to be present in those of us who may possess it as a gift from the gods. We shall have clear knowledge of this when, before we investigate how it comes to be present in men, we first try to find out what virtue in itself is. But now the time has come for me to go. You convince your guest friend Anytus here of these very things of which you have yourself been convinced, in order that he may be more amenable. If you succeed, you will also confer a benefit upon Athenians. (32)

MENO'S SLAVE AND MENO AS SLAVE

The discussion between Socrates and Meno's slave boy is a miniature version of the conversation Socrates has with Meno in the dialogue. The interlude with Meno's slave serves to reflect in microcosm the dialectical exchange between Socrates and Meno, in the way a scene depicted in a still-life painting might contain a miniature self-representation caught in the reflection of a looking-glass included among the painted objects.

If this is a plausible interpretation of Socrates' examination of Meno's slave, then Socrates in this passage might be offering a subtle and none too flattering image of Meno. Socrates appears to picture Meno as a slave in just this way, despite his claim that he will offer no image of Meno in return for Meno's comparison of Socrates with a torpedo fish. Socrates' image of Meno more directly represents the internal state of Meno's soul than his outward physical appearance. Socrates, as we know from other dialogues of Plato, is more concerned with the internal beauty of the soul than the body's external beauty, and Meno by reputation lacks the deep-shining intellectual and moral beauty that is likely to excite Socrates' admiration.

The thesis that Socrates deliberately offers the image of Meno as slave to the world of appearance or Becoming cannot be definitely proved. It is offered as an interpretation, a way of thinking about what transpires in the dialogue between Socrates and Meno that may help to illuminate certain features of the text, in part perhaps through its coherence with Plato's portrait of Socrates' character and teachings throughout the dialogues. The image of Meno as slave, and its relation to Plato's distinction between the changing world of appearance and the unchanging world of reality known to the intellect, is at least consistent with what we have learned in this chapter about Socrates' philosophy in Plato's dialogues. The confinement and limitation of Meno's thought to the world of ephemeral appearance is indicated early in the dialogue in all of his attempts to define the concept of virtue. Meno answers Socrates' questions, not by offering a definition of the one Form of virtue in its universal nature, but by mentioning many particular virtues of things experienced in the changing world of physical appearances.

Meno's first "definition" of virtue by the enumeration of multiple virtues seizes on accidental features to divide the concept of virtue into several subcategories. Each of these is linked to a particular inessential distinction of phenomena in the world of appearance, when Meno, as we have seen, speaks of the virtue of men and women, freeborn and slave, young and old. Socrates on the contrary looks for something more fundamental in common among these instantiations of virtue. He seeks the Form that transcends the distinct kinds and instantiations of virtue—a one that is exhibited or instantiated by a many, as in the one common nature by which all bees are bees, rather than a swarm of many particular bees.

For Socrates, Meno in his training by the sophists has yet to raise his sight from the changing world of appearance to the unchanging world of reality, to the Forms. Learning superficially to make speeches on various subjects without having a philosophically sound critical understanding of concepts restricts understanding to the phenomena of sense experience. It is in this realm that one's audience is most likely also to be rooted, and from which everyday examples can be drawn that are most likely to impress and persuade, rather than the abstract realm of universal truths that Socrates regards as the proper domain of knowledge.

The attempt to define the concept of virtue between Socrates and Meno proceeds, significantly, with an examination of virtue as it relates in particular to the virtue of slaves. Meno persists for a time in assuming that there are many distinct kinds of virtue, including that unique to slaves, and Socrates takes him in hand:

> SOCRATES: Since then the virtue of all is the same, try to tell me and to remember what Gorgias, and you with him, said that that same thing is.
>
> MENO: What else but to be able to rule over men, if you are seeking one description to fit them all.
>
> SOCRATES: That is indeed what I am seeking, but Meno, is virtue the same in the case of a child or a slave, namely, for them to be able to rule over a master, and do you think that he who rules is still a slave?
>
> MENO: I do not think so at all, Socrates. (6)

By interrogating Meno's slave, Socrates is able to awaken his dormant knowledge of geometry, while he makes little progress with Meno in trying to understand the concept of virtue. Meno, Socrates seems by this comparison to say, is not even as intellectually and morally attuned toward knowledge as his slave. The slave, whose thinking has not been sullied by contact with the sophists' cynical indifference to the truth, has a purity and guileless intellectual innocence that make it easier for him than for Meno to grasp eternal truths. Meno's slave is able to recognize geometrical propositions as though retrieving them from memory, whereas Meno not only cannot recollect true knowledge of the Form, but cannot even remember what Gorgias taught him to recite in speeches about virtue. All this suggests an unflattering image of the condition of Meno's soul at which Socrates indirectly but repeatedly hints.

Meno's difficulty is that he is fixed on the particular and changing. In the justly famous allegory of the cave in Plato's *Republic*, he is like a prisoner of the illusory world of appearance, a slave to sensation and contingency:

> See human beings as though they were in an underground cave-like dwelling with its entrance, a long one, open to the light across the whole width of the cave. They are in it from childhood with their legs and necks in bonds so that they are fixed, seeing only in front of them, unable because of the bond to turn their heads all the way around. Their light is from a fire burning far above and behind them. Between the fire and the prisoners there is a road above, along which see a wall, built like the partitions puppet-handlers set in front of the human beings and over which they show the puppets. (*Republic* 514a–b4)

In the three-part division of the ideal state and the soul in the *Republic*, knowledge belongs only to the highest, rational part of the soul, and slaves are excluded from the uppermost echelon of society corresponding to the rational part of the soul in the individual. In much the same way, the slaves of appearance observing only the shadows of objects in the allegory of the cave cannot partake of knowledge.

Of course, not all slaves are prisoners in shackles. Yet neither are they free to go or do what they choose; in this sense the prisoners of the cave are unwitting slaves of the limited presentations they receive. We who are ostensibly free in thought and action share an identical fate in Socrates' view, if we remain unenlightened about the distinction between appearance and reality. Only a grasp of the eternal Forms, including the Form of virtue, could free Meno from his cognitive slavery and enable him to rise above the ephemeral world of appearances. Recollection of the Forms would fasten his opinions more securely in place, like the statues of Daedalus, so as to constitute knowledge. It is hard to see how Socrates could tell Meno more plainly that Meno's soul from the standpoint of its lack of knowledge is no better than a runaway slave.

This, we might say, is Socrates' image of Meno. Although Socrates insists that he does not intend to offer an image of Meno in return for Meno's image of Socrates as a torpedo fish, he appears in the end to compare Meno's real nature, the state of his soul, to that of a slave to the world of appearance. Meno, in the course of his discussion with Socrates, is pictured as a slave and prisoner of the changing ephemeral world of Becoming. Socrates has captured a likeness, not of Meno's external aspect as it appears in the realm of phenomena, which he admits to be superficially beautiful, but of Meno's soul. From the standpoint of internal beauty, of that which matters most deeply to Socrates in his search for truth and the care of the soul, Meno's slave, with whom Meno would surely resent any comparison, must seem in Socrates' judgment to be far more beautiful than Meno as slave.

FORESHADOWINGS OF SOCRATES' FATE

At a crucial point in the latter part of the dialogue, when Socrates is trying to convince Meno that there are no teachers of virtue, another character in addition to Socrates, Meno, and Meno's slave is brought into the conversation. This is Anytus, who, along with Meletus and Lycon, by no coincidence turns out later to be one of Socrates' three prosecutors at his trial.

Socrates brings Anytus into the conversation to see whether he as an outsider to the interaction that has taken place thus far between himself and Meno happens to know any teachers of virtue. Anytus claims that any citizen of Athens by their good example would be a proper teacher of virtue. Socrates does not accept this answer, and asks Anytus to name particular persons among the citizens of Athens who Anytus thinks might be qualified to teach others to be virtuous. Anytus refuses, and after Socrates presents his catalog of famous Athenians who wanted to educate their sons to be virtuous and failed in the endeavor, Anytus becomes angry and warns Socrates not to offend against others so freely. He says:

> ANTYUS: I think, Socrates, that you easily speak ill of people. I would advise you, if you will listen to me, to be careful. Perhaps also in another city, and certainly here, it is easier to injure people than to benefit them. I think you know that yourself. (27)

Plato's dialogue lacks stage directions in the manner of an ordinary drama. It is easy to imagine, however, that Anytus after this interchange with Socrates has become so angry that he storms off and leaves Socrates and Meno by themselves. Or perhaps he decides to remain but refuses to talk. This is the obvious implication of Socrates' subsequent remarks to Meno, when he observes:

> SOCRATES: I think, Meno, that Anytus is angry, and I am not at all surprised. He thinks, to begin with, that I am slandering those men, and then he believes himself to be one of them. If he ever realizes what slander is, he will cease from anger, but he does not know it now. . . . (27)

Socrates is unwilling, in a sense unable, to heed Anytus's warning. He is personally committed to the mission to which he believes he has been ordered by the gods, as a result of the oracle at Delphi's declaration that he is the wisest person in Athens. Having been a hoplite or spear-bearing foot soldier in the Greek army who fought bravely in several of the city's wars, Socrates compares his resolution to hold his post and stand guard as a philosopher critically examining the beliefs of others in Athens to the orders given to a soldier in a war, obligated to obey regardless of the consequences.

When he is found guilty at his trial, Socrates not only refuses to use courtroom tricks to avoid the heavy sentence of death that is finally imposed, but he rejects the alternative of exile away from the city-state where he had always lived, and argues in Plato's dialogue the *Crito* against those of his friends who try to persuade him to escape. Instead, Socrates bravely accepts his punishment, maintaining that to do otherwise would be an offense to the laws of the city whose protection he had always enjoyed. In the *Phaedo*, Plato describes Socrates' final moments, willingly drinking the fatal hemlock from a small black ceramic cup and discussing philosophy and the nature of the soul with his weeping friends until the poison moving from his legs through his body finally ends his life.

As we know from Plato's *Meno*, since Socrates believes that the soul is immortal, and regards the changing world of appearance that we experience in sensation as unreal, he appears to have been not only philosophically but emotionally prepared to leave his body behind and continue his soul's journey, returning to the unchanging world of the Forms and meeting with the souls of others who have already died. Socrates' last words as recorded by Plato were to ask his friends to sacrifice a rooster to the god Asclepius, the Greek god of medicine. Socrates' request for this prescribed ritual is usually interpreted as indicating Socrates' belief that death is actually a healing from the sickness resulting from the earthly imprisonment of his immortal soul in a material body, for which the god should be thanked. Significantly, Socrates' word for soul is *psyché*, from which we derive the modern English word *psychology*, a word that in ancient Greek also means butterfly. A butterfly begins life as an earthbound caterpillar before it is transformed in a deathlike sleep within a chrysalis, reawakening and taking to the air, making it an apt metaphor for Socrates' commitment to the ultimate freedom and wisdom of the soul.

SUMMARY

What have we discovered by reading and thinking critically about Plato's *Meno*? We have learned about Socrates' method of dialectical question and answer known as the *elenchus*. Socrates searches for the meaning of general terms, for the definitions of concepts of philosophical interest, such as virtue, beauty, truth, and the good. The *elenchus* is dedicated to uncovering the meaning of such concepts. The method follows six distinct steps, beginning with a search for general meaning and ending in puzzlement. It is characteristic of Socratic irony that the process should typically end in *aporia* rather than a satisfying analysis of a concept.

Socrates argues that knowledge of the eternal Forms is an eternal possession of every immortal soul. It needs only to be awakened in memory by considering the answers to the right sort of questions. Knowledge is not just true belief or right opinion, but requires justification, a reason for believing what is true. Socrates maintains that virtue is not teachable and is not a product of nature, but a gift of the gods. The theory of Forms and the importance of mathematics are vital to Plato's philosophy, in which reason rather than sense experience is made the basis for knowledge, and in which metaphysics depends on the real existence of abstract entities that can only be known through rational reflection. Socrates is not only a master of argument but an ironic moral presence. His practice of philosophy to the day of his execution illustrates the ideal of pursuing knowledge for its own sake by following the conclusions of the strongest philosophical arguments wherever they lead.

We also learn something more in this chapter. We learn how philosophical ideas, distinctions, standpoints, assumptions, starting places, and arguments can be identified in a philosophical text, and how selected elements can be put together in a narrative exposition of a philosophical system. We have now begun the study of philosophy through its history, and we have discovered the basic thought of one the first important thinkers in Western philosophy. We have learned something about what kinds of problems interest philosophers and how they go about addressing them. We have also learned something about what we should expect from a good philosophical definition and a good philosophical argument, and how to criticize these in philosophical writings. Above all, we have laid a sound foundation for the further study of philosophy. We can expect to find philosophers after Plato disagreeing with much of what he and Socrates have to say, extending philosophical methods into other areas in pursuit of different problems and arriving at very different philosophical principles. All carry forward the project of philosophical inquiry in different directions along different pathways.

QUESTIONS FOR PHILOSOPHICAL UNDERSTANDING

1. What is a Platonic Form?
2. Why is Socrates dissatisfied with efforts to define Forms in terms of particular things?
3. How does Socrates use the method of counterexamples in criticizing definitions?
4. Why does Socrates believe that the soul is immortal?
5. What is the best explanation of Meno's slave boy's answers to Socrates' questions in the geometry lesson?
6. What is knowledge? How, if at all, can we hope and try to acquire it?
7. How can we avoid the sophist's dilemma that seems to make knowledge impossible?
8. If we already possess perfect knowledge of the Forms, how can Socrates sincerely claim

to be wise only in the sense of knowing that he does not know? Why does he say that he does not know rather than merely that he does not remember?

9. What can we conclude about Socrates' religious beliefs from his answer to the question whether virtue can be taught?

10. How does Socrates try to get around the problem of explaining whether virtue can be taught when he claims not to know what virtue is?

11. What is the force of Socrates' appeal to the fact that wealthy people were not able to find teachers who could make their children virtuous?

12. How should Meno have tried to defend his definition of virtue as enjoying beautiful things and having the power to acquire them?

13. What is a more correct definition of virtue that would satisfy Socrates' requirements?

14. What is the relationship between grasping that a particular thing instantiates a Form and being able to give a general definition of the Form in terms of its necessary and sufficient conditions?

15. How would you describe Plato's and Socrates' philosophy? What are the major contributions Socrates and Plato made to the early origins of the history of philosophy?

KEY TERMS

advocacy

anamnesis theory of knowledge

aporia

aretē

care of the soul

correct belief, correct opinion

counterexample

eidos

elenchus

erotic man

Form

geometer's method

going between a dilemma's horns

grasping a dilemma horn

horns of a dilemma

hubris

immortality of the soul

knowledge

Lethe ri ver

maieusis, maieutic

necessary condition

one and the many

Plato's theory of Forms

pragmatic reason

psyché

Socrates' geometry lesson

Socratic irony

sophism

sophist's dilemma

statues of Daedalus

sufficient condition

techné

Third Man problem

torpedo fish image of Socrates

virtue

world of Becoming

world of Being

Sources and Recommended Readings

Benson, Hugh. *Socratic Wisdom: The Model of Knowledge in Plato's Early Dialogues.* New York: Oxford University Press, 2000.

Beversluis, John. *Cross-Examining Socrates: A Defense of the Interlocutors in Plato's Early Dialogues.* Cambridge: Cambridge University Press, 2000.

Brown, Malcolm. "Socrates Disapproves of the Slave Boy's Answer." In *Plato's Meno,* ed. Brown. New York: Bobbs-Merrill, Inc., 1971.

Kerferd, G. B. *The Sophistic Movement.* Cambridge: Cambridge University Press, 1981.

Klein, Jacob. *A Commentary on Plato's Meno.* Chapel Hill: University of North Carolina Press, 1965.

Nehamas, Alexander. *Virtues of Authenticity: Essays on Plato and Socrates.* Princeton: Princeton University Press, 1999.

Phillips, Bernard. "The Significance of Plato's *Meno,*" *The Classical Weekly* 42 (1948–1949).

Plato. *The Republic of Plato,* second edition. Translated with notes, an interpretive essay, and a new introduction by Allan Bloom. New York: Basic Books, 1991.

Sternfield, Robert. *Plato's Meno: A Philosophy of Man as Acquisitive.* Carbondale: Southern Illinois University Press, 1978.

Thomas, John E. *Musings on the Meno.* The Hague: Martinus Nijhoff, 1980.

Vlastos, Gregory. "*Anamnesis* in the *Meno,*" *Dialogue* 4 (1965).

Weiss, Roslyn. *Virtue in the Cave: Moral Inquiry in Plato's Meno.* Oxford: Oxford University Press, 2001.

CHAPTER 2

SUBSTANCE AND THE CHANGING WORLD

Aristotle's *Metaphysics*

Aristotle offers a very different approach to the problems of metaphysics and theory of knowledge. His theory of substance, essence, and accident provides a solution to the ancient metaphysical puzzle of how things persisting through time can change and yet remain the same. Where Plato advocates abstract knowledge of imperceivable Forms as the only reality, Aristotle emphasizes concrete knowledge of the physical world obtained through sense experience and validated by logic and inductive reasoning. Aristotle's philosophy is interesting for its down-to-earth methods and commonsense conclusions, and is vital to understanding its continuing influence in later philosophical traditions through the medieval period to modern and contemporary philosophy.

A SCIENTIFIC PHILOSOPHY

Aristotle (384–322 B.C.E.) was a student of Plato's. He was not an Athenian like Socrates and Plato, but came to Athens from Stagira in Macedon in the northern Greek mainland to study at Plato's Academy, where he remained for twenty years. Aristotle was so well respected for his intelligence and philosophical ability that he was nicknamed "The mind of the Academy," evidently a significant distinction, given that Plato was the founder and director of the school.

Although Aristotle learned much from Plato, he did not agree with all of Plato's teachings, and in some ways their philosophies are fundamentally opposed. Whereas Plato was primarily interested in mathematics and abstract truths as a model and subject matter for philosophy, Aristotle was motivated by a love for logic and natural science. It is a popular image to think of Plato, the son of an aristocratic Athenian family, immersed in lofty contemplation of the abstract Forms, investigating a subject matter that, like pure mathematics, one can study without dirtying one's hands. Aristotle, in contrast, the founder of such scientific disciplines as physics, biology, psychology, among others, was perfectly comfortable scooping out sea creatures from a tidal pool, dissecting them and examining the functioning of their parts, touching and empirically investigating those things of the world of experience that Plato disdained as belonging only to the changing realm of appearance or Becoming. Plato's thoughts concern the objects in Platonic heaven, an unchanging world of reality or Being, the world of the untouchable Forms, of which alone, Plato believes, we can have genuine knowledge. Aristotle is more down to earth, absorbed in the things we can experience in everyday life.

The philosophical differences between Plato and Aristotle in terms of their basic philosophical perspective are illustrated in Raphael's 1510 oil painting masterpiece, *The School of Athens*. There an elderly Plato with a white beard is walking beside his brilliant student, a more youthful dark-bearded Aristotle. The differences in their gestures tells the whole story. Where Plato points with a finger toward the heavens, Aristotle makes a passing movement with the flat of his hand parallel to the earth.

Aristotle indicates the importance of sensation for his philosophy in the very first paragraph of his great work, the *Metaphysics:*

> All men by nature desire to know. An indication of this is the delight we take in our senses; for even apart from their usefulness they are loved for themselves; and above all others the sense of sight. For not only with a view to action, but even when we are not going to do anything, we prefer sight to almost everything else. The reason is that this, most of all the senses, makes us know and brings to light many differences between things. (980ᵃ20–30) (We refer throughout to Aristotle's writings by a numbering system devised for the scholarly edition of Aristotle's collected works devised by Immanuel Bekker in 1831.)

An interesting feature of Aristotle's statement is the claim that human beings desire by nature to know. The implication is that it is our natural function to seek knowledge, perhaps in much the same way that it is a natural function of bears to hibernate in winter or plants to turn toward a light source. The anthropological perspective of Aristotle's opening sentences in the *Metaphysics* sets the tone for the book's entire project of inquiry.

Aristotle begins with what we as knowers actually do when we try to secure knowledge. The answer is clear and diametrically opposed to Socrates' or Plato's. Aristotle takes it for granted that knowledge is discovered and augmented by means of the senses, whereas Socrates and Plato deny that anything can be known among the appearances of things in the changing world of Becoming through sense perception. Aristotle asserts that it is a sign of the fact that humans naturally desire to know that we regard vision in particular as intrinsically valuable, precious for its own sake and not merely as a means to another end, a type of sensation that he believes we prefer to all others. The best explanation for these facts, in turn, Aristotle maintains, is that it is through perception, and vision in particular, that we naturally derive much of our knowledge.

The contrast of Plato as mathematician and Aristotle as field biologist should not mislead us into thinking that Aristotle is any less a philosopher than Plato. The two thinkers are very different in their approaches to philosophy, but they represent equally legitimate philosophical methodologies. The starting assumptions with which they begin a philosophical inquiry, the questions they find important in understanding knowledge and the existence and nature of the world, as well as topics in moral, political, and aesthetic value, complement one another in an interesting way. We can begin to appreciate the way in which Plato and Aristotle stand for alternative ways of doing philosophy when we look at such questions as what each believes to be the real world and the ways in which we can attain knowledge. Plato, like his teacher Socrates, is in some ways more dialectical than Aristotle. If we think of dialectic as largely a matter of following the Socratic *elenchus*, then we have already seen that for Socrates and for Plato, especially in Plato's early and middle dialogues, a proper philosophical investigation typically ends in an *aporia* or puzzlement. In the *aporia*, as we have seen, Socrates induces in his interlocutors a recognition of their own ignorance, of knowing at last that they do not know that which they thought they knew. This is the state of perplexity that prompts Meno to describe Socrates as a torpedo fish that shocks and numbs its prey into stunned silence. Aristotle on the contrary is more empirical in his mode of inquiry, and, for Aristotle, a conceptual puzzle or *aporia* is not the end of philosophical inquiry, but only the beginning.

ARISTOTLE'S INVESTIGATION OF FIRST PHILOSOPHY

Aristotle writes treatises rather than dialogues. As a student of Plato's, Aristotle is supposed to have written at least one dialogue, on "The Good," which unfortunately has been lost. Some of Aristotle's writings do not seem to have been composed as unified manuscripts intended for distribution as the ancient equivalent of books, but may have been lecture notes, either written by Aristotle himself for teaching purposes, or compiled by his students. The internal evidence for the latter possibility is the occasional repetitions, lack of obvious overall organization, and other textual clues that suggest Aristotle may have been speaking before an audience who recorded his statements in a form that were later edited into separate works.

Aristotle takes philosophical problems as his point of departure in his treatises and sets about trying to solve them. He does this in a variety of ways, depending on the subject matter. He works to tailor his technique to the particular requirements of each special topic, in what we have now, partly through Aristotle's efforts, come to think of as an early precursor of modern scientific method. Aristotle typically starts his investigations by reviewing what other major philosophers have had to say that may be of relevance to the problems he is addressing. He does this for two reasons. First, he wants to make sure that he is not overlooking promising solutions in the ideas of his philosophical predecessors. Since the problems of philosophy are in many ways conceptual, and since concepts may change and evolve but still bear traces of their origins, philosophy at its best stays in contact with its history. Aristotle generally works through the suggestions to be found in philosophy's past as a way of preparing the discussion he proposes to advance. He sifts through the ideas of other thinkers and sorts them out critically, discarding ideas that seem incorrect and identifying those that might help him in his task. When he has completed this preliminary effort, Aristotle is at last prepared to move forward by making what he often explicitly calls a fresh start. Having surveyed the background to his main question, and critically evaluated alternative approaches, he puts together and develops the best suggestions from philosophy's history and supplements them with original proposals of his own in order to arrive at a unified account that he is prepared to recommend as an answer to the philosophical problems he wants to solve.

We shall be examining Aristotle's important work, the *Metaphysics*. The book has a somewhat misleading title, because Aristotle never used the word *metaphysics* to describe his teachings. The term was introduced in the first century A.C.E. by an editor who decided to assemble a folio of Aristotle's writings primarily on the concept of substance and its implications for the phenomena of matter and form, causation and change, and the existence of God. The manuscripts were presented in the collection immediately after Aristotle's treatise, the *Physics*. They were titled, *Ta meta ta physica*, meaning literally 'that which comes after the physics'. In this way, the word *metaphysics* became a permanent addition to the philosophical vocabulary. The exact subject matter of metaphysics has since come to alter its meaning many times, to be made the "Queen of the Sciences," to be rejected as meaningless or impossible, but to persist as an active area of philosophical study from Aristotle's day to contemporary times.

Aristotle's own terminology for the discipline now known as metaphysics includes three separate concepts: (1) *ontology* or theory of being, from the Greek word *ontos*, meaning "being"; (2) *theology*, as the philosophical study of the concept and existence of god, which Aristotle tends to discuss only in the singular and to equate with the *first cause* or *unmoved prime mover* of the universe that sets the entire cosmos in motion; (3) topics of substance, causation, change, identity, and the like, which Aristotle includes under the umbrella of *first philosophy*, or, in Greek, *proté philosophia*. The idea of first philosophy is that there are questions that are conceptually fundamental to any of the other investigations to be conducted in the specialized sciences or higher branches of philosophy. First philosophy is literally the set of problems that must be investigated and solved first. They are the problems to be settled before any of the other disciplines can proceed in proper order, in which we first resolve more deeply underlying conceptual difficulties and identify the most basic principles that are presupposed by the superstructure of knowledge in philosophy and science.

The treatise we now call Aristotle's *Metaphysics* appears to be a compilation of lecture notes written either by Aristotle or his students. The book as a whole, despite some problems of interpretation, is largely coherent and unified in its final message. What is challenging is to grasp the overall plan of Aristotle's development of themes. At times the text appears disconnected, repetitious, and intrinsically dense in its teachings, especially where the necessary context to the problems Aristotle investigates is not explained. It is therefore part of our task to fill in some of the gaps in the background in order to appreciate what Aristotle has to say about the nature of substance and its explanatory role in understanding the changing world of experience. Aristotle's arguments in the *Metaphysics* are among the most difficult that we shall try to interpret in this book. It is important and worthwhile to do so, however, because of the importance of Aristotle's ideas in the history of later metaphysics and epistemology. We must be patient and, if necessary, read and carefully reread Aristotle's remarks, and try to understand the point of what he is saying, remembering all along that we might be looking only at lecture notes stitched together from an oral presentation of Aristotle's ideas.

Aristotle disagrees with Plato about the existence of abstract universal Forms. Plato regards the eternal Forms as existing independently of the changing world of physical things in the world of appearance. Taking what he sees of value in another thinker's ideas without adopting its objectionable aspects, even in the case of his own teacher, Aristotle opposes Plato's theory of Forms, while preserving some of the doctrine's underlying implications and explanatory usefulness, which he reinterprets quite differently in his own terms. Aristotle reinterprets Plato's concept of the Forms as what he calls *definitions* or *secondary substances*. Aristotle's forms (with a small f), as opposed to Plato's Forms (with a capital F), are not supposed to exist independently of the world of material things in some kind of Platonic heaven. Rather, Aristotle argues that the definitions or secondary substances *inhere* or are manifested in the changing world of the physical things we directly perceive, divided up into the discrete concrete entities that we can experience, which Aristotle calls "primary substances."

To emphasize their difference on this important point, we can say that Plato believes that there would be an eternal unchanging Form of *horse*, even if there were no existent horses. Aristotle, in comparison, considers the definition or secondary substance *horse* to inhere and therefore to exist only insofar as it is exemplified in actually existent horses. If all the horses that now exist should somehow become extinct, Plato would continue to believe in the unexemplified abstract Form of *horse*, whereas for Aristotle, his equivalent of the Platonic Forms, the definition or secondary substance *horse* would no longer exist the moment the last horse perished. There is no form (with a small f) of *horse* for Aristotle if there are no actually existent horses, and in particular if there are no horses as primary substances in which the definition or secondary substance of *horse* can inhere. To understand this crucial difference between Plato and Aristotle on the basic categories of existence and the possible objects of knowledge, we must look more deeply into Aristotle's concept of substance and the changing world of empirical phenomena.

IDENTITY AND PERSISTENCE THROUGH CHANGE

The puzzle that Aristotle examines at length in the *Metaphysics* is the problem of understanding change and the identity or persistence of things through change. When a thing changes, as long as it is not completely destroyed, we ordinarily assume that somehow the same entity survives in modified form. The philosophical problem is how to understand this possibility, if it is true that at least some things persist through some kinds of change.

Consider an acorn. It is the seed of an oak tree, which, if it is properly planted, watered, and nourished by minerals and sunlight, will ordinarily grow into an oak tree. When it does so it will have undergone significant changes. Yet in another sense it will be the same acorn that has developed into a tree. This biological example is very much in keeping with the kinds of problems Aristotle finds insightful for philosophical reflection. Numerous other instances might also be given; such as a baby growing up into an adult, or a house being painted, a piece of metal rusting, or the like. All such instances are cases of changing empirical phenomena. If a change occurs, then we ordinarily believe that in some sense it is the same thing that has undergone the change, persisting through the change in a changed form or altered state. The acorn, to return to our first example, does not change so radically as to become a maple tree or a daffodil or a human being or a painted house or rusting piece of metal. It remains the original acorn, the very same thing changes from being a small, hard, roughly spherical seed into a spreading oak tree with extended roots, branches, leaves, and more acorns. The resulting oak tree is in some unspecified sense a transformed acorn, one that in a supportive environment has fulfilled its biological destiny by becoming a particular type of tree.

The question for Aristotle is not whether such things occur, or whether we ought to be suspicious of our everyday judgments about this type of event, but how exactly we are supposed to understand such occurrences philosophically. To give more poignancy to the problem Aristotle hopes to solve, we might ask what reasons we could have for accepting our commonsense judgment that the acorn really is in some sense identical with the oak tree into which it grows. Why not, for example, suppose that if anything whatsoever undergoes any sort of change, then the original acorn does not persist through the change but is completely destroyed and replaced by another similar but still not precisely identical object. The acorn, as it swells with water, for example, because of its biological genetic code, as we would say today, begins to call forth growth hormones contained within the seed, breaking through its hard shell underground and sending forth a radical that if all goes well will become the root of a future mighty oak. This seems to be a change that the acorn undergoes, being transformed from seed to tree over a relatively long period of time. On what basis, we should ask, however, would we be right to think of the identical acorn as undergoing these changes, surviving in a different form, rather than a succession of distinct and strictly speaking nonidentical acorns being substituted one after another at each stage of growth and at every alteration of properties that we might otherwise attribute to the same acorn?

Does it seem too fanciful to imagine a succession of similar acorns followed by a succession of simple tree forms followed by a succession of mature tree forms? Should we not instead simply accept the conventional wisdom whereby it is the same material thing that has been subjected to a series of perfectly natural changes and so is transformed from an acorn into an oak? It might be theoretically simpler and more economical to adopt the view that an identical acorn persists through change while being transformed from seed to tree. Perhaps that should be the end of the story, from a philosophical as well as scientific and commonsense standpoint, without any further philosophical complications.

The difficulty is that the alternative conception of change as involving a succession of distinct but similar acorns rather than a single acorn undergoing successive changes is by no means a philosophical extravagance. The more complicated model is one for which there is a very solid rational justification, which ought to lead us to very different conclusions if we cannot provide a better general theory of the identity conditions for objects undergoing change. What we shall refer to as the standard identity theory is that an entity is defined by and distinguished from other entities by virtue of its unique set of properties. Thus, the acorn has among its indefinitely many qualities the properties of being roughly round, wearing a little beret, weighing only a few grams, and being not much larger than a gumball. The fully grown oak tree, in contrast, is not round, but cylindrical, has no cap but branches with leaves, and can weigh several tons and extend a few meters in circumference and tens of meters in height. The acorn has no leaves, while the tree, at least during the summer and part of the spring and fall, on the other hand, has tens of thousands of leaves.

How, then, can the acorn be the same entity as the oak tree? Why should we agree that the oak tree is identical in any sense to the acorn? What do we mean by saying as we do in commonsense judgment that the same acorn has changed in such a way as to become an oak tree? An analogy that is sometimes made in response to similar scientific and philosophical conundrums is to say that common sense is not always an infallible guide to the conclusions that are required in exact investigations, just as we cannot uncritically take our bearings from commonsense experience and ways of speaking about the sun rising or setting in understanding astronomy. It might be harmless, then, to agree with common sense in speaking of a sunrise or sunset, provided we know that the sun does not actually move relative to the Earth, but rather that the Earth revolves around the sun. In like manner, we might come to agree that a physical entity such as the acorn does not really become an oak tree, but is successively replaced by a series of similar entities, all with distinct collections of identifying individuating properties. At the same time, speaking in a loose and popular but unscientific way of sunrises and sunsets, we might allow ourselves the convenience of referring to the acorn in a loose and popular but unphilosophical way as becoming an oak, and, indeed, of the oak later becoming a coffee table or dinette with chairs.

The deeper metaphysical challenge posed by the problem of change is thus to understand what it means to speak of an object of any kind. To do so, we should be prepared from a philosophical perspective to be able to articulate at least in general terms the identity conditions by which each entity is distinct from every other. We must be able in principle to distinguish an object as a unique individual. Otherwise, we will have no basis for referring to it as a particular thing, and we will not be entitled philosophically to think of it as a discrete entity that either survives through change or is replaced by a similar entity at each successive stage during a process of change. In that event, we must inevitably allow the object to be confused theoretically with other things to which it is not strictly identical. What is the alternative to the standard way of identifying and individuating objects by reference to their distinct sets of properties? If the acorn is simply or simply identifiable in terms of its properties, say, P, Q, and R, then acorn A = [P,Q,R], while, bearing a quite different set of properties, oak tree T = [S,U,V]. It follows immediately that acorn A $\neq$ tree T, because, obviously, [P,Q,R] $\neq$ [S,U,V].

Even if we map the genetic DNA code for the acorn and oak as individual living things, uniquely shared by no other living things, genetically identical twins and clones aside, we still will not have an exactly matching property set in the two cases to justify concluding that the acorn persists through the changes it has undergone in becoming an oak tree. Now we have instead something like [P,Q,R,C] $\neq$ [S,U,V,C], from which, despite the shared property C denoting a jointly distributed identical genetic code, it still does not follow that A = T. By itself, the fact that A and T share some but not all their properties in common is not enough to prove their identity, just as it is not enough for any two different bicycles to be identical by virtue of sharing the property of having two wheels. The same is true even if two acorns or two entities of any type share virtually all of their properties in common, but differ even in the slightest degree with respect to even so few as a single property, as when an acorn changes from one instant to the next as a result of taking on the tiniest quantity of water that it did not previously possess from the surrounding soil, sending out a root or a shoot, or even undergoing imperceptible changes in its underlying microphysical structure as the electrons in the shells of its atoms move about. In that case, we might have: [P,Q,R,C, . . . ,S] $\neq$ [P,Q,R,C, . . . ,U], from which it still follows that A $\neq$ T, *if*, and that is finally the deeper metaphysical question underlying the inquiry in Aristotle's metaphysics, in the end, A = [P,Q,R,C, . . . ,S] and T = [P,Q,R,C, . . . ,U].

The best we can do, although it is clearly not good enough, is to specify the exemplifications of properties in the corresponding property sets of the same entity as occurring at different times. Thus, we might write: A = $[P^t,Q^t,R^t,S^{t'},U^{t'},V^{t'}]$ and T = $[P^t,Q^t,R^t,S^{t'},U^{t'},V^{t'}]$, from which it now appears to follow that A = T. The acorn is thereby described over time as having the same properties as the tree, and the change in properties by which an acorn becomes a tree is explicitly registered in the distinct times at which different properties are exemplified by one and the same entity, provided that t ≠ t'. The trouble is that in order in practice to implement a theory of identity whereby changing entities exemplify different properties at different times, we need a correct metaphysical principle by which to judge that properties exemplified at different times belong to the same entity and should therefore be included together in the same property set. This is the very question at issue in Aristotle's inquiry, which we cannot assume has already been solved. As we shall see, moreover, there are other related issues and other related difficulties that stand in the way of a straightforward solution to the problems of substance, change, and identity of objects undergoing change over time.

The history of philosophical commentary on the phenomenon of change contains many different sorts of answers to the problems we have outlined. The background to Aristotle's metaphysics includes his intricate familiarity with these sources, many of which are no longer available in their original texts today. Indeed, in many cases we know about these Presocratic thinkers and their attitudes to the problem of understanding change largely through Aristotle's and other ancient writers' discussions and occasional quotations. We can familiarize ourselves with some of the pre-Aristotelian approaches to the problem of change that would have been known to Aristotle in order to understand what is new in Aristotle's metaphysics.

PLATONIC AND PYTHAGOREAN BACKGROUND TO ARISTOTLE'S INQUIRY

We should begin, as Aristotle does in the *Metaphysics*, by looking at the source of a particular philosophical problem and previous attempts at solutions. To restate the problem that motivates much of Aristotle's work in this field, for which he offers his theory of substance as a solution, it is the question of how physical things can undergo change and yet in some sense remain the same.

Plato's theory of Forms is perhaps the most obvious place to start, even though Plato is evidently not a Presocratic. We have already seen that Plato, like Socrates, does not regard the changing world of appearance as real or as a basis for genuine knowledge. The very fact that the world we experience in sensation is constantly changing makes it of negligible value for Plato, and for Socrates too, who does not attribute value to the sensible order by contrast with the eternal soul and, to the extent that he may have accepted a prototypical version of Plato's theory of Forms, to the eternal unchanging Forms.

Aristotle characterizes the Platonic Forms as numbers. He does so partly because the Forms are supposed to be abstract like mathematical entities, and partly because the principle of individuation for changing things in the world of appearance for Plato seems to involve their exact locations in space and time, which can be completely characterized geometrically. Beyond this, Plato, like Pythagoras, regards mathematical entities, and numbers especially, as possessing philosophical and almost mystical significance as representing the forces of nature in definite rational proportions and harmonies. The idea of substance, *ousia* in ancient Greek, is thus closely related in the Pythagorean and Platonic schools to numbers or the properties of numbers, as Aristotle recognizes, when he maintains:

> Further, besides sensible things and Forms [Plato] says there are the objects of mathematics, which occupy an intermediate position, differing from sensible things in being eternal and unchangeable, from Forms in that there are many alike, while the Form itself is in each case unique.
>
> Since the Forms are the causes of all other things, he thought their elements were the elements of all things. As matter, the great and the small were principles; as substance, the One; for from the great and the small, by participation in the One, come the numbers.
>
> But he agreed with the Pythagoreans in saying that the One is substance and not a predicate of something else; and in saying that the numbers are the causes of the substance of other things, he also agreed with them; but positing a dyad and constructing the infinite out of great and small, instead of treating the infinite as one, is peculiar to him; and so is his view that the numbers exist apart from sensible things, while *they* say that the things themselves are numbers, and do not place the objects of mathematics between Forms and sensible things. (987^{b}14–29)

The changes that physical things undergo in the world of Becoming for Plato are understood in terms of the Forms they are trying more or less perfectly to imitate or in which they are trying to participate. Although Plato does not mention this particular example, it is clear that he would describe the changes an acorn undergoes in becoming an oak tree as steps along the way toward perfecting its nature, an acorn being just another kind of imperfect manifestation of a certain type of tree and hence of the Form of tree.

To the extent that Plato is interested in the specific processes involved in the changing world of appearance, he would insist that when an acorn changes into a tree, the acorn and the tree all along participate in the same Form, and the successive stages of change that the acorn goes through in becoming an oak tree are developmental phases in its realizing the Form to which it belongs in the best and most complete way it can under prevailing circumstances in the world of Becoming. A changing object's participation in a particular Form explains its identity through change, while the geometrical Forms provide a more specific formal identity for a changing physical entity to be specified in terms of the continuity by which it occupies specific spatial locations at particular times. This is presumably why Aristotle refers to number and the mathematical properties of things in Plato's formalistic conception of the identity conditions for changing things.

Aristotle does not accept Plato's theory of Forms, but questions whether numbers are adequate to understand what it means for an object to change while in other ways remaining the same. He objects to Platonic Forms and numbers on the grounds that abstract entities by themselves do not adequately identify and individuate particular entities. In the first place, Aristotle does not accept the existence of abstract Platonic Forms and mathematical entities. Even if he did, Aristotle believes that Platonic Forms, including numbers, by virtue of their universality, could never adequately identify or individuate particular sensible things undergoing change by passing from one set of properties to another. Thus, Aristotle rejects Plato's theory of abstract Forms as a way of explaining identity through change, and decides that he must continue his search for a satisfactory answer to the problem.

The trouble with Forms and numbers is that, at least as Plato and Pythagoras interpret them, they are not part of the world of Becoming with which Aristotle is primarily concerned, but belong to an abstract order. They are supposed to populate the unchanging world of Being as opposed to the world of Becoming where change occurs. We know from many of Aristotle's writings that he rejects the concept of Platonic Forms, and argues at length against Plato's theory. In the *Nicomachean Ethics*, for example, Aristotle targets Plato's Form of the Good as an abstract concept which he attacks with six different criticisms. Aristotle rejects Plato's universal Form of the Good and presents an alternative concept of earthly human goods for human beings as social animals living real lives in the nonideal world as we find it, with all its problems and imperfections. Aristotle does not accept Plato's distinction between the world of Being and the world of Becoming, of real unchanging abstract Forms versus changing appearances. As a result, Aristotle is not willing to countenance the application of Forms or numbers as any part of the solution to the problem of explaining the metaphysics of change and the persistence of dynamic entities such as acorns and oak trees through change.

MATERIAL ELEMENTS IN THE PRESOCRATICS

If we turn next to the Presocratics, we find in the few surviving fragments of their writings a wide variety of proposals concerning the metaphysics of change. Some of the Presocratics were early scientific thinkers who sought to explain natural phenomena in terms of a single underlying principle. The desire to reduce the complexity of the world to a simple set of basic laws remains one of the most important driving forces in science and philosophy even today. It is amusing from a contemporary standpoint to see that some of the Presocratic solutions to the problem of change try to reduce the complexity of experienceable phenomena to so few and such overly simplified principles as to seem implausible.

Thales of Miletus, for example, taught that all things are water. Anaximenes maintained that all things are air, and Heraclitus of Ephesus, who emphasized the perpetually changing nature of the physical world, believed that all things are fire. If it is true in some sense that all physical things really are any of these elements, water, say, as Thales would have it, then, whatever scientific and philosophical explanatory problems such a theory might entail, the approach at least helps to account for how the same things are capable of undergoing change, preserving their identity throughout the process. Things can change despite remaining the same, according to some of the Presocratics, because everything is ultimately made of water (or air or fire). We know from everyday experience that water persists through drastic changes of state when it is converted from one physical form to another, changing from ice to liquid to steam and back again. It might be that Thales had these kinds of facts in mind in generalizing that all things are water.

Since Thales and most of the other Presocratics experimented with philosophical conjectures in the form of poetry or aphorisms, it is not always clear whether we are supposed to interpret their ideas literally or only metaphorically. Thales might have meant that all physical things are actually water in a larger number of different kinds of forms, so that even earth and metals and human bodies are ultimately made of nothing but different configurations of water. Alternatively, Thales might have meant that all physical things are water in an analogical sense, meaning that all things are like water in that they are all ultimately composed of a simpler element or set of elements that can be transformed in at least as many different ways as can ordinary water. Or Thales might have meant that all things are water in much the same sense that Heraclitus seems to have described all things as fire, flowing and continually in flux, a stream of physical stuff constantly changing its configuration, where differences in the arrangements of its parts can be used to explain the changing appearances of things.

Similarly with respect to other Presocratic hypotheses about the physical world as consisting ultimately of fire or air. Empedocles, as Aristotle recounts, combined several of the material first principles of other Presocratics, explaining all physical change in terms of fire, water, and air, apparently in an effort to capitalize on the advantages of all three of these elements while avoiding the explanatory limitations of relying on any single one. Aristotle expresses greater interest in theories involving such combinations of elements than in explanations involving only elements such as water, fire, or air, considered individually, although he also does not accept any of the combination of elements theories in their original formulations. He nevertheless devotes more attention to Presocratic thinkers who tried to explain the nature of substance in concrete physical terms, in contrast with Plato's theory of Forms and Pythagorean references to numbers as abstract mathematical entities.

Aristotle lumps together many of the Presocratics who tried to explain the identity, individuation, and change of physical things in the physical world. In an important passage, he contrasts Plato's solution involving Forms and numbers with matter and material elements as the opposite theory:

> Our account of those who have spoken about first principles and reality and of the way in which they have spoken, has been concise and summary; but yet we have learnt this much from them, that of those who speak about principle and cause no one has mentioned any principle except those which have been distinguished in our work on nature, but all evidently have some inkling of *them*, though only vaguely. For some speak of the first principle as matter, whether they suppose one or more first principles, and whether they suppose this to be a body or to be incorporeal; e.g. Plato spoke of the great and the small, the Italians of the infinite, Empedocles of fire, earth, water, and air, Anaxagoras of the infinity of homogeneous things. These, then, have all had a notion of this kind of cause, and so have all who speak of air or fire or water, or something denser than fire and rarer than air; for some have said the prime element is of this kind. (988ª17–35)

Aristotle regards all Presocratic attempts to understand the nature of substance as superficial. He speaks in this context of the materialist philosophy of the "Italians," by whom he means most of the Presocratic thinkers we have already mentioned living in Greek colonies on the Italian peninsula.

Aristotle accepts the existence of the material elements, earth, air, fire, and water, so important to the materialist Presocratics, to which he adds the further element of æther as the material stuff of stars and planets and other heavenly bodies. He interprets the elements as vital to an explanation of changing physical phenomena, but not yet the most ultimate substance of the experienceable realm of the senses, and as such not yet among the basic principles of a sufficiently general first philosophy. There is, in Aristotle's metaphysics, a more basic type of matter, which he calls "prime matter," *proté hylé*. Prime matter is pure undifferentiated physical stuff that underlies all physical entities, including the five elements, at their deepest level of material constitution. There is some reason to think that Aristotle might have derived his idea of prime matter from another Presocratic philosopher, Anaxagoras, who put forth the idea of the *indeterminate* that can become anything if, like a piece of clay, it is properly shaped. Aristotle seems to regard the other Presocratics as having confused four of the elements as the ultimate material principles of the changing world. He believes on the contrary that prime matter is the most fundamental material stuff from which the five elements are constituted.

Aside from the conclusions Aristotle later draws concerning the nature of matter, he criticizes the Presocratic reliance on concepts of particular experienceable material elements in order to explain the phenomenon of change and the persistence of physical things undergoing change. He faults them for making a very different mistake from that of Plato and the Pythagoreans. Whereas the theory of abstract Forms or numbers does not seem to account for the individuality of distinct material objects, Aristotle complains that the Presocratic materialism of Thales, Anaximenes, and Empedocles, leaving Anaxagoras and the concept of the indeterminate or infinite out of the picture for the moment, are unable to explain satisfactorily the metaphysics of abstract entities. Aristotle designates these as "incorporeals," in effect something like the Platonic Forms, which he does not recognize as such, but for which he again offers his own revised doctrine of definitions or secondary substances. The implication, if Aristotle's critique is correct, is that while the Platonists and Pythagoreans did not do justice to the metaphysics of corporeal or material things, the more materialistically minded Presocratics equally failed to explain the metaphysics of incorporeal or qualifiedly "abstract" things. He observes:

> Those, then, who say the universe is one and posit one kind of thing as matter, and as corporeal matter which has spatial magnitude, evidently go astray in many ways. For they posit the elements of bodies only, not of incorporeal things, though there are incorporeal things. And in trying to state the causes of generation and destruction, and in giving an account of the nature of all things, they do away with the cause of movement. Further, they err in not positing the substance, i.e. the essence, as the cause of anything, and besides this in lightly calling any of the simple bodies except earth the first principle, without inquiring how they are produced out of one another,—I mean fire, water, earth, and air. (988^b21–31)

Without elaborating on his reasons, Aristotle also finds it unsatisfactory that the Presocratics he mentions did not theorize about substance generally or the specific types of material substance that each of the Presocratic thinkers in this category individually championed as causes, formal principles, or the very "essence" of a thing. Aristotle regards this omission as a failure on the part of the early Presocratics, although in this place he does not try to say why. A more thorough examination of his first philosophy is needed in order to understand what Aristotle considers objectionable about the Presocratics overlooking this further step in trying to explain the metaphysics of change. Aristotle discovers other inadequacies in the Presocratic reliance on physical elements as explanatory principles for complete and correct first philosophical inquiry. He continues:

> For some things are produced out of others by combination, others by separation, and this makes the greatest difference to their priority and posteriority. For in a way the property of being most elementary of all would seem to belong to the first thing from which they are produced by combination, and *this* property would belong to the most fine-grained and subtle of bodies. Therefore, those who make fire the principle would be most in agreement with this argument. But each of the other thinkers agrees that the element of corporeal things is of this sort. (988^{b}31–989^{a}4)

A more satisfactory analysis of the concept of material substance than that offered by Presocratic materialists, Aristotle believes, would need to delve more deeply into the conditions for the generation of all material elements. Aristotle remarks on the anomaly that none of the Presocratics proposes earth as a basic element by which all other elements and all physical entities are produced and may be individuated, so that their changes might be traced through space and time as they are transformed in various ways.

Aristotle argues that, if anything, earth ought to be regarded as more basic than fire, water, and air, from the standpoint of how some of the elements might be produced from the others, as he says, "by combination." Apparently the reason is that earth is less dense in internal structure and composition than the other elements, which can therefore be made from it by compacting its material substances in such a way as to produce water, fire, and air. It seems strange to regard air and fire as more dense than earth, if we are meant to think of these material substances in anything like the form in which we typically encounter them. Aristotle, nevertheless, singles out fire in particular for criticism as a preferred basic element among the Presocratics, contrary to which he maintains they should instead prefer earth. A confident interpretation is difficult because we do not know exactly what Aristotle or the Presocratics meant by the concept of a material element, or in exactly what sense they spoke of water, fire, earth, and air as basic material principles underlying the world of change. It is worth noting that Aristotle rejects their materialist solution to the problems of change as thoroughly as he rejects Plato's and Pythagoras's formalist-numerical solution.

As a rather different Presocratic approach for which Aristotle has more sympathy, we should now say something more about Anaxagoras, who believed that all things are what he called the indeterminate, and which some English translations render less informatively as "infinity" or "the infinite." The concept of the indeterminate is a way of describing the potentiality of physical stuff to be configured and reconfigured in an unlimited number of ways. On such a theory, physical things change while in another sense remaining the same because at bottom they are all composed of some kind of determination being imposed on the indeterminate as an underlying undifferentiated *something*. This is a more difficult concept than that of the other Presocratics, insofar as it seems to be less concrete. Aristotle nevertheless regards the concept of potentiality as vitally important in understanding natural phenomena, and especially in explaining the changes and the persistence of identical things through change. Aristotle, despite his greater sympathy for Anaxagoras's concept, is unprepared to accept the indeterminate in its original mystical formulation. He revises the concept in his own way to fit in with the decidedly more scientific principles of his philosophy.

The final Presocratic thinker whose ideas should be considered in this context is Democritus of Abdera. Democritus as a materialist philosopher is the extreme opposite of Plato's formalism. Unlike the other materialists we have mentioned, Democritus does not commit himself to the existence of any particular element, but develops an atomic theory of physical matter, according to which all physical things are composed of tiny atoms or material corpuscles. The atoms are too small to see, inelastic, impenetrable, and capable of combining with other atoms in unlimitedly many different ways to compose the wide array of physical objects we perceive. The materialist answer to the question how sensible things can undergo change while yet remaining the same in Democritus's philosophy is that the ultimate material constitutions of these physical entities are composed of atoms in different configurations, and that change occurs when the atoms in an object are lost or change their positions in the internal configuration to which they belong, or when other atoms are added to a given configuration.

The possibility of change and the persistence of perceivable things through change is accounted for in Democritus's atomistic theory in terms of arrangements and rearrangements of atoms, provided that at least some of the original atoms in a thing are preserved from moment to moment through each phase of change. We might imagine a common core of atoms staying the course as others are shed, added, or transposed, when a physical entity undergoes change. If all of the original atoms are eventually lost, we might still think of the same object surviving through even the most drastic change, unless, of course, it is completely destroyed, by virtue of an overlap of shared collections of atoms successively reconfigured over time, or persisting distributively as a scattered object. Although Aristotle does not mention Democritus by name in this part of the *Metaphysics*, it is evident that he knew of Democritus's many writings. In considering materialist solutions to the problem of change and the identity of "bodies" or material entities through change, Aristotle probably means to include Democritus along with the other Presocratics.

The comparison of theories in Aristotle's survey of previous solutions to the problem of change opposes the formalism of Plato and Pythagoras with the materialism of the Presocratics, especially Thales, Anaximenes, Empedocles, and Democritus. Aristotle believes that they all have worthwhile if ultimately incorrect things to say about the problem of understanding change and identity through change. He further believes, when he is done, that he will have improved on their solutions, adopting the best of their ideas and developing them in his own way. If the later materialists did not arrive at exactly the right answer, Aristotle seems to believe they were at least proceeding in a more correct direction than the formalists. By critically examining the views of formalists and materialists, Aristotle sets the stage for a synthesis of their respective solutions that combines in the right way considerations of form and considerations of matter in a theory of substance.

METAPHYSICS AS A SCIENCE OF SUBSTANCE

One of the most valuable aspects of Aristotle's treatise on first philosophy is its self-conscious examination of the proper method of metaphysics. Aristotle is concerned to explain exactly how he intends to proceed in answering questions about the concept of substance. He needs to relate his way of approaching the problem of change and the persistence of physical things through change to the general knowledge-validating criteria that he endorses in opposition to those of his teacher Plato.

Aristotle requires a special method to discover and justify knowledge concerning the physical world. Plato, and Socrates, if Plato has accurately presented Socrates' views in the *Meno*, believes that the genuine knowledge does not need to be acquired at all, and may not be possible to acquire. For Socrates, knowledge is exclusively of the eternal Forms, a permanent possession of our immortal souls, that needs only to be stirred up into active memory by the right sort of dialectical stimulation, in order to be recollected. Aristotle believes that we can know about existent objects and their properties in the phenomenal world that we experience in perception. When it comes to the more "abstract" properties of things and what Aristotle generally classifies under the heading of "incorporeals," he holds that we can know about these things only through perception, in the first place, together with critical philosophical reflection on the contents of experience in an effort to discern within experience the principles needed to understand the nature of the world as it is perceived.

The first step in Aristotle's effort to delimit the field of metaphysics is to distinguish it from other disciplines such as natural science and mathematics. Aristotle begins tentatively and conditionally. He says, in effect, that if there is something "abstract," which he characterizes here as "eternal" and "immovable," then it belongs to a theoretical science. He describes the abstract as a truth or principle applying generally to phenomena we can know through experience, but that presupposes a kind of nonphysical existence, which Aristotle designates as *subsistence,* and by which he means a thing that has only a dependent kind of being by virtue of inhering in another existent thing. We have already mentioned as examples of inherence the definition or secondary substance of *horse* inhering in an existent horse. The same will be true for any universal quality or property for which Plato would posit the existence of an eternal unchanging Form. Aristotle argues that there must be a special science to investigate immovables, which no other discipline addresses. Aristotle speaks of the theory required for the investigation of extra-spatiotemporal, and hence unchanging or eternal and immovable subsistent, entities as a speculative science or ontology, and finally as "first philosophy." He briefly sketches the problem of identifying a proper subject for the study of these topics, and explains why it will not do to relegate their investigation to physics or mathematics. He remarks:

> But if there is something which is eternal and immovable and separable [from matter], clearly the knowledge of it belongs to a theoretical science,—not, however, to natural science (for natural science deals with certain movable things) nor to mathematics, but a science prior to both. For natural science deals with things

which are inseparable from matter but not immovable, and some parts of mathematics deals with things which are immovable but probably not separable, but embodied in matter; while the first science deals with things which are both separable and immovable. (1026ª10–17)

Physics is the science of motion, and as such takes movable things and the study of their changing places in space through time as its subject. Although Aristotle does not mention biology, psychology, or any of the other natural sciences in this connection, it is clear that what he says about physics applies with appropriate qualifications to any other science of changing phenomena. No natural science of movable spatiotemporal things can possibly be appropriate for the study of abstract immovables. With physics set aside, Aristotle turns next to mathematics as a science that aims at understanding at least some kinds of abstract immovables.

Mathematical objects, numbers and geometrical figures and the like, are not subject to movement or change, and as such might be thought to be a fitting arena for investigation of all subsistent abstract entities, the principles and properties of things that are in Aristotle's sense eternal and immovable. Surprisingly, Aristotle refuses to include the immovables discovered in experience as part of mathematics because mathematics in his view is not sufficiently abstract to accommodate the principles needed for the secondary substances inherent in perceivable things. He argues that only some mathematical sciences have to do with immovables, and that even these are not concerned with a subject matter that is also "separable" from movable entities.

What Aristotle means by this pronouncement is not immediately obvious, but on examination the implication is clear enough. It appears that Aristotle understands mathematics exclusively in the sense of what we would today call applied mathematics, and has no concept of pure mathematics. The difference in contemporary terms is that pure mathematics is the development of formal systems of completely abstract mathematical relations that Aristotle would describe as "separable" from movable entities, without considering their usefulness in understanding the material world, but entirely in themselves. Pure mathematics is thus the mathematical equivalent of art for art's sake, but it appears that Aristotle has no such category. Applied mathematics, on the other hand, as the name suggests, involves the use of mathematics in understanding and trying to predict and control physical phenomena in the material world. A clear-cut example of applied mathematics is the use of mathematical principles in engineering to build a bridge or design an airplane. Aristotle does not acknowledge the difference between pure and applied mathematics under any terms, and it would no doubt have been a strange idea for any thinker of his time. He appears to think of mathematics as nothing but the application of formal principles of number and geometrical shape to the movables of the spatiotemporal world. If this is not his sweeping assumption about the nature of mathematics, then it is hard to see how he could insist that mathematics, even if some of it deals with immovables, is ultimately inseparable from all movables.

Whether or not Aristotle is right to conceive of mathematics in this way, given his interpretation of the nature of mathematics, it is plain why he does not propose to include the study of the immovables discovered through reflection on experience as eternal, immovable and requiring a separable subsistence in mathematics. Physics does not involve eternal or immovable entities. Mathematics, on the other hand, as

Aristotle thinks of it, does not subsume subsistent entities that are separable from movable spatiotemporal physical entities, but always concerns numbers, shapes, and mathematical objects and relations generally that are inseparable from, presumably in the sense of being necessarily instantiated and understandable exclusively as inherent in, the dynamic movable things that we can count and whose geometrical properties, shapes, distances, and other spatiotemporal features we can perceive.

If neither physics nor mathematics is the rightful home of the most basic principles of philosophy, then a special third category of specifically philosophical discipline must be designated for the purpose of investigating inherent subsistent immovables. Aristotle accordingly establishes a new science, the science of metaphysics, which in his technical language is ontology, first philosophy, or theology. Metaphysics is the investigation of fundamental concepts, distinctions, and truths on which all the rest of philosophy, mathematics, and the physical sciences depend. What by implication is necessary and sufficient for the principles of first philosophy, marking the requirements of a discipline that is unique among the physical and mathematical sciences, is that they are eternal, immovable, and separable from the realm of movable spatiotemporal entities. The question that must eventually be considered is therefore whether Aristotle's immovables are themselves entirely separable from movable things in the way he denies that mathematical objects, properties, and principles are separable.

Interestingly, Aristotle also declares after the final sentence of the above passage that the principles of first philosophy concern matters of divinity, that the principles of first philosophy are in some sense among the divine causes of what is manifest or phenomenal. The unexpected association of the most basic principles of metaphysics in first philosophy with the concept of the divine in Aristotle's argument introduces yet another designation for the philosophical study of the ultimate principles of knowledge as theology. Aristotle explicitly distinguishes these categories of inquiry, when he adds:

> Now all causes must be eternal, but especially these; for they are the causes of so much of the divine as appears to us. There must, then, be three theoretical philosophies, mathematics, natural science, and theology, since it is obvious that if the divine is present anywhere, it is present in things of this sort. And the highest science must deal with the highest genus, so that the theoretical sciences are superior to the other sciences, and this to the other theoretical sciences. (1026ª17–23)

Having distinguished between mathematics, natural science, and theology or first philosophy, Aristotle asks which of these ought to be considered the most general. The answer turns out to be that it depends on whether or not there exist immovables. If so, as Aristotle believes, then first philosophy is first; but if it were otherwise, then natural science would be the first and most important discipline. Aristotle now adds:

> One might indeed raise the question whether first philosophy is universal, or deals with one genus, i.e. some one kind of being; for not even the mathematical sciences are all alike in this respect—geometry and astronomy deal with a certain particular kind of thing, while universal mathematics applies alike to all. We answer that if there is no substance other than those which are formed by nature,

natural science will be the first science; but if there is an immovable substance, the science of this must be prior and must be first philosophy, and universal in this way, because it is first. And it will belong to this to consider being *qua* being—both what it is and the attributes which belong to it *qua* being. (1026ª24–33)

What makes metaphysics or philosophy divine, and what qualifies it as theology or the systematic study of god or the gods, is the fact that first philosophy as a speculative science investigates concepts that are so fundamental that it must be in touch with the divine or with things in whose nature the divine resides, and as such is most deserving of the sort of respect that is usually accorded religious teachings. Metaphysics or the speculative science Aristotle projects as a necessary foundation to all philosophy and the specialized sciences is thus aptly described also as theology. Ontology in particular is explained by Aristotle as the study of being *qua* being, a Latin term introduced by Aristotle's later editors for his concept of being considered only as such. Aristotle regards first philosophy as theology in the sense that its ultimate principles lead to a distinctive conception of god in a detached metaphysical or philosophical sense, rather than as a subject of popular religious worship.

Aristotle does not believe that he is the first thinker to have advanced the study of first philosophy. He recognizes that others have come before him and made their own worthwhile contributions to the field. He is willing to incorporate some of these ideas into his own theory. The appropriate question, which Aristotle poses only much later in the text, concerning the scope and limits of first philosophy, is whether metaphysics is one science or many different sciences rolled into one. It is important for Aristotle's method to determine from the outset whether first philosophy as a single discipline is capable of dealing with all metaphysical problems, or whether a network of distinct theories is required, each corresponding to a distinct subdivision of its complete subject matter. Aristotle accordingly asks:

That Wisdom is a science of first principles, is evident from the introductory chapters in which we have raised objections to the statements of others about the first principles; but one might ask the question whether Wisdom is to be conceived as one science or as several. If as one, it may be objected that one science always deals with contraries, but the first principles are not contrary. If it is not one, what are these sciences with which it is to be identified?

Further, is it the business of one science or of more to examine the first principles of demonstration? If of one, why of this rather than of any other? If of more, which must these be said to be?

Further, does it investigate all substances or not? If not all, it is hard to say which; but if, being one, it investigates them all, it is doubtful how the same science can embrace several subject matters. (1059ª18–28)

Aristotle reasons that if first philosophy is one unified science, then it might be thought to be a science of the contraries, the concept of which remains to be explained, but concerning which Aristotle assures us there is generally understood to be just one science. The purpose of first philosophy is to identify first principles, and contraries are evidently not first principles. If first philosophy does not constitute a single unified science, then Aristotle thinks that before we can proceed to answer its questions, we must first try to specify all the various sciences that are needed to investigate its problems.

Contraries and the concept of *contrariety* are important ideas in Aristotle's metaphysics. There is a contrariety for every type of change, involving pairs of contrary properties. In the case of movement, for example, to simplify things, an object might be said to undergo change from left to right, for which the corresponding contrariety is left-right. Where the aging of a living thing is concerned, an animal might be said to undergo change from young to old, for the contrariety young-old. Similarly for all changes of which individual things are capable, as they are altered in their properties or dispositions from one contrary component of a contrariety to the other. We will need to say more about Aristotle's theory of contrariety in understanding the metaphysics of substance. For the moment, it should suffice to see that Aristotle believes that there can only be one science of the contraries. This suggests that the one and only science of the contraries might be the sought-after discipline of first philosophy. Aristotle nevertheless denies that a science of contraries could be first philosophy, because first philosophy is concerned with first principles, and contraries are not first principles. The mere fact that there is but one unified science of the contraries and that first philosophy is also supposed to be a single unified science by itself does not mean that they are one and the same. The implication is that first philosophy must be constituted as a distinct single unified science like the science of contraries, but one concerning first principles having to do with the concept and common nature of many different kinds of substances. Aristotle continues:

> Substance is the subject of our inquiry; for the principles and the causes we are seeking are those of substances. For if the universe is of the nature of a whole, substance is its first part; and if it coheres by virtue of succession, on this view also substance is first, and is succeeded by quality, and then by quantity. At the same time these latter are not even beings in the unqualified sense, but are quantities and movements—or else even the not-white and the not-straight would be; at least we say even these *are*, e.g. "there is a not-white." Further, none of the others can exist apart. (1069ª17–24)

A difficult passage, but we can make sense of it. Aristotle distinguishes between substance, which he regards as primary, and its properties, qualities, and quantities as secondary substances. If the universe is a One or whole indivisible thing, as Parmenides and his followers, including Plato, believe, then substance is still its "first part," and hence the subject of metaphysics. If, on the other hand, the universe is a successive entity, persisting through changes in space and time, then its substance is still its first part, to which the properties of quality and quantity attach to something that already exists.

The question throughout is whether anything of which philosophers speak can have priority over the concept of substance in first philosophy. Aristotle answers "no," on the grounds that none of these things can exist apart from substance. To emphasize the point, Aristotle includes even such contraries as the not-white and not-straight, which are generally related to substance in referring to *a* [something that is] not-white or *a* [something that is] not-straight as the source of the concepts or categories of properties. Without such substantializations of properties, Aristotle says, we do not speak of qualities or quantities as existing independently of the substances in which they inhere.

We see that Aristotle is in search of a single unified speculative science of substance as the proper subject matter of first philosophy. The point of Aristotle's consideration of these alternatives for the science of metaphysics is to establish the requirements of a special discipline to ask and try to answer these specific kinds of questions. There must in some sense be unity and in some sense diversity. Aristotle concludes that there is just one concept of substance, and hence justification for a single unified science of first philosophy to investigate the first principles of all other sciences, even though there are many different kinds and categories of substance. The conclusion is not that there must be different sciences for each type of substance, but different first principles that are investigated by one and the same science looking into the properties of every distinct category of substance. In the end, Aristotle classifies all substances into precisely three main categories, of which there are many first principles intended to explain substance as a factor in the phenomena of physical change.

Systematic Ambiguity of the Concept of Substance

As he does in most of his writings, Aristotle devotes considerable attention to subtle nuances of different but related ways in which a term of philosophical interest is used in everyday language. The word *substance (ousia)* is a relevant case in point. Aristotle observes that the term can have several different meanings. If there is no underlying unity to these terminological variations, and if first philosophy is supposed to explain the nature of substance or substances, then we are back to the problem of whether there is just one science or many sciences of substance. We would then need to ask again whether first philosophy as a special theory of substance is warranted, or whether the study of substances should instead be turned over to diversified physical sciences that are already in practice.

Aristotle claims that there is a unity in the concept of substance underlying the multiplicity of ways in which substance is described in ordinary thought and discourse. He talks about substance in several ways, all of which seem to reflect a single concept of substance understood from different perspectives. The first definition Aristotle considers is that substance is whatever it is that is primarily an entity, primarily an existent thing. He explains:

> Therefore that which is primarily and *is* simply (not is something) must be substance. (1028ª30)

This compact formulation conceals a double meaning. We can think of Aristotle as defining the concept of substance in simple terms as whatever is an entity "simply" or absolutely, which Aristotle also says is "primarily" an entity. Aristotle refers to substances that satisfy this definition as "primary substances." The category includes the things we ordinarily regard as discrete distinct objects, our bodies, animals, stones, books, statues, chairs, trees, and even more complex entities such as planets, stars, galaxies.

All of these are primary substances in Aristotle's sense, and as such are substances in the most basic sense of the word. Yet they are not the only kind of substance. Primary substances are said to be independent in that they do not require the existence of anything else in order to exist, and in that sense they are, as Aristotle remarks, simply or absolutely entities. All other entities and kinds of entities, Aristotle believes, are dependent for their existence or subsistence on the existence of primary substances, in which other kinds of entities inhere or in the existence of which they are exemplified.

Under this category Aristotle includes the definitions or secondary substances as forms (with a small f), in his revised conception of Platonic Forms. These kinds of substances have no independent existence despite being entities of a sort, but subsist only insofar as they inhere or are instantiated in existent primary substances. Primary substances also materially subsume more basic physical substances, including the material elements, earth, air, fire, water, and æther, as well as prime matter, the more basic material substratum of all primary substances. The concept of secondary substance and the distinction between primary and secondary substance are mentioned only indirectly, when Aristotle divides the systematically ambiguous concept of substance into these two main categories:

> It follows, then, that substance has two senses, (a) the ultimate substratum, which is no longer predicated of anything else, and (b) that which is a "this" and separable—and of this nature is the shape or form of each thing. (1017^{b}23–25)

The form and species of each thing is that which distinguishes it from every other thing. This basis for the differentiation of distinct primary substances is due to differences in their definitions or secondary substances. Secondary substances literally define the primary substances in which they inhere as the specific kinds of things they are. The properties that belong to a primary substance are definitions or secondary substances, and would not subsist if the primary substances in which they inhere did not exist; yet Aristotle remarks that both types are substances in two different senses of the word.

Aristotle also provides a useful grammatical criterion for distinguishing between primary and secondary substances. The difference is that secondary substances can be predicated of other things, in fact, only of primary substances, whereas primary substances cannot be predicated of anything, or as we might say, of any other thing. What Aristotle means is that we can predicate the secondary substance *horse* of a particular primary substance, say, Old Paint. Old Paint can have the property of being a horse. But we cannot predicate Old Paint of anything. Old Paint the horse in the barn or field is not a property to be predicated. By distinguishing between primary and secondary substances in this way, Aristotle further explains the sense in which primary substances are simply or absolutely entities. A secondary substance, form or species, definition or property of a primary substance, such as the property of being red or round or virtuous or anything else, does not subsist independently on its own, but only insofar as it is exemplified by, instantiated, or inheres in a primary substance.

The concept of primary substance as that which is capable of existing independently, of which properties, definitions, or secondary substances can be predicated, but is not in turn predicable of anything else, was to have a lasting impact on the future of metaphysics. It was widely accepted through the medieval period especially into the rise of modern philosophy in the seventeenth century, and in one form or another even in contemporary philosophical thought. Aristotle's analysis provides a single and unified concept of primary substance. It offers an intuitive commonsense basis for distinguishing between primary substances and secondary substances that seems to establish what Aristotle demands of first philosophy as a single unified speculative science. The subject matter of first philosophy, ontology, or theology, is substance, to be distinguished into primary and secondary substance according to Aristotle's criterion.

The difference between Aristotle and Plato as a result could hardly be more extreme. Whereas Plato believes that the Forms are the most real and only legitimate subject of genuine knowledge, his gaze fixed on the heavenly abstract realm of general ideal concepts that are at best only imperfectly realized in the changing world of appearance, Aristotle regards primary substances in the changing world of spatiotemporal things as the most real and important. These are the entities that we experience directly in sensation, that alone are genuinely knowable, according to Aristotle, together with the secondary substances that inhere in them and by which they are defined. The secondary substances, Aristotle's diluted reconceptualization of the Platonic Forms, are, as even the name of their category indicates, of secondary importance relative to the primary substances to which secondary substances belong and of which they are predicated, while the subsistence of secondary substances depends metaphysically on the existence of the primary substances in which they inhere.

The forked paths represented by Plato's and Aristotle's philosophies lead away in very different directions. Plato describes a route to abstract entities as the only things we can truly know, and makes pure reason the method of recollecting knowledge of the eternal unchanging Forms. Aristotle points instead to empirical knowledge of the physical entities we can know through sense experience, and relegates the Platonic Forms as secondary substances to a clearly secondary ontological and explanatory role in first philosophy. The two thinkers in their metaphysics and epistemology are thus fundamentally opposed. The future course of philosophy after Plato and Aristotle has similarly been divided time and time again into systems of thought that favor abstract ideas versus concrete sense experience.

Aristotle summarizes and extends the distinction between primary and secondary substances, relying on the criterion by which primary substances unlike secondary substances are not predicable of any other thing. He nevertheless drops an important clue about the metaphysical relationship between primary and secondary substances, remarking that some secondary substances are vital to the existence of the primary substances in which they inhere. If a certain kind of secondary substance inhering in a primary substance is removed or eliminated, Aristotle argues, the primary substance cannot continue to exist, but is destroyed and ceases to exist. Secondary substances in Aristotle's metaphysics are ontologically dependent on the primary substances in which they inhere. They do not subsist absolutely and could not subsist independently of the primary substances of which they are predicated. Aristotle also maintains, however, that the primary substances we encounter in sense experience must have properties, without which they could not exist, and may even need to be identified and individuated by reference to their predicables. It is one thing for an apple to be red or green or yellow, to be a primary substance in which these color properties or secondary substances inhere, and another thing altogether to imagine that an apple as a primary substance could exist without any color properties at all, entirely lacking, say, in those secondary substances that give it shape, taste, odor, weight, volume, and all the other qualities that we believe happen to belong to this or that particular apple as a distinct primary substance.

There is thus a kind of metaphysical reciprocity between primary and secondary substances. The subsistence of secondary substances is ontologically dependent on the existence of the particular primary substances in which they inhere. The existence of primary substances is independent of the subsistence of this or that particular secondary substance inhering in them; their existence is unthinkable without the inherence of some secondary substances or other. Aristotle hints that there may be special types of secondary substances, the subsistence of which in a certain primary substance may be indispensable to the existence or continuing existence of a given primary substance. These would then be properties without which the primary substance cannot survive or persist through change. If the primary substance in question were to be deprived of the relevant secondary substance or secondary substances, it would effectively be destroyed, at least as the same particular kind of primary substance. Aristotle refers to a secondary substance that cannot be eliminated from a primary substance without destroying it as the substance's "essence":

> We call substances (1) the simple bodies, i.e. earth and fire and water and everything of the sort, and in general bodies and the things composed of them, both animals and divine beings, and the parts of these. All these are called substance because they are not predicated of a subject but everything else is predicated of them.—(2) That which, being present in such things as are not predicated of a subject, is the cause of their being, as the soul is of the being of animals.—(3) The parts which are present in such things, limiting them and marking them as individuals, and by whose destruction the whole is destroyed, as the body is by the destruction of the plane, as some say, and the plane by the destruction of the line; and in general number is thought by some to be of this nature; for if it is destroyed, they say, nothing exists, and it limits all things.—(4) The essence, the formula of which is a definition, is also called the substance of each thing. (1017^b10–22)

If a human being is defined as a rational animal, then any particular human being is a primary substance in which the secondary substances of being rational and being an animal must inhere. If the secondary substance of being rational or being an animal is somehow taken away from a human being, then that human being would immediately cease to exist. What would remain might be an animal or something rational, but it would not be a human being.

Again, Aristotle emphasizes that physical entities or "bodies" should most properly be understood as substances, and hence as primary substances. He refers to the "simple bodies" or elements in this connection also as substances, including fire, water, and earth. There is a crucial distinction to be observed between the material elements, earth, air, fire, and water (and æther) on the one hand as the underlying physical substance of which primary substances are composed, and on the other hand as primary substances themselves.

The latter status of material entities as primary substances holds true, so to speak, for discrete and distinct samples of earth, air, fire, water, and æther. Such entities are particular quantities of a particular type of earth or air, fire, water, or æther, as opposed to such elements considered without sufficient definition or form so as to constitute a particular physical entity; earth or air or fire or water or æther in general. These are said to represent substance in another sense than that in which this or that individual quantity or portion of these elements is said to qualify as a "body" in Aristotle's technical sense. They are different in any case than primary substances construed as physical entities of which predicables can be attributed, hot or cold or wet or dry, and so on; for they are not themselves predicable, since they cannot be attributed to any other thing. Aristotle maintains:

> Substance is thought to belong most obviously to bodies; and so we say that both animals and plants and their parts are substances, and so are natural bodies such as fire and water and earth and everything of the sort, and all things that are parts of these or composed of these (either of parts or of the whole bodies), e.g. the heaven and its parts, stars and moon and sun. But whether these alone are substances, or there are also others, or only some of these, or some of these and some other things are substances, or none of these but only some other things, must be considered. Some think the limits of body, i.e. surface, line, point, and unit, are substances, and more so than body or the solid. Further, some do not think there is anything substantial besides sensible things, but others think there are eternal substances which are more in number and more real, e.g. Plato posited two kinds of substance—the Forms and the objects of mathematics—as well as a third kind, viz. the substance of sensible bodies. And Speusippus made still more kinds of substance, beginning with the One, and making principles for each kind of substance, one for numbers, another for spatial magnitudes, and then another for the soul; and in this way he multiplies the kinds of substance. And some say Forms and numbers have the same nature, and other things come after them, e.g. lines and planes, until we come to the substance of the heavens and the sensible bodies. (1028^{a}9–26)

As he often does, Aristotle begins with a rundown of ways in which other thinkers have spoken of the concept of substance. In the process, he soon identifies a choice of interesting questions with which to continue his own inquiry. The fact that there is so much disagreement on the part of his predecessors is a good enough reason for Aristotle to enter into the discussion and try to sort things out, bringing clarity to what otherwise seems to be philosophical confusion about the concept of substance. He indicates the next step to be taken:

> Regarding these matters, then, we must inquire which of the common statements are right and which are not right, and what things are substances, and whether there are or are not any besides sensible substances, and how sensible substances exist, and whether there is a separable substance (and if so why and how) or there is no substance separable from sensible substances; and we must first sketch the nature of substance. (1028^{a}27–32)

The distinction between the existence of primary substances and the subsistence of secondary substances is central to Aristotle's metaphysics. He asks whether there are any nonsensible substances, or whether all substances are experienceable, and if there are nonsensible substances whether they subsist or have some other type of being. He raises new considerations in this passage, but surprisingly restates the question of the distinction between primary and secondary substances as though the topic had not previously occurred. The passage offers the kind of evidence some commentators have thought decisive in concluding that the *Metaphysics* is an edited collection of lecture notes, on the assumption that in the case of a published manuscript we would not expect to see repetitions of previously canvassed topics and reassertions of questions that Aristotle had already mentioned earlier. The difference is that Aristotle at this stage of his inquiry is prepared to look in a more detailed and rigorous way at the nature of substance in its two main categories.

Aristotle accordingly restates his analysis of the concept of substance in the following passage. He describes a kind of ascending hierarchy of physical or natural substances, beginning with what he calls the elements or simple bodies, then bodies in the ordinary sense, including plants, animals, and the parts of these biological entities, and finally the physical entities seen above the earth in the planets and stars. All of these are said to be *natural* substances. Aristotle reaffirms his commitment to forms, as distinct from Plato's abstract Forms or Ideas, and to mathematical entities, numbers and geometrical shapes. Together, primary and secondary substances provide a comprehensive first philosophy of substance. Aristotle draws the strands of his metaphysics of substance into a unified theory:

> We have said that the causes, principles, and elements of substances are the object of our search. And some substances are recognized by all thinkers, but some have been advocated by particular schools. Those generally recognized are the natural substances, i.e. fire, earth, water, air &c., the simple bodies; secondly, plants and their parts, and animals and the parts of animals; and finally the heavens and the parts of the heavens. Some particular schools say that Forms and the objects of mathematics are substances. And it follows from our arguments that there are other substances, the essence and the substratum. Again, in another way the genus seems more substantial than the species, and the universal than the particulars. And with the universal and the genus the Ideas are connected; it is in virtue of the same argument that they are thought to be substances. (1042ᵃ4–16)

All these distinct types of substance, according to Aristotle, have in common the fact that they are subjects of predicables, of properties, qualities, or relations. Primary substances exist in the most independent way, in that an acorn could exist, for example, even if its property of being green did not exist, for example, if it were to change over time from being green to being brown. The same is true in different ways of other kinds of substances, all brought together into a unified account by the single principle or "same argument," which Aristotle mentions, through the fact that they are the subjects of properties.

FORM AND MATTER, SUBSTANCE AS INFORMED MATTER

Aristotle returns to the two principles, form and matter, suggested by his philosophical predecessors, Plato and the Presocratics. Plato's theory of the Forms is a formalist approach to the problem of understanding change and the nature of substance. The theory of Forms places all its emphasis on the formal aspect of things to the neglect of matter, which the Presocratics had emphasized. Aristotle's concept of substance combines form and matter and makes them equally important in understanding the metaphysics of change.

He objects to theorists who try simply to identify substance exclusively with either matter or form. He is evidently thinking in the first instance of the Italians or Presocratics, and, secondly, of Plato and the Academy, as though there were no material aspect of things to be taken into account. He argues that substance is form combined with matter or informed matter, matter that is defined or has a specific secondary substance imposed upon it so as to constitute substance. Aristotle's word for matter is *hylé,* which in its earlier Greek roots originally meant wood. His use of the term does not entail that all physical entities are literally wooden. The concept is metaphorical, reflecting the importance of wood in the early history of the culture and its language. The material of wood is thus made symbolic, representing whatever physical stuff comprises bodies and simple bodies as primary substances in Aristotle's metaphysics. Aristotle criticizes the materialist approach to the analysis of substance and the occurrence of change as failing to do justice to the formal aspects of entities that undergo change. He voices his objections to both extreme materialisms and formalisms in the following terms:

> For those who adopt this point of view, then, it follows that matter is substance. But this is impossible; for both separability and individuality are thought to belong chiefly to substance. And so form and the compound of form and matter would be thought to be substance, rather than matter. The substance compounded of both, i.e., of matter and shape, may be dismissed; for it is posterior and its nature is obvious. And matter also is in a sense manifest. But we must inquire into the third kind of substance; for this is the most difficult. (1029^{a}26–33)

The combination of matter and form in a correct theory of substance is applied to several well-chosen examples. Aristotle cites the case of a flat nose and a brass sphere. We cannot adequately understand a flat nose either exclusively in terms of its form or shape or exclusively in terms of its matter. Nor for the same reason can we adequately explain a brass sphere exclusively as a certain quantity of brass or exclusively as a rounded shape or form without considering its matter. The two factors must rather be brought together in a complete explanation.

The form or shape of the nose is to be flat, which we can more precisely describe in geometrical terms, and in modern mathematics could be exactly plotted on a three-dimensional grid. That is its form. From this alone, however, we do not yet know that it is a real flesh-and-blood nose as opposed to anything else with the same shape, such as a facial feature belonging to a statue rather than a living person. If, on the other hand, we make reference only to the material flesh of the nose and overlook its shape, then we are thinking of it only as an unformed quantity of living tissue without any definite shape, and so once again through the opposite failure we will have lost sight of its being a nose, consisting of the material of flesh with a definite configuration.

Aristotle likes to say that if we adopt a purely materialist metaphysics in trying to explain the flat nose or brass sphere, then we will in effect have destroyed the nose or the sphere by "corrupting" or reducing it to nothing but the matter of which it is composed, so that the nose or sphere will have vanished from the explanation. Aristotle adds the example of the clay from which a statue is sculpted, and mentions the person Callias as distinct from the flesh and bone of which the body of Callias consists. He argues:

> Therefore of some things the formula of such parts will be present, but in others it must not be present, where the formula does not refer to the concrete object. For it is for this reason that some things have as their constituent principles parts

in to which they pass away, while some have not. Those things in which the form and the matter are taken together, e.g. the snub, or the bronze circle, pass away into these material parts, and the matter is a part of them; but those things which do not involve matter but are without matter, and whose formulae are formulae of the form only, do not pass away,—either not at all or at any rate not in this way. Therefore these materials are principles and parts of the concrete things, while of the form they are neither parts nor principles. And therefore the clay statue is resolved into clay and the ball into bronze and Callias into flesh and bones, and again the circle into its segments; for there is a sense of "circle" in which it involves matter. For "circle" is used homonymously, meaning both the circle in general and the individual circle, because there is no name proper to the individuals. (1035^{a}22–^{b}2)

Turning his attention next to the pure formalists among metaphysicians, Aristotle objects that Plato and his school are unable to account for the existence of incorruptibles. The idea of Plato's formalist theory of substance is that all physical things are corruptible, by which Aristotle evidently means to say that they are changeable and constantly changing, and imperfectly imitate or participate in the eternal unchanging Forms.

Aristotle, curiously, maintains that Plato's formalism is unsatisfactory in this regard because it does not account for some physical entities that are, as Aristotle believes, incorruptible. What would such a category of physical spatiotemporal things include? Aristotle mentions the stars as physical but incorruptible entities. There is apparently a difference for Aristotle between incorruptibility and being capable of undergoing change. Aristotle believes that the stars are incorruptible, meaning that they cannot be destroyed. On the other hand, the stars evidently change in the sense of moving, if we suppose as Aristotle and many generations of his successors consistently did, that the Earth holds still at the center of the universe, and the stars change their position by moving through the heavens relative to the Earth. It must be admitted that this is a doubtful way to criticize Plato's theory of Forms and its exclusive reliance on Forms and formal principles alone as substances. Aristotle has no solid evidence that the stars are incorruptible, except for the fact that from the vast distances in space through which we perceive them we do not see them destroyed. We believe today that the stars are subject to destruction as much as any other entities down here on Earth. Aristotle weakly says only that perhaps there are some eternal entities in existence.

The assumption may or may not be true. Without conclusive reasons for agreeing that there are immutable eternal entities in the physical world, Aristotle is hardly in a strong position to refute Plato's formalism. For all its limitations, this is the argument by which Aristotle proposes to dismiss the formalist identification of substance with form:

But those who say the Forms exist, in one respect are right, in saying the Forms exist apart, if they are substances; but in another respect they are not right, because they say the one *in* many is a Form. The reason for their doing this is that they cannot say what are the substances of this sort, the imperishable substances which exist apart from the individual and sensible substances. They make them, then, the same in kind as the perishable things (for this kind of substance we know)—man himself and the horse itself, adding to the sensible things the word "itself." Yet even if we had not seen the stars, none the less, I suppose, would there be eternal substances besides those which we knew; so that now also if we do not know what eternal substances there are, yet it is doubtless necessary that some should exist. Clearly, then, no universal term is the name of a substance, and no substance is composed of substances. (1040^{b}28–1041^{a}5)

Aristotle maintains that all sensible substances are material, but not simply identical with their constitutive matter. Relying again on synonymous meanings of "formal principle," "definition," and "secondary substance," Aristotle, in the following passage, reaffirms the analysis of substance as the subject of predicables. Substances, according to Aristotle's theory, have a dual nature, material and formal. Alternatively, substances can also be considered as the subjects of any imaginable sort of change, including movement. Aristotle does not mention contrariety in this context, but it is clear from what he says that he has in mind the fact that in the case of alteration, in which an entity modifies its condition without being generated (created) or destroyed, physical things change from one state in a contrariety to a contrary state. As examples, Aristotle cites the movement of an object from here to there, from small to large, healthy to diseased, and from being whole to being corrupted, in the most extreme case. He claims that change involving physical entities cannot be adequately understood except for substances possessing both matter and form, as subjects of predicables:

But now let us resume the discussion of the generally recognized substances. These are the sensible substances, and sensible substances all have matter. The substratum is substance, and this is in one sense the matter (and by matter I mean that which, not being a "this" actually, is potentially a "this"), and in another sense the formula or form (which being a "this" can be separately formulated), and thirdly the complex of matter and form, which alone is generated and destroyed, and is without qualification, capable of separate existence; for of substances in the sense of formulae some are separable and some are not.

But clearly matter also is substance; for in all the opposite changes that occur there is something which underlies the changes, e.g. in respect of place that which is now here and again elsewhere, and in respect of increase that which is now of one size and again less or greater, and in respect of alteration that which is now healthy and again diseased; and similarly in respect of substance there is something that is now being generated and again being destroyed, and now underlies the process as a "this" and again underlies it as the privation of positive character. In this last change the others are involved. But in either one or two of the others this is not involved; for it is not necessary if a thing has matter for change of place that it should also have matter for generation and destruction. (1042^{a}24–^{b}7)

The picture of Aristotle's theory of substance that emerges from this examination of his statements about the relation of substance to form and matter is that substances necessarily consist of form and matter. Whereas the Platonists defended the view that the Forms alone were the persisting substances in a correct metaphysics, and the materialists among the Presocratics made the same claim for matter, Aristotle believes it is necessary to consider the relationship between both form and matter.

Aristotle finds extreme formalism and extreme materialism unsatisfactory. They are incomplete when considered in and of themselves. Formal and material aspects or factors of substance in Aristotle's first philosophy, as his commonsense examples reveal, must be combined. The case of Callias's flat nose and the brass sphere are perfect illustrations of the point Aristotle finds it important to make about the nature of substance. Substance is both form and matter, informed matter or matter defined by specific types of form. If we try to explain the changes that occur in the phenomenal world, Aristotle argues that we are certain to go wrong if we concentrate exclusively on either the forms of things in the sense of the secondary substances, species, or definitions of things, or in terms of their mathematical properties, number and geometrical shape, or on the material stuff of which physical entities are comprised. We need, instead, to think of substance as a synthesis of form and matter, and appeal to both formal and material considerations in explaining change as a passage between the contrary predicables in a contrariety.

ESSENTIAL AND ACCIDENTAL PROPERTIES

The distinction between *essential* and *accidental* properties is one of the most valuable innovations of Aristotle's first philosophy. The theory of substance depends heavily on the possibility of defining the *essence* of a substance. A substance's essence or essential properties are the properties that are necessary to its existence. If a substance is deprived of any of its essential properties, then, according to Aristotle, it ceases to exist as that object or as an object of the precisely specified kind. In this section, we analyze Aristotle's distinction between essence and accident, and in the following section we explain Aristotle's interpretation of essence and essential properties in terms of *natural functions*.

Essential properties, as the term indicates, are essential, vital, to a substance. An entity cannot persist, survive, or preserve its identity through changes involving the elimination of any of its essential properties. Accidental properties by contrast are those that an object has only by chance. It is accidental to a woman that she be musically talented, since some women are musical and others are not. A person does not become a woman by virtue of acquiring the ability to make music, nor does she cease to be a woman if she should somehow lose her musical skills. On the other hand, to appeal to one of Aristotle's favorite examples, if it is essential to any human being to be capable of reasoning, then reasoning, unlike musical ability, cannot be subtracted from a person without the person ceasing to exist as a human being, even if not being totally destroyed. Whatever is left behind from such a devastating change, it is anyway not a human being, if reasoning is an essential human property.

Aristotle accordingly distinguishes between two kinds of change. One type of change affects only a substance's accidental properties. Changing, say, from being musical to being unmusical is a mere alteration through which an entity persists, surviving the change as an existent thing with its identity intact. The other type of change affects a substance's essential properties. Such a change destroys the substance in a drastic elimination of its essence. The substance in that case is not merely altered but altogether annihilated, in a kind of change that Aristotle speaks of as "corruption." He draws the distinction between essential and accidental properties and provides the following examples:

I mean, for instance, the white is musical and the latter is white, only because both are accidental to man. But Socrates is musical, not in this sense, that both terms are accidental to something else. Since then some predicates are accidental in this and some in that sense, those which are accidental in the latter sense, in which white is accidental to Socrates, cannot form an infinite series in the upward direction,—e.g. Socrates the white has not yet another accident; for no unity can be got out of such a sum. Nor again will white have another term accidental to it, e.g. musical. For this is no more accidental to that than that is to this; and at the same time we have drawn the distinction, that while some predicates are accidental in this sense, others are so in the sense in which musical is accidental to Socrates; and the accident is an accident of an accident not in cases of the latter kind, but only in cases of the other kind, so that not *all* terms will be accidental. There must, then, even in this case be something which denotes substance. And it has been shown that, if this is so, contradictories cannot be predicated at the same time. (1007ª4–18)

In much the same way that the concept of substance is systematically ambiguous in Aristotle's first philosophy, so is the distinction between essence and accident. The two distinctions unavoidably go together, because the identity conditions for a substance are nothing other than the substance's essential properties together with its accidental properties, and a substance's accidental properties are defined relative to and in contrast with its essential properties.

Thus, a human being as essentially a rational animal is identifiable as such in persisting through a change from being longhaired to shorthaired after a trip to the barber. Relative to the supposed essence of a human being as a rational animal, the property of being longhaired or shorthaired and the contrariety longhaired-shorthaired is purely accidental. If you have long hair and get it cut you do not cease to be a human being; nor if you start out with short hair and let it grow long. Having short hair on the other hand is relative to the more specific essence of being a shorthaired human being, or, more generally to that of any shorthaired substance, is essential, as is the property of having some hair rather than being completely bald, while being blond, brunette, or red-haired is accidental. In the same way, relative to the essence of being a blond shorthaired substance the property of being fair-haired is essential, while relative to the substance of being a fair-haired human being or fair-haired thing, the property of being platinum blond or dishwater blond in particular is accidental. The distinction between essential and accidental properties of substances goes hand in hand with systematic ambiguities in the applications of the concept of substance itself and the precise ways in which substances are specified. Aristotle is sensitive to the nuances of language in determining the possibilities, and requires the principles of his metaphysics to reflect these differences.

Aristotle introduces the distinction between essence and accident by comparing the accidental properties of a substance to the chance occurrences that are more familiarly spoken of as accidents, relative to the pursuit of a given purpose. His first example is that of someone finding a treasure by accident while gardening. Part of what makes such an event an accident is that there is no necessary connection between digging a hole to plant a tree and coming upon a buried treasure. It does not follow generally or naturally upon opening a patch of ground for the sake of planting a tree that one happens to locate hidden valuables. We certainly cannot count on finding treasure whenever we dig up a garden; it might happen, but more often it is unlikely to happen. Moreover, as Aristotle remarks, if it were true that we frequently find a treasure when digging in the earth we would not generally be planting when engaged in such activity, but we would instead as a matter of fact be digging for treasure.

> We call an accident that which attaches to something and can be truly asserted, but neither of necessity nor usually, e.g. if one in digging a hole for a plant found treasure. This—the finding of treasure—happens by accident to the man who digs the hole; for neither does the one come of necessity from the other or after the other, nor, if a man plants, does he usually find treasure. And a musical man might be white; but since this does not happen of necessity nor usually, we call it an accident. (1025ᵃ14–20)

In keeping with his distinction between the existence of substances and the subsistence of predicables, Aristotle maintains that accidental as well as essential properties inhere in the substances of which they are truly predicated. He refers to the ambiguity we have described in distinguishing between the essential and accidental properties of a substance relative to the precise ways in which a substance might be characterized. Here he appeals again to another example of an accidental occurrence in the ordinary nonmetaphysical sense of "accident":

> Therefore since there are attributes and they attach to a subject, and some of them attach in a particular place and at a particular time, whatever attaches to a subject, but not because it is this subject, at this time or in this place, will be an accident. Therefore there is no definite cause for an accident, but a chance cause, i.e. an indefinite one. Going to Aegina was an accident, if the man went not in order to get there, but because he was carried out of his way by a storm or captured by pirates. The accident has happened or exists,—not in virtue of itself, however, but of something else; for the *storm* was the cause of his coming to a place for which he was not sailing, and this was Aegina. (1025ᵃ20–29)

Aristotle considers the accidental color of a substance when the substance is appropriately distinguished in color-neutral terms. Then he distinguishes between substances and predicables, which is to say between the existence of a primary substance and the subsistence or inherence in a primary substance of a predicable, definition or secondary substance. He illustrates the fine but metaphysically important distinction between the substance white man and the predicable, the being of a white man:

> We must inquire whether each thing and its essence are the same or different. This is of some use for the inquiry concerning substance; for each thing is thought to be not different from its substance, and the essence is said to be the substance of each thing.
> Now in the case of things with accidental attributes the two would be generally thought to be different, e.g. white man would be thought to be different from the essence of white man. For if they are the same, the essence of man and that of white man are also the same; for a man and a white man are the same, as people say, so that the essence of white man and that of man would be also the same. But probably it is not necessary that things with accidental attributes should be the same. For the extreme terms are not in the same way the same.—Perhaps *this*

might be thought to follow, that the extreme terms, the accidents, should turn out to be the same, e.g. the essence of white and that of musical; but this is not actually thought to be the case. (1031ª15–28)

Aristotle argues that the existence of a substance is indifferent to its qualification by reference to its accidental properties when the substance is indifferent, or, as he puts it, "passive," with respect to its accidents. As a rule, Aristotle observes, we cannot identify a substance with its accidents. If we overlook the accidental skin color or gender of a person *qua* human being, then there is no harm philosophically in saying, as we might do when we are speaking nontechnically, that the substance of a white man is identical with the substance of a human being. The main point Aristotle wants to make in these difficult passages concerning the multiple senses in which substance, essence and accident are applied, is that substances are generally identified by reference to their essential properties, rather than in terms of their detachable accidental properties. He collects the main points of his distinction between the essential and accidental properties of primary and secondary substances in the following comments:

(But of an accidental term, e.g. "the musical" or "the white," since it has two meanings, it is not true to say that it itself is identical with its essence; for both that to which the accidental quality belongs, and the accidental quality, are white, so that in a sense the accident and its essence are the same, and in a sense they are not; for the essence of white is not the same as the man or the white man, but it is the same as the attribute white.)

The absurdity of the separation would appear also if one were to assign a name to each of the essences; for there would be another essence besides the original one, e.g. to the essence of horse there will belong a second essence. Yet why should not some things be their essences from the start, since essence is substance? But not only are a thing and its essence one, but the formula of them is also the same, as is clear even from what has been said; for it is not by accident that the essence of one, and the one, are one. Further, if they were different, the process would go on to infinity; for we should have the essence of one, and the one, so that in their case also the same infinite regress would be found. Clearly, then, each primary and self-subsistent thing is one and the same as its essence.

Now the sophistical objections to this position, and the question whether Socrates and to be Socrates are the same thing, are obviously answered in the same way; for there is no difference either in the standpoint from which the questions would be asked, or in that from which one could answer it successfully. We have explained, then, in what sense each thing is the same as its essence and in what sense it is not. (1031ᵇ22–1032ª11)

The distinction between essential and accidental properties makes it possible to describe conditions under which an entity can persist through a change in its accidental properties while remaining the same by not changing any of its essential properties. There are several important conclusions to be derived from Aristotle's exposition for the metaphysics of change. We can summarize the significance of Aristotle's first philosophy in the following first principles of first philosophy:

Principles of Aristotle's First Philosophy

1. A substance is a combination of form and matter or informed matter.
2. There are many different senses in which different kinds or categories of substances need to be distinguished.
3. Principally, there is a distinction between primary and secondary substances; primary substances are entities that exist in their own right and are not predicated of any other thing; secondary substances are the properties of primary and other secondary substances, also known as predicables, that are truly predicated of or attributed to primary or other secondary substances, and that inhere or subsist in the substances and ultimately in the primary substances of which they are truly predicated or to which they are truly attributed.
4. Primary substances exist primarily, which is to say independently of any of their particular properties; primary substances must have some inhering secondary substances, and cannot exist without any properties, as what are sometimes called "bare particulars"; secondary substances by contrast subsist only in the primary substances in which they inhere and are incapable of independent existence without or in the absence of primary substances.
5. Secondary substances are distinguished into two categories of essential and accidental properties; essential properties are those without which a substance cannot exist as the particular kind of substance it is, but is "corrupted" or destroyed as the kind of thing it had been if deprived of any of its essential properties; accidental properties can be added to or eliminated from a substance without destroying it, resulting only in an alteration of the substance's condition.
6. The distinction between essential and accidental properties is systematically ambiguous in precisely the same ways and number of ways as substance; the identity conditions for a substance persisting through change are thereby equated with its essence or set of essential properties.

The problem of change, as we have suggested, is addressed by Aristotle within the framework of these principles of first philosophy. Aristotle argues that change can affect either the essential or accidental properties of substances, respectively corrupting or merely altering the substance. Things do not always remain the same through change; it depends on the kind of things we are talking about and the kind of change. Some things survive change, persisting or continuing to exist with their identities intact, when only their accidental properties are altered. Aristotle's answer to the problem of change is complicated, but in many ways affirms commonsense judgments about the kinds of changes a sensible, movable, physical entity is capable of undergoing.

The question that remains is how essential properties are more exactly to be characterized. What is needed in order for a property to be essential rather than accidental? If Aristotle said only that a substance's essential properties are those that cannot be changed without destroying the substance, and that accidental properties are properties that by the same standard are not essential, or those that can be changed without destroying but merely altering a substance, then his solution to the problem of understanding the persistence of some things through some kinds of change would be viciously circular. Aristotle would then be saying that substances can persist through changes of their accidental properties without loss of identity, because accidental properties are those properties through changes of which a substance can persist without loss of identity. The way out of this circle for Aristotle is found in the fact that he offers an independent analysis of the concept of a substance's essential properties as its natural function.

ARISTOTLE'S THEORY OF NATURAL FUNCTION

Aristotle distinguishes four kinds of substance, corresponding to his prior distinction between four kinds of "causes." The four causes are to be thought of as "becauses" or explanatory factors, including *formal, material, efficient,* and *final* causes. It is only efficient mechanical cause as expressed in the laws of modern physics that many philosophers and scientists think of today as causation.

A formal cause in Aristotle's first philosophy is an explanation offered in terms of the definitions and species of things, the secondary substances that exist only insofar as they inhere in primary substances. Formal causes explain phenomena in terms of the kinds of principles Aristotle derives from Plato's concept of the Forms, including or as well as number, shape, and other mathematical principles and relations. A material cause explains a phenomenon in terms of the physical stuff of which a thing is made, without which we cannot completely understand what we hope to have explained. An efficient cause involves the mechanical motions of things interacting with one another under the laws of physics in order to bring about a change in an entity. An efficient cause is whatever changes things by transfer of energy in physical events to bring it about that one object in a certain physical state at a later time is no longer in that state. The final cause of a phenomenon is the end or reason for which it was accomplished, the purpose or *telos* that explains why the caused event took place. In the case of events brought about by human agents, it is usually easy to specify a final cause, since actions are generally performed for a reason or with a certain motivation in order to achieve a certain purpose.

Aristotle interestingly maintains that all natural occurrences take place because of a final cause, even when human agency is not directly involved. Contemporary science is different among other ways from Aristotelian science primarily because of the fact that science emphasizes efficient causation, and because it includes reference to material factors and formal features of physical events, especially the mathematical properties of entities involved in efficient causal interactions, while virtually ignoring if not totally eliminating final causes from natural science.

An example that Aristotle discusses in his *Physics* to illustrate the application of the four causes is that of a statue whose complete explanation requires all four causes. The statue as it exists exists in part because it has a certain shape or form; this is its formal cause. Secondly, the statue is also made of a certain physical stuff, to be explained by what Aristotle calls its material cause. Thirdly, the statue is produced by the actions of the sculptor imposing a certain form on the chosen material, chiseling away at the stone, let us say, and polishing and in other ways shaping the substance of the statue, as an efficient causal explanation must explain. Fourthly and finally, the existence of the statue also needs to be understood in terms of the reasons why it came to be made and what purpose it is supposed to serve. Probably the statue was made to adorn a garden or a public building, so that the artist could express his or her thoughts, and perhaps to make money or win a competition or impress another person. There can be many separate purposes in the final cause of a thing's existence and condition, which is to say of the secondary substances that inhere in a given primary substance.

Aristotle similarly divides substances into four subcategories, corresponding to the four causes. These concern essence, form, matter, and the combination of form and matter in a primary substance. What is conspicuously missing from this list when compared with the four Aristotelian causes, is the final or teleological sense of substance. This, as we shall see, is significant. The reason or purpose for a thing's existing is not intuitively characterizable as a substance, but turns out to be indispensable in Aristotle's theory of the identity conditions of a substance's essence, and of the theological component of his metaphysics. He explains:

> The word "substance" is applied, if not in more senses, still at least to four main objects; for both the essence and the universal and the genus are thought to be the substance of each thing, and fourthly the substratum. Now the substratum is that of which other things are predicated, while it is itself not predicated of anything else. And so we must first determine the nature of this; for that which underlies a thing primarily is thought to be in the truest sense its substance. And in one sense matter is said to be of the nature of substratum, in another, shape, and in a third sense, the compound of these. By matter I mean, for instance, the bronze, by the shape the plan of its form, and by the compound of these (the concrete thing) the statue. Therefore if the form is prior to the matter and more real, it will be prior to the compound also for the same reason. (1028^{b}33–1029^{a}6)

The concept of natural function is explained in terms of Aristotle's four causes, and especially by reference to final or teleological causes, the purposes of things. Natural functions pervade Aristotle's discussion of substance, and as such are a main ingredient of his first philosophy. We have already seen an important example of Aristotle's use of the idea of natural functions in the very first sentence of the *Metaphysics*, in which he asserts that all persons desire by nature to know. It is thus a function of human beings to want to acquire knowledge as Aristotle thinks of the activities that characterize human life.

Nor is Aristotle's notion of natural function limited to intelligent social animals such as ourselves. Although they are different kinds of substances, human beings constitute just one category among all the existent things inhabiting the world, each of which has special distinguishing natural functions by which they are known. Aristotle regards natural functions as germane not only to living things, human beings and other animals and plants, but also to inanimate objects of every kind, and even to the material elements of which physical bodies are composed. A natural function is what an entity naturally does, left to its own devices, so to speak, without external interference in whatever it does or whatever happens to it. If it is the natural function of human beings, no doubt among other things, to know, then as long as no obstacle occurs, human beings will tend to seek and augment their knowledge. If it is the natural function of an acorn to grow into an oak tree, then, if nothing happens to prevent it, and the proper natural conditions are fulfilled, the acorn will naturally in time become an oak.

Where inanimate objects are concerned, their natural functions as Aristotle conceives them are less complicated but also less familiar and more theoretical. The natural functions of a complex nonliving physical entity are determined by the natural functions of its component material substances. That is, the natural function of something made of some combination of earth, air, fire, and water is a result of the exact proportions of these material elements combined in the thing, and of the natural functions by which each is characterized. The behavior of compound substances immediately becomes difficult to explain and predict. What we can say following Aristotle's discussion of the natural functions of the material elements is that they all tend, in the absence of interference, to move toward an appropriate characteristic part of the physical universe. Earth, for example, set free in space, has the natural function of moving toward the very center of the universe; water naturally seeks the next highest level close to earth but below the natural level of fire and air; all of which naturally gravitate toward their corresponding levels of substances below the æther, as the material element of the heavenly bodies. The natural function of a material element in every case is thus a matter of where the substances go when released. What is their destination when they are unencumbered by the presence of other kinds of substances that might otherwise block their way? Where do they naturally find their home from the center of the universe to its outermost periphery?

A natural function in this teleological sense is thus explainable in Aristotle's first philosophy as a final cause. It is the "purpose," end, or *telos* of earth, air, fire, water, and æther to move toward their respective appropriate locations in the world. The same is true of more complex kinds of primary substances. It is the purpose of an acorn to grow into an oak and produce other acorns to produce other oaks. It is among the natural purposes of human beings to know, Aristotle seems to believe, and as such prior to whatever other purposes we persons as agents of purposeful action might choose for ourselves. We cannot fully explain the existence of a primary substance unless we explain it in terms of all four causes. To explain in the most general first philosophical terms the changes that substances undergo from the standpoint of their teleological causes requires appeal to their natural functions. In every case, a natural function can be understood as the instantiation of a different contrary term in a specific contrariety according to its final cause.

An object's natural function is further understood by Aristotle as fulfilling its potential. Potentiality in this sense is not merely logical possibility, but the entire range of possibilities in which the object can actually satisfy its natural function. An acorn is potentially an oak tree, and a human being is, among other things, potentially a knower. An acorn satisfies its natural function by fulfilling its potential, which it can do in practice in a number of ways, depending on the exact circumstances that happen to prevail. An acorn can become an oak tree by growing here or there, bending its roots around a stone or by sending them straight down into the unresisting soil, and so on. A human being can become a knower, and thereby fulfill his or her potential according to this natural function, in many different ways; by learning science or mathematics or history or art. A person can acquire knowledge here or there, learning this or that in this or that way. The possibilities, in any case, even when they are many, are not limitless, but constrained within definite limits determined by an object's natural function and potential.

Aristotle explains the implications of his conception of potentiality in terms of the distinction between a substance's essential and accidental properties. Where essential properties of things are concerned, to change an object so radically as to deprive it of any of its essential properties is to annihilate it. By contrast, to change an object with respect to any of its accidental properties is merely to alter and not destroy it. An object's accidental properties can thus be defined in Aristotle's system as whatever properties can be changed in an object without destroying it. It is not every entity that survives every sort of change, but there is always a distinction to be drawn between an object's essential and accidental properties. Any primary substance has both essential and accidental properties; secondary substances considered in themselves may have only essential properties, and accidental properties only insofar as they are considered in relation to the contingently existing primary substances in which they inhere. A primary substance can undergo any change of any of its accidental properties and survive the change as the identical object, having merely been altered in its condition without vanishing from the world. Insofar as any of a primary substance's essential properties are changed, the object does not survive the change, it does not persist or preserve its identity through the change, but is so radically transformed as to cease to exist as the kind of thing it was.

If I as a human being am essentially a rational animal, and if I am also accidentally musical, I might lose my musical ability, but I will not thereby be destroyed. I will persist as the identical person I was before, minus my talent for music. As we have observed, if as a rational animal I am somehow permanently deprived of my reason or of my animality, then I must cease to exist. I will not in that case be merely altered with respect to one of my accidental properties, but so corrupted in what is indispensable to my identity as to no longer exist as a human being. Aristotle speaks in these kinds of contexts of being a human being as such, or of my identity *qua* or considered as a human being. In that case, I do not survive the change *qua* human being, although obviously something or other ordinarily survives—even if it is only a living animal that is no longer truly human, or a dead body that was once a human being by virtue of having been a rational animal—by persisting through the change.

Similarly with respect to the essential and accidental properties of every other primary substance. With respect to nonsensible things or immovables, in particular the definitions, species, or secondary substances, as well as numbers and other arithmetical and geometrical entities, they have no natural function because considered in themselves they are separable from sensibles in Aristotle's ontology, and hence altogether lacking in accidental properties. They cannot be said to possess natural functions, because as incorruptible and immovable secondary substances they are incapable of undergoing any sort of intrinsic change, and hence of no alteration or corruption within the opposing poles of a contrariety.

Aristotle explains the difference between essential and accidental properties in terms of a further distinction between productive and artless or indefinite potentialities or capacities. He states that things that exist according to accident are contingent rather than necessary, giving as a favorite example again the case of a white musician. Aristotle claims that such accidents as whiteness and being musically talented must be the result of matter, and hence require a material cause, since matter unlike form exists contingently as the stuff of logically possible but not logically necessary primary substances. He maintains:

For some accidental results sometimes tend to be produced by alien capacities, but to others there corresponds no determinate art nor capacity; for of things which are or come to be by accident, the cause also is accidental. Therefore, since not all things are or come to be of necessity and always, but the majority of things are for the most part, the accidental must exist; for instance a white man is not always nor for the most part musical, but since this sometimes happens, it must be accidental. If not, everything will be of necessity. The matter, therefore, which is capable of being otherwise than as it for the most part is, is the cause of the accidental. (1027^{a}5–15)

The connection between essential properties and natural function is clinched in the following passage when Aristotle defines essence in terms of function. The essential properties of any entity are explained teleologically as its natural function, what it is disposed to do if uninhibited. Aristotle gives an example to illustrate the relation between essence and function in the case of the soul as the essence of an animal's bodily substance. The soul of an animal as Aristotle understands it is functionally interpreted as the natural inclination for sensation and self-animated motion. Aristotle's entrenchment in the theory of natural function as the analysis of essential properties is reflected in his analogy of a dead finger. The object once part of a living hand is a finger equivocally or in name only, Aristotle believes, since it has been deprived of its essence by the loss of natural function in its power of movement. Aristotle adds:

And since the soul of animals (for this is the substance of living beings) is their substance according to the formula, i.e. the form and the essence of a body of a certain kind (at least we shall define each part, if we define it well, not without reference to its function, and this cannot belong to it without perception), therefore the parts of soul are prior, either all or some of them, to the concrete animal, and similarly in each case of a concrete whole; and the body and its parts are posterior to this its substance, and it is not the substance but the concrete thing that is divided into these parts as its matter. To the concrete thing these are in a sense prior, but in a sense they are not. For they cannot even exist if severed from the whole; for it is not a finger in *any* state that is the finger of a living thing, but the dead finger is a finger only homonymously. (1035^{b}14–25)

It is reasonable for Aristotle with his interest in biology to choose a dead finger as an example to represent his thesis that the essence of a thing is defined in terms of its natural function. The implication is that to deprive an entity of its natural function is to deprive it of its essence. This, by virtue of the distinction between essential and accidental properties, is to destroy the entity as a thing of its original kind.

There is generally something left over, which in this case we can continue to call a finger if we want. Aristotle claims, however, that we can only do so homonymously, using the same word *finger* inappropriately in both circumstances, both while it is capable and after it is no longer capable of performing its natural function. When a finger is dead and no longer able to move as a living finger it has ceased literally to be a finger, because it cannot do what fingers are supposed and defined as being able to do. The flesh and bone that remains is not really a finger, according to Aristotle, and is referred to as such only equivocally, using the word improperly when the requirements for qualifying as a genuine finger are no longer satisfied. It is accidental to a finger that it be any particular color, or even that it be human or nonhuman; but it is essential, according to Aristotle, for a finger to be able to flex and curl and move in the ways that are characteristic of a living finger. Elsewhere, Aristotle makes the identical point involving the example of a stone flute in a statue that is not really or truly a flute. It is misdescribed as such because it looks superficially like a genuine flute, despite the fact that it is unable to perform the natural function of a flute, because it is incapable of playing music.

It is therefore appropriate to refer to Aristotle's first philosophy of substance as *functionalist*. Insofar as the theory of substance is concerned with the essential properties of things, the analysis of essence as natural function in Aristotle's metaphysics provides a noncircular way of understanding essential properties. The account is independent of the main conclusion Aristotle wants to make, that changes in essential properties destroy a substance, while changes in accidental properties are tolerated as alterations that do not threaten a substance's identity. Aristotle avoids the circularity that would otherwise threaten his theory of substance and change. He offers an independent account of essential properties in terms of natural functions, and thereby frees the distinction between essential and accidental properties from the vicious circle of assuming that substances survive and persist through alterations of their accidental properties, but are destroyed if changed with respect to any of their essential properties.

Aristotle's Concept of Secondary Substance as a Solution to Plato's Third Man

We can divide Aristotle's theory of substance into two parts, one for matter and one for form. The concept of primary substance brings together the idea of form—adapted from Plato's theory of Forms and Pythagorean ontology of abstract mathematical entities—and the idea of matter, which Aristotle presents as a synthesis of several different Presocratic materialisms. If a primary substance is form and matter, then as we would expect, there must at least be formal and material causes, principles, and explanations.

There are many kinds of substances. In particular there are extreme categories in Aristotle's theory that limit the range of different kinds of substance but are not themselves substances. They either consist of pure form without matter, or of pure matter without form. The extremes in the opposition of matter and form in Aristotle's thought, pure matter and pure form, systematically delimit a space in which different types of combinations of matter with form or of informed matter can be situated. The result is a comprehensive way of understanding the nature of many different types of substance, from the standpoint of the distinction between a primary substance's form and its matter, the distinction between its essential and accidental properties, and the concept of essence as natural function. Within this framework, we can understand the logic of Aristotle's solution to the problem of corruption and alteration, and essential and merely accidental change.

Aristotle introduces the concept of nonsensible substances. These are the definitions, species of things, and secondary substances that inhere in primary substances. They presumably include all non-Platonic Aristotelian (small f) forms, numbers, and shapes, and every kind of property it is possible for a primary substance to have. He distinguishes the investigation of formal aspects of substances from that of sensible substances, including primary substances in the case of bodies and their parts, and their material components. He proceeds:

> Whether there is, apart from the matter of such substances, any other substance, and one should look for some substance other than these, e.g. numbers or something of the sort, must be considered later. For it is for the sake of this that we are trying to determine the nature of perceptible substances, since in a sense the inquiry about perceptible substances is the work of natural science, i.e. of second philosophy; for the natural scientist must not only know about the matter, but also about the substance in the sense of the formula, and even more than about the other. And in the case of definitions, how the elements in the formula are parts of the definition, and why the definition is one formula (for clearly the thing is one, but in virtue of *what* is the thing one, although it has parts?)—this must be considered later. (1037ª10–20)

Aristotle properly relegates the study of material aspects of sensible substances to *second philosophy*, which is to say the natural sciences, physics, chemistry, biology, and others. This is a reasonable division of labor for Aristotle to suggest, since much of the inquiry into the matter of primary substances is naturally an appropriate subject for the specialized sciences rather than metaphysics. He narrows the study specifically to secondary subsistent substances that, by virtue of being nonsensible, cannot be discovered by perception.

He recalls that the concept of substance has already been defined in universal terms. The example of a flat nose surfaces again. He speaks of the inherent or "indwelling" of secondary substance, the flatness of the nose, in the material substance of the nose. As a further clarification, Aristotle now indicates that secondary substance is not a part of a primary substance in anything like the way that a finger is a part of a hand or the finger and hand are parts of a complete human body. Rather, Aristotle maintains that a secondary substance pervades a primary substance which it defines and in which it inheres; it is literally part but not literally any particular part, of the primary substance in which it inheres, and it is metaphorically a part of the whole, distributed throughout and integrated in the form and definition of the primary substance in which it subsists and to which it belongs. Aristotle explains:

> What the essence is and in what sense it is independent, has been stated universally in a way which is true of every case, and also why the formula of the essence of some things contains the parts of the thing defined, while that of others does not; and we have stated that in the formula of the substance the material parts will not be present (for they are not even parts of the substance in that sense, but of the concrete substance; but of this there is in a sense a formula, and in a sense there is not; for there is no formula of it with its matter, for this is indefinite, but there is a formula of it with reference to its primary substance—e.g. in the case of man the formula of the soul—, for the substance is the indwelling form, from which along with the matter the so-called concrete substance is derived; e.g. concavity is a form of this sort, for from this and the nose arise snub nose and snubness; but in the concrete substance, e.g. a snub nose or Callias, the matter also will be present. (1037ª21–35)

Much of Aristotle's discussion is so abstract that it is difficult to follow the thread of argument from topic to topic. It is imaginable that in the course of presenting his ideas on first philosophy verbally to an audience, Aristotle might have presupposed and so not bothered to mention some of what for us is necessary background. Aristotle does not always say as much as he might to help us fully understand his assertions.

Aristotle remarks that bodies or sensible things must be composed of substances and not qualities. They cannot be composed of qualities, Aristotle contends, because qualities cannot exist independently of but can only subsist in substances. Aristotle puts the point succinctly by saying that quality, which is to say property, definition, species, or secondary substance, cannot exist prior to substance. To suppose otherwise is to pretend that a quality could have a separable subsistence independently of the existence of the substance in which it inheres or for which it is "indwelling." Aristotle illustrates the point by means of a concrete example involving Socrates. He remarks that Socrates is a substance in two senses because Socrates is first of all a primary substance in whom substance also inheres. He further reemphasizes the fact that it is only primary substances that exist entirely in themselves. Primary substances have specific qualities, essential and accidental properties, inhering in them. Aristotle commits himself to an inherence theory of secondary substance when he requires that there are no animals other than the particular animals exemplifying the definition of the property of being an animal. More importantly, Aristotle insists that the definition, species, or secondary substance of being an animal that subsists in the particular existent animals to be found in the world is not itself an animal. Aristotle writes:

> But perhaps the universal, while it cannot be substance in the way in which the essence is so, can be present in this, e.g. animal can be present in man and horse. Then clearly there is a formula of the universal. . . . And further it is impossible and absurd that the "this," i.e. the substance, if it consists of parts, should not consist of substances nor of what is a "this," but of quality; for that which is not substance, i.e. the quality, will then be prior to substance and to the "this." Which is impossible; for neither in formula nor in time nor in coming to be can the affections be prior to the substance; for then they would be separable from it. Further, in Socrates there will be a substance in a substance, so that he will be the substance of two things. And in general it follows, if man and such things are substances, that none of the elements in their formulae is the substance of anything, nor does it exist apart from the species or in anything else; I mean, for instance, that no animal exists apart from the particular animals, nor does any other of the elements present in formulae exist apart.
>
> If, then, we view the matter from these standpoints, it is plain that no universal attribute is a substance, and this is plain also from the fact that no common predicate indicates a "this," but rather a "such." If not, many difficulties follow, and especially the "third man." (1038^{b}17–1039^{a}3)

Aristotle denies that the definition, species, or secondary substance *animal* is itself an animal. This need not seem particularly noteworthy, but it has important implications for a problem in Plato's theory of Forms that Aristotle's theory of inherent or subsistent forms, definitions, species, or secondary substances, neatly avoids. It is mentioned in the final sentence as the *problem of the Third Man*.

Plato's Forms are supposed to explain the properties of particular things in the constantly changing perceivable world of Becoming. The things we experience in sensation are said to participate in or imitate ideal Forms in the rationally knowable unchanging world of Being. Plato is aware of the problem, which he discusses at length in his dialogue, the *Parmenides*. Particular flesh and blood men are men rather than horses, according to Plato, because they imitate or participate in the ideal Form of man. We might designate all Platonic Forms by capitalizing the term, in this case, as "Man." If an individual man imitates or participates in the ideal Form of Man, then a man and Man are in a more generic sense both "men." This can only be true according to Plato's theory by virtue of all men and Man imitating or participating in a yet higher ideal Form of Man. This we might distinguish from both men and Man by using all capitals, "MAN." So, a man participates in the Form of Man, and individual men and the first-order Form of Man participate in the higher-order Form of MAN. The higher-order Form of MAN is thus the Third Man. The commitment to higher and higher-order Platonic Forms of MAN must go on indefinitely. We could continue to distinguish them terminologically in further ways as needed, say, by asterisks, *MAN*, **MAN**, and so on. By supposing that there is even so much as the first-order ideal Form Man, Plato's theory of Forms appears to be committed to an indefinite regress of ideal Forms of successively higher orders of Forms, from men to Man to MAN to *MAN* to **MAN**, and so on, without limit.

The trouble is that by allowing any Forms at all, Plato seems to be stuck with unlimitedly many higher and higher orders of Forms. Yet at most it is only the first-order Form, Man, that appears to serve any useful explanatory purpose in Plato's theory if we want to understand why all things of a certain kind are men. The Platonic Form of Man is thereby supposed to unlock the mystery of the nature of man. Plato, unfortunately, is stuck in an endless regress of Forms once he admits the existence of a first-order Form of anything. The trouble is not only the wild proliferation of Forms, but the fact that none of the higher-order Forms after the first order fulfills any explanatory purpose in Plato's metaphysics. The implication is that Plato's theory of Forms is overcommitted to too many ideal Forms that do no work to earn their keep. As a result, Plato's theory of Forms appears to violate the principle of Ockham's razor, never to multiply entities beyond explanatory necessity. This is a principle accepted even in Aristotle's time, although Aristotle for obvious reasons could never have referred to it as such. The aesthetic criterion for choice among competing theories that Ockham's razor expresses is popularly formularized from its suggestive statement in the writings of fourteenth-century anti-Platonist philosopher William of Ockham. Ockham's dictum states: *Entia non sunt multiplicanda praeter necessitatem.* The problem is that Plato's theory engenders an indefinite hierarchy of ideal Forms, all of which are supposed to be real existent entities, but for which, beyond the first-level Forms such as that of Man, there is no explanatory justification.

Aristotle's doctrine of inherent or "indwelling" secondary substances avoids the regress of Forms in Plato's metaphysics. Aristotle's definitions, species, or secondary substances, forms with a small letter f, do not exist as real entities. They cannot exist independently in a Platonic heaven, but subsist only insofar as they inhere in the primary substances that they define and to which they give specific definition and form. Since Aristotle's secondary substances do not exist on their own, we do not have to worry that they might be multiplying indefinitely behind our backs with no explanatory payoff. There is no cause in Aristotle's metaphysics for thinking that there are any secondary substances other than those inhering in the primary substances they define. They provide no basis for proceeding to any higher order of forms in a hierarchy of nonsensibles, as the secondary, tertiary, and so on, definitions of primary, secondary, tertiary, and so on, substances. When Aristotle remarks that the definition, species, or secondary substance *animal* is not itself an animal, he cuts off any way to produce a third man and spares his metaphysics of substance the problem of the Third Man that affects Plato's theory of Forms.

Aristotle nevertheless maintains that the formal or definitional component of primary substances is eternal and unchanging. Despite their dependent existence subsisting only in the primary substances in which they inhere, secondary substances are immovable and separable from the world of sensible things in much the way that Formal realists such as Plato maintain. Aristotle adds this explanation to his metaphysics of inherent secondary substances:

> There are three kinds of substance—one that is sensible (of which one subdivision is eternal and another is perishable, and which all recognize, as comprising e.g. plants and animals),—of this we must grasp the elements, whether one or many; and another that is immovable, and this certain thinkers assert to be capable of existing apart, some dividing it into two, others combining the Forms and the objects of mathematics into one class, and others believing only in the mathematical part of this class. The former two kinds of substance are the subject of natural science (for they imply movement); but the third kind belongs to another science, if there is no principle common to it and to the other kinds. (1069ª30–ᵇ2)

PRIME MATTER AS PURE POTENTIALITY, GOD AS PURE ACTUALITY

Aristotle introduces the concepts of *pure* or *prime matter*, of form without matter and matter devoid of any form. Pure form and prime matter are not substances, because they are not combinations of matter with form. Let us first consider Aristotle's concept of pure or prime matter and then his concept of pure form.

Prime matter is a limit in Aristotle's first philosophy of substance. Aristotle describes matter as the underlying physical basis of all substance, from the elements to inherent secondary substances:

> Regarding material substance we must not forget that even if all things have the same primary constituent or constituents, and if the same matter serves as starting-point for their generation, yet there is a matter proper to each, e.g. the sweet or the fat of phlegm, and the bitter, or something else, of bile; though perhaps these have the same constituent. And there come to be several matters for the same thing, when the one matter is matter for the other, e.g. phlegm comes from the fat and from the sweet, if the fat comes from the sweet; and it comes from bile by analysis of the bile into its ultimate matter. For one thing comes from another in two senses, either because it will be found at a later stage of development, or because it is produced if the other is analysed into its original constituents. (1044ª15–24)

Aristotle's theory of matter distinguishes between matter in two senses. In one sense, there is matter that underlies all sensible things, common to all, while in another sense every distinct substance involves its own peculiar matter. We have already seen why Aristotle distinguishes between matter in a general sense as the underlying physical basis of all primary substances, and as it is exemplified in particular samples or quantities of a particular kind of matter. In everyday thought and language we distinguish between gold or water in a general sense and between this particular sample or quantity of water or gold. Aristotle generalizes the distinction with respect to the elements of earth, air, fire, water, and æther. There is a difference, Aristotle maintains, between fire in general as a material element of physical things that might exist in combination with other elements in a primary substance, and a particular fire considered as a primary substance in an actual concentration of flames.

Next, Aristotle proceeds to draw a surprising connection between the general concept of substance and the idea of a specific kind of substance, which he designates as "eternal substance." The following passage makes it clear that Aristotle has god or the gods in mind when he refers to this remarkable category of substance:

> It is clear then from what has been said that there is a substance which is eternal and unmovable and separate from sensible things. It has been shown also that this substance cannot have any magnitude, but is without parts and indivisible. For it produces movement through infinite time, but nothing finite has infinite power. And, while every magnitude is either infinite or finite, it cannot, for the above reason, have finite magnitude, and it cannot have infinite magnitude because there is no infinite magnitude at all. But it is also clear that it is impassive and unalterable; for all the other changes are posterior to change of place. It is clear, then, why the first mover has these attributes. (1073ª4–13)

He refers explicitly to the deity. It is clear from the first sentence that he is thinking of the theological implications of first philosophy. The idea of an eternal substance that is also immovable already suggests Aristotle's idea of a *first or prime mover itself unmoved*. This is a crucial concept in Aristotle's philosophical theology developed at greater length in the *Physics*. There Aristotle considers an argument to prove that there must exist a god or deity, in the sense of a prime mover.

The concept is of a being that causes the universe to begin to move, but is itself unmoved and incapable of being moved. The argument for the existence of a first mover itself unmoved is to consider three conceivable ways of explaining the movement that we know occurs in the universe, and then to eliminate two of the choices as impossible. Aristotle considers three patterns of movement that seem to exhaust the alternatives for understanding the nature of motion in the universe at large. The causal relations responsible for motion in the universe might be: (1) *infinitely regressive*, one motion being caused by another motion, caused by another, and so on, infinitely; (2) *circular*, one motion causing another, and so on, but ultimately circling back as the cause of the first mentioned motion; (3) *terminal and foundational*, in which one motion is caused by another, and so on, neither infinitely nor circularly, but beginning with a first mover that itself is unmoved by any other cause.

Aristotle rejects possibilities (1) and (2). If he is right that these three are the only conceivable alternatives, then we are left with (3) alone as not only the best but the only possibility for understanding motion. Aristotle's objection to possibility (1) is that there can be no actually infinite regresses, but at most only potentially infinite series, those that could in principle go on beyond any specified point. The reason Aristotle believes that there can be no actual infinity or infinite regress is that if infinities are real, then logical paradoxes such as those described by Zeno of Elea, a student of Parmenides, would obtain.

Zeno discusses several such paradoxes, of which the following is a typical example. Imagine two runners running a race. One runner has a head start on the other, however slight. If distance, as is supposed in applications of Euclidean geometry to spatial phenomena (although Euclid lived after Zeno), is infinitely divisible, then the second runner, paradoxically, running at any speed whatsoever, can never catch up to the first runner. The reason, according to Zeno, is that the second runner faces an impossibly infinite series of tasks to be fulfilled before the first runner can be reached. The second runner must first cover one-half of the distance between the starting point and the first runner. While this is happening, the first runner continues to move forward at least a little distance, so that the second task the second runner must accomplish is to cover one-half of the distance between the point the second runner has reached at that point and the new endpoint reached in the meantime by the first runner. And so on. If Zeno is right, there will be infinitely first half-lengths that the second runner must reach before completing the second half-length of any distance separating the runners. The second runner can never catch up with let alone pass the first runner.

Of course, in observing an actual race, we expect a faster second runner to pass a first slower runner. Such an observation does not embarrass Zeno, who regards the difference between what is observed in practice and what the rational thesis of the infinite divisibility of spatial extension implies as proof that the empirical evidence of the senses is illusory. The world as a whole is not as it appears, but is rather an indistinguishable One in which motion and change is impossible. This conclusion reflects Zeno's teacher Parmenides' distinction between the way of Being and the way of Seeming. As we have seen, Parmenides' philosophy is also the basis for Plato's doctrine of the one and the many, to which we have now through a circuitous route unexpectedly returned.

Aristotle's solution to Zeno's paradoxes, all variations on a similar theme, is to deny the reality of infinite divisibility. If there is no such thing as an actually infinitely divisible magnitude, then Zeno's paradoxes cannot get off the ground. To account for the mathematical concept of infinite divisibility, Aristotle strikes a compromise by considering the possibility of a potential infinity. The implication in Aristotle's proof for the existence of a first mover itself unmoved is that choice (1) is impossible if there is no such thing as an actual infinity, where an infinitely regressive series of motions or causes for motions as effects would need to be an actual rather than merely potential infinity. Pattern (2) is rejected by Aristotle for a different reason. If motion is arranged in an ultimately circular cause and effect configuration, then at least some effects must precede their causes. This, Aristotle holds, is impossible. It inverts the temporal order that governs any causally related events, whereby cause always precedes effect and never the other way around. This leaves as the only possibility (3), according to which motion in the universe, sequences of causes and effects, do not regress infinitely or loop into circles, but have a definite terminus, a first cause that is itself uncaused, which Aristotle refers to as a first mover itself unmoved. This unmoved first mover causes all motion in the universe but is not moved and so not subject to cause by anything else. Aristotle calls the unmoved first mover an eternal substance, and describes it also as deity; it is in effect a cosmic philosophical concept of god.

Aristotle describes the unmoved first mover as pure form or pure actuality. Where pure or prime matter is pure potentiality, capable of becoming any material element, god as unmoved first mover is pure actuality. The sense in which the unmoved first mover is supposed to be pure actuality remains somewhat obscure. What is easy to see is that if the unmoved first mover sets the universe in motion, then it does in one act all that is needed to bring about all the other events that will ever take place in the entire history of the entire material universe. The unmoved first mover affects all motion involving all changes, essential and accidental, all creation and generation, corruption, and alteration. As such, there is no more that will ever actually occur in the world that is not actualized, no matter how long it might take for all the causal chains to play out, bringing about motion from motion and change through change, when the prime mover in the original act of moving sets the entire universe in motion. If this is the implication of Aristotle's first philosophy as theology and of his concept of god as unmoved first mover, then there is no difficulty in appreciating the sense in which god or the unmoved mover is also rightly understood in Aristotle's terms as pure actuality.

Aristotle's Ousiology and the Metaphysics of Change

We can now think of Aristotle's first philosophy as an *ousiology*. By this is meant a systematic way of disambiguating the various systematically related meanings of substance or *ousia* to which Aristotle calls attention. Aristotle's ousiology consists of the two endpoints that set limits to the kinds of substance, bounded by nonsubstances. In the one case at the formal extreme, god or unmoved first mover is pure actuality, while prime matter at the opposite material extreme is undifferentiated material stuff requiring form or definition of some sort in order even to constitute any of the material elements that enter into the physical composition of bodies or primary substances. In between the extremes of god and prime matter, all elements, primary and secondary substances in the true sense of the word, are arranged according to their proximity either to prime matter or pure form.

Primary substances belong in the very middle of the ousiology. They are located equidistantly from the extremes of pure form or pure actuality and prime, pure undifferentiated, matter. Ranged along the ousiology between primary substances and pure form or pure actuality are the definitions, species, forms, or secondary substances. These are more formal than material, despite being substances, but as substances in Aristotle's sense they still contain matter of some kind, even if it is only a definition's subject matter. Along the other side of the ousiology in the opposite direction between primary substances and prime or pure undifferentiated matter are included the five Aristotelian material elements: earth, air, fire, water, and æther. These are more material than formal, but have at least some formal properties by which they are differentiated from prime matter as specific kinds of material stuff.

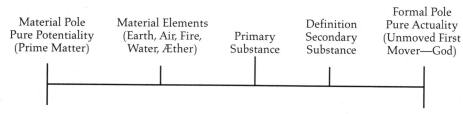

FIGURE 2.1 Aristotle's ousiology

As material elements, they are not themselves primary substances that exist independently in themselves and in the full sense of the word, but exist only insofar as they constitute the underlying material basis of all primary substances. Aristotle's ousiology is represented in Figure 2.1.

Aristotle's ousiology explains the nature of change in the theory of substance as the centerpiece of Aristotle's first philosophy. He observes that sensible substance is subject to change, implying that nonsensible substance is eternal and unchangeable. He repeats the formulation by which change is movement between opposites paired together in a contrariety. When the category of change being considered is an alteration among the accidental properties of a substance, a primary substance exchanges one secondary substance in a contrariety for its contrary. Aristotle remarks that substances undergo change with respect to contrary properties but that contraries themselves as predicables do not change.

> Sensible substance is changeable. Now if change proceeds from opposites or from intermediate points, and not from all opposites (for the voice is not-white) but from the contrary, there must be something underlying which changes into the contrary state; for the contraries do not change. . . . Further, something persists, but the contrary does not persist; there is, then, some third thing besides the contraries, viz. the matter. Now since changes are of four kinds—either in respect of the essence or of the quality or of the quantity or of the place, and change in respect of the "this" is simple generation and destruction, and change in quantity is increase and diminution, and change in respect of an affection is alteration, and change in place is motion, changes will be from given states into those contrary to them in these several respects. The matter, then, which changes must be capable of both states. (1069^{b}3–13)

Aristotle distinguishes categories of change. He defends a distinction that cuts across the more fundamental distinction between essential and accidental change. He mentions in this connection changes of essence, sometimes referred to as a thing's quiddity or "thisness," its being a "this," quality, quantity, and place, which he contrasts with alterations of affection. All such changes, Aristotle indicates, can be characterized as transitions between the opposite terms of an appropriate contrariety.

The conclusion is that change for Aristotle should be understood either as generation or corruption, creation or destruction, or identity-preserving alteration. The question that troubled the Presocratics and Plato, how something can change and yet remain the same, is answered in Aristotle's first philosophy by distinguishing between kinds of change. Like the practicing biologist he is, Aristotle proposes a taxonomy of all the related species of phenomena his theory is supposed to explain, and, proceeding scientifically, divides up his explanation according to the multiplicity of kinds of changes the theory is meant to include. Aristotle does not seek to oversimplify either the phenomena to be explained or the explanations by which he proposes to understand the nature of change.

Aristotle's first philosophy identifies every substance in terms of its essence. Each substance in each category of substance has a core of essential properties. A substance persists through change when only its accidental and not its essential properties are affected. More extreme changes result in the destruction of an entity, which Aristotle explains as the elimination of an entity's essential properties, without which the substance cannot continue to exist as the same kind of substance. The possibilities are complex, and Aristotle explains the conditions for all the variations in functional terms, as factors of the kind of natural final cause of each different species of primary substance, of each kind of discrete physical sensible object that happens to exist. It is only in such primary substances that secondary substances, the definitions and formal principles of things, subsist and inhere.

Aristotle in this way explains change as an essential or accidental movement from nonexistence to creation or from existence to corruption or destruction, or from one accidental condition to another. By observing these distinctions, Aristotle is able to answer the riddle posed by Plato and the Presocratics about how things change while remaining the same. His solution agrees with commonsense judgment in many respects. The solution to the ancient problem of understanding the nature of change is managed in Aristotle's first philosophy by bringing together the separate formal and material principles of Plato and the Presocratics in a way that neither of these extremes advanced exclusively by themselves could not hope to achieve. The ousiology in Aristotle's first philosophy provides an intuitive solution that combines form and matter in a metaphysics of primary and secondary substance, essential and accidental properties, god, pure form, or pure actuality, and prime matter or pure potentiality, and distinctions among several kinds of changes of creation, destruction and identity-preserving alteration.

SUMMARY

Aristotle defines substance as informed matter, combining form and matter. His metaphysics can be described by an ousiology that is bounded at opposite extremes by pure form or God as pure actuality and prime matter as pure potentiality. In between, there are different combinations of form and matter at distinct points along the spectrum. These include the five elements earth, air, fire, water, and æther near the material extreme, primary substances at the very center as substances in the most proper and metaphysically most basic sense, also known as individual spatiotemporal physical entities, and secondary substances or definitions that inhere in primary substances and are located closer to the formal extreme.

Aristotle distinguishes between a thing's essential and accidental qualities. A thing's essence consists of those properties without which it would not exist or could not continue to exist. Accidental properties are those that can be altered in a thing without destroying it as a thing of that general kind associated with its essence. Aristotle solves the problem of change that had perplexed Plato and the Presocratic philosophers by appealing to the distinction between a substance's essence and accidents. The question how a thing can change and yet remain the same is answered by the theory that a substance remains the same only when its accidental properties change, leaving its essence unaffected, and preserving whatever essentially makes something the particular kind of thing it is, according to its nature. A substance's essence is also independently defined in terms of its natural function. Secondary substances are Aristotle's modified version of Plato's Forms. Although Plato's Forms would exist in the abstract even if none of their instances happened to exist, Aristotle's secondary substances exist only insofar as they inhere in existent substances.

By emphasizing the importance of sense experience in knowledge of the changing physical world, Aristotle paves the way for a very different style of philosophy than Plato's, to which, despite these differences, his thought owes a significant debt. Aristotle's philosophy is an important precursor of modern scientific method and logical analysis in philosophical inquiry. Plato and Aristotle in their respective systems of thought represent a fundamental opposition in philosophical method and ideology. Their differences complement one another, and together they stand as the first great thinkers of ancient Greek philosophy. The choices in philosophical outlook that they defend are found in different forms at different times throughout the history of philosophy.

QUESTIONS FOR PHILOSOPHICAL UNDERSTANDING

1. What does Aristotle mean by a substance's essence? What is Aristotle's distinction between primary and secondary substances?

2. Can all properties of a substance be part of its essence? Why or why not?

3. Do primary substances that are made by intelligent beings like ourselves have a natural function? If not, can they have an essence according to Aristotle's metaphysics?

4. Can a person have an essence? If personal identity is determined by a thinker's memories and expectations, can any of these be essential, or must they not all be accidental?

5. Can secondary substances change?

6. Do secondary substances also have an essence and accidents?

7. How does Aristotle's attitude toward the purpose and method of philosophy differ from Plato's? How and in what ways if any are they the same or similar?

8. Would Aristotle and Plato agree on any of the same items of knowledge?

9. Does Aristotle, like Socrates, need to maintain that knowledge is an eternal possession of an immortal soul?

10. How can we tell without actually destroying a substance whether any of its properties is essential or merely accidental?

11. How might Aristotle interpret Socrates' geometry lesson with Meno's slave?

12. Where and how do secondary substances originate when a first example of a primary substance in which they inhere is first created? When the first pyramid was built, when did the secondary substance of pyramidhood or pyramidicity come into being? Did it happen when the building of the pyramid began, or only when it was com-

plete, or could it happen somewhere in between? What if later it is only partially destroyed or defaced in a minor way?

13. How would Socrates or Plato criticize Aristotle's theory of substance?

14. What is Aristotle's proof for the existence of a prime mover itself unmoved? Is the argument successful? Why or why not?

15. What would be some of the philosophical implications of denying that physical things actually undergo change? What would be some of the philosophical implications of affirming that all physical things constantly change and never remain the same or persist even through accidental change without sacrificing their identities?

KEY TERMS

accident

active phenomenon, passive phenomenon

alteration

atomic theory of physical matter

being *qua* being

causation

change

circular causation model

contingent

contrariety

definition

deity, eternal substance

earth, air, fire, water, æther

efficient cause

elements

essence

existence, subsistence

final cause

first philosophy, *proté philosophia*

formal cause

formal principle

four Aristotelian causes

functionalism, functionalist theory of substance

generation, corruption

hylé

identity

immovable

incorporeal

indeterminate

infinitely regressive causation model

inhere, inherence

material cause

metaphysics

metaphysics of change

natural function

Ockham's razor

ontology

ontos

ousia

ousiology

persistence of things through change

predicable

Presocratic thinkers

primary substance

prime matter, *proté hylé*

prime mover

problem of change

pure actuality

pure potentiality

quiddity

secondary substance

second philosophy

substance

telos

terminal and foundational model of causation

theology

vicious circularity

Zeno's paradoxes

SOURCES AND RECOMMENDED READINGS

Anton, John. *Aristotle's Theory of Contrariety*. London: Routledge & Kegan Paul, 1957.

Bäck, Allan. *Aristotle's Theory of Predication*. Leiden: E. J. Brill, 2000.

David, Charles. *Aristotle on Meaning and Essence*. Oxford: Clarendon Press, 2000.

Fine, Gail. *On Ideas: Aristotle's Criticism of Plato's Theory of Forms*. Oxford: Clarendon Press, 1993.

Furth, Montgomery. *Substance, Form, and Psyche: An Aristotelian Metaphysics*. Cambridge: Cambridge University Press, 1988.

Gill, Mary Louise. *Aristotle on Substance: The Paradox of Unity*. Princeton: Princeton University Press, 1989.

Irwin, Terence. *Aristotle's First Principles*. Oxford: Clarendon Press, 1988.

Lewis, Frank A. *Substance and Predication in Aristotle*. Cambridge: Cambridge University Press, 1991.

Scaltsas, Theodore. *Substances and Universals in Aristotle's Metaphysics*. Ithaca: Cornell University Press, 1994.

Wedin, Michael V. *Aristotle's Theory of Substance: The Categories and Metaphysics Zeta*. Oxford: Oxford University Press, 2000.

Witt, Charlotte. *Substance and Essence in Aristotle: An Interpretation of Metaphysics VII–IX*. Ithaca: Cornell University Press, 1989.

CHAPTER 3

UNIVERSALS, PARTICULARS, AND THE CONCEPT OF TRUTH

Ockham's *Summa Logicae I*

Theories of the metaphysics of things and their properties continue into the medieval period of Scholastic philosophy. Ockham develops a solution to the problem of universals that is very different from Plato's theory of Forms and Aristotle's theory of inherent secondary substances. Ockham uses principles of logical subdivision to draw metaphysical distinctions, organize the principles of a theory of universals and particulars, and elaborate criticisms of alternative theories of universals in the process of working out a theory of his own. He concludes that universals are concepts or intentions of the soul that do not exist outside the mind, but are expressed linguistically in the mind's natural signs and in the conventional signs of languages.

MEDIEVAL PHILOSOPHY

William of Ockham (c. 1280–1347) is one of the most interesting and controversial figures in the history of philosophy. He was born in England and educated at Oxford University, but never completed his formal studies. He was a Franciscan monk at a time when England was still a thoroughly Catholic country. In 1323 he was ordered to appear before the papal court at Avignon, France, and was soon brought up on fifty-six charges of religious heresy.

The incidents surrounding his trial and condemnation by the Church had a profound impact on Ockham's life and philosophical career. His interests turned from topics in logic, philosophy of language, and early scientific methodology to specific problems of religious orthodoxy, political theory, and history. Ockham and several of his friends who had all fallen under official censure escaped from the authority of the Church to Germany, seeking refuge with Emperor Ludwig of Bavaria, who was a political opponent of the pope. Ockham spent the rest of his life in exile under the protection of the German emperor at his court in Munich.

Medieval philosophy owes much to two distinct sources of ideas. Its greatest influences include Aristotle, whose writings had been preserved and translated by Arabic scholars and commentators, and the Bible. Thomas Aquinas achieved a great synthesis of Aristotle and the Bible that had a profound impact on the direction of European philosophy throughout the entire later Middle Ages to the Renaissance and into the early modern period. We have already seen that ancient Greek philosophy is diversified, and that thinkers as important to its tradition as Plato and Aristotle disagree in many ways. The same is true of medieval philosophy, which resists oversimplifying generalizations as much as any other epoch in philosophy. It is nevertheless appropriate to identify certain prevalent trends at this time, from roughly the ninth through the fifteenth century, together with a family of topics and questions that philosophers during the Middle Ages found especially deserving of attention. Philosophy in the medieval period centers around a number of distinct schools based on the teachings of Aristotle, for which reason medieval thought is also sometimes known as Scholastic philosophy.

We focus on Ockham's investigations of the metaphysics of universals, a central philosophical preoccupation of the medieval era. Ockham is surprisingly modern in his attitude toward the primacy of philosophical argument in the search for philosophical truth. An uncompromising devotion to philosophy got Ockham into conflict with the Church in his day. We are primarily concerned with Ockham's theory of properties, in the course of which we also encounter his views concerning the nature of mind, in the broader context of major developments in medieval philosophy.

THE PROBLEM OF UNIVERSALS

A *universal* is a quality or relation that is instantiated by or can be predicated of many different particular things. The property *red* or being red is an example. There are many different red things, a list of which would need to include blood drops, sunsets, roses, and rubies. The problem of universals is to understand what makes all of these things red and what kind of thing a universal is.

We have already considered two prominent attitudes concerning the existence of abstract entities in Plato's theory of Forms and Aristotle's doctrine of definitions or secondary substances inhering in other substances. Plato holds that abstract Forms are real timeless eternally existent entities that physical things in the world of appearance imitate or in which they participate. The way in which particulars imitate or participate in Platonic Forms is unclear, and Plato often resorts to metaphors to convey their exact relation. Although Plato does not usually discuss universals in the sense of ordinary qualities of things like redness, he comes very close to including universals among such Forms as the ideal city-state, ideal human being, ideal bed or couch, that in one sense seem to be abstract particulars but are multiply instantiated in the world of experience. Aristotle does not accept Plato's theory of Forms, but construes properties that can be instantiated by inhering in the physical spatiotemporal world of primary substances rather than existing in an abstract Platonic realm. Where Plato would say that redness is a real abstract universal that can be instantiated in many different particular red things, Aristotle holds that there is no redness that exists as a separate abstract entity, but that individual things are red only insofar as the definition or secondary substance redness inheres in existent things.

Ockham is familiar with both Plato's and Aristotle's solutions to the metaphysics of universals. He discusses at length Aristotle's concept of the inherence of universals as definitions or secondary substances primarily for purposes of criticism. He does not deny the existence of universals, but argues that they do not exist outside the mind. Ockham is a *conceptualist* in his metaphysics of universals, and a *nominalist* in his interpretation of universals in the mind as natural signs in the mind's innate language and of property terms as conventional signs in ordinary language.

The word *nominalism* derives from the Latin word *nomen*, meaning "name." A nominalist believes that there is nothing more to the properties of things than the fact that we use the same name to refer to similar qualities exemplified by a collection of particular things. The reason, according to most nominalists, why roses, blood drops, and sunsets are red is not that there is an abstract universal *redness* in which they all participate, nor a definition or secondary substance *redness* that inheres in particular red things and would not otherwise exist. What makes particular things red is merely the fact that we use the same word to refer to their color, to which we give the same name "red." There is nothing more to the redness of roses, blood drops, and sunsets, according to nominalism, than the common use of the name "red" and the fact that we language users choose to describe the color of a number of different things by that name. It is only a matter of how we think and speak about things, the names we give to things in describing the content of our experience of the world.

Nominalism by itself is a category but not a complete theory of universals. In addition to saying that the properties of things are explained merely as the use of the same name for the perceived qualities of a number of different things, it is also important to provide a reason or justification to explain why it is appropriate to use the same name in such situations. Ockham fills this need by offering a theory of the mind's *natural signs* that combines nominalism with conceptualism. Conceptualism is the view that universals exist within the mind rather than inhering in things or as abstract entities in a Platonic heaven of Forms. The use of the same name "red" to refer to the color quality of roses, blood, and sunsets is justified by virtue of the fact that the mind groups these things together with respect to their similarity of color. There is nothing more to the redness of different red things than the common use of the name "red." According to Ockham's conceptualist version of nominalism, the mind organizes its experiences in such a way that it groups together roses, blood drops, and sunsets under a single mental category to which the name "red" is assigned as a convenient reference tag. The fact is that a common name for the particular qualities of particular things does not point to the existence of an abstract or inherent universal, but to a universal that exists only as a concept within the mind, and that for simplicity is indicated in language by the choice of a single word to cover a variety of different but relevantly similar individual cases.

OCKHAM'S LOGIC AND METAPHYSICS OF TERMS

Ockham's primary intellectual debt is to Aristotle. He nevertheless disagrees with Aristotle in important ways. Even in the title of his *Summa Logicae*, Ockham expresses his interest in logic and scientific method. Where Aquinas writes a *Summa Theologiæ* to articulate the sum of theological knowledge, Ockham proposes to bring together the total of logical knowledge. He divides the *Summa* into two main parts, Books I and II. Book I presents a logic of terms, and Book II contains a theory of propositions constructed out of terms. We will be concerned entirely with Ockham's theory of terms in *Summa Logicae I*, since it is there that Ockham explains the meanings of universal terms. He understands the logic, semantic theory or philosophy of language, and metaphysics of terms as inextricably connected. We cannot fully understand any of these philosophical aspects of terms without looking into the others.

Ockham takes an analytic approach to the meaning of terms. Logic as the formal theory of correct reasoning and valid argument, as Aristotle taught, is at root a theory of terms, which is how Ockham accordingly begins his *Summa*:

> All those who treat of logic try to show that arguments are composed of propositions and propositions of terms. Thus, a term is simply a component part of a proposition. When he defines the notion of a term in the first book of the *Prior Analytics*, Aristotle says: "I call that a term into which a proposition is resolved (i.e., the predicate or that of which it is predicated), when it is asserted or denied that something is or is not the case." (49)

Ockham's subject matter is logic. Logic deals with arguments. Arguments consist of propositions, and propositions consist of terms. In particular, terms are the units of meaning into which propositions are "resolved." Terms belong to two categories, referring either to predicates or that of which predicates are predicated. Predicate terms are universals in the sense that the same predicate can be truly or falsely predicated of many different things. Aristotle refers to such terms as "predicables." Other terms refer to the things of which universal predicate terms are predicated. A sentence that could belong to many arguments, such as "This rose is red," is combination of terms governed by logical and grammatical rules.

Ockham is interested in a proposition's subject and predicate terms. In the true or false proposition, "This rose is red," the subject term is "rose" and the predicate term is "red." An Aristotelian logic of terms distinguishes other terms that enter into a proposition as belonging to distinct categories. The term "this" is sometimes classified in this logical tradition as *syncategorematic*, meaning that it is neither a subject nor predicate term but a word that is used to link together other referring expressions in a proposition. In this case, the syncategorematic term is also an *indexical* term, like "here," "now," "that," "I," and the like. Indexicals help to specify reference to a thing relative to a language user or language use context. To speak of "this" rose makes reference to a particular rose to which a speaker or writer stands in a specific relation. The term refers in different ways, depending on the circumstances in which it is used. If we are talking in the presence of just one rose, then by "this" rose we generally mean the one we are looking at. If we are standing in front of a long line of roses when we say, "This rose is red," our meaning might be obvious if only one of them is red, or we might need to point to a specific object in order to indicate by the indexical as we point with our index finger to indicate which particular flower we have in mind.

The other term component of the proposition is "is." Term logic standardly categorizes cognate forms of the words *to be* ("is," "are," "am") and "has" when combined with certain predicates as *copulae*. A copula is a word that literally joins or couples together a subject and predicate term in a proposition. Much like a coupler in an electrical connection or a pipe elbow in plumbing, a copula hooks up a subject term with a predicate term so that together with syncategorematic terms in a sentence they constitute a complete proposition. A proposition, in turn, can be true or false by virtue of expressing a state of affairs that either exists or does not exist. "This rose is red" is thus a combination of terms, beginning with an indexical, and proceeding to a subject term that is joined to a predicate term by means of a copula. A copula is sometimes combined with a predicate term as a more complete formulation of the predicate, so that instead of referring simply to "red" as the predicate term within a proposition the predicate in its entirety is given as "is red," "are red," "being red," "to be red," "was red," "will be red," "has the property of being red," and the like. If we combine syncategorematic reference terms with subject terms and copulae with predicate terms we can think of every proposition more simply as combining a subject and predicate.

As a follower of Aristotle's term logic but not of Aristotle's metaphysics of inherent universals, Ockham is particularly interested in predicate terms and understanding how they function in the logic of propositions and arguments. There is no deep mystery about the meanings of subject terms as far as Ockham is concerned. They refer to the things we can experience by means of the five senses, such as the rose. The meaning of predicate terms is more complicated and correspondingly more philosophically interesting. What, exactly, Ockham wants to know, do we mean by the universal predicate term "red," when we say, "This rose is red"? What kind of a thing is a universal by which many different roses can all be red, and many different kinds of things, roses, blood drops, and sunsets, can all be red? How is it that different shades and hues of color are all red or all reds?

Ockham argues that it is not enough to have a superficial understanding of universal predicate terms; a logician must also have a "deep" knowledge of such terms. He distinguishes between subject and predicate terms as terms of *first* and *second intention*. This is the difference we have previously described as that between subject and predicate terms. He charts a natural transition from logic to metaphysics, without which he seems to think that logic itself is incomplete and lacking in depth. He writes:

§14: On the Universal

It is not enough for the logician to have a merely general knowledge of terms; he needs a deep understanding of the concept of a term. Therefore, after discussing some general divisions among terms we should examine in detail the various headings under these divisions.

First, we should deal with terms of second intention and afterwards with terms of first intention. We must discuss those terms of first intention. I have said that "universal," "genus," and "species" are examples of terms of second intention.

We must discuss those terms of second intention which are called the five universals, but first we should consider the common term "universal." It is predicated of every universal and is opposed to the notion of a particular. (77)

A term of second intention is one that is predicated of other things. It might appear that terms of second intention are always predicated of terms of first intention, and while this is often true, Ockham explains that it is not generally the case. Universals as terms of second intention can also be predicated of terms of second intention, themselves and others. Thus, we could say that the term of second intention "red," which can be predicated of a term of first intention such as "rose," can also have predicated of it another term of second intention, such as "color," as in the proposition, "Red is a color." Nor is logic limited to the predication of terms of second intention to terms of first intention or to other terms of second intention. An interesting exception to which Ockham calls attention is the term *universal* itself. It is predicated of every specific universal, such as "red," "blue," "round," "square," and the like, and also of the term *universal,* in the proposition, "Any universal is or has the property of being a universal" or "This universal is or has the property of being a universal."

OCKHAM'S CRITIQUE OF UNIVERSALS AS ARISTOTELIAN SUBSTANCES

Ockham shows himself a true philosopher by insisting that philosophical conclusions must be supported by sound reasoning. He maintains that the metaphysics of universals should be upheld in two ways, by good arguments and a corroborative appeal to authority. He announces his conceptualism in the section title and again immediately after explaining how any philosophical position should ideally be defended. He prepares to argue that universals do not exist except as concepts of mind:

§15: That the Universal Is Not a Thing Outside the Mind

But it is not enough just to state one's position; one must defend it by philosophical arguments. Therefore, I shall set forth some arguments for my view, and then corroborate it by an appeal to the authorities.

That no universal is a substance existing outside the mind can be proved in a number of ways. . . . (79)

Ockham implies that he does not regard himself as an authority. We should remember throughout that he is still a graduate student when he writes the *Summa Logicae.* If he were an authority, he could simply declare his positions, which by itself would make them worthy of philosophical consideration. He does not plead youth or lack of acceptance as an authority in his own right, but maintains instead that a philosophical position should be recommended only if it can be strongly defended by philosophical reasoning. What comes first in philosophy is good philosophical argument, and only afterward is it appropriate to seek corroboration from recognized authorities.

Agreement with other thinkers, no matter how worthy of our respect, cannot settle philosophical questions. Ockham's philosophical free thinking is evident in subtle ways throughout his writings. His attitude toward philosophical method and the priority of clarifying ideas when doing philosophy, accepting only whatever conclusions are supported by philosophical reasoning, is refreshing in a medieval philosopher. The attempt to secularize philosophy by Ockham as a member of the lower clergy leaves little room for doubt about why he raised concerns among ecclesiastical authorities and in what ways he might have been perceived as a danger to religious orthodoxy. What if everyone started pursuing knowledge and making decisions on the basis of philosophical argument instead of consulting the Church-approved authorities? What if they started to think for themselves about the nature of the world and the morality of individual and social conduct?

That the universal is nothing outside the mind can also be perceived as a specific metaphysical doctrine contrary to Church dogma. If there are no universals existing outside the mind, then the world can be explained in terms of external physical objects and their properties and relations existing as concepts only within human minds. Where is the medieval Christian God supposed to be found in such a metaphysics? If there are no eternal truths needed to explain the world, then perhaps is there is also no need for the existence of a divine eternal source of eternal truths, no reason for religion to look beyond the limits of the temporal world of experience. Ockham now begins a series of arguments to prove that universals do not exist outside the mind. He strings together a number of considerations in a complex chain of inferences that first needs to be surveyed in its entirety and then taken apart and put back together in order to be absorbed. He argues:

> No universal is a particular substance, numerically one; for if this were the case, then it would follow that Socrates is a universal; for there is no good reason why one substance should be a universal rather than another. Therefore no particular substance is a universal; every substance is numerically one and a particular. For every substance is either one thing and not many or it is many things. Now, if a substance is one thing and not many, then it is numerically one; for that is what we mean by "numerically one." But if, on the other hand, some substance is several things, it is either several particular things or several universal things. If the first alternative is chosen, then it follows that some substance would be several substances; and consequently that some substance would be several men. But although the universal would be distinguished from a single particular, it would not be distinguished from several particulars. If, however, some substance were to be several universal entities, I take one of those universal entities and ask, "Is it many things or is it one and not many?" If the second is the case then it follows that the thing is particular. If the first is the case then I ask, "Is it several particular things or several universal things?" Thus, either an infinite regress will follow or it will be granted that no substance is a universal in a way that would be incompatible with its also being a particular. From this it follows that no substance is a universal. (79)

The argument has several parts. Ockham assumes an Aristotelian framework of metaphysical categories of substances and asks what kinds of things a universal would need to be in order to exist outside the mind. He eliminates each category systematically in turn and is left with no possibility for a universal to be anything other than a concept in the mind. In a way, this is only a negative result. By leaving open only the possibility of universals as existing within the mind, Ockham sets the stage for a more positive nominalist theory of universals as nothing more than concepts as the references of predicate terms, of names given to concepts that collect together similar things within the mind for the convenience of thought.

Ockham tries to prove that no universal is a particular substance, and no particular substance is a universal. To show that no universal is a particular substance, he argues that if it were true that any universal is a particular substance, then it would follow that Socrates is a universal, on the grounds that if any universals are any particular substances, then we can have no basis for excluding any particular substance as a universal. If we suppose that any universal is a particular substance, in other words, then we open the floodgates to any particular substance being a universal. Is Ockham's reasoning correct? It sounds very much as if we were to say that no horse is a particular substance, because if a horse is a particular substance, then any particular substance, say, Socrates, is a horse. The inference obviously does not follow in the case of horses, so why should it do so in the case of universals? There appears to be something flawed in Ockham's logic. To show that no particular substance is a universal, Ockham argues that every substance is numerically one and particular, together with the conclusion he thinks he has just established that no universal is particular. The argument is not entirely convincing, although its conclusion is plausible. It appears that what Ockham needs to prove in this context is that particular substances cannot be universals because if universals exist outside the mind they need to be distributed in as many different numerically distinct things as instantiate or exemplify them. No particular numerically one substance can coexist in other distinct particular substances. Perhaps this is more like the argument that Ockham could and should have given.

The proof does not end here but describes a more penetrating series of metaphysical distinctions and logical dilemmas. Ockham assumes that a substance is either one thing or many things. If a substance is one, then it is numerically one, and hence cannot be many. If, on the other hand, a substance is many, then, since all things are either particular or universal, the substance is either several particular things or several universal things. If a substance as many is several particular things, then some substance is several substances and hence, astonishingly, some substance would be several men. Ockham does not explain why he finds the conclusion absurd, but admittedly it seems impossible for one substance at the same time and in the same sense to be many substances. If that were true, then it would follow that the universal *man* as a substance that was many rather than one would be identical to whatever things had the property of being a man, and hence, as Ockham says, of several men. The conclusion is rejected because it implies that a substance at one and the same time is fundamentally metaphysically many and one. If a substance as many is several universal things, then Ockham asks whether each of these universals is itself one or many. If each universal is one thing, then the substance in question is particular rather than universal, contrary to the assumption. If each universal is many rather than one, then we can ask of it whether it is particular or universal. Ockham concludes as a result of his nested dilemmas that either no substance can be understood as a universal that would be inconsistent with its also being a particular, or else we are stuck in an infinite regress in which we can keep asking indefinitely whether a universal as many substances is many particulars or many universals. The problem

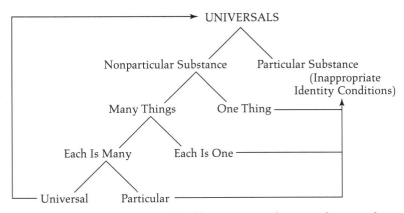

FIGURE 3.1 Logical structure of Ockham's main refutation of universals as secondary substances

with the infinite regress that results in the second case is that it means we cannot arrive at a final characterization of universals as many substances, because we can never pin down whether it exists as multiple particulars or multiple universals.

If Ockham is right, then universals are not substances in any imaginable subcategory, and no substances are universals. This would be an important conclusion, because Aristotle had held that universals are secondary substances. Ockham's argument in its application to substances generally entails that Aristotle's metaphysics of the inherence of secondary substances in primary substances is false. Universals cannot be secondary substances that inhere in other substances outside the mind because no universals are substances and no substances are universals. The proof he offers may not be as watertight as he desires, and it is a bit abstract and difficult to follow, but the basic strategy is clear. We represent the logical structure of Ockham's reasoning as in Figure 3.1.

Ockham argues by dividing up the possibilities for a theory of universals as substances outside the mind in a series of logical distinctions. He runs through the categories and subcategories, finding reasons for rejecting each possibility, as one or many, particular or universal. When he is done he believes that logically he has left no stone unturned and has given good reasons at each step for rejecting universals as substances in any sense. Along the way he refutes Aristotle's theory of universals as definitions or secondary substances inhering in primary substances.

FURTHER OBJECTIONS TO UNIVERSALS AS INHERENT SUBSTANCES

This part of Ockham's argument is complete. He supplements the reasons he has already offered with additional considerations that imply the impossibility of universals existing as substances outside the mind:

Again, if some universal were to be one substance existing in particular substances, yet distinct from them, it would follow that it could exist without them; for everything that is naturally prior to something else can, by God's power, exist without that thing; but the consequence is absurd. (79)

The idea of a universal as one substance simultaneously existing in many particular substances from which it remains distinct makes an obvious reference to Aristotle's inherence metaphysics of secondary substances in primary substances. Ockham claims that an absurdity follows from such an assumption, based on another related implication of Aristotle's distinction between substance, essence, and accident.

Aristotle characterizes a substance as that which could exist without its accidents, and defines essence and accidents as secondary substances incapable of existing except as inhering in existent primary substances. If we assume that a universal existed as a substance in other substances from which it was distinct, then as a substance it could exist without them. Ockham invokes God's omnipotence as sufficient to permit a universal existing as a substance in other substances to exist independently of the substances in which it inheres. Such a conclusion contradicts Aristotle's concept of a secondary substance as inhering in primary substances. It is tempting as a result to say that Ockham does not understand Aristotle's theory of secondary substance as something that could not exist independently of the primary substances in which it inheres.

The more likely interpretation of Ockham's objection is that he is questioning the appropriateness of referring to a universal as a secondary *substance*, given that a substance by definition is something that can exist independently of its accidental properties. It is an accidental property of the secondary substance *red* that it hypothetically inheres in a particular rose, since the rose could continue to exist even if had some other color, if its color were to change naturally or artificially. It follows in that case according to the definition of substance as that which can exist independently of its accidents that the color red should be capable of existing as a secondary substance independently of its inherence in the rose.

The implication contradicts Aristotle's theory of secondary substance as something whose existence depends on the existence of the primary substances in which it inheres. The contradiction is that the existence of universals as secondary substances is both dependent on and independent of the existence of the primary substances in which they inhere. The inconsistency is traced back to Aristotle, casting more doubt on his theory of universals as inherent secondary substances. By this reasoning, Ockham refutes Aristotle's theory of universals in two ways by two different arguments. It is Aristotle's metaphysics of universals as secondary substances that he regards as the principal obstacle to a theory of universal terms as names for mind-dependent concepts. He signals yet another argument in support of the conclusion that universals cannot be substances:

Again, if the view in question were true, no individual would be able to be created. Something of the individual would pre-exist it, for the whole individual would not take its existence from nothing if the universal which is in it were already in something else. For the same reason it would follow that God could not annihilate an individual substance without destroying the other individuals of the same kind. If He were to annihilate some individual, he would destroy the whole which is essentially that individual and, consequently, He would destroy the universal which is in that thing and in others of the same essence. Consequently, other things of the same essence would not remain, for they could not continue to exist without the universal which constitutes a part of them. (80)

Invoking God's infinite power, Ockham looks at the argument from another angle, with respect to the creation and annihilation of things. The theory of universals as secondary substances now also makes it impossible for anything to be created. The reason is that if secondary substances as genuine substances can exist independently of the primary substances in which they accidentally inhere, then a thing consisting in part of the secondary substances that inhere in it could not be created in its entirety from nothing but could only be put together out of preexisting universals.

The objection seems to be that such a conclusion would contradict the theological assumption that God can and did create the universe in its entirety out of nothing. The same kind of complaint would obviously hold if universals were preexisting abstract Platonic entities, which for practical purposes Ockham in this regard does not distinguish from inherent Aristotelian definitions or secondary substances. The same Platonic-Aristotelian theory of universals as independently existing abstract entities or secondary substances outside the mind equally places an unacceptable limit on God's ability to destroy things.

What is worse, Ockham argues, is that the metaphysics of universals as independently existing secondary substances outside the mind has the consequence that by completely destroying any particular thing, God would need to destroy its essence, where the essence of a thing is the secondary substances inhering within that thing that are necessary to its existence. Ockham reasons that God can completely destroy something, and that nothing is completely destroyed unless its essence is completely destroyed; but by completely destroying the essence of a thing the essence is unavailable for instantiation by any other particular thing that we would otherwise suppose has the same essence. If God completely destroys a particular horse, it follows that God destroys every horse, which Ockham rightly regards as an absurd implication reflecting back on the absurdity of assuming that universals are independently existing secondary substances inhering in many different particular substances. He offers two final related arguments:

Again, such a universal could not be construed as something completely extrinsic to the essence of an individual; therefore, it would belong to the essence of the individual; and, consequently, an individual would be composed of universals, so that the individual would not be any more a particular than a universal. (80)

A universal cannot be entirely excluded from a primary substance's essence, and hence must be part of its essence. It follows that an individual in its essence is composed of universals, which in a sense unspecified by Ockham is itself universal rather than particular. The undeveloped idea appears to be that if an individual's essence contains any universals, then the individual itself is essentially or in its essence universal rather than particular. The implication carried to its logical conclusion would then be that there are no particulars but only universals, which Ockham dismisses as false.

The final argument directly refutes the possibility of universals as substances existing outside the mind. Ockham illustrates the general metaphysical problem with an example from the Bible. If universals were secondary substances existing in primary substances, then it would be part of the essence of Jesus Christ to suffer the same defects as Judas Iscariot. The unpalatable conclusion, he believes, follows from the assumption that Christ and Judas share a common essence that on the theory of universals as inherent secondary substances equally inheres in both:

> Again, it follows that something of the essence of Christ would be miserable and damned, since that common nature really existing in Christ would be damned in the damned individual; for surely that essence is also in Judas. But this is absurd. (80)

The argument is not strongly compelling. Would it not be an option for an Aristotelian inherence theorist to argue in response that Christ and Judas do not share the same essence because Jesus unlike Judas is not essentially but only accidentally a human being? Judas does not share in all of Christ's essence, nor does Christ partake of all of Judas's essence. Perhaps there are individual essences, known to medieval philosophy as *haecceities*, or, literally, "thisnesses," by which the individual essence of Christ is distinct from the individual essence of Judas. The overlapping part that one has essentially and the other only accidentally is presumably not enough to justify inferring that whatever happens to affect the nature of Judas would also affect the nature of Christ. Nor is it clear in the first place that it is essential to Judas's nature that he be miserable and damned. It might be more correct for a Christian theologist to conclude that Judas is at most only accidentally miserable and damned, that he is responsible for his condition because he freely chose to betray Christ. Arguably, Judas did not need to bring these problems on himself, but acted in this way only accidentally through greed and envy and weakness of will. Ockham's point may nevertheless be well taken if it is generalized beyond the case of Christ and Judas to include the essence of any two human beings, say Judas and John or another of the original Apostles. If these two particulars share in the essence of humanity, if an identical secondary substance inheres in both as men, then anything that characterizes the essence of one as an individual, including things that happen to them as they undergo change through time, should also be part of the essence of the other. The implication seems contrary to fact if not impossible.

AUTHORITY AND THE PRIMACY OF PHILOSOPHICAL REASONING

Ockham claims that additional arguments could be adduced, but he decides to cut his criticism short and proceed to the second half of his defense, the appeal to authorities who agree with the proposition that universals cannot exist as substances outside the mind. He marks the transition in his pursuit of the question at just this point:

> Many other arguments could be brought forth, but in the interests of brevity, I shall dispense with them. Instead, I shall collaborate my account by an appeal to authorities. (80)

We are more interested in Ockham's own arguments than in his efforts to dredge up support for his conclusions in other authors. It is significant that he does not begin with the opinions of authoritative thinkers, but turns to them only after he has reasoned things through by his own lights and has investigated the strengths and weaknesses of what he takes to be the best arguments. He first considers the major reasons for and against the theory of universals as substances existing outside the mind.

Ockham does not regard himself as an authority at liberty merely to state his opinions in order for them to carry weight in the absence of sound philosophical arguments. Nor can he appeal without further ado to the authoritative views of such classical thinkers as Plato or Aristotle, unless or until their opinions are shown to stand up to rigorous philosophical scrutiny. The thoughts of respected thinkers, religious and philosophical, are not authoritative in Ockham's methodology if they cannot be independently philosophically justified. A philosopher never surrenders responsibility for evaluating the legitimacy of a philosophical position to any other thinker. It is a responsibility that extends to the need to screen received authorities on a given philosophical question and decide which among them if any deserve to be regarded as authorities. Again we see Ockham heading for trouble with the Church and its authority in endorsing particular writers as authorities in science and philosophy.

Ockham surprisingly includes Aristotle and Aquinas's commentaries on Aristotle's *Metaphysics* as his only authorities. Even here Ockham is not looking for fellow travelers merely to confirm the philosophical conclusions he has deduced through his own reflections, but cites precisely those thinkers whose metaphysics of universals as inherent secondary substances he has worked hard to reject. His purpose is to try to refute these authorities out of their own mouths, catching them upholding certain parts of his arguments that he needs in order to demonstrate the absurdity of trying to understand universals as substances existing outside the mind. He seems to believe that if only these authorities had thought through some of their philosophical commitments more clearly and carefully, they would probably have recognized the same difficulties and given up or never endorsed the idea that universals could be any category or subcategory of substance. Ockham resists the idea of authority in philosophical investigations on general grounds, and allows questions of authority only a secondary place after philosophical reasoning and philosophical criticism of purported authorities have indicated where the truth lies. More particularly, he directly challenges the Catholic Church's most deeply cherished philosophical authorities in the writings of Aristotle and Aquinas.

AGAINST UNIVERSALS AS ABSTRACT ENTITIES

Having rejected the possibility of interpreting universals as Aristotelian secondary substances inhering in primary substances, Ockham turns to consider the possibility that universals are abstract Platonic Forms. He characterizes these as existing not as substances outside the mind but as distinct from whatever particulars possess universal qualities and relations.

Ockham's main target is Aristotle's inherence theory of universals as secondary substances. When that theory is eliminated, he finds it worthwhile to move backward in time to Aristotle's teacher Plato as possibly having solved the problem of universals in a more correct way. This alternative, although less widely accepted by Ockham's contemporaries, is nevertheless important to consider. Ockham believes that when both Aristotelian and Platonic theories of universals are excluded, the only possibility that remains is the solution he accepts, according to which universals are concepts in the mind named by predicate terms in thought and language. With the definitive refutation of both Platonism and Aristotelianism, the only remaining explanation of universals is a theory that combines conceptualism with nominalism.

A universal that is distinct from particulars, as Ockham phrases it, does not inhere in another substance, but exists in another realm or abstract order that is also supposedly outside the mind. He does not mention Plato in this context, but elsewhere refers to another medieval metaphysician, Duns Scotus, as upholding a related theory of universals as inherent in but formally distinct from particulars:

> It may be clear to many that a universal is not a substance outside the mind which exists in, but is distinct from, particulars. Nevertheless, some want to claim that the universal is, in some way, outside the soul and in particulars; and while they do not want to say that a universal is really distinct from particulars, they say that it is formally distinct from particulars. Thus, they say that in Socrates there is human nature which is contracted to Socrates by an individual difference which is not really, but only formally, distinct from that nature. Thus, while there are not two things, one is not formally the other.
>
> I do not find this view tenable. (82)

Ockham questions the Platonic theory of universals as Forms understood as existences outside the mind that are "formally" independent of the existence of particulars. By the formally independent existence of a universal from the existence of particulars, Ockham relies on a popular Scholastic idea about real existence outside the mind. He considers the possibility that a universal might exist outside the mind in such a way as to be formally distinct from the particulars of which it is predicated. If the term "red" does not describe a secondary substance inhering in substances outside the mind, it might nevertheless describe a universal existing outside the mind whose existence is also at least formally independent of the existence of whatever things they qualify. The description is sufficiently general, despite their many differences, to apply to both Plato's and Scotus's metaphysics.

Ockham's first characterization of this non-Aristotelian theory of universals fits Plato's theory of Forms. He proceeds thereafter to include Scotus's modified Platonic quasi-Aristotelian theory, according to which universals inhere in but are formally distinct from particulars as real independently existing entities. The theory represents a kind of synthesis of Plato's and Aristotle's theories of universals, although in context Ockham seems interested only in its Platonic aspect. By dividing up the field of choices for a metaphysics of universals outside the mind into those that posit universals as either inhering within (Aristotle) or existing at least formally independently outside the particulars to which they are predicated (Plato, Scotus), Ockham tries to cover all logical possibilities. When he has defeated both types of classical theories, he thinks he will be in a strong position to recommend a third theory of universals as concepts of mind. A series of logical alternatives, categories, and dilemmas again describes Ockham's strategy of dividing a subject matter into opposed possibilities and rejecting each in turn as he eliminates certain theories and leaves others standing.

Plato's Forms as abstract things are supposed to exist independently of any of the particulars that imitate or participate in them. Ockham reports that he does not find the view tenable, and we have come to expect that he will reject the theory only on the basis of what he takes to be good arguments. He begins:

> First, in creatures there can never be any distinction outside the mind unless there
> are distinct things; if, therefore, there is any distinction between the nature and
> the difference, it is necessary that they really be distinct things. I prove my prem-
> ise by the following syllogism: the nature is not formally distinct from itself; this
> individual difference is formally distinct from this nature; therefore, this individ-
> ual difference is not this nature. (82)

He argues that distinctions outside of thought presuppose a mind-independent
distinction among things. It follows that the nature of a substance and the universals
or "differences" that are accidentally predicated of it must be distinct things in reality and not just in the mind. He offers a simple inference in the form of an Aristotelian three-proposition inference or *syllogism*, consisting of these assumptions and
conclusion:

Ockham's Proof That Individual Difference Is Distinct from Essence
1. The nature (essence) of a thing is not formally distinct from itself (nothing can
   be formally distinct from itself).
2. An individual difference (accidental universal property) is formally distinct
   from the thing's nature (essence).

---

3. An individual difference (accidental universal property) is distinct from a
   thing's nature (essence).

With this obvious conclusion Ockham emphasizes that some universals outside
of the mind, if they are formally distinct from the particulars they qualify, must be
different from and exist independently of the particulars. This is clearly true in the
case of universals as Platonic Forms and of any compromise theory that regards universals as existing in but as formally distinct from the particulars to which they belong. The only way they can be formally distinct from the particulars in which they
inhere in things entirely outside the mind is if universals and particulars are different independently existing things.

A second argument is offered to show that no universal is identical with any individual difference. Ockham distinguishes between an entity being "common," or
shared as one between many different particulars, and "proper," in the sense of existing as a thing's specific differences or qualifications. The argument is this:

> Again, the same entity is not both common and proper, but in their view the in-
> dividual difference is proper and the universal is common; therefore, no univer-
> sal is identical with an individual difference. (82)

The distinction in mode of existence between universals and individual differences,
distributively among many things or uniquely in each particular, implies that universals cannot be individual differences, and that they cannot exist or inhere in while yet
remaining formally distinct from particulars. The only choice logic allows according
to Ockham is for a universal's existence outside the mind to be formally dependent
on or independent of the existence of whatever particulars it is truly predicated. Again
he splits cases into contraries and deals with each in dilemma form. If the existence of
universals is formally dependent on the existence of particulars, then we are back to
the Aristotelian inherence theory that Ockham has already refuted. If the existence of

universals is formally independent of the existence of particulars, then universals are not part of and hence cannot inhere in the particulars they qualify.

Nor can a universal be formally distinct from the particulars to which it belongs. Nothing that exists formally in reality outside the mind can have contrary or opposite qualities or belong to contrary or opposite categories at one and the same time. Ockham argues that if an individual difference and a common nature were the same thing, then a universal would impossibly need to be both common and proper. What he means is that a universal is a common nature exemplified by many different things that consequently cannot also be proper in the sense of belonging exclusively as an individual difference to any particular in or as one of its constituent parts. He follows the assumption to its absurd implication:

> Again, opposites cannot be attributed to one and the same created thing, but *common* and *proper* are opposites; therefore, the same thing is not both common and proper. Nevertheless, that conclusion would follow if an individual difference and a common nature were the same thing. (82–83)

Another intolerable consequence concerns the numerical identity requirements of universals understood as formally distinct from the particulars to which they are supposed to belong. Ockham adds:

> Again, if a common nature were the same thing as an individual difference, there would be as many common natures as there are individual differences; and, consequently, none of those natures would be common, but each would be peculiar to the difference with which it is identical. (83)

He objects that if a universal as the common nature of many different things were also an individual difference, then there would impossibly need to be as many universals as there are individual differences. If every particular has its own uniquely possessed universals, however, then the universals are not really universal, for in that case they are not common natures shared by different things.

Finally, Ockham maintains that universals cannot explain the differences in particulars if they are formally distinct from the particulars that they qualify. Differences among particular things depend on differences that are intrinsic to themselves. An intrinsic property is a property that a thing would have even if so to speak nothing else were to exist. The red color of a rose is an example of a property that is intrinsic to it, by virtue of which it is distinguished from white and yellow and other roses. If we take all of an object's intrinsic properties into consideration, then, according to Ockham, we have the only possible basis for the object's distinction from every other particular. An extrinsic property in contrast is a property that a thing has only in relation to other things outside itself. A rose in a vase has the extrinsic property of being related to the vase by being contained in it, protruding from its lip, and the like. An object's extrinsic properties do not enter into its identity conditions or its distinction from other things. The rose is the particular rose it is and is different from all other things exclusively because of the intrinsic properties it has in and of itself.

If we consider the intrinsic properties of a particular as sufficient to distinguish it from other things, then there is no need to invoke universals as belonging to while remaining formally distinct from them in order to explain their identity and difference. If there is no need to postulate formally extrinsic universals in order to explain their distinction from other things, then there is equally no theoretical justification for supposing that there could be universals existing outside the mind that belong to particular things from which they are nevertheless formally distinct. This is the final argument Ockham considers in this section:

> Again, whenever one thing is distinct from another it is distinguished from that thing either of and by itself or by something intrinsic to itself. Now, the humanity of Socrates is something different from the humanity of Plato; therefore, they are distinguished of and by themselves and not by differences that are added to them. (83)

Socrates and Plato share the universal common nature of being human, but more specifically, the humanity of Socrates is distinct from the humanity of Plato. When Ockham asks what makes this so, he concludes that these differences are based entirely on the intrinsic qualities of Plato's humanity and Socrates' humanity. Those intrinsic differences are enough to understand the distinction between their respective instantiations of the common property of being human, rather than by any formally extrinsic differences that might unnecessarily be added to their self-sufficiently individuating intrinsic qualities. There is no philosophical rationale for supposing that in addition to intrinsic qualities that belong to a thing there are also formally extrinsic universal differences. Thus, universals should not be interpreted as existing outside the mind in particular things from which they are formally distinct as extrinsic to the particulars they qualify.

CONCEPTUALISM AND THE METAPHYSICS OF UNIVERSALS

After refuting the Aristotelian theory of universals as inherent secondary substances, Ockham indicates how he proposes to resolve the problem. If the leading account is false and no other received doctrines offer a better explanation of universals as existing outside the mind, then the only possibility is to try to explain universals as existing within the mind. This is Ockham's conclusion. He maintains that a universal is a concept existing only in the mind, which he refers to as an *intention of the soul.* He sketches the only alternative that remains after his devastating criticism of several forms of Platonic and Aristotelian metaphysics of universals. He offers a conceptualist theory of universals as having nothing more than a mental existence within the mind. As we have come to expect, he first states his position and then proceeds to support it by a string of arguments:

> From these remarks it is clear that the universal is an intention of the soul capable of being predicated of many. The claim can be corroborated by argument. For every one agrees that a universal is something predicable of many, but only an intention of the soul or a conventional sign is predicated. (81)

Universals exist only in the mind as intentions of the soul. There are other intentions of the soul, including passions and ideas that make reference to particulars outside the mind. What is special about universals as intentions of the soul is that they are capable of being predicated of many things. Ockham claims that only intentions of the soul are capable of being predicated of different things in the manner of universals, which he takes as an indication that universals must be intentions of the soul. He further mentions conventional signs in ordinary language as predicable of many things, thinking of the linguistic order in which language is used to predicate properties of things.

We are reminded that Ockham's primary focus is on the meaning of terms that constitute the propositions in arguments as a special topic in the metaphysics of logic and the philosophy of language. A sign in language and an intention in the thoughts of the soul are the only things that can be predicated of many things, but a conventional sign in ordinary language is predicated of many things presumably by virtue of expressing an intention of the soul. Universals are most appropriately understood conceptualistically as intentions of the soul, and universal terms in logic and language are most appropriately understood as designating universals as concepts of mind or intentions of the soul. They are nothing real in and of themselves existing outside the mind, and are not formally distinct from or extrinsic to the mind, but are rather the ways in which the mind organizes its thoughts according to categories for purposes of logical reasoning.

What remains to be explained is why Ockham believes that only an intention of the soul or linguistic sign can be predicated of many things, as is said of universals. Why is he so convinced that nothing other than an intention of the soul can in the first instance be predicated of different things in thought and expressed by the predication of a universal term to things referred to in language? He is confident in the conclusion because he is satisfied that he has just refuted every other possibility. He seems to divide existent things into two categories, substances existing outside the mind and the mind and whatever it intends, the contents and categories of thought. He thinks that, given this metaphysical division in his previous attack on substances as universals, there is no other option than to admit that only intentions of the soul can be predicated of many things. If nothing outside the mind can be universally predicated of different things, then only intentions of the soul within the mind are universal. He says:

> No substance is ever predicated of anything. Therefore, only an intention of the soul or a conventional sign is a universal; but I am not here using the term "universal" for conventional signs, but only for signs that are universals by nature. That substance is not capable of functioning as predicate is clear; for if it were, it would follow that a proposition would be composed of particular substances; and, consequently, the subject would be in Rome and the predicate in England which is absurd. (81–82)

In a reprise of his refutation of Aristotle's theory of universals as secondary substances inhering in particulars, Ockham argues that substances cannot be predicated of different things. The reasoning is obscure at first, but makes sense when we understand how literally Ockham thinks of the requirements of a substance as a predicate in thought or language. If substances are predicates, then a proposition that consists of a subject and predicate would be composed of individual substances. In that case, Ockham dramatically asserts, a true proposition about a subject in Rome having a property predicated of it in England would simultaneously exist as subject and predicate respectively in Rome and England. If substances themselves of any kind or in any category cannot be predicated of many things, and if there are only substances existing outside the mind and the mind and its contents or intentions of the soul, then the predication of universals to different things can only be understood as involving mind-dependent intentions of the soul. He splits the possibilities logically into two, and argues by dilemma that since one choice is impossible the other must be true.

Ockham distinguishes between *conventional* and *natural signs.* The expression of intentions of the soul in language occurs in a conventional linguistic sign system. Although he does not elaborate on the concept of a natural sign, he seems to have in mind something that does not represent something for purposes of communicating between persons in a social context, in the sense of ordinary convention-governed languages such as English, Latin, and German, among others. A natural sign is rather something that signifies on its own without the intervention of conventional decision making that occurs in the case of natural languages. It is presumably a sign by which thought represents things to itself for the purposes of comprehending experience, memory, and reasoning. There are also universal terms in conventional language, but here Ockham deliberately limits discussion to natural mental signs that are first predicated universally of a number of things in thought and then expressed within the conventions of a social language. In due course, Ockham adds a nominalistic theory of universal terms in logic and language to complement the conceptualistic theory of universals as intentions of the soul.

He turns next appropriately to the metaphysics of propositions. Propositions contain universal as well as particular terms among the other parts of speech analyzed by logic. The existence of propositions is confined to thought, verbal, and written language. He observes that no particular substances can exist in the mind, relying on a view of the soul as a nonphysical spiritual entity that even Socrates and Plato and Christian and other religious traditions would recognize as the metaphysical peculiarity of consciousness. If no proposition is composed of particular substances but of universals, then universals cannot possibly be substances. The only alternative is for universals to exist only within the mind as intentions of the soul:

> Furthermore, propositions occur only in the mind, in speech, or in writing; therefore, their parts can exist only in the mind, in speech, and in writing. Particular substances, however, cannot themselves exist in the mind, in speech, or in writing. Thus, no proposition can be composed of particular substances. Propositions are, however, composed of universals; therefore, universals cannot conceivably be substances. (82)

If Ockham's reasoning is correct, then universals cannot possibly exist outside the mind. Universal predicate terms in language and logic in that case are only names for universals as intentions of the soul. Conceptualism and nominalism in Ockham's metaphysics of universals and logic and theory of the meaning of universal terms provide a distinctly non-Platonic, non-Aristotelian, and non-Scotian theory of universals. Universals for Ockham are neither inherent Aristotelian secondary substances, for they are no kind of substances at all, nor are they abstract timeless Forms in a Platonic realm of Being that exist outside the mind, nor, as Scotus holds, constituents in while remaining formally distinct from existent particulars. They are instead concepts in the mind, something mental rather than anything substantial. They are intentions of the soul expressible in the mind's natural signs or in the signs of a conventional public language. If natural signs naturally designate things of which the mind is acquainted in experience, then the mind's categories which it predicates to many different things are the only universals we need or could possibly justify. The logic of universal terms involves the convenient use of names to refer to the universal intentions of soul that are predicable of different things. Logic for Ockham begins and ends with the contents, calculations, and judgments of mind.

Five Types of Universals

The theory of universals as intentions of the soul provides a foundation for Ockham's further characterization of universals and their linguistic expression in logic and language. He divides the general category of universals into five specific types. The five types of universals are conspicuously Aristotelian, including genus, species, difference, property, and accident. Ockham proceeds as he usually does through a series of logical choices distinguished by contrary subcategories:

> §18: On the Five Universals in General
>
> Now that we have shown what a universal is we ought to determine how many species of universals there are. There are five species, and this can be shown in the following way. Every universal is predicated of many either *in quid* or not *in quid.* If it is predicated *in quid,* then it can be used as an answer to the question "What is it?" (88)

Ockham arrives at an Aristotelian list of general types of universals, but does not appeal to Aristotle's authority in support of his categories. Rather, he reasons them out from a more fundamental consideration of logical distinctions. The first distinction he invokes is that between predications made *in quid,* which is to say as belonging to or in the thing, and predications that are not made *in quid.* A true predication *in quid* tells us what a thing is, because the predication predicates a universal that is constitutive of the thing. A further subdivision is then immediately identified as distinguishing another two general categories of universals:

> There are two possible cases here. In the first case the many things of which the universal is predicated are all alike so that they agree essentially, although it can happen that one of them is composed of several such similar things: here we have a lowest level species. In the second case not all the things of which the universal is predicated agree in the aforesaid way, but among them there are things which are dissimilar both as wholes and in their parts. *Animal* is an example. *Animal* is predicated of both *man* and *donkey,* but the similarity in substance between two men is greater than that obtaining between a man and a donkey. (88)

The first possibility is that a predication of a universal *in quid* is made to many different things that are all essentially alike. Ockham holds that this can only happen in the case of universals at the lowest level of species. Thus, another Aristotelian category emerges through an analysis of the logic of possible predications.

The second possibility is one in which a predication *in quid* is made to many different things, some but not all of which are essentially alike. This distinction of possibilities logically justifies introducing the Aristotelian category of genus. Ockham gives an example from zoology and another concerning colors. The species *man* is different from the species *donkey*, although both men and donkeys are animals. The predication of a universal *in quid* exclusively to things that are essentially alike, such to all men or all donkeys, involves a species type of universal. The predication of a universal *in quid* to things that are not essentially alike, such as men and donkeys, cannot be a species universal, since men and donkeys are not members of the same species, but of the same higher order universal, the genus *animal*. The same logical structure obtains with respect to black particulars as members of the species *black*, of white particulars as members of the species *white*, and of black and white particulars considered together not as members of any single species of colors but of the higher-order universal genus *color*.

> The same is true in the case of *color*. This term is predicable of both whiteness and blackness, but neither this blackness nor one of its parts agrees with another. For this reason the intention predicable of whiteness and blackness is not a lowest level species but a genus. But *whiteness* is a lowest level species with respect to all whitenesses. Admittedly, it sometimes happens that one whiteness agrees more with a second whiteness than with a third. Thus, equally intense whitenesses seem to agree more than two whitenesses of different intensities. Nevertheless, given two such whitenesses, one always agrees with some part of the other as much as any two whitenesses agree with each other. For this reason, *whiteness* is a lowest level species and not a genus with respect to whitenesses. (88–89)

Thus, Ockham offers a logical reconstruction of two of Aristotle's most important categories of universals, genus and species. We have yet to consider how difference, property, and accident are identified by a similar process of logical decomposition on the opposite side of Ockham's original distinction, concerning predications that are not made *in quid*. Species and genus evidently pick out universals that are essential to a thing, which is the real import of the concept of predication *in quid*. Predications not made *in quid* establish differences among the parts of things without attributing extrinsic qualities. An example is the predication of the universal *rational* to a human being, which only refers to a part of a human being, on the Aristotelian conception of a human being as a rational animal. Such differences can either be logically necessary or logically contingent. Logically necessary differences belong to the Aristotelian category of property as a fourth type of universals, while logically contingent differences belong to the fifth and final Aristotelian universals category of accident.

The Aristotelian list of five general types of universals is complete and shown to derive from the purely logical division and subdivision of predications as intentions of the soul. Ockham concludes:

> But if a universal is not predicated *in quid*, it can express one part of a thing and not another while expressing nothing extrinsic to the thing. In this case we have a difference. If *rational*, for example, is the difference of man, it expresses a part of man, such as the form, but not, for example, the matter. On the other hand, a universal can express something which is not a part of the thing. In that case it is predicable either necessarily or contingently. If contingently we call it an accident, if necessarily we call it a property. (89)

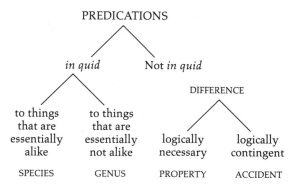

FIGURE 3.2 Ockham's logical derivation of five types of universals

The logical derivation of the five general types of universals is represented by the Ockhamesque tree diagram of logical divisions shown in Figure 3.2.

By distinguishing logically between five Aristotelian categories as general types of universals, Ockham takes the first steps toward a more detailed logical specification of the metaphysics of universals and the meaning of predicate terms.

We might nevertheless wonder how Ockham arrives at this choice of principles for logical division, between *in quid* and not *in quid*, logically necessary and logically contingent. We might also wonder why he chooses to apply them precisely as and where he does in working out his taxonomy of the five types of universals. Why does he not begin with the distinction between logically necessary and logically contingent predications, or with some entirely different set of distinctions that could equally well be raised with respect to the predication of universals from a purely logical point of view? If we started dividing universals up in another way according to a different choice of logical distinctions, we might arrive at a very different list of general universal types. Ockham nevertheless seems satisfied to have touched base with Aristotle's categories of universals, having rejected so thoroughly his metaphysics.

OCKHAM'S METAPHYSICS OF INDIVIDUALS

As a preliminary to more detailed consideration of the five types of universals, Ockham first suggests the need to look more carefully into the metaphysics of individuals as the subjects of universal predications. He marks a single concept by means of a variety of synonyms, which he says are *convertible;* by this term of medieval logic he means that they are interchangeable where they occur in most language as equivalent in meaning:

§19: On the Individual

Next we shall examine each of the five universals in some detail, but first we shall examine the notion of an individual, the notion of that which is contained under every universal. It should be noted that among logicians the following names are convertible: "particular," "individual," "suppositum," but among theologians "individual" and "suppositum" are not convertible. The reason is that while only a substance can be a suppositum, an accident can be an individual. In this chapter, however, we shall use the expressions in the way that logicians do. (90)

Ockham remarks on an interesting sidelight about divergent uses of some of the terminology for individuals between logicians and theologians. He does not explain why such disagreement occurs, and for our purposes it does not much matter. What is important is that he does not try to distinguish between the meanings of the words *particular, individual,* and *suppositum,* by all of which, still operating in a general Aristotelian Scholastic metaphysical framework, he parts company with the theologians when he tells us in advance that he does not intend only a substance. He distinguishes a number of logician's meanings of the technical term *particular:*

> In logic the term "particular" has three senses. In the first sense that is said to be a particular which is numerically one and not many. In this sense every universal is a particular. In another sense a particular is a thing outside the mind that is one and not many and not a sign of anything. In this sense every substance is a particular. In the third sense a particular is a sign proper to just one thing; it is also called a discrete term. Thus, Porphyry says that a particular is that which is predicated of one thing. But this definition does not make any sense if it is construed as a definition of something existing outside the mind, e.g., Socrates or Plato or something of that nature. Such things are not predicated either of one or of many. (90–91)

Three different senses of the word *particular* are explained. Something is particular if it is: (1) numerically one rather than many; (2) outside the mind and not a sign of any other thing; (3) a singular designating term. To be numerically one rather than many according to meaning (1) is not limited to substances, but includes also universals, each of which is always one thing rather than a plurality of different things. It is only in sense (2) that a particular is a substance, according to which a particular is supposed to exist outside the mind but is not a sign for anything else. Sense (3) appears to be a specialized meaning of the word limited to uses within the study of logic as a sign for something nonplural existing only in the mind, implying that only such things other than substances can be predicated of others.

Sense (1) is unexciting, in that every philosopher Ockham considers will agree that a particular is in some sense numerically one rather than many. This turns out to be a dull but still important requirement of particularity, although it is one that is so easily satisfied that it is not worth talking much about. A sign of this limited interest is that in Ockham's own terms we could give good reasons to interpret "numerically one rather than many" and "particular" (and "supposita") as convertible. We learn two important features of a substance in sense (2), that it exists outside the mind and that it is not a sign for anything else. The definition makes us wonder about the metaphysical status of public signs, including road signs as well as any actual linguistic expression. Is a piece of wood with an arrow and a word on it not a substance, since although it exists outside the mind it is a sign for a city? An adherent of sense (2) might draw a distinction between the substance and the signhood of the piece of wood. The signhood is not something external to the mind, but is an intention of the soul. The piece of wood used to express a certain intention of the soul is of course a substance.

Considering particulars in sense (3), Ockham maintains that these too can be divided into three further subcategories. There are three grammatical kinds of words that can all be used as signs to refer to or to be predicated of just one particular thing:

> The definition must be understood as an account of a certain kind of sign, a sign which is proper to one thing and predicated of one thing. Put in another way, "particular" is not predicated of anything which can supposit for several things in one and the same proposition.
>
> But even taking the term "particular" in this sense, it can be used in three ways. First, proper names like "Socrates" and "Plato" are particulars. Second, demonstrative pronouns are particulars. Thus, "this" when used to refer to Socrates in "This is a man" is a particular. Finally, the demonstrative pronoun, taken with some common term (e.g., "this man" and "this animal") is a particular. And just as one can distinguish senses of "particular" one can distinguish senses of the expressions "singular" and "suppositum." (91)

The three types of particulars in the sense of individually designated terms include proper names for particular substances such as "Plato" and "Socrates," indexicals or demonstrative pronouns referring to specific individuals, such as "This is a man" or "This is a red rose," and finally indexical or demonstrative pronouns combined with a universal term, as in "This man," "This rose," or "This red rose." All of these kinds of terms are particular in sense (3) in that they all represent different ways of achieving particular reference to things and are themselves in that regard also particular in the relevant sense.

Ockham collects these conclusions into a unified analysis of the concept of a particular, individual, or suppositum to which universals as intentions of the soul can be predicated. An important part of his distinction between individuals and universals in opposition to theologian's usage, is the possibility that individuals to which properties are predicated need not exist outside the mind. The contents of mind are themselves individuals that can have properties in the sense of having universals as intentions of the soul within the mind attributed to other individual items of thought. Ockham lays the groundwork for his most fundamental metaphysical distinction between individuals as either substances or intentions of the soul:

> In way of summary it should be said that a property as we have been using the term (where a property is a universal distinct from other universals) is an intention predicable of some species in quale and convertible with it. It connotes affirmatively or negatively something extrinsic to the thing which is designated by the subject. It is not, however, necessary that the extrinsic thing be some entity outside the mind and actually existing in the nature of things. It can be something which is by nature predicable, or it can be a proposition existing or capable of existing in the mind. The same point holds with regards to passions (i.e., universals predicated of a subject in the second mode of perseity); they are not things inhering in an entity outside the mind. In that case a passion could not be predicable of something, nor could it be the predicate of a conclusion in a demonstration; and both of these points hold true of passions. A passion, we must grant, is an intention of the soul. (102)

By a passion Ockham means anything the mind suffers rather than does. The distinction between active and passive phenomena is borrowed from Aristotle. Active intentions of the soul include mental acts such as decisions and resolutions; passive intentions include emotions in the sense we ordinarily think of as including feelings of love and hate and fear and joy, but also such occurrences as pains and perhaps beliefs and desires, if these are experiences that we do not actively bring about but passively suffer or live through when they occur to thought. Ockham says that intentions of the soul are also individuals and as such can be the subjects of predications, of properties and accidents and the other five types of universals. They can be qualified in different ways as occurring at a certain time, being associated with certain things or other events, of one sort or another, a pain or a decision, emotion or belief or desire, having any of a variety of different qualities. It follows that universals in Ockham's metaphysics are intentions of the soul that can be predicated of individual substances outside the mind existing in nature or of individual intentions of the soul existing within the mind.

Ockham's logic describes universals as natural signs of the many individuals to which the universal is predicated within or outside the mind. He remarks that a universal as a natural sign signifies all the things to which the universal applies. A universal as a natural sign or a universal term in logic or language as a conventional sign can therefore "supposit" for this collection of things, by which he means it can serve as a substitute in thought or language or alternative way of referring to them. Instead of referring specifically to all of the individual red things, the mind can use the universal *red* as a suppositum that naturally signifies them. The analysis of the meaning of a predicate in conventional language involving the conventional sign "red" is then that the sign makes it possible conventionally to signify all red things for purposes of thought and the expression of thought. When a universal as an intention of the soul is predicated of another intention, such as a passion or another universal, it does not predicate itself of the second intention, but to whatever things possess the universal it naturally signifies:

> In summarizing some points made about universals it should be noted that every universal is an intention of the soul which signifies many things and which can supposit for the many things it signifies. One intention is predicated of an intention distinct from it, not for itself, but for the things it signifies. Therefore, those propositions, in which one intention is predicated of another, do not assert that one intention is another, but rather that what is designated by one intention is what is designated by another. Universals of this sort are not things outside the mind. They do not belong to the essence of things outside the mind, nor are they parts of those things. They are entities in the soul different from each other and from things outside the mind. (104)

The theory permits naturally signifying intentions to refer to and be predicated of one another and even of themselves in complex ways. Ockham clarifies the ways in which universals as intentions of soul can be predicated of one another. When an intention is truly predicated of another intention, the two are not identified; rather, what is signified by one intention is in fact the same as what is designated by the other. An example is one in which a universal such as *joy* is predicated of the passion joy, as when we say that joy is *joy*. We do not say that joy and *joy* are the same thing, but that all particular things signified by the universal suppositum *joy* as an intention of soul are also things that are signified by the conventional linguistic suppositum "joy."

This tells us how Ockham thinks of the relation between natural and conventional signs. Neither intention, as Ockham observes, is the essence of anything outside the mind, but both are mental occurrences. Some universals as intentions of the soul serve as supposita for things that also exist within the mind, and others for substances as things outside the mind. Some universals can even be signs of themselves, such as the universal *universal*. There are signs of things including other signs, but he insists that no universal is a sign of itself. The universal *universal* is conventionally signified by the term "universal" which is a sign of all universals other than itself. Ockham does not explain why a sign cannot be a sign of itself, but he seems to assume as obvious to everyone that there must generally be a distinction between a sign and what it signifies, or that a sign is always a sign of something other than itself. He adds:

> Some are signs of things outside and others are signs of those very signs. Thus, the name "universal" is common to all universals; and, consequently, it is a sign of all the universals other than itself. It ought to be granted then that the universal which is predicable of the five universals, standing not for itself but for other universals, is the genus of universals in just the way an expression predicable of all expressions is a name and not a verb, particle, conjunction, or any other part of speech. (104)

Ockham concludes by observing that the universal *universal* as a natural sign is, and the term "universal" as a conventional sign designates, the genus of all five species of universals, genus, species, difference, property, and accident. An individual or particular is a relative concept for Ockham, depending on which of the three senses of the terms is intended. He stipulates that an individual can include a universal as a particular type of universal subsumed by the highest order genus of all universals other than itself. Universals are intentions of the soul and natural signs of the things they qualify. The universal *universal* as the highest genus (itself a universal) of universal subsumes the five individual subcategories of universals, each of which in turn subsumes all the individual or particular universals, which in turn qualify all other individual things, within or outside the mind, including particular substances existing in nature outside the mind and mind-dependent intentions of the soul.

What emerges from Ockham's logic and metaphysics of universals is a vast hierarchy in which particulars and universals are structurally ordered according to a rational system of logical division and subdivision. The rational order in the world of things for Ockham is the mind's rational order, the order it partly finds in and partly imposes on experience. There are no Platonic universal Forms or Aristotelian inherent secondary substances; nor are there constitutive but formally independent universals in particulars as Duns Scotus believes. There are only substances existing outside the mind in nature and the intentions of the soul that naturally signify many particulars that the mind groups together and refers to by means of universal supposita. We can refer to the same things in a public language by means of conventional signs, the meaning of which is explained by their reference to the natural signs they express and the individuals to which a universal linguistic term is predicated. The outside world is real, but the universals by which particular substances in the world are categorized exist only in the mind as intentions of the soul, designated in true linguistic predications.

MODIFIED ARISTOTELIAN INHERENCE

Ockham next develops a revisionary theory of the Aristotelian inherence of universals in particulars. He has explained the metaphysics of universals after criticizing and rejecting the theories of Plato, Aristotle, and Duns Scotus, he has divided the genus of all universals into five species or Aristotelian categories, and he has explained the nature of individuals. He is now prepared to explain how universals and particulars are related. The theory of universals requires an account of the nature of true predication and the sense in which universals qualify the features of individuals. He now pursues the analysis of universals in this direction:

§32: On Inherence and Being In

We say that predicates are predicated of their subjects; but we also say that predicates are in, belong to, and inhere in their subjects. Such locutions should not be understood to imply that predicates really inhere in their subjects in the way that whiteness inheres in the wall. On the contrary these locutions are synonymous with "predicated of." They should not be taken in any other way. (112)

Although Ockham is willing to adopt the Aristotelian terminology of inherence in understanding the relation between universals and particulars, he makes it clear from the outset that this is only a manner of speaking and is not to be taken literally. We could hardly expect otherwise, given that he has devoted so much energy to refuting the Aristotelian inherence theory of universals. There is nothing wrong or even potentially misleading about speaking of universals as inhering in their subjects as long as we interpret and apply these expressions in the right way.

When we allow ourselves to say that a universal inheres in a particular, what we mean, according to Ockham, is only that the universal is predicated of it. What this means in turn is to be understood in psychological conceptualistic terms. It is a matter of thought attributing a universal to a thing. We may find it puzzling to see that Ockham appears to regard the whiteness of a wall as something that can legitimately be said to inhere in it. For it seems that the whiteness of a wall is merely a special case of inherence as Aristotle would have understood their relation. What could be special about the inherence of the color whiteness in a wall as opposed to the predication of any other universal to any other particular?

Perhaps the best way to make sense of Ockham's exception is that he is thinking here of what an adherent of the inherence theory of universals would say about the universal whiteness inhering in a particular wall. We are not to think of it as that kind of relation even in the case of a wall's whiteness, although whiteness is a perceivable property of perceivable things like the wall, Ockham holds that there is no whiteness as an Aristotelian secondary substance that literally exists or has its being in white things. The temptation to suppose that the whiteness really inheres in the white wall is precisely the view that Ockham wants us to resist. It is true that the wall is white, which is what makes the predication true. The whiteness of the wall is nevertheless not to be understood as a matter of the universal *whiteness* literally belonging to the wall, since the universal is only an intention of the soul that exists nowhere but in the mind. The wall as a particular thing has its own particular color, among other properties, its own particular whiteness. The universal *whiteness* is not the whiteness of the wall, but an intention of the soul that intends and considers as one all particular white things. The wall is white and has its own whiteness, but its whiteness is not the universal.

More generally, Ockham states:

> Thus, all the accidents . . . can be said to be in substance as in a subject, but not because they really inhere in substance; the notion is, rather, that of inherence by way of true predication. Some who say that quantity is an accident which is in substance want to deny that quantity actually inheres in substance; they mean on the contrary that it is contingently predicated of substance so that it is possible for substances to exist when the proposition "Substance is a quantity," is false. (112)

To claim that an accidental quality is *in* a substance is not to say that it actually *inheres* in it. Inherence is an indirect way of referring to the predication of a universal such as an accident to a substance. When the mind's predication of a universal to a substance is true, then if we like we can say that the universal inheres in it. Ockham distinguishes his position from that of thinkers unidentified by name who consider quantity as an accident that is in but does not actually inhere in substances. He thinks that they make the right qualification, on the grounds that quantity does not always inhere in all substances under all circumstances, but they do so for the wrong reason and in the wrong application.

He generalizes the explanation of the wall's whiteness. He argues that what they should say instead is merely that quantity is contingently predicated of substance. It is true in some but not all circumstances that substance is or has a quantity, especially if we consider other categories of Aristotelian substances. The contingent possession of a universal, whether an essential property or contingent accident, is in any case interpreted as a matter of predication. It is the mind's attribution of a universal to a particular that is true or false depending on the state of the world within or outside the mind. Ockham deals with inherentist language as partly revealing and partly misleading if taken literally as implying an Aristotelian theory of secondary substances that inhere in other substances. All such expressions harmlessly refer to the predication of universals as intentions of the soul to other intentions or to substances in the world outside the mind. Where Aristotle and the Scholastics try to understand the metaphysics of universals exclusively in terms of different kinds and categories of substances, Ockham enlarges the terms of his explanation of universals by including intentions of the soul in addition to substances in the extramental outside world. Aristotle, from Ockham's perspective, does not pay enough attention to the mind and the possibilities it affords of explaining the metaphysics of universals conceptualistically.

Ockham reviews the kinds of linguistic expressions that can also be used to refer to the mind's predication of universals to particulars. By showing that such terms can be reduced in meaning to predication, he disarms a potential source of objections that would otherwise threaten to reinstate an Aristotelian doctrine of universals as inherent secondary substances. They are all treated instead merely as different ways of talking about the acts of thought whereby the mind predicates essences and accidents of individuals. It is important for his purposes nevertheless to show that these ways of speaking do not imply the real being or inherence of universals in particulars. He now maintains:

Similarly, other expressions like "come to," "leave," "present in," and "absent from" are frequently used in place of "predicated of." The venerable Anselm in his *Monologion* says, "While some of those things (e.g., colors) that are said to be accidents can come to or leave the thing participating in them only with some change in that thing, others (e.g., certain relations) can be present in or absent from that of which they are predicated without any change in that thing." Anselm is using the terms "come to," "leave," "present in," and "absent from" in place of "predicated of"; likewise, logicians frequently use "participate in" for "to be a subject of." (112–13)

Anselm gives a concise exposition of the basic principles of Aristotle's metaphysics of change. He recites Aristotle's distinction between alterations in which things persist through changes, the "comings and goings" of their inherent accidental properties, and the total destruction of things that results from changes in their inherent essential properties. Referring here only to accidental changes, Anselm like most Scholastic metaphysicians unsurprisingly relies on a distinctively Aristotelian terminology of accidental universals coming to, departing from, being present in or absent from a substance. This makes it sound superficially as though accidents are literally injected into or extracted from a substance in which they either inhere or from which they are removed more or less like substantial self-contained physical parts.

Ockham allows the language but explains its meaning in terms of predication, thereby avoiding commitment to a theory of real inherence. He explains how Anselm's use of literal inherence-sounding language can be reinterpreted in terms of the predication of universals to individuals. To say that an accident comes to a substance, as when a wall is painted white, is not to say that *whiteness* has come to inhere within the wall, but only that the universal *whiteness* as an intention of the soul is truly predicated of the wall at the time when it is painted. Similarly when Anselm and other Aristotelians say that an accident leaves or is taken away from a substance, relying on the same spatial component metaphor to describe what Ockham believes to be merely a matter of the mind's true predication of universals to individuals. He also reinterprets what he characterizes as a logician's way of referring to the relation between a universal and a subject as the subject's "participation in" the universal in terms of "being a subject of," which he has already explained as a matter of the mind's predicating universals of substances. He does not name the logicians he has in mind, but it is noteworthy that the language of a subject "participating in" a universal is the way in which Plato describes the relation between sensible things in the world of appearance or Becoming and the abstract universal Platonic Forms in the unchanging eternal world of Being. It is possible as a result that Ockham means to refer in this place to logicians in a medieval Platonic tradition.

NOMINALISM AND UNIVERSAL TERMS

The conceptualist theory of universals as intentions of the soul and the relation between universals and particulars as the mind's predication of universals to individuals stands in need of a further explanation of the meaning of universal terms in language. We have already seen that Ockham distinguishes between natural and conventional linguistic signs and between the natural and conventional signifying of universals.

Natural signs are the mind's own devices for referring to things, primarily its own contents or intentions. Conventional signs are terms in social language developed for the sake of communication in speech and writing. Ockham seems to regard the mind's natural signs as taking precedence over conventional signs. Thought with its natural signs comes first, at the most primitive linguistic level in which universals as intentions of the soul are designated. Why does the mind need naturally to name its own intentions? Ockham does not say, but we can imagine that thought must be able to refer to other things for the purpose of memory and reasoning and other cognitive functions, including the predication of universals to particulars, which can also be expressed in the social conventions of a public language.

The mind translates from its native natural signs into the socially conventional signs of an ordinary language, such as English or Chinese or Arabic, when language is learned. When we predicate universals of particulars in ordinary language, we express the mind's predication of certain intentions of soul to certain substances or other intentions of soul. The mind accomplishes this feat by intending, meaning, referring to, and expressing judgments about states of affairs in which judgments of mind predicate universals of things that can be expressed in natural or conventional signs as the linguistic predication of a universal term as a natural or conventional sign for a psychological entity, a certain intention of the soul, to a particular term as a natural or conventional sign for something within or outside the soul. In effect, the particular terms of a natural or conventional language designate individual substances outside the mind or other individual states of mind, Ockham's intentions of the soul. The metaphysical distinction between substances and intentions of the soul is supported by a more fundamental logical distinction between things existing within or outside of the mind. Indeed, for Ockham, these should just be two different ways of drawing what amounts to the same distinction.

The transition from a conceptualist metaphysics of universals as intentions of the soul to a nominalist philosophy of language is the next important step in Ockham's logic of terms. He must consider the meaning of a proposition in which a universal is linguistically predicated of something. The question is how the meaning of universal and particular terms in a proposition are to be understood. Ockham interprets all terms as designating individual things, either within or outside the mind. There are particular and universal terms in propositions. Particular terms designate either individual substances or individual intentions of the soul as predication subjects; universal terms always designate intentions of the soul. When judgment affirms the truth of predicating a certain universal to a certain individual substance or intention of the soul, then the judgment and propositions expressing the judgment are true.

When a judgment (truly or falsely) combines a universal with a particular in thought, it predicates a particular intention of the soul to an individual thing. The same is true linguistically for the judgment itself as a predication in thought of universal to particular natural signs, and for its expression in the form of a proposition in which universal terms are conventionally linguistically predicated of particular terms in everyday language. Ockham shows that we do not need to suppose that universal terms ever refer to anything substantial; we can treat them instead as no more than convenient categories of mind. They are things of thought rather than mind-independent substances in the world of nature or beyond the world of Becoming in a Platonic world of Being equally outside the mind.

Ockham interprets the language of universal terms nominalistically, as nothing more than names of certain intentions of the soul. A name must name something, but it need not be something in the world of substance outside the mind. To say first that a universal term in one sense is merely a name means only that a universal is not something independent of thought. Second, universal names as natural signs exist within the mind, and as such they are identical with universals as intentions of the soul. Universal names in conventional languages designate the same intentions of the soul, and as such they refer to nothing outside the mind in Platonic heaven or inherent Aristotelian or Scotian earth. We need not suppose that there are any other kinds of things than those that exist within or outside the mind, and we need not and should not suppose that universals exist outside the mind. If universal names as natural signs are themselves universals within the mind, and if they do not designate anything outside the mind, then Ockham's theory of universal terms is nominalist in both senses.

Ockham begins a detailed consideration of the logic of signs. A term in the most general meaning of the word is a sign that signifies something. Signs signify by virtue of designating something, which they can do linguistically and contextually in a number of ways. Terms designate as propositions or parts of propositions. We can think of an entire proposition as a term, or more typically as the individual terms that make up a proposition, such as subject, predicate, copulae, and syncategorematical terms. These notably include universal predicate and particular subject terms in linguistic predications expressing judgments of mind. Ockham defines the terms of any logic or language as signs that can signify in several ways:

> In the broadest sense of all we say that a term signifies provided it is a sign which is capable of being a part of a proposition or a whole proposition and designates something, whether primarily or secondarily, whether in the nominative or one of the oblique cases, whether by actually expressing or merely connoting something, whether by signifying affirmatively or merely negatively. In this sense we say that the name "blind" signifies sight because it does so negatively, similarly, that "immaterial" signifies matter negatively and that both "nothing" and "nonbeing" signify being but in a negative way. Anselm discusses this mode of signifying in *On the Fall of the Devil.* (114)

He finds occasion here to refer to Anselm authoritatively rather than argumentatively as before. He illustrates the point that terms can signify negatively as well as positively by implying a complementary or contrary universal or particular. We can designate sight either positively by the word "sight," or negatively by the word "blind." We refer negatively to everything by implication in using the words "nothing," "nonbeing," and the like. If we are sensitive to the variety of ways in which terms signify, then we should not be shocked by Ockham's inference that every universal signifies. The reason for this assessment is that every universal as an intention of the soul is also a natural name:

> Therefore, in some sense of "signify" every universal can be said to signify. In chapter 8 of *Logic,* Damascene says, "The universal is what signifies many, for example, 'man' and 'animal.' " Every universal signifies many in the first or second way since every universal is predicated of many others in a *de inesse* present

tense proposition or in a past, present, or future proposition or in a modal proposition. Clearly then those are wrong who say that the word "man" does not signify all men. According to the aforementioned authority the universal term "man" signifies many things; but since it does not signify many things which are not men, it must signify many men. This point must be granted; for nothing is signified by "man" except men, and not one man more than another. (114)

Universals are themselves signs because they signify their instances. Ockham appeals to the authority of Damascene, the Catholic saint and philosopher St. John of Damascus (c. 675–749), for corroboration on the thesis that universals signify. The universal *red* naturally signifies all red things or at least as many of them as the mind imagines. The universal term "red" conventionally does the same. This is the primary sense in which Ockham's theory of universal terms is nominalist. It follows immediately that the theory is nominalist also in the technical secondary sense that it does not imply that universal terms refer to anything substantial outside the mind.

A *de inesse* present tense of a predication is abstract rather than committed to any existent states of affairs at any particular time or place expressed by a past, present, future tense, or modal proposition. A modal proposition, to mention just one of the most important types of a proposition's modality, qualifies the truth of a categorical proposition as necessarily, contingently, or possibly true. We say, categorically, "It is raining," but also, modally, "It is possible that it will rain." Ockham's theory recognizes many categories of ways in which universals can signify, but the fact that universals are themselves signs makes Ockham's conceptualism, his theory of universals as intentions of the soul, a distinctively nominalist metaphysics of universals. Universals for Ockham are natural names for the things they signify, the individuals to which they are truly predicated. The important conclusion is that universals are names because they signify the things to which they apply:

Therefore every universal signifies many things. Genera and species, since they can be predicated of a pronoun referring to some object, do not signify many except in [a specialized sense]. But of the remaining universals many signify in [that] sense only; whereas others signify in [other] senses as well. Thus every universal that is not a genus or species, while signifying many things in the nominative case, also signifies something else in one of the oblique cases. This is clear with "rational," "risible," and "white," and similarly of course with other universals. (114)

The fact that universals signify in any of the senses Ockham distinguishes is enough to qualify universals as names. Universal terms as signs in an ordinary language conventionally signify universals, and universals as intentions of the soul naturally signify all the individual things to which they are capable of being truly predicated in judgments of mind. Thus, universal terms conventionally also indirectly signify all the particular things designated by particular terms to which they are capable of being truly linguistically predicated.

Ockham builds on the conclusion of his previous argument that universal terms do not signify a common nature constitutive of particulars in the Aristotelian sense of inhering in primary substances. They signify instead the individuals they qualify, the particulars to which universal terms are truly predicated. He appeals again to John of Damascus as his authority on matters of logic and the meaning and metaphysics of language:

> The name "man" does not signify primarily one nature common to all men, as many mistakenly think; it signifies on the contrary all particular men primarily as we earlier showed by an appeal to Damascene. (136)

Here in the most general terms, Ockham declares on the strength of previous arguments that universal terms do not signify universal properties instantiated as the common nature of all particular things of a relevant kind, but to the particular things themselves. The universal *red* and the universal term "red" signify all red things, naturally or conventionally. There is no abstract or inherent universal property or common nature instantiated by all and only those things, because a universal is not a Form or substance outside the mind, but an intention of the soul. Ockham combines his metaphysics of universals with a speculative anthropological account of the origin of universal terms in conventional language. He sketches a plausible story of how the universal term "man" is first introduced to ordinary language:

> Whoever it was that first instituted the first use of the term "man" saw some particular man and coined the term to signify that man and every substance like him. It was not necessary that the common nature occur to the person instituting the use of the term for the simple reason that there is no such common nature. But even though it signifies indifferently many men, "man" is not equivocal, for in signifying indifferently many men it is a sign subordinated to just one concept and not many. (136)

It seems reasonable enough to remark that actual language users when they first use a universal term do not consult or make contact with the universal common nature of a thing to be subsumed by the term. If you encounter a fish for the first time and decide to use the word "fish" for things of that kind you are not necessarily in touch at any cognitive level with the essence of all fish as a higher abstract metaphysical Form or inherent secondary substance. The experience on which the basis of a language user adds a new universal term to a language is a sensory encounter with a particular thing or things, which is to say either a primary substance in the physical world outside the mind or another intention of the soul.

Common natures in the sense of Plato's theory of Forms or Aristotle's metaphysics of inherent secondary substances are not perceived by language users who take it upon themselves to name all relevantly similar individuals by means of a universal term. Ockham adds that universal terms nevertheless do not signify equivocally, even though they signify many different particulars to which a universal is predicated rather than just a single thing. Their signifying is equivocal because a universal term is a sign that is "subordinated" to a single concept. It is not entirely clear what Ockham means by this, but he evidently intends to relate a universal term as a linguistic sign to an individual, a single something, probably psychological, such as a concept or universal in the sense of an intention of the soul and natural name for the individuals to which the universal is truly predicated.

UNIVERSALS IN TRUE AND FALSE PREDICATIONS

It is not enough for Ockham's purposes to be able to refer generally to judgmental predications of universals to particulars or generally to linguistic predications of universal to particular terms. He cannot interpret the relation of universals to particulars merely in terms of predications, since predications can be true or false and do not always correctly describe the state of the world. Someone can predicate the universal *red* of snow, by judging or entertaining the proposition that snow is red, which obviously does not make it the case that snow in fact is red. The judgmental predication of the universal *red* to snow is therefore no sound basis on which to conclude that the universal *red* or universal term "red" naturally or conventionally signifies, among other things, snow. We can only base such interpretations more specifically on *true* predications. This makes it indispensable for Ockham to explain the semantics of true and false judgmental and linguistic predications.

Ockham again makes Aristotle his touchstone as he considers the truth values of predications in thought and language. What makes a proposition true? What makes it false? How are true predications determined, and what are the truth makers by which some predications turn out to be true and others false? For one thing, it will not be the inherence of truth or falsehood in a predication or proposition. Ockham notes that even Aristotle does not imagine that truth and falsehood are qualities that inhere respectively in true and false judgments or propositions. If this were true, then the same proposition could be true or false as its inherent truth or falsehood was added and removed like plug-in, plug-out values, truth replaced with falsehood at different times, and falsehood with truth. As further intolerable implications, Ockham argues cryptically that if truth and falsehood were qualities inhering in a proposition, then as circumstances in the world change, new qualities are added to the mind that formulates propositions describing the change and previous qualities of the mind disappear. He states:

> In the process of making his point Aristotle makes it clear that the truth and falsity of propositions are not qualities of propositions which actually inhere in propositions. If they were it would follow that a proposition which is at one time true and at another time false would really admit contraries. It would also follow that in the case where something is first moving and afterwards at rest, a new quality would come to exist in the soul of the person who forms the proposition, "This thing is moving" and another quality would be lost. It would even follow that some written proposition would be changed by the mere fact that a fly moves. But these things are false and absurd. (140)

Ockham's concluding objection to the inherence of truth and falsehood in propositions requires explanation. He seems to think that a written proposition would be changed in some way although to all appearances it remains precisely the same, as he puts it, "by the mere fact that a fly moves." He claims that these implications are "false and absurd," but he leaves it to the reader to figure out why. It is hard to know exactly what he might have in mind, although we can make a good guess that makes a sensible objection to the thesis he is attacking. We can say that a written proposition that seems unchanged from moment to moment is in fact changed if the proposition says, "A fly moves," both before and after the fly moves. The inherence of truth or falsehood in the written proposition accordingly changes depending on whether it is or is not the case that the fly moves. Imperceptibly, the written proposition undergoes a transformation from having falsehood inhere in it before the fly moves to having falsehood vanish and replaced with truth when the fly moves and thus brings it about that now truth instead of falsehood inheres within the inscription of the proposition.

If truth and falsehood are not inherent qualities in propositions, as even Aristotle admits, the question remains what kinds of things they are and what it takes for a predication to be true or false. Ockham sides with Aristotle on the interpretation of truth and falsehood. He maintains that the truth values of propositions are nothing different than the propositions themselves in relation to the state of the world. He asks:

> What then are truth and falsehood? Like Aristotle I hold that truth and falsity are not really distinct from the true or false proposition. Thus, if the abstract terms "truth" and "falsity" do not incorporate any syncategorematic terms or expressions equivalent to such, one must grant the following propositions: "Truth is a true proposition" and "Falsity is a false proposition." (141)

Ockham is caught in an interesting dilemma. He needs to distinguish between true and false predications as part of his theory of universals. He needs to do this in order to prevent false predications from contaminating the analysis of universals, as in the problem of falsely predicating *red* to snow and concluding that *red* and the universal term "red" signify (among other things) snow. If Ockham says that truth and falsehood are themselves universals that can belong to or be superadded to qualify predications in propositions, then he faces a vicious circularity. He must know which predications are true in order to determine the analysis of any universal, and, if truth and falsehood are universals, he must have already determined the analysis of the universals *true* and *false* in order to know which predications are true.

The only solution is to deny that truth and falsehood are universals, which he promptly does. The noninherence metaphysics of truth he adopts claims that there are no universal true or false values, but that truth is nothing other than a true proposition and falsehood is nothing other than a false proposition. Ockham collapses truth and falsehood into true and false propositions, but in the process he acquires a related explanatory obligation. He must now say what it means for a proposition to be true or false. What makes a proposition true is its positive correspondence with the states of affairs it expresses, and what makes it false is it failure to positively correspond. Ockham pauses to consider a number of related issues in the proposal to reduce truth and falsehood to true and false propositions, and poses a strange question:

> But does the preceding argument not also work against my construction of truth and falsity? The answer is no, for if it is assumed that the following propositions are true: "Truth is a true proposition" and "Falsity is a false proposition," it follows that the following is false: "Wherever this falsity exists, this is true, 'This falsity exists.' " Therefore, it must be granted that the falsity of the proposition "God creates something from nothing" can be created by God from nothing. Nevertheless, it can be held that the proposition "This falsehood is created by God" is impossible. In the same way, while "The white can be black" is true, "The white is black" is impossible. (141)

He draws an analogy with color qualities that can be one thing or another, as long as they are not both at once. The puzzle arises on the assumption that from nothing God can create the falsity of the proposition that God creates something from nothing. The view to be resisted in Ockham's opinion is that the same proposition is both true and false. It is no challenge to his theory of truth as true propositions and falsehood as false propositions that the same proposition, depending on circumstances, can be true and can be false. The application in the case of God's omnipotence to create from nothing the falsity of a proposition that God can create something from nothing is to say that the proposition both can be true and can be false because God can either create or not create the falsehood of the relevant proposition. There is no contradiction if God merely can but does not actually create from nothing the falsehood of the proposition that God can create something from nothing, so the problem is nullified.

Ockham explains that his theory can escape the difficulty because it does not presuppose that "truth" and "falsity" or "falsehood" are universal terms. He does not further explain what makes a proposition true or false in this context, but he leaves open the possibility of interpreting truth as in Aristotle and as is customary today in terms of a positive correspondence between the existence of the state of affairs that a proposition asserts. Again, Ockham exits from the dilemma facing his analysis of universals in terms of true predications by invoking Aristotle's reduction of truth to true propositions and falsehood to false propositions:

> The reason my view can hold this and the preceding view cannot is that in my view "truth" and "falsity" are not absolute names but connotative names. In the former view, however, they must be construed as absolute names like "whiteness" and "blackness" and "cold" and "heat." I agree with Aristotle's view that except for substance, nothing can admit contrary qualities by way of inherence. Thus, at the end of the chapter on substance he says, "Thus, it is peculiar to substance that while being numerically one and the same, it can, because of a change on its own part, admit contraries. . . . " (141)

There are true and false propositions, but truth and falsehood are not universals to be predicated of particular propositions. Truth makers for propositions can be understood as the states of affairs expressed by propositions that can alternatively turn out to exist or not to exist, in the case of true and false propositions, respectively. True predications can then be safely appealed to without risk of circularity in determining the content and meaning of a universal as signifying all the things to which the universal is truly predicated.

OCKHAM'S RAZOR

It would be remiss in a discussion of Ockham's philosophy not to mention the methodological principle that has come to be known as Ockham's razor. We have already described Ockham's razor in connection with the Third Man argument in light of Plato's theory of Forms and Aristotle's theory of inherent secondary substances.

The simplest formulation of Ockham's razor is that we are not to multiply entities beyond explanatory necessity. The principle is that we require a solid reason for saying that something exists and including it in a theory's domain of existent entities. Ockham's razor tells us that, other things being equal, if two theories are equally explanatorily adequate, we should prefer whichever theory is more economical in the sense of involving commitment to fewer entities or kinds of entities in order to make its explanations work.

The difficulty in applying Ockham's razor in a given case is always that of determining what is and is not an explanatory necessity, and what does or does not need to be explained. The standard applications are usually more straightforward than the real situations in which the principle is applied. We are invited to consider alternative explanations of such phenomena as the origin of species, which we can try to explain in at least two different ways. One explanation involves natural selection of mutations that turn out to be beneficial to survival and reproduction under environmental pressures, and are thereafter passed on genetically to offspring. Another explanation includes all of the biological entities and facts that are posited by evolutionary theory but says that the origin of species is due to God's divine intervention creating distinct species of each kind of living thing that never evolve into other species, or at least do not do so in the case of the special creation of human beings.

If these are our choices and if in some sense the two theories provide equally satisfying explanations of the origin of species, then we may decide to prefer one to the other on the basis of the existence commitments each requires in its explanations. We can specify the choices in this way. Natural selection theory implies the existence of all biological entities and facts interpreted in a certain way; divine creationist theory also implies the existence of all biological entities and facts interpreted in a different way, and in addition implies the existence of God and God's freewill decisions to create distinct species in populating the world with living things. Ockham's razor in this case recommends natural selection theory over divine creationism as a theoretically more economical explanation of the origin of species. The choice may seem straightforward in this situation, but in many other applications there are subtleties and opportunities for the defenders of a theory to argue that the explanatory necessity requirement is not actually met by the more economical theory. They can often try to show that a competing theory despite being more economical does not adequately explain all the things that strictly need to be explained, or that its explanations are not as satisfactory as those afforded by a theory that admits the existence of additional entities.

More importantly, there is no guarantee that the most economical explanatorily adequate theory will also be true. What if the truth is that God did create distinct species, even though it is less economical to accept divine creationism than natural selection? Following Ockham's razor uncritically to approve the most theoretically economical explanation does not necessarily lead to the truth, even if in some sense it leads to a more desirable theory. Naturally, if we know that God exists and created each immutable species, then we have an extra fact to be included in our explanations, and no explanation of the origin of species that ignores this hypothetical truth can possibly be adequate. The usefulness of Ockham's razor as a metatheoretical criterion for choosing between theories is more apparent when we are not in the possession of such decisive information. When we need to make up our minds about two or more theories, each of which in its own way is agreed to be explanatorily adequate to the data we actually have but one of which is theoretically more economical than the other, then Ockham's razor can help us to decide which theory to prefer. With no other basis for decision, Ockham's razor provides a valuable guide.

The popular application of Ockham's razor assumes that the principle is wielded to eliminate Platonic Forms from the nominalistic metaphysics he prefers. It is sometimes said in this connection that Ockham's razor shaves Plato's beard. Plato's beard is the excessive growth of Forms in the Third Man, Fourth Man, and so on. There seems to be no explanatory justification or purpose served by these higher Forms, but Plato's theory of Forms appears to be logically committed to all of them without end once we allow that there is an ideal form of Man which all individual men imitate or instantiate or in which they participate. Ockham's razor slices off any such infinite regress of higher and higher Forms by denying that we need even the first ideal Form. All we need instead is a nominalist theory of universals as intentions of the soul. We notice, contrary to this commonly told story about Ockham's razor and Plato's beard, that Ockham says relatively little about Plato or Plato's theory of Forms in the *Summa Logicae*, nor does he introduce the principle of economy in the *Summa* in the context of his discussion of universals. Perhaps he regards Plato's theory of Forms as having been so definitively refuted by the Third Man objection that he sees no particular need to say anything more about it. It is clear in any case that Ockham does not use his razor to criticize Plato nor to defend his own nominalist theory of universals as a theoretically more economical alternative.

The principle of explanatory economy appears in several forms in Ockham's book *On the Principles of Theology*. Here, in the *Summa Logicae*, he complains in connection with the metaphysics of universals about the practice on the part of some philosophers to assume that every term signifies an entity. We have already seen that Ockham is unwilling to say that the terms "truth" and "falsehood" represent universals or qualities of propositions. He deplores the trend toward multiplying entities beyond necessity, particularly when to do so saddles us with theoretical commitments whose existence cannot be independently verified. In the theory of meaning, Ockham as we have seen has an additional reason for resisting the idea of understanding truth and falsehood as universals. The determination of true predications is needed in Ockham's theory in order to explain what each universal signifies as a natural sign. As a result, he can hardly allow truth itself to be classified as a universal. Although Ockham does not mention the problem, avoiding circularity provides a solid motive for him to reject the idea that truth and falsehood are universal qualities of propositions.

The general problem Ockham mentions is what is sometimes known as *reifying* the meanings of terms. This is a matter of attributing existence to the meanings of terms or treating them as though they are things that exist or must exist in order for the terms to have meaning. The word derives from the Latin *res*, meaning "thing." Ockham disputes such an oversimplified attempt to interpret the meanings of terms as things, when he writes:

[A] source [of theoretical error] consists in the tendency to multiply entities according to the multiplicity of terms, so that for every term there is a thing. This is a wrong-headed approach, and more than any other it leads one from the truth. For one should not ask in the case of every term what the relevant thing is. In the case of many terms the question is what the term means. Examples include all relative terms and some other terms which are equivalent in signification to longer expressions. Therefore, propositions in which they play a role have to be analyzed and broken down replacing a name sometimes by a description, for words and concepts by themselves can deceive. (171)

The idea of Ockham's razor is related to his general objections to the reification of universals and other explanatorily unnecessary theoretical objects. If there is not a sufficient justification for supposing that something exists in terms of the explanations we require and expect to be able to give, then Ockham's methodological criterion for the comparative evaluation and preference among competing theories favors a metaphysics that excludes from its theoretical existence domain any kinds of entities that are not strictly needed for the satisfactory explanation of any phenomenon.

As a remedy, Ockham recommends not automatically asking what every term *designates,* but what it *means.* The proposal implies that the meaning of some but not all terms will involve the designation of a thing. An obvious comparison is that between the name of any substance or universal and the terms "truth" and "falsehood." Ockham advances a nuanced semantic analysis that does not try to reduce all meaning to the designation of things, regardless of their metaphysical status, but locates meaning in a variety of categories for different kinds of linguistic expressions. The kind of theory that interprets the meaning of every term as naming a thing is described in contemporary semantics as a "Fido"-Fido theory. By this is meant the theory that a term such as "Fido" has meaning by virtue of naming a thing, in this case, the dog Fido. Ockham does not accept a simplistic theory of meaning such as the "Fido"-Fido theory, but understands meaning as a variegated relation of words and their several kinds of meanings.

Ockham's Conceptualism and Nominalism in the Metaphysics of Universals and Logic of Universal Terms

We have seen that Ockham's metaphysics of universals is both conceptualist and nominalist. The logic of universal terms in Ockham's philosophy has two aspects, the analysis of universals as intentions of the soul and as signs naturally signifying all things capable of having the universal truly predicated of them.

Ockham does not deny the existence of universals. On the contrary; he argues that universals exist as intentions of the soul, by which he means concepts within the mind or ideas. Universals in Ockham's metaphysics are psychological, creatures of thought or mental "names" referring to many different things, which he also refers to as "passions of being." He is most concerned to show by appeal to authority that Aristotle's logic and metaphysics entail that universals and relations do not exist outside the mind. Unlike contemporary universals theory, Ockham does not include relations in the category of universals, which he follows Aristotle in interpreting in a purely linguistic or syntactical way. He concludes that numbers, lengths, geometrical figures, and the like, which are otherwise interpreted as formal abstract entities or inherent secondary substances, which he collects together under the category of "quantity," also do not exist outside the mind.

This is what we should expect from Ockham as both a nominalist and conceptualist with respect to the metaphysics of universals. Plato and Aristotle in their very different ways similarly treat universals and mathematical objects by including them together under the same metaphysical categories. Plato regards both universals and mathematical objects as abstract Forms residing in the unchanging world of Being, while Aristotle regards both universals and mathematical objects as formal secondary substances inhering in primary and other secondary substances. Ockham in a comparable way also lumps together universals with mathematical "quantity" as intentions of the soul existing only within the mind and expressed linguistically as natural or conventional signs in a nominalist theory of the meaning of mathematical terms in language. He could hardly say anything different about the existence of mathematical properties than about universals generally, particularly if, as some philosophers have argued, purported mathematical entities can be reduced to mathematical properties. If the triangle can be understood as the universal *triangle* or *triangularity*, and if the numbers 1, 2, 3, and so on can be interpreted as the universals *unity, duality, trinity*, and so on, then there may be no justification, especially given an Ockhamesque principle of theoretical economy, for adding mathematical entities to metaphysics in addition to mathematical universals understood as intentions of the soul.

The conceptualist theory of universals and quantities in Ockham's philosophy has many advantages over its competitors. The theory is metaphysically economical by comparison with the leading alternatives, especially Plato's, Aristotle's, and Duns Scotus's, to which Ockham's analysis explicitly refers or implicitly applies. These accounts of universals additionally have serious drawbacks that Ockham identifies in his criticisms. His doctrine of universals as intentions of the soul emerges as superior to other leading theories in the field in these and other respects. It is more economical to interpret universals and quantities as intentions of the soul than as independently existent abstract Platonic Forms or even as inherent or formally independent Aristotelian secondary substances. It also avoids other kinds of problems to which the standard theories are subject. Plato's theory of Forms is freighted with the Third Man problem, and Aristotle's inherence concept of universals as secondary substances has the theoretical embarrassment of trying to explain how substances can be predicated of other substances. If we do not need to posit the existence of Platonic Forms or Aristotelian secondary substances in order to understand the logic of universals in predications, but can do so conceptualistically on the basis of intentions of the soul, why should we not adopt Ockham's ontically less profligate nominalism?

There is nevertheless also a difficulty in Ockham's conceptualism that he does not acknowledge or try to address. This is the problem of trying to explain how the same universal referred to by the same universal term in conventional language can simultaneously belong to different minds. If it is explicitly assumed that each mind possesses its own distinct universals, then there are even worse problems for Ockham's theory. If two persons communicate by means of the same social language in which a universal term is linguistically predicated of a particular term, as in the sentence, "This rose is red," how are we to understand the meaning of the universal term "red"? It is one thing for Ockham to say that the term refers to all red things, which it can do for both language users. How, on the other hand, in that case is the universal term supposed to be related to the universal?

If the universal term "red" is the expression of the universal *red*, and if *red* is supposed to be an intention of the soul, which intention in which of the two persons' souls does it express? There does not seem to be any good reason to suppose that it expresses one person's rather than another's, say, on the basis of age or rank in the military. Why should a word in a language shared by several language users express only one of their ideas in particular? How can we then explain the meaning of their predications and their understanding of language? Why would it express the intentions of Mary's soul instead of Jane's? If, on the other hand, the term expresses intentions of neither of their souls, then Ockham's conceptualistic metaphysics of universals seems redundant, fulfilling no necessary explanatory purpose. If we can explain the meaning of universal terms exclusively as names that refer to all things to which the universal is capable of being truly linguistically predicated, then we cut intentions of the soul entirely out of the explanatory loop and have no need to include them in the theory of universals. By Ockham's razor, in that case, it would appear that we should prefer a different theory than Ockham's that is not committed to his analysis of universals as intentions of the soul.

Finally, if the universal term "red" expresses the universal *red* construed as an intention of both language users' souls, how are we to know whether the term is predicated univocally? How can it have one and the same unequivocal meaning if different thinkers have different intentions? How in that case is communication and logically valid inference possible? If the term "red" simultaneously expresses *red*-in-subject-S's-soul and *red*-in-subject-S^*'s-soul, where $S \neq S^*$, then *red* for all we know has as many different meanings as there are different souls with different intentions. We can illustrate the problem in connection with Ockham's theory of quantity as existing also within the mind, and then recognize the same difficulty with respect to universals. If the number term π represents the quantity as a numerically distinct intention in every different language user's soul, then there is not just one number π, as we ordinarily think and as most metaphysicians have assumed, but as many different πs as there are persons who think about π or refer to π in language. Moreover, Ockham has given us no reason to expect that a universal or quantity existing as an intention in the soul will even be the same from moment to moment within the same person's soul. The problem presumably holds with respect to any universal, such as *red, round, democratic*, and the like. The magnitude of Ockham's difficulty is clear when we consider that a universal in some sense or other is supposed to be the same predicable predicated of many different things. This is precisely what Ockham's theory of universals as intentions of many different souls seems to make impossible, if the universal term "red" simultaneously refers to the intentions of many different persons' souls.

A version of the paradox confronts any conceptualist metaphysics of universals and mathematical objects. What is universal about universals if they exist only in every different thinker's thoughts? The fact that Mary and Jane can both predicate the universal term "red" of several things is among the things that non-negotiably need to be explained by an adequate theory of universals. If the explanation is supposed to be that the word refers to both Mary's and Jane's intentions as distinct psychological occurrences, then what Ockham calls a universal seems to be no different than a particular existent psychological thing. If Mary and Jane can somehow both have the very same identical intention of soul, even though their souls and thoughts are manifestly different from one another, then we are back to the problem of trying to understand how it is possible for the same thing to be multiply instantiated or to be present in or exemplified by many different things, here, in the distinct souls of two or more thinkers. This, we should recognize, is nothing other than the original problem of universals. If Ockham's conceptualist and nominalist theory is to provide an adequate solution to the problem of universals it must satisfactorily answer these kinds of objections.

SUMMARY

Ockham is an important figure in the history of philosophy not only because of his philosophical methods and conclusions, but because of his attitude toward the primacy of philosophical argument over appeals to authority in the pursuit of philosophical truth. Ockham is much like a contemporary philosopher in this regard, and his deep commitment to philosophy explains the biographical fact that he was summoned to appear before a papal commission and censored for his unorthodox philosophical and theological beliefs.

Through a complicated series of arguments, Ockham criticizes theories of universals as things existing in different ways outside the mind. His opposition to three kinds of metaphysics of universals applies logical divisions to expose their weaknesses through a succession of dilemmas. He rejects Aristotelian theories of universals as secondary substances inhering in other substances and ultimately in primary substances. He criticizes Duns Scotus's variation of an inherence metaphysics of universals that makes inherent secondary substances formally distinct from the substances in which they inhere. Although he does not mention Plato in this context, he also raises objections to the theory of universals as abstract eternal and unchanging Forms. He proposes a conceptualist theory of universals as mind-dependent intentions of the soul. Conventional linguistic predicates for qualities and relations do not represent universals outside the mind in the natural world or in a realm of abstract Platonic entities, but express the possibility of something being predicated by thought to many different things. Universals as predicative intentions of the soul are natural signs, which makes Ockham's metaphysics of universals not only conceptualist but nominalist. Universals as natural names or naturally signifying intentions of the soul can also be publicly expressed in the conventional signs of ordinary language.

An interesting problem for Ockham's conceptualism is how a universal can be expressed in a public conventional language if it exists as a distinct intention of the soul in each individual mind.

QUESTIONS FOR PHILOSOPHICAL UNDERSTANDING

1. What should we expect and require of an adequate metaphysics of universals?

2. What is a universal? What is a particular? How should they be thought to be related?

3. How does Ockham use logic as a method of metaphysics? What, generally, is the relation between logic and philosophy?

4. What is Ockham's objection to Plato's theory of universals as abstract eternal unchanging Platonic Forms?

5. What is Ockham's objection to Aristotle's theory of universals as inherent secondary substances?

6. What is Ockham's objection to Duns Scotus's theory of universals as inherent but formally distinct from the substances in which they inhere?

7. How would you characterize Ockham's attitude toward philosophical inquiry in relation to theological and other recognized philosophical authorities?

8. Why does Ockham believe that universals are intentions of the soul?

9. In what sense can an intention of the soul be universal if a universal is supposed to be a property of many different particular things?

10. What is meant by Ockham's razor? How is it supposed to function as a metatheoretical criterion of preferred theory choice?

11. Is there any reason to think that of two explanatorily adequate theories the simpler or theoretically more economical theory is more likely to be true?

12. Can Ockham's razor provide a reason other than truth to prefer one theory over its competitors?

13. What is the metaphysical relation between an intention of the soul and the mind that thinks or contains it?

14. Can Ockham fully understand the metaphysics of universals without satisfactorily explaining the metaphysics of intentions of the soul?

15. What does Ockham mean by intentions of the soul as natural signs? What is a natural sign? In what sense is it natural, and in what sense is it a sign? How are natural signs related to conventional signs in ordinary language?

KEY TERMS

abstract entity

accident

appeal to authority

common nature

conceptualism

conventional sign

convertible term

copula

de inesse predication

extrinsic property

five types of universals

formally independent existence of inherent secondary substance

genus

haecceity

indexical term

inhere, inherence

intention of the soul

intrinsic property

logic of terms

natural sign

nomen

nominalism

nonparticular substance

particular, particular substance

passion

predication in quid

primacy of philosophical reasoning

proper nature

property

reifying meanings of terms

reism

species difference

suppositum

syllogism, syllogistic logic

syncategorematic term

term of first intention

term of second intention

true, false predication

universal

Sources and Recommended Readings

Adams, Marilyn McCord. "Ockham's Nominalism and Unreal Entities." *The Philosophical Review* 86 (1977): 144–76.

Adams, Marilyn McCord. *William Ockham*. Notre Dame: University of Notre Dame Press, 1987.

Goddu, André. *The Physics of William of Ockham*. Leiden: E. J. Brill, 1984.

Henry, Desmond Paul. *Medieval Logic and Metaphysics*. London: Routledge & Kegan Paul, 1972.

Lahey, Stephen. "William of Ockham and Trope Nominalism," *Franciscan Studies* 55 (1998): 105–20.

Leff, Gordon. *The Dissolution of the Medieval Outlook: An Essay on Intellectual and Spiritual Change in the Fourteenth Century*. New York: New York University Press, 1976.

Maurer, Armand A. *The Philosophy of William of Ockham in the Light of Its Principles*. Toronto: Pontifical Institute of Mediaeval Studies, 1999.

Ockham, William of. *Ockham's Theory of Propositions: Part II of the Summa Logicae*. Translated by Alfred J. Freddoso and Henry Schuurman; Introduction by Freddoso. Notre Dame: Notre Dame University Press, 1980.

Ockham, William of. *Predestination, God's Foreknowledge, and Future Contingents (Tractatus de Praedestinatione)*. Translated with notes by Marilyn McCord Adams and Norman Kretzmann; Introduction by Adams. Indianapolis: Hackett Publishing, 1983.

Spade, Paul Vincent. "Ockham's Nominalist Metaphysics: Some Main Themes." In *The Cambridge Companion to Ockham*, ed. Spade, 100–17.

Spade, Paul Vincent, ed. *The Cambridge Companion to Ockham*. Cambridge: Cambridge University Press, 1999.

Tachau, Katherine H. *Vision and Certitude in the Age of Ockham: Optics, Epistemology, and the Foundations of Semantics, 1250–1345*. Leiden: E. J. Brill, 1988.

Tweedale, Martin M. "Ockham's Supposed Elimination of Connotative Terms and His Ontological Parsimony," *Dialogue* 31 (1992): 431–44.

Weinberg, Julius R. *Ockham, Descartes, and Hume: Self-Knowledge, Substance, and Causality*. Madison: University of Wisconsin Press, 1977.

Wood, Rega. *Ockham on the Virtues*. West Lafayette: Purdue University Press, 1997.

CHAPTER 4

REASON, KNOWLEDGE, AND CERTAINTY

Descartes's *Meditations* on *First Philosophy*

We turn now from ancient and medieval thought to the first major philosopher in the period of modern philosophy. Descartes is well known in his day as a mathematician, scientist, and philosopher. He proposes to establish knowledge on absolutely certain foundations, and to raise the level of epistemic certainty in the empirical sciences to that of mathematics. In the course of carrying out his project, he produces two proofs for the existence of God and two proofs for the distinction between mind and body. He offers an argument for what he takes to be the strongest possible basis for skepticism, which he then shows can be overcome by relying entirely on the resources of pure reason. As the first premier philosopher of the era, Descartes's method typifies the seventeenth century as the epoch of modern rationalism.

ARISTOTELIAN METAPHYSICAL BACKGROUND

René Descartes (1596–1650) is the first major thinker in the time of "modern" philosophy, which is standardly said to cover the seventeenth and eighteenth centuries. Descartes's ideas continue to interest and motivate contemporary theory of knowledge, metaphysics, philosophy of mind, philosophy of science, philosophy of mathematics, and philosophy of religion.

Descartes was not only a philosopher, but a mathematician and scientist. He made contributions to all of these disciplines at a time when revolutionary developments in all branches of learning were being made. In mathematics, Descartes invented new uses for variables and a graphic method of representing algebraic relations on a two-dimensional grid of axes that have since come to known as "Cartesian" coordinates. Descartes's methods permitted him to clarify and solve long-standing problems in mathematics. He introduced a constructivist way of doing mathematics, in which the proving of theorems from mathematical axioms became less important than solving problems by using mathematical instruments and rigorously building up mathematical systems from basic concepts.

In natural science, Descartes made original findings in optics, physics, cosmology, biology, anatomy, and medicine. Although Descartes's scientific reputation has not withstood the test of time as well as his work in mathematics, and has been in many ways superseded by the work of Isaac Newton and numerous others in ensuing centuries, it is still widely respected for its groundbreaking approach to the study of physical phenomena. The seventeenth century, emerging from the late Renaissance, laid the foundations for contemporary science and philosophy. Descartes is very much at the forefront of these developments that helped so dramatically to set the stage for today's scientific culture.

Above all, Descartes is a philosopher. When he remarks, as he frequently and with great elaboration does in many of his philosophical treatises, on the nature of scientific method, he speaks as a philosopher, but with the experience of a practicing mathematician and scientist. He articulates an approach to the theory of knowledge from the standpoint not merely of an abstract familiarity with mathematics and science, but reflecting on his own years of successful inquiry in these fields. Descartes's philosophy is one manifestation of a widespread intellectual current that gained extraordinary momentum in the seventeenth century. In order to understand the scientific and philosophical climate of which Descartes's thought is a vital part, we need to consider the Aristotelian background to Descartes's philosophy. We are already familiar with Aristotle's first philosophy, and in particular with his metaphysics of substance, from which a general sense of Aristotle's approach to ways of doing philosophy can be gathered. Descartes's *Meditations on First Philosophy* is evidently a response to Aristotle, as Descartes's choice of the distinctive Aristotelian phrase "first philosophy" reveals even in the title.

It would be hard to exaggerate the importance of Aristotle's influence on the course of science and philosophy between the Renaissance, in the fifteenth and sixteenth centuries, and the early part of the seventeenth century. Aristotle and Aristotelianism as it came to be interpreted in the teachings of Thomas Aquinas and other medieval thinkers was the dominant philosophical school during the birth of early modern philosophy, when Descartes was beginning to make his mark in mathematics, science, and philosophy. Although we have also seen that Ockham was prepared to challenge Aristotle on many key points of his logic and metaphysics, the fact remains that Aristotle was the most highly regarded philosopher at the time when Descartes began to write. We also recall that Ockham was driven from England to the protection of a German prince by the Church's persecution not only because of his free thinking about papal infallibility, but because he had criticized some of Aristotle's doctrinally approved teachings.

Aristotle's scientific and philosophical writings almost disappeared in late antiquity, particularly after the burning in Roman times of the great library at Alexandria, Egypt. That Aristotle's philosophy survived at all, and that his texts were available to be passed along to future generations, is due to Arabic scholars who preserved many of Aristotle's most important works in translations and philosophical commentaries. Arabic culture, reaching from the Mideast as far as Spain at the time, was in the glory days of its civilization in the fourteenth and fifteenth centuries, and had made numerous advances in the arts and sciences, especially engineering and medicine. Arabic thinkers concerned themselves with literature, philosophy, and fine art, and made great efforts to locate and translate into Arabic whatever documents could be found from great civilizations of the past, including those of ancient Greece. When the late Middle Ages and early Renaissance reawakened to philosophy, Aristotle's writings were recovered by a new generation of thinkers who were hungry for knowledge of the past.

The appearance of Aristotle's virtually complete system of thought made a powerful impact. The comprehensiveness of Aristotle's works and the depth of his philosophical reflections at the time caused many less independent thinkers to revere Aristotle's ideas as the final word on scientific questions. It is an oversimplification, but one that still makes an important point, to say that, after the reemergence of Aristotle's writings in the fourteenth century, Aristotle was treated as an almost unquestioned authority in all secular intellectual matters. Contrary to scientific method, and especially to Aristotle's own commitment to empirical evidence as a way of discovering scientific truths, the early European Renaissance maintained an extraordinary degree of confidence in Aristotle's conclusions. Instead of conducting experiments or organizing observations to settle a scientific problem, or consulting Aristotle's texts as a source of ideas with which to begin scientific inquiry, Renaissance humanism turned to Aristotle's writings more often than not as the definitive solution. This, from a contemporary perspective, was not a healthy situation for science, one with which Aristotle himself would surely never have agreed. It took several centuries of trying to reconcile new emerging knowledge with Aristotle's philosophy before the limitations of answering all scientific problems by appeal to his authority finally became intolerable.

The invention of the telescope enabled researchers for the first time to study the stars and planets surrounding us in space. As Galileo, a contemporary of Descartes, reports in his pamphlet *The Starry Messenger*, the moon is pitted with craters and filled with mountains, much like the Earth, and planets in the distant reaches of the solar system, Jupiter and Saturn, have moons, again very much like the Earth. The implication is that other heavenly bodies are not entirely different from the Earth, which seems to make the Earth just one planet among others. As a consequence of his analysis of essence as natural function, Aristotle concludes that it is the nature of the material element earth to go to the center of the universe. He reasons that therefore the Earth as the only repository of earth must be located at the center of the universe, so that all heavenly bodies, made of æther rather than earth, move about in space above the Earth. The fact that these inferences are all mistaken, and that Aristotle despite his genius had gotten things wrong, was now plain for anyone to see with their own eyes through an eight-power telescope. Nor was this Aristotle's only false conclusion based on false assumptions, as we might expect of early attempts to explain the world of nature.

The rediscovery of Aristotle and his prestige as an infallible scientific authority, followed by his failure to correctly answer all scientific problems, is crucial background to

Descartes's *Meditations on First Philosophy*. Where authority fails, as a general rule, it becomes necessary to search for new and better methods of establishing truths. Descartes is one of a number of philosophers at roughly this time who reacted to the new scientific discoveries of Galileo and other protomodern scientists. We find a similar response on the part of Francis Bacon, whose *Novum Organon*, literally, the "new machine," like Descartes's reflections on first philosophy, makes an explicit reference to Aristotle. Aristotle's treatises on logic and methodology were collected by a first century editor under the title, the *Organon*, and Bacon proposes to replace it with a *new Organon*. Bacon's treatise proposes what by contemporary standards appears to be a rather naive method of empirical discovery. The idea is to collect and organize data for the sake of solving scientific problems without offering guidelines about how to choose what is relevant and ignore what is irrelevant or how in the absence of theory to organize whatever data is collected so that a theory can emerge.

Bacon's recipe for advancing knowledge nevertheless seemed revolutionary at the time, rather than simply looking for the answers in Aristotle's writings. Similarly, Descartes's *Discourse on the Method of Rightly Conducting Reason in the Search for Truth* (1637) and *Meditations on First Philosophy* (1641) fit into this same category of methodological manifesto for the new age of modern post-Aristotelian science. Here also Descartes, as a distinguished philosopher and practicing mathematician and scientist of the time, rethinks the requirements of successful scientific methodology from a philosophical standpoint and charts a new course for scientific philosophical inquiry as a reaction against an entrenched Aristotelian scientific orthodoxy. Descartes's philosophy and his program for revitalizing natural science are nevertheless different from Bacon's in many ways.

RELIGIOUS DIMENSIONS OF DESCARTES'S PHILOSOPHY

The other crucial factor in understanding the philosophical context of Descartes's *Meditations* is religious. The European Middle Ages after the fall of the Roman Empire to the Renaissance to Descartes's time in the seventeenth century and beyond was dominated by Christian and especially Roman Catholic ideology.

The fourteenth-century theologian Thomas Aquinas brought together Aristotle's metaphysics with the teachings of the Bible and Catholicism in his masterwork, the *Summa Theologiæ*. To give an idea of one aspect of Aquinas's project, his synthesis of Aristotle and the Bible includes a solution to the problem of understanding the Catholic sacrament of the holy eucharist, in which communion bread and wine is supposed to be transformed into the body and blood of Jesus Christ. Although Aristotle died several hundred years before the time of Christ, Aquinas adapts Aristotle's theory of substance to argue that the communion sacraments when blessed are, in Aristotelian terms, *essentially* Christ's body and blood and only *accidentally* bread and wine.

Descartes officially embraces the religious component of this tradition. The Catholic Church is an integral part of Descartes's life, having been raised a Catholic and educated by Jesuits at the college of La Fleche. Descartes detaches Christianity, which he accepts, from the Aristotelian science and metaphysics he does not accept. We can think about Descartes's philosophy as trying to replace Aristotle's metaphysics in the grand Scholastic synthesis of Aristotle and Catholic theology effected by Aquinas. Descartes leaves the religious component in place, but substitutes for Aristotle's metaphysics a new theory of knowledge and first philosophy. Descartes in this sense wants to become a new Aristotle, much as Bacon wants to replace Aristotle's methodology with an improved way of practicing the sciences. Descartes understands the precariousness of his situation perfectly well. He understands the political dangers he risks by opposing the conservative forces of established religion. Although Descartes does not directly speak against Saint Thomas Aquinas, it is implicit in his philosophical program that by superceding Aristotle in Catholic philosophical theology, he in effect proposes to replace Aquinas.

Descartes manifests his caution in several ways. He moves from his native Catholic France, where the Inquisition had recently spread its persecutions in the name of religious orthodoxy in Italy and Spain. Descartes relocates to the more hospitable liberal and tolerant shores of seventeenth-century Netherlands. Here he spends the major part of his philosophical career in Amsterdam before moving to another Protestant country, Sweden. Descartes self-consciously meant to avoid the fate that had befallen Galileo in Italy. After publishing his discoveries about the moons of distant planets, Galileo was brought to trial before the Inquisition, his books were banned and burned, and he was placed under house arrest, being allowed to teach only the uncontroversial implications of his new physics at the University of Padua. Another sign of Descartes's efforts to stay out of trouble with the Church is indicated by his "Letter of Dedication" to the *Meditations*, addressed *To the Wisest and Most Distinguished Men, the Dean and Doctors of the Faculty of Sacred Theology of Paris*. Descartes commends his work to their judgment and explains his purpose, hoping to solicit the support or at least to mollify any hostility of the Catholic intellectual hierarchy toward his philosophy. Thus, Descartes declares:

> I have always thought that two questions—that of God and that of the soul—are chief among those that ought to be demonstrated by the aid of philosophy rather than of theology. For although it suffices for believers like ourselves to believe by faith that the soul does not die with the body and that God exists, certainly no unbeliever seems capable of being persuaded of any religion or even any moral virtue, unless these two are first proven to him by natural reason. And since in this life there are often more rewards for vices than for virtues, few would prefer what is right to what is useful, if they neither feared God nor hoped for an afterlife. And although it is utterly true that God's existence is to be believed in because it is taught in the Holy Scriptures, and, on the other hand, that the Holy Scriptures are to be believed because they have God as their source (because, since faith is a gift from God, the very same one who gives the grace that is necessary for believing the rest, can also give us the grace to believe that he exists); nonetheless, this cannot be proposed to unbelievers because they would judge it to be a circle. (1)

Descartes articulates the two main goals of his treatise. The same two purposes are emphasized in his work's subtitle: *Meditations on First Philosophy in Which the Existence of God and the Distinction of the Soul from the Body are Demonstrated.* Descartes argues that religious faith, despite its importance in the lives of the faithful, does not offer philosophical reasons for believing in the existence of God and the soul's immortality. He accordingly sets himself the tasks of proving the religious tenets of the existence of God and the distinction between body and soul on philosophical grounds.

The problem is formulated by Descartes as a dilemma. Believers in God and the basic principles of (Catholic) Christianity already believe by faith. Unbelievers are unlikely to be convinced by theology alone, Descartes maintains, for two reasons. First, because, in the absence of faith, unbelievers on their own will not come to accept what Descartes regards as the two philosophically most important articles of faith, that God exists and that the soul as distinct from the body is immortal. An atheist will only come to accept religion if these two main theses can first be *demonstrated,* in the exact phrase of Descartes's subtitle, to natural reason, much as in the case of a geometrical theorem in mathematics, by rational proof. Second, theology fails in this effort because unbelievers object to the viciously circular reasoning implied by those who believe in the existence of God because it is taught in Scripture, and believe that Scripture is true because it is the inspired word of God.

Descartes argues that philosophy must step in to lend its persuasion to support the teachings of religious faith. Philosophy complements faith when it serves as intellectual scaffolding for the faithful, and as a way for unbelievers to be brought to the Church's truths. He adds that without a sound basis in reason there can be no adequate motivation for religious unbelievers even to accept moral principles as opposed to prudential considerations for their actions. He says that the unfaithful have no incentive for being guided by what it is right to do rather than what it is smart to do in view of their self-interests. If atheists have no compelling justification for believing that God exists to judge their actions and reward or punish them in an afterlife, then Descartes imagines that they will conduct themselves immorally. This, in itself, is a highly controversial proposition that we shall not pause now to evaluate. We should remark contra Descartes that it is by no means even widely agreed that morality depends on religion. If reason, as Descartes says, is needed in order for unbelievers to accept the existence of God and immortality of the soul in the service of morality, other thinkers in the history of philosophy and in contemporary philosophical thought have held on the contrary that reason can lead directly to an adequate rationale for ethical conduct that is altogether separable from religious belief.

Descartes's desire to advance a new philosophy for the sake of religion and morality must be taken seriously in reading his *Meditations.* If we are going to measure the success or failure of Descartes's project, we must try to do so in terms of the book's purpose and the work Descartes sets himself to accomplish. Descartes's promise to *demonstrate* the existence of God and the distinction of the body from the soul commits him to the highest standards of mathematical justification. Descartes proposes by this yardstick to prove the existence of God, the distinction between body and soul, and to secure the rational foundations for rebuilding knowledge in the sense and with the justificational strength of a formal mathematical demonstration. Whether Descartes's project lives up to its own standard is a question that only a critical exposition of his argument in its entirety can answer.

DESCARTES'S QUEST FOR CERTAINTY

In order to understand Descartes's quest for epistemic certainty, we distinguish two different meanings of "certain" and "certainty": *psychological* and *epistemic.* Descartes, although he does not use this precise terminology, is clearly interested in attaining epistemic rather than mere psychological certainty in the sciences.

To be psychologically certain is to be firmly convinced that a belief is true. I am psychologically certain when I do not doubt and cannot imagine a sound basis for doubting a proposition's truth. Psychological certainty is a state of mind, a fixed commitment that is unshaken and appears unshakeable as a person reflects on what he or she takes to be its truth. It is with a sense of psychological certainty that a religious believer feels the most powerful convictions in an article of faith. Nor is psychological certainty unique to religious sentiments. Any belief can be held with psychological certainty, if the believer has the right sort of assurance in its truth. Psychological certainty can be experienced as a powerful emotional attitude toward a belief's truth, even when a belief is false. The trouble with psychological certainty is that merely feeling strongly that a belief is true does not by itself guarantee that the belief is actually true. The inner impression that a proposition must be true that comes with psychological certainty can sometimes be an indication that the proposition is true, or that we might be wise to take the belief seriously as having a strong presumption in favor of its truth—but it is no indication that the proposition is in fact true.

Where psychological certainty is a subjective state of mind, epistemic certainty is an objective feature of the most strongly possible justified beliefs. Philosophers define epistemic certainty in a number of different ways, but in connection with Descartes's philosophy, again, although he does not use this terminology, we can think of epistemic certainty as the degree of epistemic justification a belief has when no other belief can be more strongly justified. Epistemic certainty, by contrast with psychological certainty, guarantees the truth of an epistemically certain belief, assuming as we do in mathematics that the strongest possible rational justification justifies a belief as true.

Searching for certainty in knowledge, Descartes seeks epistemic rather than mere psychological certainty. The irrelevance of psychological certainty to the needs of science in validating the truth is more easily seen in extreme cases. If it is logically possible to artificially induce a subject's mental state of psychological certainty in any true or false belief by use of hypnosis, drugs, or brainwashing, then psychological certainty by itself is never an adequate sign of truth. Descartes needs something stronger for the certainty of knowledge. He is interested in epistemic rather than psychological certainty because he has set his sights on the same standards of certainty to be found in mathematical demonstrations of mathematical truths.

METHODOLOGICAL DOUBT AND SKEPTICISM

The overall structure of Descartes's plan in the *Meditations* includes three distinct parts. In order to establish knowledge on epistemically certain grounds, Descartes believes he must first go back to the beginning, find a way to destroy the old edifice of knowledge, resecure the foundations of knowledge on rational grounds, and then start to rebuild a new edifice of knowledge that will have throughout its principles and conclusions the same epistemic certainty as mathematics.

Descartes proposes to raze the old edifice of knowledge not one brick at a time, but with a heavy-duty demolition ball. He considers a single source of doubt that if it were to prevail would plunge us deeply into universal skepticism. By overturning this strongest possible basis for doubting the evidence of the senses, Descartes believes he has shown that perception can afford the same high degree of epistemic certainty as the strength of the reasoning by which the basis for doubt was imagined and disarmed.

Descartes's strategy is to tear down the old system of knowledge and replace it with science based on mathematically certain clear and distinct perceptions. He argues that his own existence is not subject to doubt even by the most powerful doubt-casting possibility. From the contents of his own thoughts together with principles of what he calls "the light of nature" *(lumen naturale),* he then proves the existence of God as our perfect truth-loving creator who has faultlessly designed the equipment by which we perceive the world. If these momentous inferences are correct, then Descartes will have attained his goal of proving that knowledge, even the everyday perceptual knowledge we ordinarily believe ourselves to possess, can have the same high degree of epistemic certainty as a mathematical proof. No atheist, he believes, can demand a higher standard for philosophical or theological argument. The most important metaphysical questions of religion will thereby be settled from the standpoint of pure reason reflecting on the epistemically certain existent contents of thoughts. Descartes thus accords the same high degree of epistemic certainty to all experiential knowledge that is generally expected to apply only in mathematics. If his project is successful, he will have extended the possibility of attaining the same degree of rational epistemic certainty that characterizes mathematics to all of science or natural philosophy, philosophical theology, and philosophical psychology.

Descartes accordingly titles the first Meditation: "Concerning Those Things That Can Be Called into Doubt." He considers virtually all of his beliefs as belonging to one encompassing category, including those he acquired through sensation and those he has uncritically absorbed as part of his education. He begins with an autobiographical statement of what he now takes to be his youthful naivety concerning the beliefs he acquired during his first years of study. He immediately goes beyond the faulty theories of phenomena that he might have been wrong to accept to the much more general philosophical problem of whether or not we can believe anything that we learn through perception about the presumed outside world. He opens Meditation One with these words:

> Several years have now passed since I first realized how many were the false opinions that in my youth I took to be true, and thus how doubtful were all the things that I subsequently built upon these opinions. From the time I became aware of this, I realized that for once I had to raze everything in my life, down to the very bottom, so as to begin again from the first foundations if I wanted to establish anything firm and lasting in the sciences. But the task seemed so enormous that I waited for a point in my life that was so ripe that no more suitable a time for laying hold of these disciplines would come to pass. For this reason, I have delayed so long that I would be at fault were I to waste on deliberation the time that is left for action. Therefore, now that I have freed my mind from all cares, and I have secured for myself some leisurely and carefree time, I withdraw in solitude. I will, in short, apply myself earnestly and openly to the general destruction of my former opinions. (13)

This is an astonishing declaration, and one worth considering in detail as a clear announcement of Descartes's starting place. The beginning remarks have somewhat the tone of a philosophical confession. Descartes confides in the reader that in the past he had accepted many beliefs that he since has come to recognize as false, and that it seems reasonable to infer that he must have built many false opinions on the weak foundations of even more basic falsehoods. He invokes an architectural metaphor when he says that he recognized the need to "raze" his previous beliefs. This is the phrase used in building trades when one says of an unsafe building that it must be razed down to the ground, so that we can begin again with more secure groundwork. What other course could a sane person follow when a building has faulty foundations and its superstructure is in danger of collapsing? The wise policy is surely to knock down the old building and start all over again, after providing a sound foundation on which to rebuild. That is what Descartes says he recognized the need to do with respect to the beliefs he had accumulated throughout his life.

He explains that because of the sheer magnitude of the task he had hesitated to undertake the undoing of all his previous beliefs and the providing of new more secure foundations for knowledge. He waited, he tells us, until he had reached such a point in life that he had the opportunity to do what he deemed necessary to rethink all of his prior presumed knowledge. He has waited, he says, until he believed himself to be of such an age that he could no longer postpone the project with any prospect of successfully completing it within his remaining lifetime. What Descartes does not say is that by waiting until the time of writing the *Meditations*, or at least until he began to reason through its principal themes, he had had a chance to discover and perfect the methods he had successfully used in mathematics and science. Descartes writes his methodological treatises after the early part of his most productive career, when he has already made significant contributions to mathematics and science. The implication is that Descartes developed his method on purely rational grounds many years earlier during a cold winter's retreat when he was still a soldier with a unique opportunity to withdraw from the activity of the world and simply think.

An anecdote surrounding Descartes's discovery of his method helps to illustrate the difference between reason and perception that pervades his philosophy. When still a young man, Descartes like most of his well-born contemporaries trained as a soldier. He enlisted in the private army of Maurice of Nassau, and saw action in the Thirty Years War in Europe, between Protestants, largely from Sweden and northern Germany, and Catholics, primarily from southern Germany. Descartes probably did not engage directly in the conflict, but took the opportunity to travel with the army as part of his education. During one such campaign in Prussia, during a blizzard, Descartes is supposed to have bivouacked in a cottage. In a medieval-style bed, in an opening in a wall enclosed with a heavy curtain and heated by a fire on the other side of the wall, Descartes shut himself off from the rest of the world under his blankets in an otherwise very cold room. As the title of his treatise suggests, Descartes was free to meditate on the problem of the nature and limitations of knowledge, and the doubtfulness of everything he believed himself to know up until that point. He took the opportunity to devise a plan for the improvement of the sciences that would be based on pure reason in such a way as to avoid the uncertainty of experiential knowledge as it is usually understood.

The image of Descartes absorbed in philosophical meditations about the nature of knowledge quickly becomes the dominant theme of his most famous work. In several places, Descartes describes himself as involved in reflections on philosophy and science in a sequence of six days. We know, however, that Descartes wrote and rewrote and labored heavily on the *Meditations* over a period of eight years. Moreover, Descartes was so concerned about the reception his book would receive, particularly in light of the difficulties encountered by Galileo in his confrontations with Church authorities, that he took enormous care not to offend against the religious establishment. To improve the final statement of his argument, he also circulated copies of his text to many of the leading intellectual figures of the day for their comments and criticisms, which he then published in an expanded first edition of the work, along with his replies. The compilation of the text itself with objections and replies makes an effective rhetorical statement of the main theses of Descartes's treatise. It anticipates many of the criticisms that other readers are likely to want answered, thereby strengthening the force of Descartes's conclusions by solving certain problems in advance.

As Descartes undertakes the "general destruction" of his "former opinions," he stands in need of an effective method. He explains that he was unable in one stroke simply to discard all of his beliefs as false. For one thing, he does not yet know enough, if he is going to question his beliefs, even to know that his prior opinions are false. Some might be true, others false, and he will have to decide which are which. At this stage of his inquiry he is no more in a sound position to be able to discredit than he is able confidently and definitively to affirm any of his previous beliefs. What, then, is he to do? Descartes thinks that it will be good enough, in lieu of finding that all his beliefs are definitely false, merely to find a strong reason to regard them all as doubtful. Furthermore, he remarks that he has no need actually to proceed one by one through all of his beliefs and find a motivation for doubting each individually, which, he explains, would be a difficult and potentially infinite labor. Instead, he proposes to find a single justification for doubting the basis of his previous beliefs. If he can undermine the foundation of his knowledge, it will bring down the entire edifice. He states:

> Yet to this end it will not be necessary that I show that all my opinions are false, which perhaps I could never accomplish anyway. But because reason now persuades me that I should withhold my assent no less carefully from things which are not plainly certain and indubitable than I would to what is patently false, it will be sufficient justification for rejecting them all, if I find a reason for doubting even the least of them. Nor therefore need one survey each opinion one after the other, a task of endless proportion. Rather—because undermining the foundations will cause whatever has been built upon them to fall down of its own accord—I will at once attack those principles which supported everything that I once believed. (13)

DESCARTES'S FIRST—ILLUSION—RATIONALE FOR SYSTEMATIC DOUBT

To accomplish this purpose, Descartes first tries to discover a common element in the beliefs he has accepted. Eventually, he considers four different grounds for doubting all of his previous held beliefs. The first rationale depends on the fact that all of his previous opinions were derived from the senses, and that, since he has sometimes been deceived by his senses, as in the case of optical illusions, it is possible that his senses always deceive him. If so, then perhaps he has already hit upon a powerful reason to doubt all of his earlier beliefs insofar as they may depend on the evidence of the senses. He continues:

> Whatever I had admitted until now as most true I took either from the senses or through the senses; however, I noticed that they sometimes deceived me. And it is a mark of prudence never to trust wholly in those things which have once deceived us. (13)

Descartes's first rationale for skepticism can be reconstructed as an inference from the fact that some perceptions are illusory to the conclusion that perhaps all sense experience is false and mistaken about the true state of the world:

Descartes's Illusion Rationale for Skepticism
1. I have sometimes been deceived by sensory illusions that were not veridical sensations.

2. For all I know, all of my sensations are illusory.

The fact that some perceptions are illusory, Descartes soon realizes, does not provide a strong enough reason for doubting all of his previous beliefs. The mere possibility of being deceived by sensory illusion cannot be sufficient to make a rational person conclude that all sense experience is illusory. He maintains that at most we might be deceived by our sensations applied to "very small and distant things," and, we might add, considering for the moment only visual illusions, to things that are not clearly perceived, as through a fog or haze or under dim or unusual lighting conditions. The examples that come to mind at once under this category include optical tricks and mirages or the *fata morgana*. Against these, Descartes argues that in ordinary perceptual circumstances objects seen plainly or experiences that are immediate and undeniable in their crystal clarity cannot reasonably be doubted. He argues:

> But perhaps, although the senses sometimes deceive us when it is a question of very small and distant things, still there are many other matters which one certainly cannot doubt, although they are derived from the very same senses: that I am sitting here before the fireplace wearing my dressing gown, that I feel this sheet of paper in my hands, and so on. But how could one deny that these hands and that my whole body exist? Unless perhaps I should compare myself to insane people whose brains are so impaired by a stubborn vapor from a black bile that they continually insist that they are kings when they are in utter poverty, or that they are wearing purple robes when they are naked, or that they have a head made of clay, or that they are gourds, or that they are made of glass. But they are all demented, and I would appear no less demented if I were to take their conduct as a model for myself. (14)

It will not do for Descartes to challenge his ordinary beliefs on the basis of the fact that sensations are sometimes illusory. To reason in that way would amount to claiming that something that is not actually doubtful is doubtful. In that case, Descartes says, he would be no better off than the insane who believe themselves to be gourds or made of glass, apparently a common delusion among the mentally ill. If the only motivation Descartes can give for doubting the evidence of his senses is as extreme as that, then he cannot hope eventually to answer the objection and restore knowledge. He cannot proceed rationally to evaluate each step of the argument in advancing from doubt to the razing of the old edifice of knowledge to the securing of epistemically certain foundations and rebuilding of a new superstructure of knowledge if he is required to begin with the kinds of assumptions shared by the insane.

Whatever justification Descartes finally settles on to raise doubts about the experiential basis of his previous beliefs, it must be strong enough to provide a good reason to doubt, but not so strong that it would be available only to someone whose judgment in general was so impaired as to make reasoning impossible. If Descartes's only ground for doubting his prior beliefs is irrational, then he can never reason his way back to knowledge. We must recall that by raising skeptical doubts about his previous knowledge, Descartes is not, so to speak, a confirmed skeptic who wants to remain permanently in doubt. On the contrary, Descartes wants to use doubt and skepticism only temporarily and provisionally as a method to arrive at a way of tearing down the old structure of his beliefs so as to establish better foundations for a new more perfect science and philosophy with the same high degree of epistemic certainty as mathematics.

Another consideration that Descartes does not consider that would imply the futility of doubting all sensory beliefs by virtue of the fact that our senses sometimes deceive us is seen in the following analogy. Imagine someone reasoning as follows:

Art Forgeries Analogy for Descartes's Illusion Rationale
1. I have sometimes been deceived by clever art forgeries that were not genuine artworks.

---

2. For all I know, all artworks are clever art forgeries.

This appears to be a very similar argument. It more clearly expresses the problem that invalidates Descartes's first rationale for doubting the truth of all his beliefs originating in sense experience. The inference is clearly deductively invalid, since the assumption in (1) might be true, but the conclusion in (2) false. It might well be true that I have sometimes been deceived by clever art forgeries that were not genuine artworks, just as I might have been sometimes deceived by sensory illusions that were not veridical sensations. The conclusion of the art forgeries analogy, on the other hand, cannot be true, since it is impossible for all artworks to be forgeries. There must be at least some genuine artworks in order for forgeries to be made. It is sometimes said that the concept of an art forgery is *parasitic* on the concept of a genuine artwork, in the sense that if there were no genuine artworks then there would be nothing for forgeries to imitate. If the analogy between Descartes's first rationale and the art forgeries analogy holds, then there must be veridical perceptions just as there are genuine artworks, that not all perceptions can be illusory just as not all artworks can be forgeries, and that the concept of a perceptual illusion is equally parasitic on the concept of a veridical perception.

The difficulty remains in that case of trying to distinguish any particular perception as veridical or illusory. The same is true for the art connoisseur who must confront the problem of deciding about any given painting whether it is genuine or a fraud. Merely to know that there must exist at least some genuine artworks is not enough to determine whether this or that particular object is a genuine artwork, nor similarly whether this or that particular sense experience is veridical or illusory. The logical requirements of genuine artworks and veridical perceptions are so minimal that they do not help us to decide which items are the genuine article. All that needs to be true is that there is at some time in some place for some sentient creature at least one original artwork and at least one veridical perception. Where sense experiences are concerned, the perception need not even be the veridical sensation of any human being, let alone of Descartes. In an obvious way, as we consider the truthfulness of any particular perception, we are no better off recognizing that the possibility of illusions depends on veridical perceptions than if we had never admitted the existence of veridical perceptions at all.

DESCARTES'S SECOND—DREAMING—RATIONALE

Descartes does not accept the first rationale for doubting his perceptions, but turns from it to another possibility, which he also criticizes. All told, Descartes considers four reasons for doubting the veridicality of perception, rejecting all but the last. The second rationale for maximum doubt Descartes expresses in these terms, concerning the indistinguishability of waking perceptions from the contents of very vivid dreams. Descartes asks of any perception we might have, for example, right here and now: How do we know that we are not dreaming? If we do not or perhaps cannot know that we are having a waking perception rather than dreaming, then we can have no solid reason to judge of any perception whether it reveals the true nature of things or like dream images is only a creation of fantasy and digestion. Descartes remarks:

> All of this would be well and good, were I not a man who is accustomed to sleeping at night, and to undergoing in my sleep the very same things—or now and then even less likely ones—as do these insane people when they are awake. How often has my evening slumber persuaded me of such customary things as these: that I am here, clothed in my dressing gown, seated at the fireplace, when in fact I am lying undressed between the blankets! But right now I certainly am gazing upon this piece of paper with eyes wide awake. This head which I am moving is not heavy with sleep. I extend this hand consciously and deliberately and I feel it. These things would not be so distinct for one who is asleep. But this all seems as if I do not recall having been deceived by similar thoughts on other occasions in my dreams. As I consider these cases more intently, I see so plainly that there are no definite signs to distinguish being awake from being asleep that I am quite astonished, and this astonishment almost convinces me that I am sleeping. (14)

Descartes tries to infect the reader with the same uneasiness of doubt about the reality of our perceptions. If we cannot prove with epistemic certainty that we are not at this moment merely dreaming rather than perceiving an external world, then how can we be justified in knowing any of the things we believe ourselves to know? He observes:

> But arithmetic, geometry, and other such disciplines—which treat of nothing but the simplest and most general things and which are indifferent as to whether these things do or do not exist—contain something certain and indubitable. For whether

I be awake or asleep, two plus three makes five, and a square does not have more than four sides; nor does it seem possible that such obvious truths can fall under the suspicion of falsity. (15)

Interestingly, although Descartes ultimately wants to make perceptual knowledge as epistemically certain as the demonstrations of mathematics, he complains that the second rationale for maximum skepticism is not powerful enough to set aside beliefs in basic mathematical truths. He claims that the belief that $2 + 2 = 4$ can be just as indubitable whether we consider the proposition when we are wide awake or in a dream. The possibility that he might be dreaming when he thinks he is awake as a result is therefore not a powerful enough wrecking ball to knock down all of his previous beliefs, if we now insist that it must also demolish even his beliefs in the simplest propositions of mathematics.

How else, we must ask, could we ever justify extending the epistemic certainty of mathematics to all natural science and philosophy if we did not also reconsider the epistemic status of mathematical truths? Descartes raises the stakes significantly in this part of his effort to impose maximum skepticism limitations on all of his previous knowledge. Descartes had not previously included extra-perceptual basic beliefs about arithmetic and geometry as targets for maximum skepticism along with perceptual beliefs. Arithmetic and geometry are only mentioned when Descartes rejects the possibility of dreaming as grounds for maximum skepticism on the complaint that it is not strong enough to cast doubt on our belief in their truth. It is not strange to find Descartes arguing that mathematical beliefs can be just as justified in or out of dreams, but it is intriguing to learn for the first time that he proposes also to investigate the epistemic status of mathematics. If mathematical truths are derived entirely from reason, ultimately from the definitions of mathematical concepts, then they are not justified by perception in the first place, and can only have their epistemic credentials verified if we can prove their dependence on something that is epistemically incapable of doubt. Descartes needs a basis for doubt that is so powerful as to overshadow the absolute maximum of everything he previously regarded as knowledge, including his beliefs in many ordinary things.

Does Descartes too quickly reject the possibility that he is dreaming when he believes himself to be perceiving the world? The fact, if it is a fact, that we do not always doubt the truths of mathematics in the dreams we happen to remember does not by itself show that we can never doubt such beliefs when we are dreaming, nor that we can always rightly judge whether or not we are dreaming when we believe during the course of a dream that we are veridically perceiving a real world beyond the dream. Descartes's argument that we do not always doubt the truths of mathematics when we are dreaming appears to be an inadequate reason for dismissing the possibility of dreaming as a basis for general skepticism about the truth of perceptions. To uphold his criticism, Descartes would need to know with epistemic certainty when he is dreaming about the propositions of mathematics and when he is not dreaming but considering them in waking self-conscious life, in order to know with epistemic certainty whether or not we ever mistakenly dream mathematical falsehoods, and whether we might not be doing so now.

Descartes identifies the foundations of all his beliefs that he hopes to upset as involving the fact that all such beliefs are based on perception. The possibility of not doubting mathematical truths when we are dreaming as a result at first seems irrelevant to Descartes's effort to find a reason for universally doubting all his prior perceptual beliefs, and we are surprised to find without warning that he now wants to include extra-perceptual mathematical beliefs along with perceptual beliefs in the limbo of maximum doubt. Descartes cannot simply assume the epistemic certainty of mathematics as a standard for the rest of philosophy and science. He must rather try to demonstrate in terms of reason alone that mathematics too can withstand the full onslaught of the strongest possible argument for doubt. He is surely right to conclude that no one reflecting on the kinds of simple mathematical truths he mentions would be dissuaded from their beliefs by the possibility that they are dreaming. If extra-perceptual mathematical beliefs are to be included along with perceptual beliefs in the reach of maximum skepticism, then he is also right that we must go beyond the dreaming rationale and try to find a more powerful reason for doubting mathematics as well as the truthfulness of perceptions.

DESCARTES'S THIRD—GOD'S OMNIPOTENCE—RATIONALE

Descartes rejects the first, illusion, rationale because it is too strong, bordering on madness. He rejects the second, dreaming, rationale because it is not strong enough, leaving mathematical truths untouched. He next examines the possibility that God as an omnipotent spirit might be able to deceive him whenever he exercises his senses or considers a mathematical belief, and concludes in a moment of apparent enthusiasm that God's omnipotence would make it possible for a person to be deceived even when considering basic mathematical propositions fully awake and with good concentration. He now writes:

> All the same, a certain opinion of long standing has been fixed in my mind, namely that there exists a God who is able to do anything and by whom I, such as I am, have been created. How do I know that he did not bring it about that there be no earth at all, no heavens, no extended thing, no figure, no size, no place, and yet all these things should seem to me to exist precisely as they appear to do now? Moreover—as I judge that others sometimes make mistakes in matters that they believe they know most perfectly—how do I know that I am not deceived every time I add two and three or count the sides of a square or perform an even simpler operation, if such can be imagined? But perhaps God has not willed that I be thus deceived, for it is said that he is supremely good. Nonetheless, if it were repugnant to his goodness that he should have created me such that I be deceived all the time, it would seem from this same consideration, to be foreign to him to permit me to be deceived occasionally. But we cannot make this last assertion. (15)

God by virtue of omnipotence in Descartes's judgment could deceive any thinker about perceptual or mathematical truths. Whenever we believe ourselves to perceive the actual state of the outside world, for all we know, according to Descartes's rationale, God as an infinitely powerful spirit could be deceiving us, planting in our minds false ideas about the real state of the world. Descartes seems briefly satisfied with this hypothesis. The possibility of God's intervention in our cognitive lives might lead us to falsely believe virtually everything we now believe ourselves to know, including mathematical truths as he makes a special point of mentioning. The deceiving God hypothesis allows Descartes to go beyond the limits of the possibility of dreaming rationale, as he must do if he cannot simply take the epistemic certainty of mathematics for granted.

Despite its attractions, Descartes also dismisses the third rationale, on the grounds that objectors might point out that God is supposed to be perfectly benevolent or infinitely good, as well as infinitely wise and powerful. Descartes remarks that while it can appear to be a sign of power to be able to deceive another person, the will to deceive might be regarded as incompatible with God's nature as a perfectly good being. For God to will to deceive us or even to be able to will to deceive us, Descartes suggests, would be a defect in moral character rather than an indication of perfect strength. Accordingly, Descartes sets aside the hypothesis that all of his sense experiences might be deceptively intervened in by God. This, in Descartes's judgment, leaves only one other possibility for general skepticism concerning perception and mathematical thinking, which he finally accepts as the most powerful rationale for maximum skepticism.

DESCARTES'S FOURTH—EVIL DEMON—RATIONALE

Descartes's fourth and final rationale for doubt is the hypothesis that, rather than God, whose perfect benevolence might be incompatible with the will to deceiving us when we perceive, there might be an *evil demon* or *evil genius*, or, as in some translations, a *malignant spirit*. The demon is hypothesized to be as powerful as God in the relevant respects, but has no moral impediments to deceiving us in all the ways Descartes considers in the third rationale. Descartes adds:

> Thus I will suppose not a supremely good God, the source of truth, but rather an evil genius, as clever and deceitful as he is powerful, who has directed his entire effort to misleading me. I will regard the heavens, the air, the earth, colors, shapes, sounds, and all external things as nothing but the deceptive games of my dreams, with which he lays snares for my credulity. I will regard myself as having no hands, no eyes, no flesh, no blood, no senses, but as nevertheless falsely believing that I possess all these things. I will remain resolutely fixed in this meditation, and, even if it be out of my power to know anything true, certainly it is within my power to take care resolutely to withhold my assent to what is false, lest this deceiver, powerful and clever as he is, have an effect on me. (16)

The evil demon hypothesis in Descartes's *Meditations* provides him with what he takes to be the strongest possible justification for doubting all his previous beliefs. Although it had seemed that Descartes had advanced from the dreaming rationale to the God and evil demon rationales in order to have a strong enough reason for doubting even the most basic propositions of mathematics, when he describes the extent of the evil demon's mischief in our cognition he mentions only sensible objects of perception. These doubts are already covered by the dreaming rationale, and Descartes leaves us to wonder exactly how the evil demon could deceive us about the proposition that $2 + 2 = 4$ or that a triangle has three sides. If told that he was only dreaming these things, Descartes says, he would not give up his belief in these truths. Why then would he give them up if told that there is an evil demon interfering with his thoughts? The demon's unlimited power over our thinking, and the fact that the demon as another thinker can choose to deceive us in any of our beliefs, makes the fourth rationale strong enough to cast doubt on perceptual and mathematical beliefs. Descartes nevertheless does not mention mathematical beliefs in his endorsement of the evil demon hypothesis as his final rationale for maximum skepticism. More remarkably, he compares the evil demon's deceptions to the "deceptive games of my dreams." Again, we must consider why Descartes does not simply accept the possibility that we might be dreaming whenever we think we are perceiving an outside world.

Descartes concludes this section of his treatise by remarking that no matter what the evil demon does, the demon cannot prevent Descartes from withholding his assent from any proposition concerning which the demon might deceive him. He emphasizes three possibilities an epistemic agent has with respect to a proposition considered as a potential belief. An agent might accept, reject, or withhold judgment about a belief, neither accepting nor rejecting it. Withholding judgment about the truth or falsehood of a belief is comparable to religious agnosticism. Where religious beliefs are concerned, a person might similarly be a believer in the existence of God, an atheist, or agnostic. An agnostic admits that God might exist, but maintains that there is not enough evidence or good reason to go so far as to accept the proposition that God definitely does exist. If we want to avoid all error in epistemology, then we can accomplish this goal by refusing to accept any belief, either through positive disbelief or suspension of all belief. If we want to maximize knowledge, on the contrary, then we can also do that easily enough by accepting belief in every proposition.

The first choice, sometimes known as *radical skepticism*, completely rules out mistaken beliefs, but does so at the cost of precluding all knowledge. We have no false beliefs, in that case, only because we have no beliefs whatsoever, including true ones, and therefore no knowledge. The second choice, sometimes described as *radical syncretism*, guarantees all knowledge, omniscience in a sense, or at least a full acceptance of all true propositions as beliefs. Unfortunately, it does so only by embracing every belief in every proposition, so that to follow this strategy is to accept all false beliefs equally alongside of all true beliefs, without discrimination. The trick, to find the contested middle ground between these two extremes that epistemology should want to occupy, is to maximize knowledge while minimizing error, maximize the total number of accepted true beliefs, and minimize, and preferably eliminate, the total number of accepted false beliefs.

In order to attain the ideal of maximal knowledge and minimal error, Descartes, intuitively directed toward this same kind of goal in the theory of knowledge, begins at least with a commitment to a methodological skepticism justified by the evil demon hypothesis. When he has cleaned house of all of his formerly potentially erroneous beliefs, he then prepares to rebuild a new edifice of knowledge brick by individually justified brick. Descartes first remarks on his tendency to lapse back into his former acceptance of comfortable familiar beliefs. He feels the need to guard himself from taking the easy route and to encourage vigilance with respect to the restrained epistemic attitude he has at this point only recently cultivated in response to the evil demon hypothesis. This attitude provides a first plank in Descartes's methodological skepticism, the doubt by which he proposes to raze the old edifice of knowledge. He remarks on the psychological difficulties of sustaining this disciplined attitude of agnosticism toward his previous beliefs:

But this undertaking is arduous, and laziness brings me back to my customary way of living. I am not unlike a prisoner who might enjoy an imaginary freedom in his sleep. When he later begins to suspect that he is sleeping, he fears being awakened and conspires slowly with these pleasant illusions. In just this way, I spontaneously fall back into my old beliefs, and dread being awakened, lest the toilsome wakefulness which follows upon a peaceful rest, have to be spent thenceforward not in the light but among the inextricable shadows of the difficulties now brought forward. (16)

The evil demon hypothesis is Descartes's way of driving a distinction between what can and cannot be doubted. Descartes does not suppose that there actually exists such a demon, nor that an evil demon ever actually deceives him. The mere possibility of the demon is enough to challenge the justification of any doubtable knowledge. If an evil demon deceives us, how can we trust the truth of any of our beliefs?

How might we imagine the evil demon deceiving us about the truth of the belief that $2 + 2 = 4$, or that a triangle always has three sides? The demon supposedly must somehow cloud our judgment as we perform these mathematical operations or reflect on the meanings of terms and their conclusions and try to draw inferences; or perhaps the demon plays havoc with our reliance on memory in moving from step to step in any of this mathematical thinking. Whatever explanation is given, it seems we might reasonably ask why our judgment could not equally be clouded simply through the effect of a dream.

More importantly, if the evil demon is able to disrupt even the simplest mathematical reasoning, how can we place any trust in our ability to reason as we work through all the parts of the argument that has taken us this far in following Descartes's search for a rationale for maximum skepticism? If the demon can cast doubt on extra-perceptual thinking about doubt as well as extra-perceptual thinking about mathematics, then the evil demon might be too powerful. Descartes, having let the skeptical genie out of the bottle, might find it impossible to get him back inside. It seems the evil demon might confuse and deceive us when we consider how many conceivable rationales there might be for doubt, which things we can or cannot doubt, whether or not this or that particular basis for doubt, the illusion, dreaming, deceiving God, or evil demon rationales, are strong enough for maximum skepticism without slipping into irrationality.

AN ARCHIMEDEAN POINT—*COGITO, SUM*

In invoking the possibility of an evil demon, Descartes believes he has conjured up the strongest possible basis for doubt. If he is right, then there can be no stronger reason for doubting the truth of any beliefs, perceptual or extra-perceptual. Descartes must raze mathematics along with the old edifice of knowledge in order to make sure that it is on sound foundations before trying to rebuild. The proposition that the evil demon hypothesis is the strongest possible basis for doubt is crucial. It is only by defeating the strongest possible basis for doubt that Descartes believes he can make empirical knowledge epistemically certain.

The more demanding the grounds of skepticism, the stronger the epistemic status of beliefs needed to overcome doubt. After scolding himself for not being able to stick to his resolve to suspend commitment to all beliefs subject to the evil demon's dirty work, Descartes now observes that when he takes the evil demon hypothesis seriously he is overwhelmed by doubts and finds no firm platform for his reasoning. He compares his situation to that of a drowning swimmer caught in whirling water between the bottom he cannot touch and the air above he cannot reach. He makes all his perceptual and mathematical thought precarious when he hypothesizes the evil demon as a rationale for maximum skepticism:

> Yesterday's meditation filled my mind with so many doubts that I can no longer forget about them—nor yet do I see how they are to be resolved. But, as if I had suddenly fallen into a deep whirlpool, I am so disturbed that I can neither touch my foot to the bottom, nor swim up to the top. Nevertheless I will work my way up, and I will follow the same path I trod yesterday, putting aside everything which admits of the least doubt, as if I had discovered it to be absolutely false. I will go forward until I know something certain—or, if nothing else, until I at least know for certain that nothing is certain. Archimedes sought only a firm and immovable point in order to move the entire earth from one place to another. Surely great things are to be hoped for if I am lucky enough to find at least one thing that is certain and indubitable. (17)

The idea of establishing an Archimedean point is to identify a fixed and immovable foundation. Archimedes was an ancient Greek mathematician and engineer who claimed that if he could find a single fixed point in outer space to act as a fulcrum, and a sufficiently long and perfectly rigid lever, then he could, as an application of basic physical principles, move the entire planet Earth merely by exerting human energy at the opposite end of the lever. Descartes remarks that he is similarly in search of an immovable point, by which he means an indubitable belief, something that is epistemically certain in the sense that its truth cannot rationally be doubted. With such an Archimedean point in hand, Descartes believes he can reconstruct a modern edifice of epistemically certain mathematical and scientific knowledge.

The evil demon hypothesis, as powerful as it is, cannot justify doubt about a philosophically important belief. Descartes reasons that at least whenever he is thinking, he exists, and in particular that he exists whenever he considers the proposition that he exists or that he thinks. Thinking for Descartes is meant to include any mental occurrence, including belief, doubt, pain, joy, reflecting on the content of a thought or its expression, and the like. Descartes summarizes the principle, in a form adapted from Saint Augustine, as the *Cogito, sum*—meaning, in Latin, literally, "I think, I am."

The belief that Descartes exists whenever he thinks is supposed to be epistemically certain in the sense that the proposition holds up even under the evil demon hypothesis. The evil demon hypothesis is supposed to be the strongest rationale for maximum doubt. The worst mischief the evil demon can inflict on Descartes is to cause him to doubt the truth of his beliefs. Descartes argues that if he doubts then he thinks and if he thinks then he exists, so it is epistemically certain that he exists whenever he thinks, including whenever he doubts or is deceived. The epistemically certain belief that he exists while he is thinking in the subjectivity of his mental life is Descartes's Archimedean point from which he proposes to rebuild all genuine knowledge.

DESCARTES'S MEDITATION TWO PROOF
THAT HIS SOUL ≠ HIS BODY

The title of Meditation Two, "Concerning the Nature of the Human Mind: That the Mind is More Known Than the Body," introduces the second main promise in Descartes's treatise, to prove that the soul is not identical with the body. He argues that the self, soul, ego, person, or subject is an essentially thinking thing, and that the body is only accidental and not essential to the existence of thought and hence to that which thinks. He asks whether his existence depends on that of his body, and quickly decides that he must be something other than and different from his physical flesh and blood. In this respect, Descartes is more closely in agreement with Socrates and Plato than Aristotle. He nevertheless adopts Aristotle's terminology for the distinction between essential and accidental properties of substances in arguing that he is essentially a thinking thing that is only accidentally united with a material body. He asks:

> Am I so tied to the body and to the senses that I cannot exist without them? But I have persuaded myself that there is nothing at all in the world: no heaven, no earth, no minds, no bodies. Is it not then true that I do not exist? But certainly I should exist, if I were to persuade myself of something. But there is a deceiver—I know not who he is—powerful and sly in the highest degree, who is always purposely deceiving me. Then there is no doubt that I exist, if he deceives me. And deceive me as he will, he can never bring it about that I am nothing so long as I shall think that I am something. Thus it must be granted that, after weighing everything carefully and sufficiently, one must come to the considered judgment that the statement "I am, I exist" is necessarily true every time it is uttered by me or conceived in my mind. (17)

Descartes promises to prove the existence of God and the distinction between mind and body. In Meditation Two, he makes the first installment toward demonstrating a distinction between body and soul. He argues that there must be a difference between body and soul because the existence of the body can be rationally doubted as a consequence of the evil demon hypothesis, but that the existence of the soul cannot rationally be doubted because of the *Cogito, sum*.

Descartes relies on sense perception for his belief that he has a physical body. He sees his torso and limbs when he looks down or in a mirror. At the same time he experiences other perceptual aspects of his body by means of his other senses, including proprioception as an extension of the sense of touch. The evil demon hypothesis is meant to cast doubt on all sensation-based perceptual belief. If the demon is at his deviltry when Descartes consults his senses for evidence of his possession of a body, then any of the data by which Descartes comes to believe in the existence of his body can be doubted. He must then, in keeping with his resolve to rein in knowledge to the limits of the evil demon hypothesis, adopt an attitude of doubt or at least agnostic suspension of belief with respect to the existence of his body or any of its perceived parts.

The existence of Descartes's mind is a different matter. Descartes argues that, unlike the existence of his body, he cannot rationally doubt the existence of his mind. There may be no stronger basis for doubt than the evil demon hypothesis, but the evil demon can at worst do no more than cause Descartes to think false beliefs. If Descartes doubts, then he thinks; and if he thinks, then he exists. He exists in that event as a combination of body and spirit. He is not essentially body, but only accidentally embodied. His mind is not simply his body or a part of his body, because he has epistemically certain knowledge that his mind exists, but not that his body exists. Body and mind therefore cannot be the same. To believe that an evil demon deceives him about the truthfulness of his perceptions as information about the real state of the world, Descartes must still exist as essentially a thinker, a thinking thing that can be deceived.

With the difference between the better knowability of mind and the lesser knowability of body as background, Descartes begins to reflect on what kind of thing he is, whether essentially material or immaterial, or something else again. "But I do not yet understand well enough who I am," he admits, "—I, who now necessarily exist" (17). He pauses to reconsider some of his previously unquestioned beliefs about himself, prior to taking up the evil demon hypothesis as a challenge to the truth of his beliefs. He questions himself introspectively:

> What therefore did I formerly think I was? A man, of course. But what is a man? Might I not say a rational animal? No, because then one would have to inquire what an "animal" is and what "rational" means. And then from only one question we slide into many more difficult ones. Nor do I now have enough free time that I want to waste it on subtleties of this sort. But rather here I pay attention to what spontaneously and at nature's lead came into my thought beforehand whenever I pondered what I was. Namely, it occurred to me first that I have a face, hands, arms, and this entire mechanism of bodily members, the very same as are discerned in a corpse—which I referred to by the name "body." (18)

He recalls that none of these properties can justifiably be predicated of himself, and that none of his beliefs in this category can be sustained in opposition to the evil demon hypothesis while it remains in place. If he is ever to restore belief in the existence of his body, Descartes makes clear, it can only be by first arriving at good reasons for rejecting the evil demon hypothesis not only as false but as impossible, as an epistemically certain conclusion that logically no evil demon can diabolically instill our cognition with confusion, falsehood, or deceit. The argument continues:

> These are surely nothing but illusions, because I do not have a body. How about sensing? Again, this also does not happen without a body, and I judge that I really did not sense those many things I seemed to have sensed in my dreams. How about thinking? Here I discover that thought is an attribute that really does belong to me. This alone cannot be detached from me. I am; I exist; this is certain. But for how long? For as long as I think. Because perhaps it could also come to pass that if I should cease from all thinking I would then utterly cease to exist. I now admit nothing that is not necessarily true. I am therefore precisely only a thing that thinks; that is, a mind, or soul, or intellect, or reason—words the meaning of which I was ignorant before. Now, I am a true thing, and truly existing; but what kind of thing? I have said it already: a thing that thinks. (18–19)

The implication is that Descartes believes with epistemic certainty that he exists, but does not know, while the evil demon hypothesis yet prevails, that his body exists. Therefore, he concludes, he is not identical with his body nor is he essentially an embodied thing. Rather, he is an essentially thinking thing, because, although he can rationally doubt the existence of his body, he cannot rationally doubt the existence of his mind. If it is true that Descartes can know with epistemic certainty that he is essentially a thinking thing that is only accidentally embodied in a perceivable flesh and blood body, then the soul as the thinking part of a person must be distinct from the physical body, and hence in principle capable of surviving the body's death. This is just as orthodox Christianity and other traditional religions teach their followers as an article of faith, but which Descartes believes he has now rationally justified.

The demonstration of a difference between body and soul in Descartes's Meditation Two depends on the evil demon hypothesis and the *Cogito, sum.* Were it not for the *Cogito, sum,* Descartes would succumb entirely to what he calls the "whirlpool" of doubt. The fact that he exists whenever he thinks, and can know this to be epistemically certain for at least as long as he thinks, is the Archimedean point with which Descartes expects to attain "great things" in his project to establish a new and revolutionary first philosophy to replace Aristotle's, and to establish new and revolutionary epistemically certain foundations for all empirical scientific knowledge.

COGITO, SUM AS INFERENCE OR PRINCIPLE

In the *Discourse on Method,* Descartes formulates the *Cogito* in something more like an inference, which he writes as: *Cogito, ergo sum.* The *ergo* term is significant, because it means "therefore" in Latin, suggesting that in that context Descartes understands the *Cogito* as a deductive argument. In the *Meditations,* Descartes says only that whenever he thinks about the question he knows with absolute epistemic certainty that he exists. The distinction between whether the *Cogito* is intended as an inference or principle is important, because many critics have objected that it would be circular reasoning to infer from the assumption "I think," the conclusion, *therefore,* "I exist." The question is, What could entitle Descartes to begin with the premise that anything at all is true of an "I," an ego, self, person, or soul that thinks, without assuming from the outset that an "I" exists? What or who is this "I" that Descartes believes thinks, and how does the epistemic certainty that such a thing exists contribute to Descartes's goal of rebuilding all of knowledge with the same degree of certainty?

In Descartes's defense it might be said that even if he is not justified in immediately accepting the assumption "I think" unless or until he establishes the conclusion "I exist," he can nevertheless infer the proposition without much difficulty. The problem is much the same even in Descartes's *Cogito, sum* formulation in the *Meditations* as in the *Cogito, ergo sum* version in the *Discourse.* The issue is whether Descartes is correct to speak of an "I," of whether or not an assumption about the "I" can justifiably be incorporated into Descartes's reasoning as part of a deductive inference. Reference to the "I" is explicit even by the inflected Latin ending "o" in the term "*Cogito,*" which is literally translated "I think."

Critics of Descartes's *Cogito, ergo sum* in the *Discourse* and of the *Cogito, sum* in the *Meditations* often allow that Descartes is justified in beginning with the assumption "Thinking occurs," even if it is not the thinking specifically of an "I," ego, person, self, or soul. The proposition might nevertheless be all that Descartes needs in order to work his way back to the original assumption, "I think," in which reference to the first person thinker appears. In anything resembling an Aristotelian framework of substance and properties, it seems unavoidable to conclude that if thinking occurs, then the predicable thinking must apply to a substance, a subject or thinking thing.

What harm, let us ask rhetorically, can there then be in stipulating that such a thinking substance, the only one that each of us experiences directly rather than infers from the external behavior of others, the subject of thinking or thinking thing as we can only directly know it, be called "I," purely as a linguistic convention? If this is not unreasonable, then Descartes is in a comfortable position from which to deduce "I think" from the more cautious pronouncement that "Thinking occurs." Descartes reaffirms his commitment to the first-person subject of experience and its psychological states as something whose existence is incapable of being rationally doubted, when he inquires:

> But what then am I? A thing that thinks. What is that? A thing that doubts, understands, affirms, wills, refuses, and which also imagines and senses. It is truly no small matter if all of these things pertain to me. But why should they not pertain to me? Is it not I who now doubt almost everything, I who nevertheless understand something, I who affirm that this one thing is true, I who deny other things, I who desire to know more things, I who wish not to be deceived, I who imagine many things against my will, I who take note of many things as if coming from the senses? Is there anything in all of this which is not just as true as it is that I am, even if I am always dreaming or even if the one who created me tries as hard as possible to delude me? Are any of these attributes distinct from my thought? What can be said to be separate from myself? (19–20)

Descartes's final question sets the problem for the next step in his program. If he has demonstrated his own epistemically certain existence as a thinking thing, then the further task for his first philosophy, as he clearly recognizes, is to determine what if anything can be known to the same high degree of epistemic certainty as existing outside himself, beyond the limits and contents of his thoughts. He proposes in a series of steps to prove the existence of God.

DESCARTES'S PIECE OF WAX

To pursue his strategy to the next level, from the immovable epistemically certain Archimedean point of his own existence to epistemically certain beliefs about the existence of things outside himself, Descartes first attempts to establish a distinction between the degree of certainty afforded by two kinds of experiential belief. He begins with the mind's experience of itself, of the immediately experienced contents of its own thoughts, as contrasted with sense experience of things that appear to exist outside itself. Descartes accordingly proposes to prove that the mind is better knowable than the body. In a way, this conclusion is already available from the combined force of the evil demon hypothesis and the *Cogito, sum.* Descartes now makes the implication explicit.

He brings us into his study as he examines an ordinary object, a piece of wax, from a desktop candle, perhaps, or a piece of sealing wax. He reflects on what we can believe about the wax and how we come to believe it, and the source of our justifi-cation. The passage in the *Meditations* where Descartes describes the features of the piece of wax is a vivid portrayal of a philosopher's thought processes as he muses over an object he is holding in his fingers. He writes:

> Let us consider those things which are commonly believed to be the most dis-tinctly comprehended of all: namely the bodies which we touch and see. But not bodies in general, for these generic perceptions are often somewhat more con-fused; rather let us consider one body in particular. Let us take, for instance, this piece of wax. It has very recently been taken from the honeycombs; it has not as yet lost all the flavor of its honey. It retains some of the smell of the flowers from which it was collected. Its color, shape, and size are obvious. It is hard and cold. It can easily be touched, and if you rap on it with a knuckle it makes a sound. In short, everything is present in it that appears to be needed in order that a body can be known as distinctly as possible. (20)

The piece of wax we believe to have all the properties Descartes describes as he turns it over in his hand. Since it is a small easily scrutinized object, it is as clearly and distinctly perceived as any physical entity we might imagine. We can not only see its color, shape, and so on, just as Descartes says, but he brings it to life as we read about its flavor of honey and smell of blossoms, texture and temperature, and even the sounds it makes. If we cannot reach clarity about the physical properties of such an immediately perceivable object, then we cannot hope to focus our senses more concentratedly on any other more elusive and questionable object of experience. Descartes quickly shifts to a consideration of what happens to the wax when it is heated beyond its melting point, and changes all of the properties he had previously listed as belonging to it. We can easily perform the experiment ourselves with little trouble if we can only find an ordinary piece of wax. Descartes explains:

> But notice that while I am speaking, it is brought close to the fire; the remaining traces of the honey flavor are purged; the odor vanishes; the color is changed; the original shape disappears. Its magnitude increases, it becomes liquid and hot, and can hardly be touched; and now, when you knock on it, it does not emit any sound. Up to this point, does the same wax remain? One must confess that it does: no one denies it; no one thinks otherwise. What was there then in the wax that was so distinctly comprehended? Certainly none of the things that I reached by means of the senses. For whatever came under taste or smell or sight or touch or hear-ing by now has changed, yet the wax remains. (20–21)

Descartes draws several important conclusions about the wax as it is transformed by its proximity to the fire. His interest in the problem of change and in what Aris-totle would call an alteration in a primary substance is clearly related to what we have previously discussed as the main underlying problem of Aristotle's first philosophy. It should come as no surprise then that Descartes turns to the same subject in his meditations on first philosophy.

Although in broad outline and despite other significant disagreements with Aris-totle's metaphysics, Descartes appears at least to accept Aristotle's concept of primary substance and the distinction between essential and accidental properties. He differs from Aristotle also in his theory of the requirements under which the properties of the object can be known. Descartes maintains that when the wax changes all its immediately perceptible properties, the wax, as Aristotle would also undoubtedly agree, persists through the accidental changes of its original color, shape, size, texture, odor, taste, and sound. Descartes appeals to common sense in arguing that no one denies that the wax survives these presumably accidental changes, that "no one thinks otherwise."

The question Descartes raises that does not seem to have occurred to Aristotle is how or why we believe that it is the very same piece of wax that undergoes these changes. He assumes that there are only three possibilities, and he eliminates two of them, leaving only the third. The choices are that the wax is determined to be the same either by the senses, imagination, or by the judgment of mind, which is to say by reason. Sensation is ruled out by Descartes when he argues that there is no single continuously sensible property of the piece of wax that is experienced before and after the change brought about by its proximity to the fire. The color, taste, shape, size, odor, and so on, everything he posits as having been altered; so we cannot appeal to these perceptible properties as evidence that it is the same piece of wax that has undergone a series of accidental changes. Imagination is ruled out by Descartes on the grounds that we understand that the wax is capable of undergoing indefinitely many more changes than we are capable of imagining.

If it is not through sensation or imagination that we believe the wax to remain the same through its changes of state, but we are correct in thinking that the original piece has not been replaced by another piece of wax with totally different perceivable properties, then, as Descartes argues, we can only arrive at the belief that the wax persists as the same thing through the alteration of all of its perceptible properties as a conclusion of reason or judgment of mind. He writes:

> It remains then for me to concede that I in no way imagine what this wax is, but perceive it by the mind only. I am speaking about this piece of wax in particular, for it is clearer in the case of wax in general. But what is this wax which is perceived only by the mind? It is the same that I see, touch, and imagine; in short it is the same as I took it to be from the very beginning. But we must take note of the fact that the perception of the wax is neither by sight, nor touch, nor imagination, nor was it ever so (although it seemed so before), but rather an inspection on the part of the mind alone. (21)

Descartes offers next to draw a further conclusion about the knower, the I or subject of knowledge who comprehends the piece of wax by means of an "inspection of the mind alone." By this Descartes must mean a faculty of reason or rational intuition or reflection other than ordinary sensation or imagination. There is something worthwhile to be learned, Descartes thinks, from the fact that the piece of wax is better known by mind than by perception.

What follows from the fact that we know the wax persists through changes of all its perceptible properties is that the mind knows itself even more certainly than it knows anything whatsoever about the wax. By implication, the mind knows itself more truly and with greater certainty than it knows anything about any other perceivable thing external to the mind. The conclusion is a further inference of the evil demon hypothesis that casts doubt on belief in the existence of the wax or any perceivable object and the *Cogito, sum,* by which the existence of the mind, self, or soul remains indubitable in spite of the imaginable deceptions of a hypothetical evil demon. Descartes offers the illustration as an opportunity to reflect on the nature of the thinking self:

> What, I say, am I who seem to perceive this wax so distinctly? Do I not know myself not only much more truly and with more certainty, but also much more distinctly and evidently. For if I judge that the wax exists from the fact that I see it, certainly it follows much more evidently that I myself exist, from the fact that I see the wax. For it could happen that what I see is not truly wax. It could happen that I have no eyes with which to see anything. But it could not happen that, while I see or think I see (I do not now distinguish these two), I who think am not something. Likewise, if I judge that the wax exists from the fact that I touch it, the same thing will again follow: I exist. If from the fact that I imagine, or from whatever other cause, the same thing readily follows. But what I noted regarding the wax applies to all the other things that are external to me. Furthermore, if the perception of the wax seemed more distinct after it became known to me not only from sight or touch, but from many causes, how much more distinctly I must be known to myself; for there are no considerations that can aid in the perception of the wax or any other body without these considerations demonstrating even better the nature of my mind. (22)

Descartes summarizes the moral of the piece of wax story in the following paragraph, and on this note concludes Meditation Two:

> Since I know that bodies are not, properly speaking, perceived by the senses or by the faculty of imagination, but only by the intellect, and since, moreover, I know that they are not perceived by being touched or seen, but only insofar as they are expressly understood, nothing can be more easily and more evidently perceived by me than my mind. But because an established habit of belief cannot be put aside so quickly, it is appropriate to stop here so that by the length of my meditation this new knowledge may be more deeply impressed on my memory. (23)

EXISTENCE AND VERACITY OF GOD

Meditation Three is titled, "Concerning God, That He Exists." Descartes is ready at this stage to study himself, that is to say his mind, in greater detail, as the only thing of whose existence he is epistemically certain. The demon hypothesis and *Cogito* are supposed to have shown that he can know the existence of his own mind with absolute certainty, and the piece of wax example is supposed to have shown that the nature of his mind is better known internally to itself than it can possibly know anything else.

Descartes begins to examine his thinking in order to better understand his essence as a thinking thing. These reflections lead him to a demonstration of the existence of God. The proof that God exists in Descartes's *Meditations* is supposed to establish the first entity outside his own mind as he turns outward from the resources of his immediate consciousness to certify his perceptual beliefs in the existence and condition of the external world. The necessary existence and absolute truthfulness of God are central to Descartes's efforts to rebuild epistemically certain knowledge on epistemically certain foundations. He first suspends his usual reliance on the senses and his ordinary commonsense belief in the sensible things that appear to exist, and looks more deeply into himself and the contents of his ideas. He reinforces his earlier impressions of what the evil demon can and cannot cause him to doubt:

> Now I will shut my eyes, I will stop up my ears, I will divert all my senses, I will even blot out from my thoughts all images of corporeal things—or at least, since the latter can hardly be done, I will regard these images as nothing, empty and false as indeed they are. And as I converse only with myself and look more deeply into myself, I will attempt to render myself gradually better known and familiar to myself. I am a thing that thinks, that is to say, a thing that doubts, affirms, denies, knows a few things, is ignorant of many things, wills, rejects, and also imagines and senses. As I observed earlier, although these things that I sense or imagine may perhaps be nothing at all outside me, nevertheless I am certain that these modes of thinking—which I call sensations and imaginations—insofar as they are only modes of thinking, are within me. (23)

We might think of Descartes entering more deeply into himself as he waits out the storm in his heated cabinet during the war in Germany, much as if he were in a sensory deprivation booth. Here he concentrates on the contents of his thoughts without the distractions of the senses. He takes inventory again of the things of which he is epistemically certain that he believes he has already established in his meditations. He appears to have made good progress in articulating general principles for the attainment of knowledge, making his first reference to the suggestion that whatever he clearly and distinctly perceives must be true:

> I am certain that I am a thing that thinks. But do I not therefore also know what is required so that I may be certain of something? Surely in this first instance of knowing, there is nothing else than a certain clear and distinct perception of what I affirm. Yet this would hardly be sufficient to render me certain of the truth of a thing, if it could ever happen that something that I perceive so clearly and distinctly were false. And thus I now seem to be able to posit as a general rule that what I very clearly and distinctly perceive is true. (23)

Attracted as he appears to be to this general epistemic principle, Descartes finds that he cannot accept it in view of the evil demon hypothesis. Oddly, he puts the objection to the principle in terms of his third rationale for doubt, the deceiving God hypothesis, although he speaks of "some God" rather than simply of "God," indicating that he might want to include the evil demon as a very powerful spirit under this same category.

He explains that in the past he had accepted the clear and distinct perception principle. Perhaps this explains what were actually his earlier successes in mathematics and the sciences, which he now questions in light of the evil demon hypothesis. He identifies a connection between epistemically certain belief and the principle of clear and distinct perception. He tries to justify the truthfulness of clear and distinct perceptions in spite of the possibility of an evil demon on the grounds that God exists and is no deceiver, and is the perfect designer of our perceptual and cognitive faculties. He describes the argument in these terms:

To be sure, I did decide later on that I must doubt these things for no other reason than that it entered my mind that some God could have given me a nature such that I might be deceived—even about matters that seemed most evident. For every time this preconceived opinion about the supreme power of God occurs to me, I am constrained to admit that, it he wishes, it is very easy for him to cause me to err, even in those matters that I think I have intuited as plainly as possible with the eyes of the mind. Yet every time I turn my attention to those very things that I think I perceive with such great clarity, I am so entirely persuaded by these things that I spontaneously burst out with these words: "let him who can deceive me; as long as I think that I am something, he will never bring it about that I am nothing, or one day make it true that I never existed, because it is true now that I am; nor will he ever bring it about that two plus three yield more or less than five or that similar matters, in which I recognize an obvious contradiction exist." (24)

Descartes refers to the power of God in order to dramatize the power he imagines the evil demon to exercise over his thoughts. Having invoked the concept of God, he takes the opportunity to point out that the threat of godly power as a basis for maximum skepticism is not established as anything more than a hypothesis. He has said nothing thus far to discourage even the possibility that it is God or a god who might deceive him, and he explains that in order to eliminate the basis for such doubt he must next examine the question of whether there is a God and whether God could be a deceiver. He makes a subtle slide from speaking of an evil demon who might deceive him in his perceptual beliefs and God or a god who might or might not be capable of such deception:

And, certainly, because I have no occasion for thinking that there is a God who deceives, and because I am not certain whether there even is a God, the reason for doubting—depending as it does on the above hypothesis—is very tenuous and, so to speak, metaphysical. Moreover, in order to remove this doubt, I ought at the first opportunity to inquire if there is a God, and, if there is, whether or not he can be a deceiver. If I am ignorant of these matters, I do not think I can ever be certain of anything else. (24)

The important connection between the evil demon and the concept of God in Descartes's Meditation Three is the power they are imagined to possess in equal measure. The only difference separating God and the evil demon is that the demon is evil whereas God is supposed to be infinitely good. Where the question of the potential to be deceived by some kind of spirit is concerned, God and the evil demon are on precisely equal terms. This makes it appropriate from Descartes's perspective to speak of the two together and to consider them both as relevant to the problem of attaining epistemic certainty. If the evil demon is so powerful, then God, and perhaps only God, could be powerful enough to thwart the possibility that an evil demon could deceive us in our efforts to attain perceptual knowledge. This is the line of argument Descartes undertakes. By proving that God exists and is no deceiver he hopes to lay to rest the strongest possible challenge to the veridicality of clear and distinct perceptions, and thus to make sensation-based knowledge epistemically certain, resistant to the greatest conceivable challenge to the truthfulness of clear and distinct perception in the form of the evil demon hypothesis.

Descartes proceeds from his conclusion in the piece of wax example by examining the contents of his ideas, recognizing that he is essentially a thinking thing and that his mind is better knowable to itself than it can possibly know anything outside itself. He orients the discussion in these terms, concerning the distinct sources of several kinds of ideas:

> Among these ideas, some seem to me to be innate, some seem to be derived from an external source, and some seem to be produced by me. I understand what a thing is, what truth is, what thought is—I do not seem to have derived these from any source other than from my very own nature. But now I hear a noise, I see the sun, and I feel a fire; until this point I judged that these things proceeded from certain things existing outside me. Finally, I judged that sirens, hippogriffs, and the like have been formed by me. Or perhaps I could also suppose that all of these ideas are derived from an external source, or are innate, or are produced, for I have not yet ascertained clearly their true origin. (25)

Descartes divides the ideas he finds in himself into several categories, according to their origins. Some are innate, some manufactured by him, which is to say by his reason or imagination, as in the case of ideas of mythological creatures, and some, significantly, seem to derive from an external source. Descartes is not yet in a position to say that he knows with epistemic certainty where his ideas come from, especially in the case of ideas he believes to have external sources outside his own mind. Nor does he know that his ideas have such a wide diversity of sources, although the piece of wax example is supposed to show that the mind has a special epistemic intimacy with its own nature and its own contents. Conceivably, all of Descartes's ideas, at this stage of his inquiry, might derive from the malicious activity of the evil demon, imprinting thoughts on Descartes's internal psychology that do not correspond with any external reality. It is enough for Descartes's immediate purposes that these ideas appear to have such a diversity of sources.

Against the possibility that any of his ideas are owing to the evil demon, Descartes advances the most important principle of his Meditation Three proof for the existence and veracity of God. He argues that whatever the source of any of his ideas, it is a general truth, revealed by the light of nature or *lumen naturale*, that the cause of an idea must have at least as much *formal reality* as the idea has *objective reality*. These are technical terms with an Aristotelian-Scholastic flavor that Descartes does not say much to explain. By "formal reality," Descartes means actuality or real existence, and by objective reality, despite the misleading character of the name, he means the degree of completeness and vividness of an idea considered a particular object of thought. Although we are accustomed to think of anything objective as real, public, and independent of subjective attitude, Descartes uses the term *objective reality* in another of its senses with reference to the objects of thoughts that might but need not exist. We can think of an object either in perception, memory, or imagination and regard it as having a certain internal degree of completeness and vividness. If I consider an imaginary beast, such as a winged horse, I might imagine it as being more or less complete, in greater or less detail. I might imagine the animal in very general terms simply as a horse with wings, or I might imagine it as having a definite color, wings with feathers or fur, a stallion or a mare, an Arabian or a Clydesdale, and so on. The more completely and vividly I imagine the winged horse, the greater its degree, Descartes will say, of objective reality.

Descartes posits a principle about the source of ideas by which the cause of any idea must have at least as much formal reality or actuality as the idea has objective reality or degree of completeness and vividness as an object of thought. Descartes maintains that the principle is revealed by the light of nature; a highly significant admission that must be more thoroughly considered. The principle seems to be recommended on the grounds that to deny the principle would be unintelligibly to assert that the objective reality of an idea can be uncaused or lack an adequate or sufficient cause, which is to say that something can be produced from nothing. The standard Latin phrase, which Descartes does not use here, is: *Ex nihilo nihil fit.* It means literally that from nothing nothing comes or nothing can be made. The idea in Descartes's application is that if we have an idea of God, then the idea must have some definite cause, for otherwise it must come from nothing whatsoever, which is impossible.

Having suspended belief in the truth of any of his perceptual beliefs, Descartes has not suspended his commitment to reason. Indeed, his entire way of proceeding in the *Meditations* would not be possible except as an exercise of reason. If reason supports the principle that the cause of any of our ideas must have at least as much formal reality as the idea has objective reality, then Descartes is prepared to consider a number of alternative causes in particular of the idea of God which he claims to discover within himself as he reflects with the aid of the light of nature on the contents of his mind's most intimately known thoughts. Descartes takes the next step in the development of his proof for the existence of God:

> But still another path occurs to me for inquiring whether there are some objects, from among those things of which there are ideas in me, that exist outside me. Now, insofar as these ideas are merely modes of thought, I do not see any inequality among them; they all seem to proceed from me in the same way. But insofar as one idea represents one thing and another idea another thing, it is obvious that they are very different from one another. There is no question that those ideas that exhibit substances to me are something more and, as I phrase it, contain more objective reality in themselves than those which represent only modes or accidents. Again, the idea that enables me to understand a highest God, one who is eternal, infinite, omniscient, omnipotent, and creator of all things other than himself, has more objective reality in it than those ideas through which finite substances are exhibited. (26–27)

The principle about the metaphysical status of the cause of an idea on which he relies is clearly stated, as he continues:

> But it is evident by the light of nature that at the very least there must be as much in the total efficient cause as there is in the effect of that same cause. For, I ask, where can an effect get its reality unless it be from its cause? And how can the cause give that reality to the effect, unless the cause also has that reality? Hence it follows that something cannot come into existence from nothing, nor even can what is more perfect, that is, that contains in itself more reality, come into existence from what contains less. But this is clearly true not merely for those effects whose reality is actual or formal, but also for ideas in which only objective reality is considered. (27)

It might be wondered whether the evil demon could not also confuse Descartes and lead him to draw incorrect inferences about the causes of his ideas, much as Descartes is supposed to be capable of being deceived when he perceives and tries to discover empirical truths about the outside world. This, Descartes argues, would be going too far; he does not imagine that the evil demon could have power over his reason.

If the demon could deceive Descartes's reason as well as his perceptual and mathematical judgment, then Descartes would have no possibility of rebuilding knowledge, or even of arriving at a rational way of tearing down the old edifice of knowledge. Descartes rejects the second rationale for maximum skepticism based on the possibility that he is always deceived by perceptual illusions. He does not want to reduce his state of mind to that of deranged persons who are convinced that they are gourds or that their heads are made of glass, and for the same reason he will not allow the evil demon to have control over his reason in addition to the truthfulness of his sense perceptions.

If reason or the light of nature is protected from the evil demon, and if the purely rational principle that the cause of any of our ideas must have at least as much formal reality as the idea has objective reality so that theoretically we do not try to get something for nothing, then Descartes can proceed to apply the principle to any of his ideas. He begins with an illustration and analogies involving the causes of ordinary physical objects, which he then applies to the reality requirements of his ideas:

> This means, for example, that a stone, which did not exist before, can in no way begin to exist now, unless it be produced by something in which there is, either formally or eminently, everything that is in the stone; nor can heat be introduced into a subject which was not hot before unless it is done by something that is of at least as perfect an order as heat—the same holds true for the rest. Moreover, in me there can be no idea of heat, or of a stone, unless it comes to me from some cause that has at least as much reality as I conceive to be in the heat or in the stone. (27)

Descartes thinks that from the light of nature alone he can prove that if he has any ideas whose cause entails greater formal reality than can be provided by his own mind, its faculties, or any of its ideas, then there must exist something beyond or outside of his mind as the cause of its ideas. This is the essential next step in Descartes's efforts to rebuild knowledge, extending epistemic certainty by the light of nature, first, to the epistemically certain existence of his own mind in the *Cogito, sum*, and now to the equally epistemically certain existence of something outside of his own mind. All of this is supposed to occur in spite of the evil demon, or at least of the hypothesis that there could be an evil demon who acts viciously to confuse and deceive our minds. As Descartes puts it, in that case he will have proved from the light of nature and his mind's examination of its own intimately known ideas, that he himself cannot be the cause of the idea, and that therefore he is not alone in the world. He argues:

> Why, if the objective reality of one of my ideas is such that I am certain that the same reality is not formally or eminently in me, and that therefore I myself cannot be the cause of the idea, then it necessarily follows that I am not alone in the world, and that something else—the cause of this idea—also exists. If in fact no such idea is found in me, I shall plainly have no argument to make me certain

of the existence of something other than myself. For I have looked at all of these arguments most diligently and so far I have been unable to find any other. (28)

With the framework in place, Descartes turns to consider his idea of God. He asks whether his own mind or something else other than God could possibly be the cause of his idea of God. Given the principle revealed by the demon-proof light of nature that the cause of any of his ideas must have at least as much formal reality as the idea has objective reality, Descartes argues that no other candidate cause has enough formal reality to possibly be the cause of his idea of God. The particular content of his idea of God and its particular degree of objective reality, considered in the first instance merely as an object of thought, could not be caused by anything other than God. Descartes opens this next part of the argument by introducing the fact that among his many ideas as he reflects on the contents of his thoughts is the idea of God:

> Among my ideas, in addition to the one that represents me to myself—about which there can be no difficulty at this point—there are some that represent God, others that represent inanimate, corporeal objects, others that represent angels, others that represent animals, and finally others that represent men like myself. (28)

The causes of most, even virtually all, of his ideas, Descartes acknowledges, need not be the things represented by or in the ideas. The idea of God, on the contrary, for very interesting reasons, turns out to be the only exception. If the idea of God cannot be caused by anything with less formal reality than God, then God exists:

> As to the ideas that represent other men, animals, or angels, I easily understand that they can be formed from the ideas that I have of myself, or corporeal things, and of God—even if no men except myself, no animals, and no angels were to exist in the world. . . . Thus there remains only the idea of God. We must consider whether there is in this idea something which could not have originated from me. I understand by the word "God" an infinite and independent substance, intelligent and powerful in the highest degree, who created me along with everything else—if in fact there is anything else. Indeed all these qualities are such that, the more diligently I attend to them, the less they seem capable of having arisen from myself alone. Thus, from what has been said above, we must conclude that God necessarily exists. (28–30)

This is a startling result. It is a momentous occasion in philosophy when a thinker proposes to prove the existence of God. Historically, there have been a number of highly contested efforts to demonstrate that God exists, by comparison with which Descartes's argument in Meditation Three stands out as original and unique. To secure his conclusion, Descartes examines alternative answers about the source and cause of his idea of God, and rejects each in turn as inadequate for one specific reason or another, all lacking sufficient formal reality to serve as the cause of his idea of God, given its high degree of objective reality. Thus, to survey the main alternative explanations, Descartes argues:

> For although the idea of substance is in me by virtue of the fact that I am a substance, nevertheless it would not for that reason be the idea of an infinite substance, unless it proceeded from some substance which is in fact infinite, because I am finite. (30)

> Nor should I think that I do not perceive the infinite by means of a true idea, but only through a negation of the finite, just as I perceive rest and shadows by means of a negation of motion and light. On the contrary, I clearly understand that there is more reality in an infinite substance than there is in a finite one. Thus the perception of the infinite somehow exists in me prior to the perception of the finite, that is, the perception of God exists prior to the perception of myself. Why would I know that I doubt and I desire, that is, that I lack something and that I am not wholly perfect, if there were no idea in me of a more perfect being by comparison with which I might acknowledge my defects? (30)

Descartes rejects the suggestion that his idea of God might have been assembled from a number of distinct sources. Suppose that each source has just enough formal reality to account for the objective reality of its corresponding part in the resulting composite idea of God. Could Descartes's idea of God have derived from separate causes of the ideas of power, knowledge, and goodness, as found in objects of his experience, together, perhaps, with the idea of infinity as expressed in mathematics, to synthesize an idea of an infinitely powerful, knowledgeable, and perfectly benevolent God? Descartes denies the possibility, arguing that it is an indispensable aspect of his idea that God is a unified entity, in which all of these infinite properties are exemplified in a single thing. Although it should be possible in principle to assemble an idea of a being with any choice of the properties associated with God, as Descartes himself presumably does in imagining the idea of an evil demon when he formulates the evil demon hypothesis, he insists that his idea of God is different because of the inherent unity he believes to be implied by the concept of God. Descartes maintains:

> Nor can one imagine that perhaps several partial causes have concurred to bring me into being, and that from one cause I have taken the idea of one of the perfections I attribute to God and from another cause the idea of another perfection; so that all of these perfections are found somewhere in the universe, but not all joined together in one thing, which would be God. On the contrary, unity, simplicity, or the inseparability of all those things which are in God is one of the principal perfections that I understand to be in him. Certainly the idea of the unity of all these perfections could not have been placed in me by a cause from which I do not also have the ideas of the other perfections; for it could not bring it about that I would instantaneously understand them to be joined to one another inseparably, unless it brought it about instantaneously that I recognize which ones these are. . . . Rather, one has no choice but to conclude that, from the simple fact that I exist and that an idea of a most perfect being, that is, God, is in me, it is most evidently demonstrated that God exists. (33)

Instead of looking critically in detail at each of the alternative explanations of the cause of Descartes's idea of God and his reasons for rejecting them, let us consider instead where he goes next, assuming he is right that God exists. Let us simply grant Descartes's conclusion that God exists because only God can be the cause of his idea of God. The further consequences of this proof for the existence of God for epistemology are even more far-reaching. After dismissing other explanations of the origin of his idea of God that do not imply God's existence, Descartes concludes that deception would be a sign of defect, from which it follows that God, a perfect being in

Descartes's idea of God, is no deceiver. His reasoning has this structure, by which he concludes that God exists and is no deceiver:

Descartes's Argument That God Exists and Is No Deceiver

1. I have the clear and distinct idea of God as an essentially unified being of infinite perfection.
2. The cause of any idea must have at least as much formal (extramental) reality as the idea has objective (mental) reality (as the light of nature reveals, on the grounds that nothing comes from or can be made by nothing, *Ex nihilo nihil fit*).
3. There can be no other cause than God of my clear and distinct idea of God as an essentially unified being of infinite perfection (collapsing Descartes's examination and rejection of what is supposed to be an exhaustive consideration of conceivable alternative explanations of the cause of his idea of God).
4. Deception is the sign of a defect, and as such is incompatible with the nature of a being of infinite perfection.

5. God could be the cause of my clear and distinct idea of God.   (1,2)
6. God must be the cause of my clear and distinct idea of God.   (3,5)
7. God as an essentially unified being of infinite perfection exists, and creates me as an essentially thinking thing (is causally responsible for my cognition).   (6)
8. God is no deceiver.   (4,7)

If the proof is sound, it accomplishes two purposes. It establishes that God exists as a being of infinite perfection, and, as the cause at least of Descartes's cognition as an essentially thinking thing, links God as creator directly to the veracity of Descartes's perceptions. God causes Descartes to have the clear and distinct idea of God. From the proof of God's existence as his creator, Descartes infers that an infinitely perfect God is causally responsible for constituting all his sense modalities and cognitive abilities.

Together with the assumption that deceit is a sign of defect, it follows that God is no deceiver. The evil demon hypothesis is overcome, and clear and distinct perceptions are justified as epistemically certain. God's causal responsibility for Descartes's cognitive abilities supports God's moral responsibility as a perfectly good being whose nature is incompatible with deception for the essentially thinking things God creates. Descartes concludes that he could not be so constituted by an infinitely perfect veracious God that he could be deceived by clear and distinct perceptions. As a suppressed (and questionable) premise, indicated in brackets below as item [10], Descartes needs to assume that his thinking is not constituted by a collaboration of God and the evil demon, but that if God is his creator, then the demon cannot have deceitfully constituted or interfered even in part with his way of knowing.

The implication is that the evil demon hypothesis is false, that Descartes in advancing his epistemic project can know with epistemic certainty that his clear and distinct perceptions are demon-proof, and that his clear and distinct perceptions truthfully represent the true condition of an external real world. The argument continues:

Descartes's Argument Against the Evil Demon Hypothesis

  9. I am rationally justified in doubting the truthfulness of the representations of reality in my clear and distinct ideas if and only if it is possible that my sense modalities and cognitive abilities are deceitfully constituted or interfered with by an evil demon (collapsing Descartes's consideration and rejection of three alternative bases for methodological doubt).

[**10.** If God creates me as an essentially thinking thing (is causally responsible for my cognition), and if God is no deceiver, then my cognitive abilities cannot be constituted or interfered with even in part by an evil demon.]

  11. My cognitive abilities cannot be deceitfully constituted or interfered with by an evil demon. (7,8,9)

  12. I am not rationally justified in doubting the truthfulness of the representations of reality in my clear and distinct perceptions; my clear and distinct perceptions are epistemically certain. (9,11)

The conclusion in (12) clears away the only rational basis for methodological doubt of which Descartes approves in Meditation One. If there is no possibility for Descartes's cognitive abilities to be constituted by or interfered with by an evil demon, then there remains no rational justification for methodological doubt about the truthfulness of clear and distinct perceptions. The foundations for epistemically certain empirical knowledge are established when Descartes demonstrates that the thinking subject is not deceived by the only available evidence of an external reality by truthful representation in clear and distinct ideas.

It is worth remarking, as we conclude this section on Descartes's proof for the existence and veracity of God, that Descartes offers a more conventional proof for the existence of God later in the treatise, in Meditation Five. We shall not consider Descartes's second argument for God, except to note that it is similar in form to what is usually called Saint Anselm of Canterbury's or G. W. Leibniz's *ontological proof* for the existence of God. The essence of an ontological proof is to say that God exists because the definition or concept of God is of a divine person possessing all perfections, and that for such a person it would be a perfection to exist rather than not exist, or that God must exist in order to be the greatest conceivable being. Descartes offers a version of this style of proof, arguing that to think clearly and distinctly of God as a being with all perfections who nevertheless does not exist would be tantamount to thinking of a mountain without a valley.

The argument is meant to bolster Descartes's position that an existent God who is no deceiver would not permit us to be confused or deceived by an evil demon. He thereby provides another reason to eliminate the strongest imaginable basis for doubting perceptual evidence about the existence and condition of the external world. It is also worth remarking, in connection with the relation between his two proofs for the existence of God, that Descartes regards the inference in Meditation Three as the main and most important of the two. In the "Synopsis of the Following Six Meditations" that appears immediately after the "Preface" to the treatise, Descartes unequivocally states: "In the Third Meditation I explained at sufficient length, it seems to me, my principal argument for proving the existence of God" (9).

PROBLEM OF THE CARTESIAN CIRCLE

The quest for certainty leads Descartes to attempt to prove that God exists and is no deceiver. He hopes in this way to justify clear and distinct perceptions as truthful representations of external reality. Whether and in what sense Descartes's proof for the existence of God also presupposes the prior justification of clear and distinct ideas is the problem of the *Cartesian circle*.

It has appeared to many critics, even in Descartes's own day, that the argument in Meditation Three is circular. The trouble is that Descartes's proof for the existence of God seems to assume the prior justification of his clear and distinct ideas of God. That God exists and is no deceiver is supposed to justify clear and distinct ideas. The proof that there exists a perfectly veracious God is itself not epistemically certain unless its assumptions are beyond doubt, beyond the demon's reach. For this, it seems, it must already be known with epistemic certainty that God exists and is no deceiver.

In other words, Descartes seems to assume what he needs to prove in demonstrating that clear and distinct perceptions are truthful because God exists and is no deceiver. The objection is that Descartes must know the truth of key propositions with epistemic certainty prior to establishing the grounds for epistemic certainty of any such beliefs. These include the *Cogito, sum*, by which his own existence as an essentially thinking thing survives the evil demon hypothesis, the assumption that the cause of any idea must have at least as much formal reality as the idea has objective reality, that there is no satisfactory alternative explanation for the cause of his clear and distinct idea of God, and that deception is the sign of a defect rather than of perfection or strength. Descartes must also know with epistemic certainty that all of the connecting steps of inference in his proof for the existence of a veracious God are logically valid. Unless or until Descartes knows beyond the shadow of a doubt that he has not been so constituted or interfered with in his thinking by an evil demon in such a way that even his clear and distinct ideas misrepresent the truth, he cannot, according to his own ground rules, be epistemically certain about any of the assumptions by which he tries to prove that God exists and is no deceiver. It nevertheless appears that Descartes cannot know that these things are true with epistemic certainty unless or until he has first proved that a veracious God exists and that God divinely constitutes him as an essentially thinking thing.

The circularity objection appears in the above reconstruction in the claim that Descartes must appeal to the truth of his conclusion in (12) in order to uphold the truth of at least some of the assumptions in (1)–(4). The Cartesian circle in its simplest terms has the form shown in Figure 4.1.

The Cartesian circle has also been interpreted as a symptom of a deeper difficulty that plagues knowledge theory. This is known as the problem of the criterion, *diallelus* or wheel. There is a circle in the justification of particular beliefs on the basis of whether or not they fall under sound epistemic principles, where the soundness of epistemic principles depends on whether or not they support all and only justified beliefs. The Cartesian circle seems to be a special instance of the *diallelus*. Here the particular beliefs to be justified are the beliefs that God exists and is no deceiver, and the epistemic principle whose soundness is at issue is that clear and distinct ideas are truthful.

Many solutions to the Cartesian circle have been proposed. The objection once clearly expressed seems so obvious that some commentators have doubted whether a

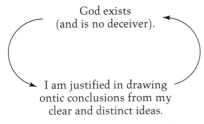

FIGURE 4.1 Cartesian circle

thinker as astute as Descartes could have blatantly begged what is perhaps the central question of his epistemic enterprise. Other critics find no particular difficulty in the assumption that Descartes like any thinker might be capable even of the most whopping logical howler. They interpret the circle as an instructive mistake that could only occur in the effort to develop a subtle and sophisticated philosophy, or of the philosophical risks Descartes is willing to take in exploring the limits of knowledge.

It is even harder for some defenders to believe that Descartes could have continued to uphold the framework of his theory after the circularity had been called to his attention twice in the *Objections and Replies,* and later again in his "Conversation with Burman." In the latter correspondence, Burman writes: "It seems there is a circle. For in the Third Meditation the author uses axioms to prove the existence of God, even though he is not yet certain of not being deceived about these" (Descartes, *Correspondence,* 16 April 1648, translated in collaboration with Anthony Kenny, *Writings,* 3, 334). The circularity objection supports the claim that Descartes through an unnoticed distinction does not actually involve himself in the Cartesian circle, or that there is a solution available by which he can escape. The challenge, since his official answer is often judged unsatisfactory or at least in need of a better explanation, is to discover the solution Descartes might have had in mind, or that might be offered on his behalf consistently within the main outlines of his reform of first philosophy.

Some commentators have tried to defend Descartes's reasoning against the circularity objection by insisting that God's guarantee of the veracity of clear and distinct ideas is not needed for the proof of God's existence while Descartes is carefully attending to the proof. Afterward, when the proof is completed and the conclusion is proved, God's existence and perfect veracity uphold the truthful representations of all previous clear and distinct perceptions, thereby exiting the circle. Such a solution to the Cartesian circle is doubtful for several reasons. To topple the edifice of Aristotelian science presumably calls for more than doubt about the truth of demonstrations whose conclusions were perfectly certain when attended to, but may afterward have become hazy. It would be extraordinary to bring God into epistemology merely in order to uphold the conclusions of clearly and distinctly perceived demonstrations only later when the demonstrations themselves are no longer fully present to mind. Nor, as several critics have rightly observed, is the existence and veracity of God sufficient to overcome a faulty memory, if, say, Descartes were clearly and distinctly to misremember the conclusion of a geometrical proof he had once correctly demonstrated while attending more closely to its assumptions and inferences. In matters such as this, God's existence and veracity do not seem to help.

What the atheist claims to know in any area can be overturned by the kinds of doubts Descartes raises concerning the possibility of an evil demon. Only God is powerful enough to defeat the evil demon. If God exists and is no deceiver, then clear and distinct perceptions take on the same demon-proof epistemic certainty that is otherwise thought to belong only to knowledge of the simplest necessary truths in elementary mathematics. The possibility of extending epistemic certainty to all of Cartesian science is limited by the role of freewill judgment in interpreting data, drawing less than epistemically certain conclusions about the nature of reality from the epistemically certain content of clear and distinct perceptions, and constructing explanatory and predictive theories from the infallible raw evidence of perception. It is misjudgment rather than perception that Descartes believes leads to error in the sciences.

If the solution to the Cartesian circle is to prove God's existence and veracity with something less than epistemic certainty in order to uphold the epistemic certainty of clear and distinct ideas for knowledge as science, then at best at the end of the proof Descartes still does not know with epistemic certainty that a veracious God exists. If he does not know with epistemic certainty that God exists and is no deceiver, then he remains subject to the possibility of the evil demon's doubt-inducing deceptions, and the whole system of knowledge he is trying to construct cannot attain epistemic certainty because its foundations in that case are less than epistemically certain. The objection undermines any effort to avoid the Cartesian circle by drawing inferences that step up the epistemic status of beliefs from less than epistemic certainty in the proof of God's existence to full epistemic certainty. If we know with less than epistemic certainty that God exists and is no deceiver, then we cannot know with epistemic certainty that clear and distinct ideas are truthful representations of reality.

The proposal to advance from beliefs with less than epistemic certainty to beliefs with epistemic certainty commits the fallacy of trying to derive stronger from weaker justification. If Descartes's proof does not begin with epistemic certainty, it cannot produce it, on pain of violating an epistemic version of the principle that *Ex nihilo nihil fit.* The demon, for all that Descartes knows with certainty at the first stages of his proof, could mislead the thinker about the *Cogito, sum,* the metaphysical maxim that the source of any idea must have at least as much formal reality as the idea has objective reality, the principle that God's nature is incompatible with deceit, the refutation of alternative explanations of the source or cause of his clear and distinct idea of God, and the soundness of any of the inferences by which Descartes goes from step to step in the proof.

LIGHT OF NATURE

A more promising solution to the problem of the Cartesian circle is suggested by Descartes's references to necessary truths as revealed by the *light of nature.* The light of nature is a mysterious intuitive faculty by which the truth of certain kinds of propositions is supposed to be indubitably and infallibly understood. These are the elementary ideas Descartes alternatively designates as "axioms," "simples," "first principles," or "common notions."

Descartes significantly mentions the *lumen naturale* as the unfailing source of his knowledge of the assumptions in his first proof for the existence of God. The solution to the Cartesian circle afforded by Descartes's concept of the light of nature requires that whatever is revealed by the light of nature is clearly and distinctly perceived, but that not all clear and distinct perceptions are indubitably true or epistemically certain as truths revealed by the light of nature. If the light of nature supports Descartes's proof that God exists and is no deceiver, then he does not need to step up the level of justification from less than epistemic certainty to full epistemic certainty. Nor does Descartes then need to reason in a circle by assuming that clear and distinct perceptions are epistemically certain in order to prove that clear and distinct perceptions are epistemically certain. The light of nature, if we can accept its epistemic credentials, shows us a way out of the Cartesian circle.

Descartes does not discuss the light of nature in detail. The concept first appears in the writings of the medieval philosophers Aquinas and Ockham. Descartes introduces the concept in the *Meditations*, where most of his references to it appear in his Meditation Three proof that God exists and is no deceiver. In the "Synopsis" of the *Meditations*, Descartes dissociates the light of nature from any connection with revelations from God or matters of faith, when he claims, probably to ease the censorial concern of the Church authorities in Paris, "Nor do I [in Meditation Four] examine those matters pertaining to religious faith or to the conduct of life, but only those speculative truths that are known by the aid of the light of nature" (9). Indeed, the point of referring to the faculty as a light *of nature* is presumably to distinguish it from any supernatural connection. The most important premises in Descartes's Meditation Three proof are explicitly said to be justified by the light of nature. These include the assumption that the cause of an idea must have at least as much formal reality as the idea has objective reality, and of its derivation from the principle *Ex nihilo nihil fit*, together with the claim that God is no deceiver, and that the concept of deceit is "repugnant" to the idea of God.

Descartes does not claim that the metaphysical maxim about formal and objective reality, and God's essence as nondeceiver, are not justified merely by being clearly and distinctly perceived. He says specifically that these conclusions are justified by the light of nature, suggesting the possibility that the light of nature is a different and prior source of knowledge than clear and distinct perception. Truths revealed by the light of nature, even if also clearly and distinctly perceived, are not justified only by virtue of being clear and distinct ideas, but by the light of nature as the faculty of reason. Descartes can no more consider the evil demon hypothesis as calling into question the conclusions of the light of reason than he can accept a basis for maximum skepticism that amounts to abandoning reason like the severely insane.

If the light of nature is indubitable even under the evil demon hypothesis, then the assumptions in Descartes's proof that God exists and is no deceiver need not presuppose God's vindication of what is clearly and distinctly perceived. Descartes distinguishes knowledge obtained by the light of nature from clear and distinct perception when he indicates that he has a natural inclination to accept clear and distinct perceptions as truthfully representing the world, but that this natural inclination is different from the light of nature. The structure of Descartes's argument in the *Meditations* indicates that his acceptance of clear and distinct perceptions stands in need of justification, while the natural light is intrinsically rationally indubitable. Importantly, he also attributes the epistemic certainty of the *Cogito* to the light of nature prior to his proof of the existence and veracity of God.

The light of nature by itself confers epistemic certainty on the truths it reveals. The mere inclination to accept clear and distinct ideas as representative of reality does not carry epistemic certainty, unless or until it can be proven with epistemic certainty that an undeceiving God exists who has creative and sustaining responsibility for all our cognition. Descartes's task is to justify clear and distinct ideas as epistemically certain truthful representations of the real external world. Hence, we can also think of his epistemic project as one of extending the epistemic certainty of truths revealed by the light of nature to clear and distinct perceptions generally. The dubitability of clear and distinct ideas under the demon hypothesis is overcome only when Descartes proves with epistemic certainty that God exists and is no deceiver.

It is thus a mistake to hold, as some commentaries have, that the existence of the self or thinking subject is the ultimate egocentric foundation of Descartes's philosophy. Such a suggestion is implausible, because Descartes must first be justified in the reasoning by which he rejects the three alternative rational grounds for maximum skepticism, and by which he concludes that the ego's existence cannot be doubted as long as and whenever it thinks. He cannot justify these inferences by the appeal to an undeceiving God, because he needs demon-proof reason in order to prove that God exists and is no deceiver. He explicitly claims that the ego's existence is established by surviving the demon hypothesis according to the light of nature. It follows that the light of nature is a prior source of epistemic certainty. The real foundation of Descartes's system is not the ego or *Cogito, sum,* but the light of nature as the ultimate indubitable foundation of all epistemic certainty. Since Descartes supposes that any philosophical system worthy of the name must share the same commitment to the light of nature in order to develop or defend any of its principles, it remains meaningful to describe what is distinctively egocentric about his theory of knowledge and how it relates to the *Cogito, sum* as its immovable Archimedean point.

The assumptions of the evil demon hypothesis and the reasoning whereby alternative justifications for maximum skepticism are rejected might be directly justified by the light of nature. What about the deduction of conclusions from assumptions in Descartes's meditations? Descartes is relatively silent about the epistemic status of logical implication. He maintains that while attending to mathematical demonstrations the mind can be sure of its clear and distinct perceptions, though the memory of these may later become blurred and doubtful. What does Descartes regard as justifying deductive inference? There are three possibilities, none of which has definitive textual support, but any of which is consistent with the light of nature solution to the Cartesian circle: (1) The truths of logic and validity of logical inference are justified by the light of nature as indubitably self-evident at least during those times when the mind attends to them. (2) The truths of logic and the validity of logical inference are self-justifying in somewhat the way Aristotle in *Metaphysics* 1006^{a}11–1007^{a}20 argues that there need and can be no proof of the law of noncontradiction, independently of the epistemic certainty of truths revealed by the light of nature. (3) The truths of logic and the validity of logical inference are self-justifying in roughly the way that Aristotle describes, and they thereby mediately justify the epistemically certain truths of other propositions that are ultimately justified by the light of nature.

The attraction of (1) is that it attributes no special status to logical propositions and inferences, but regards their certainty as deriving from the light of nature as a single faculty by which the mind discerns certain truth from possible falsehood. The advantage of (3) is that it partially explains what must otherwise remain mysterious about the illumination of truth by reason's natural light. Logical noncontradiction is reasonably well understood, which makes it plausible to suppose that Descartes might have regarded the light of nature as clicking on when the mind detects a contradiction in conceptual analysis, say, in the idea of God as a deceiver, or in the juxtaposition of the evil demon hypothesis with the nonexistence of the thinking ego. The disadvantage in (3) is the lack of explanation of how the mind detects such contradictions, an omission that might make us go back in yet another vicious justificatory circle to the light of nature as the faculty by which contradictions are distinguished with absolute certainty from noncontradictions. The remaining choice in (2) postulates that Descartes has two independent and irreducible certainty principles, in relying separately on both logic and the light of nature. In what follows, no commitment to the options presented in (1)–(3) is assumed. The light of nature as the source of absolute certainty in Descartes's argument prior to his proof of the existence of a veracious God can be understood as combining logic and the light of nature, with no preference for their dependence or independence.

The assumptions of Descartes's proof that God exists and is no deceiver are rationally revealed by the light of nature. As such, they do not presuppose the existence of a veracious God for their justification, but can be advanced as Descartes offers them in a noncircular epistemically certain demonstration supported by the light of nature. Clear and distinct ideas as opposed to truths disclosed by the light of nature are justified as truthful representations of external reality by the existence of a veracious God. The epistemic certainty of the light of nature, is thereby extended, first, to the existence of the thinking subject in the *Cogito, sum,* then to the existence (but not the prior justification) of the thinker's clear and distinct idea of God as an essentially unified being of absolute perfection, then to God's essential veracity, and finally to the epistemically certain truthful representation of the thinker's clear and distinct ideas, thanks to the God-given constitution of the thinker's mode of cognition. There is no need for God's justification of clear and distinct ideas to circle back in support of the premises by which God's existence and veracity are proved. For these assumptions were never meant to be upheld merely as clear and distinct ideas, but as indubitable revelations of the light of nature. The argument of Meditation Three, interpreted in this way, allows an atheist lacking the theist's epistemic certainty of knowledge as science to enjoy what Descartes calls the same "awareness" of truth. An atheist capable of arriving even at an epistemically uncertain awareness of these truths nevertheless unknowingly has in hand all the elements of an epistemically certain proof that God exists and is no deceiver, by which a stubborn persistence in atheism would be irrational. Descartes believes that his reasoning in this way fulfills the exhortation of the Lateran Council to employ philosophy in the service of religion. As he announces in the prefatory "Dedicatory Letter" to the *Meditations* (2–3), Descartes has fused philosophy and theology by providing a noncircular argument to persuade even the atheist of the fundamental truths of religion.

Descartes is not trapped inside the Cartesian circle. There is an escape that accords with his pronouncements about the proof for the existence of God as warrant for the truthful representation of reality by clear and distinct ideas. It is, moreover, a solution that makes sense of Descartes's philosophy as a foundationalist epistemology. The foundational structure of Descartes's system has already been sketched. We can graphically depict the relation between Descartes's proof for the existence of a vera-

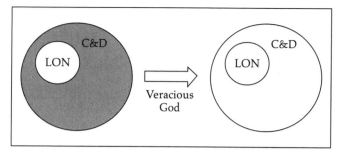

FIGURE 4.2 Descartes's epistemic project

cious God and the justification of clear and distinct ideas ultimately by logic and the light of nature. In Figure 4.2, the sphere on the left indicates Descartes's understanding of his epistemic situation prior to proving that God exists and is no deceiver. He accepts the indubitable truths available to him as to any philosophical theory by the light of nature (LON). The hatching represents the demonic doubt that haunts clear and distinct (C&D) ideas unless or until they are shown to be epistemically certain. The unshaded arrow indicates an absolutely certain light of nature transition in the epistemic status of clear and distinct perceptions from admitting of doubt prior to the proof that God exists and is no deceiver, to the situation depicted in the sphere on the right, in which clear and distinct perceptions, like the truths revealed by the logic and the light of nature, are also indubitable and epistemically certain.

The main task to which Descartes dedicates Meditation Three is to extend the epistemically certain foundations of knowledge from whatever is revealed by the light of nature to clear and distinct perceptions generally. The reliance ultimately on logic or noncontradiction and the light of nature makes Descartes's foundationalism distinctively rationalistic. The solution to the Cartesian circle, interpreted either as a way out, or as an argument to the effect that Descartes avoids circular reasoning in the first place, is that the purpose of Descartes's foundational project is to upgrade the epistemic status of all clear and distinct ideas by removing them from the possibility of skepticism entailed by the evil demon hypothesis.

The noncircularity of Descartes's integrated theological-epistemic-metaphysical foundationalism can be seen in the following reconstruction. His appeal to the light of nature is indicated as an epistemically certain foundation that does not depend for its epistemic status on the later conclusion that other clear and distinct perceptions are justified as epistemically certain by the epistemically certain proof of the existence of a veracious God. The light of nature is numbered (0), to indicate that it is a common foundation belonging to any rational philosophy. It is the justificatory bedrock that underlies Descartes's commitment to the *Cogito* in light of the evil demon hypothesis. As such, the light of nature underlies even Descartes's epistemically certain conclusion that a thinking self provides an Archimedean point on which the remaining epistemically certain substructure and superstructure of Cartesian knowledge depends, and that characterizes Descartes's foundationalism as distinctly egocentric:

Bruno
Michel

Alain
Beaulieu

9:30   PHIL-1105   — 114

1087

UNIVERSITÉ DE SUDBURY
PROJET ÉTHIQUE
UNIVERSITY OF SUDBURY
ETHICS PROJECT

15 sept - Linda
    2:30   Black Rose Books
    1 - How academic ?
    ②- WORD COUNT

Linda 4506214187

234   H - P

Sudbury (Ontario) Canada, P3E 2C6   (705) 673-5661
Sudbury, Ontario, Canada, P3E 2C6   (705) 673-4912

Foundational Structure of Descartes's Philosophy

0. Light of Nature (rational epistemic faculty)
   Justifies *a priori* matters of conceptual analysis and logical inference while the thinker attends to the demonstration; supports (1)–(7).
   Epistemically certain foundation (of any philosophical system).
1. Conceivability of Evil Demon
   Light of nature reveals no contradiction in concept; rational basis for doubting clear and distinct ideas if and only if evil demon is possible.
2. Existence of Ego or Thinking Subject *(Cogito, ergo sum)*
   Light of nature reveals contradiction in hypothesis that evil demon might deceive thinker about the thinker's existence.
   Nominal epistemic foundation.
   Archimedean point of Descartes's egocentric foundationalism.
3. Existence of Clear and Distinct Idea of God
   Discovered in thought as possession of thinker, whose existence and the existence of whose ideas are guaranteed by (2); a clear and distinct idea that is not justified here as supporting ontic conclusions by virtue of being clear and distinct.
4. Metaphysical Principle *(Ex nihilo nihil fit)*
   The cause of an idea must have at least as much formal (extramental) reality as the idea has objective (mental) reality (degree of completeness or perfection of detail).
   Revealed by light of nature.
5. Existence of God
   From (3) and (4), together with elimination of alternative explanations of origin of (3).
   Meditation Three proof.
6. Veracity of God (God no deceiver)
   Revealed by light of nature; independent of proof of (5).
7. Justification of Clear and Distinct Ideas
   From (1), (5), and (6), together with suppressed assumption about the exclusion of the evil demon from any role in constituting or interfering with the thinker's sense modalities and cognitive abilities if a veracious God exists as the thinker's creator.
   Epistemic foundational substructure.
8. Cartesian Science
   Metaphysics; mathematics; natural philosophy.
   Epistemic superstructure.

The noncircularity of Descartes's foundationalism is even more apparent in Figure 4.3. It diagrams the relation between the several components of his system identified by the same numbers as in the reconstruction above. Here single shaft arrows indicate epistemic dependence, while double shaft arrows indicate logical implication, all of which under the light of nature are supposed to hold with epistemic certainty.

Figure 4.3 presents Descartes's system in the manner of most foundationalist epistemologies as an inverted pyramid. The one point on which all else rests is Descartes's

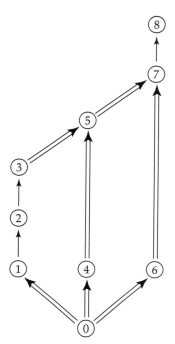

FIGURE 4.3 Foundational structure (inverted pyramid) of Descartes's epistemology

acceptance of truths revealed to reason by the light of nature. From this, the proof that God exists and is no deceiver, the epistemically certain justification of clear and distinct ideas, is supposed to uphold the superstructure of a Cartesian system of science, including metaphysics, mathematics, and natural philosophy.

In Meditation Five, Descartes summarizes and reiterates the conclusion of Meditation Three's demonstration of the existence and veracity of God. He extends to all knowledge in his epistemology the same epistemic certainty we expect of mathematics to our knowledge about the existence and veracity of God, and thereafter to "other intellectual matters" and to all knowledge about the external physical world or "corporeal nature," revealed by proper use of sense perception. He reflects:

> And thus I plainly see that the certainty and truth of every science depends upon the knowledge of the true God, to such an extent that, before I had known him, I could not know anything perfectly about any other thing. But now it is possible for me to know certainly and fully countless things—both about God and other intellectual matters, as well as about all corporeal nature, which is the object of pure mathematics. (45)

We have now considered an interpretation of Descartes's foundationalist epistemology, according to which the problem of the Cartesian circle is avoided by appealing to the light of nature. The light of nature is a more fundamental rational principle of knowledge than Descartes's defense of the epistemic certainty of clear and distinct ideas. Showing that God exists and is no deceiver is supposed to overcome the evil demon hypothesis in a way that only God through perfect knowledge, power, and goodness can do. The light of nature thereby acquires enormous importance in Descartes's system; it is what makes Descartes, as the history of philosophy rightly judges him, a paradigmatically rationalist thinker.

What is the light of nature, and what are the implications of solving the problem of the Cartesian circle in Descartes's foundationalism in terms of the light of nature? We can, for what it is worth, say that the light of nature is a faculty of reason, the mind's ability to grasp connections and distinctions and principles that cannot be denied without contradiction. Descartes excludes the light of nature from the principles and abilities of mind that fall under the evil demon's deceptions. This is for good reason, since in order to challenge any part of our presumed knowledge by such a rationale, we need to be able to draw on our reasoning abilities in order to see that this is a possible or conceivable basis for maximum skepticism. If we cannot consider the possibility of doubting everything that can be doubted without including reason and the light of nature, then we can have no sound justification for doubting in the first place.

Veridical Perception and Errors of Judgment

In Meditation Four, "Concerning the True and the False," Descartes considers the conditions under which it is possible to make errors in knowledge, and offers general epistemic advice about how to avoid them. If God exists and is no deceiver, and stands behind all our clear and distinct perceptions to guarantee their epistemic certainty as truthful representations of an external world, then how is it possible for any of us to be mistaken? Descartes explains that God's perfection precludes the possibility of willful deception:

> To begin with, I acknowledge that it is impossible for him ever to deceive me; for in every trick or deception some imperfection is found. Although the ability to deceive seems to be an indication of cleverness or power, nevertheless, willful deception evinces maliciousness and weakness. Accordingly, deception is not compatible with God. (35)

Descartes remarks that in addition to cognition, thinkers such as ourselves are also provided by God with a faculty of judgment. Infallible perception by itself is not enough, and cannot lead to epistemically certain knowledge, unless it is accompanied by correct judgment. Judgment is essential to knowledge, and yet it is also the potential source of error, insofar as it is exercised by individual free will.

As in the moral sphere, free epistemic judgment always has the possibility of getting things right or going astray and leading us into error, depending on whether we use it properly or improperly. How we exercise epistemic judgment is up to us, something we can learn to control. If all perceptual mistakes are due to the will rather than our epistemically certain clear and distinct perceptions, then we should in principle be able to avoid all errors of knowledge by controlling the will and directing it in accord with a correct method. It is no different than fallibility trying to conduct our lives according to moral precepts and willful moral judgment. Our perceptual like our moral mistakes are always our own fault, willfully misapplying judgment in evaluating the information contained in epistemically certain clear and distinct perceptions to draw conclusions that do not accord with the truth or are unsupported by the evidence.

God's perfection guarantees the epistemic certainty of our perceptions considered in themselves. What we judge about them can but need not lead us into error rather than toward greater epistemically certain knowledge, for the sake of which we must properly discipline our willful epistemic judgment. In general, if we want to avoid errors we must not jump to conclusions when judging the epistemically certain data of perception. This is a category of advice that can be finely subdivided in many ways for many kinds of different cases. Descartes remarks:

> Next I observe that there is in me a certain faculty of judgment that I undoubtedly received from God, as is the case with all the other things that are in me. Since he has not wished to deceive me, he certainly has not given me a faculty such that, when I use it properly, I could ever make a mistake. (35)

Of course, we do make mistakes, as Descartes freely admits in his own case. The argument that God exists and is no deceiver, and that God is the perfect author of our epistemic abilities, should imply that in some sense we are incapable of error. There must therefore be some other source of our mistakes, which Descartes as we have explained attributes to the willful faculty of judgment. He argues:

> Finally, focusing closer on myself and inquiring into the nature of my errors (the only things that argue for an imperfection in me), I note that these errors depend on the simultaneous concurrence of two causes: the faculty of knowing that is in me, and the faculty of choosing (in other words, the free choice of the will), that is, they depend on the intellect and will at the same time. Through the intellect alone I perceive only ideas concerning which I can make a judgment; no error, properly so-called, is to be found in the intellect thus precisely conceived. For although countless things about which I have no idea perhaps exist, nevertheless I must not be said, properly speaking, to be deprived of them. I am bereft of them only in a negative way, because I can give no argument by which to prove that God ought to have given me a greater faculty of knowing than he has. (36)

What, then, is the remedy for the excesses of willful judgment that lead us from God-given-and-guaranteed demon-proof, infallible, and epistemically certain clear and distinct perceptions to mistaken judgments? Can we avoid making judgment errors of perceptual knowledge? Descartes believes that we can avoid mistakes by restraining judgment and never going beyond the contents of clear and distinct perceptions in a bid for knowledge. Thus, he says:

> But if I hold off from making a judgment when I do not perceive with sufficient clarity and distinctness what is in fact true, I clearly would be acting properly and would not be deceived. But were I to make an assertion or a denial, then I would not be using my freedom properly. If I turn in the direction that happens to be false, I am plainly deceived. But if I should embrace either alternative, and in so doing happen upon the truth by accident, I would still not be without fault, for it is manifest by the light of nature that the intellect's perception must always precede the will's being determined. Inherent in this incorrect use of the free will is a privation that constitutes the very essence of error: a privation, I say, is inherent in this operation insofar as the operation proceeds from me, but not in the faculty that was given to me by God, nor even in the operation of the faculty insofar as it depends upon God. (38–39)

We avoid errors of judgment by confining it to the limits of clear and distinct perceptions. This does not mean that we can never infer that the world actually is as it appears to be in perception, but only that we are not to make such judgments when our perceptions are anything less than clear and distinct. Descartes maintains that we can correctly judge the existence and condition of things in the world, provided we limit ourselves to the information contained in clear and distinct perceptions.

The difficulty is to be able to tell the difference between when we are and when we are not experiencing clear and distinct perceptions. These would appear to be a matter of degree. Some perceptions will be more or less clear and distinct than others, so that it may be hard to draw a sharp line between those that are and those that are not clear and distinct in the way Descartes requires. If we wish to apply Descartes's epistemic principles effectively and with good result, therefore, we must be able to correctly judge when a perception is clear and distinct in the highest, epistemically certain knowledge-conferring degree, and when it is not. Since this is itself a matter of judgment, there might be insuperable difficulties in trying to contain willful judgment within the inexact limits Descartes requires in order to know with epistemic certainty that we have not arrived at false beliefs mistaken for knowledge.

Descartes's proposal for gathering empirical knowledge now begins to show its weaknesses. We must exercise judgment concerning whether and which of our perceptions are clear and distinct in order to know when and to what extent we are epistemically entitled to correctly judge the condition of the external world. If we make the right choices, we arrive at knowledge, and if we make the wrong choices, we fall into error. We must restrain the will to keep from jumping to conclusions that are not adequately supported by epistemically certain perceptions. The problem once again is to know when we have and when we have not properly restrained the will to judge, so as to avoid error at the same time that we do not fail to judge a given perception true. Nor is the will in these matters easily restrained, otherwise there would not be so much error in the history of knowledge. In judging the nature of the world, it is always possible to deceive ourselves if not to be deceived by the epistemic pranks of an evil demon, into misjudging that a particular perception is clear and distinct, or that it possesses the requisite degree of clarity and distinctness, in order to allow the will to judge that the perception warrants the judgment that the state of the world is actually as it is perceived.

Promise and Limitations of Descartes's Rationalist Epistemology

If Descartes escapes the Cartesian circle, there are other difficulties in his theory of knowledge and metaphysics.

To begin with the proof for the existence of a veracious God, it should be noted that it is not enough for Descartes to prove that God exists and is no deceiver. God must also be shown to be Descartes's creator, causally responsible for his sense modalities and cognitive abilities as an essentially thinking thing. This part of the argument is vulnerable to the objections raised against mind-body dualism, as well as the complicated proof that Descartes's clear and distinct idea of God can have no other cause than God.

Descartes claims that the idea of God cannot be synthesized by the mind out of separately acquired clear and distinct ideas of power, knowledge, goodness, and infinity, because a clear and distinct idea of God is the idea of an essentially unified being. The objection is supposed to preclude the possibility of the mind's fabricating the concept of God by piecing together God's properties from several sources and then imagining them to obtain in one being to infinite degrees of perfection. If the mind has the idea of essential unity derived from some nondivine source, however, then God's essential unity might be thrown into the imagination's crucible as well, in order subconsciously to manufacture a clear and distinct idea of God as an essentially unified being of infinite perfection.

Suppressed premise [10] in the reconstruction of Descartes's main argument is also questionable. The assumption states that if Descartes's sense modalities and cognitive abilities are created by a veracious God, then they cannot also be partially constituted or interfered with in any way by the evil demon. Descartes assumes that the demon can only threaten the truthfulness of clear and distinct ideas if the demon rather than God controls a thinker's cognition. A stronger rational basis for doubt, which Descartes does not consider, is a scenario in which God constitutes the thinker in such a way that the demon can freely interfere with the thinker's cognition so as to produce perfectly clear and distinct ideas that radically misrepresent reality.

Perhaps God allows the demon to intervene in our perceptions despite having first constituted his thinking creatures with truth-discerning clear and distinct ideas, in the way that God is said to permit Satan to tempt our once perfectly made souls with false promises as a trial of faith. Perhaps God constitutes Descartes as an essentially thinking thing, but restricts Descartes's reality-representing clear and distinct ideas to the empty truths of logic, excluding even whatever else is revealed by the light of nature. It would then be accidental to Descartes's essential thinking nature whether or not his clear and distinct ideas truthfully represent reality. God, for reasons unfathomable to finite minds, might for all we know relinquish responsibility for the truth or falsehood of clear and distinct ideas relating to the reality of the external world, and allow the principles of natural philosophy to be systematically misrepresented by the evil demon. God might conceivably do so in order to cause humankind to turn away from the worthless things of the empirical world to spiritual values. Or, perhaps God's epistemic righteousness like God's perfect moral justice is not meted out in this world, but only in the afterlife. Then it could be true that God's veracity guarantees the truthfulness of Descartes's ideas, but not of any thoughts he has during his embodied sojourn in his life on Earth.

How are we to restrain the will to avoid mistakes in judgment from epistemically certain clear and distinct perceptions? To do so we would first need to know when we were and when we were not clearly and distinctly perceiving the world. Is this so obvious? Am I clearly and distinctly perceiving the world right now as I look about the room in which I am writing? Perhaps so. But what can I judge of it if I am not to go beyond the limits of the clear and distinct perceptions themselves? Can I conclude that there actually exists a room with the colors and shapes and other perceived properties of things? Are these judgments about the external world epistemically certain, such that no belief could possibly be more strongly justified than my belief that 2 + 2 = 4? It is hard to see how we have made any progress at all in this regard, even if we agree that Descartes proves with epistemic certainty that God exists and is no deceiver. God's perfect goodness requires God to thwart the demon's mischief. But how, where, when does God do so, and can I know that he is doing so right now as I look at what I take to be the real physical entities around me?

In all of these scenarios, the evil demon deprives Descartes of certitude, even on the assumption that Descartes is an essentially thinking thing created by a veracious God. God in Descartes's conception is powerful enough to contain the evil demon, and to Descartes it may appear that God's infinite goodness requires him to prevent the demon's mischief. But God's ways are inscrutable, and God's humanly incomprehensible intentions and unlimited free will lend a further rational basis for skepticism about the truthfulness of clear and distinct ideas, despite the noncircular proof that God exists, is no deceiver, and has creative and sustaining responsibility for all our perceptual cognitive abilities.

Finally, what does Descartes mean by a truthful representation? The idea presumably involves a positive correspondence between world and idea. What is the possible application of the concept, however, if we are never in a position to see around the corners of appearances to judge them as representative or misrepresentative? Descartes's argument might avoid circularity by appealing to the light of nature as an epistemically certain foundation for the proof that God exists and is no deceiver. How does he know prior to this point in the argument that the demon has not mischievously provided him with a faulty light of nature or a faulty sense of noncontradiction, or that, although God has perfectly constituted these faculties, the demon interferes with their normal operations? If this is conceivable, and it is hard to deny that it might be, then all of Descartes's conclusions are subject to the same maximum degree of skepticism that is supposed to prevail in his argument only prior to proving that God exists and is no deceiver.

SUMMARY

The desire to make knowledge epistemically certain is a long-standing ambition in philosophy. Descartes offers a model of certainty that begins by projecting the most powerful imaginable basis for doubt, and then explains how to overcome the methodological skepticism that results. He proposes to show that even under the strongest reason for doubting whatever it is possible to doubt one still cannot doubt one's own existence. From this immovable Archimedean point Descartes attempts to ground all of knowledge on absolutely secure foundations.

Taking mathematical certainty as his standard, he tries to raise the epistemic status of all perceptual knowledge to the level of mathematics. He argues that God must exist in order to explain the content of his idea of God, on the principle revealed by the light of nature that the cause of any idea must have at least as much formal reality as the idea has objective reality. If the idea of God were to lack an adequate explanation, then we would be violating the necessary general principle that you cannot make something from nothing, *Ex nihilo nihil fit*. The idea of God as a spirit with all perfections is understood by Descartes as implying that God is no deceiver. As Descartes's perfect creator, God provides him with infallible cognition. It follows, if Descartes is right, that all his clear and distinct perceptions have the same high degree of epistemic certainty as mathematics.

Descartes explains the possibility of error as a matter of judgment rather than perception. Clear and distinct perception considered in and of itself is infallible, provided that God exists and is no deceiver. We get into trouble epistemically only when we fail to restrain willful judgment in jumping to conclusions that go beyond the evidence of the senses. Descartes accordingly offers practical advice for avoiding error by overreaching what can be known with epistemic certainty in perception.

The problem of the Cartesian circle suggests a logical difficulty in Descartes's epistemology and metaphysics. The problem is that he seems to need to assume that God exists in order to uphold the proposition that his clear and distinct ideas are certain, which he needs in turn to prove that God exists. The problem might be solved by emphasizing his reliance throughout the meditations on the light of nature as a faculty of reason that does not need to be validated by any external justification and is needed even to decide upon the strongest basis for systematic doubt. Descartes's legacy in metaphysics and theory of knowledge makes him one of the most important thinkers even among those contemporary critics who accept few if any of Descartes's conclusions.

QUESTIONS FOR PHILOSOPHICAL UNDERSTANDING

1. What does Descartes mean by knowledge?

2. How does Descartes understand the relation between God's goodness and the correspondence of our perceptions with reality?

3. Does Descartes successfully avoid the problem of the Cartesian circle?

4. Why is certainty important to Descartes's philosophy?

5. What is the point of Descartes's trying to bring empirical science up to the same level of epistemic certainty as mathematics?

6. Is Descartes correct to reject the possibility that he might be dreaming or subject to illusion in all his perception as a basis for maximum skepticism?

7. How would you compare Descartes's philosophy with Plato's, Aristotle's, and Ockham's?

8. What are the consequences of Descartes's attempt to distinguish between the body and mind?

9. Why does Descartes trust the light of nature to be certain even if there is a deceitful evil demon?

10. What can we learn from Descartes's proposal to ground all of philosophy and science on the indubitable existence of the self?

11. How should we understand Descartes's first proving the indubitable existence of the self and only then proving the existence of God? Can the choice in the order of topics in these proofs be detached from the fact that according to Descartes God creates the self?

12. What is the significance of Descartes's offering two different proofs for the existence of God? How are they supposed to be related?

13. How is Descartes's concept of the role of will in making perceptual judgment errors supposed to cohere with the proposition that our divinely created cognitive faculties are infallible?

14. Could God have created human beings so perfectly that their wills would never make false judgments on the basis of clear and distinct perceptions?

15. How can we decide whether or not a particular perception is clear and distinct? Could the evil demon deceive us about whether a perception that seems to be clear and distinct is actually so?

KEY TERMS

Archimedean point

Cartesian circle

clear and distinct perception

Cogito, sum

diallelus

dreaming rationale for
maximum skepticism

edifice of knowledge

egocentric foundation of
Descartes's philosophy

epistemic certainty

evil demon rationale for
maximum skepticism

Ex nihilo nihil fit

formal reality

foundationalist epistemology

free will

God rationale for maximum
skepticism

illusion rationale for
maximum skepticism

illusory perception

judgment error

light of nature *(lumen
naturale)*

material substance

objective reality

ontological proof for the
existence of God

parasitic concept

piece of wax example

psychological certainty

rationalism, rationalist
philosophy

skepticism

spirit, spiritual substance

syncretism

systematic doubt

truthful representation

veridical perception

Sources and Recommended Readings

Beck, L. J. *The Metaphysics of Descartes: A Study of the Meditations.* Oxford: Clarendon Press, 1965.

Broadie, Frederick. *An Approach to Descartes' Meditations.* London: Athlone Press,
1970.

Cottingham, John, ed. *The Cambridge Companion to Descartes.* Cambridge: Cambridge University Press, 1992.

Curley, Edwin M. *Descartes Against the Skeptics.* Cambridge: Harvard University
Press, 1978.

Descartes, René. *The Philosophical Writings of Descartes (Writings).* Translated by
John Cottingham, Robert Stoothoff, and Dugald Murdoch. 3 volumes. Cambridge:
Cambridge University Press, 1984.

Dicker, Georges. *Descartes: An Analytical and Historical Introduction.* New York:
Oxford University Press, 1993.

Feldman, Fred. *A Cartesian Introduction to Philosophy.* New York: McGraw-Hill,
1986.

Gaukroger, Stephan. *Descartes: An Intellectual Biography.* Oxford: Clarendon Press,
1997.

Kenny, Anthony J. P. *Descartes: A Study of his Philosophy.* New York: Random House, 1968.

Smith, Norman Kemp. *Studies in the Cartesian Philosophy.* New York: Russell & Russell, 1962.

Spinoza, Benedictus de. *The Principles of Descartes' Philosophy.* Translated by Halbert Hains Britan. Chicago: Open Court Publishing Company, 1905.

Williams, Bernard. *Descartes: The Project of Pure Enquiry.* Atlantic Highlands: Humanities Press, 1978.

Wilson, Margaret D. *Descartes.* London: Routledge & Kegan Paul, 1978.

CHAPTER 5

EXISTENCE AND NATURE OF GOD

Berkeley's *Three Dialogues Between Hylas and Philonous*

W e conclude this section with an introduction to one type of empiricist epistemology and metaphysics. Berkeley opposes the possibility of mind-independent matter, which he sees as a source of skepticism and atheism. He refutes materialism and claims to prove God's existence as he unites the metaphysical basis of science and religion in a radically empiricist theory of knowledge. Berkeley's empiricism leads him to adopt an idealism that regards all existence as consisting of either minds or ideas. God as an infinite mind must exist, according to Berkeley, in order to explain the fact that sensible things exist independently of the will of any particular finite mind, and that the sensible things we finite minds intermittently perceive exist continuously even when we are not perceiving them.

BERKELEY'S IDEALISM

As modern philosophy advanced from the seventeenth to the eighteenth century, many philosophers came to reject the predominance of pure reason in epistemology and metaphysics exemplified by Descartes's thought. The focus of the new philosophy in certain quarters, despite these differences, remained fixed on some of the same problems and modified methods from the earlier period. A noteworthy example is the effort to prove the existence of God as a basis for philosophical explanation. We shall consider in depth a post-Cartesian approach of this kind in a demonstration of the existence of God by one of the most important but frequently misunderstood philosophers of the eighteenth century, George Berkeley (1685–1753).

Berkeley was an Irish clergyman and Bishop of Cloyne, who was personally and professionally interested in the applications of philosophy to questions of religion.

More importantly, Berkeley was a gifted philosopher who was also adept in mathematics and had a good grasp of the predominant Newtonian physics of his day. Berkeley was a prodigy well versed in classical and European languages at an early age, and was well equipped for a career in philosophy, which he understood as inseparable in some ways from theology. For Berkeley, philosophical justification for belief in the existence of God is essential as a way of defeating atheism and skepticism in philosophy and the sciences. The connection between religion and science is deep and pervading in Berkeley's philosophy.

Berkeley is an *idealist* philosopher. This does not mean, as the word is sometimes popularly understood, that he has a naive optimistic view about the good inherent in people or the positive outcome of events that otherwise seem hopeless. To be an idealist in Berkeley's sense is to hold for philosophical reasons that the only things that exist are ideas and the minds in and to which ideas occur. Berkeley sums up his idealist philosophy in the Latin principle, *Esse est percipi aut posse percipere*. The translation is, "To be is to be perceived or a perceiver." Ideas are perceived by minds, which are in a sense mutually dependent. There are no ideas that exist independently of minds, and presumably there can be no minds that are completely empty of any ideas. What is significant about Berkeley's formulation is that Berkeley does not acknowledge the existence of anything different than, beyond or outside of, the mind and its ideas. This is a remarkable, and, to many critics, controversial, even philosophically insupportable, concept. It implies that the physical objects we ordinarily believe ourselves to perceive outside of ourselves and that we assume would exist even if we did not happen to be there to perceive them are nothing but ideas in the mind.

Ideas in Berkeley's technical terminology, in a quite different sense than Plato spoke of Ideas or Forms as ideal abstract entities, are the contents of sense perceptions. If I experience an apple, I can see its red color, taste its sweet or tart flavor, smell its delicious aroma, feel its waxy skin, and hear the satisfying crunch it makes when I bite into its fruit. All of these experienced qualities of the apple in Berkeley's language are *ideas*. The perceived redness, flavor, smell, touch, and sounds of the apple are among its many ideas, which is to say simply that they are perceptions or sensations associated with the apple. Berkeley uses the phrase "congeries of ideas" to describe the integrated collections of ideas that constitute the physical objects experienced in thought, and that, for Berkeley, exist only in the mind. Berkeley can thus maintain that the physical entities we perceive by means of sense perception are congeries of ideas, and, we might even say, *mere* congeries of ideas. If Berkeley is right, then the physical objects that we experience in sensation are not external to thought, and do not exist, as Berkeley also likes to say, "without" the mind, but exist as congeries of ideas within the mind.

Our main purpose in this chapter is to understand Berkeley's idealism as it relates to his attempts to prove the existence of God. We shall begin by explaining the general features of his philosophy, and then concentrate on his proposal to demonstrate the existence of God as an all-powerful creative mind. When we have outlined Berkeley's two arguments to prove that God exists and their implications for his philosophical system, including the problem of free will and the creation of the world, we will be in a position to criticize his idealist metaphysics and epistemology, and to consider the alternative way of thinking about the existence and nature of the world represented by Berkeley's metaphysics as opposed to Plato's, Aristotle's, Ockham's, and Descartes's.

BERKELEY AND DESCARTES ON GOD IN PHILOSOPHY

Berkeley's metaphysics flies in the face of a realist assumption about the nature of the world. Aristotle and Ockham would agree that physical objects are independent of thought, and exist "out there" in the external world that is perceived rather than as a congeries of ideas "within" the mind. Berkeley's philosophy as such offers an exciting challenge to realist assumptions in the philosophy of science, philosophy of mind, metaphysics, theory of knowledge, and philosophy of religion.

Berkeley's attempt to prove the existence of God highlights the differences between his philosophy and Descartes's. Descartes imagines that an evil demon might deceive him into thinking that there are external existent entities when in fact the world of experienced things exists only in his mind. He then offers a purely rational demonstration that God exists and is no deceiver as a way of rescuing us from the evil demon's clutches. Berkeley, by contrast, argues that sensible things exist only as ideas in a mind, and seeks to show that God must exist as a greater mind within which sensible things exist even when they are not being perceived by any human or lesser finite mind. As Berkeley writes in the Preface to his *Three Dialogues Between Hylas and Philonous* (1713), the work that we will be considering:

> If the principles which I here endeavour to propagate are admitted for true, the consequences which, I think, evidently flow from thence are that Atheism and Scepticism will be utterly destroyed, many intricate points made plain, great difficulties solved, several useless parts of science retrenched, speculation referred to practice, and men reduced from paradoxes to common sense. (376)

If Berkeley is right, then he will have united science and religion, and avoided both skepticism and atheism, in a way that is unique in the history of philosophy. The details of Berkeley's arguments, partly because his conclusions are so unexpected and extreme, require sympathetic exposition, at least until we have understood them and are ready to raise criticisms.

Berkeley was one of the most intelligent and well-educated thinkers of his generation. While this by itself is no assurance that his philosophical positions are correct, it suggests that his reasoning is worth taking seriously, if only for the value of ferreting out his mistakes and trying to learn from them. When we have worked through the major elements of Berkeley's idealist philosophy, we will see that he has good if not conclusive grounds for holding that sensible things are congeries of ideas in the mind, and that God exists as a divine mind in which all sensible things are more fully, properly, and creatively apprehended by comparison with their occurrence in human minds. If we are not prepared as a result of these reflections to follow Berkeley's lead toward idealism, we will at least be in a better position to understand why Berkeley chose such a path, and how he unflinchingly accepted the conclusions of a starting point and direction that are in many ways attractive for philosophers who do not accept the opposite assumptions represented by rationalist epistemologists and metaphysicians such as Descartes.

It is not only for the sake of attaining a more complete understanding of the history of philosophy that it is important to study Berkeley. Berkeley is an intellectual curiosity; yet he is something much more. Mastering his theory would hardly be worth the trouble if it were merely a strange chapter in the course of philosophy.

Rather, Berkeley is important because he pursues an apparently reasonable line of inquiry to its ultimate extraordinary implications. Berkeley thereby explores the outcome of a promising theory of knowledge to its distant metaphysical and theological shores, presenting along the route many ingenious concepts, distinctions, and inferences, with an integrity and singleness of vision that has seldom been repeated in the history of philosophy.

EMPIRICISM CONTRA RATIONALISM

The eighteenth century, in the period following Descartes's era, underwent a second philosophical revolution against entrenched Aristotelianism that was fundamentally different than Descartes's. Descartes and other so-called rationalist philosophers, following mathematics as a model, had emphasized the role of pure reason as a mode of knowledge in arriving at philosophically significant metaphysical truths, such as the nature of substance, the existence of God and the distinction between body and soul. Philosophers who followed later in their footsteps came to see the methodology of pure reason as too impoverished to attain scientifically respectable results.

It would distort the complicated history of rationalism and its aftermath to suppose that philosophers suddenly changed their minds when the new century dawned. We cannot draw a neat demarcation between seventeenth-century rationalist philosophy and the opposing trends that arose later in the eighteenth century. We must resist the idea that the eighteenth century rejected all of the major philosophical conclusions of the seventeenth and started all over again with a clean slate as though Descartes and other rationalist thinkers such as Baruch de Spinoza and Leibniz, among many others, had never existed. Although we can plot a kind of choppy progress from identifiable features in philosophical movements during this time, we must bear in mind that the eighteenth century is enormously indebted to the intellectual advances made by the rationalists, whose ideas they do not always reject even if they transform and use them in another way.

Thus, it would be impossible to imagine the unfolding of eighteenth-century philosophy without the profound influence of Isaac Newton's researches in physics, kinematics, cosmology, and optics. Newton's scientific method served as a paradigm or exemplary model for much of eighteenth-century philosophical thought. Newton's discoveries would nevertheless not have been possible in turn in the absence of Galileo's and Descartes's innovations in science and philosophy. To mention just one crucial example, Newton's famous First Law of Motion, that a body moving in space unimpeded by impressed forces continues infinitely in a straight line, is found in and was first articulated and made widely known in Descartes's physics. Newton declared that he was able to achieve great things in science because he "stood on the shoulders of giants," by whom he meant to include not only scientific researchers in the narrow sense like Copernicus, but also pioneering philosopher-physicists such as Galileo and Descartes.

What, then, characterizes the period of philosophy that is somewhat arbitrarily associated with the onset of the eighteenth century? It is frequently identified as a time of great interest in a countermovement to rationalism known as *empiricism*. The word "empiricism" derives from the name of an important ancient philosopher, Sextus Empiricus, who criticized the conclusions of excessively rationalist thinkers in his own day. Sextus wrote an important manuscript titled *Adversus Mathematicos*, which is to say, *Against the Mathematicians*. Although Sextus did not dispute the usefulness of mathematics as a tool for acquiring and validating scientific information, he argued against efforts in philosophy to base all knowledge on the kind of abstract general reasoning that one typically finds in mathematically minded philosophers such as Pythagoras, Parmenides, Zeno of Elea, and Plato, whose rationalist mantle was taken up in later times, among others, by Descartes.

Historical parallels in philosophy are often problematic. There are, nevertheless, interesting similarities in the opposition between, say, Plato and Aristotle, and between the mathematicians against whom Sextus says we should try to base knowledge on experience. It is in honor of Sextus's contributions to the discussion that we refer specifically to the experiential data provided by sense perception as empirical evidence. We see many of the same differences that divide Plato and Aristotle, or Plato and Sextus Empiricus, and the latter day rationalists and empiricists of the seventeenth and eighteenth centuries, such as Descartes and Berkeley. In the period of modern philosophy, it is common to speak of a trio of thinkers on each side of this divide, usually considering together among others Descartes, Leibniz, and Spinoza as representative rationalist philosophers, and, on the other side, also among others, John Locke, Berkeley, and David Hume.

We want to avoid oversimplifications in the history of philosophy. We nevertheless recognize that we must start somewhere in order to piece together a picture of how philosophical inquiry has developed. We can then correct and refine our rough historical outline as we proceed and as our knowledge of specific figures in the chronology of philosophy and their interrelation improves. If we begin with a sense of the contrast between seventeenth-century rationalism as represented by Descartes and eighteenth-century empiricism as represented by Berkeley, then we can construct a basic framework within which to examine Berkeley's theory of sensible things and proof for the existence of God. We will then be able to take first steps in understanding Berkeley's philosophical orientation in part as a reaction to what he perceived as the limitations of rationalism and the course he and others in the eighteenth century hoped to chart in philosophy, leading in his case to idealism.

The essential feature of empiricism as distinct from rationalism is its emphasis on sense experience as a source of knowledge. We have already seen that both Plato and Descartes, rationalist thinkers in individual ways, are suspicious of experience as a source of knowledge. Plato goes so far as to deny that we can have any knowledge in the true sense of the word concerning the changing world of experience. He reserves the word "knowledge" exclusively for true justified beliefs concerning the unchanging ideal world of the abstract Forms. Plato describes physics as at most a "likely story" about the nature of things. He contrasts the genuine knowledge that is supposed to be possible of the Forms with what is merely and can at most be the right opinion or correct beliefs concerning sensible things encountered in sense experience. Descartes does not draw quite the same extreme conclusion, but in the piece of wax example he argues that even ordinary physical bodies are better known by the mind's faculty of judgment than by the senses. He also insists that the senses considered by themselves cannot lead us to epistemically certain empirical knowledge, in the absence of a sound rationalist foundation based in pure reason. He maintains that the senses are subject to doubts based on the logical possibility that there might be an evil demon who deceives us whenever we try to gather knowledge about the world. In different ways, reason for rationalist philosophers such as Plato and Descartes inevitably triumphs over sense experience. As a matter of emphasis and methodological priority, rationalist thinkers in any generation regard reason as philosophically more valuable than sensation.

A greater distinction between rationalists and empiricists such as Berkeley could hardly be imagined. While Plato and Descartes argue that because of illusions and subjective differences in perspective, changing phenomena in the world of experience cannot be trusted to provide knowledge, Berkeley and other empiricists maintain that pure reason by itself is too empty. Their objection is that reason at most guarantees that a theory will be free of contradictions or logical inconsistencies. They urge that the mere lack of inconsistency is not itself a positive thing that guarantees truth. If we are looking to a philosophical methodology as a way of discovering and adding to our knowledge, we cannot hope that any method based in pure reason will yield truth. A theory that says only that grass is white and snow is green is justified by pure reason in the sense that it is internally logically consistent; there are no contradictions in asserting the two claims. The mere logical consistency or noncontradiction of such a theory does not make it true, however, where we believe from our experience of grass and snow that the two assertions are false and have the color properties of snow and grass reversed.

As a further sign of the limitations of a rationalist methodology in trying to acquire or justify beliefs in knowledge, empiricist critics of rationalism sometimes object that pure reason cannot be an adequate method of knowledge because numerous rationalist philosophers, all of whom claim to be following the method of pure reason, reach diametrically opposed conclusions in the articulation of their respective rationalist philosophical systems. If pure reason offered more than the mere freedom from logical inconsistency, if it provided a method of discovering truths, then one might expect that anyone following the same method ought to achieve the same results. Such agreement, notably, is not found in the legacy of seventeenth-century rationalism when we consider the disparate conclusions of, say, Descartes, Leibniz, and Spinoza, who defended radically opposed results about the concept of substance, and the nature of God, the soul, and freedom of the will.

Where rationalism at best produces only internally consistent free-floating grandiose metaphysical systems, such as those found in the writings of the great rationalist system builders, there the empiricists urgently wanted to find a way to anchor philosophy and science to the real world. They accordingly followed a variation of the philosophical method of Aristotle. At this time, Aristotle was no longer taken as an absolute authority as in the late Middle Ages and Renaissance, but rather as a proponent of the view that we must bring philosophy back down to earth by using empirical observation of the state of the world as a source of information and ideas, and as a basis for philosophical reasoning. The rationalists had their chance in the seventeenth century to establish the virtues of pure reason as a method of knowledge. Their grand experiment inadvertently proved just the opposite, that knowledge cannot rest entirely or exclusively on reason, and that reason is not a sufficiently powerful basis for knowledge. The pendulum in some ways predictably swings far in the opposite direction in the eighteenth century as a result, supporting contrary philosophical assumptions and methodology based on experience rather than pure reason, as we find in Berkeley's philosophy.

Berkeley's idealism is a consequence of his radical empiricism. Berkeley's radical empiricism, in turn, while possessing methodological advantages of its own, is by no means the uncritical experientialism that Descartes rightly criticizes, and is in part at least a reaction to the failings of rationalism. The shortcomings of rationalism give rise to empiricism, and empiricism in the radical form Berkeley espouses in turn entails idealism. How does this happen? We can follow the philosophical development from rationalism to empiricism and idealism by considering the principal arguments presented in Berkeley's *Three Dialogues.*

RHETORICAL PURPOSE OF BERKELEY'S DIALOGUES

Let us turn now to Berkeley's text and see how his radically empiricist methodology leads to an idealist theory of knowledge, metaphysics, and philosophy of religion, and to a combined refutation of skepticism and atheism. The common philosophical error that leads to skepticism and atheism, Berkeley believes, is an ultimately unintelligible commitment to the existence of mind-independent *substance* or *matter* as the underlying *substratum* of sensible things and the sensible properties we experience in sense perception.

Berkeley's *Three Dialogues Between Hylas and Philonous* emphasizes the contrast between *materialism* and *idealism* even in its title. The name *Hylas*, with its classical connotations, is chosen by Berkeley not only for literary effect, but as representing materialism. As we remarked in discussing Aristotle's theory of substance, the ancient Greek word *hylé* means matter, which Aristotle incorporates in his account of *proté hylé* or prime matter. Hylas, an imaginary composite character in Berkeley's dialogue, is a materialist, a thinker who, at the outset of the book at least, accepts the existence of mind-independent matter. Exactly what this belief amounts to we shall have to come more gradually to understand as the arguments on both sides of the dispute unfold. Scholars have conjectured that Hylas among other thinkers represents the materialist metaphysics of Locke and Nicolas Malebranche. Philonous, on the other hand, is an eloquent spokesman for Berkeley's idealism and antimaterialism, and ultimately for Berkeley's empiricism. The name *Philonous* is equally significant for Berkeley in its language roots. The name combines the Greek words *philo* and *noûs*. The word *philo* means love of. We find it in the word *philosophy*, where, together with the word *sophia*, it means love of wisdom. Combined here with *noûs*, meaning mind, the name *Philonous* refers to the love of the mind. It is a perfect designation for the Berkeleyan idealist stridently opposed to materialism in Berkeley's dialogue.

The fact that Berkeley chooses to express his theory in the form of a dialogue is also noteworthy. Berkeley wrote a previous philosophical book, *A Treatise on the Principles of Human Knowledge* (1710), at the age of twenty-five, arguing that sensible things or physical objects are congeries of ideas in the mind rather than material entities existing external to all thought. The theory he presented there was greeted with incomprehension, misunderstanding, and even ridicule. Berkeley accordingly resolved to present his views again in a different format that he hoped would receive a friendlier reception by philosophical critics and the general educated reading public. The dialogue format, as we know from Plato's example, tracing dialectical twists and turns in trying to arrive at the truth about a philosophical concept or to resolve a philosophical problem, is especially suited also to Berkeley's purposes. Berkeley reports, again in the Preface to *Three Dialogues:*

> This design I proposed in the First Part of a treatise concerning the *Principles of Human Knowledge*, published in the year 1710. But, before I proceed to publish the Second Part, I thought it requisite to treat more clearly and fully of certain Principles laid down in the First and to place them in a new light. Which is the business of the following *Dialogues.* (376)

The advantage Berkeley sees in the use of dialogue is primarily rhetorical. The dialogue communicates the principles of his idealist philosophy in the give-and-take between Hylas and Philonous. There is an opportunity in following their exchange for the reader to examine objections to Berkeley's position that might also occur to an unsympathetic critic represented in the person of Hylas, and, more importantly, for criticisms to be answered and refuted by Philonous. There is also a theatrical effect that Berkeley expects to achieve in the drama portrayed as Hylas initially expresses disagreement with Philonous, but, being reasonable and open-minded, as Berkeley expects an intelligent reader to be, Hylas progressively accepts first some of Philonous's main contentions, retrenches and tries in various ways to reassert materialism as against idealism, and is finally if reluctantly convinced.

Berkeley hopes that the gentle reader who might at first be unpersuaded or even hostile to idealism, like so many of those who objected to or simply could not understand his *Principles*, will also gradually come around to accepting his antimaterialism. By identifying with Hylas, critics may find that they cannot do any better in trying to support his objections to Philonous, and in the end will be won over to Berkeley's philosophy despite their original misgivings. Philonous challenges Hylas at a critical juncture in their exchange in this spirit, when Philonous has answered Hylas's criticisms, but Hylas remains unwilling to admit defeat:

> PHILONOUS: I would fain know what more you would require in order to a perfect conviction. Have you not had the liberty of explaining yourself all manner of ways? Were any little slips in discourse laid hold and insisted on? Or were you not allowed to retract or reinforce anything you had offered, as best served your purpose? Hath not everything you could say been heard and examined with all the fairness imaginable? In a word, have you not in every point been convinced out of your own mouth? And, if you can at present discover any flaw in any of your former concessions, or think of any remaining subterfuge, any new distinction, colour, or comment whatsoever, why do you not produce it? (418–19)

If Berkeley has done his work well, then at the end of the dialogue, even a reader predisposed to disagree with Berkeley's conclusions should be in no stronger philosophical position than Hylas to object to Berkeley's radical empiricism and the idealism it entails, in exasperation at his inability to refute Philonous. Berkeley expects to give his theory a new life by presenting it in this argumentatively more effective version, to win more advocates for a position that he thinks is necessary in order to maintain the tightly interwoven connection between science and religion, and between the refutation of skepticism and atheism, and to demonstrate in a different way than Descartes the dependence of all knowledge and the existence and nature of the sensible world on the existence of God.

Skepticism, Atheism, and Godless Materialism

Berkeley thinks that skepticism and atheism are two sides of the same coin. He believes that both can be defeated if materialism is refuted in favor of idealism. The connection between these conclusions is that if we accept a theory of material entities existing independently of mind, that are not congeries of ideas existing in a mind, then science has no reason to assume that God exists and we are in that case metaphysically committed to the existence of entities that we cannot know, because their properties are necessarily hidden from perception.

The problem with materialism, according to Berkeley, is that science can in principle explain all physical phenomena without making reference to the existence of God. Science as a rule adopts a minimalist attitude with respect to the entities that are strictly needed in order to make its explanations work. If we can explain physical events in the material universe without referring to the existence or will of God, then, following the principle of Ockham's razor, it would seem to imply that God is unnecessary to science. If that is true, then there is no reason from the standpoint of science as the most complete and correct system of knowledge to accept the existence of God. The linking of the topics of skepticism, atheism, and science in Berkeley's project is revealed in the extensive original title of his book: *Three Dialogues Between Hylas and Philonous. The Design of Which is Plainly to Demonstrate the Reality and Perfection of Human Knowledge, the Incorporeal Nature of the Soul, and the Immediate Providence of a Deity in Opposition to Sceptics and Atheists. Also to Open a Method for Rendering the Sciences more Easy, Useful, and Compendious.*

If natural science grounded on a materialist metaphysics offers satisfactory explanations of physical phenomena without making reference to the existence of God, then materialism provides a powerful scientific rationale for atheism as the positive disbelief in God's existence. If we deny materialism, and conclude instead with Berkeley's idealism that sensible things exist as congeries of ideas in the mind, then it may be reasonable to suppose that God exists as an infinitely powerful mind that comprehends all sensible things that we can at best only partially experience. Science based on Berkeley's idealist assumptions requires the existence of God. Natural science as Berkeley thinks of it cannot offer explanations of even the most basic physical phenomena without supposing that sensible things exist as congeries of ideas in God's mind, and that what we think of as causal connections in the physical world are God's choices concerning successions of events. We shall need to inquire more closely into the reasons for these conclusions in Berkeley's philosophy. For the time being, it is worth remarking that from Berkeley's perspective science cannot succeed except on the assumption that God exists.

It follows, if Berkeley is right, that science contradicts atheism and skepticism. For this, science must be based on an idealist rather than materialist philosophy. Near the end of Berkeley's *Three Dialogues,* in the Third Dialogue, Berkeley's character Philonous states:

> PHILONOUS: . . . But allowing Matter to exist and the notion of absolute existence to be as clear as light; yet, was this ever known to make the creation more credible? Nay, hath it not furnished the atheists and infidels of all ages with the most plausible arguments against a creation? That a corporeal sub-

stance, which hath an absolute existence without the minds of spirits should be produced out of nothing, by the mere will of a Spirit, hath been looked upon as a thing so contrary to all reason, so impossible and absurd, that not only the most celebrated among the ancients, but even divers modern and Christian philosophers have thought Matter co-eternal with the Deity. Lay these things together and then judge you whether Materialism disposes men to believe the creation of things. (477–78)

Skepticism is also directly related to materialism in Berkeley's view. Materialism acknowledges the existence of nonsensible things beyond the contents of the mind, and about which the mind literally has no idea. It follows in that case that philosophy is committed to the existence of things that are unknowable. There are entities or parts or aspects of entities that we can never know. If we did know about them, then, Berkeley argues, we can know about them only by virtue of entertaining ideas of their properties, in which case they would once again exist within the mind.

The concept of a material entity that exists entirely without or independently of the mind, and does not consist of any idea or congeries of ideas, is the idea of something that, by virtue of existing beyond thought, is necessarily unknowable, unexperienceable. A dilemma therefore confronts the idealism-materialism dispute. If we accept Berkeley's idealism, then we must admit the conclusion that sensible things are mental, existing in the mind, as Berkeley says. Berkeley is delighted with this conclusion, but many anti-idealist thinkers find it paradoxical to imagine that physical entities could exist only in the mind, even if the mind in question turns out to be God's. If, on the other hand, sensible things are material, in the sense of being nonmental, metaphysically independent existences that do not require or presuppose the existence of any mind, then philosophy is committed to the existence of something for which we can have no empirical evidence. The properties of a material entity must then remain unknowable, inscrutable to perception and inaccessible to the mind. If there is nothing more to sensible things than the sensible properties experienced by a mind, then the mind can at least in principle have a complete grasp of an entity's properties, with no unknowable remainder. In this respect, materialism entails skepticism in Berkeley's critique, while idealism in principle has transparent access to all the properties of any sensible thing, and need not acknowledge that there is anything inherently unknowable about the existence and nature of physical entities.

The dialogue takes place against this background of issues. It begins with Hylas questioning Philonous about a rumor he has heard, according to which Philonous is supposed to hold extravagant philosophical conclusions and to be a kind of skeptic. Philonous rejects the charge, but requires Hylas to clarify the meaning of skepticism before answering the criticism. This question sets the tone for discussion in which Hylas and Philonous engage throughout the dialogue. Hylas accuses Philonous of being a skeptic in the sense of denying the existence of matter, on the unexamined but supposedly commonsense assumption that matter exists. To reject the existence of anything so apparently indispensable to understanding the nature of the world, Hylas believes, is to be guilty of some form of skepticism; to be doubtful about things whose existence is obvious. Philonous rightly counters that skepticism is more properly a term reserved for those who are doubtful about the existence of anything or about the possibility of any kind of knowledge. With respect to the first meaning of "skepticism," Philonous denies being skeptical in this sense, since he fully acknowledges the existence of sensible things, interpreting them as congeries of ideas; nor is he skeptical about the existence of minds as thinking things that think ideas. As to the second meaning of "skepticism," concerning the possibility of knowledge, Philonous argues that it is Hylas and materialists generally who deny the possibility of knowing sensible things in their entirety. Hylas and Philonous set the stage for their exchange throughout the dialogue in these remarks:

> HYLAS: I am glad to find there was nothing in the accounts I heard of you.
>
> PHILONOUS: Pray, what were those?
>
> HYLAS: You were represented, in last night's conversation, as one who maintained the most extravagant opinion that ever entered into the mind of man, to wit, that there is no such thing as *material substance* in the world.
>
> PHILONOUS: That there is no such thing as what *philosophers* call *material substance*, I am seriously persuaded: but, if I were made to see anything absurd or sceptical in this, I should then have the same reason to renounce this that I imagine I have now to reject the contrary opinion. (380–81)

The connection between materialism and skepticism is featured from the beginning of the dialogue. Philonous admits that if he believed that his rejection of materialism amounted to skepticism, then he would need to rethink his antimaterialism. As things stand, the very opposite is true. Philonous maintains that materialism entails skepticism, and that, far from being a skeptic himself, he denies materialism in order to avoid being skeptical about the possibility of knowledge. Hylas fires back with an astonished counterassertion that it is skeptical to question the existence of matter. The question turns naturally to the meaning of "skepticism":

> HYLAS: What! can anything be more fantastical, more repugnant to Common Sense, or a more manifest piece of Scepticism, than to believe there is no such thing as *matter*?
>
> PHILONOUS: Softly, good Hylas. What if it should prove that you, who hold there is, are, by virtue of that opinion, a greater sceptic and maintain more paradoxes and repugnances to Common Sense, than I who believe no such thing? (381)

Dispute over the question of who is the greater skeptic, one who accepts or one who denies the existence of matter, epitomizes the opposition between Hylas and Philonous. Their discussion is pursued at many depths and through many side-issues. Philonous first denies being a skeptic, and demands that Hylas explain clearly what he means by the concept; he flatly rejects the label if it is taken to mean denying the possibility of knowledge. He rightly objects that if that were the proper meaning of the word, then Hylas, by denying the contrary view that Philonous accepts, would be just as much a skeptic. By denying the existence of matter, Philonous rather affirms an item of knowledge, namely, that matter does not exist, and so cannot reasonably be accused of denying the possibility of any and all knowledge. He asks:

> PHILONOUS: How cometh it to pass then, Hylas, that you pronounce me a *sceptic*, because I deny what you affirm, to wit, the existence of Matter? Since, for aught you can tell, I am as peremptory in my denial, as you in your affirmation.
>
> HYLAS: Hold, Philonous, I have been a little out in my definition; but every false step a man makes in discourse is not to be insisted on. I said indeed that a *sceptic* was one who doubted of everything; but I should have added, or who denies the reality and truth of things.
>
> PHILONOUS: What things? Do you mean the principles and theorems of sciences? But these you know are universal intellectual notions, and consequently independent of Matter. The denial therefore of this doth not imply the denying them. (382)

A skeptic in the sense of someone who denies the "reality and truth of things" perhaps comes closer to a correct definition of the term. Philonous clearly does not doubt everything, or even everything it is possible to doubt, in the manner of Descartes in the *Meditations* before he has disposed of the evil demon.

Hylas nevertheless accuses him of being a skeptic in the sense of denying things that he along with every other person of sound judgment ought to accept. Philonous accordingly denies being a skeptic in this redefined sense also, since he accepts the principles and conclusions of science. He is no opponent of scientific knowledge as such. His quarrel is with what he regards as the extravagant philosophical conjecture that sensible things are supported by an insensible mind-independent material substratum. Philonous considers himself as a result to be the true philosophical defender of scientific and religious knowledge against the skepticism he believes is entailed by materialism.

In Berkeley's Third Dialogue, Philonous summarizes the debate as it stands after lengthy efforts on Hylas's part to convince Philonous that matter exists, and by Philonous to persuade Hylas of the opposite. Hylas maintains a succession of alternative interpretations of the concept of matter, in an attempt to make a stronger case for the existence of an underlying material substance as the metaphysical foundation for ideas of the sensible properties experienced in the perception of physical things. Philonous believes he has refuted every one of these proposals, and has thereby exhausted Hylas's ability to sustain the concept of matter against his philosophical objections. The two now say:

> PHILONOUS: Pray tell me if the case stands not thus:—At first, from a belief of material substance, you would have it that the immediate objects existed without the mind; then, that they are archetypes; then, causes; next, instruments; then, occasions: lastly, *something in general*, which being interpreted proves *nothing*. So Matter comes to nothing. What think you, Hylas, is not this a fair summary of your whole proceeding?
>
> HYLAS: Be that as it will, yet I still insist upon it, that *our* not being able to conceive a thing is no argument against its existence. (437)

Having reduced Hylas to this precarious conclusion, Philonous runs through a list of possible interpretations of the concept of matter, all of which Hylas admits are inappropriate to his purpose, and concerning none of which he thinks it is possible to have knowledge. Trying to make a virtue out of this calamity, Hylas argues that ignorance and skepticism are the proper conclusions of true philosophy. Later, again, at the beginning of the Third Dialogue, he is driven to admit:

> HYLAS: There is not that single thing in the world whereof we can know the real nature, or what it is in itself.
>
> PHILONOUS: Will you tell me I do not really know what fire or water is?
>
> HYLAS: You may indeed know that fire appears hot, and water fluid; but this is no more than knowing what sensations are produced in your own mind, upon the application of fire and water to your organs of sense. Their internal constitution, their true and real nature, you are utterly in the dark as to *that*.
>
> PHILONOUS: Do I not know this to be a real stone that I stand on, and that which I see before my eyes to be a real tree?
>
> HYLAS: *Know?* No, it is impossible you or any alive should know it. All you know is that you have such a certain idea or appearance in your own mind. But what is this to the real tree or stone? I tell you that colour, figure, and hardness, which you perceive, are not the real natures of those things, or in the least like them. (442–43)

Hylas, in desperation, clinging still to his commitment to the existence of material substance, declares that we cannot know anything about the real nature of perceived entities; we can only know the ideas that such things produce in our minds. Here again is a perfect statement of the philosophical disagreement between Hylas and Philonous. Hylas begins by accusing Philonous of skepticism, or at least of wondering whether the reports he has heard are true that Philonous is a skeptic who denies the existence of matter. Philonous turns the tables on Hylas by forcing him to admit that it is the materialist rather than the idealist who is driven to skepticism. The materialist believes that there is a hidden aspect to sensible things. The sensible properties of sensible things are perceived, but according to the materialist, there is also supposed to be an underlying material substance or substratum that by definition remains imperceivable and hence unknowable. Hylas tries to promote this consequence of materialism as a philosophical virtue, but Philonous does not agree:

> HYLAS: . . . Hence, the vulgar retain their mistakes, and for all that make a shift to bustle through the affairs of life. But philosophers know better things.
>
> PHILONOUS: You mean they know that they *know nothing*.
>
> HYLAS: That is the very top and perfection of human knowledge.
>
> PHILONOUS: But are you all this while in earnest, Hylas; and are you seriously persuaded that you know nothing real in the world? Suppose you are going to write, would you not call for pen, ink, and paper, like another man; and do you not know what it is you call for? (443–44)

There is an echo of Socrates' irony in Philonous's challenge to Hylas concerning the materialist philosopher's superiority of knowledge. Philonous asks in disbelief whether according to Hylas materialists have higher knowledge in knowing that they know nothing. This is much like Socrates' assertion in Plato's dialogues, interpreting the oracle at Delphi's pronouncement that he is the wisest man in Athens in knowing that he does not know, whereas others think they have knowledge but do not really know.

Philonous rejects the skepticism implied by materialism. He reaffirms the commonsense view that the world is known through perception. He attacks Hylas's materialism because of the skepticism he believes it entails, and reversing the objection with which Hylas originally charged him, claiming:

> PHILONOUS: You amaze me. Was ever anything more wild and extravagant than the notions you now maintain: and is it not evident you are led into all these extravagances by the belief of *material substance?* This makes you dream of those unknown natures in everything. It is this occasions your distinguishing between the reality and sensible appearances of things. It is to this you are indebted for being ignorant of what everybody else knows perfectly well. Nor is this all: you are not only ignorant of the true nature of everything, but you know not whether any thing really exists, or whether there are any true natures at all; forasmuch as you attribute to your material beings an absolute or external existence, wherein you suppose their reality consists. And as you are forced in the end to acknowledge such an existence means either a direct repugnancy, or nothing at all, it follows that you are obliged to pull down your own hypothesis of material Substance, and positively to deny the real existence of any part of the universe. And so you are plunged into the deepest and most deplorable scepticism that ever man was. Tell me, Hylas, is it not as I say?
>
> HYLAS: I agree with you. . . . (444–45)

A materialist metaphysics also contributes to atheism according to Berkeley and his spokescharacter Philonous. Berkeley's attempt to prove the existence of God within his antimaterialist philosophical framework is intended not only as a refutation of skepticism of the sort Hylas is finally compelled to admit, but equally as a refutation of atheism. The two positions, anti-skepticism and anti-atheism are closely linked together in Berkeley's antimaterialism.

The argument Philonous develops is that the world of sensible phenomena, if it is not upheld by an underlying material substratum that is altogether insensible and unknowable, must exist primarily in the infinite mind of God, and only secondarily, partially, and incompletely in our finite minds, as we experience sensible things. If Berkeley is right, then all problems of metaphysics and epistemology boil down to the fundamental opposition between sensible things as material or ideal. The world of experience either has an unknowable material substratum or it does not. If the world has an unknowable material substratum, then skepticism is entailed and there is no need to bring the concept of God into scientific explanations of physical occurrences. If sensible things consist only of ideas in the mind, whether God's mind or ours, then the universe in all its properties is in principle knowable, so that refuting atheism is equally a refutation of skepticism.

Matter as the Substratum of Sensibles

The concept of matter, despite Berkeley's criticisms, has been attractive to many philosophers. Hylas says much to explain why material substance as the substratum of sensible things has a powerful appeal.

One popular argument for the existence of mind-independent matter depends on the assumption that sensible things would exist even if there happened to exist no minds to perceive them, and that they continue to exist even when no one is actually perceiving them. We do not ordinarily imagine that physical objects pop in and out of existence depending on whether or not someone is there to perceive them. Perception is the method by which we learn about the properties of sensible things, but we do not ordinarily imagine that perception brings sensible things into existence and can cause them to disappear when they are not being perceived. Berkeley eventually wants to explain this expectation as a natural consequence of our limitation to immediate experience of our own finite human minds. If God exists, and this is precisely what Berkeley through Philonous proposes to prove, then sensible things even in the most remote parts of the physical universe where human minds will never travel to perceive them, and at all times when human minds only intermittently perceive them, are completely and continuously perceived by the infinite mind of God. As Hylas remarks:

> HYLAS: I acknowledge, Philonous, that, upon a fair observation of what passes in my mind, I can discover nothing else but that I am a thinking being, affected with variety of sensations; neither is it possible to conceive how a sensation should exist in an unperceiving substance. But then, on the other hand, when I look on sensible things in a different view, considering them as so many modes and qualities, I find it necessary to suppose a *material substratum*, without which they cannot be conceived to exist.

> PHILONOUS: *Material substratum* call you it? Pray, by which of your senses came you acquainted with that being?

> HYLAS: It is not itself sensible; its modes and qualities only being perceived by the senses.

> PHILONOUS: I presume then it was by reflexion and reason you obtained the idea of it.

> HYLAS: I do not pretend to any proper positive *idea* of it. However, I conclude it exists, because qualities cannot be conceived to exist without a support. (408)

Later, Hylas elaborates on the concept of a material substratum as the insensible metaphysical platform supporting sensible qualities. Philonous presses Hylas for a further explanation of the concept, and Hylas retreats to the implications of the terminology, suggesting that a material substratum must be spread beneath or underlie the sensible qualities of sensible things. He answers:

> HYLAS: Is it not sufficiently expressed in the term *substratum*, or *substance*?

> PHILONOUS: If so, the word *substratum* should import that it is spread under the sensible qualities or accidents?

HYLAS: True.

PHILONOUS: And consequently under extension?

HYLAS: I own it.

PHILONOUS: It is therefore somewhat in its own nature entirely distinct from extension? (409)

It is not hard for Philonous to persuade Hylas that the position is absurd. If material substance or substratum is entirely distinct from extension, then it cannot literally be true that a material substratum is spread beneath or underlies sensible qualities in anything like the way one physical thing can be placed under another.

The metaphor is that of a material substratum being "spread" underneath the sensible properties of things experienced in sensation. Matter thereby lends sensible qualities support as a kind of surface to which they may attach. The concept of something's being spread under another thing, however, is one that is derived from sense experience, where we see or feel a sensible thing such as butter being spread on a piece of bread and in turn spread under a layer of peanut butter or jam. Material substance as a substratum for all perceivable properties, on the contrary, must itself be totally insensible and imperceivable. It is unclear, as Philonous observes, whether we can think of matter as a substratum in anything like the sense of a platform or subsurface to which sensible qualities of sensible things adhere.

Another important role that the concept of matter is supposed to play in a materialist metaphysics is as a unifying foundation for sensible properties. The problem that materialism hopes to solve in this way is that of accounting for the fact that the ideas we associate with a particular sensible thing must somehow be bound together as the sensible properties of a single sensible entity. Consider again the example of an apple. The apple, we say, is red, sweet, aromatic, waxy and firm, and crunchy-sounding. What makes all of these sensible properties properties of the same sensible thing? What ties them together? We experience them as distinct categories of sensible qualities. There is no necessary connection, it would seem, between color and taste or smell, texture or sound. We nevertheless believe that they are all properties of the same apple, and we think of an apple as a unified entity that possesses all of these among other sensible properties. What philosophical principles can be adduced to justify belief in the unity and integrity of a single apple? How do I know when I see the apple's color and taste its flavor that I am experiencing properties of the same thing? What if anything is the connection between an apple's color and its flavor, or any of its other sensible properties? What justifies us in believing that all of these properties belong together as properties of one and the same object?

Materialists answer this question by saying, as Philonous gets Hylas to admit, that a material substratum underlies the sensible properties of sensible things. The materialist explanation of why the several properties of the apple all belong together as properties of the same thing is by allowing that all the sensible properties literally attach to the same underlying substratum or material base. The concept of a material substratum in turn is that of an insensible and for that reason entirely mind-independent foundation or support for the sensible properties that we experience in sensation. A sensible thing, such as the apple, according to materialism, is not merely an integrated assemblage or congeries of ideas, but rather an underlying insensible substance that is in some sense spread out under the sensible qualities of sensible things, to which the object's sensible properties are all inextricably linked.

The apple is red and sweet, in the materialist conception, because redness and sweetness are both sensible properties superimposed on the same underlying insensible material foundation. They are properties of the same thing, not merely because there is nothing more to say than that they are experienced in proximity, seeing the color of the apple in a continuous series of experiences that is also found together in roughly the same space-time frame in which we experience the apple's taste and aroma, textures, and sounds, but because they all belong and are all attached as multimodal sensible qualities to one and the same underlying insensible material entity. It is the apple's insensible matter or material substratum that is metaphorically spread out underneath the apple's sensible properties. We must, for consistency's sake, speak of the material substratum of the apple as only metaphorically spread out beneath the apple's sensible properties. As an insensible entity, the material substratum of the apple is not distributed in space and time in the way that sensible things are literally described as spread out, such as a blanket or a layer of cake frosting.

The material substratum of sensible things to which all sensible properties of the same sensible thing are ascribed according to materialism is supposed to exist in space and time, and presumably never occurs except as the foundation of sensible qualities. It is not supposed to be experienced in space and time like other spatiotemporal entities. It is, rather, like Hylas's namesake in Aristotle's concept of prime matter or *proté hylé*, altogether lacking, when considered in itself, in any individuating definition, species, secondary substance, or form. It is also related for this reason to what contemporary metaphysicians sometimes speak of as *bare particulars*. A bare particular is similarly supposed to be an individuated thing that has no properties of its own, but to which sensible qualities attach. It is also never found by itself, but is assumed to provide an explanation of the identity and individuation of sensible things. The concept of a sensible thing is understood on a variation of the materialist model as an individual mind-independent entity to which a particular set of ideas or sensible properties attach, rather than a mere congeries of mind-dependent ideas. This is the concept of matter as the material substratum of sensible things that Hylas defends and Berkeley through Philonous rejects.

SENSIBLE THINGS AS CONGERIES OF IDEAS

Discounting the existence of a material substratum of sensible things, Berkeley speaks of the apple as nothing more than a congeries of ideas. The problem is whether or not the concept of a congeries of ideas explains how it is that the many sensible properties of a sensible thing all go together as the properties of one thing. What, exactly, is a congeries in Berkeley's metaphysics, and how does it help us to understand the unity of sensible things and the sensible properties we associate with an individual object belonging to one and the same entity?

It might be useful to begin by asking how well the materialist concept of matter as the underlying substratum of sensible things works in trying to explain the identity of sensible things. We should recall that the substratum proposed by materialists is entirely insensible. We cannot experience it by means of any of the senses. How then does it help to provide identity conditions for sensible things? How does it help us to understand the reason why the redness and sweetness of the apple are properties of the same thing to say that these particular qualities somehow "attach" to the same underlying material substratum or bare particular? We cannot see (or hear or touch or taste or smell) the insensible substratum, nor can we see (etc.) the insensible connections by which the sensible properties of sensible things that the materialist says are attached to an underlying material substratum. In practice, the materialist hypothesis does not seem to represent any sort of gain in understanding how the apple's redness and sweetness can be thought of as properties belonging to the same thing. Philonous in Berkeley's dialogues makes the same point in two important passages in the Third Dialogue, with respect to the example of a cherry:

> PHILONOUS: What you call the empty forms and outside of things seem to me the very things themselves. Nor are they empty or incomplete otherwise than upon your supposition—that Matter is an essential part of all corporeal things. We both, therefore, agree in this, that we perceive only sensible forms: but herein we differ—you will have them to be empty appearances, I real beings. In short, you do not trust your senses, I do. (463)

> PHILONOUS: . . . I see this cherry, I feel it, I taste it: and I am sure *nothing* cannot be seen or felt or tasted: it is therefore *real*. Take away the sensations of softness, moisture, redness, tartness, and you take away the cherry, since it is not a being distinct from sensations. A cherry, I say, is nothing but a congeries of sensible impressions, or ideas perceived by various senses: which ideas are united into one thing (or have one name given them) by the mind because they are observed to attend each other. Thus, when the palate is affected with such a particular taste, the sight is affected with a red colour, the touch with roundness, softness, &c. Hence, when I see, and feel, and taste, in sundry certain manners, I am sure the cherry exists or is real; its reality being in my opinion nothing abstracted from those sensations. But if by the word *cherry* you mean an unknown nature, distinct from all those sensible qualities, and by its *existence* something distinct from its being perceived; then, indeed, I own neither you nor I, nor anyone else, can be sure it exists. (469)

If the matter underlying a sensible thing is entirely without sensible properties, then there do not seem to be any recognizable identity conditions by means of which we can distinguish the material substance to which the redness and sweetness of the apple belong, as opposed, say, to the greenness and mellowness of a pear. How, if material substrata have no distinguishing sensible properties, does the hypothesis that there exists an insensible mind-independent underlying material substratum serve to avoid mixing up these sensible qualities, grouping the redness of the apple with the mellowness of the pear and the greenness of the pear with the sweetness of the apple? It appears that the best a materialist might be able to do is to say that the material substratum of the apple is the particular substratum that supports the sensible properties of redness and sweetness that are associated with the apple, while the material substratum of the pear is the particular substratum that supports the sensible properties of greenness and mellowness associated with the pear. This is clearly no advance over the immaterialist assertion that the apple is just defined as the congeries of sensible properties that include redness and sweetness and the others, which col-

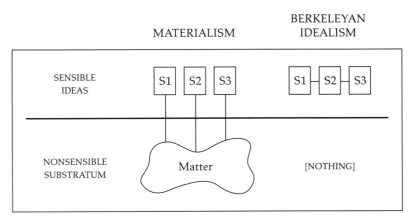

FIGURE 5.1 Materialism versus Berkeleyan idealism

lectively distinguish it from the congeries of sensible properties that include greenness and mellowness and the other properties of the pear.

We can compare the difference between the materialism Berkeley opposes and Berkeley's own idealism in the metaphysics of an apple. For simplicity sake, we imagine an apple to have only three sensible qualities, S1, S2, and S3, such as the qualities of being red, sweet, and crunchy. We see the contrast between materialism's commitment to an underlying material substratum as binding these sensible qualities together as the properties of a single thing, of an apple or other sensible thing as its sensible qualities plus a nonsensible material substratum. The materialist position can then be contrasted with the view that Berkeley accepts, according to which an apple or other sensible thing is a mere congeries of sensible qualities. We illustrate the difference between materialism and idealism pictorially in Figure 5.1. The horizontal line in the diagram distinguishes between the sensible and nonsensible aspects of a sensible thing such as an apple according to materialism and Berkeley's antimaterialist idealism. For materialism, there is an underlying nonsensible material substratum that supports the apple's sensible qualities, whereas for Berkeley there is nothing that is neither nonsensible nor unthinking, and, in particular, no nonsensible unthinking material substratum underlying or spread out beneath the sensible qualities of a sensible thing such as an apple. The apple, in Berkeley's idealist metaphysics, is nothing over and above the congeries of its sensible qualities.

If the hypothesis of an insensible underlying material substratum does not offer any advantage over the concept of sensible things as distinct congeries of ideas or sensible qualities, then the congeries account need not be on the defensive. The congeries theory that Berkeley accepts in that case is at least no worse off than materialism. As we shall see, the congeries theory, also sometimes known for obvious reasons as a *bundle theory* of sensible things, can be seen in fact to have more to recommend it than the hypothesis of a material substratum.

Philonous upholds the concept of sensible things as congeries of ideas on the grounds that it accords more fully with common sense. A nonphilosopher relying on sense experience to get along in the world does not suppose that there is anything more to sensible things than the sensible properties experienced as constituting spatiotemporal objects. The apple we see is the apple we taste. The entity with the shape and size and color that we hold in our hand is experienced as the same object that is brought to the mouth and nose to taste and smell. There need be nothing more to the apple, and nothing further to explain about the identity conditions for the apple than to say that the sensible qualities of the object are experienced as belonging together in a single spatiotemporal package. If Berkeley is right, then there is no more to a sensible thing than this close association of sensible qualities experienced as spatiotemporally continuous and contiguous, which is what he means by a congeries of ideas. Philonous explains his position to Hylas in precisely these terms:

> PHILONOUS: I assure you, Hylas, I do not pretend to frame any hypothesis at all. I am of a vulgar cast, simple enough to believe my senses, and leave things as I find them. To be plain, it is my opinion that the real things are those very things I see, and feel, and perceive by my senses. These I know; and, finding they answer all the necessities and purposes of life, have no reason to be solicitous about any other unknown beings. A piece of sensible bread, for instance, would stay my stomach better than ten thousand times as much of that insensible, unintelligible real bread you speak of. It is likewise my opinion that colours and other sensible qualities are on the objects. I cannot for my life help thinking that snow is white, and fire hot. (445)

Philonous now extends his commonsense theory of the nature of sensible things to the question of their existence. He denies that there is anything more to a sensible thing than its congeries of ideas, and he argues that there is no underlying material substratum, nor any quality or substance of a sensible thing that is in principle mind-independent, insensible, imperceptible, or incapable of being experienced by sensation. Philonous continues:

> PHILONOUS: . . . And, as I am no sceptic with regard to the nature of things, so neither am I as to their existence. That a thing should be really perceived by my senses, and at the same time not really exist, is to me a plain contradiction; since I cannot prescind or abstract, even in thought, the existence of a sensible thing from its being perceived. Wood, stones, fire, water, flesh, iron, and the like things which I name and discourse of are things that I know. And I should not have known them but that I perceived them by my senses; and things perceived by the senses are immediately perceived; and things immediately perceived are ideas; and ideas cannot exist without the mind; their existence therefore consists in being perceived; when, therefore, they are actually perceived, there can be no doubt of their existence. Away then with all that scepticism, all those ridiculous philosophical doubts. What a jest is it for a philosopher to question the existence of sensible things, till he hath it proved to him from the veracity of God; or to pretend our knowledge in this point falls short of intuition or demonstration! I might as well doubt of my own being, as of the being of those things I actually see and feel. (445–46)

The reference to justification for belief in the existence of sensible things by appealing to the veracity of God is evidently a criticism of Descartes's solution to the evil demon hypothesis, and possibly also to Malebranche as a follower of Descartes. Berkeley, in the person of Philonous, argues in effect that it is simpler and as such theoretically preferable to avoid the complications of resorting to the truthfulness of God as a guarantee that we experience a real world of external entities possessing the properties we perceive. If sensible things are just congeries of sensible qualities, the qualities we directly experience in sensation, then there is no more to be said about the existence of sensible things in the sensible world. It is only if we suppose that there is also imperceivable matter underlying the ideas or sensible qualities of things that we open the door to doubts about whether the world is actually as it is perceived.

Would Berkeley's theory then be embarrassed by the possibility of sensory illusions? The answer is that Berkeley can regard any experience of any object as a sensible quality belonging to its constitutive congeries of ideas. If I see a stick in a glass of water that appears to be bent when in fact it is straight, it is still one of the sensible properties of the stick and of the water for the stick *to appear* bent when viewed at a certain angle. The existence and identity of the stick considered as a congeries of ideas in the mind is not compromised by the fact that some of these ideas do not agree with others. The same sensible thing can appear red in sunlight and grey at night, the same sensible thing can appear bent in water and straight in the open air. The redness in sunlight and the greyness at dusk can equally be included in the congeries of ideas that constitutes a given sensible thing, and similarly for the distinct ideas of the stick in or out of water as bent or straight.

Different appearances of things belong to the respective congeries by which sensible things are distinguished. Whereas there do not seem to be any identity conditions for a totally insensible unexperienceable material substratum, there are straightforward identity conditions for any sensible thing considered as a congeries of ideas. Congeries of ideas are distinguished from one another by virtue of the fact that each uniquely consists of a different combination of ideas. The apple, according to Berkeley's metaphysics, is identical with the redness, sweetness, and other ideas or sensible qualities with which it is identified; the pear is and consists of greenness, mellowness, and the other ideas or sensible qualities with which it is identified. If the apple and pear and other sensible things are nothing other than particular distinct congeries of ideas, then there is nothing further to know in determining what an apple or pear is, or what identity conditions these entities must satisfy in order to possess the qualities that belong together in their respective identifying and individuating congeries of ideas.

BERKELEY'S CANDLE

We have now considered the main tenets of Berkeley's idealism and antimaterialism. Berkeley rejects empirically unsupported speculation that the sensible properties of sensible things are upheld by insensible material substrata, and the conclusion that sensible things are mere congeries of ideas lacking any underlying material substance as their metaphysical foundation. Berkeley's philosophy is so unusual, and it has been the subject of so much misunderstanding, that is necessary to clarify his position before considering his arguments in order to avoid distortions. It is appropriate to recount the chain of reasoning by which Berkeley proposes to deny the existence of insensible unthinking matter, and to defend the existence of God and the concept of sensible things as congeries of ideas.

Philonous first requires Hylas to explain the nature of sensible things. He elicits from Hylas an important concession, a point with which Berkeley also firmly agrees, that sensible things are immediately perceived by sensation. This may seem like an obvious enough assumption, but it turns out to have crucial implications for Philonous's conclusion that sensible things are congeries of ideas existing only in the mind with no underlying material substratum. It follows as a consequence of the proposition that sensible things are immediately perceived by sense that we do not see stars but bright pinpoints of colors, that we do not hear carriages in the street but rather characteristic sounds that we associate with moving carriages along cobblestones as their causes. Hylas admits the point readily enough:

> PHILONOUS: It seems, then, that by *sensible things* you mean those only which can be perceived *immediately* by sense?
>
> HYLAS: Right.
>
> PHILONOUS: Doth it not follow from this, that though I see one part of the sky red, and another blue, and that my reason doth thence evidently conclude there must be some cause of that diversity of colours, yet that cause cannot be said to be a sensible thing, or perceived by the sense of seeing?
>
> HYLAS: It doth. . . . To prevent any more questions of this kind, I tell you once for all that by *sensible things* I mean those only which are perceived by sense; and that in truth the senses perceive nothing which they do not perceive *immediately:* for they make no inferences. The deducing therefore of causes or occasions from effects and appearances, which alone are perceived by sense, entirely relates to reason. (383)

It seems reasonable to say, as Hylas and Philonous agree, that the senses make no inferences. This is especially true if we agree with Berkeley's widely held eighteenth-century belief that sensation is passive, receiving only such data as are made available to it, and incapable of reasoning, whereas judgment is active and capable of inference. If sensation is passive, then sensation considered in itself cannot deduce the existence of any of the causes of sensible qualities, but can at most passively perceive whatever sensible qualities are presented immediately to it without inferring their causes. The implication is that sensible things are immediately perceived, directly experienced in sensation, rather than inferred from what is sensed as the causes of sensation. Hylas's and Philonous's agreement on this point can be understood as a clarification of what it means for something to be a sensible thing, given the concept of sensation and of what it means to be a sensible thing.

With this preliminary admission in hand, Philonous proceeds to offer one of his most important demonstrations. He proposes to show that sensible things exist only as congeries of ideas in the mind. Although Berkeley does not mention any particular source of flame, it is convenient to think of his example in this section of the First Dialogue as Berkeley's candle. The argument takes this form. Hylas and Philonous agree that heat is a sensible thing, but Hylas at first insists even in the case of heat that there is a difference between existing and being perceived:

> PHILONOUS: *Heat* is then a sensible thing?
>
> HYLAS: Certainly.

PHILONOUS: Doth the *reality* of sensible things consist in being perceived? or, is it something distinct from their being perceived, and that bears no relation to the mind?

HYLAS: To *exist* is one thing, and to be *perceived* is another. . . .

PHILONOUS: Heat therefore, if it be allowed a real being, must exist without the mind?

HYLAS: It must. (384)

Hylas articulates the materialist position that Philonous rejects. Philonous holds that if heat is a sensible thing that exists in objects outside the mind, then it must do so regardless of its exact degree, whether it is merely warm or burning hot. Hylas agrees:

PHILONOUS: Tell me, Hylas, is this real existence equally compatible to all degrees of heat, which we perceive; or is there any reason why we should attribute it to some, and deny it to others? And if there be, pray let me know that reason.

HYLAS: Whatever degree of heat we perceive by sense, we may be sure the same exists in the object that occasions it.

PHILONOUS: What! the greatest as well as the least? (384)

Hylas grants the assumption of Philonous's rhetorical question. This is all that Philonous needs in order to close the jaws of his trap on the materialist thesis. He is ready to reveal an absurdity in the belief that sensible things as immediately perceived in sense experience nevertheless exist outside the mind. Hylas continues to claim that to exist is one thing and to be perceived is another altogether different thing.

Philonous leads Hylas to question the assumption that heat in particular exists independently of the mind that perceives it. He poses a series of questions in which he gets Hylas to admit that there is no discernible difference between great heat and pain, and that pain undoubtedly exists in the mind. Wherever great heat exists, it must exist in the same place as the pain that is indistinguishable from it. Since the sensation of pain is evidently something mental, it does not exist outside the mind in the candle flame as a material substance. If great heat is indistinguishable from pain, then they must exist together, wherever that turns out to be. If pain is mental, then great heat must also be mental, existing as pain within the mind. Nor is there an important difference in principle, as Hylas admits, between great heat and heat of any lesser degree. It follows, if what has gone before is correct, that heat as a sensible thing exists only in the mind. Hylas and Philonous arrive step-by-step at the idealist conclusion:

PHILONOUS: But is not the most vehement and intense degree of heat a very great pain?

HYLAS: No one can deny it.

PHILONOUS: And is any unperceiving thing capable of pain or pleasure?

HYLAS: No, certainly. . . .

PHILONOUS: Upon putting your hand near the fire, do you perceive one simple uniform sensation, or two distinct sensations?

HYLAS: But one simple sensation.

PHILONOUS: Is not the heat immediately perceived?

HYLAS: It is.

PHILONOUS: And the pain?

HYLAS: True.

PHILONOUS: Seeing therefore they are both immediately perceived at the same time, and the fire affects you only with one simple or uncompounded idea, it follows that this same simple idea is both the intense heat immediately perceived, and the pain; and, consequently, that the intense heat immediately perceived is nothing distinct from a particular sort of pain.

HYLAS: It seems so. (384–85)

Philonous begins to break the hold that the materialist way of thinking about the existence and perception of sensible things has had on Hylas. In the case of intense heat and the pain produced in touching a flame, Philonous maintains, and Hylas is finally compelled to yield, that there is a sensible thing that exists only in the mind. If Hylas had assumed that no sensible things exist entirely within the mind, or that there is always a difference between a sensible thing's existing and its being perceived, then Philonous has at least succeeded in disabusing him of this materialist assumption. Philonous follows up the heat-pain argument with a similar illustration from Locke's (1700) *Essay Concerning Human Understanding.* The example is meant to show that sensible qualities do not always exist independently of sensation, but are sometimes a function of preconditioning. Philonous relies on Hylas's knowledge of a common experience:

PHILONOUS: Suppose now one of your hands hot, and the other cold, and that they are both at once put into the same vessel of water, in an intermediate state; will not the water seem cold to one hand, and warm to the other?

HYLAS: It will.

PHILONOUS: Ought we not therefore, by your principles, to conclude it is really both cold and warm at the same time, that is, according to your own concession, to believe an absurdity?

HYLAS: I confess it seems so. (388)

By preparing the same person's two hands, placing one in hot water and the other in cold, and then plunging them into the same vessel of lukewarm water, the heated hand, as we can easily verify for ourselves, will feel cool and the chilled hand will feel warm. If the heat of the lukewarm water cannot be regarded as belonging outside the mind in the water as a mind-independent material substance, then it must belong instead to the mind. At least this must be true if, as Hylas also believes, the same external thing such as the water in a bowl cannot simultaneously uniformly possess the contrary properties of being both warm and cool. The warmth and coolness, Philonous concludes, must instead reside in the subject's mind as distinct ideas of the same thing. Philonous generalizes the conclusion, arguing that it applies to other sensations produced by other kinds of interactions with the senses:

> PHILONOUS: When a pin pricks your finger, doth it not rend and divide the fibres of your flesh?
>
> HYLAS: It doth.
>
> PHILONOUS: And when a coal burns your finger, doth it any more?
>
> HYLAS: It doth not.
>
> PHILONOUS: Since, therefore, you neither judge the sensation itself occasioned by the pin, nor anything like it to be in the pin; you should not, conformably to what you have now granted, judge the sensation occasioned by the fire, or anything like it, to be in the fire.
>
> HYLAS: Well, since it must be so, I am content to yield this point and acknowledge that heat and cold are only sensations existing in our minds. But there still remain qualities enough to secure the reality of external things. (388)

While Philonous by means of these examples may have opened the door to counterexamples to the general materialist thesis that all sensible things exist outside the mind and that there is always a distinction between the existence and perception of a sensible thing, it is not clear that Hylas must admit that the conclusion holds in every case. Hylas indicates in his final remark that although he grudgingly grants the idealist antimaterialist conclusion in the case of such sensible qualities as heat and cold, the candle flame and the basin of water, he still believes that there are other sensible qualities existing outside the mind in external material or mind-independent sensible things.

PRIMARY AND SECONDARY QUALITIES

Hylas retreats to a distinction between types of qualities made famous by Galileo, Locke, and others. The distinction between *primary* and *secondary qualities* marks a difference between qualities of things that seem to be subjective or conditioned by the individuals who perceive something on the one hand, and qualities that appear to be more objective, that obtain if they obtain at all regardless of the condition of the perceiving subject.

We begin by giving a rough idea of how the distinction is supposed to divide properties into two categories. Secondary qualities are supposed to include colors, tastes, smells, feels, and sounds, whereas primary qualities are meant to classify extension or size, figure, shape, gravity, weight, motion, mass, and the like. We can see that the category of primary qualities includes the sort of properties that are studied in the natural sciences such as physics, whereas the secondary qualities seem to be more readily included as topics for psychology. Locke, indeed, proposes to distinguish physics and psychology precisely on the basis of the distinction respectively between primary and secondary qualities. We tend to think of secondary qualities as subjectively variable in the same way as Locke's example of the hot and cold hands submerged in lukewarm water. We know, for example, that some persons see colors differently than others, that they are what is called color-blind, and that some persons perceive tastes and smells and other properties differently than others.

Hylas has now been forced to admit that heat and cold, the degree of warmth or lack thereof that sensible things appear to the senses to possess, exist within the mind rather than externally or mind-independently in an external material world. He digs in his heels, and tries to preserve at least a modified version of the materialist thesis. He clings to the possibility of some properties of sensible things existing outside the mind. If there are such properties of things, then sensible things are not merely constituted as ideas within the mind. Hylas adopts the distinction between primary and secondary qualities to this purpose, and grants Philonous only the conclusion that secondary qualities are mind-dependent, while continuing to insist that primary qualities exist independently of thought.

Hylas proposes to qualify the concept of heat and cold *as* experienced by a subject in contrast with heat and cold *as* existing externally in sensible things. Philonous correctly resists this dodge, on the grounds that it goes against Hylas's previous admission that sensible things are immediately experienced in sensation. It is the difference again between what is passively perceived as ideas and what is inferred about the causes of ideas. Their discussion proceeds in this way, as they continue agreeing to disagree:

> HYLAS: Hold, Philonous. I now see what it was [that] deluded me all the time. You asked whether heat and cold, sweetness and bitterness, were not particular sorts of pleasure and pain; to which I answered simply that they were. Whereas I should have thus distinguished:—those qualities, as perceived by us are pleasures or pains; but not as existing in the external objects. We must not therefore conclude absolutely, that there is no heat in the fire, or sweetness in the sugar, but only that heat or sweetness, as perceived by us, are not in the fire or sugar. What say you to this?

> PHILONOUS: I say it is nothing to the purpose. Our discourse proceeded altogether concerning sensible things, which you defined to be, *the things we immediately perceive by our senses.* Whatever other qualities, therefore, you speak of, as distinct from these, I know nothing of them, neither do they at all belong to the point in dispute. (389)

Hylas now takes the necessary further step, explicitly introducing the distinction between primary and secondary qualities. He declares:

> HYLAS: I frankly own, Philonous, that it is in vain to stand out any longer. Colours, sounds, tastes, in a word, all those termed *secondary qualities,* have certainly no existence without the mind. But by this acknowledgment I must not be supposed to derogate anything from the reality of Matter, or external objects; seeing it is no more than several philosophers maintain, who nevertheless are the farthest imaginable from denying Matter. For the clearer understanding of this,

you must know sensible qualities are by philosophers divided into *Primary* and *Secondary*. The former are Extension, Figure, Solidity, Gravity, Motion, and Rest; and these they hold exist really in bodies. The latter are those above enumerated; or, briefly, *all sensible qualities besides the Primary*; which they assert are only so many sensations or ideas existing nowhere but in the mind. But all this, I doubt not, you are apprised of. For my part, I have been a long time sensible there was such an opinion current among philosophers, but was never thoroughly convinced of its truth until now. (397–98)

The distinction between primary and secondary qualities lends Hylas's position the authority of scientific philosophy from the work of Galileo and Locke. It enables Hylas to grant Philonous's conclusion about the properties of the candle in its original form, concerning the perception of heat. At the same time, Hylas's use of the distinction implies that at least some kinds of properties of sensible things exist outside the mind and independently of thought.

The difference between the subjectivity in experience of secondary qualities and the objectivity of primary qualities is seen even in Philonous's example involving Berkeley's candle and Locke's basin. If we distinguish between *warmth* as a subjective secondary quality of feeling and *temperature* as an objective primary quality involving the speed of molecular motion in the candle flame and the lukewarm water bath, then we can hold both that warmth exists in the mind, while insisting that temperature exists outside the mind. We expect to be able to obtain objective information about temperature that is not directly associated with the experience of pain or the variable sensation of coolness or warmth to hot and cold hands by checking the objects with a nonthinking instrument such as a thermometer. A thermometer provides an unambivalent reading with no feeling and no subjective variability. We need only look at the scale on the thermometer to know what objective temperature the candle flame or vessel of water has, regardless of whatever subjective sensations of warmth are experienced. Philonous is not deterred by Hylas's maneuver, but meets the objection by arguing that in the end there is really no difference between primary and secondary qualities.

THE MITE'S FOOT

To undermine Hylas's appeal to primary and secondary qualities, Philonous attacks the objectivity of exemplary primary quality, involving the size or extension of a sensible thing. Philonous's strategy is to persuade Hylas that judgments of size are just as subjective and hence just as mind-dependent as judgments of so-called secondary qualities. Philonous describes a tiny insect, a mite, and its experience of the size of its own foot by contrast with our perception of its size. Philonous further questions Hylas in this way:

PHILONOUS: Besides, it is not only possible but manifest, that there actually are animals whose eyes are by nature framed to perceive those things which by reason of their minuteness escape our sight. What think you of those inconceivably small animals perceived by glasses? Must we suppose they are all stark blind? Or, in case they see, can it be imagined their sight hath not the same use in preserving their bodies from injuries, which appears in that of all other animals? And if it hath, is it not evident they must see particles less than their own bodies; which will present them with a far different view in each object from that which strikes our senses? Even our own eyes do not always represent objects to us after the same manner. In the jaundice everyone knows that all things seem yellow. Is it not therefore highly probable those animals in whose eyes we discern a very different texture from that of ours, and whose bodies abound with different humours, do not see the same colours in every object that we do? From all which should it not seem to follow that all colours are equally apparent, and that none of those which we perceive are really inherent in any outward object?

HYLAS: It should. (394–95)

Philonous repeats a common misconception about the experience of colors by persons diseased with yellow jaundice. He says that they perceive everything as though tinged with yellow. The illness causes the whites of the eyes to become yellowed, but there is no evidence to indicate that victims afflicted with the disease see things as though through yellow lenses. The general point Philonous wants to make is nevertheless correct, that by special conditioning it is possible for different subjects to experience colors differently, as we have seen already in the case of color blindness. With variable color perception as the basis for analogy, Philonous now suggests the possibility of variable size or extension perception on the part of human subjects and of tiny creatures like the mite. Hylas agrees that mites have eyes much as we do, and that their vision is used like ours among other ways to help inform them about the state of the world around them, and in particular about potential dangers they need to avoid. Philonous presses the point:

PHILONOUS: You are still then of opinion that *extension* and *figures* are inherent in external unthinking substances?

HYLAS: I am.

PHILONOUS: But what if the same arguments which are brought against Secondary Qualities will hold good against these also?

HYLAS: Why then I shall be obliged to think, they too exist only in the mind.

PHILONOUS: Is it your opinion the very figure and extension which you perceive by sense exist in the outward object or material substance?

HYLAS: It is.

PHILONOUS: Have all other animals as good grounds to think the same of the figure and extension which they see and feel?

HYLAS: Without doubt, if they have any thought at all. (398)

Admitting that insects are able to perceive figure and extension or shape and size much as we do and for similar purposes, Hylas opens himself to an obvious objection. Philonous observes that in that case a mite should be able to perceive its own foot, which to the mite must appear roughly as large to it as our feet do to us. The mite's foot as the mite experiences it is relatively large, while the mite's foot as we perceive it is miniscule, barely visible, if visible at all without the aid of a magnifying glass. The difference in subjective sensation of the size or extension of the mite's foot as we see it and as the mite sees it is thus just as variable in the case of this supposedly primary quality as Hylas and Philonous have already admitted with respect to the subjective experience of secondary qualities such as hot and cold, warm and cool, colors, tastes, and smells. Philonous interrogates Hylas:

PHILONOUS: Answer me, Hylas. Think you the senses were bestowed upon all animals for their preservation and well-being in life? or were they given to men alone for this end?

HYLAS: I make no question but they have the same use in all other animals.

PHILONOUS: If so, is it not necessary they should be enabled by them to perceive their own limbs, and those bodies which are capable of harming them?

HYLAS: Certainly.

PHILONOUS: A mite therefore must be supposed to see his own foot, and things equal or even less than it, as bodies of some considerable dimension; though at the same time they appear to you scarce discernible, or at best as so many visible points?

HYLAS: I cannot deny it.

PHILONOUS: And to creature less than the mite they will seem yet larger?

HYLAS: They will.

PHILONOUS: Insomuch that what you can hardly discern will to another extremely minute animal appear as some huge mountain?

HYLAS: All this I grant.

PHILONOUS: Can one and the same thing be at the same time in itself of different dimensions?

HYLAS: That were absurd to imagine.

PHILONOUS: But, from what you have laid down it follows that both the extension by you perceived, and that perceived by the mite itself, as likewise all those perceived by less animals, are each of them the true extension of the mite's foot; that is to say, by your own principles you are led into an absurdity. (398–99)

The implication is that there is no real distinction between primary and secondary qualities. Both alike are equally subjectively variable, and as such equally mind-dependent. After momentarily acknowledging defeat, Hylas thinks again and resorts to another distinction that he believes might still save the materialist thesis, at least with respect to their primary qualities. The further distinction concerns a difference between *absolute* and *sensible* primary qualities. Hylas reports:

HYLAS: It is just come into my head, Philonous, that I have somewhere heard of a distinction between absolute and sensible extension. Now, though it be acknowledged that *great* and *small,* consisting merely in the relation which other extended beings have to the parts of our own bodies, do not really inhere in the substances themselves; yet nothing obliges us to hold the same with regard to *absolute extension,* which is something abstracted from *great and small,* from this or that particular magnitude or figure. So likewise as to motion; *swift* and *slow* are altogether relative to the succession of ideas in our own minds. But, it doth not follow, because these modifications of motion exist not without the mind, that therefore absolute motion abstracted from them doth not. (402)

The distinction between absolute and sensible primary qualities is the same that we have already considered in connection with the indistinguishable heat and pain experienced in touching a candle flame. There is at least an apparent difference between the subjective way a flame feels and its temperature objectively determined by a thermometer or other scientific instrument, or between subjective qualitative judgment and objective quantitative measurement.

The same might now be said in the example of the mite's foot. There is an apparent difference between the subjective way a mite and a human percipient might qualitatively perceive the size of the mite's foot as great or small, and the objective quantitative determination of the size or extension of the mite's foot as determined by a measuring stick. If a human perceiver and the mite were both to look at the scale of distance values on a ruler held alongside the mite's foot they could equally agree, differences in qualitative judgments of the foot's size as great or small aside, that the foot is objectively quantitatively speaking of precisely the same size, say, so many microns or millimeters or other subunits long. We need only hold up a ruler to the mite's foot, Hylas seems to imply, just as we need only place a thermometer in the candle flame, for the mite and the human perceiver, despite subjective differences in their qualitative experiences of the mite's foot, to agree in their judgments that the foot has a certain definite size, exactly and objectively quantitatively measurable.

AGAINST ABSTRACT GENERAL IDEAS

It is crucial for Hylas's purposes in this part of his defense that the distinction between absolute and sensible qualities not be confused with the distinction he has previously tried and failed successfully to apply between existent and perceived heat. Hylas has already admitted that the latter distinction is incompatible with the definition of sensible things as whatever is immediately perceived rather than their inferred causes. The distinction between absolute and sensible qualities is different in that an absolute quality, as Hylas indicates in the passage quoted in the last section, is supposed to be *abstracted* from particular sensible qualities or their instantiations in the perceptions of sensible things.

Philonous's objection to the distinction is of more general interest than its use in Hylas's defense of materialism. As an empiricist, Berkeley, much like Aristotle and Sextus Empiricus, is opposed to the existence of any abstract ideas. This is as true of absolute magnitudes of temperature or extension or any other so-called primary quality as it is of any abstract entity. We can consider a dilemma in connection with Philonous's example of the mite's foot or Berkeley's candle. When we imagine putting a thermometer into the candle flame or setting a ruler against the mite's foot and reading the results, we might interpret the procedure in several ways. If we consider looking at the scale on the thermometer or ruler as another perception involving visual or other sense experience, then we are back where we started with respect to the subjective variability of secondary quality generally. The measuring stick will look bigger to the mite than to a human observer, and its markings so differently perceived from its standpoint are also sure to be differently read and differently judged with respect to the exact size of the mite's foot. The use of scientific measuring equipment in this sense offers another set of perceptual objects to be evaluated in judging primary qualities, but does not avoid any of the subjectivity that affects determinations of values in the case of secondary qualities.

If, on the other hand, as the terminology by which Hylas characterizes the distinction strongly suggests, absolute, by contrast with sensible primary qualities, are supposed to be nonsensible, then they can only be so by virtue of involving *abstract ideas*, abstracted as generalizations from particular sensible primary qualities in particular perceptions of sensible things. Philonous argues against the possibility of absolute primary qualities in this sense, on the grounds that there can be no abstract ideas, and that the concept of an abstract idea is unintelligible. Philonous first challenges Hylas to try to think of an abstract general idea, an idea that has no particular sensible qualities, and is altogether abstracted from any particular application. Philonous says:

PHILONOUS: These [absolute] qualities, therefore, stripped of all sensible properties, are without all specific and numberical differences, as the schools call them.

HYLAS: They are.

PHILONOUS: That is to say, they are extension in general, and motion in general.

HYLAS: Let it be so.

PHILONOUS: But it is a universally received maxim that *everything which exists is particular*. How then can motion in general, or extension in general, exist in any corporeal substance?

HYLAS: I will take time to solve your difficulty.

PHILONOUS: But I think the point may be speedily decided. Without doubt you can tell whether you are able to frame this or that idea. Now I am content to put our dispute on this issue. If you can frame in your thoughts a distinct *abstract idea* of motion or extension, divested of all those sensible modes as swift and slow, great and small, round and square, and the like, which are acknowledged to exist only in the mind, I will then yield the point you contend for. But if you cannot, it will be unreasonable on your side to insist any longer upon what you have no notion of.

HYLAS: To confess ingenuously, I cannot. (403)

As a last-ditch effort, Hylas suggests that abstract ideas might be entertained by what he proposes to call *pure intellect*. Philonous replies that he cannot consider abstract ideas by any faculty, regardless of how they are designated. Thus, Philonous dispenses with the possibility of abstract ideas, and therewith Hylas's attempt to defend the distinction between primary and secondary qualities. At the same time, he refutes the concept of abstract ideas generally in mathematics and all other areas of science and philosophy. Later, Philonous argues somewhat like Ockham that what is called abstract reasoning involves the delegation of particular ideas to stand for a collection of other similar particular ideas. He holds that the imagination resists mistaken attempts to draw false generalizations based on the particular properties and peculiarities of a chosen example to represent all others grouped together in the same category. The imagination spontaneously produces counterexamples in such cases to alert us to the fact that our thinking has gone astray. In the meantime, Philonous insists that there are no such things as abstract ideas on which to sustain the distinction between absolute and sensible primary qualities:

> PHILONOUS: Consequently, the very same arguments which you admitted as conclusive against the Secondary Qualities are, without any further application of force, against the Primary, too. Besides, if you will trust your senses, is it not plain all sensible qualities coexist, or to them appear as being in the same place? Do they ever represent a motion, or figure, as being divested of all other visible and tangible qualities? (405)

Although Hylas later makes several efforts to resuscitate the possibility of mind-independent matter or the material substratum of sensible things, it is clear at this stage of the dialogue that he has lost the war. From this point onward he can only fight a rearguard action against the conclusions Philonous begins to draw from the idealist proposition that sensible things are mere congeries of ideas existing in the mind.

BERKELEY'S PROOF FOR THE EXISTENCE OF GOD

We are at last in a position to understand Berkeley's proof for the existence of God. The argument he offers depends on the metaphysical thesis Philonous believes he has satisfactorily established, that sensible things are mere congeries of ideas. If so-called secondary qualities exist in the mind, and if there is no essential difference between primary and secondary qualities, then the qualities of things generally exist only in the mind. It follows, remarkably enough, if Berkeley is right, that God exists.

Hylas engages in a certain amount of backpedaling in his discussion with Philonous, attempting to resurrect the materialist thesis about the mind-independence existence of sensible things. Philonous counters these efforts by refuting additional distinctions and proposals for reconstruing the concept of matter or material substance or substratum as causes or occasions, or as standing in other relations to the ideas or sensible qualities, of sensible things. When he has discounted all of these retrenchments by Hylas, Philonous believes he has satisfactorily proved the idealist position that there is no such thing as matter or the material substratum and that sensible things are mere congeries of ideas existing in the mind.

Philonous reminds Hylas that materialism, as a result of its commitment to the existence of an unknowable insensible material substratum underlying or "spread" beneath the sensible properties of sensible things, rather than idealism, in which all sensible things are directly and in principle completely knowable through their sensible experienceable properties, entails skepticism. The sense in which Philonous accuses Hylas of skepticism is not a suspension of belief in propositions that are widely conventionally accepted, but a commitment to the existence of an inherently unknowable reality. Philonous argues that the concept of a material substratum, by virtue of having no sensible properties, but serving supposedly instead as the foundation or support of sensible properties, is unknowable; it appears to follow then that the nature of reality is ultimately unknowable, according to materialism, and hence that materialism rather than idealism is embroiled in skepticism. Philonous objects:

> PHILONOUS: I deny that I agreed with you in those notions that led to Scepticism. You indeed said the *reality* of sensible things consisted in an *absolute existence out of the minds of spirits,* or distinct from their being perceived. And pursuant to this notion of reality, *you* are obliged to deny sensible things any real existence: that is, according to your own definition, you profess yourself a sceptic. (424)

Philonous now indicates in broad outline the reasoning by which he proposes to demonstrate the existence of God from the idealist thesis that sensible things are mere congeries of ideas. The reasoning is that sensible things must sometimes exist as constitutive congeries of ideas in the mind of a spirit greater than any finite human mind, and hence that a divine infinitely powerful Spirit exists.

Philonous agrees with Hylas that sensible things are not dependent on our minds. We cannot will what we experience, and thereby bring sensible things into existence. If that were possible, then we would all be wealthy and supplied with whatever sensible things we desire, freely available merely by an act of will. We know from experience that sensible things are not subject to our wills in this way, and so we conclude that perception is passive, receiving information about whatever is there to be perceived, rather than creating sensible things, as Hylas and Philonous both concur. Where they part company is in trying to explain the independence of sensible things from the willful control of finite minds. Hylas interprets the facts as proving that sensible things are altogether mind-independent, whereas Philonous interprets them as proving that sensible things do not merely exist in human finite minds, but in the infinite mind of God. The independence of sensible things from our human thought leads Philonous to conclude that God must exist in order for human perception to be passive and for the existence of sensible things to be beyond the willful control of finite human minds. Philonous argues:

> PHILONOUS: . . . But I neither said nor thought the reality of sensible things was to be defined after that manner. To me it is evident, for the reasons you allow of, that sensible things cannot exist otherwise than in a mind or spirit. Whence I conclude, not that they have no real existence, but that, seeing they depend not on my thought, and have an existence distinct from being perceived by me, *there must be some other Mind wherein they exist.* As sure, therefore, as the sensible world really exists, so sure is there an infinite omnipresent Spirit who contains and supports it. (424)

The infinite omnipresent Spirit is none other than God, as Hylas immediately acknowledges. Hylas is surprised that Philonous has invoked the existence of God at this point in the argument, since everyone admits that God is an all-powerful and all-knowing spirit who is capable of perceiving more completely and comprehensively the same mind-independent sensible things we human beings perceive.

Philonous replies that Hylas has misunderstood. Philonous is proposing something different and philosophically novel. He attempts to prove the existence of God as that infinite spirit whose existence can be deduced from the assumption that sensible things exist only as congeries of ideas in a mind, and that we know from personal experience that sensible things are independent of our finite minds in the sense that they are not subject to our will. If sensible things must exist as congeries of ideas in a mind, and if they are independent of finite minds, then they must reside as congeries of ideas in the infinite mind of God as an "omnipresent Spirit." Hylas voices surprise and Philonous informs him that he has got things reversed:

> HYLAS: What! this is not more than I and all Christians hold; nay, and all others, too, who believe there is a God and that He knows and comprehends all things.

> PHILONOUS: Aye, but here lies the difference. Men commonly believe that all things are known or perceived by God, because they believe the being of a God; whereas I, on the other side, immediately and necessarily conclude the being of a God, because all sensible things must be perceived by Him.

> HYLAS: But, so long as we all believe the same thing, what matter is it how we come by that belief? (424–25)

God, as Philonous now more fully explains, is the divine infinite mind wherein sensible things as congeries of ideas are perceived, and on which our finitely limited human perceptions of sensible things depend for their existence. He argues:

> PHILONOUS: But neither do we agree in the same opinion. For philosophers, though they acknowledge all corporeal beings to be perceived by God, yet they attribute to them an absolute subsistence distinct from their being perceived by any mind whatever, which I do not. Besides, is there no difference between saying, *There is a God, therefore He perceives all things*; and saying, *Sensible things do really exist; and, if they really exist, they are necessarily perceived by an infinite Mind: therefore there is an infinite Mind, or God?* This furnishes you with a direct and immediate demonstration, from a most evident principle, of the *being of a God*. Divines and philosophers had proved beyond all controversy, from the beauty and usefulness of the several parts of the creation, that it was the workmanship of God. But that—setting aside all help of astronomy and natural philosophy, all contemplation of the contrivance, order and adjustment of things—an infinite Mind should be necessarily inferred from the bare *existence of the sensible world*, is an advantage peculiar to them only who have made this easy reflection: That the sensible world is that which we perceive by our several senses; and that nothing is perceived by the senses besides ideas; and that no idea or archetype of an idea can exist otherwise than in a mind. (425)

The argument Philonous offers in this first part of his demonstration of the existence of God is sometimes known as Berkeley's *dependence proof*. It is reconstructed by means of the following assumptions:

Berkeley's Dependence Argument for the Existence of God

1. Sensible things are mere congeries of ideas.
2. Ideas have no independent existence but exist only in a mind.
3. Experience shows that sensible things are independent of all finite minds, in the sense that their existence is independent of finite human will.
4. Logically, there can only be either finite or infinite minds.
5. An infinite mind is an omnipresent Spirit or God.

6. There must exist an infinite mind in which the existence of sensible things as congeries of ideas primarily exists, and on which the perception of sensible things by finite minds depends.
7. God exists as an infinite mind or omnipresent Spirit.

Berkeley's dependence proof for the existence of God is unique in the history of philosophy. This is true in part because no other thinker has embraced the radical idealism the argument requires. The proof is interesting for all the reasons Philonous mentions. If it has truly been shown that sensible things exist merely as congeries of ideas, and that ideas have no metaphysically independent existence but exist only in a mind, and if, furthermore, sensible things are independent of finite human minds by virtue of being independent of human will, then there must exist an infinite mind, God, as Berkeley and Philonous contend, on which the existence of sensible things, and the congeries of ideas in perception by which each is constituted, ontologically depends.

Before trying to decide whether the proof is logically correct, we first consider another related proof that occurs subsequently in Berkeley's *Three Dialogues*. We find Philonous arguing later in the Third Dialogue:

> PHILONOUS: . . . When I deny sensible things an existence out of the mind, I do not mean my mind in particular, but all minds. Now, it is plain they have an existence exterior to my mind; since I find them by experience to be independent of it. There is therefore some other Mind wherein they exist, during the intervals between the times of my perceiving them: as likewise they did before my birth, and would do after my supposed annihilation. And, as the same is true with regard to all other finite created spirits, it necessarily follows there is an *omnipresent eternal Mind* which knows and comprehends all things, and exhibits them to our view in such a manner, and according to such rules, as He Himself hath ordained, and are by us termed the *laws of nature*. (446–47)

In a way, Berkeley's second argument is a variation or extension of his first dependence proof for the existence of God. Philonous again maintains, for a slightly different reason, that the existence of sensible things that are also experienced at least partially and at particular times by finite minds depends on the existence of an infinite mind or omnipresent Spirit usually known as God.

The argument is similar in structure to the dependence proof. The central idea of the inference is that God exists because at least some sensible things continuously exist even when they are not perceived by finite minds. Since ideas and sensible things as congeries of ideas do not have independent existence in Berkeley's view, but exist only in a mind, Philonous concludes that some sensible things must exist continuously in the infinite mind of God, at least during those intervals of time when they are not perceived by any finite minds, and that, therefore, God, as a being of infinite mind, exists.

The main difference between the second and first proofs for the existence of God in Philonous's reasoning is the reason for concluding that the existence of sensible things depends on the existence of God. In the first proof, the argument is that we know sensible things to be independent of our thought because they are independent of our will. If I could create a sensible thing such as a pile of gold to exist merely by willing it, then perhaps I would do so. I try, and I discover it does not work. Thus, I conclude that my ideas of sensible things are dependent on some source other than my own mind. If, however, sensible things are congeries of ideas that must exist in some mind, and if their existence is not dependent on my or any other finite mind, then they must exist in an infinite mind, which is to say in the mind of God. The second proof offers a different reason for thinking that the existence of sensible things as congeries of ideas is not dependent on any finite minds, and must therefore once again be dependent for their existence on God's infinite mind. The justification is that we have good reason to think that sensible things continue to exist even when they are not being perceived by any finite minds.

What is meant is something very commonplace. We suppose that when all perceivers exit the room, close the doors, and shutter the windows behind them, then, discounting perception by tiny unnoticed creatures such as mice or mites that might remain in the room, we do not suppose that the furniture and other objects in the room cease to exist as soon as we depart. The sofa and chairs or whatever else is in the room do not disappear the moment they are no longer perceived; at least, that is what we generally assume. If we are right in making such an assumption, then, if sensible things in such situations do not cease to exist and then pop back into existence when we enter the room again and are there to perceive its contents, we may need to conclude, as Philonous argues, that an infinite spirit or God exists in order to continuously perceive the sensible things that finite minds only intermittently perceive. Berkeley's or Philonous's second argument can therefore be reconstructed in this way:

Berkeley's Continuity Argument for the Existence of God
1. Sensible things are mere congeries of ideas.
2. Ideas have no independence existence but exist only in a mind.
3. Some sensible things continue to exist even when they are not being perceived by any finite minds.
4. Logically, there can only be either finite or infinite minds.
5. An infinite mind is an omnipresent Spirit or God.

6. There must exist an infinite mind that continuously perceives the sensible things as congeries of ideas that are only intermittently perceived by finite minds.
7. God exists as an infinite mind or omnipresent Spirit.

The only difference, although it is an important one, between this, Berkeley's or Philonous's second argument for the existence of God, and the first, is seen in assumption (3) and conclusion (6). Assumption (3) provides a different reason for regarding the existence of sensible things that human finite minds perceive as dependent on the existence of the infinite mind of God. If it is true that sensible things continue to exist even when they are not being occurrently perceived by any finite minds, then, together with the rest of the structural framework that is identical in the two arguments, it appears to follow that God exists as an infinite spirit that continuously perceives the sensible things that finite minds only intermittently perceive. The argument thus describes another way in which the sensible things perceived by finite human perceivers are dependent on the existence of God.

COLLECTIVE UNCONSCIOUS WILL AND CIRCULARITY OBJECTIONS

Are Philonous's arguments correct? Hylas does not inquire too critically into the conclusions Philonous defends, perhaps because he is already persuaded of the religious truth that God exists and is prepared to accept a variety of philosophical justifications for the existence of God without deep reflection. The importance of the argument as an attempt to philosophically demonstrate the existence of God nevertheless deserves the most painstaking study. As we saw in the case of Descartes's attempt to prove the existence of God in his *Meditations on First Philosophy*, it is no easy task to prove that God exists. The unique perspective that Berkeley's radical empiricism and idealism offers in philosophy might nevertheless afford a special way of proving that God exists, which other philosophers such as Aristotle and Descartes, beginning from different starting places, cannot achieve.

Let us begin with the dependence argument. The assumption that experience shows that sensible things are independent of all finite minds, in the sense that their existence is independent of finite human will, might be questioned in several ways. It is true that we cannot successfully consciously will the existence of sensible things. It need not follow for that reason, however, that the existence of sensible things is not dependent in some other way on finite minds rather than on the infinite mind of God. What are the alternatives? If we accept a more modern concept of the complexity of human thought, we might consider that our finite minds might be capable of subconsciously willing the sensible things we perceive. A picture of the mind layered into conscious and subconscious as well as unconscious faculties of this sort is provided by Sigmund Freud's theory and clinical practice of psychoanalysis. Such an account could explain the fact that sensible things are independent of our conscious wills, as we know from experience, while allowing for a mundane nondivine explanation of the existence of sensible things within the general framework of Berkeley's idealism through the acts of our subconscious wills.

A difficulty to be addressed in any such explanation is the fact that there seems to be large-scale agreement among finite minds about the sensible things that are publicly perceived. We could accommodate even this problem by adopting a position known as *solipsism*. According to solipsism, only the first-person subject exists or can be known to exist, and what appear to be other persons are fabrications of the first-person subject's possibly subconscious imagination, projections of appearances rather than real existent other minds. This would obviously be a desperate effort merely for the sake of resisting Philonous's dependence argument for the existence of God. It would need to be evaluated in comparison with Philonous's comparatively less bizarre conclusions. Another, arguably more plausible, possibility is that the sensible things that are publicly experienced by different minds are the product not of God but of a *collective unconscious*, such as Carl Jung, a follower of Freud, postulated. If a society of finite human perceivers in its collective unconscious wills the existence of sensible things, then it would follow again that sensible things are independent of the will of any particular finite mind, but not necessarily dependent on the infinite mind of God.

Such a criticism of the dependence argument for the existence of God need not be far-fetched, depending on the independent scientific support offered for the concept of a collective unconscious. Perhaps it is unfair to criticize Berkeley and more directly Philonous for not having anticipated and answered an objection the basis for which was not explicitly hypothesized until the twentieth century. On the other hand, the concept of a collective unconscious might have occurred to Berkeley and hence to Philonous in Berkeley's dialogues, and is therefore a reasonable ground for criticism. The existence of an alternative explanation of the fact that sensible things are not subject to individual finite human will is sufficient to show that Berkeley's dependence argument for the existence of God is deductively invalid. The conclusion of the argument is not logically guaranteed, and does not necessarily follow from the assumptions Berkeley makes, even if they all turned out to be true, if there is another reasonable explanation of the independence of sensible things on individual or collective finite human will.

Berkeley's continuity argument for the existence of God is sometimes said to be subject to another kind of objection. The criticism is that, much like Descartes's attempt to prove the existence of God in Meditation Three, Berkeley's continuity argument is caught in a vicious circularity. In order to support assumption (3), that some sensible things continue to exist even when they are not being perceived by any finite minds, it appears that Berkeley must appeal to the truth of the conclusion of the inference, that God exists. What, otherwise, would entitle Berkeley to believe that sensible things continue to exist when they are unperceived by finite minds? If sensible things are mere congeries of ideas that exist only in a mind, and if there are times when no finite minds are perceiving a given sensible thing, why suppose that the sensible thing continues to exist? If the conclusion of the continuity argument must be assumed in order to uphold the truth of any of its assumptions, and in particular of assumption (3), then the argument is viciously circular by virtue of assuming what it is supposed to prove.

The premise might be independently defended as intuitively obvious. Since, in some ways, however, Berkeley's radical idealism is so counterintuitive in concluding that sensible things exist only as congeries of ideas in a mind, it might be inappropriate to appeal without further ado to intuitive judgment about the truth of other assumptions. Another way out of the circle is to provide independent support for the truth of assumption (3) by arguing that it is simpler and hence theoretically preferable to suppose that sensible things continue to exist even when no finite perceiver is actually perceiving them. It is a more complicated, and as such less attractive, hypothesis to suppose that sensible things go in and out of existence depending on whether or not someone happens to be there. Are considerations of simplicity enough to uphold the truth of Berkeley's assumption that sensible things continue to exist even when they are not being perceived by any finite minds? Not if it also turns out to be simpler or just as simple or complex, other things being equal, to assume that there is a material substratum underlying sensible things as it would be to conclude that God exists and that God continuously perceives the sensible things that are only intermittently perceived by finite minds. In that case, the simplicity of the assumption that sensible things continue to exist even when no finite minds are occurrently perceiving them is counterbalanced by equal or greater complexities in Berkeley's argument.

There remains at least one other suggestion for lending independent external support to Berkeley's third assumption, and thereby for extricating his continuity argument from circularity. We should take note first of the fact that all Berkeley absolutely needs in order to uphold the assumption is a good reason to believe that there exists at least one sensible thing that continues to exist even when it is not being perceived by any finite mind. A single example is all that is strictly required. It might then be possible to provide such an example that indicates a large class of similar cases, any of which would independently support the truth of assumption (3) without having to assume that God exists.

We might accordingly begin with the fact that all three-dimensional objects are such that, if they have an outside surface, then they also have an inside. This proposition might be regarded as a necessary truth, an implication of what it means for something to be a three-dimensional object, or as a highly confirmed empirical truth about the three-dimensional objects we have experienced. As an example, we might consider again an apple, a typical three-dimensional object with an outside and an inside. The outside of a whole unsectioned apple might be perceived by a finite mind even though no finite mind occurrently perceives its inside. Suppose that an apple is sectioned, the inside immediately perceived, and then closed up again so that only the outside is perceived. Afterward, the sections can be separated and the inside again immediately perceived. The question is whether in following Berkeley's principles the inside of the apple continues to exist between those times when it is immediately perceived as the apple is repeatedly opened for inspection and reclosed.

It seems reasonable to conclude that an apple has an unperceived inside that continues to exist as a sensible thing even when only its outside or exterior surface is perceived. At least it appears that we are justified in believing this during those intervals of time when the apple halves are closed up and only the outside is immediately perceived. If so, then there is good justification backed up by positive reliable inductive evidence that the inside of the apple immediately perceived when the apple is cut open and examined continues to exist unperceived by any finite mind when the sections are closed together and only the outside or exterior surface is perceived. Since the inside of the apple by hypothesis is not actually immediately perceived by any finite mind when the halves are closed, assumption (3) in Berkeley's continuity argument can be independently justified without simply assuming the conclusion that God exists.

This is not to say that Berkeley or Philonous have satisfactorily proved the existence of God. At most, even if it is correct, the apple defense only preserves the continuity argument against the circularity objection. There are other deeper difficulties in Berkeley's idealism, especially concerning the main question of whether sensible things are mere congeries of ideas existing only in the mind. If the truth of

Berkeley's antimaterialism as a whole remains open to doubt, then to that extent so does the soundness of Berkeley's continuity argument. Even if either the dependence or the continuity arguments in Berkeley's dialogues is correct, it still does not follow that God exists in anything like the sense that God is understood in traditional religions, including Berkeley's own Irish Anglican church. At most, it follows that at least one divine thinker exists, but not necessarily the single all-powerful all-knowing God of monotheism. For all that the dependence and continuity arguments show, there might be many gods, even infinitely many. Nor does it follow from either of Berkeley's proofs that the infinite spirit on whose perceptions the existence of all sensible things depends for their existence and continuity is anything like the God worshipped by religions as perfectly benevolent, perfectly good, or even as having a moral nature of any sort at all. Berkeley's God, whose existence is supposed to be proved by the dependence and continuity arguments, is only a perceiver of the sensible properties of sensible things, and cannot be known by Berkeley's reasoning to have any of the other properties usually associated with the nature of God.

This is an appropriate point at which to consider the age-old question: If a tree falls in a forest and there is no one there to hear it, does it make a noise? The question sums up the dispute between idealism and materialism in a nutshell. If a falling tree makes a noise even when no one is there to hear it, then it appears that materialism and the mind-independence of sensible things must be true. If the tree makes no noise, if, indeed, we cannot even intelligibly speak of a tree existing let alone falling outside of all minds and all thought, then idealism is true and all sensible things, as Berkeley insists, must be mind-dependent. The standard answers that have been given suggest that if a tape recorder were left in the woods when the tree falls, then it would record the sounds made in the absence of any immediate perceiver. This is a reasonable but inconclusive response to the real philosophical difficulty. The evidence of the tape recorder is certain to be less than decisive, because if the existence of unperceived things generally is in doubt, then we cannot simply assume that the tape recorder continues to exist along with the falling tree when there is no perceiver to perceive the objects in the woods. We would then have no way to know for sure in the absence of perceivers present on the scene when the tree falls whether the sounds that later appear on the tape recorder's tape are evidence of something that happened when no perceiver was there, because we cannot know whether the tape recorder and its tape existed during that time, let alone what might have caused the sounds it later contains.

Berkeley's and Philonous's solution to the question of whether a tree falling in the forest makes a noise when there is no one there to hear it is that there is always someone there to see and hear the tree if it falls. God as an omnipresent spirit in Berkeley's conception is always in the woods to perceive what happens to the tree even when no finite minds are present to perceive its fate. A tree falling in a forest when there are no finite minds there to experience it makes a noise in God's infinite mind. If Berkeley is right, then God's infinite mind perceives all the sensible properties of things that enter into their complete individuating congeries. God perceives all sensible things in all of their dimensions at all magnifications, their insides and outsides, like the inside and outside of the apple and all other three-dimensional physical objects, in all their aspects, under all lighting conditions, and under all circumstances. We finite human subjects can at most perceive only certain of the sensible properties of sensible things. We can never experience as many as God does simultaneously and from all perspectives. This, according to Berkeley, is just the difference we should expect there to be between the capabilities of finite minds and God's infinite mind.

ECTYPAL AND ARCHETYPAL IDEAS

Philonous presents two apparently conflicting if not contradictory arguments concerning the sensible qualities of sensible things experienced by unaided vision and under the microscope. By addressing this difficulty we can shed greater light on Berkeley's concept of God as well as his idealist metaphysics of sensible things.

The first account of sensible things experienced at different magnifications occurs in the First Dialogue. There Philonous argues against the objective reality of color external to the mind, on the grounds that surfaces appear differently colored to the naked eye than they do under the microscope. For this proof, Berkeley must assume that it is the same object examined by the naked eye and by a microscope. Otherwise, if these sensible things are distinct, there is no reason to conclude that color is subjective and does not occur beyond the mind. It is only if the same object, such as a drop of blood, appears bright red to the naked eye but not when magnified by observation under the microscope that Berkeley can justify his idealist conclusion that the blood is neither simply red nor nonred in itself, but that the color of the object as a secondary quality belongs to or is a property rather of the perceiver's mind. Philonous seeks to persuade Hylas in this way:

PHILONOUS: And those [colours], I suppose, are to be thought real which are discovered by the most near and exact survey.

HYLAS: Right.

PHILONOUS: Is the nearest and exactest survey made by the help of a microscope, or by the naked eye?

HYLAS: By a microscope, doubtless.

PHILONOUS: But a microscope often discovers colours in an object different from those perceived by the unassisted sight. And, in case we had microscopes magnifying to any assigned degree, it is certain that no object whatsoever, viewed through them, would appear in the same colour which it exhibits to the naked eye.

HYLAS: And what will you conclude from all this? You cannot argue that there are really and naturally no colours on objects: because by artificial managements they may be altered, or made to vanish.

PHILONOUS: I think it may evidently be concluded from your own concessions, that all the colours we see with our naked eyes are only apparent as those on the clouds, since they vanish upon a more close and accurate inspection, which is afforded us by a microscope. (394)

If it were maintained on the contrary that a sensible thing such as a drop of blood seen by the naked eye is in some sense different than that seen under the microscope, then there would be no reason to suppose that the object's color is not objective, nor for denying that its color exists outside or independently of the mind. The burden of proof in that case must shift to the idealist to provide adequate reasons for thinking that color cannot belong to the object itself. Berkeley's argument from microscopes in the First Dialogue achieves its purpose only if the very same object seems to have different colors at different magnifications.

This, remarkably, is precisely the position that Philonous later denies, in the Third Dialogue. There he asserts that an object seen by the naked eye is not strictly identical when seen under the microscope. Philonous describes this as a special instance of the more general claim that what is commonly called "the same object" is not strictly identical even as seen from different angles or in different lights, by the same perceiver at different times, or by different perceivers at the same time. The reason is that for the perceivers the objects experienced from those perspectives consist of different distinct congeries of ideas. Hylas takes the offensive by raising a criticism against Philonous's naive perceptual "realism":

> HYLAS: You say you believe your senses; and seem to applaud your self that in this you agree with the vulgar. According to you therefore, the true nature of a thing is discovered by the senses. If so, whence comes that disagreement? Why is not the same figure, and other sensible qualities, perceived all manner of ways? and why should we use a microscope, the better to discover the true nature of a body, if it were discoverable to the naked eye?

> PHILONOUS: Strictly speaking, Hylas, we do not see the same object that we feel; neither is the same object perceived by the microscope, which was by the naked eye. . . . And, when I look through a microscope, it is not that I may perceive more clearly what I perceived already with my bare eyes; the object perceived by the glass being quite different from the former. (463–64)

The conclusion follows directly from Berkeley's idealism. If a sensible thing exists only as a congeries of ideas, then by altering the congeries ever so slightly, the sensible thing must also change, sacrificing its identity in the reconstitution of another thing. The difficulty is not merely that Berkeley makes superficially inconsistent remarks about the identity of objects seen by the naked eye and under the microscope in the First and Third Dialogues. More importantly, the problem is that the discrepancy cannot straightforwardly be resolved because of the incompatible purposes, each crucial to Berkeley's philosophy, to which the conflicting positions on the reality of microscopic subjects are addressed.

This makes the microscope passages in the First and Third Dialogues of interest not only as a puzzle for understanding Berkeley's metaphysics of sensible things, but as a symptom of potential logical inconsistency within his theory, an indication of deep incoherence in the conceptual basis of his idealism. Berkeley simultaneously wants his immaterialist system to agree with commonsense judgments about the real (ultimately ideational) properties of things presented to immediate sensation, and he wants to conclude that the perceived properties of sensible things do not belong to things themselves existing outside the mind. The two microscope arguments are important because they emphasize this tension in Berkeley's thought, showing in a single application, all the more revealing if Berkeley was careless enough to overlook it, that not both requirements can easily be satisfied.

The same difficulty occurs with respect to telescopes or other scientific instruments believed to give more or more detailed information about the same objects than the unaided senses. In this way, Berkeley's microscope arguments conveniently stand for a larger set of inconsistencies that may run through his empiricist epistemology and metaphysics. Berkeley offers his brand of immaterialism in the service both of natural science and common sense. Minimally, the apparent inconsistency requires a reevaluation of Berkeley's dialogues, to decide whether the contradiction is real, sufficient to reject Berkeley's idealism on logical grounds, apart from its unwelcome consequences, or whether the contradiction is apparent only, and somehow resolvable within the main lines of his philosophy. Berkeley's microscope arguments thus provide the occasion for a necessary reinterpretation of his radical idealist empiricism that may broaden our understanding of its underlying strengths and weaknesses.

Fortunately, there is a consistent way to understand and reconcile Philonous's remarks about sensible things perceived with or without a microscope. It is unlikely in the first place that Berkeley would have simply failed to notice a conflict in the two passages, especially since each stands out and recalls the other by its unusual references to observations made under the microscope. It appears more probable as a result that Berkeley in this way means to underscore a feature of his idealism that might otherwise be disregarded, that in a sense confers objectivity on the mind's constitution of sensible things as congeries of ideas. This is the role of God as an infinite mind in which sensible things have an existence outside of particular finite human minds, and in terms of which sensible things, though still existing within a mind, need not be regarded as limited to subjective experience or willful control of individual finite human minds. The apparent conflict in Berkeley's two microscope arguments is resolved by appeal to God's infinite mind as the repository of all ideas constituting identical sensible things, including those that constitute it as distinct objects for finite minds experiencing it by the naked eye and under the microscope. From this standpoint, it is no accident that Philonous in his Third Dialogue discussion with Hylas surrounding the second microscope passage, reflects at length, in response to Hylas's challenges, on the nature of God's infinite mind and the identical archetypes of sensible things contained in God's mind as opposed to their distinct limited appearances in finite human minds.

If Berkeley speaks of the strictly different objects seen by the naked eye and under the microscope, he also recognizes the connections linking them. By considering these, Philonous maintains, we may better get to know "the nature of things." This in turn indicates a solution to the problem raised by the *Esse est percipi* principle. The solution is given by Berkeley's distinction between the more complete objects identically constituted by congeries of ideas occurring *archetypally* in God's infinite mind, and objects known or constituted by comparatively limited congeries of sense impressions existing only *ectypally* in finite minds. There are several interrelated principles in Berkeley's elaboration of this part of his philosophy. We reconstruct the entire chain of reasoning as a series of steps, before turning to textual evidence in support of the distinction. It will be useful at the outset to refer in a general way to an unspecified C-relation by which sensible things can be connected. We later explain the concept of a C-relation more fully, after distinguishing between the ectypal existence of sensible things as partial congeries of ideas in finite minds, and their archetypal existence as complete congeries of ideas in God's infinite mind. The argument has this structure:

Berkeley's Microscopes Argument

1. To be is to be perceived or a perceiver, an idea or immediate sense impression, or a mind.
2. Sensible things are mere congeries of ideas.
3. Sensible things seen by the naked eye and under the microscope are constituted by distinct congeries of ideas, and are themselves therefore distinct *in sensu strictu.*
4. Sensible things distinct *in sensu strictu*, as when seen by the naked eye and under the microscope, are sometimes referred to as identical only as a practical matter of convenience in "vulgar acceptation" where words are of "arbitrary imposition," if they are observed to be C-related (see below), or to have some connection with respect to coexistence or succession.
5. The study of C-related distinct sensible things *in sensu strictu* under different conditions or by different means, including naked eye and microscopic inspection, is therefore not *in sensu strictu* for the purpose of learning more about the same sensible thing, but for the purpose of learning about the connections among distinct sensible things or the ideas of which they are constituted.
6. The better connections among sensible things or ideas are understood, the more is understood about "the nature of things."
7. To suppose that C-related sensible things are identical in any stronger sense by reference to or participation in an identity archetype *outside the mind* implies the intelligibility of abstract general ideas.
8. Abstract general ideas are unintelligible; the concept of an abstract is an incoherent philosophical fiction.
9. The identity archetype of C-related sensible things distinct *in sensu strictu* can only reside *within a mind*; but as the archetype by hypothesis does not reside within any finite human mind, it can only reside in God's infinite mind.
10. Sensible objects have an eternal archetypal existence in God's infinite mind, but only a relative ectypal natural existence in finite human minds, sharing at most in a proper subset of the complete sets of ideas that constitute the object in God's mind.

---

11. A sensible thing viewed by the naked eye can therefore be the same as that viewed under the microscope, not *in sensu strictu* as a natural ectypal existent known to and residing as a congeries of ideas or immediate sense impressions in a finite mind, but *in sensu strictu* as parts or proper subsets of the complete sets of ideas or immediate sense impressions that constitute the eternal identity archetypal existent known to and residing in God's infinite mind.

The propositions in (1) and (2) are underlying principles of Berkeley's idealism and immaterialism; (2) follows from (1). Proposition (3) in turn follows directly from (2), where if sensible things are congeries of ideas, then the identity principle for sensible things derives from the identity of their congeries. Proposition (4) blunts the edge of objections to the counterintuitiveness of the conclusion in (3), by allowing that sensible things that are strictly distinct can be referred to as identical on pragmatic grounds to avoid the "inconveniencies" of everyday communication.

Philonous in a sense is justified in adopting a nonchalant attitude toward the exact specification of these conditions, since he regards the attribution of identity to strictly distinct objects in all such cases as philosophically mistaken. He is not obligated to speak for the misinformed who find it necessary to treat nonidentical things as identical. Philonous wants to establish a connection between this technically misguided ordinary usage, and the identity even of objects constituted by distinct congeries of immediate sense impressions in God's infinite mind when they are properly related.

In a complete presentation of his theory, Berkeley must be able to specify the precise conditions to be satisfied by distinct congeries of ideas in finite minds when object identity is pragmatically attributed to distinct congeries of ideas. In the reconstruction of this part of Philonous's argument, the unspecified connection needed by Berkeley's metaphysics as a refinement of these first approximations accordingly is referred to schematically as a *C*-relation for objects that are *constituted* by distinct congeries of ideas in finite minds, but that belong as constituents to the same completed congeries of ideas in God's infinite mind and designated as identical in vulgar usage, are said to be *C*-related.

Propositions (5) and (6) summarize Berkeley's position on the meaning and purpose of scientific investigation. They further deflect commonsense criticisms of the nonidentity of differently perceived but *C*-related objects that are distinct *in sensu strictu*. Hylas had asked Philonous: "Why is not the same figure, and other sensible qualities, perceived all manner of ways? and why should we use a microscope, the better to discover the true nature of a body, if it were discoverable to the naked eye?" (463). This, after all, is what the interlocutors had agreed in the First Dialogue. The fact that it is at this juncture that Philonous insists on the "strict sense" perception of distinct objects by the naked eye and under the microscope should make us wary of the claim that Berkeley unwittingly falls into inconsistency in his two microscope discussions. To Hylas's question, Philonous now further explains:

> PHILONOUS: Hence it follows that when I examine, by my other senses, a thing I have seen, it is not in order to understand better the same object which I had perceived by sight, the object of one sense not being perceived by the other senses. . . . But, in both cases, [perceiving what is vulgarly referred to as the "same" object by different senses, or by the naked eye and under the microscope] my aim is only to know what ideas are connected together; and the more a man knows of the connexion of ideas, the more he is said to know of the nature of things. (464)

The point of (6) is that knowledge is increased through inquiry into connections among ideas. This assumption can be true no matter whether distinct congeries of ideas are believed to constitute the same or strictly nonidentical objects. What the empiricist investigator wants to know is how ideas or sense impressions are related one to another. Philonous expresses the fundamental motivation of empiricism in its most basic terms, turning aside the commonsense objection that if these objects were not identical or regarded as identical, then there would be no reason to have different persons examine them under different conditions, or with different perception-enhancing instruments.

With proposition (7), a new line of argument begins. The development of previous inferences leads Hylas and Philonous to conclude that distinct congeries of ideas constitute distinct sensible objects *in sensu strictu*. The discussion now shifts to a consideration of extramental identity archetypes for *C*-related strictly distinct objects, a concept Hylas introduces from the teachings of unidentified "materialists":

> HYLAS: But they suppose an external archetype, to which referring their several ideas they may truly be said to perceive the same thing.
>
> PHILONOUS: And (not to mention your having discarded those archetypes) so may you suppose an external archetype on my principles;—*external, I mean, to your own mind:* though indeed it must be supposed to exist in that Mind which comprehends all things; but then, this serves all the ends of *identity*, as well as if it existed out of a mind. And I am sure you yourself will not say it is less intelligible. (468)

Philonous appeals to Hylas's previous rejection of extramental archetypes as abstract general ideas. He assumes that they are in no position to return to extramental material substance or substrata as a justification for identity attributions to distinct congeries of ideas. The subargument is completed by step (8), in which the rejection of abstract general ideas is made explicit. Together with proposition (7), the conclusion entails that strictly distinct but *C*-related objects cannot be identical in any stronger sense by virtue of participation in an extramental identity archetype.

If there is to be an external identity archetype for sensible objects, there is only one remaining possibility, involving a mental rather than extramental identity archetype, as proposition (9) states. Since by hypothesis the *C*-related objects in question are strictly distinct for finite minds, the external identity archetype must reside in God's infinite mind. Philonous refers to God as "that mind which comprehends all things." If there is at most one such mind (which, as we have seen, is not proved by Berkeley), Philonous can conclude that an infinite divine external but decidedly mental identity archetype for strictly distinct but *C*-related sensible objects would "serve all the ends of identity, as well as if it existed out of a mind." That is to say, the identity archetype for strictly distinct but *C*-related sensible objects in God's mind is *objective despite being mental*, since it is external to every finite mind.

This assumes again without proof that there is or can be at most one God, one divine infinite mind with a single identity archetype consisting of the complete congeries of ideas or immediate sense impressions constituting each object. Why should there not, however, for all that Berkeley says, be a different god who entertains a different archetype of each sensible thing for every distinct congeries of ideas of a sensible thing in the thoughts of every finite mind? Berkeley denies such a possibility, but does not try to argue against it. This is evident in his distinction, expressed in proposition (10), between the eternal *archetypal* existence of objects in God's infinite mind, and their relative *ectypal* natural existence in finite minds. Philonous responds to Hylas's challenge that his immaterialism appears inconsistent with the biblical account of God's creation of the world, and the calling into existence of things by divine fiat, when he explains the contrast and relation between the existence of things in God's mind and finite human minds:

> PHILONOUS: . . . All objects are eternally known by God, or, which is the same thing, have an eternal existence in His mind: but when things, before imper-

ceptible to creatures, are, by a decree of God, made perceptible to them, then they are said to begin a relative existence, with respect to created minds. Upon reading therefore the Mosaic account of the creation, I understand that the several parts of the world became gradually perceivable to finite spirits, endowed with proper faculties; so that, whoever such were present, they were in truth perceived by them. (472)

The objective existence of an identity archetype for strictly distinct C-related sensible things in God's mind provides the glue needed to attach multiple perceptions of sensible things to a single entity. Thus, Philonous explains the view of a drop of blood by the naked eye and under the microscope as different perspectives of the same sensible thing existing archetypally in God's mind.

Berkeley thereby explains the commonsense attribution of identity to different perceptions of objects on higher metaphysical grounds. From the standpoint of finite minds limited to knowledge only of proper subsets of the complete congeries of ideas that constitute each object, there is on the contrary no justification for regarding different perceptions as belonging to the same sensible things. There is an interesting transition in Philonous's commitment to the distinction between the ectypal or natural existence of objects as congeries of ideas exhibited to finite minds, and their archetypal existence as complete congeries of ideas in God's infinite mind. After introducing the concept and using it to defend the biblical orthodoxy of immaterialism against Hylas's objections, Philonous increasingly insists on the archetypal identity in God's mind of objects perceived as distinct congeries of ideas by finite minds. Hylas and Philonous pursue the topic in this way:

HYLAS: I must acknowledge, the difficulties you are concerned to clear are such only as arise from the non-existence of Matter, and are peculiar to that notion. So far you are in the right. But I cannot by any means bring myself to think there is no such peculiar repugnancy between the creation and your opinion; though indeed where to fix it, I do not distinctly know.

PHILONOUS: What would you have? Do I not acknowledge a two-fold state of things—the one ectypal or natural, the other archetypal and eternal? The former was created in time; the latter existed from everlasting in the mind of God. (475)

Rather than suggesting as before that Hylas "may . . . suppose an external archetype" that is minimally "intelligible," Philonous now urges with some insistence the distinction between an object's ectypal natural existence in finite human minds and its eternal archetypal existence in God's infinite mind. It seems reasonable to conclude that Berkeley is not merely experimenting with the distinction as a way in which an objection about the coherence of idealism with the Genesis account of God's creation of the world might be answered, but that he fully accepts the concept as an essential part of his philosophy.

Even if Berkeley's position were only that on his principles we *can* accept the archetypal existence of complete congeries of ideas that constitute sensible objects, that would still not be sufficient to reconcile his discussion of the objects seen by the naked eye and under the microscope in the First and Third Dialogues. First, Berkeley believes that God knows and in his mind "comprehends" all things, which for Berkeley means that all things exist or reside in God's infinite mind. Second, Berkeley holds that God exhibits partial congeries of these complete sets of ideas to finite minds, presumably because these are all that finite minds by definition are capable of experiencing. Philonous states, earlier in the Third Dialogue: "[T]here is an *omnipresent eternal Mind*, which knows and comprehends all things, and exhibits them to our view in such a manner, and according to such rules as He Himself hath ordained, and are by us termed the *laws of nature*" (447).

The distinction between the ectypal and archetypal existence of sensible objects makes it possible for Philonous to resolve the apparent inconsistency in his discussion of the objects of unaided and microscopic perception. An object seen by the naked eye, as the conclusion in step (11) affirms, *can* be the same as that viewed under the microscope, whether or not human finite minds are ever in a position to know it with certainty. The objects can even be identical in the strict sense, *provided* that each is a partial set belonging to the complete congeries of ideas constituting an identical object archetypally in God's infinite mind. God then chooses selected partial subsets of the complete congeries of a sensible thing to be perceived ectypally in finite minds both with and without the use of a microscope. The appearance of inconsistency results only from equivocation on two different meanings of sensible object as a congeries of ideas. In one sense, as ectypal congeries of ideas accessible to and residing in finite minds, microscopic and naked eye objects are strictly distinct. Insofar as they belong together in and are constituted by the same identity archetype or complete congeries of ideas in God's infinite mind, they are also, at least for God, strictly identical.

GOD'S CREATIVITY AND THE FREE WILL PROBLEM

Although Hylas at this stage of Berkeley's dialogues has granted many if not most of Philonous's most important conclusions, he continues to express reservations about other aspects of the proof for the existence of God. More particularly, Hylas seems concerned that the way in which Philonous tries to prove the existence of God as a divine perceiver of archetypal congeries raises paradoxes about the nature of God's creativity and the free will of human minds as God's creations. The relation between finite human minds and God's divine infinite mind is at the root of both controversies. Hylas begins this new debate in the Third Dialogue:

> HYLAS: It cannot be denied there is something highly serviceable to religion in what you advance. But do you not think it looks very like a notion entertained by some eminent moderns, of *seeing all things in God?*

> PHILONOUS: I would gladly know that opinion: pray explain it to me.

> HYLAS: They conceive that the soul, being immaterial, is incapable of being united with material things, so as to perceive them in themselves; but that she perceives them by her union with the substance of God, which, being spiritual, is therefore purely intelligible, or capable of being the immediate object of a spirit's thought. Besides, the Divine essence contains in it perfections correspondent to each created being; and which are, for that reason, proper to exhibit or represent them to the mind.

PHILONOUS: I do not understand how our ideas, which are things altogether passive and inert, can be the essence, or any part (or like any part) of the essence or substance of God, who is an impassive, indivisible, pure, active being. Many more difficulties and objections there are which occur at first view against this hypothesis; but I shall only add, that it is liable to all the absurdities of the common hypothesis, in making a created world exist otherwise than in the mind of a Spirit. Beside all which it hath this peculiar to itself that it makes that material world serve to no purpose. And, if it pass for a good argument against other hypotheses in the sciences, that they suppose Nature or the Divine wisdom, to make something in vain, or do that by tedious roundabout methods which might have been performed in a much more easy and compendious way, what shall we think of that hypothesis which supposes the whole world made in vain? (426–27)

To see all things in God, in Hylas's phrase, is to be involved in a kind of "union with God," which Hylas attributes to certain "modern" philosophers, undoubtedly including Malebranche. This sort of mystical union with God, Philonous maintains, is not only not implied by but is strictly incompatible with his idealism. The reason is important and instructive in trying to understand Berkeley's philosophy of religion. Philonous explains that the only sense in which a perception can occur is when a thinker, an active entity, entertains ideas of the sensible qualities of things, which in contrast are entirely passive. If the mind is active and its ideas are passive, then there is no possibility of literally seeing all things in God or achieving any sort of mystical union merging the finite minds of individual human beings with the infinite mind of God. It would be equally impossible, according to Berkeley's distinction, for two or more human minds to be fused together into mystical union. The reason, Philonous explains, is that no mind can have among its ideas an idea of another mind, finite or infinite and divine. If minds are always active rather than passive, then no active thing can contain an active mind among its purely passive ideas. Philonous develops the distinction:

PHILONOUS: . . . Take here in brief my meaning:—It is evident that the things I perceive are my own ideas, and that no idea can exist unless it be in a mind: nor is it less plain that these ideas or things by me perceived, either themselves or their archetypes, exist independently of my mind, since I know myself not to be their author, it being out of my power to determine at pleasure what particular ideas I shall be affected with upon opening my eyes or ears: they must therefore exist in some other Mind, whose Will it is they should be exhibited to me. The things, I say, immediately perceived are ideas or sensations, call them which you will. But how can any idea or sensation exist in, or be produced by, anything but a mind or spirit? This indeed is inconceivable. And to assert that which is inconceivable is to talk nonsense: is it not?

HYLAS: Without doubt.

PHILONOUS: But, on the other had, it is very conceivable that they should exist in and be produced by a Spirit; since this is no more than I daily experience in myself, inasmuch as I form a great variety of them, and raise them up in my imagination: though, it must be confessed, these creatures of the fancy are not altogether so distinct, so strong, vivid, and permanent as those perceived by my senses—which latter are called *real things*. From all which I conclude, *there is a Mind which affects me every moment with all the sensible impressions I perceive*. And, from the variety, order, and manner of these, I conclude the *Author of them to be wise, powerful, and good, beyond comprehension.* Mark it well; I do not say, I see things by perceiving that which represents them in the intelligible Substance of God. This I do not understand; but I say, the things by me perceived are known by the understanding and produced by the will of an infinite Spirit. And is not all this most plain and evident? Is there any more in it than what a little observation of our own minds, and that which passes in them, not only enables us to conceive, but also obliges us to acknowledge? (427–28)

The difference is subtle but important. A human thinker cannot literally share in God's thoughts, but at best experiences some of the ideas that constitute sensible things that are perceived in their entirety by God. We do not perceive sensible things by taking part in God's thoughts. The sensible things that we experience ectypally as congeries of ideas are nevertheless the partial contents of the complete archetypal congeries of ideas existing in God's mind, seen from every perspective and under every condition and magnification. We experience parts of the same things not by being a part of God's mind or sharing in God's thoughts, even though we partially experience many of the same things that God's ideas creatively constitute. God, according to Philonous, creates the universe of sensible things by directly willing the congeries of ideas that we can also experience in sensation. Philonous remarks:

PHILONOUS: . . . We indeed, who are beings of finite powers, are forced to make use of instruments. And the use of an instrument sheweth the agent to be limited by rules of another's prescription, and that he cannot obtain to be limited by rules of another's prescription, and that he cannot obtain his end but in such a way, and by such conditions. Whence it seems a clear consequence, that the supreme unlimited Agent useth no tool or instrument at all. The will of an Omnipotent Spirit is no sooner exerted than executed, without the application of means; which, if they are employed by inferior agents, it is not upon account of any real efficacy that is in them, or necessary aptitude to produce any effect, but merely in compliance with the laws of nature or those conditions prescribed to them by the First Cause, who is Himself above all limitation or prescription whatsoever. (433)

The world of sensible things is brought into existence by an all-powerful act of divine creative will. Philonous's interpretation reaffirms received religious teachings about God's creation of the universe. Indeed, if the world were not a complex network of sensible things, constituted by congeries of ideas in God's mind, then it is hard to understand how a material world could have been caused to exist by the all-powerful will of an immaterial spirit.

There is a metaphysical difficulty in that case of grasping how it could happen that an immaterial spirit that is literally nowhere in space or time, existing at no particular place and at no particular time, even if omnipotent and omniscient as God is supposed to be, could have caused the material world to exist. We do not ordinarily suppose that something nonspatiotemporal can bring about changes in something spatiotemporal. If we think of causation in the usual way, as efficient mechanical causation, then it requires something to impart motion to something else by touching it. A spirit cannot literally touch something material. This is another sense in which Berkeley regards materialism as godless, inviting atheism by positing mind-independent material substance and making it impossible to comprehend God's creation of a material universe. It is also the reason why Descartes, who makes similar materialist assumptions, is accused on a lesser scale of endorsing a metaphysically insupportable distinction between body and soul, while at the same time expecting that physical events involving the body can causally affect the soul, and that occurrences such as decisions and acts of will in the soul can causally bring about changes in the body, as when a subject chooses to move a limb.

Berkeley's concept of causation is also explained philosophically and theologically by Philonous in the Third Dialogue. Philonous understands causation in the world of empirical phenomena as the result of God's freely willing certain sequences of events involving sensible things, construed again as congeries of ideas, to follow other sequences of events with perfect regularity. Berkeley's theory of causation explains the necessity that seems to attend causation in the world. It is the result of God's will. It also explains the logical contingency of causal connections, or the fact that causation is actual and hence logically possible, but not logically necessary. When we place a teapot filled with water over a fire, the water becomes heated and steam soon issues from the spout. Why does this happen, and what does it mean? According to Berkeley, the fire causes the water to turn to steam, which means only that God has willed one type of event involving the sensible teapot on the fire to be regularly followed after a certain length of time by another type of event involving sensible steam issuing from the teapot's spout.

That is all there is to causation, according to Berkeley. He concludes that any causal sequence of events that actually occurs in the phenomenal world could be different than it is, depending on God's free choice. There is no reason why God might not have willed that a teapot filled with water and placed on the fire after a certain period of time should not freeze or bubble over with champagne, or turn into a hedgehog and scamper away. If so, then the discoveries of natural science would be different than they are, but they would in every case constitute an attempt to understand the will of God. Science for Berkeley in this sense is nothing other than an effort to reconstruct the decisions God has made for the existence and nature of the world of sensible things and physical events. To be a Berkeleyan natural scientist is to follow in the directions God has set for physical things as regular sequences of sensible occurrences, any of which could have been different than they happen to be discovered in experience. A scientific causal law is nothing other than a regularity among sensible events that God has freely willed.

Philonous reaffirms the idealist conclusion that we can have no idea of God's or any other mind, in the technical sense of the word, because of the active nature of minds and the passive nature of ideas. He somewhat awkwardly co-opts the word *notion* to cover the thoughts and concepts we have of other minds, including God's, in philosophy and religion. Philonous and Hylas engage in the following further discussion of this important point in Berkeley's philosophy of mind and religion:

HYLAS: Answer me, Philonous. Are all our ideas perfectly inert beings? Or have they any agency included in them?

PHILONOUS: They are altogether passive and inert.

HYLAS: And is not God an agent, a being purely active?

PHILONOUS: I acknowledge it.

HYLAS: No idea, therefore, can be like unto, or represent the nature of God.

PHILONOUS: It cannot.

HYLAS: Since therefore you have no *idea* of the mind of God, how can you conceive it possible that things should exist in His mind? Or, if you can conceive the mind of God, without having an idea of it, why may not I be allowed to conceive the existence of Matter, notwithstanding I have no idea of it?

PHILONOUS: I own I have properly no *idea*, either of God or any other spirit; for these, being active, cannot be represented by things perfectly inert, as our ideas are. I do nevertheless know that I, who am a spirit or thinking substance, exist as certainly as I now my ideas exist. Further, I know what I mean by the terms *I* and *myself*; and I know this immediately or intuitively, though I do not perceive it as I perceive a triangle, a colour, or a sound. The Mind, Spirit, or Soul is that indivisible unextended thing which thinks, acts, and perceives. I say *indivisible*, because unextended; and *unextended*, because extended, figured, moveable things are ideas; and that which perceives ideas, which thinks and wills, is plainly itself no idea, nor like an idea. Ideas are things inactive, and perceived. And Spirits a sort of beings altogether different from them. I do not therefore say my soul is an idea, or like an idea. However, taking the word *idea* in a large sense, my soul may be said to furnish me with an idea, that is, an image or likeness of God—though indeed extremely inadequate. For, all the notion I have of God is obtained by reflecting on my own soul, heightening its powers, and removing its imperfections. I have, therefore, though not an inactive idea, yet in *myself* some sort of an active thinking image of the Deity. And, though I perceive Him not by sense, yet I have a notion of Him, or know Him by reflexion and reasoning. My own mind and my own ideas I have an immediate knowledge of; and, by the help of these, do mediately apprehend the possibility of the existence of other spirits and ideas. Further, from my own being, and from the dependency I find in myself and my ideas, I do, by an act of reason, necessarily infer the existence of a God, and of all created things in the mind of God. (447–48)

With this clarification in hand, Hylas feels emboldened to pose his most difficult and potentially damaging objection to Philonous's concept of God. Hylas asks a poignant question, for which Philonous has a ready answer:

HYLAS: You are not aware, Philonous, that, in making God the immediate Author of all the motions in nature, you make Him the Author of murder, sacrilege, adultery, and the like heinous sins.

PHILONOUS: In answer to that I observe, first, that the imputation of guilt is the same whether a person commits an action with or without an instrument. In case therefore you suppose God to act by the mediation of an instrument of occasion called *Matter*, you as truly make Him the author of sin as I, who think Him the immediate agent in all those operations vulgarly ascribed to Nature. I further observe that sin or moral turpitude doth not consist in the outward physical action or motion, but in the internal deviation of the will from the laws of reason and religion. This is plain, in that the killing an enemy in a battle, or putting a criminal legally to death, is not thought sinful; though the outward act be the very same with that in the case of murder. Since, therefore, sin doth not consist in the physical action, the making God an immediate cause of all such actions is not making Him the Author of sin. Lastly, I have nowhere said that God is the only agent who produces all the motions in bodies. It is true I have denied there are any other agents besides spirits; but this is very consistent with allowing to thinking rational beings, in the production of motions, the use of limited powers, ultimately indeed derived from God, but immediately under the direction of their own wills, which is sufficient to entitle them to all the guilt of their actions. (453–54)

Philonous invokes several important commonsense distinctions. Hylas has tried to argue that God, as the creator of the universe of sensible things and the "Author" of the world with all of its causal regularities reflecting divine will, is thereby made morally responsible for all of the crimes that human beings commit. This, needless to say, is a conclusion that Philonous is anxious to avoid.

The solution has several parts. Philonous first asserts that the same could be said on the hypothesis that there is such a thing as mind-independent matter rather than mind-dependent congeries of ideas. The problem, therefore, if it is a problem, does not cut uniquely against Philonous's idealist metaphysics and philosophical theology as opposed to Hylas's materialism. Second, Philonous argues that moral responsibility is not simply a matter of causing events to occur, but of the agent's intentions. The fact that a person is killed by another does not automatically mean that a wrongful act has been done; it depends on the circumstances and the intentions of the persons involved. As Philonous controversially asserts, the killing of a person in war or in a legal execution is not necessarily morally objectionable.

The fact that God is metaphysically responsible for all physical occurrences in the phenomenal world by willing regular successions of events does not make God morally responsible for the evils that human agents perpetrate. Importantly, Philonous reminds Hylas that he has not said that God is the only cause of events in the world. The agency of finite human will is also causally responsible for much that happens in the world. Since our active minds are no more contained in God's mind as passive ideas than God's mind is contained in ours, we as minds, active agents in the world, are just as capable on a lesser scale of producing changes in the world for which we are individually responsible. Philonous offers a similar line of reasoning to blunt Hylas's objection that it would be an imperfection in the nature of God to suffer pain and other mental infirmities that afflict human thought. God is the greatest mind, according to Philonous, but still only one mind among others. Each mind has its own content, and each mind is responsible for its actions and the subject of its own experiences—despite the fact that God creates the universe and is the divine thinker within which all sensible things archetypally exist as complete congeries of ideas.

Hylas's final challenge for Philonous takes the form of a criticism of another apparent inconsistency between Philonous's espousal of Berkeleyan idealism and the Scriptural account of the creation of the world. Philonous believes he is on firm ground, and takes the opportunity to reiterate the consequences of his view that God exists as the archetypal originator of the world of sensible things. As he does throughout the dialogues, in what might be described as Berkeley's rhetorical signature, Philonous reverses the force of Hylas's objection by turning the tables. The objection and reply are stated in this passage:

> HYLAS: . . . But there still remains one great difficulty, which I know not how you will get over. And, indeed, it is of such importance that if you could solve all others, without being able to find a solution for this, you must never expect to make me a proselyte to your principles.

> PHILONOUS: Let me know this mighty difficulty.

> HYLAS: The Scripture account of the creation is what appears to me utterly irreconcilable with your notions. Moses tells us of a creation: a creation of what? of ideas? No, certainly, but of things, of real things, solid corporeal substances. Bring your principles to agree with this, and I shall perhaps agree with you.

> PHILONOUS: Moses mentions the sun, moon, and stars, earth and sea, plants and animals. That all these do really exist, and were in the beginning created by God, I make no question. If by *ideas* you mean fictions and fancies of the mind, then these are no ideas. If by *ideas* you mean immediate objects of the understanding, or sensible things which cannot exist unperceived, or out of a mind, then these things are ideas. But whether you do or do not call them *ideas*, it matters little. The difference is only about a name. And, whether that name be retained or rejected, the sense, the truth, and reality of things continues the same. In common talk, the objects of our senses are not termed *ideas* but *things*. Call them so still: provided you do not attribute to them any absolute external existence, and I shall never quarrel with you for a word. The creation, therefore, I allow to have been a creation of things, of *real* things. Neither is this in the least inconsistent with my principles, as is evident from what I have now said; and would have been evident to you without this, if you had not forgotten what had been so often said before. But as for solid corporeal substances, I desire you to show where Moses makes any mention of them; and if they should be mentioned by him or any other inspired writer, it would still be incumbent on you to show those words were not taken in the vulgar acceptation, for things falling under our senses, but in the philosophic acceptation, for Matter, or *an unknown quiddity, with an absolute existence.* When you have proved these points, then (and not till then) may you bring the authority of Moses into our dispute. (471–72)

We note that by describing sensible things as congeries of ideas in the mind, Philonous by no means refers to objects of fantasy or creations of the imagination, but to real things, the very same real things in which a materialist believes. The essential point is that Philonous and Berkeley as idealists are not proponents of a theory of ir-reality, but, on the contrary, believe themselves to be the defenders of the true and correct theory of the real existence of the sensible physical world.

Philonous is not the advocate of mystery or skepticism or confusion, but sees himself as upholding the commonsense view that the things we experience in sensation are real things, perceived just as they exist in reality. It is, on the contrary, the position of those who accept the existence of something imperceivable, of matter or material substance or the substratum, who are committed to the existence of something mysterious, unknowable, and impenetrable to the senses. It is materialists who deserve to be regarded as skeptics, accepting a version of the unknowability of ultimate reality that further entails atheism. For they endorse a metaphysics that pretends that all physical occurrences can be explained without referring to the infinite mind of God as ultimate cause of the ideas we experience. Philonous sees no reason to abandon his principles in light of the Old Testament account of God's creation of the world:

> PHILONOUS: Why, I imagine that if I had been present at the creation, I should have seen things produced into being—that is become perceptible—in the order prescribed by the sacred historian. I ever before believed the Mosaic account of the creation, and now find no alteration in my manner of believing it. When things are said to begin or end their existence, we do not mean this with regard to God, but His creatures. . . . This is the literal obvious sense suggested to me by the words of the Holy Scripture: in which is included no mention, or no thought, either of *substratum*, instrument, occasion, or absolute existence. And, upon inquiry, I doubt not it will be found that most plain honest men who believe the creation, never think of those things any more than I. What metaphysical sense you may understand it in, you only can tell. (472–73)

The reversal of burden of proof between idealism and materialism is complete when Philonous argues that it is the materialist rather than the idealist who has the greater theoretical difficulty in light of the biblical account of the creation. Certainly, Philonous is right that the biblical story of the creation of the world by God does not mention matter, material substance, or material substratum as required by the opponents of idealism. Instead, the authors of the Old Testament speak of the origin of the world we all experience in sensation, which is to say a world consisting of congeries of sensible qualities, of sensible things constituted by congeries of ideas, light and water, the heavenly bodies, plants and animals, and human beings. This is nothing other than the sensible world in all its glory that the Berkeleyan idealist celebrates, as Hylas, despite his usual sour diffidence, finally admits:

> PHILONOUS: Moses tells us of a creation. A creation of what? of unknown quiddities, of occasions, or *substratum*? No, certainly; but of things obvious to the senses. You must first reconcile this with your notions, if you expect I should be reconciled to them.
>
> HYLAS: I see you can assault me with my own weapons. (477)

We must nevertheless wonder whether Hylas's concerns about the free will of finite minds are adequately answered by Berkeley's idealism. If the active minds of finite human agents are not simply incorporated as passive ideas in God's infinite mind, it remains true presumably that the physical bodies of finite human agents are complete congeries of ideas in God's infinite mind. Is it thinkable, then, that a finite mind could will the body to perform an action that is contrary to God's will in determining the course of events that are caused to occur in the sensible world? Suppose that God has archetypally willed the congeries of ideas that constitute my body, including my brain and nervous system, and that a neurophysiological event transpires in my brain resulting in body movements that bring about the wrongful death of another person.

There is a dilemma. Either I willed the act or I did not. If I willed the act, then either I did so because my will itself, despite being active, is caused by the electrochemical events in my neurophysiology, for which, as sensible occurrences, God is again morally responsible. Or, perhaps, I willed the act in a way that is causally independent of the physical events occurring in my brain and nervous system. The result in that case is the same as if I did not will the act, but it happened anyway, so to speak, despite and even against my will. My body in either case is not responsive to my will, suggesting that I can never be morally responsible for my body's actions. If I am not morally responsible for what my body does, and if God is the author of the universe of sensible things including my body and all that happens to it, then, again, much as Hylas complains to Philonous, God appears to be morally responsible for whatever we God-created human beings do.

The motions human bodies as sensible things are subject to, the movements they undergo in making decisions and taking actions, are congeries of ideas that are created by and exist archetypally in God's infinite mind, and are subject to the causal regularities determined by God's free will. It does not appear consistent to imagine that God could both will the existence of all sensible things including human bodies and the causal laws by which all sensible events are determined and at the same time permit the actions of human bodies to be under the potentially contrary control of human thought. How can we poor mortals oppose what an all-powerful God has ordained, at least where our bodies as sensible things, congeries of ideas existing archetypally in God's infinite mind, are concerned? If God rules the universe of sensible things as Berkeley and Philonous contend, then it appears that God's will must extend even through all the actions of our bodies. God's free will, at least insofar as it concerns the movements and actions of our bodies, appears incompatible in Berkeley's idealist metaphysics with free will and the moral responsibility of finite human agents.

IDEALIST METAPHYSICS AND EMPIRICIST EPISTEMOLOGY

To this point we have sidetracked the difficult but most interesting question of whether Berkeley's idealism is philosophically correct. We have seen that idealism follows from Berkeley's methodological commitment to radical empiricism, but we have not asked whether or not radical idealism is advisable in epistemology, or whether it must be accepted in a form that entails idealism. If we want to include only those concepts in our philosophy that can be supported by perception, then we may need to admit that there is no insensible unthinking underlying material substratum that serves somehow as a support for sensible qualities. Are we philosophically obligated also to accept the conclusions that sensible things are mere congeries of ideas that exist only in the mind, and that, given the independence and presumed continuity of sensible things, they exist archetypally in the infinite mind of God, and only ectypally in our finite minds, as Berkeley concludes?

The challenge of radical empiricism is raised by the consideration that if we do not limit knowledge to what can be experienced then we seem driven to a form of mysticism, in which we accept the existence of things for which we have no experience and can have no scientific knowledge. It is no accident that Berkeley closely links the topics of skepticism, atheism, and the content and philosophical orientation of the natural sciences. We must nevertheless ask whether it is true that devotion to the rigorous methods of empirical science inevitably points in the direction of the view that sensible things exist only in a mind, and ultimately in the mind of all-powerful God. If anything, this appears to be an extraordinary paradox for epistemology, metaphysics, and the philosophy of science. We begin with the epistemological requirements of rigorous science, and wind up with idealism and theology. It is part of the historical and philosophical importance of Berkeley's idealism to have pointed out this unexpected connection of philosophical implications, so different in obvious ways from the metaphysics and epistemology of Plato, Aristotle, Ockham, and Descartes, to mention only those major thinkers in European philosophy that we have so far considered. Where Berkeley warmly embraces the implications of idealism, others have reacted against the poverty of radical empiricism in Berkeley's philosophy. The main lesson of Berkeley's idealism has accordingly more often been to cast doubt on the adequacy of radical empiricism, and the limitations of relying exclusively on sensation and the data of experience in philosophy.

What is the alternative? If we think narrowly of our choices in metaphysics and epistemology in terms of the polar opposites of rationalism and empiricism, then we may have no option except to live with the alternatives proposed by Plato and Aristotle, Ockham, Descartes and Berkeley, or variations of their respectively relatively pure forms of rationalism and empiricism. Fortunately, there are other possibilities. We discover one such alternative in the chapter on the philosophy of Immanuel Kant, where it appears, surprisingly, in the context of his moral philosophy. The metaphysical and epistemological background of Kant's ethics is neither exclusively rationalist nor empiricist, but in a way combines features of both in a radically new philosophical method. We can think of the deadlock between rationalism and empiricism as forcing a new direction in philosophy, the need for which was recognized and taken up by Kant. As we conclude this section on Metaphysics and Epistemology, and prepare to begin the study of Ethics and Political Philosophy, we reflect on the fact that Berkeley's idealism, the theory in particular that sensible things are mere congeries of ideas existing in the mind, is a dramatic illustration of philosophy's long-standing concern with problems of method in securing the principles of what appears to be the best, and sometimes the only, way of acquiring knowledge, and following its metaphysical conclusions logically wherever they lead.

SUMMARY

By limiting knowledge to what can be experienced in sensation, Berkeley leaves no possibility for philosophers to know about the existence of anything other than minds and their ideas. To be, for Berkeley, is to be perceived or a perceiver, excluding any concept of matter, substratum, or mind-independent substance. Hylas and Philonous in Berkeley's dialogues debate these topics at length and in depth, looking into many different aspects of the assumption that knowledge can only depend on sense experience. We experience the sensible qualities that Berkeley calls ideas, but we do not experience other minds, of which we can only have notions, and above all we do not experience matter existing, in Berkeley's terminology, outside the mind. Berkeley's radical empiricism for this reason leads directly to idealism.

Philonous presents a battery of objections to Hylas's materialism, arguing in particular that the doctrine leads to skepticism and atheism. Skepticism arises from materialism because it entails the existence of something of which we can have no experiential knowledge, so that we can never know the true nature of things. Atheism arises from materialism because it implies that the real material world exists outside of all thought, including the mind of God. If we do not need to mention God in order to account for the existence of the world, then we need not suppose that God exists in order to provide a metaphysical grounding for natural science. If Berkeley's or Philonous's immaterialism is true, on the other hand, we cannot plausibly explain the objective existence of the world or the nature of causation, so vital to the sciences, without supposing that God exists.

To prove that God exists, Berkeley in the person of Philonous offers two related arguments, referred to by some commentators as the dependence and continuity arguments. Philonous says that God as an infinite mind must exist in order to explain the fact that the existence of sensible things is independent of finite human thought, and in particular of finite human will, and that sensible things sometimes continue to exist even when they are not being perceived by any finite minds. An apparent circularity threatens the continuity argument if there is no way to support the assumption that sensible things continue to exist when they are not perceived by finite minds except by presupposing that they exist continuously in the infinite mind of God. The circularity objection to Berkeley's continuity argument for the existence of God can be avoided by calling attention to the interior parts of three-dimensional sensible things that we know continue to exist even when they are not perceived by any finite minds, provided that their external surfaces are perceived.

Berkeley's eighteenth-century idealism and empiricism stand in sharp contrast to Descartes's seventeenth-century rationalism, in much the same way that Aristotle's essentialism and Ockham's conceptualism and nominalism are diametrically opposed to Plato's realism in ancient and medieval philosophy. Although we may find Berkeley's idealism far-fetched, it conveys valuable lessons about the implications of a strictly empiricist philosophical methodology when taken to extremes.

QUESTIONS FOR PHILOSOPHICAL UNDERSTANDING

1. What is meant by empiricism? How is it different from rationalism?

2. How does an empiricist theory of knowledge differ from a rationalist theory of knowledge such as Plato's or Descartes's?

3. Is there a fundamental metaphysical distinction between primary and secondary qualities?

4. Why does Berkeley believe that we can have no idea of any mind?

5. What is the significance of Berkeley's distinction between archetypal and ectypal existence?

6. Is it reasonable to interpret sensible things as congeries of ideas?

7. If there is no such thing as a material substratum, what holds a congeries of ideas together so as to constitute an individual sensible thing?

8. Does Berkeley make a strong case for the conclusion that materialism entails skepticism and atheism?

9. What are the philosophical implications of Berkeley's thesis that sensible things exist only in the mind?

10. Can human beings have free will if God exists as the creator of all sensible things, including our bodies, and of all causal connections, including all our body movements?

11. How does Berkeley's theory of causation relate to his argument for the existence of God?

12. Does Berkeley successfully prove the existence of God? Why or why not?

13. Why does Berkeley believe that things seen by the naked eye are not the same as when seen under a microscope?

14. How would you compare Berkeley's philosophy to Aristotle's and Ockham's?

15. Does Berkeley offer a convincing disproof of the existence of abstract general ideas such as the triangle? How does Berkeley's metaphysics compare with Plato's?

KEY TERMS

absolute primary quality

abstract general idea

antimaterialism

archetypal existence

atheism

bare particular

Berkeley's candle

bundle theory of sensible things

collective unconscious

congeries of ideas

continuity argument for the existence of God

dependence argument for the existence of God

ectypal existence

empiricism

Esse est percipi aut posse percipere

idea

idealism

immaterialism

materialism

matter

mind-independent entity

mite's foot

notion

perception

primary quality

pure intellect

secondary quality

sensible primary quality

sensible property

sensible thing

skepticism

solipsism

subjective sensation

substratum

Sources and Recommended Readings

Atherton, Margaret. *Berkeley's Revolution in Vision*. Ithaca: Cornell University Press, 1990.

Bennett, Jonathan F. *Locke, Berkeley, Hume: Central Themes*. Oxford: Clarendon Press, 1971.

Berkeley, George. *The Works of George Berkeley Bishop of Cloyne*. Edited by A. A. Luce and T. E. Jessup. 9 Volumes. London: Thomas Nelson & Sons, 1949–1958.

Berman, David. *George Berkeley: Idealism and the Man*. Oxford: Clarendon Press, 1994.

Bracken, Harry M. *The Early Reception of Berkeley's Immaterialism, 1710–1733*. The Hague: Martinus Nijhoff, 1965.

Broad, C. D. *Berkeley's Argument About Material Substance*. London: H. Milford, 1942.

Brook, Richard J. *Berkeley's Philosophy of Science*. The Hague: Martinus Nijhoff, 1973.

Luce, A. A. *Berkeley and Malebranche: A Study in the Origins of Berkeley's Thought*. London: Oxford University Press, 1934.

Pappas, George S. *Berkeley's Thought*. Ithaca: Cornell University Press, 2000.

Sillem, Edward Augustus. *George Berkeley and the Proofs for the Existence of God*. London: Longmans, Green, 1957.

Tipton, I. C. *Berkeley: The Philosophy of Immaterialism*. London: Methuen Press, 1974.

Turbayne, Colin M., ed. *Berkeley: Critical and Interpretive Essays*. Minneapolis: University of Minnesota Press, 1982.

Urmson, J. O. *Berkeley*. Oxford: Oxford University Press, 1982.

Warnock, G. J. *Berkeley*. Melbourne: Penguin Books, 1969.

Wild, John Daniel. *George Berkeley: A Study of His Life and Philosophy*. New York: Russell & Russell, 1964.

Winkler, Kenneth P. *Berkeley: An Interpretation*. Oxford: Clarendon Press, 1989.

Wisdom, J. O. *The Unconscious Origin of Berkeley's Philosophy*. London: Hogarth Press, 1953.

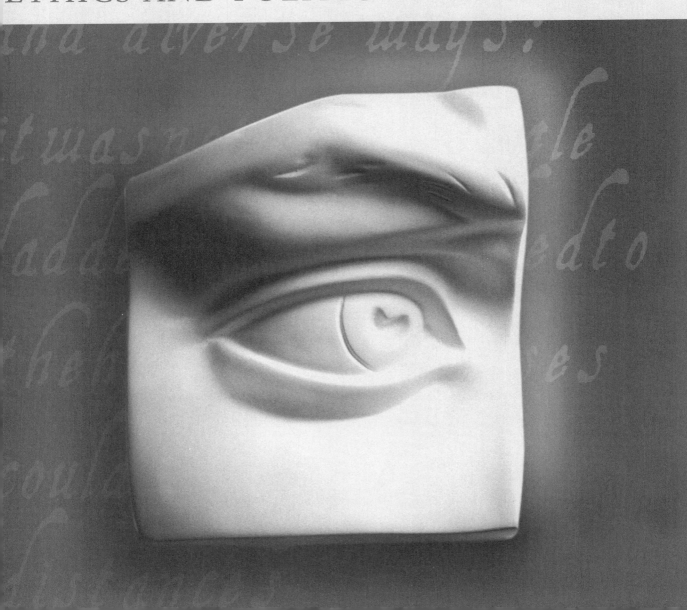

PART 2

ETHICS AND POLITICAL PHILOSOPHY

MORAL RIGHTS, OBLIGATIONS, AND RESPONSIBILITY

Kant's *Grounding for the Metaphysics of Morals*

W̲e now begin the study of ethics and political philosophy. Turning from metaphysics and epistemology in theoretical philosophy, we embark on topics of normative philosophy. Kant as a major thinker of the German Enlightenment made important contributions to every area of philosophy. We shall consider Kant's transcendental grounding of the metaphysics of morals, in which he develops a deontological theory of ethics. Kant emphasizes moral duty as determined by what he calls the categorical imperative. He further interprets the freedom presupposed by moral responsibility in a theory of moral autonomy, in which reason dictates to itself a rational principle of moral conduct in the form of the categorical imperative.

MORAL PHILOSOPHY

The historical topics we have now investigated in the philosophy of Plato, Aristotle, Ockham, Descartes, and Berkeley all belong to the general category of *theoretical philosophy*, including epistemology and metaphysics. These subjects are complemented by the study of *normative philosophy*, including ethics or moral and political philosophy, the subject of the next five chapters.

Theoretical philosophy primarily concerns questions of fact, while normative philosophy primarily concerns questions of value. Moral philosophy in particular does not attempt to explain what is true or false and how we can come to know what is true and distinguish it from what is false. It offers insights into what ought or ought not to be the case; not what things are or the way they are, but what they should be, and what we as moral agents should and should not do. In political philosophy it raises questions about social values in law, government, public policy, and international relations.

Disagreements about matters of value seem different than disagreements about matters of fact, both in number and difficulty. The differences between theories of fact and value have discouraged some thinkers from supposing that there could ever be objective answers to moral and political problems. We cannot simply calculate or perform laboratory experiments to solve moral problems as we can in mathematics and science. We can nevertheless apply the time-honored philosophical methods of clarifying concepts, drawing distinctions to avoid paradoxes and inconsistencies, and following the best arguments to whatever conclusions they lead. We neither downplay nor overemphasize the impression that philosophical problems in metaphysics and epistemology often seem answerable with enough patience and ingenuity, whereas controversies about whether, say, capital punishment or abortion is morally permissible, whether democracy or aristocracy is a morally preferable form of government, and whether capitalism or socialism is a morally justifiable form of political economy, are problems of a different order and higher magnitude, about which we can imagine long-standing oppositions that may never be resolved, that will always divide the opinions of philosophers and the moral attitudes and ethical conduct of persons in all walks of life.

The differences between fact and value do not prevent philosophical inquiry in ethics and political philosophy from reaching worthwhile conclusions. They do, however, suggest that the modes of argument to be followed in normative philosophical disciplines are likely to be different in some ways than those we have found useful in metaphysics and epistemology. Aristotle, in his great work, the *Nicomachean Ethics*, maintains that we should not expect the same degree of precision in moral philosophy that we find in mathematics and natural science. The wisdom of this word of caution is easily appreciated by anyone who has pondered the problems of deeply rooted moral and political disputes. We shall consider Aristotle's advice as we prepare to begin the study of ethics and political philosophy. We shall continue to expect that philosophical methods of analysis and argument will remain the best way to understand philosophical problems of moral and political value.

The issues here are among the most important and difficult questions for an integrated theoretical and normative philosophy. As Socrates reminds his friends discussing the nature of virtue in Plato's dialogue, the *Republic,* the topics of moral and political philosophy deserve our greatest attention and care, because they concern how we are to live. We can easily see why Socrates attaches such significance to the challenges of moral and political philosophy. What can be more important, and, therefore, understandably, more disputatious, than philosophical problems about the nature of moral and political good, what we ought and ought not to do in living our lives, the sort of political and social arrangements by which human beings are best organized and governed, and that affect every other practical aspect of our existence? Our lives are not personally affected by whether or not Plato's Forms exist, or whether the sensible properties of sensible things are supported by an underlying insensible unthinking material substratum, or, as Berkeley argues, are mere congeries of ideas. On the other hand, it makes a very tangible difference in our daily lives whether we decide that it is morally permissible or impermissible to steal or kill, or whether we believe that political institutions should be tolerant or intolerant of religious differences, discriminative or nondiscriminative against persons because of their gender, race, ethnicity, sexual orientation, or lifestyle. For these are among the ways in which we and those we care about can be directly affected, in which the quality of our lives can be made better or worse for us as individuals.

We are now ready to address problems of moral and political value, beginning with Immanuel Kant's (1724–1804) masterwork, the *Grounding for the Metaphysics of Morals* (*Grundlegung zur Metaphysik der Sitten*, 1785), and turning thereafter to philosophers of ethical and political value who profoundly disagree with Kant's approach. We shall try in this way to obtain a well-rounded perspective on the central questions of moral and political value from leading thinkers in the history of philosophy.

KANT'S OBJECTIONS TO RATIONALISM AND EMPIRICISM

Kant's philosophical method is an outgrowth of the difficulties encountered by the two major movements in the seventeenth and eighteenth centuries. Working during the middle and later part of the eighteenth century, Kant is the premier representative of the German Enlightenment or *Aufklärung*. His great treatise, the *Critique of Pure Reason*, or *Kritik der reinen Vernunft*, in which he describes a new method for philosophy, appeared in two editions in 1781 and 1787.

As Kant explains in his *Prolegomena to Any Future Metaphysics that Can Come Forth as Science* (1783), he was dissatisfied with both the rationalism that typified seventeenth-century philosophy and the empiricism that characterized the earlier part of the eighteenth century. Kant remarks that rationalism as we find it in Descartes, Spinoza, and Leibniz *is dogmatic* rather than scientific, because it does not offer a repeatable method by which different rationalists claiming to follow the same method are likely to arrive at the same conclusions. Where science, with its procedures of hypothesis, testing, and refinement of hypotheses, is not practiced, there, Kant observes, a thinker can only resort to dogma, scientifically unsupported speculation, and authoritative pronouncement, in the pejorative sense of the word. These qualities make rationalism unattractive to Kant. He also finds empiricism, in the forms articulated by Locke, Berkeley, and Hume, also to be unsatisfactory for a different reason, because it leads to skepticism.

Kant observes that if we are going to limit philosophical knowledge to what can be experienced empirically in perception or constructed by reason, imagination, and memory from the contents of immediate sense experience, then many important philosophical propositions cannot be upheld. He has in mind here specifically beliefs in the necessity of causation and the existence of material substance, both of which Berkeley denies, and the existence of the person, self, or soul as a unified substantial subject of experience, about which Hume in *A Treatise of Human Nature* (1739–40) raises interesting doubts. All of these tenets of rationalist philosophy are disputed by empiricism because they cannot be directly experienced, and are not constructible by the other faculties of mind from the data of perception. As a result, Kant finds modern philosophy caught between the two extremes of rationalist dogmatism and radically empiricist skepticism.

To implement a new method for philosophy that will overcome the limitations of rationalism and empiricism, Kant proposes to make metaphysics scientific in a revolutionary way. The solution Kant offers to the impasse between rationalism and empiricism, and so between dogmatism and skepticism, has two parts, both of which he pursues in his theoretical and normative philosophical inquiries, which he refers to respectively as *speculative* and *practical* philosophy. We are interested in Kant's ethics, but since to this point we have been considering problems of epistemology and metaphysics, and are more familiar with its territory, it will be useful to begin by explaining Kant's scientific method in philosophy, first, with respect to theoretical or speculative philosophical topics, and then describe how the method is supposed to apply to practical philosophy in ethics and politics.

METAPHYSICS AS A SYSTEM OF SYNTHETIC *A PRIORI* PROPOSITIONS

Kant's philosophical method has two principal tasks. The first task is to identify the specific kinds of judgments or beliefs that philosophy must try to establish. Kant expresses surprise that such a basic question about the purpose of philosophy had never previously been asked, but simply taken for granted. The second task he sets is to describe a way of discovering and justifying the particular kinds of judgments at which philosophy aims.

Like many philosophers before him, Kant distinguishes between *a priori* and *a posteriori* propositions. An *a priori* proposition cannot be justified empirically by perception, whereas an *a posteriori* proposition can only be justified in this way. Kant further distinguishes between *analytic* and *synthetic* propositions. Following an analogy with the division of labor in analytic and synthetic chemistry, Kant describes analytic judgments as predications of properties to subjects in which the concept of the property is already contained in the concept of the subject. An analytic judgment analyzes or breaks down the concept of a subject by unpacking its set of properties, some or all of which are then attributed to the subject in a proposition that cannot fail to be true. An example is the analytic judgment that "Red is a color," where the property of being a color is already contained in the concept "red" as part of its meaning or analysis.

When we assert that red is a color, according to Kant, we are only putting together a subject with a predicate that already belongs to the subject. The property of being a color is not something that we need to add to the concept red in order to judge that red is a color, because red is defined as a particular color or range of colors. Whereas analytic statements involve predications in which the concept of the predicate is contained in the concept of the subject, synthetic propositions are nonanalytic assertions in which a predicate that is not part of the analyzed subject is added to, put together, or literally synthesized with the concept of the subject. Thus, to judge that "Blood is red" is synthetic. The concept of blood does not contain in its analysis the concept of being red; instead, the predicate "red" is added to or combined synthetically with the concept of blood in order to assert that blood is red.

Kant considers the possibility of analytic *a priori*, synthetic *a posteriori*, and synthetic *a priori* propositions. There can be no analytic *a posteriori* propositions, so this category is empty and eliminable. An analytic *a posteriori* proposition would be a proposition in which the concept of the predicate was already contained in the concept of the subject, but which required sense experience in order to be justified. Such a cross-section of judgment categories clearly does not make sense, since if the concept of a predicate is already contained in the concept of the subject, then the predication does not require experience to be justified, but is justified when conceptual analysis reveals that the predicate is contained in the subject, independently of experience. Analytic *a priori* and synthetic *a posteriori* judgments are the most straightforward categories, the usual and expected combinations, in which an analytic proposition, true or false, is justified as such by conceptual analytic methods that do not involve an appeal to perception, and in which a synthetic judgment, true or false, is justified by empirical evidence ultimately dependent on sense experience. The way we find out that blood is red, for example, is to observe a sample of blood under normal conditions (leaving aside the fact that unoxygenated venous as opposed to oxygenated arterial blood is dark blue) and see that it is red, or to test its color by other reliable means.

The remaining category of synthetic *a priori* propositions is the most interesting for Kant's purposes. Although it is standardly supposed that all analytic propositions are *a priori* and all synthetic propositions are *a posteriori*, Kant argues that synthetic *a priori* judgments is the appropriate category for the principles of philosophy, including the metaphysics of morals. The conclusion that there are synthetic *a priori* propositions is often regarded as one of Kant's most valuable philosophical discoveries. Kant believes that identifying the proper subject matter of the judgments of philosophy as synthetic *a priori* is vital to establishing metaphysics as a science, including the metaphysics of morals, in opposition to dogmatism and skepticism. The possibilities are represented in Figure 6.1.

To understand what Kant intends by the category of the synthetic *a priori* judgments, it is useful to begin with Kant's favorite example in mathematics. Kant explains the concept as it applies to the elementary arithmetical proposition that $7 + 5 = 12$. What makes the proposition *a priori* is perhaps obvious enough. The truths of mathematics do not require observation for their justification, even though we may learn about or otherwise acquire the knowledge that $7 + 5 = 12$ through experience. Kant's innovation is in recognizing that $7 + 5 = 12$ is synthetic rather than analytic.

	a priori	*a posteriori*
Analytic	Conceptual and Definitional Truths	
Synthetic	Mathematics Metaphysics of Science and Morals	Natural Science

FIGURE 6.1 Kant's table of judgment types

He argues that when we analyze the concept 7 + 5, we find nowhere concealed within it the concept of 12. If we construe the proposition as a predication in which the property of being equal to 12 is predicated of the subject 7 + 5, then there are no grounds for thinking that the concept of 7 + 5 contains the concept 12. We do not find the concept of 12 in the concepts of 7, or +, or 5, into which the concept 7 + 5 is analyzed.

Kant argues that all of mathematics is concerned with just such synthetic *a priori* propositions, and, he maintains, the same is true of the metaphysics of science and foundations of the metaphysics of morals. Metaphysics, in the scientific mode to which Kant aspires, is concerned with the discovery of true synthetic *a priori* propositions. It is a tremendous advance, Kant believes, to have finally identified the proper subject matter of metaphysics. We thereby take an important first step toward making metaphysics scientific in the search for genuine metaphysical knowledge that stands opposed to both dogmatism and skepticism. Kant in the *Prolegomena* reports that it was reading Hume in particular and Hume's account of the empirical origin of the idea of causation that, as Kant says, "awakened" him from his "dogmatic slumbers." By this Kant means his previous uncritical acceptance of rationalist doctrines concerning the logical necessity of causal connections advocated by Leibniz and the later Leibnizian philosopher Christian Wolfe.

METAPHYSICS AS TRANSCENDENTAL GROUND OF THE GIVEN

Having identified the proper sphere of metaphysical inquiry and its purpose as the discovery of true synthetic *a priori* judgments of metaphysics, it remains for Kant to explain the exact method by which synthetic *a priori* principles are to be discovered. If we define the work of scientific metaphysics as justifying a system of synthetic *a priori* propositions, how does Kant propose to do it? What is the proper method of metaphysics by which synthetic *a priori* judgments can be recognized and confirmed?

Kant outlines a *transcendental methodology* for metaphysics. The method has a specific starting place and a specific question it asks, together with a definite way of trying to answer its questions and verify the correctness of its answers. Transcendental reasoning in Kant's metaphysics is an effort to uncover synthetic *a priori* propositions that are presupposed by different types of judgment, for present purposes, in science and ethics and politics, but also in aesthetics and other areas of human knowledge. Metaphysics in the ordinary sense, as Plato, Aristotle, Ockham, Descartes and Berkeley, among other thinkers in the pre-Kantian history of philosophy practice it, is for Kant an investigation of the most basic underlying assumptions or *presuppositions* of the sciences, which Kant describes as their *transcendental ground.*

Kant's transcendental method begins with something that is *given,* and then asks the transcendental question, What *must* be true in order for what is given even to be *possible?* The answer that is uncovered as the presupposition or ultimately underlying assumption of the given, if Kant is right, is a synthetic *a priori* proposition that is presupposed by knowledge, in this case, of the relevant science. In the case of moral philosophy and Kant's excavation of the transcendental ground of morals, the given is the ethical judgments we make, for which the transcendental question is, What *must* be true in order for moral judgments to be possible? The given in Kant's meta-

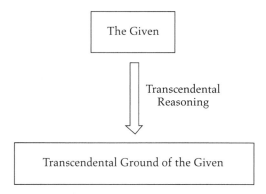

FIGURE 6.2 Kant's method of transcendental reasoning

physics takes several forms, depending on Kant's division of the project of metaphysics into a complex of related preliminary investigations. In the section on the Transcendental Aesthetic in the *Critique of Pure Reason*, Kant begins with sense, especially visual, experience of objects in space and time, and asks what must be true in order for our experience of such objects even to be possible. As part of his overall program in metaphysics, he takes as his starting place all of Newtonian science, and identifies the purpose of metaphysics as uncovering the transcendental ground of synthetic *a posteriori* propositions that must be true in order for the world of phenomena explained in Newtonian science to be possible. The structure of Kant's transcendental methodology is seen in Figure 6.2.

The way in which we are supposed to recognize the synthetic *a priori* transcendental ground of science is by looking for and confirming conditions whose existence cannot be denied except on pain of contradiction with the given. Thus, if the given is *G*, and Kant asks the transcendental question, What must be true in order for *G* to be possible?, then the correct transcendental answer, the transcendental ground or ultimate foundation of *G*, which we might call *T*, will be a presupposition of *G* without which *G* would not be possible. The sign of the dependence of *G* on *T* is the fact that *G* is made impossible if *T* is not presupposed, or that asserting *G* while denying *T* produces an outright logical contradiction. Then we can say that *G* is impossible in lieu of or without the truth or occurrence of *T*.

Although Kant's transcendental reasoning in all its details is complicated to explain, a relatively good idea of Kant's method can be gathered from the fact that, in the case of our visual experience in the Transcendental Aesthetic, Kant concludes that space and time are not external properties to be discovered in the world, but are rather pure forms of intuition with which thought must be innately pre-equipped, and without which we could never experience the world as divided up into distinct objects, foreground and background, and the like, as given to experience. If we did not already have spatiotemporal forms for the mind to impose on its experience of the phenomenal world, then we could never discover space and time in the external realm of sensation, because we would not be capable in the first place of distinguishing objects as spatiotemporally discrete things separated from one another in what Kant calls the "manifold of experience."

The world that would appear to us in that case when we opened our eyes would be nothing but a chaos with no definite spatial shape, and no possibility of mentally clocking whatever passes through consciousness in time as occurring at different times. What would that be like? It is unthinkable, unintelligible for us even to imagine anything we would be prepared to recognize as *experience*, as Kant says, without shape or color, and unaccompanied by any sense of the passing of time in which we ordinarily live through a conscious stream of sequentially ordered thoughts and images. The experienceability of things in space and time and in particular places in space is a function of the perception of extended sensible things persisting or disappearing from moment to moment in thought. If we were not already pre-equipped with space and time as pure forms of intuition, our minds would never be capable of discovering them in the meaningless inarticulated flux of experience for which no sense of persistence or change, no places, sizes, or colored shapes of things, could possibly be discerned. Kant concludes that space and time do not exist externally in the world of objective facts to be experienced by a thinking subject, but belong to the thinking subject's built-in experiential apparatus. Space and time as pure forms of intuition are among the transcendental grounds of sense experience, according to Kant, and by implication constitute part of the speculative metaphysics of Newtonian science.

A similar mode of reasoning is offered by Kant in the *Grounding for the Metaphysics of Morals* in order to uncover the synthetic *a priori* propositions that constitute the transcendental ground of moral judgments. The conceptual foundations of ethical reasoning provide an answer to the transcendental question Kant poses with respect to the presuppositions of moral judgment: What must be true in order for moral judgments to be possible? The complicated answer to this question is the subject of the present chapter as we delve into Kant's transcendental foundations of the metaphysics of morals. The given for Kant's transcendental method in investigating the metaphysics of morals is the fact that we make moral judgments and that we make sense, whether morally right or wrong, when we do so. What must be true in order for these judgments to be possible, what synthetic *a posteriori* principles constitute the conceptual foundations of morality, and what implications if any they have for ethical theory and the practical conduct of our moral lives, if we adhere to the correct principles of moral philosophy, Kant proposes to explain as the transcendental ground of morality.

STOIC BACKGROUND TO KANT'S ETHICS

The first step in Kant's project is to identify the proper subject matter of ethics. Kant argues that we must distinguish between genuine moral judgments and related considerations that are not strictly moral. Kant begins his treatise with what might seem to be a kind of historical digression, but which actually turns out to be crucial to his method. He refers obliquely to the division of three subject matters within "Ancient Greek philosophy." He clearly has in mind more specifically the Stoics, a school of philosophy founded by Zeno of Citium, and his students Chrysippus and Cleanthes, who taught under the colonnaded covered walkways of the marketplace in ancient Athens, known in Greek as a *stoa*. Kant states:

> Ancient Greek philosophy was divided into three sciences: physics, ethics, and logic. This division is perfectly suitable to the nature of the subject, and the only

improvement that can be made in it is perhaps only to supply its principle so that there will be a possibility on the one hand of insuring its completeness and on the other of correctly determining its necessary subdivisions. (1)

The Stoics were famous for teaching and practicing a philosophy that emphasized living a morally good life that was indifferent to the ups and downs of fortune. Even in the worst of calamities, if one loses all one's wealth, becomes enslaved or captured by pirates, has one's city invaded by enemies, is imprisoned, tortured, or even put to death, nothing that is done to a person need take away the only true value available to human beings, which is to preserve a good will and good intentions, to act rightly insofar as one is able, and never to will evil. Kant's works on the foundations of morals in some ways belong to the tradition of Stoic handbooks on moral philosophy, including Marcus Aurelius's *Meditations* and Epictetus's *Enchiridion*. It was specifically in order to advance an ethical philosophy of life that the Stoics and Epicureans divided all knowledge into the three categories Kant mentions in the opening lines of his treatise. To live the morally good life, the Stoics in particular believe, one must begin by applying logic and science to understand that death and the gods are nothing to fear.

The interrelation of these subject matters in philosophy, and, more importantly in some ways, their distinction and the differences between them, are of vital concern to Kant's efforts to uncover the transcendental grounds of morals. Without distinguishing correctly between the proper subject matter of empirical science and ethics, identifying the field of ethics and moral judgment, we cannot isolate the appropriate given required by Kant's transcendental method, in order to proceed to the transcendental question and its synthetic *a priori* answers in a metaphysics of morals.

Kant next proceeds to divide up the disciplines of the natural sciences and moral philosophy. The distinction he offers follows a basic Aristotelian division between the *formal* and *material sciences*. Logic is identified as formal philosophy, concerned with the structure of reasoning, while material philosophy is dedicated to the content of thought, which Kant further divides into two subcategories. Material philosophy involves specific objects of study, distinguished by Kant according to their respective laws, designated by Kant as *laws of nature* and *laws of freedom*. He writes:

All rational knowledge is either material and concerned with some object, or formal and concerned only with the form of understanding and of reason themselves and with the universal rules of thought in general without regard to differences of its objects. Formal philosophy is called logic. Material philosophy, however, has to do with determinate objects and with the laws to which these objects are subject; and such philosophy is divided into two parts, because these laws are either laws of nature or laws of freedom. The science of the former is called physics, while that of the latter is called ethics; they are also called doctrine of nature and doctrine of morals respectively. (1)

Laws of nature are studied by physics, Kant remarks, also designated as natural philosophy or the empirical sciences. Ethics, by contrast, Kant describes as concerned with laws of freedom. The contrast Kant evidently means to invoke is that between the deterministic laws that govern natural physical phenomena and the principles of moral decision making involving free choice for which moral agents are morally responsible.

Physical phenomena are unfree, since we do not imagine that events in the material world come about through the exercise of free choice, at least on the part of the physical order or physical entities in the physical world. Moral phenomena, by comparison, are often assumed to result from freewill moral decision making. Whether it is accurate to portray ethics as involving laws of freedom, according to the common conception that there are free agents who freely choose their actions and are thereby morally responsible for their conduct, should remain an open question until Kant has completed his inquiry. For the time being, it should suffice to note that, roughly following the same division as the Stoic philosophers, Kant draws a sharp distinction between the natural empirical sciences and ethics. This distinction turns out to be essential for Kant's specification of ethical judgment as the given for his exploration of the transcendental ground of morality. Kant's reference to theoretical ethics as the study of the laws of freedom is crucial in turn for his foundations of the metaphysics of morals.

RATIONAL AND EMPIRICAL ASPECTS OF ETHICS

As a necessary prerequisite to isolating the given in ethics, to distinguish a specifically ethical given and purify it of any nonethical ingredients in moral reasoning, Kant further articulates a division between rational and empirical aspects of ethics. He argues that the proper subject matter of logic has no empirical aspect, but is purely rational, because it has to do with universal and necessary laws of thought. In contrast with logic, Kant asserts that ethics has both an empirical and nonempirical component. Were it not for the fact that morality like natural philosophy has both an empirical and nonempirical side, there could be a difficulty in distinguishing ethics from logic. More significantly, there would then be no problem distinguishing between ethics and physics, and no need to purify ethics of empirical elements in order to arrive at the given in ethics. Kant accordingly explains:

> Logic cannot have any empirical part, i.e., a part in which the universal and necessary laws of thought would be based on grounds taken from experience; for in that case it would not be logic, i.e., a canon for understanding and reason, which is valid for all thinking and which has to be demonstrated. Natural and moral philosophy, on the contrary, can each have an empirical part. The former has to because it must determine the laws of nature as an object of experience, and the latter because it must determine the will of man insofar as the will is affected by nature. The laws of the former are those according to which everything does happen, while the laws of the latter are those according to which everything ought to happen, although these moral laws also consider the conditions under which what ought to happen frequently does not. (1)

Kant's reference to the exact role for empirical considerations in ethics, determining the human will insofar as it is affected by nature, makes it clear that he recognizes the psychological dimension of ethical judgment. We as willful moral thinkers are determined in various ways by psychological factors, including our empirical psychological natures and the impact of environment. These influences in turn depend on social interactions with others and the ways in which these influences shape our desires, inclinations, and ultimately our moral values, decisions, and actions. All this,

Kant says, is an inextricable part of our moral lives, and hence an inextricable part of ethics; in particular, it is the empirical part of ethics that must be distinguished from its rational part. Kant distinguishes between the rational and empirical elements of ethics, bringing ethics into the same orbit as physics and separating both method-ologically from logic as a purely formal science:

> All philosophy insofar as it is founded on experience may be called empirical, while that which sets forth its doctrines as founded entirely on *a priori* principles may be called pure. The latter, when merely formal, is called logic; but when lim-ited to determinate objects of the understanding, it is called metaphysics. (1)

Physics and ethics alike, therefore, each require a specialized metaphysics. The empirical element of ethics Kant refers to as "practical anthropology," emphasizing its empirical nature as a study of human moral behavior. As practical anthropology, the empirical component of morals in Kant's theory is directed toward the human moral condition, including ethical activity, inclinations, and proclivities:

> In this way there arises the idea of a twofold metaphysics: a metaphysics of na-ture and a metaphysics of morals. Physics will thus have its empirical part, but also a rational one. Ethics will too, though here the empirical part might more specifically be called practical anthropology, while the rational part might prop-erly be called morals. (1–2)

Kant nevertheless believes that morality transcends specifically human limitations. What other subjects of moral reasoning other than human beings could there possibly be? How can there be a purely rational aspect of morality to be distinguished from the empirical side of practical anthropology? Kant elsewhere mentions the moral require-ments of a purely rational ethical theory that would need to apply to angels as well as human beings. In more contemporary terms, we might imagine that a correct moral the-ory should not be confined exclusively to principles based on human psychology if there could be extraterrestrial aliens who would also be bound by appropriate moral laws.

The point is that we cannot assume a correct theory of ethics will apply only to human agents. The principles of a pure moral philosophy in Kant's conception should therefore not depend on the empirical facts of human psychology. An angel or ex-traterrestrial might not have anything relevantly like a human psychological makeup, but might, for example, be incapable of pleasure or pain, lacking human emotions of compassion, envy, greed, or the like. What, then, would human, angelic, and alien moral agents all have in common by virtue of which their behavior is governed by moral law?

Kant thinks the answer in every case is their ability to reason. For it is only by virtue of rationality that moral agents can be subject to principles of any kind, in-cluding the principles of ethical conduct and moral philosophy. We do not attribute moral responsibility to inanimate objects or to nonhuman terrestrial animals insofar as they are unable to reason. When we consider rational nonhuman beings, on the other hand, we expect, if we ever directly encounter them, that in their actions they will be subject to the same moral principles that govern human moral conduct. Since such creatures by hypothesis need not have anything resembling a human psychol-ogy, aside from being rational agents, the principles of a correct moral theory must also be predicated exclusively on reason, eliminating reference to any other aspect of specifically human psychology. If Kant is right, then reason is both necessary and sufficient for an agent to be subject to the moral law.

Kant accordingly argues that ethics just like physics is supported by a special type of metaphysics. The metaphysics of natural science and of ethics in Kant's terminology must be "purified" of empirical elements in order to determine the applicable range of moral principles. Kant marks the distinction between "all moralists" as opposed to only those who "feel a call thereto." The difference emphasizes the full generality that Kant maintains must hold for true moral principles versus the inclinations of a limited number of persons who by virtue of their psychologies are inclined to live their lives according to prescribed moral rules. The idea is that even persons who through accidents of psychology are not inclined to accept moral precepts, but are outside the circle of moral involvement, should still be regarded as subject to the moral law. Kant first makes a case for the need to identify the underlying metaphysical principles of empirical physics and practical anthropology or empirical ethics, asking:

> Should not physics proper (i.e., empirical physics) be preceded by a metaphysics of nature, and practical anthropology by a metaphysics of morals? Both of these metaphysics must be carefully purified of everything empirical in order to know how much pure reason can accomplish in each case and from what sources it draws its *a priori* teaching, whether such teaching be conducted by all moralists (whose name is legion) or only by some who feel a call thereto. (2)

As an essential preliminary, Kant argues that the metaphysics of morals is altogether nonempirical. The metaphysics of morals as a discipline must correspondingly be freed of all empirical elements. From the standpoint of modern philosophical opposition between reason and experience, rationalism and empiricism, Kant proposes to eliminate all empirical elements from ethical thinking, which he describes as "practical cognition," to concentrate on what is "purely" moral. This, it turns out, is equivalent to saying, the rational part of ethics. Kant recognizes the empirical component of ethics as indispensable to its practical applications, making its principles available to human decision making. He further identifies such practical reasoning in ethics as "a power of judgment sharpened by experience." A complete and correct moral theory must finally integrate rational and empirical elements. The rational foundations of ethics, the grounding or groundwork of morals, Kant asserts, in order to constitute the metaphysics of morals, by analogy again with the metaphysics of physical science, must be purified of all empirical elements, so as to provide a foundation for the practical empirical superstructure. Kant states:

> Thus not only are moral laws together with their principles essentially different from every kind of practical cognition in which there is anything empirical, but all moral philosophy rests entirely on its pure part. When applied to man it does not in the least borrow from acquaintance with him (anthropology) but gives *a priori* laws to him as a rational being. To be sure, these laws require, furthermore, a power of judgment sharpened by experience, partly to gain for them access to the human will as well as influence for putting them into practice. For man is affected by so many inclinations that, even though he is indeed capable of the idea of a pure practical reason, he is not so easily able to make that idea effective *in concreto* in the conduct of his life. (3)

Thus, Kant distinguishes between the abstract theory of ethics and the practical application of moral principles. He defines the abstract theory as the metaphysics of morals, which he requires to be purified of all empirical elements as a purely rational discipline. The practical application of moral principles evidently involves a relation to the empirical psychology of human moral agents, and in particular to their will, desires, and inclinations by which they are motivated to act.

Although reason must be combined with emotion and will in a complete moral philosophy, just as they must in a complete human moral agent, the metaphysics of morals, according to Kant, must be purely rational. Kant's method of purifying ethics of its empirical components is to identify a purely rational principle or set of principles to explain moral decision making in general terms that do not appeal to any empirical facts about the moral psychology of human agents. The principles of moral judgment that he is prepared to invoke must therefore be evaluated from a standpoint of pure reason as contributions to pure moral philosophy. The informal test of whether Kant has succeeded in articulating the grounding of the metaphysics of morals is whether the moral laws he prescribes would be just as applicable to nonhuman as to human moral agents. We can judge the effectiveness of Kant's moral theory in Kant's own terms by this standard, asking whether at any stage Kant's principles would apply only to human beings with their particular type of moral psychology, human will, and emotions, or whether the same principles hold, to the extent that they do, to any rational agents, regardless of their biology or psychology, and independently of all empirical experience.

Acting from as Opposed to Merely in Accord with Moral Laws

To explain the importance of purifying the metaphysics of morals by eliminating all empirical elements, Kant, in a frequently misunderstood passage, highlights the difficulty in practice of distinguishing between morally correct actions that are done "from" as opposed to merely "in accord with" moral laws.

Kant's distinction reflects the opposition between rational and empirical elements that guides every phase of the development of his moral philosophy. To act *from* the moral law is to act with the purpose, not just primarily, but exclusively of fulfilling the ethical requirements dictated by a correct moral principle. In contrast, to act *in accord* or *in agreement* with moral laws is to do what is right, although not exclusively for the sake of doing what is right, but for some motivation other than fulfilling the moral law. Kant collects together the alternative motives that might direct a person to do what is also prescribed by correct moral principles as "inclination" or what such moral agents are "inclined" to do. The difference between acting from as opposed to merely in accord with the moral law is a matter of intent, whether an agent acts in order to meet the obligations of morality, or in order to satisfy a desire. Kant argues:

> For, in the case of what is to be morally good, that it conforms to the moral law is not enough; it must also be done for the sake of the moral law. Otherwise that conformity is only very contingent and uncertain, since the non-moral ground may now and then produce actions that conform with the law but quite often pro-

duces actions that are contrary to the law. Now the moral law in its purity and genuineness (which is of the utmost concern in the practical realm) can be sought nowhere but in a pure philosophy. Therefore, pure philosophy (metaphysics) must precede; without it there can be no moral philosophy at all. That philosophy which mixes pure principles with empirical ones does not deserve the name of philosophy. . . . (3)

To consider an example relevant to Kant's distinction, imagine the following case. Suppose there are three persons who undertake what from an observer's perspective appear to be the identical action of contributing pocket change to a worthy charity. The three might have had lunch together at a restaurant and as they are paying the check and leaving, each drops the same amount of coins into a container provided to raise money for the cure of a disease such as cancer, AIDS, or diabetes.

Let us further stipulate for the sake of argument that there is a moral principle that requires moral agents to donate surplus wealth to such causes. There appears to be no difference as seen between the actions of the three persons, each of whom is doing what is required of them by the appropriate moral principle. Now, however, suppose that the three persons have significantly different reasons for what they do. The first person donates the money because she understands the ethical law that implies it is morally right to donate surplus wealth to the needy. The second person donates the money because she feels sorry for persons who suffer from such diseases, and wants to do something out of compassion to help ease their pain and spare other persons from a similar plight, but has no knowledge of or consideration for the moral principle that entails what is morally required of moral agents. The third person donates the money because her two friends have done so and she wants to appear to be morally good and to sustain a reputation for being concerned about the welfare of others.

Kant would insist that at most only the first moral agent has acted *from* the moral law, acting for no other reason or ulterior motive or inclination than to do what the moral law requires. The other two persons, although they perform precisely the same action, do not act from the moral law, but merely in accord with it, doing the kind of action that the moral law prescribes, but without regard for the requirements of the law. From the standpoint of fulfilling our moral obligations to satisfy correct moral principles, their situation is no different than if they were to do something that happens to be morally right inadvertently and entirely by accident, as if they dropped a coin through sheer clumsiness and it fell into the slot in the donations container. Human motives are more complicated than any of these three cases adequately represents. It is rare for anyone to do anything for a simple pure reason, as opposed to a mixture or combination of reasons. If a person drops a coin into a relief box, it is likely to be because she partly understands that it is morally right to do so, partly because she feels sorry for persons who are less fortunate than herself, and partly, in some cases, because she wants to feel good about herself, to cultivate a self-image of someone who acts charitably on behalf of others, or in order to cultivate that impression in others.

Kant claims that we cannot generally know whether someone is acting from or merely in accord with the moral law. For that, we would need to be able to perceive their intentions. This is difficult if not impossible in the case of discerning the motives of another person, but may also be opaque for any individual with respect to his or her own reasons for acting. Can I be sure when I pay my taxes that I do so because I believe that it is morally right for me to obey the law of a legitimately elected government whose benefits I enjoy and whose services I require or find advantageous, or because I want to avoid legal penalties? If I do not use illegal drugs, is it because I want above all things to observe the law, or because I fear the enforcement of law and the possibility of going to prison, or simply because I have no interest in or inclination to use drugs? If I have no inclination to use drugs, could it be in part because I know that there are legal risks involved if I should get caught?

Inclination and ulterior motives as opposed to doing whatever morality requires are sometimes distinguished as *prudential* versus purely *moral* considerations. The distinction is roughly between what is smart or in one's best interests to do in contrast with what it is unqualifiedly morally right to do. To draw the distinction in the abstract, obviously, is one thing, and to be able to discriminate between prudential and purely moral considerations as reasons for acting, knowing ourselves well enough to judge whether and when we are doing what is right purely for the sake of doing what is right as opposed to doing what serves our interests, is something else again. Kant says that the metaphysics of morals must be concerned exclusively with the principles of what he calls a "possible pure will." A possible pure will is distinguished from the inclinations and other psychological factors involved in the complex motivations that sometimes direct moral agents to act either from or merely in accord with moral principles. Kant adds:

> For the metaphysics of morals has to investigate the idea and principles of a possible pure will and not the actions and conditions of human volition as such, which are for the most part drawn from psychology. Moral laws and duty are discussed in this universal practical philosophy (though quite improperly), but this is no objection to what has been said about such philosophy. (4)

The starting place for the metaphysics of morals, purified, as Kant believes it must be, of all empirical elements, is the pure or morally good will. It is the only thing, considered in the abstract, regardless of how difficult it may be to isolate in practice, that satisfies Kant's requirement for a moral philosophy purified of all empirical elements, or as we might also say of all prudential as opposed to purely moral considerations.

However hard it may be in practice to identify an agent's real intent in acting from rather than merely in accord with the moral law, Kant insists that the metaphysics of morals must take the concept of the pure morally good will as the only rational basis of morality. All other goods and morally good attitudes are potentially contaminated by extraneous psychological factors. Identifying the requirements of a pure morally good will as distinct from inclination is essential to Kant's program of purifying moral philosophy of empirical elements. Kant begins with the concept of a pure morally good will, because it alone considered in the abstract is purged of all inclination, and is therefore the only proper subject for the metaphysics of morals in explicating the synthetic *a priori* principles that constitute the transcendental ground of moral judgment.

CONCEPT OF A MORALLY GOOD WILL

What, then, is a morally good will? Kant characterizes the morally good will as unqualifiedly good, and as the only possible thing that is good in itself without qualification. All other goods, Kant maintains, are good in some other way as a means to an end, or are otherwise blended with other empirical or prudential conditions, or whose goodness is subject to compromise by wrongful abuse. Kant makes the point clearly:

> There is no possibility of thinking of anything at all in the world, or even out of it, which can be regarded as good without qualification, except a *good will*. Intelligence, wit, judgment, and whatever talents of the mind one might want to name are doubtless in many respects good and desirable, as are such qualities of temperament as courage, resolution, perseverance. But they can also become extremely bad and harmful if the will, which is to make use of these gifts of nature and which in its special constitution is called character, is not good. The same holds with gifts of fortune; power, riches, honor, even health, and that complete well-being and contentment with one's condition which is called happiness make for pride and often hereby even arrogance, unless there is good will to correct their influence on the mind and herewith also to rectify the whole principle of action and make it universally conformable to its end. (7)

Moral virtues such as courage, justice, and the like are not unqualifiedly good, because they can be wrongfully practiced by a morally corrupt will. Thus, a good will is the key to moral goodness. If a morally good will is at work, it can turn virtues and other kinds of assets, commonly called goods, to good intent, whereas a will that is not morally good cannot make anything, even the best of so-called goods, unqualifiedly good. All of these qualified goods are affected by the less than absolutely purely good will by which they are used in trying to achieve a certain end.

Kant's point is well taken. If we think about the ways in which various things are described as morally good or bad, it appears that anything other than a good will is good or bad depending on whether or not it is made to serve the ends of a morally good will. There is nothing, Kant declares, other than a good will itself, that cannot be diverted to evil purposes by an evil will. Whatever we think of as good or a good, therefore, other than a pure morally good will, is good only to the extent that it is properly used by a pure morally good will, and as result is only qualifiedly good. Another reason for regarding a morally good will as unqualifiedly good is that a pure morally good will is independent of all empirical psychological factors of inclination. This, we have already seen, Kant regards as an impurity in the source of moral good and theoretically in moral philosophy, and as something to be excluded from the metaphysics of morals. Kant takes the next step in identifying the proper subject matter for an exposition of the grounding of the metaphysics of morals by recognizing the pure morally good will as the only thing that can be seen as unqualifiedly morally good or morally good in and of itself. He explains the distinct roles of a pure morally good will and inclinations that might be in accord with moral good and moral law in this way:

> A good will is good not because of what it effects or accomplishes, nor because of its fitness to attain some proposed end; it is good only through its willing, i.e., it

is good in itself. When it is considered in itself, then it is to be esteemed very much higher than anything which it might ever bring about merely in order to favor some inclination, or even the sum total of all inclinations. (7)

If only a morally good will is unqualifiedly good, and hence independent of such psychological factors that are otherwise thought to be vital to moral decision making and ethical conduct, then a morally good will can only be understood in relation to moral duty. Kant's concept of the moral duty of a morally good will as the only unqualifiedly good thing is explained as he continues:

> The concept of a will estimable in itself and good without regard to any further end must now be developed. This concept already dwells in the natural sound understanding and needs not so much to be taught as merely to be elucidated. It always holds first place in estimating the total worth of our actions and constitutes the condition of all the rest. Therefore, we shall take up the concept of *duty*, which includes that of a good will, though with certain subjective restrictions and hindrances, which far from hiding a good will or rendering it unrecognizable, rather bring it out by contrast and make it shine forth more brightly. (9)

Duty or obligation, what is required of a morally good will, stands in opposition to inclination. The contrast is between what we are morally required to do and what we may for one reason or another want or desire or be psychologically inclined to do. The first charity donor in our example acts from the moral law, which is to say from a sense of duty; whereas the second and third charity donors are motivated by inclination of one sort or another. The second donor feels sorry for the suffering, and is inclined to relieve their pain if she can, at least in a small way, by donating extra pocket change to a good cause. The third donor is also inclined to act in a way that is in accord with the proposed moral law, although for a different and arguably less noble reason, in order to appear to others to be charitable, and for the sake of feeling good about herself in maintaining a charitable self-image. An average person, as a mixture of these and other motives and inclinations, presents even more difficulties in discerning the underlying motives that issue in moral or immoral action.

The idea in Kant's theory is that moral duty is something the agent knows must be done even when it conflicts with inclination. I do not want to pay my taxes. I am on the contrary strongly inclined not to pay them, because I would prefer, other things being equal, to preserve as much of my earnings as possible for my personal use. If I regard it is a moral duty as well as a legal obligation to pay my taxes, and I pay them for that reason rather than for prudential considerations, because I want to avoid legal penalties by complying with the law, then I am acting from a sense of moral duty in a situation where it is relatively clear that my motivations are unclouded by considerations of inclination or desire, precisely because by hypothesis I am acting contrary to my inclinations. Kant offers a scenario similar to the three charity donors case that we have now looked at from several standpoints:

> For example, that a dealer should not overcharge an inexperienced purchaser certainly accords with duty; and where there is much commerce, the prudent merchant does not overcharge but keeps to a fixed price for everyone in general, so that a child may buy from him just as well as everyone else may. Thus customers are honestly served, but this is not nearly enough for making us believe that the

merchant has acted this way from duty and from principles of honesty; his own advantage required him to do it. He cannot however, be assumed to have in addition [as in the third case] an immediate inclination toward his buyers, causing him, as it were, out of love to give no one as far as price is concerned any advantage over another. Hence the action was done neither from duty nor from immediate inclination, but merely for a selfish purpose. (10)

We imagine a child, an "inexperienced purchaser," entering a market to buy something. The shopkeeper could easily cheat the child, say, by overcharging or short-changing, or by selling inferior goods. If the shopkeeper does not do this, it might be for at least the two reasons Kant considers. The shopkeeper might have acted from a sense of moral duty embodied in what Kant calls "principles of honesty," or the shopkeeper might refrain from cheating the child because of a sense of his own advantage.

There are several ways in which the advantage of the shopkeeper might be injured by cheating any customer, even if he can get away with it in his transactions with an inexperienced buyer. The shopkeeper's prosperity depends on maintaining good relations with all customers, preserving a reputation for honesty that encourages business in healthy competition with other merchants who will similarity see it in their best interests to maintain everyone's confidence. The small gain to be had by cheating a single customer is therefore outweighed by the risk of damaging good business relations in the community generally. The shopkeeper knows this, Kant imagines, and accordingly resolves not to cheat anyone, but to follow the principle that honesty is the best policy, not as a moral principle motivated by considerations of duty, but rather as a prudential measure to help assure making more money honestly in the long run. The essential contrast between moral duty and psychological inclination in Kant's account is an interesting expression of the distinction between reason and emotion or feeling, and between rational and empirical elements of moral decision making.

The case of the second imagined charity donor in the illustration is also noteworthy in this regard. A person in this category, motivated by compassion and a desire to help others because of a deeply felt sense of their suffering, might regard herself as doing her duty rather than following an inclination. Indeed, the donor might find herself psychologically conflicted, if she is not wealthy and if even the spare change she considers contributing to the charity represents a hardship for her to contribute to others in need. She might find her inclinations at odds with her decision to follow the requirements of duty to help those whom she finds herself compassionately moved to help. Her situation is not like that of the hypothetical third donor who just wants to feel good about herself and maintain a reputation of being a good person. Rather, the second donor is not just inclined to turn over her spare change, but believes it is her duty to act when and as moved by compassionate feeling.

What would Kant say about the second charity donor? Kant does not explicitly consider the possibility that in certain circumstances it might be a moral duty to follow one's inclinations, particularly if the inclinations at issue are moved by the emotion of compassion for the suffering of others. Undoubtedly, Kant would want to focus attention on the exact relation between the emotion of compassion and the inclination the donor experiences as a result, in order to judge whether the donor is acting from the moral law as a matter of moral duty, rather than from inclination and merely in accord with moral law. It might be said that a very strong inclination connected with a powerful emotion such as compassion is likely to be confused with and expressed as a sense of moral duty. If that were true, then the motive of action would actually be inclination rather than moral duty. There is no problem for Kant's distinction, in that case, or at most only a superficial problem that is quickly dissolved when the donor's reasons for acting are clarified. If there is a duty to follow inclination, on the other hand, then, since Kant has not at least as yet prescribed any specific limited content for moral duty, the donor is acting from a sense of duty and from rather than merely in accord with the moral law.

MORAL DUTY VERSUS INCLINATION

The distinction between moral duty and psychological inclination, between what Kant regards as the legitimate rational basis for morality and the empirical impurities that are no part of morality, construed as the duty to act from rather than merely in accord with the moral law, can now be more thoroughly examined. Kant argues that duty-directed action is necessarily altogether distinct from matters of inclination:

> Now an action done from duty must altogether exclude the influence of inclination and therewith every object of the will. Hence there is nothing left which can determine the will except objectively the law and subjectively pure respect for this practical law, i.e., the will can be subjectively determined by the maxim that I should follow such a law even if all my inclinations are thereby thwarted. (13)

Kant invokes the same criterion we have previously considered in connection with his distinction between acting from as opposed to merely in accord with the moral law. The test is to ask whether the action would be undertaken contrary to inclination, or, in the extreme case, as Kant says above, "even if all my inclinations are thereby thwarted." Importantly, Kant argues that the moral value of what an agent does is not a function of the consequences it produces. This makes Kant's moral philosophy fundamentally different from ethical systems that determine moral value on the basis of whether they produce greater total happiness than unhappiness, which Kant emphatically opposes. He concludes:

> Thus the moral worth of an action does not lie in the effect expected from it nor in any principle of action that needs to borrow its motive from this expected effect. For all these effects (agreeableness of one's condition and even the furtherance of other people's happiness) could have been brought about also through other causes and would not have required the will of a rational being, in which the highest and unconditioned good can alone be found. Therefore, the preeminent good which is called moral can consist in nothing but the representation of the law in itself, and such a representation can admittedly be found only in a rational being insofar as this representation, and not some expected effect, is the determining ground of the will. This good is already present in the person who acts according to this representation, and such good need not be awaited merely from the effect. (13–14)

A standard terminology for distinguishing Kantian ethics from those that attribute moral value to the consequences of actions is that between *deontology* and *con-*

sequentialism. The Kantian deontologist maintains that morality is derived from the intentions or moral psychological state of an agent, and not from the effects of the actions that the agent decides to perform. The consequentialist holds just the opposite, that intentions are irrelevant to the morality of an action except insofar as they contribute to the overall effect it produces in creating more happiness or unhappiness or the like psychological consequences, an empirical aspect of morality that Kant must disavow as irrelevant to questions of morality.

The concept of moral good, Kant believes, is found only in the mind's internal "representation" of the moral law as the "determining ground" of the will. The will represents to itself the moral law, and in so doing, fixes its resolve on achieving the moral law for its own sake. If there is anything else other than the representation of the moral law in the will, then the will is not pure, and in particular it is not the pure moral will. The will, in that case, as already indicated, is contaminated by the other empirical psychological factors that can affect its decisions, such as inclination, desire, concern for the consequences of an action, or the like, any and all of which transform an action undertaken from and exclusively for the sake of the moral law into something that Kant is committed to classifying as strictly extra-moral. Kant considers the case of someone who knowingly makes a false promise, and applies the standard of whether the action is motivated entirely and exclusively by the will's internal representation of the moral law:

> The most direct and infallible way, however, to answer the question as to whether a lying promise accords with duty is to ask myself whether I would really be content if my maxim (of extricating myself from difficulty by means of a false promise) were to hold as a universal law for myself as well as for others, and could I really say to myself that everyone may promise falsely when he finds himself in a difficulty from which he can find no other way to extricate himself. Then I immediately become aware that I can indeed will the lie but can not at all will a universal law to lie. For by such a law there would be professed to other people who would not believe what I professed, or if they over-hastily did believe, then they would pay me back in like coin. Therefore, my maxim would necessarily destroy itself just as soon as it was made a universal law. (15)

Kant makes several important points in this passage. He indicates the way in which the will's internal representation of the moral law is supposed to exclude all empirical psychological factors, and in particular all aspects of inclination. The morally pure will has regard for moral duty as the only remaining basis for judging the moral value of the action, while concentrating exclusively on internal representation of the moral law as the only principle by which to determine whether the action is properly moral or has some other motivation.

Kant gives specific content to the form in which the will represents the moral law, thereby foreshadowing the most important moral principle of his ethical theory. He speaks of this as a universal law in a very definite sense. What makes the moral law universal in Kant's theory is that the agent can will the "maxim" or particular principle that guides the action to be accepted and followed by every moral agent. We shall need to look more carefully at Kant's reference to this statement of universal law. The important conclusion at this stage of Kant's investigation is that the will's internal representation of the universal moral law is supposed to be the only determinant of a genuinely moral action that falls properly under the metaphysics of morals. If the will's internal representation of universal moral law is in fact the only thing that determines an action, then all extraneous empirical psychological and prudential considerations, especially those connected with desire or inclination, are necessarily excluded, as Kant requires. The proper subject of moral philosophy is thereby purified of any nonrational elements, particularly because the judgment that the moral maxim is universalizable, as we shall further see, is based entirely on reason and involves no element of passion or emotion. The action will also necessarily then be undertaken from and not merely in accord with the moral law, reflecting the agent's commitment to moral duty as opposed to feeling, inclination, or expectation of consequence. Kant summarizes the significance of the agent's intentions and the will's internal representation of the universal moral law in designating an act as genuinely moral. These are the only circumstances in which the will can be regarded as unqualifiedly good, and hence as the only thing that is purely, unqualifiedly, or intrinsically good:

> Therefore, I need no far-reaching acuteness to discern what I have to do in order that my will may be morally good. Inexperienced in the course of the world and incapable of being prepared for all its contingencies, I only ask myself whether I can also will that my maxim should become a universal law. If not, then the maxim must be rejected, not because of any disadvantage accruing to me or even to other, but because it cannot be fitting as a principle in a possible legislation of universal law, and reason exacts from me immediate respect for such legislation. Indeed I have as yet no insight into the grounds of such respect (which the philosopher may investigate). But I at least understand that respect is an estimation of a worth that far outweighs any worth of what is recommended by inclination, and that the necessity of acting from pure respect for the practical law is what constitutes duty, to which every other motive must give way because duty is the condition of a will good in itself, whose worth is above all else. (15)

To emphasize the extent to which it is difficult to determine in practice whether an action is undertaken exclusively from duty or respect for the moral law by means of the will's internal representation of a universal moral principle, Kant states that we can never be sure that an action is undertaken for purely moral reasons as opposed to inclination. The assertion has frequently been misunderstood by commentators, for which Kant is no doubt partly to blame. Let us first consider what he says:

> In fact there is absolutely no possibility by means of experience to make out with complete certainty a single case in which the maxim of an action that may in other respects conform to duty has rested solely on moral grounds and on the representation of one's duty. It is indeed sometimes the case that after the keenest self-examination we can find nothing except the moral ground of duty that could have been strong enough to move us to this or that good action and to such great sacrifice. But there cannot with certainty be at all inferred from this that some secret impulse of self-love, merely appearing as the idea of duty, was not the actual determining cause of the will. We like to flatter ourselves with the false claim to a more noble motive; but in fact we can never, even by the strictest examination, completely plumb the depths of the secret incentives of our actions. For when

moral value is being considered, the concern is not with the actions, which are seen, but rather with their inner principles, which are not seen. (19)

Kant's remarks have been understood as meaning that it is impossible or virtually impossible to act in a morally correct way, as though Kant was imposing impossible standards that human moral agents could never satisfy. What Kant actually claims, however, on a close and careful even if philosophically unsympathetic reading, is rather that it is virtually impossible to *determine experientially* whether or not an action is undertaken from respect for the moral law or as a result of inclination.

He asserts that we cannot always tell, even in the most astute cases of self-examination, whether we are acting from a sense of duty or by or because of some other motivation. Hence, according to the moral principle he has advanced, we cannot always tell whether we are acting morally or, let us say, prudentially or emotionally or by some other spur to action. Experientially, we cannot judge whether another person is acting from moral duty or from some other private motive, because we cannot see into their hearts; and for much the same reason we cannot even tell in our own case exactly why we do what we choose to do. If we could know ourselves well enough to discover our true motives, then we could know in a given case whether we act from duty toward rather than merely in accord with the moral law. Unfortunately, persons and their hidden motives are not so transparent even to themselves. We are much more complex creatures than that, and we cannot always discover the real workings of our psyches. That, in any case, is Kant's conclusion as he contemplates the depths of human will.

If we do not know whether a person is acting from a sense of duty to or merely in accord with the moral law, then we cannot decide what in any particular instance is moral behavior. To recognize this limitation is not to contradict the theoretical truth that morality consists of a certain state of mind, an intention with which action is pursued that makes it the product of a good will as the only unqualifiedly good thing. Kant, with remarkable, almost twentieth-century, insight argues that even when we can discover in our own motives nothing more self-serving than the desire to act in accord with the demands of moral duty, we still cannot be sure that we are not driven by a secret impulse of self-love. The real reasons why we do what we do may be disguised even from the most searching scrutiny, and may involve motives that have more to do with inclination than we may be willing to acknowledge. We are capable of subconsciously deluding and deceiving ourselves with respect to our motivations to such an extent that we cannot always know whether we are acting morally or for reasons that are logically irrelevant to considerations of morality.

HYPOTHETICAL IMPERATIVES AND THE CATEGORICAL IMPERATIVE

The distinction between duty and inclination required by Kant's concept of morality is further exemplified by the difference between *hypothetical imperatives* and the *categorical imperative.* An imperative is a command, a duty of precisely the sort Kant says is inextricably linked to genuine moral motives for action. Kant's concept of the categorical imperative is one of the most important and controversial contributions ever to have been made in the history of ethics. The categorical imperative lays ra-

tionalist foundations for a metaphysics of deontological moral philosophy uncondi-
tioned by empirical contingencies of interest or circumstance. It crystallizes a single
rule of ethical conduct, presented in relation to the will as practical reason dictating
the law of reason to itself, which Kant interprets as the transcendental ground of free
morally responsible action.

The categorical imperative is expressed by Kant in no less than three distinct forms,
which he regards as different compatible formulations of an identical underlying principle. It is crucial, first of all, to understand Kant's distinction between hypothetical
and categorical imperatives, both of which make different types of commands governing moral decision making. Kant characterizes the general category of imperatives
in this fashion:

> The representation of an objective principle insofar as it necessitates the will is
> called a command (or reason), and the formula of the command is called an im-
> perative. (24)

The general idea of an imperative is a principle that commands action. It requires
those subject to its principle to do something, and hence provides the occasion and
justification for the action that is commanded. Kant explains:

> All imperatives are expressed by an *ought* and thereby indicate the relation of an
> objective law of reason to a will that is not necessarily determined by this law be-
> cause of its subjective constitution (the relation of necessitation). Imperatives say
> that something would be good to do or to refrain from doing, but they say it to
> a will that does not always therefore do something simply because it has been
> represented to the will as something good to do. That is practically good which
> the will by means of representations of reason and hence not by subjective causes,
> but objectively, i.e., on grounds valid for every rational being as such. It is dis-
> tinguished from the pleasant as that which influences the will only by means of
> sensation from merely subjective causes, which hold only for this or that person's
> senses but do not hold as a principle of reason valid for everyone. (24)

The relevance of imperatives to ethics according to Kant is that they command
the will for the sake of the good. An imperative in the ordinary grammatical sense is
merely an order to do something. We are familiar with the concept from such contexts as the claim that it is imperative to wear your seatbelt, to practice gun safety,
to reconfirm your flight departure time. The word *imperative* in all of these cases
means something it is vitally important to do. Its urgency seems understated by Kant's
formulation that an imperative is something it is simply good to do, although this is
obviously also true. Kant next explains that there are two fundamentally different
types of imperatives:

> Now all imperatives command either hypothetically or categorically. The former
> represent the practical necessity of a possible action as a means for attaining some-
> thing else that one wants (or may possibly want). The categorical imperative would
> be one which represented an action as objectively necessary in itself, without ref-
> erence to another end. (25)

The distinction between hypothetical imperatives and the categorical imperative
parallels Kant's division between empirical and rational elements of ethics and be-

tween psychological inclination and moral duty. The difference is that a hypothetical imperative is conditional. It tells what we ought to do or commands a specific action *if* or *in case* we want to achieve some other end. What makes an imperative hypothetical is that it requires that a certain action be informed on the hypothesis that we want to attain another definite end. *If* you want to avoid automobile injury, *then* it is imperative that you buckle your seatbelt; *if* you want to hunt or target shoot without causing injury, *then* it is imperative that you practice gun safety; *if* you want to be assured that your airplane will depart as scheduled, *then* it is imperative that you reconfirm your flight at least forty-eight hours in advance. And so on.

Significantly, hypothetical imperatives are conditional on desires or inclinations. If a certain end is desired, such as avoiding injury, then a certain means to that end is imperatively prescribed by a hypothetical imperative. More generally of interest for Kant is the application of hypothetical imperatives combined with conditional motivations of inclination as they figure in the empirically tainted impure moral systems that his unconditional moral deontology opposes. A moral consequentialist says conditionally in effect that if we want to promote the greatest happiness of the greatest number, then it is imperative that we strive through our actions, moral conduct, and legislation, and the like, to maximize pleasure and minimize pain and displeasure.

It is also significant that Kant from the outset in introducing the distinction between the two types of imperatives speaks of hypothetical imperatives in the plural and of the categorical imperative uniquely in the singular. The reason for this is clear if we consider the fact that there are many different desires and many different ends and inclinations, each of which can conceivably require multiple hypothetical imperatives as means to an end. The categorical imperative by contrast commands unconditionally. It is not something we must do if we want to achieve some other end, but something we are required to do no matter what other purposes we may have, as the end in itself of an unqualifiedly good will. The categorical imperative as such is not determined by the many different alternative purposes or ends toward which our actions are sometimes directed.

Although the categorical imperative can be variously formulated, as Kant eventually does, and although the categorical imperative can have unlimitedly many applications, alternative expressions of the principle must all finally come to the same thing. The categorical imperative, as Kant implies, is therefore necessarily unitary, individual, and unique.

Kant has yet to explain what the categorical imperative is, or how it is to be understood. He has provided a strong hint in his statement concerning the universalizability of maxims in the case of moral principles that are represented by the will in the case of actions directed by duty rather than inclination. It is evident from what we have already seen Kant saying that the categorical imperative is a moral command of duty that does not depend conditionally on the desire or inclination of any particular moral agents to attain any other end, or on any particular circumstances that happen to prevail, such as the existence of automobiles, firearms, or airplanes, among others, and hence is not subject to the empirical factors that Kant argues must be purged from the metaphysics of morals in pure moral philosophy. The categorical imperative commands us unconditionally to act in a certain way.

In Kant's ethical theory, empirical considerations of inclination and desire are associated with hypothetical imperatives, whereas moral duty and the requirements of pure reason in moral judgment are expressed by the categorical imperative. The categorical imperative is the universal moral law that Kant maintains is represented by the will in the case of actions motivated by moral duty. Kant underscores the necessity of the categorical imperative by referring to it as "apodeictic." By this he means a principle of practical moral reasoning that is justified by pure reason independently of experience, and in fact as synthetic *a priori*. It is just the sort of principle Kant requires of metaphysics generally, including the metaphysics of morals. Kant gives this further characterization of the distinction between hypothetical imperatives and the categorical imperative:

> A hypothetical imperative thus says only that an action is good for some purpose, either possible or actual. In the first case it is a problematic practical principle; in the second case an assertoric one. A categorical imperative, which declares an action to be of itself objectively necessary without reference to any purpose, i.e., without any other end, holds as an apodeictic practical principle. (25)

The multiplicity of hypothetical imperatives is defended by Kant on the grounds that although there are many different ends that rational agents may choose or otherwise be conditionally directed to attain, there is only one end or purpose shared in common by all rational agents as such. Kant, remarkably, identifies the end or purpose of all rational agents as happiness. He argues that taking happiness as the end of all rational agents makes any imperative commanding the will toward this or that good is still at best a means to the universal psychological end of achieving happiness, and hence remains formally distinct from the categorical imperative. It is worthwhile to clarify what Kant means by hypothetical imperatives in order to better understand the categorical imperative. To the extent that Kant acknowledges a shared, even universal, end at least of all human rational agents with the happiness-oriented psychology that seems to typify our species, imperatives for action that are directed toward the attainment of happiness remain always merely a means to an end, no matter how common an end, and as such are hypothetical rather than categorical. Kant contends:

> There is, however, one end that can be presupposed as actual for all rational beings (so far as they are dependent beings to whom imperatives apply); and thus there is one purpose which they not merely can have but which can certainly be assumed to be such that they all do have by a natural necessity, and this is happiness. A hypothetical imperative which represents the practical necessity of an action as means for the promotion of happiness is assertoric. It may be expounded not simply as necessary to an uncertain, merely possible purpose, but as necessary to a purpose which can be presupposed *a priori* and with certainty as being present in everyone because it belongs to his essence. Now skill in the choice of means to one's own greatest well-being can be called prudence in the narrowest sense. And thus the imperative that refers to the choice of means to one's own happiness, i.e., the precept of prudence, still remains hypothetical; the action is commanded not absolutely but only as a means to a further purpose. (26)

After elaborating on the means-to-end nature of hypothetical imperatives, Kant turns his attention to the categorical imperative. He begins by maintaining that there is only one such imperative because there is only one unconditional purpose of moral action. Kant describes the categorical imperative as concerned exclusively with the form of moral judgment and moral conduct as opposed to its matter or content. For this reason, Kant's pure moral philosophy and metaphysics of morals is often said to be a *formal* moral theory or *formalist* ethical system. Kant draws a sharp distinction between the empirical or psychological content-orientation of hypothetical imperatives and the purely formal character of the one and only categorical imperative:

> Finally, there is one imperative which immediately commands a certain conduct without having as its condition any other purpose to be attained by it. This imperative is categorical. It is not concerned with the matter of the action and its intended result, but rather with the form of the action and the principle from which it follows; what is essentially good in the action consists in the mental disposition, let the consequences be what they may. This imperative may be called that of morality. (26)

Kant's moral formalism and deontology go hand in hand. The formal nature of the categorical imperative and its exclusion of the means-ends contents or matter of all hypothetical imperatives is inimical to consequentialist concerns about the results or outcomes of actions as a measure of their morality. If a formalist ethical theory is incompatible with the effects or consequences of conduct in assessing moral value, then deontology as an anti-consequentialist moral philosophy is formalist. We have yet to discover everything that is implied by a Kantian deontological moral philosophy, but it is important to appreciate the extent to which Kant's formalist morality is consistently throughout a rejection of empirical elements in moral reasoning, not only in a subject's will and intent, but also in every aspect of the actions undertaken by a moral agent.

CATEGORICAL IMPERATIVE AND THE METAPHYSICS OF MORALS

We can anticipate Kant's formulation of the categorical imperative as an unconditional universal moral law. The principle is that we are to act always and only in such a way that we can will the maxim of our action to be a universal law for all rational beings.

The interpretation and implications of the categorical imperative must be developed at length. The principle applies unconditionally to all rational agents regardless of their circumstances, and makes it morally obligatory to do whatever actions are required by whatever moral maxims can be universalized in the sense of being willed universally as a law to be followed by all rational beings.

To understand how Kant arrives at this crossroads in his metaphysics of morals, and is able to put forward the categorical imperative as the universal law represented by the will in the pursuit of moral duty, we should first consider Kant's several formulations of the categorical imperative in its most general terms. Kant proceeds by posing a transcendental question about the conditions of possibility for the categorical imperative or "imperative of morality":

> On the other hand, the question as to how the imperative of morality is possible is undoubtedly the only one requiring a solution. For it is not at all hypothetical;

and hence the objective necessity which it presents cannot be based on any pre-supposition, as was the case with the hypothetical imperatives. Only there must never here be forgotten that no example can show, i.e., empirically, whether there is any such imperative at all. Rather, care must be taken lest all imperatives which are seemingly categorical may nevertheless be covertly hypothetical. For instance, when it is said that you should not make a false promise, the assumption is that the necessity of this avoidance is no mere advice for escaping some other evil, so that it might be said that you should not make a false promise, lest you ruin your credit when the falsity comes to light. But when it is asserted that an action of this kind must be regarded as bad in itself, then the imperative of prohibition is therefore categorical. (28)

Kant predictably concludes that the categorical imperative cannot be fully or correctly explained by empirical methods, but must be understood *a priori*. He warns against mistaking hypothetical imperatives for the categorical imperative, thus recognizing the problem of correctly construing the categorical imperative to avoid hidden conditionalization. He downgrades all such principles as mere "principles of the will," which he distinguishes from genuine moral laws, when he writes:

We shall, therefore, have to investigate the possibility of a categorical imperative entirely *a priori*, inasmuch as we do not here have the advantage of having its reality given in experience and consequently of this being obligated merely to explain its possibility rather than to establish it. In the meantime so much can be seen for now: the categorical imperative alone purports to be a practical law, while all the others may be called principles of the will but not laws. (29)

As a further basis for distinguishing between hypothetical imperatives and the categorical imperative, Kant mentions that the content of a hypothetical imperative is obscure unless or until its condition is clarified. The problem is that hypothetical imperatives are often formulated without making their conditions explicit. In the case of the examples we have already considered, these might include: "Always wear your seatbelt!" "Practice gun safety!" "Check and reconfirm your flight!" A more complete and correct statement of these imperatives would need to be preceded by the appropriate conditions under which each of these imperatives becomes a command as a means to an end in the service of the good. We need in all these cases to add the clause, "If you want to avoid injury," and so on. If Kant is right, all such means-ends imperatives fall under the general condition or hypothesis, "If you want to be happy and promote the happiness of others." In contrast with this situation involving hypothetical imperatives, Kant says that the entire content of the categorical imperative is transparent immediately upon grasping any of its formulations. The obvious reason is that the categorical imperative unlike hypothetical imperatives is unconditional, and thus, if adequately expressed at all, has no component of its expression that can remain hidden or implicit. Thus, Kant states:

If I think of a hypothetical imperative in general, I do not know beforehand what it will contain until its condition is given. But if I think of a categorical imperative, I know immediately what it contains. For since, besides the law, the imperative contains only the necessity that the maxim should accord with this law, while the law contains no condition to restrict it, there remains nothing but the universality of a law as such with which the maxim of the action should conform. This conformity alone is properly what is represented as necessary by the imperative. (29–30)

Summarizing this line of argument, Kant concludes again that there can only be one categorical imperative. He presents the categorical imperative in the form we have already seen in his discussion even prior to his introduction of the distinction between hypothetical imperatives and the categorical imperative. This is the formula by which the moral law, as opposed to appeals to inclination in motivating moral action, is supposed to be universalizable. The categorical imperative accordingly requires that we act only according to those maxims or moral rules guiding our moral conduct that can be universalized in the sense of being such that we can will the rules in question to be universally followed by all rational moral agents. Kant presents the principle in this way:

Hence there is only one categorical imperative and it is this: Act only according to that maxim whereby you can at the same time will that it should become a universal law. (30)

The purely formal nature of Kant's categorical imperative is manifest in the following characterization. Kant now maintains:

The universality of law according to which effects are produced constitutes what is properly called nature in the most general sense (as to form), i.e., the existence of things as far as determined by universal laws. Accordingly, the universal imperative of duty may be expressed thus: Act as if the maxim of your action were to become through your will a universal law of nature. (30)

The categorical imperative is expressed in Kant's passage in its most familiar and informative version. Kant declares that we are unconditionally morally obligated as a matter of duty, regardless and independently of any inclination or accompanying feeling or emotion, to act only from those maxims that can be willed to be universal laws.

What exactly does this mean, and in what exact sense is the categorical imperative in this formulation supposed to be a formalistic moral principle? To answer these questions, we should next consider four applications of the categorical imperative which Kant describes, in order to see how the categorical imperative works when it is put to practical use. When we have clarified Kant's concept of the categorical imperative and understood the logical mechanism of universalizability that makes his moral philosophy formalist, we will finally be in a position to evaluate his deontological ethics from the standpoint of criticisms that have sometimes been raised against the categorical imperative.

FOUR APPLICATIONS OF THE CATEGORICAL IMPERATIVE

Kant's four applications of the categorical imperative are intended to showcase the principle's practical conclusions. We need to explain his examples in order to arrive at a correct understanding of how Kant interprets the principle as an expression of unconditional moral duty purified of all empirical elements, despite its ability to guide specific concrete decision making in everyday moral situations.

He begins by indicating that the categorical imperative supports the same sort of ethical judgments and justifies the same types of moral actions that are often accepted as implications of conventional morality. These are divided in a way that is also standard in other moral systems, between duties we owe personally to ourselves and those we owe to others, and into perfect and imperfect duties. It will be worthwhile to say something about the two overlapping categories of duties, which are not always observed in contemporary moral philosophy.

The distinction between duties owed to oneself by contrast with others is clear enough from its terminology, and marks an obvious division in Kant's four examples. The first and third examples in Kant's analysis, not to commit suicide and to develop one's talents, are duties to oneself, whereas the second and fourth examples, repayment of debts and charitable donation of surplus wealth, concern duties to others. The distinction between perfect and imperfect moral duties is less common in modern ethics, but involves the difference between what is morally obligatory to do by contrast with what it is morally permissible to do. The idea is that a perfect moral duty is one that describes something definite that we are morally required to fulfill, whereas an imperfect moral duty does not command but permits action, and hence is less definite and positive in its command, prescribing only what is morally allowed or unforbidden. By this account, Kant's first and second examples involving moral permissibility are imperfect, and his third and fourth examples involving moral obligation are perfect.

Kant initiates this part of his discussion by stating his purpose in offering illustrations of how the categorical imperative can be applied:

> We shall now enumerate some duties, following the usual division of them into duties to ourselves and to others and into perfect and imperfect duties. (30)

Kant's four applications of the categorical imperative include the question of whether it is morally permissible to commit suicide in dire circumstances; whether it is morally permissible to accept a loan of money falsely promising to repay it and knowing in advance that one will not be able to repay; whether it is morally obligatory to develop one's natural talents as opposed to living an unproductive life of lazy pleasure; and whether it is morally obligatory to donate surplus wealth to others in need as an act of charity.

The first example in Kant's account is explained in these terms. Kant presupposes throughout that the persons who are contemplating the morality of a certain action are faced with specific circumstances that require a moral action, and that they accept the categorical imperative as the principle by which to arrive at a morally correct decision. The categorical imperative is supposed to determine what the agents are morally obligated or permitted to do, whether to themselves or others as a perfect or imperfect moral duty. Kant elsewhere refers to the bridge principles required for such real-time applications of the abstract principle of the categorical imperative as "typics." Here, in his first application of the categorical imperative, Kant invites us to consider the question that many persons confront during especially difficult episodes in their lives, in the case study of a potential suicide:

> 1. A man reduced to despair by a series of misfortunes feels sick of life but is still so far in possession of his reason that he can ask himself whether taking his own

life would not be contrary to his duty to himself. Now he asks whether the maxim of his action could become a universal law of nature. But his maxim is this: from self-love I make as my principle to shorten my life when its continued duration threatens more evil than it promises satisfaction. There only remains the question as to whether this principle of self-love can become a universal law of nature. One sees at once a contradiction in a system of nature whose law would destroy life by means of the very same feeling that acts so as to stimulate the furtherance of life, and hence there could be no existence as a system of nature. Therefore, such a maxim cannot possibly hold as a universal law of nature and is, consequently, wholly opposed to the supreme principle of all duty. (30–31)

Kant's method in applying the categorical imperative is easily identified in this first example, as is the sense in which his deontological ethics is rational, formalistic, unconditional, and free of any empirical impurities. The procedure is first to identify the maxim or ethical rule of guidance that a moral agent is considering as justifying a contemplated action. In this case, the act under review is committing suicide, and the relevant moral maxim, at least as Kant characterizes it in this instance, is "to shorten [one's] life when its continued duration threatens more evil than it promises satisfaction."

The second step is to determine whether or not the moral maxim in question can be willed to be a universal moral law for all rational beings. This is equivalent to the question whether the agent can will the maxim to be a universal law of nature. What makes these two formulations of the second step of Kant's method of applying the categorical imperative equivalent is that if a maxim can be willed to be universal for all rational subjects, then it is an unconditional law like a law of physics, but one that holds, despite the terminology of Kant's earlier distinction between laws of nature and laws of freedom, for all rational beings as moral agents, regardless of their species or psychologies. By analogy, a law of physics such as the universal law of gravity in Newton's mechanics is indifferent to the specific substances to which it applies, holding alike with respect to iron and copper, to wood and water and fire, to apples dropping from apple trees, and so on. A universalizable moral maxim, on Kant's theory, is one that a moral agent can will to be a natural law in the sense of providing moral guidance as a law of freedom for all rational beings and all moral agents. If a moral maxim is universalizable in this sense, as the general form of the categorical imperative prescribes, then the agent who is considering adopting a course of action falling under a moral maxim is supposed to be able to will that the maxim be adopted as a universal principle of action for all individuals capable of reasoning.

The question that remains unanswered, but which holds the clue to understanding Kant's categorical imperative, is precisely what it means to ask whether the moral maxim at issue in an application of the categorical imperative *can* be willed to be a law of nature or universal principle of moral judgment. How do we decide, if we are any of the moral agents trying to make use of the categorical imperative in any of Kant's applications, whether we can or cannot will that the relevant moral maxim be a universal law for all rational decision makers? The answer is not fully elaborated in Kant's exposition, but is clear enough from what he says. The idea is that a maxim is universalizable in the sense of being such that it can be willed to be a universal law of nature, or, better, a universal law of freedom, just in case there is no contradiction or logical inconsistency in willing that the maxim be adopted by all rational beings.

Kant says that if the maxim that is supposed to justify a decision to commit suicide were universally accepted, then an outright contradiction would result. To repeat the essential passage, Kant states: "One sees at once a contradiction in a system of nature whose law would destroy life by means of the very same feeling that acts so as to stimulate the furtherance of life, and hence there could be no existence as a system of nature." If a contradiction obtains, then, of course, the moral agent cannot will the maxim to be a universal law to be adopted by all rational beings. Logical inconsistency in that case effectively and in the strongest imaginable way prevents the agent from willing that the maxim of self-love implying the permissibility of committing suicide when life threatens more dissatisfaction than satisfaction be universally accepted. There can be no more powerful inhibition to willing that such a maxim be universally adopted than encountering an outright logical contradiction when making the attempt. Since logical inconsistency is a purely formal matter, it is also clear why and in what sense Kant's moral philosophy is formalistic. Kant's ethics, resting on the categorical imperative and the formal universalizability of moral maxims, is a purely rational moral philosophy from which empirical elements are eliminated. It all comes down to logic, a formal question of contradiction or noncontradiction, in the attempt to will that a moral maxim be universally accepted by all rational agents.

We must nevertheless ask whether Kant is right to claim that a contradiction results in the case he describes when an agent tries to universalize the moral maxim. We must also ask whether Kant identifies the right moral maxim as the principle that would justify a decision to commit suicide under the circumstances he describes. We might observe, as other critics of Kant's principle have also commented, that the maxim he takes as the basis for a judgment of universalizability or nonuniversalizability is rather weak. There are few persons contemplating a decision as drastic as whether or not to commit suicide that would be guided by the principle that suicide is justified merely when the continuance of life threatens more dissatisfaction than satisfaction. The usual scenario in which suicide is considered is one in which a person faces excruciating pain or humiliation with no possibility of relief. A standard case is that in which an agent is suffering from an incurable disease that will slowly bring about a prolonged death anyway, and in the meantime cause unbearable suffering. It is usually the avoidance of that extreme type of misery, rather than mere avoidance of dissatisfaction with life, that outweighs by however small an amount the satisfaction to be enjoyed if one continues to live.

It seems correct to conclude, despite these objections, that if Kant's purpose is merely to provide examples to indicate how the categorical imperative is supposed to work, then there is nothing wrong with his deliberately choosing an overly simplified case. The suicide example involves an unrealistic moral maxim that is easily seen to be ununiversalizable by virtue of engendering a formal logical contradiction that prevents the agent from willing that all rational agents accept and act on the same principle. We might therefore agree with Kant that *if* a moral agent contemplates suicide as an act to be justified by the moral maxim to end life whenever its continuation threatens more dissatisfaction than satisfaction, *then* the action would not be morally justified by the categorical imperative, and probably should not be. *If* anyone were to reason in this way along these lines and on the basis of such a flimsy moral maxim, without asserting that this is the only or even the primary maxim that a potential suicide might invoke in order to try justifying such a decision, and *if* a moral maxim reflecting what

Kant calls this principle of self-love cannot be willed to be universally accepted because it is internally logically self-contradictory, promoting and at the same time eliminating the possibility for the furtherance of life, *then* the action is undoubtedly morally unjustified, as the categorical imperative rightly implies.

As we shall see, the other examples in Kant's four applications of the categorical imperative involve even more inventive discoveries of contradictions. The search for inconsistencies that block an agent from willing a moral maxim to be universally accepted by all rational beings sometimes requires Kant to cast about for background assumptions. Such assumptions involve purposes that might be but are not always obviously analytically contained in the concept of a rational moral agent. It is only in connection with these assumptions that a given moral maxim runs into some kind of apparent conflict that Kant then characterizes as a contradiction to willing the universal acceptance of a moral maxim for a prohibited action. The remaining three examples in Kant's repertoire are also problematic, although the second case is often admitted to be the most intuitive. Kant offers the dilemma of a person who needs to borrow money that he knows he cannot repay:

> 2. Another man in need finds himself forced to borrow money. He knows well that he won't be able to repay it, but he sees also that he will not get any loan unless he firmly promises to repay it within a fixed time. He wants to make such a promise, but he still has conscience enough to ask himself whether it is not permissible and is contrary to duty to get out of difficulty in this way. Suppose, however, that he decides to do so. The maxim of his action would then be expressed as follows: when I believe myself to be in need of money, I will borrow money and promise to pay it back, although I know that I can never do so. Now this principle of self-love or personal advantage may perhaps be quite compatible with one's entire future welfare, but the question is now whether it is right. I then transform the requirement of self-love into a universal law and put the question thus: how would things stand if my maxim were to become a universal law? He then sees at once that such a maxim could never hold as a universal law of nature and be consistent with itself, but must necessarily be self-contradictory. For the universality of a law which says that anyone believing himself to be in difficulty could promise whatever he pleases with the intention of not keeping it would make promising itself and the end to be attained thereby quite impossible, inasmuch as no one would believe what was promised him but would merely laugh at all such utterances as being vain pretenses. (31)

Again Kant declares that the attempt to will a morally problematic moral maxim as a universal law for all moral agents is stymied by entailing a logical self-contradiction. In this situation, a contradiction is supposed to arise between the agent's willing to avoid a tight financial fix by taking unfair advantage of the expectation that a person who promises in good faith to repay a loan will actually do so.

The ability to borrow money depends on a social institution in which persons enter into an agreement whereby money on loan is eventually returned, typically with an agreed amount of interest. Otherwise, if this were not assumed, why would anyone ever choose to lend money? More importantly from Kant's purposes, if the violation of this normal expectation on which the possibility of borrowing money is predicated were taken to its extreme, then there would not only be a cultural breakdown of the institution of lending, but there would in fact be no such thing as lending or borrowing. What would replace it in that case instead would at most be the stealing or giving away of money.

Kant argues that the person who is thinking of borrowing money under false pretenses should be deterred from doing so by the proper application of the categorical imperative. To will to obtain a loan by promising to repay but without any intention of repaying cannot be justified by a moral maxim that an agent can logically consistently will to be a universal law for all rational beings, because it would mean the end of the institution of lending. The contradiction Kant claims to identify in the bad loan example can be more explicitly articulated as the agent's willing on the one hand to be able to borrow money and on the other hand to do so by appeal to a moral maxim that, if it were to become a universal practice on the part of all potential loan recipients, would have the practical effect of making it impossible to borrow money. The moral agent who tries to borrow money under false pretenses appears inconsistently as a result to will to borrow money and to will to be unable to borrow money. The contradiction prevents the agent from consistently willing the principle of action to be a universal law for all rational beings, and as such is formally prohibited by Kant's categorical imperative. Thus, the agent for formal reasons logically cannot will as a universal principle the moral maxim that would otherwise authorize the decision to accept a loan with no intention to repay.

Kant's third case involves a person of talent who has the opportunity to live without exercising or developing these talents. Many moralists have maintained that we all have a duty to self and others to make the best we can of our abilities, for our own good and for the benefits they might make available. If I have a rare talent as a brain surgeon, for example, but I suddenly come into a vast fortune that would enable me to live a life of luxury without lifting a finger in honest toil for the rest of my life, it might still be thought that it is morally obligatory for me to develop my ability as a surgeon for the sake of self-fulfillment and for the benefits that my skills might bestow on those in need of my professional services. Whether or not we agree with Kant's moral assessment of the obligations of a talented individual, it is interesting also in this third application to see how Kant arrives at his conclusion, and how he proposes to identify a formal logical inconsistency in an agent's attempt to universalize the relevant moral maxim. Kant describes the third case in these terms:

> 3. A third finds in himself a talent whose cultivation could make him a man useful in many respects. But he finds himself in comfortable circumstances and prefers to indulge in pleasure rather than to bother himself about broadening and improving his fortunate natural aptitudes. But he asks himself further whether his maxim of neglecting his natural gifts, besides agreeing of itself with his propensity to indulge, might agree also with what is called duty. He then sees that a system of nature could indeed always subsist according to such a universal law, even though every man (like South Sea Islanders) should let his talents rust and resolve to devote his life entirely to idleness, indulgence, propagation, and, in a word, to enjoyment. But he cannot possibly will that this should become a universal law of nature or be implanted in us as such a law by a natural instinct. For as a rational being he necessarily wills that all his faculties should be developed, inasmuch as they are given him for all sorts of possible purposes. (31)

The application of Kant's categorical imperative in the third case is probably the most problematic. It is certainly the example that has generated the most criticism and raised the most doubts about whether Kant has properly identified the principles for a plausible rationalist moral philosophy.

Kant's system presumably need not stand or fall with the failure of a single example. It is significant, however, that Kant appears to regard the example as every bit as correct as the others. If it does not appear as such to our judgment, then we might need to reflect further and more deeply on how the categorical imperative is supposed to work. The concluding sentence in the passage from Kant's third example is particularly unconvincing. Kant says in effect that any rational being considered as such necessarily wills to develop all the faculties with which he or she has been endowed, since they can serve "all sorts of possible purposes." It appears at best circular, asserting what Kant needs to prove, that rational moral agents should develop their talents. Why should Kant suppose that this is true?

First, it is worth remarking that no persons can develop all of their potential abilities. Talented individuals have many possibilities for perfecting their skills, and time does not permit making the most of all their natural gifts. In order to truly develop a talent, for brain surgery or painting or music or poetry or philosophy or acting or sports or dance, a person must choose and concentrate on some restricted range of abilities in order to devote the time and discipline required to bring them to a higher state of perfection. If this is true, then the implication is that whatever we do and no matter how talented and energetic we are, we have no choice but to neglect some talents for the sake of others. As a result, it cannot reasonably be expected that any rational being will develop all the talents at his or her disposal. Kant's argument that all talents might be useful for a variety of possible purposes nevertheless would presumably still apply, even to those talents an individual must inevitably allow to remain undeveloped.

Kant, however, maintains that it would be formally logically inconsistent for a rational being to will that the principle of allowing any talents to remain undeveloped hold universally with respect to all persons and all talents. Kant seems to regard it as essential to a rational being that they not neglect all their talents, and that to do so would be irrational. The scant attention that Kant gives to this example suggests that he finds it sufficiently obvious to require little comment and no further explication. It would be irrational, Kant implies, to neglect all of one's talents, presumably because one could not survive without exercising at least some natural abilities, even if these are limited in scope to whatever is minimally required to receive nourishment and avoid dangers. If it is irrational in the universal case to refuse to develop and exercise all natural talents, then it is equally inconsistent with the exercise of will generally not to attempt to develop as many of our natural talents as we realistically can, maximizing our abilities to fulfill as many essential purposes as possible. If this is correct, then Kant may after all be right in insisting that it is morally impermissible according to his interpretation of the categorical imperative to neglect the development of talents, and morally obligatory within reason to try to maximize skill in as many abilities as we can.

What is crucial in understanding Kant's concept of the categorical imperative and the universalizability of maxims as moral laws is the fact that he does not deny that there could be a natural condition in which all persons neglect the development of all their talents. Instead, his application of the categorical imperative turns specifically on the claim that a rational agent cannot consistently *will* that such a state of nature occur. Nature itself does not prohibit the universal neglect of natural talent, but the will, Kant says, rebels against the universal acceptance of the moral maxim that would allow everyone to neglect all their abilities. The contradiction in question is supposed to hold in the will of the moral agent considering the action, rather than in the world itself. Kant believes that it would be a contradiction within the will of the moral agent contemplating a life of ease to desire that all rational agents fail to develop their talents. If Kant is right, then no rational being considered as such can consistently will all persons to neglect their abilities, presumably because to do so would run counter to a rational being's willing anything whatsoever. Although Kant does not specify a reason for this conclusion beyond what we have conjectured, it might be imagined that to will at all is an expression of desire that cannot be realized or implemented except by the exercise of at least some natural talent or natural ability. To will laziness is therefore not universalizable, according to Kant, because it is logically incompatible with the requirements of will. It is irrational to will anything whatsoever at the same time as willing that there be no ability to realize whatever is willed.

Finally, Kant considers a fourth example involving charitable donations of surplus wealth to the needy. He explains:

> 4. A fourth man finds things going well for himself but sees others (whom he could help) struggling with great hardships; and he thinks: what does it matter to me? Let everybody be as happy as Heaven wills or as he can make himself; I shall take nothing from him nor even envy him; but I have no desire to contribute anything to his well-being or to his assistance when in need. If such a way of thinking were to become a universal law of nature, the human race admittedly could very well subsist and doubtless could subsist even better than when everyone prates about sympathy and benevolence and even on occasion exerts himself to practice them but, on the other hand, also cheats when he can, betrays the right of man, or otherwise violates them. But even though it is possible that a universal law of nature could subsist in accordance with that maxim, still it is impossible to will that such a principle should hold everywhere as a law of nature. For a will which resolved in this way would contradict itself, inasmuch as cases might often arise in which one would have need of the love and sympathy of others and in which he would deprive himself, by such a law of nature springing from his own will, of all hope of the aid he wants for himself. (32)

The inconsistency that Kant supposes to obtain within the will of a person willing a universal acceptance of the moral maxim in this case is also rather tenuous. The maxim would justify refusing ever to donate surplus value charitably to other persons in need. Kant claims that it would be self-contradictory to will that no one ever give charitably to others because it is rational to assume that anyone at some point or other in life might also be in need. It would be irrational to will that assistance of the required sort not be available as a result of every rational agent accepting the moral maxim never to offer charity to others. The fourth application of the categorical imperative in Kant's choice of examples is thus a moral obligation to be charitable toward others and a moral prohibition of total selfishness.

Kant identifies the common features of the four applications of the categorical imperative, and indicates the unity by which all examples, despite their diversity, are implications of the same underlying principle. He recognizes that there are different ways in which contradictions can arise within the thought of a moral agent trying to will that a given moral maxim be a universal law of nature or universal moral principle for all rational beings. He catalogs a number of possibilities under which a moral agent is blocked in trying to universalize a particular moral maxim. The limitation of will by formal inconsistency, according to Kant, can happen in several ways, any and all of which preclude a moral maxim from universalizability. The contemplated action is morally prohibited or at least not morally permitted by the categorical imperative when any of these kinds of contradictions arise within the will. Kant offers the following overview:

> These are some of the many actual duties, or at least what are taken to be such, whose derivation from the single principle cited above is clear. We must be able to will that a maxim of our action become a universal law; this is the canon for morally estimating any of our actions. Some actions are so constituted that their maxims cannot without contradiction even be thought as a universal law of nature, much less be willed as what should become one. In the case of others this internal impossibility is indeed not found, but there is still no possibility of willing that their maxim should be raised to the universality of a law of nature, because such a will would contradict itself. There is no difficulty in seeing that the former kind of action conflicts with strict or narrow [perfect] (irremissible) duty, while the second kind conflicts only with broad [imperfect] (meritorious) duty. By means of these examples there has thus been fully set forth how all duties depend as regards the kind of obligation (not the object of their action) upon the one principle. (32)

The unity and uniqueness of the categorical principle is emphasized again by Kant in summarizing the various applications he has presented. We have seen that the categorical imperative offers plausible solutions to traditional moral problems that are largely in accord with received ethical attitudes, also supported by non-Kantian, nondeontological moral theories. The answers Kant proposes are controversial, but not obviously more so than those offered by other ethical systems concerning what are, after all, difficult moral problems.

Kant by no means suggests that these four are the only or even the most important applications of the categorical imperative. We have already indicated that Kant might regard at least some of the examples in this section of his treatise as deliberately simplified illustrations of how the method is supposed to work. The interesting thing about the categorical imperative is how neatly it falls into place in Kant's formalism and deontological ethics. Kant asserts from the outset that moral philosophy and the metaphysics of morals are to be purified of empirical elements as an essential first step in clarifying its subject matter. He distinguishes thereafter between acting from a sense of duty toward rather than merely in accord with the moral law, between rational morality and psychological inclination, and between consequentialism and deontology, which he does not refer to as such by name. The categorical imperative fits exactly into this crucial set of distinctions in Kant's moral theory.

As distinct from hypothetical imperatives, the categorical imperative unconditionally prescribes moral duties, and as such is logically independent of the empirical circumstances that Kant believes must be eliminated from pure moral philosophy.

The logical mechanism of the categorical imperative by which its applications involving circumstantial typics are negotiated fits the bill by being purely formal, and hence nonempirical. The absence of formal logical contradiction when an agent attempts to will that a moral maxim justifying a contemplated action be made a universal law for all rational beings is Kant's criterion for an action commanded by the categorical imperative. The will's representation of the rational principle of the categorical imperative and its implications for moral conduct in turn is the prerequisite for Kant's concept of acting from rather than merely in accord with the moral law, and for following the dictates of moral duty rather than psychological inclination. The categorical imperative commands unconditionally, and as such is indifferent to what we want to do, what might be in our personal self-interests to do or refrain from doing, the life experiences of any particular moral agent, or the circumstances in the world that happen to prevail.

CATEGORICAL MORAL MAXIMS IN KANT'S CATEGORICAL IMPERATIVE

Kant's concept of the categorical imperative is a remarkable achievement in moral philosophy. There is much to recommend Kant's discovery. Despite its explanatory power and intuitive appeal, however, there are also many philosophical objections to the categorical imperative. Some criticisms are misguided and demonstrably unsound, while others are more pointed and difficult to answer.

We begin with an objection that reflects a basic misunderstanding of the categorical imperative. It is a necessary reminder, but one all too easily lost sight of in discussions of Kant's moral philosophy, that Kant does not propose to defend the categorical imperative by arguing that it would be desirable or undesirable if a certain maxim in question were to become universal. He does not suggest that the agent contemplating suicide or reneging on a promise to repay a debt would be unhappy with the predictable result if everyone were to adopt the practice. If that were Kant's point, his moral philosophy would reduce simply to a form of consequentialism. Kant does not offer yet another version of the Golden Rule or Confucian edict to "Do unto others as you would have others do unto you." The question of what the agent would or would not like to have others do to him cannot possibly be relevant to Kant's formalist ethics. That would be a matter of empirical psychology involving desire or inclination and the expectation of consequences to accrue to certain actions, in this world or another to come. The categorical imperative boils down instead to a question of what is or is not formally contradictory in attempts to universalize a moral maxim, or what a rational moral agent logically can or cannot will.

Much as the ancient Stoa taught that morality is entirely independent of contingent circumstances, so that the wise man can be happy in his virtue even on the rack, so Kant holds that an agent from the viewpoint of ethical evaluation is enslaved by considerations of what may promote or frustrate happiness. The determination of individual or collective happiness is the source at most of an external basis for moral decision making and action that is not grounded on reason alone. Kant believes that reason must break free of empirical contingencies by accepting its own law of practical reasoning in the categorical imperative. Kant more completely analyzes the essential features of the moral maxims to be universalized in correct applications of the categorical imperative. He distinguishes between three ways of thinking about the categorical imperative, when he states:

> The aforementioned three ways of representing the principle of morality are at bottom only so many formulas of the very same law: one of them by itself contains a combination of the other two. Nevertheless, there is a difference in them, which is subjectively rather than objectively practical, viz., it is intended to bring an idea of reason closer to intuition (in accordance with a certain analogy) and thereby closer to feeling. All maxims have, namely,
>
> 1. A form, which consists in universality; and in this respect the formula of the moral imperative is expressed thus: maxims must be so chosen as if they were to hold as universal laws of nature.
>
> 2. A matter, viz., an end; and here the formula says that a rational being, inasmuch as he is by his very nature an end and hence an end in himself, must serve in every maxim as a condition limiting all merely relative and arbitrary ends.
>
> 3. A complete determination of all maxims by the formula that all maxims proceeding from his own legislation ought to harmonize with a possible kingdom of ends as a kingdom of nature. There is a progression here through the categories of the *unity* of the form of the will (its universality), the *plurality* of its matter (its objects, i.e., its ends), and the *totality* or completeness of its system of ends. But one does better if in moral judgment he follows the rigorous method and takes as his basis the universal formula of the categorical imperative: Act according to that maxim which can at the same time make itself a universal law. But if one wants also to secure acceptance for the moral law, it is very useful to bring one and the same action under the three aforementioned concepts and thus, as far as possible, to bring the moral law nearer to intuition. (41–42)

There are formal, material, and legislative styles of characterizing the categorical imperative. We can think of the categorical imperative as formal when we emphasize the logical compatibility or incompatibility of the rational will willing a given moral maxim to be a universal law for all rational beings. We can also do so in terms of its material aspect in obligating moral agents to treat all rational beings as ends in themselves and never merely as means to another end. We can finally do so also legislatively, from the standpoint of the requirements of an ideal kingdom of ends, which we consider further below.

The question whether the promise maker's prior intent not to repay a debt violates the categorical imperative, to reconsider Kant's second example, cannot be determined on the basis of whether the promise maker would be happy or unhappy with the results if everyone acted in accord with the same maxim. The problem is to be decided on rational grounds, by logic alone. The mechanism is the procedure of examining the will for contradictions. Can the dishonest promise maker with logical consistency simultaneously will not to repay the debt and also will that all rational beings act in accord with the same maxim? No, says Kant, for then the institution of promising itself would collapse, and gestures to promise the repayment of debt would be met only by ridicule. It is therefore strictly inconsistent to will both things at once, to obtain a loan fraudulently and to will that everyone do so. The categorical imperative implies that the bad faith will to promise and that everyone adopt the same principle are logically inconsistent in their ultimate consequences. Reason proves to reason by the categorical imperative that it is morally wrong to make false promises, and when reason accepts reason's judgment, it acquiesces to an *autonomous* law, thereby securing the very foundations or ultimate presuppositions of free and morally responsible action.

There is nevertheless a potential counterexample to Kant's principle of the categorical imperative. We are supposed to ask whether a moral maxim justifying a contemplated action can be willed to be a universal moral law for all rational beings, and we are supposed to judge whether or not a contemplated action can be rationally willed to be a universal law for all rational beings by determining whether or not the attempt rationally to will the universality of the maxim is formally consistent or entails some type of logical contradiction. The categorical imperative itself is, needless to say, categorical. What, however, if the moral maxims to be considered for consistent universalizability by rational will are themselves conditional? Here, it appears, Kant's principle is vulnerable to criticism.

Suppose that a moral maxim entertained by the rational will has this form, making specific reference to the unique situation in which the moral agent in question happens to be Immanuel Kant, and has the form: "*If* you are Immanuel Kant, *then* commit as many crimes against humanity as you desire." There appears to be no contradiction whatsoever at least in Immanuel Kant's rationally willing that the conditional maxim personalized to his particular case be universally adopted by all rational beings, since the maxim does not authorize wrongdoing by anyone other than himself. The trouble is that as Kant defines the categorical imperative, only the imperative itself is explicitly required to be unconditional. He leaves unsaid what particular type of logical structure if any the maxims to which the imperative refers may or must have. This leaves the thesis open to a host of similar objections. To close the gap, moreover, takes Kant's theory in a direction he might not have approved.

Despite these cautions, there is good reason to think that a solution is available that is largely in keeping with Kant's statement of the categorical imperative. Since the categorical imperative itself is unconditional, it may seem natural to extend the same logical form to the maxims of moral conduct to which it refers. It cannot be argued that if the maxims mentioned in the categorical imperative are not also unconditional, then the categorical imperative itself cannot be unconditional, since the mere reference to another class of propositions by a proposition does not imply that the two share the same logical status. This makes it necessary, if the solution is regarded as the most promising method of preserving Kant's doctrine against this kind of criticism, to add the assumption that not only is the categorical imperative unconditional, but the moral maxims referred to in the universalizability requirement of the categorical imperative must also be unconditional.

The most persuasive internal evidence in favor of the proposal is that it not only solves objections involving conditional personalized moral maxims, but preserves Kant's characteristic central claim that nothing empirically contingent or conditional must be allowed to taint the rationalist foundations of ethics. If the moral maxims referred to in the categorical imperative are not themselves unconditional, then Kant's ethical system as a whole is not purely rationalist, but is compromised at its very foundations in the law of reason by such contingencies of empirical circumstance as whether or not the agent contemplating the principle happens in this case to be Immanuel Kant. This suggests but certainly does not prove that Kant may have intended all along for the moral maxims referred to in the categorical imperative to be absolutely unconditional. The final test of the solution is whether unconditional moral maxims are adequate to capture ethical conclusions otherwise thought to be entailed by the categorical imperative. The place to begin may be with Kant's four applications, to see how his illustrations work when limited exclusively to unconditional maxims. Even without reexamining these deductions, it is possible to suggest in a general way how unconditional moral maxims, together with another of Kant's principles that "ought" implies "can," may do justice to the most problematic intuitions about morally correct action in a formalist deontological ethics.

It is sometimes said that Kant's moral system cannot satisfactorily explain obligations related to contingent abilities like medical expertise, typically expressed by conditional principles, such as, "If you are an able physician (compare: "If you are Immanuel Kant . . . "), then whenever someone is injured, you ought to respond by giving appropriate assistance." Certainly, qualified physicians alone should apply their training in such circumstances, while those without the requisite knowledge, who are likely to do more harm than good if they try to help, ought not directly to intervene. Can the moral content of this apparently conditional obligation be maintained by an unconditional maxim? The principle might be preserved by invoking the unconditional maxim to preserve and protect human lives as intrinsically valuable ends in themselves, supplemented by Kant's principle that "ought" implies "can," this time reading "can" not as logical possibility but manifest physical ability. The principle itself remains unconditional, but is imposed in applications under particular circumstances on all and only those who have the ability to act in its accord. If I am a qualified physician, then, other things being equal, I am morally obligated to help an accident victim. If I lack the necessary training for a medical procedure, if in that sense I cannot do what is needed, then I am under no direct obligation to become involved beyond calling for others to help.

MORAL MEANS AND THE KANTIAN KINGDOM OF ENDS

Kant provides what might be considered either an alternative formulation or major implication of the categorical imperative. He says that according to the categorical imperative we are to treat all rational beings as *ends in themselves* and never merely as *means to another end*. This is a useful version of the categorical imperative that further facilitates its application in moral decision-making situations. The connections Kant draws are difficult to understand, but he emphasizes the unconditionality of the categorical imperative as a moral command that is supposed to be obeyed as an end in itself, and not for any further reason or to achieve any further end. Since the categorical imperative is a rational principle, Kant argues that the categorical imperative presupposes that the rational will also exists as an end in itself, and not merely as a means available to serve the purpose of achieving any other end. He maintains:

> If then there is to be a supreme practical principle and, as far as the human will is concerned, a categorical imperative, then it must be such that from the conception of what is necessarily an end for everyone because this end is an end in itself it constitutes an objective principle of the will and can hence serve as a prac-

tical law. The ground of such a principle is this: rational nature exists as an end in itself. In this way man necessarily thinks of his own existence; thus far is it a subjective principle of human actions. But in this way also does every other rational being think of his existence on the same time an objective principle, from which, as a supreme practical ground, all laws of the will must be able to be derived. The practical imperative will therefore be the following: Act in such a way that you treat humanity, whether in your own person or in the person of another, always at the same time as an end and never simply as a means. We now want to see whether this can be carried out in practice. (36)

It is interesting to note that Kant does not try to explain why the assumption that rational beings are ends in themselves is the transcendental ground of the categorical imperative. In trying to reconstruct his reasoning, it appears he may have in mind the fact that only a rational being is capable of representing a rational principle, and can only represent a principle as commanding a moral action by the rational will unconditionally as an end in itself if the rational will is itself an end in itself. Why this should be so is not entirely clear, but, again, trying to fill in some of the blanks in Kant's reasoning suggests that perhaps it is because, by virtue of being capable of representing within itself a principle that requires obedience unconditionally as an end in itself rather than merely as a means to another end, the will must itself be an end in itself rather than merely a means to any other end. It is as though the ability to represent such a principle automatically qualifies the rational will as an end in itself.

The further implications of Kant's commitment to the rational will as an end in itself are important in his moral theory. Kant argues in particular that we are morally obligated to treat all rational beings as ends in themselves and never merely as means to another end. This implies that we cannot under any circumstances, according to Kant, use other persons for any purpose without respecting them also as ends in themselves. What this moral injunction entails is in some ways left indeterminate in Kant's discussion. The clear implication is nevertheless that we as moral agents are unconditionally morally obligated to treat all other rational beings as ends in themselves, morally valuable without qualification regardless of whatever else they may do or however they might be useful to us. To give just one example, it would be morally wrong on Kant's interpretation of the categorical imperative, under any circumstances, to subject persons to experimental substances in order to discover what effects or side-effects might result without their knowledge, even under conditions of national emergency when there is a catastrophic threat to the welfare of all other citizens. We show the requisite moral respect to such individuals by not involving them in dangerous situations against their will or without their voluntary participation and informed consent; otherwise, we would just be using them as experimental subjects as means to another end, no matter how important, rather than as ends in themselves.

Kant introduces the concept of a "kingdom of ends," which he explains as a "systematic union" of all rational beings. The *kingdom of ends* in Kant's conception is an ideal that we as moral agents are unconditionally morally obligated by the categorical imperative to try to achieve. It is a moral state of affairs in which all rational beings treat one another with due moral respect, acknowledging one another as deserving of proper moral treatment, and interacting in all things with regard for every person as an end in himself or herself, and never merely instrumentally as a means to another end. If such an ideal could be achieved in the actual personal relationships between all rational beings, then obviously there would be no lying, theft, murder, treason, marital infidelity, war, or any of the other moral infractions that occur in transactions between persons. Kant thereby describes a logical transition from individual personal morality to an ideal social order with extensive familial, legal, and political ramifications:

> For all rational beings stand under the law that each of them should treat himself and all others never merely as means but always at the same time as an end in himself. Hereby arises a systematic union of rational of beings through common objective laws, i.e., a kingdom that may be called a kingdom of ends (certainly only an ideal), inasmuch as these laws have in view the very relation of such beings to one another as ends and means. (39–40)

What makes the ideal social fabric a "kingdom" rather than a democracy in Kant's moral-political philosophy is not merely his deep commitment to the monarchy and aristocracy, personified in the enlightened Enlightenment prince, Frederick the Great of Prussia. The kingdom of ends is a kingdom more specifically and philosophically for Kant because he holds that within the interrelationships of persons who regard themselves and every other rational being as ends in themselves and not merely means to any other end, each person is a sovereign lawgiver. In effect, every rational being in the kingdom of ends is a king. The moral law that each king in the kingdom of ends legislates is not capriciously mandated like those of many ordinary kings in the popular sense. The kingdom of ends is one in which each person accepts, represents, and acknowledges the categorical imperative unconditionally as the moral law by which all rational beings are to live. Kant clarifies the conditions under which a rational moral agent enters as a king into the kingdom of ends:

> A rational being belongs to the kingdom of ends as a member when he legislates in it universal laws while also being himself subject to these laws. He belongs to it as sovereign. The position of the latter can be maintained not merely through the maxims of his will but only if he is a completely independent being without needs and with unlimited power adequate to his will. (40)

The idea that each rational being as moral agent legislates the moral law to be followed in the kingdom of ends and as such is a king among kings in the kingdom of ends turns out to have a deeper implication. Kant directs his attention at last from morality and the metaphysics of morals to the transcendental grounding of the metaphysics of morals at the deepest level of critical investigation into the synthetic *a priori* presuppositions of ethics. The freedom that is assumed by the sovereign kingly participation of every rational moral agent in the Kantian kingdom of ends in Kant's inquiry is finally theorized by Kant as that which makes morals possible and without which moral judgment would be unthinkable. Kant claims that the sovereignty of each moral agent entering into the kingdom of ends by self-prescribing the universal moral law derives from the individual's will, freely choosing to follow the categorical imperative and abide by its implications in treating all rational beings as ends in themselves and never merely as means to an end. Kant pursues the argument in a way that seems surprising until we look more closely at its exact terms:

> Hence morality consists in the relation of all action to that legislation whereby alone a kingdom of ends is possible. This legislation must be found in every rational being and must be able to arise from his will, whose principle then is never to act on any maxim except such as can also be a universal law and hence such as the will can hereby regard itself as at the same time the legislator of universal law. (40)

Kant could hardly make a stronger statement of his basic conclusions in this part of the text. He should be taken literally when he says that morality "consists" in the relation of all actions to "that legislation" through which the kingdom of ends is possible. The legislation Kant speaks of here is the rational will's lawgiving to itself of the unconditional universal moral law expressed by the categorical imperative.

The idea of a kingdom of ends is thus made the sum total and philosophical analysis of the concept of morality. If we consider what is morally obligatory and morally forbidden, the perfect and imperfect moral duties unconditionally required by the categorical imperative, there is a good case to be made in defense of Kant's conclusion that everything involved in morality is packed into the concept of the kingdom of ends. The kingdom of ends includes every moral duty to ourselves and others, from which the transcendental ground of moral philosophy and the metaphysics of morals can supposedly be deduced. As such, it is the indispensable underlying condition for the possibility of all morality, as the free law-giving sovereignty of each rational being participating as a moral agent in the Kantian kingdom of ends.

MORAL AUTONOMY AND HETERONOMY

Kant understands moral judgment as grounded transcendentally in what he designates as the "Autonomy of the Will as the Supreme Principle of Morality." The articulation of this synthetic *a priori* principle, together with all that has led to it in his thinking, is in a sense the final goal of the book. The word *autonomy* in English as in Kant's German derives from a combination of two Greek words, *auto* meaning "self," and *nomos* meaning "law."

The concept of *autonomy* is thus the property of being self-law-ruled. Those who are autonomous give the law to themselves, legislate their own legal or moral principles, rather than having them dictated to them from an external source. The idea of autonomy clearly goes together with Kant's ideal of the kingdom of ends and with the idea of every rational being in the kingdom of ends as a sovereign moral agent, each legislating the universal moral law for his or her own moral conduct in the form of the categorical imperative. If we legislate the moral law to and for ourselves in Kant's theory, then we are *autonomous*, while if we receive the moral law from an outside source other than ourselves, then in Kant's terminology we are *heteronomous*, meaning other-law-ruled.

If the moral law comes from without in Kant's grounding of the metaphysics of morals, then those who are subject to its requirements are not free and hence not sovereign in the moral conduct they undertake, but are rather under the moral jurisdiction of something other than themselves. In particular, in that case, they place themselves under the moral rule of something other than their own reason, and in that sense are not free. Kant explains:

Autonomy of the will is the property that the will has of being a law to itself (independently of any property of the objects of volition). The principle of autonomy is this: Always choose in such a way that in the same volition the maxims of the choice are at the same time present as universal law. That this practical rule is an imperative, i.e., that the will of every rational being is necessarily bound to the rule as a condition, cannot be proved by merely analyzing the concepts contained in it, since it is a synthetic proposition. For proof one would have to go beyond cognition of objects to a critical examination of the subject, i.e., go to a critique of pure practical reason, since this synthetic proposition which commands apodeictically must be capable of being cognized completely *a priori*. This task, however, does not belong to the present section. But that the above principle of autonomy is the sole principle of morals can quite well be shown by mere analysis of the concepts of morality; for thereby the principle of morals is found to be necessarily a categorical imperative, which commands nothing more nor less than this very autonomy. (44–45)

Importantly, Kant distinguishes between volition and autonomy. Reason exercises autonomy when it governs itself rather than being governed by another, by giving the moral law to itself as the principle it wills to follow. This, as Kant rightly remarks, is not at all the same thing as the issue of whether the will is free as opposed to being causally determined by physical events in the world.

As a matter of fact, Kant believes that human moral agents are causally determined rather than contra-causally free in all their actions, or, as we might better say, in all that happens to them. He nevertheless maintains that a rational moral agent is free in the sense of moral autonomy if the agent accepts the universal moral law of the categorical imperative, and is thereby self-law-ruled rather than other-law-ruled. The possibility of a rational moral agent acting autonomously according to a self-given law of moral conduct in the form of the categorical imperative provides the required freedom from external or other-law-rule by a source of moral law other than the moral agent, is sufficient in Kant's view to make morality logically possible, and as such constitutes the underlying transcendental ground of all morality.

Kant describes the "Heteronomy of the Will as the Source of All Spurious Principles of Morality." This is the counterpart of Kant's conclusion that all morality is contained in the concept of the kingdom of ends. What are the heteronomous sources of moral principles that can coerce the will to act in unfree ways? How can the will be ruled in ways that are incompatible with the kind of freedom presupposed by moral judgment? There can be many different kinds of heteronomy, and Kant does not try to offer a complete list or any general principles by which they might all exhaustively be included. The kinds of things Kant has in mind as heteronomous moral principles are indicated by the alternative moral theories against which Kant's formalist deontology stands opposed. High on the list of heteronomous moral principles must be included anything that is not justified by pure reason, including emotion, desire, inclination, or a concern for the psychological consequences of an action, particularly as any of these are connected with what Kant identifies as the universal rational human motivation of happiness, and in general anything that serves conditionally as a means to an end rather than a moral end in itself.

All of the considerations that are typically ranged under the title of self-interest are various ways and means of achieving happiness. The desire for happiness makes the motivation for an action contributing to the attainment of a good, generally, an emotion rather than a matter of pure reason, and hence a heteronomous rather than autonomous source of moral law. Despite the feeling of freedom we might enjoy psychologically when we do what we want, pursuing pleasure or happiness or understanding our moral obligations as linked together as means-to-ends, we are motivated in so acting heteronomously rather than autonomously, according to Kant, and as such, we are not really free and do not satisfy the transcendental grounds of morality. We are in any such case of heteronomous motivation not acting morally according to moral duty, but according to inclination; we are not acting from the moral law but at best and at most merely in accord with moral law.

Even if it should turn out, so to speak, by accident that we do the morally right thing as required by the universal moral law of the categorical imperative, say, refraining from committing suicide, accepting a loan only when we intend to repay, developing our talents and natural abilities, and charitably donating surplus wealth to those in need, we do not do so for the right reason. We are not acting autonomously in that case, but heteronomously. The consequences of our actions might be indistinguishable from the consequences of actions undertaken by autonomous moral agents following the obligations of the categorical imperative, but that is not the point. The consequences of actions, particularly as they contribute to pleasure or displeasure, are altogether morally irrelevant for Kant, the morality of which he maintains is exclusively a function of the intentions and moral attitudes of rational will on the part of rational moral agents, which he believes constitutes the only possible moral justification.

Kant argues that heteronomous motivations for actions, those that obtain when a moral agent goes outside or beyond the resources of the rational will to find a reason to act, can at best issue in a hypothetical imperative that cannot morally justify our conduct, and not in the required categorical imperative. Thus, he writes:

> If the will seeks the law that is to determine it anywhere but in the fitness of its maxims for its own legislation of universal laws, and if it thus goes outside of itself and seeks this law in the character of any of its objects, then heteronomy always results. The will in that case does not give itself the law, but the object does so because of its relation to the will. This relation, whether it rests on inclination or on representations of reason, admits only of hypothetical imperatives: I ought to do something because I will something else. On the other hand, the moral, and hence categorical, imperative says that I ought to act in this way or that way, even though I did not will something else. (45)

The reason for Kant's conclusion should be obvious when we reflect that the categorical imperative is supposed to be an unconditional moral law of pure reason. A hypothetical imperative is always a means-end relation of one sort or another, usually involving a desire or inclination to attain happiness as a good. It commands us conditionally to do something for the sake of securing other values rather than as a good in itself.

Thus, a hypothetical imperative can only justify heteronomously. Its commands are not issued by reason but by emotion or another factor other than reason. It does not autonomously impose obligations on reason, which only reason can do in the form of categorical imperative. The rational will acts autonomously only when it legislates the moral law to and for itself as a principle to follow in trying to attain moral good. Kant maintains that the rational will's autonomous lawgiving remains essentially determinate, and does not in itself prescribe any particular action to be undertaken by a rational moral agent. Here again Kant's deontological ethics is formalist, avoiding specific content or commitment to any particular course of action when considered in its most general terms. All that matters is a morally good will, which Kant repeatedly says is the only thing that is unqualifiedly good, giving to itself and being willing to follow the categorical imperative, representing the universal moral law and thereby making adherence to it a moral duty, regardless of the specifics of its applications. Kant declares:

> An absolutely good will, whose principle must be a categorical imperative, will therefore be indeterminate as regards all objects and will contain merely the form of willing; and indeed that form is autonomy. This is to say that the fitness of the maxims of every good will to make themselves universal laws is itself the only law that the will of every rational being imposes on itself, without needing to assume any incentive or interest as a basis. (48)

KANT ON REASON'S FREEDOM AND MORAL RESPONSIBILITY

To complete the exposition of the transcendental grounding of the metaphysics of morals, Kant establishes a vital connection that we have previously mentioned and must now consider in greater detail. This is the relation between moral autonomy and freedom as an absolute presupposition of morality and the possibility of moral judgment.

The inference is that the will is a special type of causation that brings about changes indirectly through controlled body movements. I can raise my arm, and the movement of my arm can cause unlimitedly many other things to happen that would not otherwise occur. Kant says that the will as a kind of causation is free just in case it can effect its purposes independently of any external causes. This sense of freedom of will is analogous to the concept of free action that is attributed to many things other than the will, and also to inanimate entities, when their movement is unrestricted by anything outside themselves. It is in roughly the same sense that a path is said to be free when there are no obstacles blocking movement along its route, or a flywheel is free when it is unstuck and can spin without hindrance.

The will is free, according to Kant, only when it can function independently. This is to say, only when there is no external impediment to the will's causation. The kind of impediments Kant is thinking about with respect to the free action of the rational will include anything that influences or commands the rational will to act other than the rational will itself. Limitations on the rational will as such are heteronomous motivations that can be expressed as hypothetical imperatives. The will is free, and an agent is morally responsible, only to the extent that reason chooses autonomously. Kant writes:

> The will is a kind of causality belonging to living beings insofar as they are rational; freedom would be the property of this causality that makes it effective independent of any determination by alien causes. Similarly, natural necessity is the property of the causality of all non-rational beings by which they are determined to activity through the influence of alien causes. (49)

Kant denies that freedom of will is lawlessness. He interprets freedom in the morally relevant sense as the autonomy of reason dictating the moral law to itself by accepting a purely rational principle of conduct in the form of the categorical imperative. The freedom-conferring autonomy that makes an agent morally responsible is compatible with the body's natural necessity subject to the laws of physics. Kant argues:

> The concept of causality involves that of laws according to which something that we call cause must entail something else—namely, the effect. Therefore freedom is certainly not lawless, even though it is not a property of will in accordance with laws of nature. It must, rather, be a causality in accordance with immutable laws, which, to be sure, is of a special kind; otherwise a free will would be something absurd. As we have already seen [in the preceding paragraph], natural necessity is a heteronomy of efficient causes, inasmuch as every effect is possible only in accordance with the law that something else determines the efficient cause to exercise its causality. What else, then, can freedom of the will be but autonomy, i.e., the property that the will has of being a law to itself? The proposition that the will is in every action a law to itself expresses, however, nothing but the principle of acting according to no other maxim than that which can at the same time have itself as a universal law for its object. Now this is precisely the formula of the categorical imperative and is the principle of morality. Thus a free will and a will subject to moral laws are one and the same. (49)

Kant holds that freedom in the sense of autonomy is presupposed by the possibility of morality. The categorical imperative is a universal law for all rational beings, and, since its acceptance presupposes autonomy, it follows according to Kant that all rational beings are free and morally responsible. All rational beings are free either to accept and live their lives in accord with the moral law as represented by the categorical imperative, or to renounce morality by rejecting the categorical imperative. Kant distinguishes:

> It is not enough to ascribe freedom to our will, on whatever ground, if we have not also sufficient reason for attributing it to all rational beings. For inasmuch as morality serves as a law for us only insofar as we are rational beings, it must also be valid for all rational beings. And since morality must be derived solely from the property of freedom, one must show that freedom is also the property of the will of all rational beings. It is not enough to prove freedom from certain alleged experiences of human nature (such a proof is indeed absolutely impossible, and so freedom can be proved only *a priori*). Rather, one must show that freedom belongs universally to the activity of rational beings endowed

with a will. Now I say that every being which cannot act in any way other than under the idea of freedom is for this very reason free from a practical point of view. This is to say that for such a being all the laws that are inseparably bound up with freedom are valid just as much as if the will of such a being could be declared to be free in itself for reasons that are valid for theoretical philosophy. (50)

At last Kant announces that he has all the elements of his transcendental inquiry in place from which to derive the grounding of the metaphysics of morals. He claims that the concept of morality presupposes the freedom of will of all rational beings in the sense of the autonomy or self-moral-lawgiving of the rational will, the rational will's sovereignty in legislating for itself the moral principle by which it is to be ruled in the form of the categorical imperative. He identifies the underlying assumption of moral judgment:

We have finally traced the determinate concept of morality back to the idea of freedom, but we could not prove freedom to be something actual in ourselves and in human nature. We saw merely that we must presuppose it if we want to think of a being as rational and as endowed with consciousness of its causality as regards actions, i.e., as endowed with a will. And so we find that on the very same ground we must attribute to every being endowed with reason and a will this property of determining itself to action under the idea of its own freedom. (51)

Kant distinguishes two aspects of the nature of human rational agents. They have simultaneously a sensible nature governed heteronomously by external natural laws, and an internal rational or intelligible nature that is ruled autonomously by the rational will's dictating to itself the principle by which its decisions are determined, in the form of its internal representation and acceptance of the categorical imperative. Kant believes that it is only in this way that the will is capable of acting from and not merely in accord with the moral law. It is thus that the will is able to do what is morally obligatory as a matter of moral duty rather than psychological inclination, even in the guise of the desire to do what is morally right or to achieve the greatest happiness for the greatest number. Kant maintains that there must ultimately be a way to reconcile the freedom presupposed by the possibility of moral judgment, and the determination of body motion by external laws of nature as they affect even conscious volition and the contents of thought. He argues:

There arises from this a dialectic of reason, since the freedom attributed to the will seems to contradict the necessity of nature. And even though at this parting of the ways reason for speculative purposes finds the road of natural necessity much better worn and more serviceable than that of freedom, yet for practical purposes the footpath of freedom is the only one upon which it is possible to make use of reason in our conduct. Therefore, it is just as impossible for the most subtle philosophy as for the most ordinary human reason to argue away freedom. Hence philosophy must assume that no real contradiction will be found between freedom and natural necessity in the same human actions, for it cannot give up the concept of nature any more than that of freedom. (56)

Kant's reasoning is transcendental. We begin with the fact of moral judgment as something given to experience. We know that we make moral decisions. Kant asks what must be true in order for such moral judgments to be possible. Since the possibility of morality presupposes the freedom of the rational will, we know with the full confidence of transcendental inference that rational moral agents are free. The only question is whether and in what sense the freedom of the rational will is logically compatible with the physical determination of the will by its heteronomous control by natural law.

Kant concludes that there must be a dialectic in which these apparent conflicts of freedom and unfreedom are reconciled. The solution is reminiscent of Descartes's mind-body distinction, although Kant unlike Descartes does not maintain that there is an essential difference between physical and spiritual substances. The difference between the rational will's freedom through its sovereign autonomous legislation of the categorical imperative, and the heteronomous determination of the physical nature of the human will as psychological rather than purely rational, is all that Kant believes he needs in order to sustain his dialectical reconciliation of free will and determinism in grounding the metaphysics of morals. By securing a relevant appropriate sense of freedom at the transcendental foundations of morality, despite the physical determinism of other aspects of rational will, Kant explains the metaphysical presuppositions of moral judgment that make possible in the same way the moral responsibility of rational moral agents for their decisions and actions.

If Kant is right, then he has explained the morality of actions deontologically, in terms of the intentions and states of mind of a moral decision maker. He thus avoids defining morality in terms of an action's consequences or psychological motivations. Kant's discussion of the grounding of the metaphysics of morals finally brings him back full circle to the observation with which his transcendental inquiry began, with the analysis of a good will as the only unqualifiedly good thing:

> We can now end where we started in the beginning, viz., the concept of an unconditionally good will. That will is absolutely good which cannot be evil, i.e., whose maxim, when made into a universal law, can never conflict with itself. This principle is therefore also its supreme law: Act always according to that maxim whose universality as a law you can at the same time will. This is the only condition under which a will can never be in conflict with itself, and such an imperative is categorical. Inasmuch as the validity of the will as a universal law for possible actions is analogous to the universal connection of the existence of things in accordance with universal laws, which is the formal aspect of nature in general, the categorical imperative can also be expressed thus: Act according to maxims which can at the same time have for their object themselves as universal laws of nature. Thus, then, the formula for an absolutely good will is constituted. (42)

The theory of a good will as the only unqualified good requires an analysis of the concept. What does it mean for the will to be good? If the morality of actions is not judged by their consequences, since we cannot always predict the consequences of our actions, and since intuitively evil actions sometimes turn out accidentally to have beneficial results, we must try to say what is required of a good will.

Kant returns to this difficult question only after he has tried to explain the logic of the categorical imperative. He first explores the categorical imperative's implications for treating all rational beings as ends in themselves in a kingdom of ends, rather than merely as means to an end, and uncovers the transcendental ground of morality as the sovereign autonomy of the rational will to self-legislate the categorical imperative as universal moral law. The morally good will in Kant's deontological ethics is the autonomous rational intent to accept the categorical imperative as its basis for morality. It is only in this way, Kant believes, that we can act from rather than merely in accord with the moral law, that we can act dutifully rather than through mere desire or inclination, and that we can act freely, regardless of the moral status of what we do. It is only in this way, therefore, if Kant is right, that we can act morally at all.

The Kantian ideal of the kingdom of ends posits an imaginary realm in which all rational beings act morally according to the principles he has articulated in all personal and social interrelations with others. If the kingdom of ends were to be achieved, it is clear, everyone would treat everyone else with the utmost moral respect, and there would be no immoral conduct as Kant understands the concept.

SUMMARY

Kant's grounding of the metaphysics of morals lays rationalist foundations for ethics. Kant disavows all empirical elements in ethics, which he believes constitute theoretical impurities. When ethics is purged of empirical ingredients, Kant stands ready to reject all consequentialist morality based on the experience of pleasure or inclination. Kant is so convinced of the distinction between ethics and any empirical facts that he argues we cannot be known to act morally correctly when there is any possibility of a conflicting motivation of desire. He formulates this conclusion in the thesis that the only thing that is unqualifiedly good is a good will.

Kant's transcendental methodology is meant to overcome both the dogmatism of rationalism and the skepticism of empiricism. He achieves a synthesis of these two philosophical methodologies in his critical idealism. Kant's technique of transcendental reasoning begins with a given and asks what must be true in order for what is given to be possible. The answer to a Kantian transcendental question identifies synthetic *a priori* judgments that Kant says constitute the proper subject matter of metaphysics. He applies the same mode of reasoning to ethical problems in the transcendental grounding of the metaphysics of morals. He distinguishes between hypothetical imperatives and the categorical imperative as the one and only purely rational principle of ethics. The categorical imperative states that we are to act always according to that moral maxim that we can will to be a universal principle of conduct for all rational beings. In four applications, Kant makes it clear that violations of the categorical imperative involve moral maxims or special rules of conduct that we cannot will to be followed universally, because when we try to do so we encounter logical contradictions. The enforcement of the categorical imperative by logical consistency and inconsistency is what makes Kant's deontology a purely formal rationalist ethics purged of empirical factors.

Kant distinguishes between moral autonomy and heteronomy. Autonomy is self-governance or self-rule, and heteronomy is governance by something other than and outside the self. Kant's transcendental grounding of the metaphysics of morals identifies freedom in the sense of moral autonomy as presupposed by the possibility of moral responsibility. Moral autonomy is achieved when reason gives the moral law to itself, as when a rational agent accepts the categorical imperative. Moral heteronomy as something inconsistent with the requirements of moral responsibility occurs when a moral law is given to reason by something other than reason outside itself, such as passion, emotion, inclination, or empirical considerations of such psychological factors as pleasure.

QUESTIONS FOR PHILOSOPHICAL UNDERSTANDING

1. What does Kant mean by transcendental reasoning?

2. What does Kant mean by the category of synthetic *a priori* propositions as the proper subject matter of metaphysics?

3. How is Kant's transcendental method supposed to overcome the dogmatism of rationalism and the skepticism of radical empiricism?

4. What is Kant's philosophical justification for the conclusion of a transcendental inference?

5. Is Kant's transcendental metaphysics an alternative to or just another special form of rationalism?

6. Why does Kant claim that the only thing that is unqualifiedly good is a good will?

7. Why does Kant disregard the inclination to do good as morally irrelevant?

8. Why does Kant think it is important to establish the transcendental grounding of the metaphysics of morals? What does he mean by this? Why can we not simply develop a theory of ethics without a metaphysics or grounding of a metaphysics of morals?

9. What is Kant's distinction between hypo-

thetical imperatives and the categorical imperative?

10. Are Kant's four applications of the categorical imperative convincing? Why, in each case, or why not?

11. What is a moral maxim? What does Kant mean by universalizing a moral maxim?

12. How does Kant's categorical imperative relate to his principle that we are always to treat all rational beings with moral respect as ends in themselves and never merely instrumentally as means to an end?

13. What is the difference between treating someone as an end in himself or herself rather than merely as a means to an end? What is required when we treat a person as a means to an end so as not to treat the person merely as a means to an end?

14. What does Kant mean by the distinction between moral autonomy and heteronomy?

15. Why does Kant argue that moral autonomy is necessary for the possibility of moral obligation and moral responsibility? How is Kant's discussion of moral autonomy related to his application of transcendental reasoning to the transcendental metaphysics of morals?

KEY TERMS

acting from moral law

acting in accord with moral law

analytic judgment

apodeictic judgment

a posteriori judgment

a priori judgment

Aristotelian distinction between formal and material sciences

categorical imperative

consequentialism

critical idealism

deontology

dogmatism

formal, material, and legislative styles of characterizing the categorical imperative

formal or formalist ethical system

four applications of the categorical imperative

freedom

given

good will

hypothetical imperative

inclination

instrumental value

internal representation of the moral law

intrinsic value

kingdom of ends

manifold of experience

moral autonomy

moral duty, moral obligation

moral heteronomy

moral judgment

morally good will

moral maxim

moral responsibility

normative philosophy

"ought" implies "can" principle

possible pure will

practical anthropology

practical cognition

presupposition

prudential consideration

purely moral consideration

rational will

skepticism

Stoic philosophy

synthetic a priori judgment

synthetic judgment

transcendental ground of morals

transcendental ground of science

transcendental reasoning

typic

universalizability

universalizable moral maxim

unqualified good

SOURCES AND RECOMMENDED READINGS

Acton, H. B. *Kant's Moral Philosophy*. New York: St. Martin's Press, 1970.

Allison, Henry E. *Idealism and Freedom: Essays on Kant's Theoretical and Practical Philosophy*. New York: Cambridge University Press, 1996.

Atwell, John E. *Ends and Principles in Kant's Moral Thought*. Dordrecht-Boston: M. Nijhoff, 1986.

Aune, Bruce. *Kant's Theory of Morals*. Princeton: Princeton University Press, 1979.

O'Neill, Onora. *Constructions of Reason: Explorations of Kant's Practical Philosophy*. Cambridge: Cambridge University Press, 1989.

Paton, H. J. *The Categorical Imperative: A Study in Kant's Moral Philosophy.* New York: Harper & Row, 1967.

Ross, W. D. *Kant's Ethical Theory: A Commentary on the Grundlegung zur Metaphysik der Sitten.* Oxford: Clarendon Press, 1954.

Stratton-Lake, Philip. *Kant, Duty, and Moral Worth.* London: Routledge, 2000.

Sullivan, Roger J. *Immanuel Kant's Moral Theory.* Cambridge: Cambridge University Press, 1989.

Williams, T. C. *The Concept of the Categorical Imperative: A Study of the Place of the Categorical Imperative in Kant's Ethical Theory.* Oxford: Clarendon Press, 1968.

Wood, Allen W. *Kant's Ethical Thought.* Cambridge: Cambridge University Press, 1999.

CHAPTER 7

CONSEQUENCES OF ACTIONS IN ETHICAL CONDUCT

Mill's *Utilitarianism*

Mill presents an interesting alternative to Kant's moral philosophy. Mill's utilitarianism is a form of consequentialism that bases moral value on the consequences of actions with respect to the pleasure or happiness versus pain or unhappiness that they produce. As such, Mill's consequentialist utilitarianism is in direct opposition to Kant's deontology. Mill's utilitarianism is a kind of ethical empiricism whereas Kant's deontology is a kind of ethical rationalism. As such, their differences illustrate the rationalism-empiricism dichotomy projected into the moral domain. Mill explains utilitarianism as a theory that interprets moral value in terms of the usefulness of an action in promoting the greatest good interpreted as pleasure for the greatest number.

UTILITARIAN ETHICS

A very different approach to the problems of ethics is represented by the philosophy of John Stuart Mill (1806–1873). Mill's influential booklet *Utilitarianism* (1861) is in some ways the antithesis of Kant's *Grounding for the Metaphysics of Morals.* Mill does not share Kant's transcendental methodology, and disagrees with Kant's moral philosophy on virtually all of its most fundamental principles. It would be hard to find two thinkers more diametrically opposed to one another in their approaches to the problems of ethics. The differences between Mill and Kant, moreover, are highly instructive; we acquire a better sense of the positions each develops and of extremes among alternatives in moral theory by comparing and contrasting their respective views.

Mill is a *utilitarian.* The word derives from "utility," meaning usefulness. A utilitarian ethics is a theory of moral philosophy that emphasizes the consequences of actions, and evaluates their morality according to their usefulness in contributing to a given purpose. Mill's ethics is therefore consequentialist, in the sense explained in the previous chapter. As the name implies, to be a consequentialist is to understand the moral dimensions of decisions and actions in terms of their consequences. Utility as Mill defines the concept concerns a particular way of thinking about the consequences of what people do, and in particular the usefulness of their actions in contributing to or subtracting from the total amount of resulting happiness and pleasure in the world. Kant, we have seen, regards the consequences of actions as morally irrelevant, and establishes moral value instead on the basis of the intentions and motives of individual agents, recognizing that only a good will is unqualifiedly good. Mill, in contrast, explicitly maintains that moral attitude is altogether irrelevant to the ethical worth of an agent's acts. He argues that what matters is only the effects that are brought about or reasonably expected to occur as the result of an action.

The question for any consequentialist is to explain how the consequences of actions are related to moral value. An action and the agent who performs the action are morally good or bad, according to consequentialism, depending on the action's effects. What effects of an action make the action good, and what effects make it bad? Different consequentialists answer this question in different ways. Mill meets the challenge by defining utilitarian moral value in terms of pleasure and happiness. The utility or usefulness of an action, by which an action acquires positive moral value in Mill's utilitarianism, is its promotion of happiness, and more specifically of greater happiness than unhappiness, since many actions are mixed in the psychological effects of their consequences. Mill further interprets happiness more specifically as the experience of pleasure. Although Mill does not use this terminology, his particular brand of consequentialism, adapting a Greek word, is a version of *hedonistic* utilitarianism.

Consequentialism as such need not be utilitarian, and utilitarianism need not be pleasure-oriented or hedonistic. Mill makes both of these choices in the development of his ethics. Mill's utilitarianism implies that an action is morally justified as morally obligatory if and only if it tends to promote more happiness than unhappiness. The utility or usefulness of an action according to Mill is its value in producing more pleasure than pain or displeasure. We must try to see how and why Mill proposes this type of moral philosophy, to understand his solution to objections to the theory and efforts to defend it against criticisms, his opposition to Kant's formalist deontology, and the exploration of utilitarianism's practical implications in moral decision making, individual virtue, political interaction and social policy, and the concepts of justice and moral rights.

GREATEST HAPPINESS PRINCIPLE

The roots of Mill's utilitarianism go back to Aristotle's theory of the morally happy life articulated in *Nicomachean Ethics*. Aristotle's concept of happiness or *eudaimonia* advises individuals to perfect their virtues so as achieve their natural function as social beings through the highest type of friendship. Mill's moral philosophy is not primarily concerned with Aristotle's concept of personal happiness, nor with moral happiness in the sense of fulfilling the natural social function by which human beings are defined as a biological species. There are nevertheless important similarities between Aristotle and Mill in their general philosophical methodologies and ethical outlooks.

Mill, like Aristotle, is an empiricist, taking his philosophical orientation from sense experience rather than pure reason. Aristotle, Ockham, Berkeley, and Mill, despite significant differences, are fellow travelers in their overall philosophical ideology, by contrast with Plato, Descartes, and Kant. Mill, in some ways, is even more empiricist than Aristotle, although he is not an idealist like Berkeley. Mill nevertheless believes that philosophy depends for its truths ultimately on empirical experience, and, in rough agreement with Aristotle, he regards happiness as the standard of utility by which the consequences of actions are to be morally appraised. Whereas Aristotle is largely indifferent to the happiness of moral agents as an occurrent psychological state, or to happiness in the sense of an experience of pleasure or joy, Mill understands happiness in precisely these terms as a psychological state of pleasure. As we shall see, Mill does not limit pleasure to sensual pleasures only, although these are also meant to be included, but recognizes the extent of pleasure for human beings as featuring especially intellectual pleasures of many different kinds, and sources of distinctively human noble pleasurable satisfactions that go far beyond what Mill speaks of as "swinish" pig pleasures, in the sense of base pleasures that often come to mind in thinking of the word "pleasure."

The strength of Mill's hedonistic pleasure-oriented ethics is its connection with the motivations that seem naturally to govern human actions commonly approved of as morally justified. Mill can point to the fact that we ordinarily describe actions as infractions of morality when and because they cause pain or frustrate the normal and natural desires of beings capable of pleasure. Is this not, Mill or a defender of utilitarianism might reasonably ask, what makes murder morally objectionable, and lying and theft, and treason, marital infidelity, cheating on exams and taxes and in business transactions, and the like, insofar as these acts are deemed unethical? Why else are they morally wrong than for the fact that they cause displeasure and do not contribute to pleasure? If, by comparison, we consider the kinds of things we judge morally praiseworthy, these acts generally involve effects that contribute to happiness, to persons being happier than they would otherwise be if the actions were not undertaken. When we help people, we generally make the world a better place by promoting their happiness, thereby, in Mill's sense of the term, doing something useful, beneficial, or utilitarian. The ends of happiness are served when we teach a child or adult to read, donate to a worthy charity, cure a disease, enact legislation that protects persons physically and prevents misery, and even when we do such things as observing traffic laws to minimize accidents, injury, and loss of life or destruction of property, and of any of the practices we follow to make everyone's lives better, more rich and satisfying, and, in a word, happier in the sense of pleasure.

Mill's utilitarianism is a commonsense morality. While Kant denies that inclination provides a legitimate motivation for morality, Mill accepts the psychological basis of ethical judgment as a reason for acting and a guide to what we as moral agents ought and ought not to do. According to Mill, we ought to do whatever promotes happiness, or, recognizing the complexity of most of our actions, it is perhaps more accurate to say that Mill's utilitarianism prescribes that we are morally obligated to do whatever promotes more overall happiness than unhappiness, when the two are mixed together as opposing consequences of the same act.

As an example, consider the choice about whether or not to have an operation in order to relieve a medical ailment. The surgery obviously is not a desirable thing in and of itself; few people if any would choose to undergo an operation for its own sake. It is usually expensive, there is psychological trauma involved, and in most instances at least some pain later during recovery, not to mention the time taken away from other potentially more pleasurable activities. As a rule, there is a considerable amount of displeasure involved in surgery. If a person decides to have an operation, therefore, it is not as an unconditional or unmixed blessing, but is usually chosen because it is judged that in the end the overall result will be to produce more happiness than unhappiness—and, we might also say with Mill, more pleasure than displeasure or pain. A necessary operation might save one's life or help to avoid future pain, or make it possible to maintain better body functioning leading to a more active and in that sense happier life. This, commonsense tells us, would be a good thing, even a morally good thing, and hence the morally preferred action under the circumstances.

Mill can offer this kind of example in support of his conclusion that moral value is generally a matter of acting in such a way as to maximize the resultant amount of happiness in the sense of pleasure over unhappiness in the sense of displeasure or pain. Mill believes not only that happiness in the sense of pleasure generally motivates our actions, but that it ought to do so, as the only legitimate foundation of morality. It is much in keeping with Mill's empiricism that he begins and ends with the psychological experience of pleasure as the standard of morality. We are to do what brings pleasure and avoids unnecessary pain, morally obligated to act in such a way that we maximize happiness and minimize unhappiness. This is a psychological, and hence empirical, experiential basis for moral judgment, appropriate to Mill's philosophical outlook. As further empirical evidence for utilitarianism, Mill's thesis draws on the observable fact that when we think and talk about ethical problems, and when we judge the actions of ourselves and others, we often make reference to the happiness or unhappiness an action causes or is expected or intended to cause. We also usually interpret happiness as Mill does in terms of pleasure of one sort or another and unhappiness as displeasure or pain.

Unlike Aristotle, again, and unexpectedly more like Kant, Mill argues that the resulting happiness by which the morality of actions is to be judged is not the happiness or pleasure of any single person. Mill, unlike Aristotle, is not a perfectionistic *moral egoist* (not the same as being an egotist, which is to say an arrogant self-important personality type). Mill subscribes to the thesis that the morality of an action is a function of the total resulting happiness produced in the world as a whole, as it affects every psychological subject capable of experiencing pleasure and pain. It is not just the agent's happiness or pleasure that matters, according to Mill, but the happiness or pleasure of every sentient being capable of being affected by the agent's action or contemplated action. If we accept Mill's utilitarianism, then we are not concerned exclusively or even primarily with our own happiness, but with the happiness or unhappiness, pleasure or pain, of every sentient being potentially affected by an action's outcome. The utilitarian principle that Mill maintains is that the measure of the morality of an action is the pleasure or pain it produces or is judged likely to produce for all psychological subjects. The agent is not supposed either to discount or attach any special value to his or her own happiness, but to treat the expected resultant happiness or unhappiness of a contemplated action as it might affect each and every individual. It is the sum total of happiness or unhappiness, pleasure or displeasure and pain that determines whether an action is morally justified or unjustified, morally obligatory, forbidden, or indifferent.

This statement of utilitarian ethics is known as the *greatest good principle,* or *principle of the greatest good for the greatest number.* The idea is that we are to act in such a way that our actions produce the greatest happiness for the greatest percentage of sentient beings, treating each as one and none as more than one. This formulation was first made by a utilitarian philosopher who preceded Mill, Jeremy Bentham, in his (1789) book *An Introduction to the Principles of Morals and Legislation.* Bentham was a close personal friend of Mill's father, James Mill, who was also a utilitarian moral philosopher, but whose writings on ethics did not have as powerful an impact on the history of philosophy and the course of social policy as that of his son, John Stuart Mill. Mill was reared and educated in an environment of family and friends that was strongly imbued with utilitarian ideals. We find an account of these influences, and the pressures they exerted on Mill's psyche, in his fascinating intellectual *Autobiography* (1867). Bentham argues, and Mill evidently agrees, that the principle of the greatest good for the greatest number implies that moral agents such as ourselves also have moral obligations toward nonhuman animals, provided only that they are capable of experiencing pleasure and pain. Mill identifies the principle of utility with the greatest happiness principle, which he attributes to Bentham:

> Although the non-existence of an acknowledged first principle has made ethics not so much a guide as a consecration of men's actual sentiments, still, as men's sentiments, both of favour or aversion, are greatly influenced by what they suppose to be the effects of things upon their happiness, the principle of utility, or, as Bentham latterly called it, the greatest happiness principle, has had a large share in forming the moral doctrines even of those who most scornfully reject its authority. Nor is there any school of thought which refuses to admit that the influence of actions on happiness is a most material and even predominant consideration in many of the details of morals, however unwilling to acknowledge it as the fundamental principle of morality and the source of moral obligation. (5)

The greatest good for the greatest number is not only not limited to the happiness or unhappiness, pleasure or pain and displeasure, of the agent personally, but is not even restricted, according to Bentham and Mill, to human beings. If we accept utilitarianism as a moral theory, then our moral obligations and prohibitions extend beyond our species to include all sentient beings. We must then consider the likely impact of our actions on the total happiness or unhappiness that follows as the predictable result of what we do on all psychological subjects capable of experiencing pleasure or pain, regardless of their species. Their pleasure and pain must also be included in calculating the utility of a contemplated action in deciding whether it is morally justified or unjustified on utilitarian grounds. Mill regards humanitarian attitudes toward the treatment of nonhuman animals as ultimately justified by at least an intuitive grasp of and moral commitment to the general principle of utility.

Consider the question of whether or not to allow lumbering in a certain wooded lot. Insofar as the morality of the decision is at issue, the question is supposed to be evaluated in Mill's utilitarian framework as a matter not only of how the decision would affect people, the happiness or unhappiness, pleasure or pain, that will accrue to the human beings affected, including workers in the lumber industry, persons who need wood products, the economy in general that might be improved or diminished by a decision to permit or forbid lumbering, and the way in which the action might have an impact on the ecology that could affect other people over a wider sphere, both in the short term and the long run. A utilitarian ethics must also consider the effect of proposed lumbering on the animal population living in the woods and elsewhere insofar as they might be positively or negatively affected in the quality of their lives, the happiness they might enjoy or the pain they might suffer as a result. If we are truly to consider the consequences of our actions on all sentient beings, then we must take into account their potential effects on animals too, also treating each as one and none as more than one, while taking into account the real psychological differences in the quality of and degree to which each is capable of experiencing pleasure or pain.

The utilitarian principle of the greatest good for the greatest number is democratic in important ways. The thesis that we are to treat all sentient beings as one, so to speak, as having one vote or requiring collective consideration for the effects of an action on each individual psychological subject of pleasure or pain, as we have seen, brings nonhuman as well as human beings into the realm of moral concern. The thesis that we are not to treat any sentient being as more than one establishes a kind of sovereign utilitarian moral equality in moral decision making.

To appreciate the importance of this part of Mill's ethics, we should recall its historical situation. At the time when the utilitarians were writing, much of Europe was a monarchy, even if a constitutional parliamentary monarchy of one sort or another, in which an aristocracy had ruled for so long that its members were considered to have special privileges and to have interests of greater value and importance than those of ordinary untitled citizens who were not of royal descent.

Imagine entering a court of law in a conflict with members of an aristocratic house, in which the cards are all stacked in their favor, in which it is virtually impossible to obtain justice if you are considered a "commoner." The assumption is always that a person of royalty has more legal and moral as well as societal standing, that their interests should carry more weight than those of anyone else. Bentham and Mill's utilitarian principle of treating each sentient being as one and none as more than one, by opposing the idea that privileged classes have inherently greater moral interests, was socially and politically revolutionary. What matters for Mill is not whether a person is a member of royalty or not, which from the standpoint of utilitarianism is altogether morally irrelevant, but only whether the subjects involved are equally capable of happiness or unhappiness, interpreted as the capacity for pleasure or pain, along with the facts about how the decision would affect their happiness or lack thereof, along with that of every other sentient being that might be affected by the action. The principle, again as Bentham formulated it, is that the interests of all sentient beings are to be treated as equally important; each is to be counted as one and none as more than one in tallying up the total happiness or unhappiness, pleasure or pain, that is to result from an action, social policy, or judicial decision.

CONSEQUENTIALISM VERSUS DEONTOLOGY: MILL'S OBJECTION TO KANT'S CATEGORICAL IMPERATIVE

Mill regards happiness construed as pleasure as the basis for morality. Kant also recognizes that happiness and the inclination toward and desire for happiness is the primary motive for human action. Kant, however, disapproves of happiness as a genuinely moral justification, which he thinks has nothing to do with morality in the true sense of the word. Inclination, for Kant, as we have seen, is no part of the morally good will, which is supposed to be moved exclusively by reason and the acceptance of moral duty represented within the rational will in the form of the categorical imperative. Mill, on the contrary, as a consequentialist, offers a utilitarian critique of the categorical imperative.

Clearly, Mill thinks it is necessary to distance himself from Kant's deontology, and from transcendental investigations of the grounding of the metaphysics of morals. Kant's moral theory was well known and widely received in Mill's day. Writing in the nineteenth century, approximately one hundred years after Kant, it is incumbent on Mill to explain why he does not agree with Kant, and why he finds it necessary to adopt a radically different approach to moral philosophy. Part of the justification for introducing a new theory of ethics is the failure of a well-established but objectionable prior theory that stands in the way of the alternative morality Mill believes is preferable to Kant's formalism. The effect of Mill's objection to Kant is to distinguish the two theories, and, if Mill is correct, to show that in the large-scale philosophical conflict between utilitarian consequentialism and Kantian deontology, utilitarianism is the only real choice. Mill's reasoning is that Kant's deontology is not an alternative to consequentialism, because, in order to arrive at plausible conclusions, deontology as much as consequentialism equally depends on considerations of the greatest good. If Mill is right, then even Kant's moral philosophy, insofar as it reaches morally correct conclusions, is also ultimately utilitarian.

Mill's objection is presented in general terms, although he obviously has Kant's theory specifically in mind, and soon mentions it by name. The criticism is that in trying to apply the categorical imperative, Kant claims that the implications of his moral system are determined in a purely formalistic way by noncontradiction, and that actions morally prohibited by the categorical imperative are identified by logical inconsistency. According to Mill, the contradictions Kant proposes to discover in the case of actions forbidden by the categorical imperative do not really exist, and the attempt to uncover concealed contradictions in such situations is a mere show. What actually does the work of establishing moral inferences in Kant's applications of the categorical imperative, Mill suggests, is a tacit appeal to utilitarian consequentialist values. Mill begins by paying homage to the importance of Kant's moral philosophy, and then proceeds to explain what he finds incorrect:

> I might go much further and say that to all those *a priori* moralists who deem it necessary to argue at all, utilitarian arguments are indispensable. It is not my present purpose to criticise these thinkers; but I cannot help referring, for illustration, to a systematic treatise by one of the most illustrious of them, the *Metaphysics of Ethics* by Kant. This remarkable man, whose system of thought will long remain one of the landmarks in the history of philosophical speculation, does, in the treatise in question, lay down a universal first principle as the origin and ground of moral obligation; it is this:—"So act that the rule on which thou actest would admit of being adopted as a law by all rational beings." But when he begins to deduce from this precept any of the actual duties of morality, he fails, almost grotesquely, to show that there would be any contradiction; any logical (not to say physical) impossibility, in the adoption by all rational beings of the most

outrageously immoral rules of conduct. All he shows is that the *consequences* of their universal adoption would be such as no one would choose to incur. (5–6)

In the end, Mill might have a valid point. There is, unfortunately, an inaccuracy in his criticism that should first be addressed. Kant's categorical imperative, as previous discussion has emphasized, is not limited to the irrationality, inconsistency, or logical impossibility in the actual adoption by all rational beings of any moral maxim. Kant could and probably would agree that there is no contradiction in the supposition that all rational beings might adopt even what Mill calls "the most outrageously immoral rules of conduct." What the categorical imperative prohibits is any practical maxim or rule of conduct that cannot consistently be willed by an agent to be universally adopted as a moral law by all rational beings. There is an enormous difference between the question of whether a rule of conduct could logically be adopted by every rational being, on the one hand, and whether a subject contemplating a certain course of action could logically consistently will that every rational being adopt the maxim by which the action is to be justified.

The confusion is crucial for Mill's criticism, and indicates that he may have badly misunderstood Kant's ethics. It is also a sign of how little Mill is in sympathy with Kant's categorical imperative. An agent can consistently will things that cannot consistently occur, and presumably states of affairs can consistently occur which no agent can consistently will to occur. One can, without inconsistency or contradiction, for example, will that the measure of every diagonal of every square be a whole number or fraction of whole numbers. There is no logical impossibility about one's willing such a thing, and the will does not thereby lapse into inconsistency or contradiction. As the followers of Pythagoras showed in the time of Greek mathematics, however, the unit square is an exception, so that it is not possible for the diagonal of every square to be a whole number or fraction of whole numbers. Similarly, it is possible for every rational being to commit suicide or will to commit suicide. Kant does not deny this, but rather asserts that it is not possible on pain of logical contradiction for anyone to will that every rational being adopt a universal rule of ethical conduct based on considerations of self-love that sanctions suicide. Mill's objection fails to defeat Kant's categorical imperative, because it projects only the possibility of all rational beings adopting an immoral rule of conduct, not the possibility of consistently willing that all rational beings adopt such a rule.

Mill nevertheless has located an apparent difficulty, a weakness in the categorical imperative, that threatens to dilute and pervert its evident ethical intent and its central role in Kant's grounding of the metaphysics of morals. The objection needs to be more carefully stated, but in that form it is directly related to Mill's explicit assertion, and in this form poses a serious problem for Kant's theory. When Kant claims that by the categorical imperative we are to act only according to that maxim which at the same time we can will to become a universal law for all rational beings, he undoubtedly means to emphasize "can" as the operative term. Mill allows the possibility implied by Kant's use of "can" to be either logical or physical. However, since Kant is elaborating the foundations for a purely rationalist system of ethics, in which empirical contingencies have no place, it appears more appropriate to regard "can" as signifying logical rather than *nomic* possibility within the constraints of natural law. To be justified in any action, a deed must be warranted by the agent's acting from a maxim of moral conduct which the agent can logically consistently will to be practiced by all rational beings.

What, therefore, can we say in conclusion about Mill's criticism of Kant's categorical imperative? Although Mill misinterprets Kant's principle in an important respect, is it nevertheless true that Kant's efforts to apply the principle are all sham, and that Kant relies only on considerations of utility dressed up as implications of the categorical imperative? From Mill's perspective, beginning with his misunderstanding precisely how the categorical imperative is supposed to work, he cannot imagine any other justifications for the moral judgments Kant defends as implications of the principle other than the utility or disutility of an action's consequences. If Mill's objections depend on such a serious mischaracterization of Kant's theory, then he might not be right to hold that Kant's only resort is to fall back on the utility or disutility of an action or its psychological consequences for the world's total amount of happiness or unhappiness, pleasure or displeasure and pain.

On Mill's behalf, by way of upholding his objection to Kant, it might still be said that the criticism is warranted to the extent that it is implausible to specify a contradiction or logical inconsistency or incompatibility in the rational will's efforts to universalize a moral maxim in the case of considered actions that are supposed to be prohibited by the categorical imperative. Kant, to be candid, is more convincing in this regard in some applications of the principle than in others. Where there is no clearcut contradiction in trying rationally to will the universalization of a moral maxim,

TABLE 7.1 *Comparison of Mill's and Kant's Moral Philosophy*

Mill	Kant
Empiricist	Critical idealist (rationalist)
Nontranscendental	Transcendental
Consequentialist	Deontological
Nonformalist ethics	Formalist ethics
Psychological (anthropological)	Nonpsychological (nonanthropological)
*Happiness is recognized as a motivation for action	*Happiness is recognized as a motivation for action
Nothing Is morally unqualifiedly good	Morally good will is the only unqualifiedly good thing
Means-ends relations are morally salient	Means-ends relations are morally irrelevant
Inclination and desire are morally salient	Inclination and desire are morally irrelevant
Happiness is morally salient	Happiness is morally irrelevant
Moral attitude and will are morally irrelevant	Moral attitude and will are morally salient
Greatest good for greatest number	Categorical imperative (moral duty)
Utility of actions or rules	Justice and moral rights
Moral rights can be overridden by utility	Moral rights are absolute and can never be overridden
Social collectivity is justified by utility	Kingdom of Ends

there it may be tempting as Mill argues to suppose that Kant, despite his official explanations, is actually making use of utilitarian reasoning to decide what is morally permitted or morally forbidden, and then dressing it up in the language of the categorical imperative.

The major differences between Mill's utilitarianism and Kant's deontology are presented in Table 7.1. Here we list some of the disagreements we have already described, and anticipate others yet to be explained throughout the chapter. The chart thereby serves as a preview of the main points of opposition between Mill and Kant. The asterisk indicates the only item of theoretical agreement among these two philosophers singled out for consideration, concerning their agreement that happiness is the main motivation for human action.

PLEASURE AS MORAL GOOD

The centerpiece of Mill's utilitarianism is the thesis that pleasure is happiness, and that happiness is the moral good. The implication is that pleasure is good, which as we have said is a form of hedonism. Mill's ethics is not hedonistic in the sense of promoting only individual egoistic pleasure, but of the greatest pleasure for every sentient being. The equation of morality with pleasure is nevertheless bound to seem controversial. Mill is aware of the problem, and goes to considerable lengths to anticipate and answer objections, to make as strong a case as he can for his utilitarian version of consequentialism.

Mill begins by observing that ultimate ends or final purposes cannot be proved. He maintains in effect that moral justification depends on undemonstrated moral values. The model is like that found in mathematics, in which theorems are derived from axioms, while axioms are assumed without proof as intuitively true. We must start somewhere in trying to offer demonstrations of any conclusion, and Mill is right to hold that not everything can be proved, on the grounds that whatever is proved must be proved from something else. There is a chain of inferences that extend backward through intermediary results, building on previous conclusions, but ultimately reaching down to propositions, truths, or values that are not themselves proved. The ends to which all actions are directed, Mill argues, like axioms in mathematics, have the status of ultimate unprovable truths. The final purposes of action, by which actions are to be morally evaluated, are to be identified as undemonstrably good. Mill explains that:

> Questions of ultimate ends are not amenable to direct proof. Whatever can be proved to be good must be so by being shown to be a means to something admitted to be good without proof. (6)

Whereas Kant claims that means-ends relations are irrelevant to pure moral philosophy and the metaphysics of morals, Mill maintains that there is no other place to look for ultimate moral values. The method he proposes is one in which we consider means-ends relations and distinguish those in which all means point to the same end. We cannot directly prove the ultimate ends of action; yet we can recognize the ends or purposes to which actions are directed as means, which, by definition, are the values for the sake of which actions are undertaken. If we want to understand the good that moral agents strive to achieve, we must consider their actions and their goals, linking means to intermediate ends and finally to ultimate ends or an ultimate end. Mill, as we have remarked, agrees in general terms with Aristotle and Kant that all actions are directed toward the ultimate end of happiness. The utility or usefulness of action, and hence the moral standard by which the ethics of actions are to be evaluated, according to Mill, is its contribution as a means to the ultimate end of achieving happiness.

Mill identifies happiness with pleasure. He states that the prior ethical tradition, from ancient Greece to the British utilitarians, all recognized utility as pleasure, thereby explaining moral good in terms of happiness and happiness in terms of pleasure. What is useful in moral reasoning, Mill argues, at least for the thinkers to whom he defers, and in his own opinion, is psychologically experienced pleasure. Mill states:

> Those who know anything about the matter are aware that every writer, from Epicurus to Bentham, who maintained the theory of utility meant by it, not something to be contradistinguished from pleasure, but pleasure itself, together with exemption from pain; and instead of opposing the useful to the agreeable or the ornamental, have always declared that the useful means these, among other things. (8–9)

Utilitarianism is explained by Mill as the principle that evaluates the morality of an action according to its tendency to produce happiness construed as pleasure. Mill's utilitarianism holds that an action is morally justified to whatever extent it leads to pleasure rather than pain, and as such to greater happiness as opposed to unhappiness. To sloganize Mill's theory, at the risk of misunderstanding, it might be said that utilitarianism implies that moral good is whatever makes us feel good. Mill's tasks in the text are largely concerned with efforts to counter some of the misinterpretations that are likely to arise in connection with this stark statement of hedonistic utilitarianism, and to answer objections and blunt criticisms that might otherwise disincline serious moralists to accept the doctrine. Mill associates utilitarianism with the greatest happiness principle, and understands happiness as pleasure and avoidance or alleviation of pain:

> The creed which accepts as the foundation of morals Utility or the Greatest Happiness Principle holds that actions are right in proportion as they tend to promote happiness; wrong as they tend to produce the reverse of happiness. By happiness is intended pleasure and the absence of pain; by unhappiness, pain and the privation of pleasure. To give a clear view of the moral standard set up by the theory, much more requires to be said; in particular, what things it includes in the ideas of pain and pleasure, and to what extent this is left an open question. But these supplementary explanations do not affect the theory of life on which this theory of morality is grounded—namely, that pleasure and freedom from pain are the only things desirable as ends; and that all desirable things (which are as numerous in the utilitarian as in any other scheme) are desirable either for pleasure inherent in themselves or as means to the promotion of pleasure and the prevention of pain. (9–10)

In this passage, Mill presents the core thesis of utilitarianism and outlines the major part of his program to explain and defend the theory. There is, as he remarks, much more to be said. Having characterized moral value as usefulness or utility, and interpreted utility as whatever is productive of happiness understood as pleasure and avoidance or minimization of displeasure and pain, Mill must next systematically define the nature of pleasure and pain, to present criteria for distinguishing between pleasures and articulate methods of calculating the resultant pleasure versus pain or displeasure resulting from an action. He must provide a more complete detailed theory of the pursuit of pleasure as the only real ultimate moral good.

Mill refers to the view that pleasure is the end of all action as a "theory of life," which he intends as an empirical anthropological observation about the purpose of human behavior. It is worth reminding ourselves that this is precisely the kind of information that Kant in his criticisms of consequentialism objects to under the label "practical anthropology." Kant regards such factors as significant only in understanding the relation of the will to circumstances in exercising moral decision making that is morally irrelevant to pure moral philosophy and the metaphysics of morals. For Mill, as an empiricist in contrast with Kant as a critical rationalist or idealist, the anthropological facts about the ends of human behavior directed toward the fulfillment of the natural desire for pleasure, for happiness interpreted hedonistically as pleasure, are the only place at which a correct moral philosophy can begin. Mill explains an action's morality in terms of whether or not it produces more pleasure than pain or displeasure, whether it makes the world a better place in the sense of improving the quality of life from the standpoint of greater happiness for every sentient being affected by an agent's actions and by the social policies of larger decision-making entities.

A convenient way to summarize the opposition between Mill and Kant on this point is to say that for Kant moral agents are essentially rational, capable of reason, whereas for Mill moral agents are essentially sentient, capable of experiencing pleasure and pain. Kant regards the morality of an action as a function of the agent's rational will in relation to a purely rational formalist principle of moral duty expressed as the categorical imperative. Mill evaluates morality exclusively in terms of the pleasure or pain, the positive or negative experiences in natural animal sensations produced psychologically by an action as among its empirical causal consequences. The debate between Mill and Kant turns on such problems from Mill as why we ought to consider the morality of nonhuman moral agents such as angels and aliens if we do not even have any good reason to suppose that they exist. Why should they enter into our moral reflections at all, he asks, especially when there remain so many moral difficulties and problems here at hand involving the suffering of individuals and the ethical choices of actual human moral agents? Kant, for his part, challenges Mill to explain why a logically possible rational nonhuman agent individually incapable of pleasure or pain would have any utilitarian reason to act morally. Thus, the conflict between deontology and consequentialism persists.

HEDONISM AND UTILITY

The intuitive justification for Mill's hedonistic account of utility is likely to be most persuasive for anyone who is already sympathetic to Mill's empiricism. If we consider what moral agents do and how we generally assess the morality or immorality of actions, then it is hard to deny that the pursuit of happiness and avoidance of pain are powerful motivations for ethical conduct, and that they must therefore be included as important principles in the assessment of an action's morality. Why do we think it is a morally admirable thing to alleviate hunger and cure diseases, to build schools and hospitals and libraries, to improve the quality of food and water and air, and the like, except as a way of increasing happiness in the sense of greater pleasure for as many persons as possible?

What kinds of pleasures are morally valuable? Are any and all pleasures necessarily ethically good? Is not the point of many moral virtues intended precisely to encourage persons to curb their appetites for pleasure, to control their desires and limit their pleasures for the sake of a higher good? If we regard it as good to experience pleasure in having nourishing food, is it morally acceptable to be a glutton, or even to cultivate an excessive interest in gourmet preparations, as some people say, to live for our stomachs, or to live to eat rather than eat to live? Similarly with respect to any of the pleasures of life. If it is more pleasurable than displeasurable to provide for basic human needs, and morally desirable to that extent, and if it is morally obligatory to maximize happiness over unhappiness in the sense of maximizing pleasure over pain and displeasure, then it should presumably be morally obligatory to carry all of our pleasures to the greatest practically possible degree.

Mill might reply that the greatest happiness principle does not condone excessive pleasures while other sentient beings are suffering from want. It would not be justified on utilitarian grounds for some persons to indulge in extravagant feasts if other persons are starving. Suppose, however, that no one were starving and that all other social ills had already been remedied. Would it then not only be morally permissible but morally obligatory on utilitarian principles to maximize pleasure by wanton intemperance?

Or, to consider yet another obvious and ethically interesting example, if it is morally valuable, even morally obligatory, to feel pleasure, then why not achieve pleasurable sensations by taking certain drugs? Several objections immediately occur. A utilitarian such as Mill might maintain that drugs are morally improper because of other consequences that inevitably accompany their use. In that case, it might not actually be productive of utility understood as real total pleasure for all sentient beings in the long run to seek pleasure in mind-altering substances. Some of the problems associated with drugs include addiction, and with it a consuming involvement that can prevent persons from devoting time and energy to other necessary and equally if not morally more obligatory activities, neglect of one's health and family, and other violations of ethical demands. Suppose, however, that there is a drug that is extremely pleasurable but has no side-effects, is nonaddictive, inexpensive, and has no attendant health risks, and that everyone can enjoy without any moral downside. If there were such an imaginary substance, would it not be not only morally permissible according to Mill's hedonistic utilitarianism but morally obligatory to use the drug as frequently as possible, provided we could do so in balance with other moral obligations in order to maximize happiness interpreted as pleasure?

Mill does not consider this specific kind of example. He is nevertheless alert to the objection that utilitarian ethics entails the pursuit of pleasure, and that pleasures, if morally good, are also at least potentially if not often morally equivocal and a source of moral iniquity rather than of positive moral virtue. Mill is sensitive to criticisms of hedonistic utilitarianism, but he is firm in his commitment to the idea that morality in the end is nothing but a function of happiness, and that happiness is nothing but pleasure. He must accordingly find ways to deal with the criticism that utilitarianism in fact if not directly in intent is guilty of prescribing a doctrine of morally questionable pure pleasure seeking. If some pleasures are of doubtful morality, the issue naturally arises whether pleasure generally can possibly provide a correct standard of moral justification. Perhaps the right account is more like Kant's theory, in which pleasure is ruled out as morally irrelevant along with desire and inclination, and the appeal of morality should be pitched instead exclusively to a moral agent's rationality rather than capacity for sensations of pleasure and pain.

Mill brings together some of these concerns about the hedonism entailed by his interpretation of utility. He considers whether utility promotes the kinds of pleasures appropriate to swine, sensual pig pleasures of various types. Despite many differences, here is yet another respect in which Mill and Kant overlap to a limited extent in their moral judgments even if they do not fully agree. It is, as so often in philosophy, largely a question of interpretation and emphasis, and of finding a different place for the same or much the same considerations within a different philosophical outlook. Mill wants to mitigate misunderstandings of hedonistic utilitarianism, by showing that it does not advocate excessively sensual lower pleasures. In this limited way, his argument is similar to Kant's third application of the categorical imperative, where Kant asks whether there is a moral obligation to develop one's talents as opposed to merely living a comfortable unproductive life of lazy leisure. It has often been argued that it is morally objectionable to neglect the greater perfection of our abilities for the sake of the pleasures of an easygoing idleness. Mill opens his defense of hedonistic utilitarianism by acknowledging the problem of swinish pleasures:

> Now, such a theory of life excites in many minds, and among them in some of the most estimable in feeling and purpose, inveterate dislike. To suppose that life has (as they express it) no higher end than pleasure—no better and nobler object of desire and pursuit—they designate as utterly mean and groveling; as a doctrine worthy only of swine, to whom the followers of Epicurus were, at a very early period, contemptuously likened; and modern holders of the doctrine are occasionally made the subject of equally polite comparisons by its German, French, and English assailants. (10)

Mill mentions Epicurus, whose philosophy gave rise to the terms *epicurean* and *epicureanism*. The moral hedonism of this ancient school, Mill remarks, was also misunderstood in its day in a caricature of the position Epicurus actually held. Epicurus did not recommend the mindless pursuit of pleasure, but rather a calm "philosophical" attitude inspired by an understanding of the nature of the world, the will of the gods, and the goal of seeking pleasure primarily in the sense of avoiding pain and psychological distress. Mill goes beyond Epicurus in attaching positive moral value to many kinds of pleasures of a higher than sensual type, endorsing those especially having to do with intellectual and other enjoyable experiences that are not limited to food, sex, and inactivity. It is significant in this regard that Socrates in Plato's dialogue the *Republic* describes a city-state founded on the principle of pleasure and the pursuit of material gain as a "city of pigs." Mill follows the Epicureans in trying to turn the tables on critics who take a negative view of the human capacity for pleasure and the direction of human appetites allowed to seek its natural objects:

> When thus attacked, the Epicureans have always answered that it is not they, but their accusers, who represent human nature in a degrading light; since the accu-

sation supposes human beings to be capable of no pleasures except those of which swine are capable. (10)

The question is, Who has a more negative outlook on human nature: the hedonist or the critic of hedonism? The critic, Mill claims, is rather quick to believe that human beings naturally desire only base pleasures and would primarily try to achieve sensuality rather than the higher pleasurable goods of which people are also capable. Mill refutes the complaint that hedonistic utilitarianism promotes only swinish sensual pleasures. He argues that the objection betrays itself as internally inconsistent. He claims that crude bestial pleasures, appropriate for nonhuman animals such as pigs, are seen as degrading for human beings precisely because we all recognize that human beings are by nature not fitted for that kind of life and are not naturally inclined toward the kind of happiness that would satisfy a pig. Mill states:

> If this supposition were true, the charge could not be gainsaid, but would then be no longer an imputation: for if the sources of pleasure were precisely the same to human beings and to swine, the rule of life which is good enough for the one would be good enough for the other. The comparison of the Epicurean life to that of beasts is felt as degrading, precisely because a beast's pleasures do not satisfy a human being's conceptions of happiness. Human beings have faculties more elevated than the animal appetites, and when once made conscious of them, do not regard anything as happiness which does not include their gratification. (10–11)

Mill has more to say on this topic. It is important to appreciate in the first place that he recognizes the problem, and sees it as a source of misunderstanding of the doctrine of utility that has a long history, going back at least to the time of Epicurus as a kind of hedonistic utilitarian or proto-utilitarian. Part of Mill's solution, in an important first step, is to point out that human pleasures are by definition different from those of nonhuman animals, and that we do the other members of our own species a moral injustice if we assume without investigation that the kinds of pleasures human moral agents will naturally pursue are those appropriate for beasts.

Unfortunately, it is not that difficult to find instances in which human beings do in fact choose to pursue pleasures that are more naturally associated with animals. There is an ingrained negative attitude about the objects of many human desires that reflects a predisposition to undervalue human potential. Mill prepares to take the higher ground and to see empirically for himself what human moral agents actually choose as pleasures before he decides whether and to what extent they are in this regard better in their choice of pleasures than nonhuman animals. Mill, in any case, does not assume in the absence of strong evidence that pleasure for human beings is the same or even relevantly similar to that of beasts. If anything, he is on more secure ground, given other differences dividing the species, in presuming that there is likely to be a substantial difference between the pleasures that would satisfy a human being as opposed to those that would satisfy a pig.

Although Mill does not take the argument in this further direction, it is plausible to understand the conclusion he endorses as supported also by our knowledge of changing tastes in pleasures that we experience personally as we mature from childhood to adults. There are many kinds of things that we regard as pleasures when we are younger that we no longer find pleasurable when we have had more years of experience. A time generally comes when we set aside the pleasures we enjoyed as children and acquire new, different, and more appropriate pleasures, giving up toys for adult pursuits, or at least for other kinds of toys. The point, which Mill would also probably emphasize, is not that we surpass more basic for more sophisticated pleasures because we think we need or are supposed to, but because it feels right and natural to do so. The difference in pleasures as they are actually experienced is purely a matter of inclination and disposition in which we do what we prefer to do as contributing to what we genuinely feel to be pleasurable. If this is true in the case of the development of mature pleasures in an individual person over time, the same conclusion about the inherent differences among kinds of naturally sought pleasures is likely to be true to an even greater degree where species as different as human and nonhuman animals are concerned.

EXPERIENTIAL CRITERIA OF COMPARATIVE PLEASURES

The next step for Mill is to take notice of the empirical fact that there are different kinds of pleasures. He argues that different kinds of pleasures are deemed more worthy of pursuit, not because of overarching moral principles that are meant to limit our interest in them, but on their own terms, experienced as more or less pleasurable to different persons because of differences in their desires and inclinations. Again, Mill is on relatively sound empirical footing. He can rely on the collective experience of persons who choose different pleasures and report different preferences and levels of satisfaction. It is a fact of psychology that some persons subjectively enjoy particular kinds of experiences that others do not enjoy, or enjoy to a different degree or in a different way. Mill remarks that the experience of pleasure is a complex psychological phenomenon with multiple dimensions that can affect the overall quality of pleasure. He describes experiential criteria for comparing pleasures:

> It is quite compatible with the principle of utility to recognize the fact that some *kinds* of pleasure are more desirable and more valuable than others. It would be absurd that while, in estimating all other things, quality is considered as well as quantity, the estimation of pleasure should be supposed to depend on quantity alone. (11–12)

With respect to one of the most basic spectra of factors that enter into the experience of pleasure, the difference between quality and quantity, Mill reasonably argues that quantity is not always preferable to quality. An example for the sake of illustration is when we find that while light tickling is ordinarily a pleasure, excessive tickling, increasing the quantity alone with no concern for the sensation as it is actually experienced, is not necessarily a proportionally increased pleasure. An excessive quantity of what is otherwise a pleasure might not even be a pleasure at all, but a displeasure or pain. A bowl of ice cream under the right circumstances is a definite pleasure, but wolfing down four or five gallons of the stuff is not likely to simply increase the pleasure proportionally by that greater quantity. It is a well-known phenomenon that there is an inhibitory effect in pleasure that comes about from excess, in which less is often more.

If the quality of pleasure is at least sometimes more important than quantity, then it is necessary to consider standards whereby differences in the qualities of pleasures

can be judged. Mill acknowledges variability in the pleasures of which human subjects are capable, and combines this recognition with what he maintains is the only
conceivable test of the differences in qualities among different pleasures. The test is
simple, according to Mill, in deciding which of two pleasures under comparison is
preferable. It is entirely a matter of experiencing both and discovering which one if
either is actually preferred to the other. He continues:

> If I am asked, what I mean by difference of quality in pleasures, or what makes
> one pleasure more valuable than another, merely as a pleasure, except its being
> greater in amount, there is but one possible answer. Of two pleasures, if there be
> one to which all or almost all who have experience of both give a decided prefer-
> ence, irrespective of any feeling of moral obligation to prefer it, that is the more
> desirable pleasure. If one of the two is, by those who are competently acquainted
> with both, placed so far above the other that they prefer it, even though know-
> ing it to be attended with a greater amount of discontent, and would not resign
> it for any quantity of the other pleasure which their nature is capable of, we are
> justified in ascribing to the preferred enjoyment a superiority in quality so far
> outweighing quantity as to render it, in comparison, of small account. (12)

The basis that Mill prescribes for distinguishing the qualities of pleasures accords
with his empiricism. He argues that in order to decide which of several pleasures is
preferable we must ask those who have experienced them all in order to determine
which kinds of experiences they find or continue to find pleasurable or more pleasurable than the others. Mill's point is not that this is the best way to judge which
pleasures are better in the sense of being more pleasurable, but that it is absolutely
the only way to make such judgments. There is no other method of deciding about
the relative values of pleasures, no other authority or procedure for calculating a ranking of pleasures. Mill applies the criterion of comparable pleasures to the original
problem about swinish preferences as an objection to hedonistic utilitarianism:

> Now it is an unquestionable fact that those who are equally acquainted with, and
> equally capable of appreciating and enjoying both, do give a most marked prefer-
> ence to the manner of existence which employs their higher faculties. Few human
> creatures would consent to be changed into any of the lower animals, for a prom-
> ise of the fullest allowance of a beast's pleasures; no intelligent human being would
> consent to be a fool, no instructed person would be an ignoramus, no person of
> feeling and conscience would be selfish and base, even though they should be per-
> suaded that the fool, the dunce, or the rascal is better satisfied with his lot than
> they are with theirs. They would not resign what they possess more than he for
> the most complete satisfaction of all the desires which they have in common with
> him. If they ever fancy they would, it is only in cases of unhappiness so extreme,
> that to escape from it they would exchange their lot for almost any other, how-
> ever undesirable in their own eyes. (12–13)

There is no other way of determining which of two pleasures is preferable than
by appealing to the actual preferences of those who have experience of both types.
What we discover empirically, so to speak, or anthropologically, in the actual choices
that knowledgeable persons make, according to Mill, is that higher intellectual pleasures are inevitably judged preferable to pig pleasures or purely sensual appetites.

The conclusion is supported by a kind of sociological survey. Mill briefly summarizes what he takes to be the preferences of persons with experience of both sensual and intellectual pleasures. He claims that experience shows that higher intellectual pleasures as a matter of fact are generally preferred to lower purely sensual pleasures. We might question whether or to what extent Mill has correctly assessed the true preferences of a majority of the population, many of whom seem all too interested in the pleasures of the flesh rather than the mind. Mill, however, is convinced that the opposite is true.

He further defends his comparative evaluation of intellectual versus bestial sensual pleasures in another way, by offering an imaginative thought experiment. He asks whether an average person would prefer to accept the highly pleasurable life of a nonhuman animal, possibly experiencing continuous pleasure as a pig while being denied the capacity for thought and the experiences of pleasure available to an intelligent human being. He thinks it is obvious that few if any human beings would accept that kind of bargain, giving up their human qualities of higher reason for the pleasures of a pig. Who, Mill asks, would consent to be a pig, no matter how pleasurable a life the pig leads, rather than a human being? As Mill summarizes the preference for human pleasures:

> It is better to be a human being dissatisfied than a pig satisfied; better to be Socrates dissatisfied than a fool satisfied. And if the fool, or the pig, is of a different opinion, it is because they only know their own side of the question. The other party to the comparison knows both sides. (14)

There is an important point in Mill's example, but it is not clear to what extent he establishes the conclusion he needs to defend by what we would say about a pig's imagined life of pleasure. As human beings we are naturally familiar with and fondly attached to the kinds of pleasures we are used to experiencing. How, on the contrary, do we know that a continuous life of the kind of pleasure available to a pig would be worse than the hypothetically less sensually but more intellectually pleasurable life of a human being?

For one thing, we are constitutionally incapable of experiencing both kinds of pleasures and then making a comparative assessment of the life of a human being and that of a pig. At best, we can only try to project what a pig's pleasures would be like on the basis of the pig-like sensual pleasures of which we are capable. These include eating and sex and the like. We know what it would be like for a human being to live like this, which we may agree with Mill does not sound very attractive. We cannot, however, imagine what a pig would think of a pig's life, given the pig's admittedly more limited but in any case nonhuman point of view. As human beings, we would not like to live the mentally more limited life of a pig. Still, we cannot make this judgment on the basis of knowing both what it is like to be a human being and to be a pig, because we do not know and can at best only try to imagine the life of a pig. We must try to understand the life of a pig through the colored lenses of our human point of view, which, unlike spectacles, we cannot put on and take off at will. For that matter, if we could transcend our human perspective in order to compare our lives with a pig's, it is unimaginable that we should thereafter be able to recall what it was like being a pig, in order to arrive at a competent comparative evaluation of the two, as Mill requires.

Of course, *we* think it would be better to be Socrates dissatisfied than a pig satisfied, even immensely satisfied within the capabilities accessible to a barnyard animal. That, however, is undoubtedly because we are human beings and have come to prefer the pleasures that are actually within our grasp. It appears doubtful whether, as Mill says, the other, human, party to the comparison between human and pig pleasures knows both sides of the distinction. Where the qualities of a very different psychology are concerned, it is unclear that anyone can ever know enough about the way another, alien, kind of mind functions, and in particular what its pleasures are like and whether or not they would actually be preferable to those of the thinker trying to evaluate and compare them. In particular, it is not obvious whether any attempt at such evaluation could possibly judge the difference. Mill proceeds as though the moral agent's comparative assessment of the preferability of higher human pleasures by contrast with lower sensual animal pleasures were not only unproblematic but unanswerable, affording no opportunity for refutation or reconsideration. He contends:

> From this verdict of the only competent judges, I apprehend there can be no appeal. On a question which is the best worth having of two pleasures, or which of two modes of existence is the most grateful to the feelings, apart from its moral attributes and from its consequences, the judgment of these who are qualified by knowledge of both, or, if they differ, that of the majority among them, must be admitted as final. And there needs be the less hesitation to accept this judgment respecting the quality of pleasures, since there is no other tribunal to be referred to even on the question of quantity. What means are there of determining which is the acutest of two pains, or the intensest of two pleasurable sensations, except the general suffrage of those who are familiar with both? (15–16)

The same is true by analogy for my preference not to be a well-pleasured fool. It is one thing to know that, with the same intelligence and mental framework that we happen to have, we prefer the pleasures of classical music to heavy metal, or, just the opposite, since we can compare the two listening experiences as the same "I." It is another proposition altogether to wonder whether we would prefer to be another mind, let alone a different kind of mind, possibly even belonging to a different species without a sufficiently similar human psychology.

It is not clear that we can imagine such a thing at all. Hence, it is not clear whether we could conceivably impartially evaluate the two possibilities of being an intelligent pleasure seeker or a fool, as though tasting two wines one after another to decide which has the better flavor. This in itself, it should be remarked, can also be a difficult business, once we have replaced the taste of one with that of the other, and must try to remember exactly what the first was like as we try to compare it mentally with the wine we are now swirling around in our mouths. If or to the extent that Mill's argument in support of the higher intellectual pleasures as inherently comparatively preferable to lower sensual pig pleasures depends on being able to actually make such comparisons in order to judge their respective values, it might be said that Mill does not offer a sound philosophical or psychological basis for reaching any such evaluation. Mill is perhaps perfectly correct when he asks, rhetorically:

> What is there to decide whether a particular pleasure is worth purchasing at the cost of a particular pain, except the feelings and judgment of the experienced? (16)

There is, unfortunately, no good basis for choosing between widely separated types of pleasures that are preferred by radically remote psychologies, as in the case of pigs and human beings. The problem to a lesser extent may even too severely limit the ability of human beings from different cultures to evaluate the comparative advantages and disadvantages of the pleasures afforded by the different societies with their different cultural and historical contexts to which they belong. If we try to compare the pleasures of persons in societies very different from our own, we might find it difficult or even impossible to imagine that anyone could evaluate the choices fairly if they are so deeply integrated in a way of life to which we find it difficult at many levels to relate.

To illustrate the problem, consider the challenge of comparing the pleasures of eating steak or deliciously prepared vegetables with the raw and still living grubs that are judged a delicacy by persons in some lands. It is not enough simply to take a bite of steak or carrots and then to bite a grub in two and see which we like better and which confers greater pleasure in the experience. If a kind of experience is so different from our own, we may not be able accurately to assess the merits of the two on anything like an even playing field. We do not doubt that we would not like the grub at all. But on that basis we could not regard the comparative taste test as determining in a meaningful way that steak or carrots were somehow preferable to grubs. We are not part of a culture in which we grew up surrounded by persons extolling the pleasures of eating grubs, in the way that the enjoyment of steak and cooked vegetables has frequently been lauded by persons in our background. So the test is not really fair.

Nor would it help, as Mill also seems to indicate, if we had the vast majority of culturally biased food tasters on our side who agreed that steak or carrots were more pleasurable than grubs; for example, if one culture just happened to significantly outnumber the other. What do sheer differences in numbers signify? Meanwhile, the members of the other culture who try steak and vegetables might still continue to prefer grubs, with no clear-cut justification in Mill's empiricist methodology for judging that their preferences are somehow less correct or revelatory than those of persons who continue to prefer steak or carrots. Such conflicts of opinion are the source of the commonplace that there is no accounting for tastes, and that people simply prefer whatever they are accustomed to prefer.

MORAL PREFERABILITY OF PLEASURES

The problem calls attention to another difficulty in Mill's empiricist criterion for comparing the relative preferabilities of different kinds of pleasures. It is sometimes alleged that Mill commits a fallacy in referring to actual preference as a measure of preferability among pleasures in a morally relevant sense.

There is at least an apparent grammatical distinction between judging that a pleasure is preferable in the sense of its being *capable* of being preferred, and of its being *worthy* of being preferred. If something actually happens, then it is undeniably capable of happening, which Mill's criterion clearly if trivially establishes. The latter sense, involving the question of what ought to be or is worthy of being preferred, is philosophically more difficult to decide.

Preferability in the sense of what is worthy of being preferred is a different kind of category that does not appear to be as straightforwardly answerable by empirical

sociological or anthropological study as the question of what is capable of being preferred. To be capable of being preferred is a necessary but not a sufficient condition
for a pleasure's being such that it ought to be or is worthy of being preferred. Mill's
argument in support of his criterion seems to involve assumptions concerned exclusively with preferability in the sense of being capable of being preferred, whereas his
conclusions, insofar as they are supposed to have moral relevance for his defense of
hedonistic utilitarianism, must somehow bridge the gap between the two senses of
preferability by saying something positive about preferability in the sense of being
morally worthy of being preferred.

The strongest case that Mill can make for preferability of higher intellectual pleasures over base sensual pleasures is based on the fact that intellectual pleasures are
highly valued by those capable of experiencing them. He can try to argue that intellectual pleasures would not be given up in exchange for the most intensely pleasurable physical sensations of nonhuman animals like pigs. We must nevertheless remember that pigs for their part do not envy human beings for the intellectual pleasures
that pigs themselves are incapable of enjoying or even imagining. Perhaps we can extrapolate what it would most likely be like to live entirely and exclusively in the way
of a pig without any of the higher human intellectual pleasures. Although we cannot know exactly what it is like to be a pig, we can know immediately from our own
experiences what it is like to experience sensuous pleasures like eating slops, drinking swill, and wallowing in the mud all day. That does not sound better than spend-
ing the day in pajamas before a warm fire with something delicious, artfully and hy-
gienically prepared to eat, reading Shakespeare and listening to Beethoven, and later
sharing stimulating conversations with a friend.

A pig's life, indeed, includes none of the obligations or opportunities that give
each individual human life meaning. If, however, we truly became pigs, would we
necessarily choose to go back to being human? The difficulty, again, is that we cannot help imagining as part of the picture that we would be trying to live such a life
as human beings, with a human psychology and all of our memories and expectations of things that are available to us and not to pigs, and then mentally translating
ourselves from our actual cultural situation into that of the pigsty. Probably no one
would choose it. If we truly became pigs, however, would we necessarily choose to
go back to being human? The problem with the logic of Mill's thought experiment
is that the choice between being a pig and being human can only be made by human
beings and not by pigs, but it is only pigs who actually know what it is like to be a
pig. Human beings who have lived a pig's life for a time, at least in their imagina-
tions, can only judge as human beings from their memories of having been a pig and
what it felt like, which is not the same at all as actually being a pig. A better question to ask about another thought experiment might then be: What if a pig could live
as a human being and then decide to stay in the human world or go back to being a
pig? As a reflection of human self-satisfaction, we might not be able to imagine that
a pig would voluntarily choose to go back to being a pig. From a pig's perspective,
however, for all we know, a human existence might be a living hell. It might be painful
beyond measure for a pig, in ways that we can scarcely imagine, to wear clothes or
eat with utensils or be mindful of the time.

Mill's argument is supposed to defend intellectual over purely sensual pleasures
on the basis of the comparison of pleasures by those who have experience of both

kinds. The reasoning appears inconsistent with Mill's empirical methodology, because the example both requires and excludes the possibility of any individual subject actually having the empirical experience of both the pleasures of a pig's and a human being's life and then being able to say which is more pleasurable. The truth, Mill seems not to notice, is that no one will ever be in a position to make that kind of empirical judgment.

A more convincing thought experiment might then be this. Suppose we have a choice between the most sensual human life devoid of as many intellectual pleasures as possible, and a life of daily intellectual challenge and enjoyment of thoughtful conversation, literature, and the arts. Perhaps we can relate better to another human being who has perhaps chosen to maximally pursue sensual pleasure and maximally avoid intellectual pleasure. Then if we think we would prefer a life with more rather than less intellectual pleasure, even at the expense of some sensual pleasure, then we will have empirically proven that intellectual pleasures are preferable to sensual pleasures. Is this enough to make Mill's point without crossing the species limit from human to nonhuman pleasures? Or does a different version of the pig-human transspecies imagination and judgment problem also limit our ability with respect to different ways of human life? If we merely try out being as purely sensualist and nonintellectualist in our pleasures as possible, like many tourists on vacation, then we will not have the empirical experience we would need in order to consider and judge the choices competently. Again, if we are now thinking about the alternatives intellectually as part of a thought experiment, then we probably cannot imagine living with less or fewer possible intellectual pleasures. We are in that case at best picturing instead a life in which certain sensual pleasures predominate, and perhaps occupy a greater part of our time, but in which our cultivated intellectual lives also continue as they are. After all, we can always intellectualize about our sensual pleasures, and doing so might even synergistically enhance the overall experience of pleasure. If Mill's thought experiment requires us absolutely to cut out all or even minimize intellectual pleasures for the sake of sensual pleasures, then we might be as much at a loss to truly experience or make an empirically sound comparison of the two kinds of pleasures with respect to such another human being as with respect to a pig.

What then of Mill's apparent confusion between preferability in the capability versus worthiness senses? Mill might offer the following reply. He need not deny that preferability in the sense of being capable of being preferred is an implication of his experiential criterion of the preferability of pleasures. It can be taken for granted that whatever is preferred is capable of being preferred, which is not part of the more important philosophical conclusion Mill is trying to establish. Mill can argue that, in considering the pleasures that a wide range of subjects do in fact prefer, he is providing, just as he says, the only kind of evidence that could possibly be presented to determine whether one kind of pleasure is preferable to another. Set aside the question of preferability in the sense of a pleasure's being capable of being preferred, which Mill does not mention or explicitly try to demonstrate, and consider only the question of a pleasure's being morally preferable. What can we say about Mill's argument on its own terms if we do not assume that he is fallaciously trying to infer the preferability of intellectual to purely sensual pleasures in the worthiness sense from the capability sense?

Perhaps Mill is not trying to say what choices among pleasures morally ought to be preferred, but has another aim in view. It might be said that he is proposing empirically to discover what we moral agents do in fact value, recognizing that there is no higher court of appeal than what human beings actually do find preferable among the pleasures they have actually experienced. This would be as true, Mill might insist, whether it happens to turn out that human beings prefer intellectual to sensual or sensual to intellectual pleasures. If we are to understand the values that are actually at work in human moral decision making, then there may be no other way to determine what we find morally valuable than from the preferences we actually make. Could this more modest purpose be Mill's goal in this part of the text? Even if the answer is yes, we still face the problem of explaining the relation that is supposed to hold between what we actually prefer and what a hedonic utilitarian moralist must eventually describe as morally worthy of being preferred or such that it ought to be preferred. Mill would then be required to say that there is no further point to be made about what we ought to do than what we do in fact. This defense, while at least internally logically consistent, would not enable Mill to recommend utilitarian moral obligations or prohibitions as different in any way from what people do in fact prefer. It seems to follow, then, that what we do is morally right because that is what we or the significant majority of us choose to do. If an individual or a society happens to prefer to do things that run counter to the requirements of utility, then there will be nothing Mill can say to argue that moral agents ought not to prefer what they do in fact prefer, in order to bring their actions into line with the prescriptions of a specifically hedonic pleasure-oriented utilitarianism. In that case, Mill can only stand back and adopt the morally neutral attitude of the empirical anthropological observer, with no basis for trying to change the world for the better according to utilitarian standards or to redirect preferences in morally preferable ways.

All of these theoretical pitfalls can be avoided by Mill if we reconsider and take more fully into account the exact context in which he introduces the experiential criterion of comparative pleasure preferences. Why does Mill propose to evaluate alternative pleasures? Why does he care about the rank ordering of pleasures, if not to argue that we ought to prefer and ought to act in such a way as to bring about preferred pleasures and to avoid less preferred or rejected pleasures?

To begin, it may be worthwhile to remark that Mill nowhere suggests that we ought not to indulge in pig pleasures, if that is what we really choose. In opposition to Kant's third application of the categorical imperative, Mill does not say that we have a moral obligation to be productive in our lives and to avoid leisurely inactivity, if that is what we truly prefer to do and truly find pleasurable. If we are utilitarians, and there is more work to be done in the world to help increase the total amount of pleasure for everyone, then we ought not to remain idle. Otherwise, it is not intrinsically morally problematic for utilitarians to shun activity and allow their talents to remain undeveloped. For the same reason, we do not find Mill criticizing the lives of pigs that are simply pursuing their natural inclinations within their more limited capabilities. Mill believes that as a matter of fact there will be few if any human beings who can truly live the life of a pig, who would prefer and freely choose to live that way, although he acknowledges that not all persons are capable of the highest aspirations of intellectual pleasures. It is an empirical fact about human nature that on the whole we do not actually prefer pig-like pleasures. If human psychology were so constituted that human beings as moral agents actually did prefer to live like pigs and to pursue the pleasures enjoyed by pigs, Mill could have no utilitarian moral objection to raise, for in that case he would presumably be in pretty much the same situation himself.

What Mill argues instead is different, more limited and specific in its purpose than criticisms of his experiential criterion of comparative pleasure preferabilities acknowledge. Mill's aim is only to defend utilitarianism on very general grounds from the anti-hedonistic objection that a morality based on pleasure is inherently directed toward the worst or lowest or most bestial of pleasures. It is to answer such criticisms that Mill remarks that there is no better way to judge what psychological subjects find preferable, the pleasures to which they are inclined, than to discover empirically what individuals actually prefer. We can only observe what people do and use that data to inform moral reasoning about the pleasures that a certain class of psychological subjects actually find pleasurable, and that they find comparatively more pleasurable than other pleasures they might in principle prefer but do not actually choose.

If Mill is right to say that human beings on the whole do not and would not prefer exclusively or even predominantly to indulge in the subhuman pleasures more appropriate to animals, then he has in hand the only answer he needs in order to respond to the objections of anti-hedonists who regard the pursuit of pleasure as inescapably immoral because it is bound to lead to pursuit of the lowest sort of pleasures. Mill reasonably replies that this is simply not the case, either as a matter of fact or as a matter of the meaning or the necessary implications of the concept of pleasure. There are all kinds of pleasures, and the human pursuit of higher intellectual pleasures is at least as much if not more important to human beings on average than the lower sensual pleasures. Furthermore, Mill argues, judging empirically by the preferences humans on the whole actually make, the higher intellectual pleasures are if anything more endemic to human nature than are the exclusively sensual pleasures of nonhuman animals.

The objection is therefore no serious obstacle to the acceptance of a hedonic utilitarian morality. To repel the criticism as Mill does is not meant to be a positive argument in support of utilitarianism, but at most only the clearing away of an objection that would otherwise rule out the pursuit of pleasure as a morally worthy occupation of genuinely moral agents. Mill, at this stage of his exposition, has not yet sought to justify but only to explain a hedonic utilitarian morality, and does not offer reasons to accept the theory until much later in the book, in Chapter IV, "Of What Sort of Proof the Principle of Utility is Susceptible." Mill's tactic at this stage, in Chapter II, "What Utilitarianism Is," as the title suggests, is only to outline utilitarian moral theory and argue that it is a possible foundation for ethical philosophy.

UTILITY AS THE GENERAL HAPPINESS

Mill next elaborates on the greatest happiness principle by which hedonic utilitarianism is defined. The equation of happiness with pleasure is not supposed to describe the pleasure in particular of the utilitarian moral agent contemplating an action and proposing to apply Mill's principles in a moral decision-making situation. He maintains that we are not to consider only our own individual pleasures, no matter how high or intellectual or in other ways noble, but to consider the happiness in the sense of pleasure of all sentient beings who might be affected by the consequences of any agent's actions. He explains the generality with which the standard of hedonic utility is supposed to apply in all moral decision making:

> I have dwelt on this point, as being part of a perfectly just conception of Utility or Happiness, considered as the directive rule of human conduct. But it is by no means an indispensable condition to the acceptance of the utilitarian standard; for that standard is not the agent's own greatest happiness, but the greatest amount of happiness altogether; and if it may possibly be doubted whether a noble character is always the happier for its nobleness, there can be no doubt that it makes other people happier, and that the world in general is immensely a gainer by it. Utilitarianism, therefore, could only attain its end by the general cultivation of nobleness of others, and his own, so far as happiness is concerned, were a sheer deduction from the benefit. But the bare enunciation of such an absurdity as this last, renders refutation superfluous. (16)

Mill not only argues that the agent's pleasures are not to have any more importance attributed to them than that of all psychological subjects, but observes that in many actions morally approved by utilitarianism the agent is obligated to and may act in accord with the moral requirements of hedonic utility as Mill understands it in such a way as to accept a life of personal pain or displeasure for the sake of the greater good. Mill's hedonic utilitarian morality does not necessarily or even typically lead to acts of personal selfishness or any less appreciation for the sacrifices that some moral agents undertake in order to procure more happiness for others. Nor is a moral agent supposed to discount his or her pleasure, or always act in such a way that the consequences of the action go against personal happiness. Rather, the idea is that, however the final calculations of resulting pleasure versus pain or displeasure turn out, the agent on Mill's utilitarian principles is supposed to consider everyone's happiness in general as the standard by which to evaluate the morality of what is done, and to decide what it would be morally justified to do.

Mill distinguishes his moral philosophy from that of ethical egoism. Utilitarianism evaluates all actions with respect to their consequences not just for the agent but insofar as they affect all psychological subjects capable of experiencing pleasure or pain. Mill holds that utility as much concerns pleasure in the traditional Stoic or Epicurean sense of absence of pain, as in that of positive pleasure in any of its sensual or intellectual manifestations:

> According to the Greatest Happiness Principle, as above explained, the ultimate end, with reference to and for the sake of which all other things are desirable (whether we are considering our own good or that of other people), is an existence exempt as far as possible from pain, and as rich as possible in enjoyments, both in point of quantity and quality; the test of quality and the rule for measuring it against quantity, being the preference felt by those who, in their opportunities of experience, to which must be added their habits of self-consciousness and self-observation, are best furnished with the means of comparison. This, being, according to the utilitarian opinion, the end of human action, is necessarily also the standard of morality; which may accordingly be defined, the rules and precepts for human conduct, by the observance of which an existence such as has

been described might be, to the greatest extent possible, secured to all mankind; and not to them only, but so far as the nature of things admits to the whole sentient creation. (17)

By drawing these implications, Mill directly associates utilitarianism with liberal social practices that strive to improve the quality of life for all persons. Mill specifically mentions the eradication of disease and other improvements to material health and welfare of both our fellow human beings and whatever nonhuman animals are affected by social policies and individual actions. The "evils of the world," Mill optimistically believes, can and should be eliminated, many of them by engineering the environment and applying the results of scientific technology in medicine, housing, water and waste treatment, and unlimitedly many other practical ways. Mill argues that it is a consequence of utilitarianism that we should try to do these things and many others besides for the sake of maximizing the total amount of pleasure versus pain and displeasure. We can and should make the world a better place by acting in ways that will benefit ourselves indirectly by benefiting all other sentient beings. Mill enthusiastically invokes a hedonic utilitarian vision of the greatest happiness for the greatest number:

> Yet no one whose opinion deserves a moment's consideration can doubt that most of the great positive evils of the world are in themselves removable, and will, if human affairs continue to improve, be in the end reduced within narrow limits. Poverty, in any sense implying suffering, may be completely extinguished by the wisdom of society, combined with the good sense and providence of individuals. Even that most intractable of enemies, disease, may be indefinitely reduced in dimensions by good physical and moral education, and proper control of noxious influences; while the progress of science holds out a promise for the future of still more direct conquests over this detestable foe. And every advance in that direction relieves us from some, not only of the chances which cut short our own lives, but, what concerns us still more, which deprive us of those in whom our happiness is wrapt up. (21–22)

Historically, it must be remarked that utilitarianism as a social movement had an enormous positive impact on the improvement of social conditions for countless numbers of persons and even of nonhuman animals. The moral force for carrying out programs of social improvement for all people that is so much a part of contemporary ethics is largely owing to the major figures of utilitarianism. There is always more work to be done in these directions, since war and physical abuse and hunger and disease still exist and will no doubt always exist to a greater or lesser extent. Mill nevertheless believes he has pointed the right way toward positive action leading to the reduction of these moral problems, and his and Bentham's followers in the nineteenth and twentieth centuries did much to contribute to making the world a better place in the sense of increasing happiness and diminishing pain. The extent to which we do not regard Mill's moral theory and social program revolutionary is testimony to the widespread acceptance of the theory and the impact and influence it has had on the social consciousness of our time and the practices we regard as so obviously morally correct as to be almost taken for granted today, even while we continue to pursue utilitarian values.

Mill regards the other-directedness of utilitarianism as important enough to deserve this recapitulation:

> I must again repeat, what the assailants of utilitarianism seldom have the justice to acknowledge, that the happiness which forms the utilitarian standard of what is right in conduct, is not the agent's own happiness, but that of all concerned. As between his own happiness and that of others, utilitarianism requires him to be as strictly impartial as a disinterested and benevolent spectator. (24)

The impartiality that Mill requires of utilitarian decision making is emphasized again because its hedonic interpretation of happiness as pleasure invites misinterpretation that might cast the theory in a morally objectionable light. Pleasure is experienced by each individual, so that the endorsement of pleasure is bound to seem like a recommendation for every person to pursue their own individual personal enjoyment, even in a frivolous morally irrelevant or morally objectionable way.

This Mill strongly denies. The concept of happiness in the sense of pleasure that he defends is not selfish or egoistic, but directed toward all persons and finally all sentient beings capable of pleasure and pain that might potentially be affected by the consequences of a moral agent's actions. If pleasure is a good, Mill goes even farther by arguing that pleasure is the only ultimate good. He seems to mean this in the Aristotelian sense that all action is done for the sake of something else as a means to an end, except for happiness understood as pleasure. Properly construed, pleasure is not valued for the sake of anything else as a means to another end, but as an end that is morally valuable in and of itself.

What makes an action morally good, according to Mill, is just its additions to or subtractions from the common happiness, the pleasure experienced in the psychological lives of all sentient beings. Mill believes that this is the often unspoken purpose with which morally relevant actions are undertaken and judged. He thinks that the effectiveness of pleasure-promoting actions can be enhanced by making our ethical choices more self-consciously directed toward the goal of improving the quality of life for all psychological subjects of sensation. According to utilitarianism, we are morally obligated to maximize happiness in the sense of pleasure by working to achieve the greatest pleasure-promoting good for the greatest number.

IRRELEVANCE OF MORAL INTENT IN MILL'S UTILITARIAN ETHICS

To further compare Kant's deontology with Mill's consequentialism, it is worth considering the degree to which Mill regards the moral intent of moral agents as morally irrelevant to the moral value of an action. Kant, we have seen, makes moral intent the basis for moral evaluation. The only unqualifiedly good thing according to Kant is a morally good will, from which standpoint Kant interprets moral value as a function of the attitude with which an action is decided upon and undertaken.

We cannot know and cannot always control the consequences of our actions, and hence we cannot generally be morally responsible for what we do because of their effects. We can, however, and Kant believes we should, morally evaluate actions according to the standard of the moral intent with which the rational will decides what to do. In particular, we are to judge the morality of an action on the basis of whether it is supported by the rational will's representation of the categorical imperative as the unconditional principle of moral duty. For only this state of mind guarantees freedom in the sense of autonomy presupposed by moral responsibility. Mill is vehemently opposed to Kant's insistence on moral intent as relevant to moral judgment. Mill and Kant are diametrically opposed on this issue. Whereas Kant regards the consequences of actions as morally irrelevant, in deference to moral attitude, Mill regards the moral attitude with which an action is undertaken as morally irrelevant, in deference to an action's consequences. There is much of philosophical interest to learn in this fundamental opposition between Kant and Mill.

From Mill's standpoint as a proponent of hedonic utilitarianism, moral attitude does not make a difference in whether an action has consequences that enhance rather than diminish the total amount of happiness in the world. If the utility or disutility of an action is the factor by which an action earns its status as morally valuable or negligible, then we need not take into moral consideration the state of mind with which the action is performed. If the action produces more happiness than unhappiness, then the action is morally good, regardless of intent. If the action produces more unhappiness than happiness, then the action is morally wrong, no matter how noble the agents' intentions. What difference does it make in evaluating an action as promoting utility that an agent is or is not thinking of the categorical imperative or representing that unconditional rational law of moral duty? What difference does it make to the morally relevant consequences of an action, even if the agent is or is not thinking of the principle of utility or greatest happiness principle? How many moral agents ordinarily judged even by philosophers as doing the morally right thing have even heard of the categorical imperative or any equivalent formulation of that principle? If intent is important to moral judgment and decisions for action, why not describe the morally relevant intent of an agent as the wish to promote general utility or universal happiness in the sense of pleasure?

Mill explains what he sees as the moral irrelevance of moral intent in determining moral value:

> He who saves a fellow creature from drowning does what is morally right, whether his motive be duty or the hope of being paid for his trouble; he who betrays the friend that trusts him, is guilty of a crime, even if his object be to serve another friend to whom he is under greater obligations. But to speak only of actions done from the motive of duty, and in direct obedience to principle: it is a misapprehension of the utilitarian mode of thought, to conceive it as implying that people should fix their minds upon so wide a generality as the world, or society at large. The great majority of good actions are intended, not for the benefit of the world, but for that of individuals, of which the good of the world is made up; and the thoughts of the most virtuous man need not on these occasions travel beyond the particular persons concerned, except so far as is necessary to assure himself that in benefiting them he is not violating the rights—that is, the legitimate and authorized expectations—of anyone else. (26–28)

Mill judges an action, such as saving a drowning person, as morally valuable because of its contribution to the sum total of happiness in the world. There is more pleasure, other things being equal, if the drowning victim is saved than not saved.

Why should anyone care if the rescuer saves the victim because of a desire to be honored as a hero in the newspapers, or because of an expectation of feeling good afterward, or because of a preference for the occurrence of more happiness than unhappiness in the world, or because of a rational commitment to the categorical imperative as the unconditional principle of moral duty?

Mill answers that attitude and intent add nothing to an action's morality. The action has moral value solely and exclusively on the basis of whether it makes a difference to the world's total amount of pleasure and pain. What matters is that the life of a person who would otherwise have drowned has been saved, along with all the pleasure that would have been lost. A utilitarian calculation of the greater pleasure resulting from saving the person's life must include the pleasure that the person would have experienced in a normal lifetime beyond the near-drowning incident, along with all the suffering of the persons whose lives would have been made less happy by the person's death. How can it matter, especially in the split-second during which agents must sometimes decide whether and how to act, what if any specific intent motivates the decision to try to save the drowning victim? Contrary to Kant's declaration that only a morally pure rational will representing to itself the categorical imperative is morally good, and is otherwise at best morally indifferent, Mill thinks the attitude of the agent is altogether morally irrelevant. Mill wants to improve the pleasurable quality of life for every sentient being inhabiting the planet, and, perhaps, beyond. In this practical effort, the internal mental states of persons who act, unknowable to others anyway in trying to morally evaluate their actions, seems very far removed from questions about the moral good or evil that is done.

The point at this stage of the argument is not that Mill is right and Kant is wrong, or that Kant is right and Mill is wrong. What is important is the two stand for interesting alternatives at opposite extremes in the range of theoretical choices available to moral philosophy. The question of whether the ethics of an action depend on or are independent of the moral attitude of an agent, or whether the ethics of an action depend on or are independent of the consequences they produce with respect to happiness or unhappiness, pleasure or pain, or other psychological effects, is a fundamental division in ethics, a branching of main pathways in normative thinking. We must wrestle with the attractions, advantages, and disadvantages of both sides in order to see our way clear to a proper understanding of moral obligation and what is morally required of each morally responsible agent.

CALCULATING UTILITARIAN CONSEQUENCES

There are special difficulties in calculating the moral implications of complex kinds of actions on the basis of their consequences for pleasure and pain. Potential hazards for Mill's utilitarianism in this category of Mill's theory include the tabulation of the reasonable expectations of resulting happiness or unhappiness, pleasure or pain or displeasure, brought about by a contemplated action on the part of a moral agent. Mill runs through a catalog of objections to his utilitarianism and tries to neutralize the criticisms:

Again, defenders of utility often find themselves called upon to reply to such objections as this—that there is not time, previous to action, for calculating and weighing the effects of any line of conduct on the general happiness. This is exactly as if anyone were to say that it is impossible to guide our conduct by Christianity, because there is not time, on every occasion on which anything has to be done, to read through the Old and New Testaments. The answer to the objection is, that there has been ample time, namely, the whole past duration of the human species. During all that time mankind have been learning by experience the tendencies of actions; on which experience all the prudence, as well as all the morality of life, is dependent. (34)

The first objection Mill considers has to do with the practical circumstances under which utilitarian values can be decided in determining whether or not an action contributes to or detracts from the sum total of happiness in the world. He emphasizes what might be called the mathematics of moral decision making in a utilitarian framework.

We are expected to add up the happiness and unhappiness resulting from an action to determine whether it is morally justified or not. This is the equivalent of punching in the plus and minus values on a keypad until we hit the sum total and see whether a contemplated action is expected to produce more happiness than unhappiness or the reverse, or more pleasure than pain or displeasure, or the reverse. We need then only follow the means-to-ends procedures specified in the relevant calculations to bring about whatever actions are prescribed as producing the greatest happiness for the greatest number. If Mill is right, we will thereby have done what is morally required and avoided all that is morally prohibited. We will have done what is morally right and refrained from what is morally wrong, contributed to moral good in the world and acted in such a way as to prevent or inhibit moral evil. The theory, like that of many moral philosophies, sounds promising in abstract terms. When we think about the complications involved in trying to put the theory into practice, sometimes unexpected difficulties emerge.

Mill's answer to this challenge is typical of the problems he considers and the kinds of solutions he proposes. His reply is commonsensical, and has much in common with other attempts he makes to rebuff criticisms of utilitarianism. He argues that the objection is of the same kind that might be raised with equal justice or injustice against other moral theories. Thus, Mill remarks rhetorically that other moral philosophies face precisely the same problem in trying to evaluate the options they have on the basis of any set of principles. If it is objectionable in utilitarian ethics that there is an inevitable and potentially action-crippling delay during the time it takes to calculate whether an action is likely to produce more happiness than its opposite, more pleasure than pain or displeasure, then, as Mill justly remarks, the same complaint might be raised against Christian ethics, in which it might be said that a practitioner of that religious morality must read through and interpret hundreds of pages of holy Scripture in order to decide what is or is not morally obligatory or morally forbidden.

Mill's point is not that religious ethics is limited in this way. Rather, he argues that utilitarian ethics is no more limited in this respect than the theory with which he compares his principle of the greatest good. As a Christian ethicist has a practical sense of what is morally obligated or forbidden without consulting the Scriptures page by page, so a utilitarian knows what the principle of utility demands of us, in a rough and ready but perfectly adequate mental calculation of what kinds of actions are likely to produce more happiness than unhappiness in the sense of promoting more pleasure than pain or displeasure. We do not need to take time out from the exigencies of rapid-fire moral decision making in order to determine that it is likely to cause more pain than pleasure if we run traffic lights without regard for other motorists, or that it is likely to cause more pleasure than pain if we were to spend spare change on a worthy charity as opposed to giving it over to a person who has indicated a self-destructive desire for drug abuse. The careful calculations that are presupposed as part of utilitarian moral theory do not hinder commonsense reliance on basic considerations of utilitarianism as a compass for orienting ourselves toward moral good and avoidance of moral evil.

The same method of defending utilitarianism occurs in Mill's consideration of another objection. Mill is understandably impatient with criticisms that seem to apply peculiarly to utilitarianism but that if valid would have negative implications for all moral doctrines. He refuses to require utilitarianism to be held to a higher standard of practical applicability than any other moral philosophy. He argues that:

> There is no difficulty in proving any ethical standard whatever to work ill, if we suppose universal idiocy to be conjoined with it; but on any hypothesis short of that, mankind must by this time have acquired positive beliefs as to the effects of some actions on their happiness; and the beliefs which have thus come down are the rules of morality for the multitude, and for the philosopher until he has succeeded in finding better. (35)

Mill's conclusion is that any moral theory can appear to be unworkable if we imagine it applied by persons who are so incompetent that they cannot rely on reasonable judgment in order to apply its principles. Mill perhaps overemphasizes the degree to which lack of sympathy with any moral theory is likely to make its principles appear inept. He wants to say that the criticisms of utilitarianism considered in this category would all apply with equal force to any other moral philosophy, and to that extent are not problems with which the theory of the greatest good for the greatest number need be especially concerned. The opponents of utilitarianism assume that some alternative to the theory will fare better against their criticisms, whereas Mill's defense of the greatest good principle is that all such moral philosophies are precisely on a par when it comes to the problem of putting their principles into practice without a more sympathetic understanding of how they are supposed to guide moral decision making.

ACT AND RULE UTILITARIANISM

There is a difference in the level of generality at which the greatest happiness principle can be applied in moral judgment and decision making. Mill does not explicitly draw the distinction, which is sometimes described as that between *act* versus *rule* utilitarianisms. *Act utilitarianism* is an ethical theory by which the morality of each individual action is evaluated on the basis of whether it produces greater happiness. *Rule utilitarianism* does not try to evaluate the morality of individual acts, but of general policies, procedures, rules of conduct, and moral maxims, which if followed tend to produce greater happiness.

The difference is that it is often impractical to judge the pleasure produced by a particular act. In many cases it is difficult if not practically impossible to predict the long-term worldwide effect of an action on the pleasure or pain resulting from the behavior of any moral agent on all sentient beings. This is the objection Mill considers as threatening to make act utilitarianism hopelessly impractical. Rule utilitarianism may appear to avoid such difficulties by considering general rules under which particular actions are categorized, and which rules are justified in case they fall under the principle of being the sort of actions that have a high probability of attaining greater happiness than unhappiness. In adopting a rule utilitarianism, we do not always need to calculate the effect of an action on the resulting happiness or unhappiness, but we can justify an action if it is of the kind that is morally obligatory according to a general rule by virtue of contributing positively to the sum total of utility. A utilitarian moral philosophy thereby achieves an economy in its justification of actions and practical moral decision making, by appealing to rules as principles with general application to the morality of individual actions.

Mill does not establish a sharp distinction between act and rule utilitarianism. He nevertheless argues in effect that utilitarian rules should be invoked when act utilitarianism is rendered impractical, without finding it necessary to eliminate act utilitarianism in favor of rule utilitarianism. He explains:

> But to consider the rules of morality as improvable, is one thing; to pass over the intermediate generalization entirely, and endeavour to test each individual action directly by the first principle, is another. It is a strange notion that the acknowledgment of a first principle is inconsistent with the admission of secondary ones. To inform a traveller respecting the place of his ultimate destination, is not to forbid the use of land-marks and direction-posts on the way. The proposition that happiness is the end and aim of morality, does not mean that no road ought to be laid down to that goal, or that persons going thither should not be advised to take one direction rather than another. (35–36)

He offers a more flexible combined version of act and rule utilitarianism. There is no incompatibility between both ways of applying utilitarian principles. When actions are directly comparable as involving the greatest happiness for the greatest number from an individual standpoint, Mill applies utilitarian principles to particular actions, and otherwise invokes general utilitarian rules as moral justification. Mill thereby avoids criticisms that would refute act utilitarianism, and makes it possible to defend a more plausible rule utilitarianism that is more appropriate in many instances. Arguing that applications of utilitarianism need not always be evaluated as individual acts makes Mill's moral philosophy more flexible and adaptable to difficult applications.

MORAL SANCTIONS OF UTILITARIANISM

Mill also considers the question of why a moral agent ought to do whatever is morally obligated on utilitarian principles. The problem of providing *sanctions* for a moral philosophy is one of explaining why an agent ought to follow any given moral rules of conduct. It is one thing to determine what it is morally correct to do as a purely theoretical matter, and quite another to establish a convincing reason that will motivate moral agents to actually do what utilitarianism morally requires in practice. There is always a potential discrepancy between knowing what we ought to do and choosing to do it. We might know the traffic laws so thoroughly that we can pass a written driving test with flying colors, but choose not to follow the law when we get behind the wheel. We need a motivation to do what is obligated by law or moral principles in order to realize an ethical system's ideals.

Mill describes utilitarian sanctions for observing the theoretical moral implications of utilitarianism. He first explains the importance of having adequate motivations for implementing utilitarian principles:

> The question is often asked, and properly so, in regard to any supposed moral standard—What is its sanction? what are the motives to obey it? or more specifically, what is the source of its obligation? whence does it derive its binding force? It is a necessary part of moral philosophy to provide the answer to this question; which, though frequently assuming the shape of an objection to the utilitarian morality, as if it had some special applicability to that above others, really arises in regard to all standards. It arises, in fact, whenever a person is called on to *adopt* a standard, or refer morality to any basis on which he has not been accustomed to rest it. (39)

The need to provide a reason for agents to do what is morally correct has always been recognized as an important part of moral philosophy.

Socrates, in Plato's *Republic,* maintains that we ought to do what is morally obligatory because it is healthy for the harmony and proper order of parts within the soul to act justly. Even if we can morally misbehave without being discovered or punished, it remains in the rational self-interest of our immortal souls to be reincarnated in a favorable embodiment, which Socrates believes will be decided according to whether we have acted morally or immorally.

Aristotle, in his *Nicomachean Ethics,* offers another motivation for acting rightly on the grounds that it is only through virtue that we become capable of the highest form of friendship, dedicated to the love of friends for their own sakes, and hence to promoting the perfection of their virtues. Aristotle argues that the highest third of three types of friendship is one of the greatest goods for all persons, and as such it is also in our rational self-interests to do what is morally right even if we can escape punishment when we act immorally. For otherwise we are incapable of the highest form of friendship, and it is only through such friendship that we can fulfill our natural human potential as rational social animals.

Kant, in the *Grounding,* argues that the motivation for observing the categorical imperative is that it is an act of moral duty that does not necessarily confer happiness, but that by doing so we make ourselves worthy of happiness.

Mill takes another distinctively utilitarian approach to the problem of motivating moral action in conformity with the greatest happiness principle. Mill insists that in the first place the same reasons that apply as sanctions for the pursuit of other moral principles laid down by other ethical systems are also available to utilitarianism. He distinguishes between two main categories of moral sanctions, *internal* and *external.* External sanctions include wanting to preserve a good reputation and avoid bad opinions and punishments that otherwise accrue to persons who do not follow recognized moral obligations. An external sanction is any reward for doing what is morally good and any punishment for doing what is morally wrong. As in Socrates' reference to the rewards or punishments of the eternal soul, and for those who believe that God exists and stands in judgment of moral agents in an afterlife, these can include a similar motivation for following the principles of utilitarianism. Mill maintains:

> The principle of utility either has, or there is no reason why it might not have, all the sanctions which belong to any other system of morals. Those sanctions which are either external or internal. Of the external sanctions it is not necessary to speak at any length. They are, the hope of favour and the fear of displeasure from our fellow creatures or from the Ruler of the Universe, along with whatever we may have of sympathy or affection for them, or of love and awe of Him, inclining us to do His will independently of selfish consequences. There is evidently no reason why all these motives for observance should not attach themselves to the utilitarian morality, as completely and as powerfully as to any other. Indeed, those of them which refer to our fellow creatures are sure to do so, in proportion to the amount of general intelligence; for whether there be any other ground of moral obligation than the general happiness or not, men do desire happiness; and however imperfect may be their own practice, they desire and commend all conduct in others toward themselves, by which they think their happiness is promoted. (40–41)

Whatever sanctions motivate morally correct behavior generally, according to Mill, can equally apply in the case of utilitarianism. From the standpoint of assuring conformity with utilitarian principles, any of the reasons that move agents to follow moral requirements prescribed by other moral theories can also presumably be brought to bear in the service of utilitarian values. The utilitarian consequence is what matters to a utilitarian, by which any morally permissible sanction is justified as a means to the end of attaining the greatest happiness for the greatest number. Mill concludes that utilitarianism does not suffer from any disadvantage with respect to the sanctions available to motivate actions in accord with its principles when compared with those of other traditional non-utilitarian moral doctrines. He argues that:

> The whole force therefore of external reward and punishment, whether physical or moral, whether proceeding from God or from our fellowmen, together with all that the capacities of human nature admit, of disinterested devotion to either, become available to enforce the utilitarian morality, in proportion as that morality is recognised; and the more powerfully, the more the appliances of education and general cultivation are bent to the purpose. (41)

The internal sanctions of morality Mill regards as identical in the case of all moralities, including utilitarianism. Internal motivations for following moral requirements have to do with feelings of conscience whereby we can only remain in peace with ourselves if we live up to our moral obligations. It is an internal sanction of utilitarian morality that agents who accept its principles believe they are morally obligated to do what promotes the greatest good for the greatest number, and believe themselves not to be acting rightly if they do not do whatever they can to help promote the world's sum total of pleasure. There is thus a powerful internal feeling that drives utilitarians to act, if they recognize the moral duty to do what utility requires, in wanting to make the world a better place for all sentient beings. Mill explains that the internal sanction of conscience is rarely found in its pure form, but is typically combined in complicated ways with other psychological factors:

> The internal sanction of duty, whatever our standard of duty may be, is one and the same—a feeling in our own mind; a pain, more or less intense, attendant on violation of duty, which in properly-cultivated moral natures rises, in the more serious cases, into shrinking from it as an impossibility. This feeling, when disinterested, and connecting itself with the pure idea of duty, and not with some particular form of it, or with any of the merely accessory circumstances, is the essence of Conscience; though in that complex phenomenon as it actually exists, the simple fact is in general all encrusted over with collateral associations, derived from sympathy, from love, and still more from fear; from all the forms of religious feeling; from the recollections of childhood and of all our past life; from self-esteem, desire of the esteem of others, and occasionally even self-abasement. (41–42)

Although Mill does not offer an argument, he clearly implies that the internal sanction for morality is more basic and in that sense more important than any external sanction. He speaks of the subjective feeling of conscience as the "ultimate sanction" of morality. The sanction of conscience is as freely available to utilitarians as to the followers of other moral doctrines. The most powerful reason for acting morally therefore leaves utilitarian principles at no disadvantage. Mill admits that the internal sanction of conscience has no force for persons who do not share the feeling, for whom only external sanctions can motivate their actions by threat or reward, hope or fear. He reminds us that the same is true of any moral theory.

> The ultimate sanction, therefore, of all morality (external motives apart) being a subjective feeling in our own minds, I see nothing embarrassing to those whose standard is utility, in the question, what is the sanction of that particular standard? We may answer, the same as of all other moral standards—the conscientious feelings of mankind. Undoubtedly this sanction has no binding efficacy on those who do not possess the feelings it appeals to; but neither will these persons be more obedient to any other moral principle than to the utilitarian one. On them morality of any kind has no hold but through the external sanctions. Meanwhile the feelings exist, a fact in human nature, the reality of which, and the great power with which they are capable of acting on those in whom they have been duly cultivated, are proved by experience. No reason has ever been shown why they may not be cultivated to as great intensity in connection with the utilitarian, as with any other rule of morals. (42–43)

Mill's strategy is to prove that utilitarianism is no different than and at no comparative disadvantage with respect to other ethical theories. The same internal and external sanctions that provide rational agents with reasons for doing what is right apply in the case of utilitarianism as in any moral philosophy. There are no grounds for discrediting utilitarianism on the basis of a lack of moral sanctions if utilitarianism can be as strongly motivated as any of its competitors. If anything, the fact that utilitarianism harnesses morality to considerations of the pleasure and pain of all sentient beings provides a greater sanction for ethical action in the form of compassion for the sufferings of others, and a desire to increase one's own and one's friend's and family's happiness along with improvements in the greater general good.

JUSTIFICATION OF UTILITARIANISM

After explaining the principle of utility and offering a comparison of utilitarianism with non-utilitarian moralities, Mill is prepared to argue in defense of the truth of the greatest happiness principle and to discuss the extent to which it may be possible to prove that the theory is correct. He repeats his previous assertion that it is impossible to prove the first principles of any theory; first principles generally are to be assumed rather than proved. He raises an important methodological question about the ways in which it may nevertheless be possible to argue on behalf of moral conclusions, and about whether the appropriate types of evidence for justifying ethical principles might be the same as or relevantly similar or related to those required in the natural sciences, or whether they must be significantly different. He poses these questions about justifying a system of ethics:

> It has already been remarked, that questions of ultimate ends do not admit of proof, in the ordinary acceptation of the term. To be incapable of proof by reasoning is common to all first principles; to the first premises of our knowledge, as well as to those of our conduct. But the former, being matters of fact, may be the subject of a direct appeal to the faculties which judge of fact—namely, our senses, and our internal consciousness. Can an appeal be made to the same faculties on questions of practical ends? Or by what other faculty is cognizance taken of them? (52)

He takes another step toward answering the problem by identifying the exact kind of information required to make a moral theory plausible. He observes that moral philosophy concerns the ends of actions, which, true to his hedonistic consequentialism, he interprets as involving inclination or desire. Utilitarianism implies that pleasure is the only ultimate end, the only thing that is finally desirable, for the sake of which all actions are undertaken. With this additional clarification, Mill then inquires about what is needed in order to justify the truth of the thesis that happiness in the sense of pleasure is in fact the only ultimate end and that all actions insofar as they are desirable are means to that final end:

> Questions about ends are, in other words, questions what things are desirable. The utilitarian doctrine is that happiness is desirable, and the only thing desirable, as an end; all other things being only desirable as means to that end. What ought to be required of this doctrine—what conditions is it requisite that the doctrine should fulfil—to make good its claim to be believed? (52)

He reverts to a previous line of argument that now finds a new application. He earlier claims that the only way to determine what is preferable is to discover empirically what is actually preferred by all or at least a large percentage of knowledgeable persons with experience of whatever multiple pleasures are being compared. It was in this way that Mill proposed to justify the conclusion that higher intellectual pleasures are preferable to lower sensual pleasures. He applies much the same empirical reasoning with respect to the present question of whether, to what extent, and in what way it may be possible to justify the truth of utilitarianism as a correct moral theory. The task for Mill's moral philosophy is, accordingly, to provide proof for the truth of the greatest happiness principle, which is to say for hedonic utilitarianism, insofar as it can be justified by reason or evidence. He maintains:

The only proof capable of being given that an object is visible, is that people actually see it. The only proof that a sound is audible, is that people hear it; and so of the other sources of our experience. In like manner, I apprehend, the sole evidence it is possible to produce that anything is desirable, is that people do actually desire it. If the end which the utilitarian doctrine proposes to itself were not, in theory and in practice, acknowledged to be an end, nothing could ever convince any person that it was so. No reason can be given why the general happiness is desirable, except that each person, so far as he believes it to be attainable, desires his own happiness. This, however, being a fact, we have not only all the proof which the case admits of, but all which it is possible to require, that happiness is good: that each person's happiness is a good to that person, and the general happiness, therefore, a good to the aggregate of all persons. Happiness has made out its title as *one* of the ends of conduct, and consequently one of the criteria of morality. (52–53)

As before, it is crucial to appreciate the precise kind of question Mill is asking, the precise context of argument in which it arises, and the precise sense in which Mill introduces empirical evidence about what is actually desired as a reliable indication of what is morally preferable. We have seen that there is a fallacy in trying to infer that something is morally preferable or that it should be preferred from the fact that it is actually preferred. The problem for Mill is whether utilitarianism commits this fallacy.

We have already observed how the difficulty arises. Preferability in the sense that can be logically supported and documented in experience by proof of the fact that something is in fact preferred appears only to establish that it is capable of being preferred. The evidence does not establish the normative preferability of whatever is actually preferred as something morally worthy of being preferred. It is therefore essential to consider Mill's words carefully when he says that the only proof that something is desirable is that people actually desire it.

Mill invokes an analogy between experiential evidence for the actual desirability of happiness and the visibility and audibility of sensible things and sensible properties. Here the word clearly has to do with the ability of something visible to be perceived rather than the moral value of whatever is perceived. It is reasonable as a result to suppose that Mill intends by his appeal to what is actually desired to prove only that happiness in the sense of pleasure is desirable in the sense of being capable of being desired. All that he seems to want at this stage of the argument is a recognition that happiness is in fact desired as an end and is thus in fact desirable in the sense of being capable of being desired. Whether happiness should be the ultimate end of all action is a different question that Mill does not immediately address.

The additional moral connection he needs depends on an analysis of what it means for something to be good or a good. This Mill understands in terms of what persons actually choose for themselves. His purpose is not to ask what ought to be good or a good for the persons who choose whatever they choose. He seeks only to determine what moral agents actually regard as good, which he maintains is the only avenue by which we can come to know what is good. This is because the meaning of "good" on Mill's account is whatever is pursued as an ultimate end. Moral subjects will presumably select some type of happiness, if he is right, as the ultimate end of action, leaving it as an open question in what form they will try to attain pleasure. As a further argument, Mill mentions that if it were not acknowledged that happiness is the ultimate end of all action by virtue of the ends that agents actually pursue, then nothing else could persuade anyone of its truth. The idea seems to be that only the fact that happiness is the ultimate end of action makes it possible for philosophers such as Aristotle, Kant, and Mill, among others, to be convinced that happiness is the end or motivation of action. There is no other reason that could possibly be produced to prove that happiness generally is desired, according to Mill, other than the empirical fact that each person considered individually does in fact desire his or her own individual happiness.

There is no other necessary or possible evidence that could establish happiness as a good, even if it is not the only good. To be a good in this sense is identified in meaning with the fact that people in fact value happiness. Happiness is a good in the same sense and by the same justification that reveals other actually chosen things as goods or values. Mill would presumably include such things as health, family, opportunity to improve experience and education, and other manifest goods as means freely chosen to attain another end. Ultimately, again, if Mill is right, they are goods for the sake of and because they contribute to our happiness. He argues that since, empirically speaking, every person ultimately desires his or her own happiness, it follows that the general good, the greatest happiness for all persons, is the aggregate collectively considered of all the individual happiness chosen as a good by each individual. From this, Mill does not yet conclude that happiness is the only end of action, but only, as he says with explicit emphasis, that it is *one* of the ends of action and as such *one* of the standards by which to judge morality.

The next step for Mill is to maintain that happiness is the *only* thing that is desired. He asserts that whatever is desired is desired at least in the individual case as a means to the ultimate end of attaining happiness. He argues that virtue is valued either because it is itself pleasurable, or its absence is painful, or both. Some virtues might also be desired as means to another end, ultimately, because they help to make us happy not for their own sake, but instrumentally because of other ends to which the cultivation, practice, and experience of virtue contribute. Virtue is a particularly important case, because critics of consequentialism such as Kant have sometimes insisted that virtue is a perfection of moral attitude that as a duty is not only irrelevant to and not undertaken for the sake of pleasure or happiness, but is frequently opposed to desire and inclination. Mill, on the contrary, believes that there is no conflict:

> It results from the preceding considerations, that there is in reality nothing desired except happiness. Whatever is desired otherwise than as a means to some end beyond itself, and ultimately to happiness, is desired as itself a part of happiness, and is not desired for itself until it has become so. Those who desire virtue for its own sake, desire it either because the consciousness of it is a pleasure, or because the consciousness of being without it is a pain, or for both reasons united; as in truth the pleasure and pain seldom exist separately, but almost always together—the same person feeling pleasure in the degree of virtue attained, and pain in not having attained more. If one of these gave him no pleasure, and the other no pain, he would not love or desire virtue, or would desire it only for the other benefits which it might produce to himself or to persons whom he cared for. (57–58)

If, in fact, the ultimate end of all action is happiness, then it is reasonable, and even, arguably, as Mill holds, the only standard by which to evaluate the morality of an action, in terms of its aim or end. The inference is much the same as in other kinds of evaluations. We judge contests on the basis of a stated goal, and we decide who has won or succeeded on the basis of what the purpose of the activity is and how well participants on trial have achieved or failed to achieve their respective ends. It may therefore be appropriate to apply the same kind of measure to the moral evaluation of actions or rules, all of which, Mill concludes, are ultimately directed toward the general end of happiness.

Any action is successful, then, a moral as opposed to an immoral action, insofar as and to the degree that it contributes successfully to the end of all action. This is to say, judging by the only possible evidence, the pursuit of happiness interpreted as pleasure, as Mill's utilitarianism holds. An action is morally wrong or morally indifferent to the degree that it does not promote the general happiness or greatest good for the greatest number. Mill links general happiness as the end of all action attested by the freely chosen desires and preferences of agents manifested in their actions to the principle of utility as a proof that the theory provides a correct moral philosophy. He concludes:

> We have now, then, an answer to the question, of what sort of proof the principle of utility is susceptible. If the opinion, which I have now stated is psychologically true—if human nature is so constituted as to desire nothing which is not either a part of happiness or a means of happiness, we can have no other proof, and we require no other, that these are the only things desirable. If so, happiness is the sole end of human action, and the promotion of it the test by which to judge of all human conduct; from whence it necessarily follows that it must be the criterion of morality, since a part is included in the whole. (58)

The clue to understanding Mill's proof of utilitarianism is signposted in his assertion that the empirical psychological evidence to which he appeals establishes that happiness is the *only* thing that is desirable, and hence the *only* ultimate end of action. If this is true, which for Mill stands, if at all, as a distinctively experiential thesis about the ends that agents actually choose, then utility is the only standard by which an action can be morally justified. An action or rule of conduct is morally correct to the extent that it contributes to the general happiness, interpreted as pleasure, and morally wrong to the extent that it detracts from the general happiness. An action or rule is morally justified to whatever extent it produces or tends to produce more happiness than unhappiness, more pleasure than displeasure or pain. If there is no other end of action than happiness, then, according to Mill, it is only by reference to concerns about the general happiness that the morality of actions and rules can be morally judged.

UTILITARIAN ANALYSIS OF JUSTICE

An important implication of Mill's utilitarianism is its analysis of the concept of justice. The idea of justice is often raised as an objection to consequentialism. Deontology, as the polar opposite moral theory, emphasizes the moral rights of all rational beings. Kant, as a prime exemplar of deontological ethics, interprets justice as an implication of the categorical imperative, according to which all rational beings are to be treated as moral ends in themselves and not merely as the means to any other end. If deontology morally obligates moral agents never to treat others as mere means to an end, then considerations of justice are absolute, and violations of a person's rights can never be morally justified for the sake of achieving greater happiness.

Mill responds directly to this challenge. He meets the objection by offering a utilitarian explanation of the nature of justice, and arguing that other moral theories have no comparable explanation to give. He not only answers the objection directly by analyzing the concept of justice from within the resources of a utilitarian moral theory and explaining why justice is morally obligatory according to utilitarian principles. He goes farther by taking the offensive against the contrary anti-utilitarian ethics, arguing that whereas utilitarianism provides a plausible explanation of the meaning of justice, non-utilitarian theories cannot explain the concept of justice without invoking the concept of utility and greatest happiness principle. Mill acknowledges that utilitarianism has sometimes been criticized on the grounds that the pursuit of happiness often appears to be morally opposed to considerations of justice. If we do not understand the utilitarian concept of justice, then we might imagine situations in which utilitarian principles seem to make acts of injustice directed against a minority of individuals morally permissible or even morally obligatory in order to achieve the greater happiness. Mill observes:

> In all ages of speculation, one of the strongest obstacles to the reception of the doctrine that Utility or Happiness is the criterion of right and wrong, has been drawn from the idea of Justice. The powerful sentiment, and apparently clear perception, which that word recalls with a rapidity and certainty resembling an instinct, have seemed to the majority of thinkers to point to an inherent quality in things; to show that the Just must have an existence in Nature as something absolute—generically distinct from every variety of the Expedient, and, in idea, opposed to it, though (as is commonly acknowledged) never, in the long run, disjoined from it in fact. (62)

Mill's first move is to clarify the meaning of justice, and the contexts in which we refer to acts as just or unjust, in order to understand what is meant when we speak of justice. He associates standards of justice with the possession of legal or moral rights. We are treated with justice when our legal or moral rights are respected, and oppositely, we are treated unjustly when our rights are violated. Mill elaborates on the kinds of goods that are often characterized as rights, including personal liberty, property, and other qualities, conditions, states, and values that are protected by law. He acknowledges that legal rights are not absolute or unqualified, but subject to exceptions:

> In the first place, it is mostly considered unjust to deprive any one of his personal liberty, his property, or any other thing which belongs to him by law. Here, therefore, is one instance of the application of the terms just and unjust in a perfectly definite sense, namely, that it is just to respect, unjust to violate, the *legal rights* of anyone. But this judgment admits of several exceptions, arising from the other forms in which the notions of justice and injustice present themselves. For example, the person who suffers the deprivation may (as the phrase is) have *forfeited* the rights which he is so deprived of: a case to which we shall return presently. . . . (64–65)

Mill also argues at length that there are legal rights that are unsupported by moral justification, and therefore not only need not be observed, but in some cases ought not to be respected. What the law states is in some instances morally unjustified or even morally objectionable. We can easily satisfy ourselves that this is true by considering examples of laws that in the past have favored persons because of their birth or connection with a royal family, or because they are members of a particular political party that have been unfairly awarded special legal privileges. An obvious case from American history is the existence of laws that denied and deprived the right to vote to women or members of racial minorities, especially African Americans. Other societies at other times have instituted equally morally insupportable but unfortunately legal rights of the sort Mill has in mind. He continues:

> Secondly; the legal rights of which he is deprived may be rights which *ought* not to have belonged to him; in other words, the law which confers on him these rights may be a bad law. When it is so, or when (which is the same thing for our purpose) it is supposed to be so, opinions will differ as to the justice or injustice of infringing it. Some maintain that no law, however bad, ought to be disobeyed by an individual citizen; that his opposition to it, if shown at all, should only be shown in endeavouring to get it altered by competent authority. This opinion (which condemns many of the most illustrious benefactors of mankind, and would often protect pernicious institutions against the only weapons which, in the state of things existing at the time, have any chance of succeeding against them) is defended, by those who hold it, on grounds of expediency; principally on that of the importance, to the common interest of mankind, of maintaining inviolate the sentiment of submission to law. . . . When, however, a law is thought to be unjust, it seems always to be regarded as being so in the same ways in which a breach of law is unjust, namely, by infringing somebody's right; which, as it cannot in this case be a legal right, receives a different appellation, and is called a moral right. We may say, therefore, that a second case of injustice consists in taking or withholding from any person that to which he has a *moral right*. (65–66)

Mill strikes a particularly utilitarian note when he remarks above that it is not only sometimes morally permissible to violate an unjust law, but those who do so are often rightly regarded as benefactors of mankind. Those who object to the political policies of a morally objectionable government, and who protest the government's actions by civil disobedience and illegal demonstrations, often act in a morally defensible or morally obligatory way, by following the dictates of ethics even when they are contrary to law. It can be a brave action to endure legal punishments in acts of civil disobedience for the sake of promoting a higher moral good, as Mill observes.

Although Mill does not mention Kant in this context, Kant is undoubtedly the most prominent figure, who, in his essay "What is Enlightenment?" argues that there is never a moral justification for acting illegally, even when the law is morally wrong. Here is yet another stark contrast between Mill and Kant. Mill concludes that there is an important distinction between legal and moral rights, and argues that moral rights must always take precedence over legal rights whenever the two conflict. He identifies as a more important sense of injustice any action that violates an individual's moral as distinct from legal rights. This overture makes it necessary for him to explain more precisely what is meant by a moral right and the corresponding sense of moral justice. Mill was personally involved in related issues of the day, especially the problems of race and women's rights, as evidenced by the publication of his book *The Subjection of Women* (1869) and essays on social equality, political and economic questions, and the morality of British conduct with respect to its colonies.

Mill adds two further interpretations of the concepts of justice and moral rights to his analysis. They concern that which is deserved by persons and the obligation to keep faith, promises, and obligations to others. Mill explains the third and fourth senses of justice in expositions that are supposed to exhaust the possibilities for justice and rights, including legal and moral rights, and matters of desert and faith keeping. The concept of desert is presented as follows, when he argues:

> Thirdly, it is universally considered just that each person should obtain that (whether good or evil) which he *deserves;* and unjust that he should obtain a good, or be made to undergo an evil, which he does not deserve. This is, perhaps, the clearest and most emphatic form in which the idea of justice is conceived by the general mind. As it involves the notion of desert, the question arises what constitutes desert? Speaking in a general way, a person is understood to deserve good if he does right, evil if he does wrong; and in a more particular sense, to deserve good from those to whom he does or has done good, and evil from those to whom he does or has done evil. The precept of returning good for evil has never been regarded as a case of the fulfillment of justice, but as one in which the claims of justice are waived, in obedience to other considerations. (66–67)

The idea of the third category of justice, and the reason why Mill believes that it is among the most common, is that it is just for persons to get what they deserve, or to which they are entitled, in the sense of what they have in one way or another earned. For the same reason it is unjust for them to be deprived of such goods or to receive an evil that they have done nothing to deserve. Mill proceeds to consider the fourth category of justice or sense in which justice is sometimes spoken of, referring in this context as we have indicated to keeping or breaking one's word to another, holding or breaking faith or a personal or contractual agreement of one sort or another with a person to whom one has an obligation to fulfill a promise. Mill identifies the fourth sense of justice and injustice in these terms:

> Fourthly, it is confessedly unjust to *break faith* with anyone: to violate an engagement, either express or implied, or disappoint expectations raised by our own conduct, at least if we have raised those expectations knowingly and voluntarily. Like the other obligations of justice already spoken of, this one is not regarded as absolute, but as capable of being overruled by a stronger obligation of justice on the other side; or by such conduct on the part of the person concerned as is deemed to absolve us from our obligation to him and to constitute a *forfeiture* of the benefit which he has been led to expect. (67)

The fifth and final sense of justice and injustice that Mill considers concerns impartiality and its opposite, treating persons with partiality and in that way and to that extent demonstrating favoritism or unequal preference. A teacher might be partial and in Mill's fifth sense unjust, therefore, if he or she were to show special treatment to students, giving them higher grades or special opportunities, not on the basis of their conduct or academic performance, but for such extraneous reasons as their eye color or hair or skin color, or because of the clothes they wear or who their parents are. Another sense of this type of injustice is *nepotism,* from the Greek word *nepos,* meaning "nephew," in which persons are offered special job privileges regardless of their abilities because they are related by birth to persons in power. Mill maintains:

> Fifthly, it is, by universal admission, inconsistent with justice o be *partial;* to show favour or preference to one person over another, in matters to which favour and preference do not properly apply. Impartiality, however, does not seem to be regarded as a duty in itself, but rather as instrumental to some other duty; for it is admitted that favour and preference are not always censurable, and indeed the cases in which they are condemned are rather the exception than the rule. . . . Impartiality where rights are concerned is of course obligatory, but this is involved in the more general obligation of giving to everyone his right. A tribunal, for example, must be impartial, because it is bound to award, without regard to any other consideration, a disputed object to the one of two parties who has the right to it. There are other cases in which impartiality means, being solely influenced by desert; as with those who, in the capacity of judges, preceptors, or parents, administer reward and punishment as such. There are cases, again, in which it means, being solely influenced by consideration for the public interest; as in making a selection among candidates for a Government employment. Impartiality, in short, as an obligation of justice, may be said to mean, being exclusively influenced by the considerations which it is supposed ought to influence the particular case in hand; and resisting the solicitation of any motives which prompt to conduct different from what those considerations would dictate. (67–68)

With this system of categories of justice and rights in place, Mill turns next to the problem of explaining the nature of justice. He explains the moral basis for objecting to acts of moral injustice, and the reason why it is obligatory to preserve and protect the rights of all persons and to promote considerations of justice. He defends individual rights and the requirements of social justice on utilitarian grounds in terms of the consequences of respecting moral rights in any of the legitimate senses of the word he distinguishes.

Mill naturally returns to Kant as the chief defender of rights and justice and the chief opponent of consequentialism. Mill repeats his criticism that Kant's categorical imperative presupposes and depends for its conclusions on considerations involving the general happiness. His objection remains based on a misinterpretation of the categorical imperative, as we have already remarked. The proposition that an action is supposed to be justified by its capability of being adopted as law by all rational beings is simply not what Kant says, and for that reason Mill's complaint here does not constitute a relevant criticism of Kant's principle. Mill, insensitive to his misunderstanding of Kant, develops the argument as follows:

> When Kant (as before remarked) propounds as the fundamental principle of morals, "So act, that thy rule of conduct might be adopted as a law by all rational beings," he virtually acknowledges that the interest of mankind collectively, or at least of mankind indiscriminately, must be in the mind of the agent when conscientiously deciding on the morality of the act. Otherwise he uses words without a meaning; for, that a rule even of utter selfishness could not *possibly* be adopted by all rational beings—that there is any insuperable obstacle in the na-

ture of things to its adoption—cannot be even plausibly maintained. To give any meaning to Kant's principle, the sense put upon it must be, that we ought to shape our conduct by a rule which all rational beings might adopt *with benefit to their collective interest.* (78–79)

Mill's strategy is to interpret justice in terms of moral rights, and to interpret rights as interests individuals are entitled to have protected if and to the extent that they are justified on utilitarian grounds as promoting the greater social good. Mill divides the analysis of justice into two main parts:

To recapitulate; the idea of justice supposes two things; a rule of conduct, and a sentiment which sanctions the rule. The first must be supposed common to all mankind, and intended for their good. The other (the sentiment) is a desire that punishment may be suffered by those who infringe the rule. There is involved, in addition, the conception of some definite person who suffers by the infringement; whose rights (to use the expression appropriated to the case) are violated by it. And the sentiment of justice appears to me to be, the animal desire to repel or retaliate a hurt or damage to oneself, or to those with whom one sympathises, widened so as to include all persons, by the human capacity of enlarged sympathy, and the human conception of intelligent self-interest. From the latter elements, the feeling derives its morality; from the former, its peculiar impressiveness, and energy of self-assertion. (79)

It is significant and in accord with Mill's empirical methodology that, unlike Kant, he focuses here on the psychological aspects of the feeling of justice. To understand justice, Mill believes, it is necessary to appreciate the extent to which persons are motivated by powerful emotions, especially concerning acts of injustice. Mill regards our feelings about justice as an important factor in the social institutionalization of justice.

We do not understand justice as a motivation for moral behavior, he thinks, unless we know what it means for persons to be agitated as they often are about violations of justice and the desire to avoid injustice and see the requirements of justice fulfilled. The concept of justice combines a rule of conduct in the service of legal and moral rights, desert, keeping faith, and fairness or impartiality, and a certain feeling or sentiment of justice. Unlike Kant, Mill does not wish to discount the sentiment of justice, but to recognize it as integral to the idea of justice. The sentiment of justice is undoubtedly known firsthand by every person in strong feelings of indignation and hurt and all the emotions that accompany both an experience of injustice and the desire for justice in our own case and in those of others. What still remains for Mill to clarify is the utilitarian concept of rights.

MILL'S ETHICS AND THE CONCEPT OF MORAL RIGHTS

What is a right, legal or moral? Mill rejects the idea that rights are generally opposed to happiness in moral theory. He regards justice as a respect for rights that reflects a society's concern for the greatest happiness of the greatest number. He defines a right as "a valid claim on society" to be protected in the possession of a legitimate interest, the value of which is ultimately justified by utility. He says:

> I have, throughout, treated the idea of a *right* residing in the injured person, and violated by the injury, not as a separate element in the composition of the idea and sentiment, but as one of the forms in which the other two elements clothe themselves. These elements are, a hurt to some assignable person or persons on the one hand, and a demand for punishment, on the other. An examination of our own minds, I think, will show that these two things include all that we mean when we speak of violation of a right. When we call anything a person's right, we mean that he has a valid claim on society to protect him in the possession of it, either by the force of law, or by that of education and opinion. If he has what we consider a sufficient claim, on whatever account, to have something guaranteed to him by society, we say that he has a right to it. (79–80)

The rights that belong to the category of justice are interests that it serves the general happiness to protect. The right to due process under the law, the right to privacy, the right to an attorney if arrested, the right to free speech, and many others besides, are justified, to the extent that they are justified, by the fact that to accord them societal protection contributes to the general good, to the happiness of all individuals affected.

Thus, empirically, it makes a substantial majority in a society happier if citizens are able to live their lives in confidence knowing that they have certain protections of their interests that the society as a whole stands behind and helps to defend. If we believe that nonhuman animals also have moral rights and perhaps should have legal rights, then, Mill will say, it is justified by the effect of such principles on the sum total of happiness that follows as a consequence of instituting and protecting nonhuman animal interests. A right is morally justified on utilitarian principles, despite the costs of enforcing the relevant laws, provided that the overall happiness resulting from the observance of rights outweighs the unhappiness resulting from social conditions that obtain if legal and moral rights are not acknowledged.

Mill equally explains the absence of rights in terms of putative interests that are not utilitarian for a society to observe and protect. Where rights do not exist, it is because there is no identifiable general interest to be made out in support of the greatest happiness of the greatest number of members of a society. An example is the fact that there is no right for persons freely competing in an open economy to any specific amount of earnings. On the other hand, individuals have a legitimate utilitarian-justified right to ownership and control of property and the ability to compete freely with others for a fair market share in any moneymaking business. Mill offers this illustration:

> If we desire to prove that anything does not belong to him by right, we think this done as soon as it is admitted that society ought not to take measure for securing it to him, but should leave him to chance, or to his own exertions. Thus, a person is said to have a right to what he can earn in fair professional competition; because society ought not to allow any other person to hinder him from endeavouring to earn in that manner as much as he can. But he has not a right to three hundred a-year, though he may happen to be earning it; because society is not called on to provide that he shall earn that sum. On the contrary, if he owns ten thousand pounds three per cent. stock, he *has* a right to three hundred a-year; because society has come under an obligation to provide him with an income of that amount. (80)

Summarizing the utilitarian analysis of the concept of rights, Mill explains that the general happiness principle justifies the protection of interests where genuine rights obtain. He accounts for the righteous feeling that many persons associate psychologically with the observance of rights and the sentiment of justice that indicates an interest serving the general good. We have strong feelings about justice and injustice, according to Mill, because we recognize that such matters concern the happiness of all, to which all, including we as individuals, are entitled by the principle of utility. We get worked up about issues of justice and injustice because we recognize that everyone's interests are at stake, producing greater happiness or unhappiness potentially for all members of a society.

MILL'S MORAL PHILOSOPHY AND THE SOCIAL CONTRACT

Mill maintains that utilitarian ethics offers a plausible explanation of the origin and continued existence of rights, as well as the sentiment that attaches to the whole question of legal and moral rights. Non-utilitarian moral theories, in contrast, offer no comparable account of what is meant by the concept of a right, why it is worthwhile to respect and preserve and protect rights, the difference between genuine and spurious or merely ostensible moral rights, or the psychology of feelings of justice and injustice.

Utilitarians, unlike non-utilitarians, can plausibly argue that the reason why persons have such a strong sense of justice associated with powerful emotions is because the category of rights is directly connected with the preservation of an individual's most vital interests. All such interests are predicated ultimately on the right to life, but they also imply many further rights on which each subject's happiness in a social context depends, and which every person has a social stake in helping to preserve for the sake of all individuals protected by the observance of moral rights. Mill defends this utilitarian concept of legal and moral rights:

> To have a right, then, is, I conceive, to have something which society ought to defend me in the possession of. If the objector goes on to ask why it ought, I can give him no other reason than general utility. If that expression does not seem to convey a sufficient feeling of the strength of the obligation, nor to account for the peculiar energy of the feeling, it is because there goes to the composition of the sentiment, not a rational only but also an animal element, the thirst for retaliation; and this thirst derives its intensity, as well as its moral justification, from the extraordinarily important and impressive kind of utility which is concerned. The interest involved is that of security, to everyone's feelings the most vital of all interests. (80–81)

Mill discounts the myth of an originating social contract, developed in his day by such thinkers as Thomas Hobbes, Jean-Jacques Rousseau, and Locke. The idea of a social contract is that from a primitive state of nature in which all persons pursue only their individual interests, it eventually appears advantageous for them to band together into a social order, giving up being able to live without concern for the interests of others in a trade-off for the benefits obtained by living in a law-governed society. We sign on the dotted line, say social contract theorists, in order to profit from the energy, activity, and specialized abilities of others in a social group, in exchange for which each person agrees, according to a set of social rules, to cooperate together for the good of the whole.

Mill finds the fable instructive, despite its presumably false anthropology, as a philosophical story about the utilitarian justification for social organization. Mill nevertheless insists that the idea of a social contract does not really add anything to the bare-bones consequentialist account of the utility offered by complex social organization and the institution and protection of legal and moral rights:

> To escape from the other difficulties, a favourite contrivance has been the fiction of a contract, whereby at some unknown period all members of society engaged to obey laws, and consented to be punished for any disobedience to them; thereby giving to their legislators the right, which it is assumed they would not otherwise have had, of punishing them, either for their own good or for that of society. This happy thought was considered to get rid of the whole difficulty, and to legitimate the infliction of punishment, in virtue of another received maxim of justice, *volenti non fit injuria;* that is not unjust which is done with the consent of the person who is supposed to be hurt by it. I need hardly remark that, even if the consent were not a mere fiction, this maxim is not superior in authority to the others which it is brought in to supersede. It is, on the contrary, an instructive specimen of the loose and irregular manner in which supposed principles of justice grow up. (84)

The value of participating in social interaction when a system of law is rendered just according to the standard of utilitarianism can hardly be overestimated. Mill expresses the mutual observance of respect for other persons' rights as a prerequisite for being included in the social order. This is, in effect, Mill's version of Kant's kingdom of ends. The morality of observing the rights of others and the immorality of violating the interests of persons are explained by Mill's utilitarian consequentialism. We qualify as belonging to the fellowship of human beings by our willingness to protect the rights of others to the same extent that we need and want to have our rights protected by them. It is in a way membership in a social contract, although Mill has no desire to commit himself to the literal truth or even the explanatory usefulness of the idea of such an imaginary agreement. He now adds:

> Thus the moralities which protect every individual from being harmed by others, either directly or by being hindered in his freedom of pursuing his own good, are at once those which he himself has most at heart, and those which he has the strongest interest in publishing and enforcing by word and deed. It is by a person's observance of these, that his fitness to exist as one of the fellowship of human beings, is tested and decided; for on that depends his being a nuisance or not to those with whom he is in contact. Now it is these moralities primarily, which compose the obligations of justice. The most marked cases of injustice, and those which give the tone to the feeling of repugnance which characterizes the sentiment, are acts of wrongful aggression, or wrongful exercise of power over someone; the next are those which consist in wrongfully withholding from him something which is his due; in both cases, inflicting on him a positive hurt, either in the form of direct suffering, or of the privation of some good which he had reasonable ground, either of a physical or of a social kind, for counting upon. (89–90)

As further testimony to the pervasiveness of utilitarian principles, and hence to the correctness of utility as a sound basis for moral judgment, Mill alleges that most of the widely accepted "maxims of justice" are utilitarian concepts of justice in practice. Mill lists some of the most obvious of these, and explains the sense in which they are evidently intended to serve the principle of utility. The origin of such maxims and their justification are explainable in terms of their consequences as contributing to the greatest happiness of the greatest number. The fact, in turn, if Mill is right, that most of the maxims of justice are truly instrumentally valuable on utilitarian grounds is taken as yet another indication of the extent to which the greatest happiness principle is deeply ingrained in popular moral thinking, a sign, however inconclusive, of its being morally correct or at least in some ways on the right track in the social and legislative world. He states:

> Most of the maxims of justice current in the world, and commonly appealed to in its transactions, are simply instrumental to carrying into effect the principles of justice which we have now spoken of. That a person is only responsible for what he has done voluntarily, or could voluntarily have avoided; that it is unjust to condemn any person unheard; that the punishment ought to be proportioned to the offense, and the like, are maxims intended to prevent the just principle of evil for evil from being perverted to the infliction of evil without that justification. The greater part of these common maxims have come into use from the practice of courts of justice, which have been naturally led to a more complete recognition and elaboration than was likely to suggest itself to others, of the rules necessary to enable them to fulfill their double function, of inflicting punishment when due, and of awarding to each person his right. (91–92)

Mill interprets the concept of justice, moral rights, and respect for individual rights within a utilitarian moral framework in a very different way than Kant. Where Kant regards moral rights as absolute and inviolable accruing as direct implications of the categorical imperative, Mill, as a reflection of his consequentialist interpretation of rights, admits that there are extenuating circumstances under which even the most stridently entrenched moral rights can be overridden for the sake of the greater general happiness.

This is an important exception for Mill to allow. One of the standard objections to deontology in its unqualifiedly rigid adherence to the respect for moral rights is that it appears to lead to morally objectionable decisions in which devastating misery and pain must be endured for the sake of avoiding any violations of a person's moral rights. An action's consequences for a vigorous deontologist are morally irrelevant. Mill takes a more balanced stance, according to which legal and moral rights, as important as they ordinarily are, can at least in principle and sometimes in practice, be outweighed and overridden by conflicting considerations of greater overall happiness. Since for Mill moral rights are only justified by considerations of utility in the first place, they can always conceivably be overturned if greater unhappiness results from observing than from withdrawing the observance of rights. We can hope that there will be few situations in which it would be necessary to override moral rights for the sake of greater happiness. Because moral rights depend for their justification and social sanction on the utility they ordinarily produce, in Mill's view, however, they are always in principle subordinate to contrary utilitarian factors. He qualifies the observance of moral rights:

> All persons are deemed to have a *right* to equality of treatment, except when some recognised social expediency requires the reverse. And hence all social inequalities which have ceased to be considered expedient, assume the character not of

> simple inexpediency, but of injustice, and appear so tyrannical, that people are apt
> to wonder how they ever could have been tolerated; forgetful that they them-
> selves perhaps tolerate other inequalities under an equally mistaken notion of ex-
> pediency, the correction of which would make that which they approve seem quite
> as monstrous as what they have at least learnt to condemn. (94)

The principle of utility, to follow Mill farther in this direction, can theoretically
morally obligate agents even to steal, kill, or do any other ordinarily immoral action.
If what finally matters in assessing the moral value of an act or moral rule is the resultant happiness or tendency to promote pleasure, then anything whatsoever might
be justified for the sake of contributing to the greatest good for the greatest number:

> Thus, to save a life, it may not only be allowable, but a duty to steal or take by
> force, the necessary food or medicine, or to kidnap, and compel to officiate, the only
> qualified medical practitioner. In such cases, as we do not call anything justice which
> is not a virtue, we usually say, not that justice must give way to some other moral
> principle, but that what is just in ordinary cases is, by reason of that other princi-
> ple, not just in the particular case. By this useful accommodation of language, the
> character of indefeasibility attributed to justice is kept up, and we are saved from
> the necessity of maintaining that there can be laudable injustice. (95)

Mill denies that there can be such a thing as praiseworthy injustice. He appeals to
the utilitarian definition of the concept of justice, according to which a type of act that
is not justified by the greatest happiness principle is not actually an instance of justice
in the first place. We cannot violate a right if there is no right to violate, and there is
no right where utility is not served by the social protection of individual interests. Mill
does not consider such exceptions lightly, but acknowledges that utilitarian morality in
exceptional circumstances might sometimes morally obligate us to perform acts that
would more regularly be understood as disregarding an individual's moral rights. It remains possible in principle for a utilitarian ethics to morally approve the commission
of any act or the adoption of any moral rule if to do so is judged to produce more happiness than unhappiness, regardless of whatever apparent injustices might also result.
Moral rights and considerations of justice are not absolute for Mill, but are ultimately
justified only by their consequences for the greatest good of the greatest number.

SUMMARY

Mill explains moral good as pleasure. He is not an egoist interested exclusively or
even primarily in promoting his own pleasure, but that of all persons and even of all
sentient beings. The greatest good for the greatest number is the view that we ought
to do whatever increases pleasure and decreases pain for every psychological subject
capable of experiencing pleasure and pain, counting the experience of each as one and
none as more than one.

Mill answers objections to the hedonistic version of utilitarianism that defines moral
good as pleasure. He provides a criterion for comparative pleasures and argues that persons with experience of both types will generally prefer higher intellectual pleasures to
base sensual pleasures. He takes this to mean that there is nothing more to ask with
respect to which kinds of pleasures are preferable. He criticizes Kant's deontology as

dressing up utilitarian values in the disguise of universalizable moral maxims under the categorical imperative, but it is not clear that he fully understands Kant's principle.

He explores the ethical, social, and political implications of a utilitarian morality. Utilitarianism was enormously successful and influential as a practical moral philosophy with a wide-ranging impact especially on legislation and social policy. Efforts to improve education, health care, sanitation, housing, the treatment of underprivileged persons and even of nonhuman animals have been justified on utilitarian grounds. The role of sentience as opposed to reason and rationality in moral judgment is a further indication of the fundamental opposition between Mill's empiricist utilitarianism and Kant's rationalist deontology. We compare and contrast Mill's and Kant's moral philosophies on a number of scores and highlight some of the advantages and disadvantages of each for a correct understanding of moral good.

Finally, Mill proposes a utilitarian analysis of the concept of justice and respect for moral rights. It is often thought to be a weakness of utilitarianism that it does not adequately account for these social values. Far from admitting the problem as a deficiency in his theory, Mill argues that whereas utilitarianism provides a plausible explanation of the nature and origin of justice and rights, the theory's competitors offer no comparable definitions or background accounts of these moral concepts. Mill holds that rights are socially protected interests of individuals that are ultimately justified by their contribution to the greatest good for the greatest number. In contrast with deontologists who emphasize justice and moral rights as absolute and inviolable, Mill maintains that in extreme circumstances considerations of justice and respect for individual rights can be overridden in order to promote the greater welfare of all when these two categories of moral value happen to conflict. The exceptions are sometimes judged necessary in moral dilemmas, and are justified in Mill's system, where justice and rights are justified in the first place only insofar as they tend to enhance the general good.

QUESTIONS FOR PHILOSOPHICAL UNDERSTANDING

1. Why does Mill regard physical pleasure as a moral good?

2. Why does Mill equate moral good with whatever pleasures sentient beings happen to prefer?

3. Why does Mill believe that pleasure is morally superior to pain? What is the basis for a hedonic utilitarian morality of pleasure?

4. Is there any basis for Mill's claim that sentient beings with experience of both human and pig pleasures would naturally prefer human pleasures? Is there any way to test such an assertion? If not, does the assertion make any sense?

5. What reply, if any, could Mill make if it turned out that virtually all human beings preferred base sensual pleasures to higher intellectual pleasures?

6. Can we intelligibly ask whether pleasure is good? If the answer might be no, does that possibility undermine any theory of hedonic utilitarianism?

7. How does Mill interpret Kant's categorical imperative? Is his interpretation and the objection he builds on it correct? How might it be defended or criticized?

8. What are we to think of a situation in which the greatest good of the greatest number can

only be achieved by treating some persons unjustly in violation of their individual moral rights?

9. Can the moral rights of any persons ever be justifiably denied for the sake of increasing the pleasure of others? What does it mean to have a right if this can happen?

10. Should many persons needlessly suffer misery for the sake merely of respecting one person's moral rights even if these turn out to be relatively trivial?

11. Is it morally right according to Mill's utilitarianism to make a human being suffer extreme pain for the sake of producing a greater amount of total pleasure in the world among nonhuman animals?

12. What can Mill say about the morality of two incompatible courses of action that are precisely identical in their expected outcome of pleasure and pain?

13. What are Mill's and Kant's positions on the ethical treatment of nonhuman animals? How would each justify his position, and how would each criticize the other?

14. How does Mill's moral philosophy compare with the philosophical methodology of Plato, Aristotle, Ockham, Descartes, and Berkeley in metaphysics and epistemology? To which of these kinds of theories is Mill's utilitarianism most closely allied and from which is it most distant, and why?

15. If God exists and has a moral nature, would God be a Mill-type utilitarian or a Kantian-type deontologist? Would God have a moral perspective different from both of these types? Why? What are the philosophical implications of trying to evaluate an ethical system from the standpoint of an imagined divine attitude toward moral right and wrong?

KEY TERMS

act utilitarianism

base sensual pleasure

Epicurus, Epicurean philosophy

eudaimonia

experiential criterion of comparative pleasures

external sanctions of morality

four senses of justice

greatest good principle

happiness

hedonism, hedonistic egoism, hedonistic utilitarianism

higher intellectual pleasure

internal sanctions of morality

justice

maxim of justice

moral compassion

moral egoism

moral intent

moral preferability

moral right

moral sanctions of utilitarianism

nepotism

nomic possibility

perfectionism

rule utilitarianism

sentience

social contract

ultimate sanction of morality

utilitarian analysis of justice

utilitarian analysis of moral rights

utilitarianism

utility

Sources and Recommended Readings

Albee, Ernest. *A History of English Utilitarianism.* New York: Macmillan, 1902.

Alican, Necip Fikri. *Mill's Principle of Utility: A Defense of John Stuart Mill's Notorious Proof.* Amsterdam: Rodopi, 1994.

Berger, Fred R. *Happiness, Justice, and Freedom: The Moral and Political Philosophy of John Stuart Mill.* Berkeley: University of California Press, 1984.

Cook, Ian. *Reading Mill: Studies in Political Theory.* New York: St. Martin's Press, 1998.

Crisp, Roger. *Routledge Philosophy Guidebook to Mill on Utilitarianism.* London: Routledge, 1997.

Davidson, William Leslie. *Political Thought in England: The Utilitarians from Bentham to J. S. Mill.* New York: Henry Holt and Company, 1916.

Lyons, David. *Rights, Welfare, and Mill's Moral Theory.* New York: Oxford University Press, 1994.

Mill, John Stuart. *Collected Works of John Stuart Mill.* 33 volumes. London: Routledge & Kegan Paul, 1963.

Riley, Jonathan. *Liberal Utilitarianism: Social Choice Theory and J. S. Mill's Philosophy.* Cambridge: Cambridge University Press, 1988.

Ryan, Alan. *The Philosophy of John Stuart Mill.* London: Macmillan, 1987.

Semmel, Bernard. *John Stuart Mill and the Pursuit of Virtue.* New Haven: Yale University Press, 1984.

Skorupski, John, ed. *The Cambridge Companion to Mill.* Cambridge: Cambridge University Press, 1998.

CHAPTER 8

INDIVIDUAL VALUES AND THE WILL TO POWER

Nietzsche's *On the Genealogy of Morality*

I n this chapter we discover a strikingly different way of doing philosophy. Nietzsche uses rhetorical devices to present his ideas in a literary rather than argumentative expository style. He traces the genealogy of moral concepts from an earlier noble distinction between good and bad to a contemporary morally corrupt distinction between good and evil. He maintains that there has been a reversal and devaluation of moral values from an earlier time to the moral decadence of his day in the mid-nineteenth century. He renounces compassion in morality as a sign of life-denying moral ill health that threatens to prevent humankind from reaching its full potential. By forcing us to consider moral values that we might otherwise take for granted in a critical light, Nietzsche provides an enormously valuable service for ethical deliberation.

NIETZSCHE'S POLEMIC

Friedrich Wilhelm Nietzsche (1844–1900) takes a more extreme position in moral philosophy than Kant or Mill. Nietzsche criticizes both Mill and Kant in the process of establishing his own philosophical perspective. Nietzsche's background was in philology and classical languages, and he approaches the problems of ethics from the standpoint of a thorough background in and deep appreciation of history, philology, etymology and the development of languages, literature, and the fine arts. Nietzsche writes with fire and dramatic flair and is more a flamboyant poetic stylist than a careful craftsman of philosophical arguments.

The seductive packaging of Nietzsche's philosophical ideas should not obscure his message, nor our critical evaluation of what he is trying to say. We can enjoy Nietzsche's passionate rhetoric while still trying to remain objective about the content of his moral theory. It is appropriate for Nietzsche to subtitle his most famous (1887) treatise on moral value, *On the Genealogy of Morality*, "A Polemic." For it is precisely that, a polemical assault, at times a full-blown diatribe and harangue, against the conventional morality that most of his readers then and now continue to accept as the heart and soul of ethics.

Nietzsche wants to turn our moral thinking upside down so that it will finally be right side up. He makes us reconsider virtually everything that we may otherwise believe to be well established in moral thinking. His method is to investigate the origin and transformation of the meanings of key terms of ethical appraisal, especially of "good" and its cognates, and their opposites, in several different languages and across several cultures. He traces the historical development of the idea of the good for which evolving uses of terminology provide philosophically valuable clues. These etymological discoveries bolster Nietzsche's revolutionary proposal for a transvaluation of moral values, a reconsideration of what we consider to be morally good and morally bad as opposed to moral good and evil. Here he reaches striking unconventional conclusions and recommends a new direction for an egoistic moral philosophy.

Nietzsche projects the triumph of an idealized "higher man," sometimes translated from the German word *Übermensch* as "superman," who will achieve the "will to power" as a "philosopher of the future" and rise above conventional morality by arriving at a higher moral perspective that is "beyond good and evil." Nietzsche does not merely want to understand the nature of our moral thinking in the abstract, or to harness moral attitudes to the betterment of humanity or all sentient beings, in the manner of Kant and Mill, but to totally transform our moral dispositions, and to replace our way of thinking about ethical right and wrong with a radically different conception. Nietzsche wants to change our moral outlook in fundamental ways, so that we reverse not only our judgments but our deepest instincts about what is morally right and wrong.

ORIGINS OF THE CONCEPT OF GOOD

The story opens with Nietzsche's beautiful invocation of wonder at the mysteries and elusiveness of self-knowledge by those of us who in other ways are most adept at knowing other kinds of things. Nietzsche weaves his metaphors as lightly and skillfully as any naturalist when he invokes these lyrical images:

> We are unknown to ourselves, we knowers: and for a good reason. We have never sought ourselves—how then should it happen that we *find* ourselves one day? It has rightly been said: "where your treasure is, there will your heart be also," *our* treasure is where the beehives of our knowledge stand. We are forever underway toward them, as born winged animals and honey-gatherers of the spirit, concerned with all our heart about only one thing—"bringing home" something. As for the rest of life, the so-called "experiences"—who of us even has enough seriousness for them? Or enough time? (1)

Like bees, our knowledge of the world is gathered from outside ourselves, and brought back to nourish our understanding. Just as bees collect nectar which they return to the hive to make honey, we are continually in flight. Constantly moving from one place to another to gather sweet knowledge, we seldom if ever turn to ourselves, to ask who or what we knowers are. We do not have the time, and, more importantly, we may lack the seriousness required for such a task. It is the kind of inquiry that Nietzsche now dedicates himself to undertake.

As is appropriate for a personal exploration, turning inward in order for the knower to become better known to the self, Nietzsche offers an autobiographical sketch of how he came to be interested in the origins of morality. He shows his hand at the very outset of the book, "reluctantly" acknowledging a deeply ingrained skepticism especially toward ethics. Perhaps he exaggerates when he declares that his attitude is opposed to "everything on earth that has until now been celebrated as morality." He wants in any event to mark out his case as starkly as possible and to signal the reader in advance of his departure from ordinary ways of thinking about moral value. He accordingly confesses:

> Given a skepticism that is characteristic of me, to which I reluctantly admit—for it is directed towards *morality*, towards everything on earth that has until now been celebrated as morality—a skepticism that first appeared so early in my life, so spontaneously, so irrepressibly, so much in contradiction to my environment, age, models, origins, that I almost have the right to call it my "*a priori*"—it was inevitable that early on my curiosity and my suspicion as well would stop at the question: *what*, in fact, is the *origin* of our good and evil? (2)

To emphasize the extent to which Nietzsche finds himself at odds in thinking about the nature of morality, even as a child or young man, he speaks of his dissonance from conventional morality as his *a priori*. What does this mean? Nietzsche suggests that his moral attitudes were significantly different than those of everyone immediately around him and in European culture at large. He implies that his moral outlook is original and not acquired from others by emphasizing that his thinking was out of sync with any he later came to know, so unique and persistently in disharmony with received morality from such an early age, that he could not have obtained it through experience, but rather, it must have been built into his nature, his psyche, intellect, and personality. Unlike the honey gatherers of knowledge, Nietzsche achieves a moment of self-recognition and self-understanding. He narrates the events of his personal quest to understand the origin of good and evil:

> In fact, the problem of the origin of evil haunts me as a thirteen-year-old lad: at an age when one has "half child's play, half God in one's heart," I devoted my first literary child's play to it, my first philosophic writing exercise—and as to my "solution" to the problem back then, well, I gave the honor to God, as is fitting, and made him the *father* of evil. Was *this* what my "*a priori*" wished of me? that new, immoral, at least immoralistic "*a priori*" and the, alas! so anti-Kantian, so mysterious "categorical imperative" speaking through it, to which I have since increasingly lent my ear, and not just my ear? (2)

The problem obsesses Nietzsche even as a boy, if we are to believe this revisionary historical account of his early philosophical thinking. He recounts having written a child's drama, in which he "solves" the question of evil by attributing the origin of evil to God. This is in some ways a natural if fittingly juvenile conclusion even for a very gifted child to draw. If God is all-powerful and the creator of everything, then why not conclude that God is also the author of evil in the world? Theologians have not always done much better in trying to unravel these enigmas in the life of faith.

Some religious thinkers hold that there are two opposed forces caught in a perpetual conflict of good and evil. Satan or other evil forces are blamed for evil, on this conception, in a struggle with God in which we hope that God will eventually be victorious. The distinction between God and Satan and good and evil personified is regarded as a heresy in most established religions. The explanation of the origin and nature of evil nevertheless remains a stubborn problem for religion and religious philosophy. If we try to solve the problem by invoking the existence of a less powerful but supremely evil being in the form of Satan, the concept still leaves open the difficult question of the relation between God and Satan, and why God, if all-powerful and perfectly good, would tolerate the existence of an agent of evil acting freely for any length of time in the world. In his youthful desire to try his hand at dramatic composition and address a philosophical problem with which he feels a personal connection, Nietzsche cuts through the theological difficulties in his own blunt uncompromising way by arguing that God is the source of evil.

This, needless to say, implies a very different concept of God than has generally been accepted in the history of religious thought. Nietzsche has already warned us that his thinking ever since childhood has been out of step with "everything on earth" that was previously assumed about the nature of morality. To emphasize the compulsions that have driven his reflections on ethical problems, he refers to his sensed need to understand the nature of evil and the distinction between good and evil in his own way and in response to something like an inner voice. He describes the call to inquire into the source and origin of evil as a non-Kantian "categorical imperative." He thereby underscores these questions as making very personal demands; first on his thinking or inner "ear," and then not only passively listening to the commanding voice, but presumably doing something more actively about it, inquiring and expressing his thoughts, as he does in the present book. The intention in referring to his preoccupations as an "a priori" and "categorical imperative" is rhetorically to highlight an innate call to duty that Nietzsche says drew him into increasingly more active consideration of the theological and philosophical aspects of the problem of evil.

As his interests matured, he began to understand the origin and nature of evil in more philosophical terms. He describes a significant turn in his thinking about the problem of evil. At a certain point in his ongoing investigations from boy to adult, he says that he no longer imagined the origins of evil to exist "behind" the world. The a priori, categorical imperative, and reference to what transcends or occurs behind the world are all Kantian themes. Nietzsche compares himself to Kant, although his moral philosophy is diametrically opposed to Kant's; he will be an anti-Kant. He rejects transcendental unseen forces as responsible for the morality or immorality experienced in the world, and he assumes that the origins of moral aspects of the world must be found within the experienced world. He does not say why or how he came to change his views, only that he is fortunate for having seen the light.

Clarifying his mode of moral inquiry as nontheological and non-Kantian, Nietzsche pronounces his satisfaction with his historical and philological training. It provided a sound preparation for his life's work of discovering the origin of moral value.

Much of this history should probably be taken with a grain of salt. What nevertheless emerges as indisputable is that Nietzsche in his philosophical development came at length to the methodological conclusions he describes as having been shaped in his early life and student career. He concludes this section with the remarks:

> Fortunately I learned early on to distinguish theological from moral prejudice and no longer sought the origin of evil *behind* the world. A little historical and philological schooling, combined with an innate sense of discrimination in all psychological questions, soon transformed my problem into a different one: under what conditions did man invent those value judgments good and evil? *and what value do they themselves have?* Have they inhibited or furthered human flourishing up until now? Are they a sign of distress, of impoverishment, of the degeneration of life? Or, conversely, do they betray the fullness, the power, the will of life, its courage, its confidence, its future? (2–3)

In his early thinking about the problem of evil, Nietzsche considered the solution as involving higher powers, laying the blame—he says "honor"—on God, as the creator responsible for all the world. Later, as his vision matured, Nietzsche came instead to regard the answer as belonging to the empirical world of experience in which we actually encounter moral problems in practice.

Nietzsche does not say that good and evil themselves are invented by human beings. Nevertheless, he wants to begin with a manageable question that can be addressed by a sound methodology. He explains that the inquiry came into focus for him in these terms as the question of how and under what circumstances human beings are led to make *judgments* about good and evil. This is clearly quite another thing from the question of the nature of good and evil as such, and reflects the evolution of his thinking. Nietzsche believes that by resolving the question of the origin of moral judgments he can get a firm handle on the concepts of good and evil.

As a specific method of investigating the problem of the origin of moral judgments, Nietzsche proposes to look scientifically at the etymology of moral judgment language, of the terms and historical evolution of the terms in which moral judgments are expressed. When he has tracked down the origins of words of moral appraisal and condemnation to their historical roots, Nietzsche believes he will have provided the equivalent of a family tree of the generation of central ethical ideas as they arose and were transformed in the history of our species. By beginning with solid philological evidence, of the sort Nietzsche is professionally trained to study, and subjecting it to heavy philosophical interpretation, Nietzsche hopes to draw useful conclusions about the history of moral concepts. He proposes a genealogy of morals, that, in the end, with a better appreciation of its origins, will point in a revolutionary new direction for the future development of ethics.

SAYING "NO" TO LIFE: SCHOPENHAUER AND "EUROPEAN BUDDHISM"

Nietzsche characterizes his quest as one of probing the "value of morality." Put this way, the problem presupposes that morality itself is already straightforwardly identifiable. We know what morality is, and the question is what value it has or what we are to think of it. Nietzsche's project is remarkable for daring to ask, in effect, whether what passes for morality is in another possibly higher sense moral or immoral. He wants to know whether the morality that he finds preached and practiced by others around him, the conventional ethics that informs the lives and attitudes, decisions, and actions of the surrounding culture, has any real genuine moral value, and if so, what that value is and what it means. He specifically mentions the teachings of Arthur Schopenhauer in this connection, when he maintains:

> The issue for me was the *value* of morality—and over this I had to struggle almost solely with my great teacher Schopenhauer, to whom that book, the passion and the secret contradiction of that book, is directed, as if to a contemporary (—for that book, too, was a "polemic"). In particular the issue was the value of the unegoistic, of the instincts of compassion, self-denial, self-sacrifice, precisely the instincts that Schopenhauer had gilded, deified, and made otherworldly until finally they alone were left for him as the "values in themselves," on the basis of which he *said "no"* to life, also to himself. (4)

"That book" that Nietzsche mentions is Schopenhauer's monumental *The World as Will and Representation* (*Die Welt als Wille und Vorstellung*, 1818, 1844). Nietzsche says that he struggled with Schopenhauer's ideas; not, presumably, because they were difficult, but in the sense that for a time he fell under the sway of Schopenhauer's philosophy, and eventually rebelled against it.

Nietzsche expresses an extraordinary degree of passion in his love-hate relationship with Schopenhauer's ideas. We know that Nietzsche was serving in the military when he happened upon a copy of Schopenhauer's book, and that he read it with great interest and was powerfully influenced by its teachings. The spell was broken only when Nietzsche came to recognize something profoundly unacceptable that pervaded Schopenhauer's philosophical outlook. As we will see, Schopenhauer and Nietzsche are polar opposites in their philosophical approaches to ethics and the meaning of life. It is largely because Nietzsche is so repulsed by Schopenhauer's philosophy, despite his initial attraction to it, that he finds it natural to go farther and farther in the opposite direction away from Schopenhauer's views.

We can summarize the difference that eventually emerged between Nietzsche and Schopenhauer in Nietzsche's own terms as one in which Schopenhauer says "no" to life, and Nietzsche says "yes." To examine this contrast in its full implications requires a more complete discussion of Schopenhauer's philosophy, but it is clear that for whatever reasons Nietzsche interprets Schopenhauer as espousing a life-denying philosophy that Nietzsche comes to see as intellectually and in other ways unhealthy, and which he finds it necessary to oppose with a life-affirming philosophical stance. It is also clear from what little Nietzsche says in the passage that Schopenhauer's saying "no" to life is based on self-denial and self-sacrifice, which Schopenhauer, according to Nietzsche, regarded as pure moral values or values in themselves. Nietzsche, much to the contrary, identifies any such self-limiting attitudes as life-denying, and in their extreme form he characterizes them as "nihilism." This is the name for a moral outlook that expects and wants or is about nothing positive whatsoever, but is utterly pessimistic in its philosophical attitude toward life.

He describes his deepening disregard for Schopenhauer's philosophy, which he sees as a reflection of predominant moral perspectives. He identifies the extreme nihilistic implications of such attitudes as a sickness and melancholy. The conventional attitude that Nietzsche denounces in Schopenhauer's ethics is the "morality of compassion," in German, *Mitleid*. This is a remarkable charge for Nietzsche to make, since the conventional morality that is reflected even in Schopenhauer's ethical system regards compassion as the basis of all moral judgment and conduct. Nietzsche insists that just the opposite is true, that compassion for others is life-denying, and that it leads finally to a nihilistic embrace of nothingness:

> But against precisely *these* instincts there spoke from within me an ever more fundamental suspicion, an ever deeper-delving skepticism! Precisely here I saw the *great* danger to humanity, its most sublime lure and temptation—and into what? into nothingness?—precisely here I saw the beginning of the end, the standstill, the backward-glancing tiredness, the will turning *against* life, the last sickness gently and melancholically announcing itself: I understood the ever more widely spreading morality of compassion—which seized even the philosophers and made them sick—as the most uncanny symptom of our now uncanny European culture, as its detour to a new Buddhism? to a Buddhism for Europeans? to—*nihilism?* (4)

The affirmation of compassion in popular moral sentiment and ethical philosophy such as Schopenhauer's Nietzsche now characterizes as a kind of European Buddhism. Buddhism, one of the world's most widely morally respected religions, is known for its emphasis on compassion for all living things. Nietzsche speaks of a Buddhism for Europeans, by which he derides the morality of compassion that he believes has taken hold of European ethics. It is reasonable to suppose that Nietzsche is thinking of Christianity, another major world religion that stresses compassion, as the modern European "Buddhist" morality which he rejects as nihilistic.

Another aspect of Buddhism to which Nietzsche no doubt objects is its commitment to achieving *nirvana*. This ideal is closer to the desire for nothingness that Nietzsche regards as nihilistic. The state of *nirvana* is one of total annihilation, of quieting all desire and exiting from the wheel of *dharma* or endless cycle of birth and death and rebirth. Nietzsche is evidently repulsed by such a self-denying religious concept. He does not assume that the Europeans of his day are literally converting to Buddhism, although some then just as today were no doubt attracted to its principles, but that through the influence of self-denying compassion moral thinkers like Schopenhauer have created an intellectual climate that Nietzsche finds objectionable, whose continued proliferation he hopes to reverse, and which he describes rhetorically as Buddhism as a way of showing disapproval.

In keeping with the identification of his project as a polemic, Nietzsche does not try to argue that there is anything wrong with compassion, or even that it is necessarily life-denying. The defenders of a compassionate morality are likely to counter that feeling compassion and acting from compassionate motives toward less fortunate individuals is life-affirming rather than life-denying, that caring for others also enhances one's own life. If Nietzsche is to raise a convincing criticism of moral compassion, he will need to make a strong case and carry the discussion in unusual directions in order to upset the popular view according to which compassion is an ethical virtue. He proposes to do so, and he has no hesitation in identifying the feeling of compassion for others as the symptom of what he finds objectionable in conventional morality. To care for others and their welfare, to be moved emotionally by their suffering, oddly enough, Nietzsche regards as tantamount to a self-denying embrace of nothingness. Why should this be so?

Nietzsche understands moral compassion as a relatively new development in European philosophy. He insinuates that it is an aberration that does not reflect the underlying spirit of European morality. He thereby suggests that to resist and oppose compassion is not contrary to the real moral orientation of Western philosophy, but a return to its true nature. It is probably for this reason also that he labels moral compassion in non-Western terms as a grafting of Asian religion onto European stock, referring to it as a kind of European Buddhism. He now explains:

> For this preferential treatment and overestimation of compassion on the part of modern philosophers is something new: until this point philosophers had agreed precisely on the *worthlessness* of compassion. I name only Plato, Spinoza, La Rochefoucauld, and Kant, four spirits as different from each other as possible, but united on one point: their low regard for compassion. (4)

It is true that the rationalist philosophers Nietzsche names on the whole consider reason to be more important in moral theory than compassion. They emphasize logic, the analysis of concepts, and practical reasoning over feeling, and generally consider compassion to be inessential to morality. This is clear especially in Kant, who discounts emotion, along with inclination and desire, as morally irrelevant. What constitutes moral duty for Kant is the categorical imperative, as a principle of pure reason, rather than whether or not an agent feels sorry for other people and wants to do something to help them. Schopenhauer, by contrast, as Nietzsche rightly observes, regards compassion as the basis for morality and as the motivation for ethical behavior, for putting into practice what a correct morality requires in theory.

Although Nietzsche is correct to argue that rationalist philosophers downplay the role of such emotions as compassion in moral obligation, it is questionable whether it is accurate also to say that compassion is a particularly new development in European thought. If we think of European philosophy as heavily influenced by Christian theology, then it is a more difficult proposition to agree with Nietzsche that compassion is something new on the philosophical scene in the Europe of his day. On the contrary, it might be historically more accurate to conclude that compassion is part of the very fiber of European morality. What is new or old is a relative matter, but it is worth noting that to the extent Nietzsche regards a morality of compassion as something new in European thought, he is presumably thinking back almost two thousand years to the time before the spread of Christianity.

SCHOPENHAUERIAN BACKGROUND

Since Schopenhauer's philosophy is so important to understanding Nietzsche's ideas, it will be worthwhile to explain some of Schopenhauer's metaphysical and moral insights before returning to Nietzsche's genealogy of morality. Nietzsche, after struggling and finally overcoming his initial infatuation with Schopenhauer's system, declares that Schopenhauer in his philosophical theory as a whole says "no" to life, and later rejects Schopenhauer's thinking as detrimental to a healthy life-affirming outlook.

Where compassion governs morality, Nietzsche believes, the individual is denied and sacrificed for the sake of others, contributing ultimately to moral nihilism. Schopenhauer is the central figure in Nietzsche's critique of nihilistic European Buddhism. It is no accident that Schopenhauer was among the philosophers of his time who cultivated a lively interest in Eastern philosophy and religion. Schopenhauer was strongly influenced by Plato, Kant, and several strands of Asian thought, including Indian Vedism and classical Buddhism. The Vedas were just being translated from Sanskrit, which Schopenhauer did not read fluently, into Latin, which he could read very well, while Schopenhauer was working on the second edition of his masterpiece, and these classic Indian texts had an enormous impact on his thought. Schopenhauer frequently remarks on the surprising coincidences between certain aspects of Asian religion and his own philosophy. It is important, then, to gain a sense of the main lines of Schopenhauer's philosophical positions, especially as they relate to Asian ways of thinking, in order to appreciate Nietzsche's disagreement.

Schopenhauer adopts a central distinction in Kant's metaphysics, between the way the world is in reality independently of thought and as it appears to the mind. Kant rejects Berkeley's idealism, according to which sensible things are congeries of ideas. He does not simply assume contrary to Berkeley that there is such a thing as a material substratum that underlies the sensible properties of sensible things. Instead, he presents a transcendental argument of somewhat the same form as those he offers in moral philosophy. He argues that there must transcendentally exist thing-in-itself *(Ding an sich)* as a presupposition of sense experience. He designates the world as it is presented to thought as *phenomena,* which he distinguishes from *noumena* in the sense of thing-in-itself or world as it exists independently of thought. The noumenal aspect of the world is the world as it would be in itself even if there were no minds to experience it, rather than as experienced through the space-time spectacles of the mind's pure forms of intuition and categories of the understanding. The details of Kant's argument are less important than the fact that he distinguishes between the sensible world experienced in thought and thing-in-itself, which is taken over by Schopenhauer in modified form as a foundation of his metaphysics.

We cannot begin to describe what the world is like independently of thought, because whatever we say will involve our thinking about it, bringing the world as we know it under the categories of mind. All we can say is that thing-in-itself transcends the world of sense appearance, but we cannot say anything descriptively more informative about it. This is the significance of Kant's referring to thing-in-itself as *noumenal,* meaning that it is intelligible only to reason and is otherwise representationally unknowable. Schopenhauer avoids the term *noumena* in his own neo-Kantian metaphysics, but refers to the same idea exclusively as thing-in-itself. The importance of Schopenhauer's refusal to employ Kant's term *noumena* is that Schopenhauer, who regards Kant's distinction between phenomena and thing-in-itself as one of the most valuable discoveries in the history of philosophy, believes that he has made a groundbreaking advance over Kant's metaphysics by penetrating into the secret hidden nature of thing-in-itself in his theory of the world as Will.

Unlike Kant, Schopenhauer does not regard thing-in-itself as absolutely unknowable, making the term *noumena* inappropriate in his philosophy. He argues that the world in reality or as thing-in-itself is blind urging or directionless desire that he refers to as "Will." The world in itself for Schopenhauer is in essential self-conflict.

It is an endless unsatisfiable impersonal and directionless desire for nothing in particular, and is otherwise unknowable. It is a kind of force or energy, but one that is not physical and not measurable or describable. We cannot even say whether thing-in-itself is one or many, according to Schopenhauer, because the *principium individuationis* or principle of individuation does not apply to thing-in-itself or world as Will. Schopenhauer accordingly limits description and explanation to the world as it appears to us or is represented to thought, in its phenomenal aspect, rather than as thing-in-itself. Schopenhauer argues that the world as Will manifests itself in innumerable ways in the world we encounter phenomenally in sense experience. The experienceable, describable, and explainable features of the world Schopenhauer characterizes as falling under the *fourfold root of the principle of sufficient reason*, which promises a correct explanation for anything and everything that occurs in the phenomenal aspect of the world, but leaves the world as Will or thing-in-itself untouched. The fourfold root of the principle of sufficient reason in Schopenhauer's theory of knowledge distinguishes logical, mathematical, causal, and moral laws, and guarantees, if it is correct, a true account of any phenomenal aspect of the world under one or more of these principles.

Schopenhauer further distinguishes between the world as Will and the individual or empirical will that we all know from our own psychological lives, in wanting, willing, or desiring in the ordinary sense. He argues that it is through the experience of willing that we can come to know that the world in reality is Will, without being able to further characterize the nature of Will, individuate it, or explain any of its properties under the fourfold root of the principle of sufficient reason. The suffering of the empirical individual or psychological will can make us aware that there is something other than ourselves, something that opposes and frustrates our individual wills, and, like a Trojan horse, as Schopenhauer says, gives us a way of sneaking past the distinction between phenomena and thing-in-itself, which Kant could not see beyond, in order to discover that the world in reality is Will. Schopenhauer invokes the Vedic myth of the *veil of Maya* that like drapery conceals the nature of reality to mark the difference between the world as appearance and as it is in itself. He claims that by understanding the individual or empirical will philosophy can lift the veil of Maya to uncover the existence of thing-in-itself as Will.

The idea that the individual or empirical will is related to the world as Will in Schopenhauer's metaphysics is essential also to his moral philosophy. In much the same way as the rationalist tradition in ethics, Schopenhauer distinguishes between will and knowledge, and argues that knowledge is more important than will. In particular, Schopenhauer believes that knowledge is always more valuable than achieving the desires of the individual empirical will. It is more worthwhile to attain knowledge than to attain any base object of the empirical individual will. The moral orientation of Schopenhauer's philosophy therefore becomes one of subordinating the will to the higher faculties of mind, to denying desire, and subduing and controlling its demands. He repeatedly holds that we must overcome the individual will in order to advance the cause of knowledge, because desire and the effort required in trying to satisfy desires interferes with and constitutes an obstruction to knowledge. The same is true, according to Schopenhauer, of aesthetic experience, which he believes must be purified of any taint of will in order for the mind to receive the Platonic Forms represented in nature and art.

Schopenhauer maintains that all moral problems and all disturbances of thought are attributable to conflicts of the will. The way to achieve salvation and peace of mind is to deny and subjugate the will, to overcome desire, and quiet its urgings. His moral philosophy is set in firm opposition to the will. Since the individual or empirical will is also described by Schopenhauer as the *will to life (Wille zum Leben)*, he finds all psychological drives that contribute to the preservation and enhancement of life morally objectionable. Life is suffering because it is a phenomenal manifestation of the world as Will in eternal self-conflict. The purpose of life, the end toward which it aims, is death. The sense in which death is the end of life for Schopenhauer is not just that death brings an end to life, but that in death the cessation of individual consciousness brings us back to the world as Will, to reality as it is in itself independently of thought and of its manifestations in the phenomenal world of appearance that begin and end with the first and final moments of subjective thought. For much the same reason, Schopenhauer rejects Kant's program for achieving perpetual peace in the political arena as a social implication of the categorical imperative. Schopenhauer believes that peace is inherently unattainable in the world, because the phenomenal realm of human life and political affairs as a manifestation of the world as Will must in different ways inevitably exhibit the same irresolvable conflict.

The distinction between the world as Will and the individual empirical will, together with the rank ordering of the will as inferior to knowledge, leads Schopenhauer to reject the needs of the self and the value of life in the same way and for the same reason that he denies the will to life. Nietzsche, for reasons we are now in a position to understand, criticizes Schopenhauer's philosophy precisely on these grounds as saying "no" to life. Schopenhauer would not be embarrassed by this conclusion, but is fully confident that a correct philosophical account of the human condition ought to entail that life is worthless except as something to be resisted and overcome. Schopenhauer goes so far as to maintain that existence or living is a sin, the only positive aspect of which is its brief duration. We are to deny life, according to Schopenhauer, and to resist, overcome, and finally gain supremacy over whatever desires are associated with the will to life.

Schopenhauer does not conclude that we should all therefore commit suicide, because to do so would be yet another affirmation of will. He does not maintain that it is immoral for persons in extremities to kill themselves, but that suicide lacks philosophical meaning in response to the problem of attaining knowledge and mastering the individual will. To illustrate the extent to which Schopenhauer opposes life, it is worth remarking that he makes an exception to his general prohibition against the philosophical significance of suicide by morally praising the acts of ascetic saints who end their lives by gradual starvation. Schopenhauer finds this manner of death commendable as a result of a saint's supreme indifference to life or death, a self-caused death that occurs coincidentally as an unintended consequence of controlling the will to life so completely as to reject all nourishment, and perishing, not as an exercise of will, but through totally suppressing the individual will to life.

The life-denying ethical stance that Schopenhauer represents is attributed to several philosophers in Leo Tolstoy's remarkable *Confession*. Tolstoy summarizes the same nihilistic outlook in the following passages:

Thus we have the direct answers that human wisdom has to give when it answers the question of life.

> "The life of the body is an evil and a lie. And so the destruction of the life of the body is a blessing, and we should long for it," says Socrates.
>
> "Life is what it should not be, an evil; and a passage into nothingness is the only blessing that life has to offer," says Schopenhauer.
>
> "Everything in the world—both folly and wisdom, wealth and poverty, joy and sorrow—all is vanity and emptiness. A man dies and nothing remains. And this is absurd," says [King] Solomon [in the Old Testament].
>
> "It is not possible to live, knowing that suffering, decrepitness, old age, and death are inevitable; we must free ourselves from life and from all possibility of life," says the Buddha.
>
> And the very thing that has been uttered by these powerful minds has been said, thought, and felt by millions of people like them. I too have thought and felt the same way. (Tolstoy, *Confession*, 48)

We could hardly expect a more explicit statement of a thinker saying "no" to life, which Nietzsche deplores. Tolstoy gives ample testimony to the fact that it is not only Schopenhauer who represents this nihilistic view of life, but other philosophers who have reflected on the meaning of human existence.

The positive moral teaching that Schopenhauer advances as a result can be highly simplified. In his long essay, *On the Basis of Morality* (1841), Schopenhauer states in opposition to Kant's doctrine of the categorical imperative that compassion is the only motivation of morality. He holds that were it not for compassion there would be no sense of moral right and wrong and no impulse to do what is morally obligatory. Moral obligation Schopenhauer correspondingly interprets informally as nothing more than the injunction not to harm others and to try to do some good. The picture of life and of the sinfulness of the will to life, in Schopenhauer's pessimistic philosophy, despite the attractiveness of his compact principle of moral obligation, is thus appropriately summarized by Nietzsche as saying "no" to life, denying life and the self nihilistically by denying the individual will to life. Nietzsche thoroughly rejects Schopenhauer's metaphysics and moral philosophy, which he abominates as spiritually unhealthy. He is repelled by the subjection of the will in a very visceral way, at a deep level of intuition that precedes argument and signals fundamental irreconcilable differences in their respective views of life.

COMPASSION AND THE "DANGER" OF MORALITY

It is hard to overemphasize the extent to which Schopenhauer's philosophy gained popularity in Nietzsche's lifetime. Richard Wagner, the great German opera composer, librettist, and music theorist, was heavily influenced by Schopenhauer, an interest he shared with the early Nietzsche. Nietzsche and Wagner were close friends and intellectual confidants for a period of eight years, before a dramatic falling-out. Schopenhauer's philosophy was a common foundation of their friendship while it lasted, which might have been said of many other thinkers and artists in Europe at this time. Although Schopenhauer's works were largely ignored during most of his career as a writer, his thought gained a large sympathetic audience near the end of his life and for many years thereafter.

Nietzsche, immersed in a moral environment saturated with the concept of moral compassion that he finds morally repugnant, raises skeptical philosophical questions about conventional values. Where others take it for granted that feeling badly about the suffering of others and wanting to help them and alleviate their unfortunate circumstances is good, Nietzsche is prepared to ask more objectively whether this is or is not a good thing. The moral attitude that shapes the judgment of most of the ethical community, including world religions such as Buddhism, Christianity, and others, especially Schopenhauer, glorify compassion as essential to ethics. Nietzsche explains his purpose as one of challenging established morality based on compassionate feelings that he finds morally disagreeable, on the grounds that compassion is inextricably associated with the life-denying and self-denying Schopenhauerianism or European Buddhism that he believes is antithetical to sound moral health.

He observes that even to ask his questions, raising difficulties about what are ordinarily assumed to be prerequisites of morality, opens up new possibilities for moral reasoning. He eliminates the familiar underpinning on the basis of which we are accustomed to think of moral virtue and obligation, and can thereafter see things differently. He describes the situation as producing a sense of vertigo, the dizzy sense we get when we look down from great heights, when we bring long-accepted beliefs into question. The challenge is to question the real genuine value, if any, of what is ordinarily assumed to be the source of conventional moral values. He issues a call to inquire into the value of values:

> This problem of the *value* of compassion and of the morality of compassion (—I am an opponent of the disgraceful modern softening of feelings—) appears at first to be only an isolated matter, a lone question mark; whoever sticks here for once, however, and *learns* to ask questions here, will fare as I have fared:—an immense new vista opens up to him, a possibility takes hold of him like a dizziness, every sort of mistrust, suspicion, fear springs forth, the belief in morality, in all morality totters,—finally a new challenge is heard. Let us speak it aloud, this *new challenge:* we need a *critique* of moral values, *for once the value of these values must itself be called into question*—and for this we need a knowledge of the conditions and circumstances out of which they have grown, under which they have developed and shifted. . . . (5)

He invites radical inquiry into the nature of values that are otherwise assumed to be unquestionable. Nietzsche's method is in many ways a typical exercise of philosophical investigation. He begins with something that is otherwise taken for granted and stands it on its head. He asks what would follow if, and what can be learned by supposing that, compassion is not morally valued. He thereby systematically breaks the hold of a well-entrenched way of thinking about morality. He risks thinking critically about matters of ethical value in areas where thought seems to have reached an impasse. He breaks through the habits of custom in which traditional morality insulates itself from critical doubts by pointing out the failure of imagination that prevents us from questioning our most basic moral assumptions. He proposes a conceptual upheaval in the reconsideration of moral value:

> One has taken the *value* of these "values" as given, as a fact, as beyond all calling-into-question; until now one has not had even the slightest doubt or hesitation in ranking "the good" as of higher value than "the evil," of higher value in the sense

of its furtherance, usefulness, beneficiality—with respect to man *in general* (taking into account the future of man). What? if the opposite were true? What? if a symptom of regression also lay in the "good," likewise a danger, a temptation, a poison, a narcotic through which perhaps the present were living *at the expense of the future?* Perhaps more comfortably, less dangerously, but also in a reduced style, on a lower level? . . . So that precisely morality would be to blame if a *highest power and splendor* of the human type—in itself possible—were never attained? So that precisely morality were the danger of dangers? (5)

The potential danger of conventional morality, Nietzsche hints in the above passage, is one we are likely to overlook if we do not ask the kinds of questions he now demands to raise and to try seriously to answer. It is that of preventing the human species from realizing its "highest power and splendor." By sustaining a self-denying life-denying morality of compassion for others, Nietzsche suggests, we imperil the future of mankind, by impeding its development into something greater than it has thus far achieved.

Aristotle would probably recognize Nietzsche's concern as a matter of human beings attaining their true natural potential, like the acorn growing to become an oak rather than being thwarted in its full development. Nietzsche wonders whether the morality with which human societies have bridled themselves will inhibit them from actualizing their full natural development, all the greatness of which they are capable, by restraining the free exercise of will that might be needed for the blossoming of human potential.

What, Nietzsche in effect asks, is more dangerous to human existence? Is it more dangerous to question the value of compassion in conventional morality, or is it more dangerous to risk failing to understand human nature by not questioning the value of compassion? He thinks that the stakes are sufficiently high for us to be acting irresponsibly with respect to our deepest moral obligations to human potential and to the future of our species. He challenges us not to ignore the possibility that it is morally more essential to question the true philosophically defensible moral value of conventional morality than to acquiesce in an ethics of compassion that might stand in the way of humanity's achieving its greatest perfection.

Nietzsche imagines a time in the future when we look back on the morality of the present day and recognize it as false and even comical. He speaks in emotionally charged terms of the soul's "destiny," and, in conformity with his background as a classical scholar, he invokes the god Dionysus as symbolic of the unrestrained pursuit of pleasure and desire. Dionysus is the Greek good of wine and revelry, and as such represents the forces of natural inclinations to acquire and enjoy material things. Dionysus is the pagan patron saint of the erotic man, like Meno in Plato's dialogue. Nietzsche contrasts Dionysus with Apollo, the Greek god of invention, planning, and reason. Nietzsche elsewhere emphasizes the dialectical opposition between Dionysian and Apollonian forces as a fundamental choice for human morality. Apollo is the spirit of reason and Dionysus the spirit of desire and will.

Nietzsche maintains, in direct opposition to Plato, Kant, Schopenhauer, and much of the rest of Western philosophy, that Dionysian rather than Apollonian ideals are morally preferable. Such a suggestion flies in the face of conventional morality. Driven by his concern for the future fulfillment of human destiny, Nietzsche has no hesitation to follow the argument to its conclusion. He believes that humanity has failed to achieve its full potential because compassion for the suffering of others has made the heroic figures who would otherwise lead the species forward hold themselves back, restraining their desire by reason and allowing Apollo to rule over Dionysus. Elsewhere, in *The Birth of Tragedy* (1872), Nietzsche calls for a reconciliation between and overcoming of the distinction between Apollonian and Dionysian forces, but only after he has worked through their opposition. An alternative noncompassionate egoistic morality is required in order to serve the interests of a higher sense of morality, and to satisfy the nobler ethical obligations all human beings owe to the future of the species for the sake of advancing a greater good. Nietzsche predicts:

> On that day, however, when we say from a full heart: "Onward! even our old morality belongs *in comedy!*" we will have discovered a new complication and possibility for the Dionysian drama of the "Destiny of the Soul"—: and he will certainly make use of it, one can bet on that, he, the great old eternal comic poet of our existence! (6)

The classical distinction Nietzsche refers to is that between *cosmos* and *comos*. *Cosmos* stands for order, represented by Apollo, whereas *comos* represents the chaos associated with Dionysus. Nietzsche accordingly describes the god as a comic poet and champion of the erotic man. He takes his point of departure from the remark that in the future we might come to regard today's moral values as belonging only to comedy, from which standpoint he finds it natural to mention Dionysus as the god of comedy in the sense of reason-opposing chaos. He suggests that the morality of the future might come to reverse the present state of affairs in morality by elevating desire over reason.

Compassion is excluded from Nietzsche's discussion of these moral alternatives by both Apollonian rationalism in the philosophy of Plato and Kant, and by Nietzsche's advocacy of Dionysian willfulness. The only moral stance that acknowledges compassion, as Nietzsche describes the choices for moral theory, outside of Asian religions, is Schopenhauer's European Buddhism. Schopenhauer's philosophy resides in a strange inconsistent middle ground in Nietzsche's account of things, because it both emphasizes compassion as the underlying basis of morality, while at the same time it regards knowledge as superior to desire and the exercise of the empirical will. The fact that Schopenhauer as a Kantian champions knowledge over will suggests that he would be likely to favor Apollonian reason in moral philosophy, just as Kant does. Whereas Nietzsche sees the issues in extreme terms as an opposition between reason and desire or will, Schopenhauer makes what he would no doubt regard as a subtler distinction between reason, desire or will, and emotion, siding with emotion when it comes to understanding the basis of morality, as a third choice between or beyond reason and willful desire. From Nietzsche's standpoint, Schopenhauer's commitment to the concept of compassion appears as a confusion, neither a matter of reason nor of will. The idea that emotion is irrelevant to ethics is one of the few points of agreement between Nietzsche and Kant.

OBJECTIONS TO UTILITARIANISM

Turning from Kant and Schopenhauer to Mill and the other British utilitarian moral philosophers, Nietzsche raises special objections to another variety of conventional morality represented by the greatest happiness principle. Nietzsche lumps together utilitarians generally under the label of "English psychologists." As we have come by now to expect from Nietzsche's manner of addressing philosophical issues, he does not outline the basic principles of utilitarianism and raise conceptual difficulties about them, but proceeds polemically. He ridicules and casts scorn on efforts to link morality with such psychological factors as happiness interpreted by Mill as pleasure:

> These English psychologists whom we also have to thank for the only attempts so far to produce a history of the genesis of morality—they themselves are no small riddle for us; I confess, in fact, that precisely as riddles in the flesh they have something substantial over their books—*they themselves are interesting!* (9)

He contrasts his relatively higher level of interest in English psychologists such as Mill as personalities with what he alleges to be the dullness of their theories. He marshals harsh invective and cannot resist sarcasm in the cause of advancing his philosophical position. Above, he describes the utilitarians as "riddles in the flesh," meaning, apparently, that he cannot understand why they do what they do; perhaps because they advocate pleasure but live sober lives of reason in erotically suppressed Victorian England, where ironically they are followers in practice of Apollo rather than Dionysus.

He suggests but offers nothing to document the claim that the utilitarians are not entirely honest in their statements of purpose. What he seems to find morally objectionable about "these English psychologists" is that they introduce feelings into the realm of ethical judgment and evaluation, which Nietzsche regards as morally irrelevant. Although he is not entirely clear in his criticisms, he seems to believe that utilitarianism, by concentrating on emotions that are not among the highest faculties in humankind, corrupts rather than exalts morality. The idea of basing morality on fears, pains, and similar ignoble psychological occurrences that unlike acts of will are passive unthinking mechanical reactions, is morally objectionable to Nietzsche in the ethical theory of the English utilitarians Bentham and James and John Stuart Mill.

If Nietzsche has a legitimate complaint to raise against utilitarianism, it is that the greatest happiness principle attributes moral value entirely on the basis of passive psychological experiences of pleasure and pain rather than on active willful participation in life. The difference in moral outlook is fundamental, and virtually inaccessible to argument. There can only be conflict, a collision of opposing values, rather than a well-argued dispute in which sound reasoning carries the day. Such basic disagreements in philosophy of life are simply too deep between those such as Bentham and Mill who believe that morality depends on the ability to experience pleasure and suffer pain, and those such as Nietzsche who believe that moral value depends on the active choices of moral agents about what to do and how to live their lives. Nietzsche suggests that by establishing all moral value on passive psychological phenomena "these English psychologists" may have a more sinister ulterior motive, which is to diminish what is most noble and, from Nietzsche's standpoint, most morally valuable in human life. This is what Nietzsche means when he indicates that the utilitarians do not seem to be completely honest in explaining their purposes. It is not hard to read Nietzsche's sentiments between the lines:

> These English psychologists—what do they actually want? One finds them, whether voluntarily or involuntarily, always at the same task, namely of push-

ing the *partie honteuse* of our inner world into the foreground and of seeking that which is actually effective, leading, decisive for our development, precisely where the intellectual pride of man would least of all *wish* to find it (for example in the *vis inertiae* of habit or in forgetfulness or in a blind and accidental interlacing and mechanism of ideas or in anything purely passive, automatic, reflexive, molecular, and fundamentally mindless)—what is it actually that always drives these psychologists in precisely *this* direction? (9)

In the effort to achieve polemical effect, Nietzsche exaggerates the extent to which utilitarianism seeks to ground moral value exclusively on the basis of passive mechanical psychological reactions to occurrences. He goes too far in complaining that a philosophical stance indicates a negative or even nihilistic attitude toward the prospects of human life when he accuses the English psychologists of wanting to degrade humanistic moral impulses by making willful activity take second place to happiness and the avoidance of suffering. He strains credulity in railing against what he intimates may be the hidden moral-psychological motives of psychologistic moralists, and in particular the English utilitarians. Thus, Nietzsche asks:

Is it a secret, malicious, base instinct to belittle mankind, one that perhaps cannot be acknowledged even to itself? Or, say, a pessimistic suspicion, the mistrust of disappointed, gloomy idealists who have become poisonous and green? Or a little subterranean animosity and rancor against Christianity (and Plato) that has perhaps not yet made it past the threshold of consciousness? Or even a lascivious taste for the disconcerting, for the painful-paradoxical, for the questionable and nonsensical aspects of existence? Or finally—a little of everything, a little meanness, a little gloominess, a little anti-Christianity, a little tickle and need for pepper? (9)

The fantastic suggestion is that the English psychologists might be taking out their own inadequacies and frustrations in their theories by advancing principles that are implicitly humiliating to what is most distinctively and naturally human in morality. Nietzsche speculates about the deeper springs and causes of utilitarianism, which obviously puts the theory in an unflattering light, but again amounts only to a statement of opposing values rather than an argument against the greatest happiness principle.

Nor is it clear that Nietzsche is right to think that utilitarianism is uniquely committed to a purely passive, mechanistic, automatic, and reflexive kind of psychological account, as compared with a moral perspective like his own that emphasizes willful action. In lieu of sound argument, Nietzsche is in no position to maintain that what we call acts of will are not also psychological occurrences that simply happen to us or that we undergo. We may sometimes feel as though we are in control of events when our body movements are directed by our decision-making faculties, but this might be a misleading impression. To be fair to utilitarianism and the English psychologists, they do not recommend passively waiting through whatever life has to offer and merely suffering episodes of pleasure or pain as they sweep over us. On the contrary, utilitarians insist that we are to actively willfully engage in the affairs of the world in order to bring about a change of circumstances in which happiness predominates over unhappiness as a result of what we choose to do.

It is also unclear why a Nietzschean moralist engaged in willful activity is motivated to act if not for the sake of promoting happiness and minimizing unhappiness.

If there is a difference between Nietzsche's moral philosophy and that of the English utilitarians whom he attacks, it has yet to emerge in anything we have so far seen in Nietzsche's work. He objects to utilitarianism because it looks to the happiness and unhappiness of others and not just egoistically to the agent's own desires. This is ultimately what Nietzsche finds morally objectionable about the compassionate moral attitude of utilitarianism.

For the moment, Nietzsche criticizes the English psychologists for what he maintains is their incompetent attempt to explain the origins of moral concepts. It is his task to provide a genealogy or family tree explaining the sources of morality, and he perceives a rival account in the utilitarian thesis that moral values originated in the pursuit of pleasure and the overall enhancement of happiness that occurs through altruistic behavior. Nietzsche does not cite text, but seems to be quoting from the English utilitarian writers when he offers this critique of the utilitarian analysis of the origin of the concept of moral good:

> The ineptitude of their moral genealogy is exposed right at the beginning, where it is a matter of determining the origins of the concept and judgment "good." "Originally"—so they decree—"unegoistic actions were praised and called good from the perspective of those to whom they were rendered, hence for whom they were *useful*; later one *forgot* this origin of the praise and, simply because unegoistic actions were *as a matter of habit* always praised as good, one also felt them to be good—as if they were something good in themselves." One sees immediately: this first derivation already contains all the characteristic traits of the idiosyncrasy of English psychologists—we have "usefulness," "forgetting," "habit," and in the end "error," as a basis for a valuation of which the higher human being has until now been proud as if it were some kind of distinctive prerogative of humankind. (10)

Nietzsche skillfully extracts from the language in which utilitarians try to justify the derivation of moral concepts those key terms that indicate the explanatory framework in which psychological principles are brought into play. He does not make his criticism fully explicit, but appears to regard it as historically inadequate to impose ideas from a philosophical theory such as utilitarianism on an account of the origins of basic concepts that must first be understood on their own terms before a correct ethical system can be proposed. If this is in fact Nietzsche's criticism of the utilitarian account of the origin of moral values, then he may be reacting to an apparent circularity in the utilitarian genealogy of morals. The same objection might nevertheless be raised against any doctrinaire account of the historical origins of any concept, including Nietzsche's, unless, as he is about to argue, there is independent scientific evidence for an interpretation of the anthropological source of moral values.

Nietzsche claims that the utilitarian genealogy of morality must be mistaken because it attributes an emotionless calculation of the utility of an act to matters of moral value that are anything but unemotional. Perhaps he confuses the warmth of emotion associated with the actions in question, their effects, and what is at stake in their outcome for participants in moral decision making, with the cold calculation of pleasure and pain resulting from an action that the theory requires. Nietzsche nevertheless makes this criticism the next point of his assault on the English psychologists:

> The viewpoint of utility is as foreign and inappropriate as possible, especially in relation to so hot an outpouring of highest rank-ordering, rank-distinguishing value judgments: for here feeling has arrived at an opposite of that low degree of warmth presupposed by every calculating prudence, every assessment of utility—and not just for once, for an hour of exception, but rather for the long run. As was stated, the pathos of nobility and distance, this lasting and dominant collective and basic feeling of a higher ruling nature in relation to a lower nature, to a "below"—*that* is the origin of the opposition "good" and "bad." (The right of lords to give names goes so far that we should allow ourselves to comprehend the origin of language itself as an expression of power on the part of those who rule: they say "this *is* such and such," they seal each thing and happening with a sound and thus, as it were, take possession of it.) (10–11)

Although Nietzsche is strenuously opposed to utilitarianism, and to the supine passive values of pleasure and pain, and the neural mechanisms by which psychological experiences are made the basis of moral right and wrong, he turns the fact that the utilitarians have tried, unsuccessfully in his opinion, to explain the origins of the concept of morality, to his advantage. Their failure provides an occasion for him to introduce a contrary method for detailing the lineage of the moral categories of good and evil, circling back to his early interest in the ultimate source of evil, and by extension of all moral judgment. He slams the English utilitarian psychologists because of their efforts to explain the origin of moral concepts in nonegoistic terms, referring to the good as that which benefits others. He seizes the opportunity to present his own very different philological account of the genealogy of morality. He goes to great lengths to lambaste the utilitarians on the grounds that the greatest good principle does not recognize a hierarchy of individuals belonging to a nobility or ruling or dominant class of lords, the natural aristocrats who by moral right exercise power over those who are naturally submissive and subservient. The idea that there is such a natural division between persons who are destined to rule or be ruled is crucial to Nietzsche's genealogy of morals.

NIETZSCHE'S MORAL ETYMOLOGY

The heart of Nietzsche's discussion is his explanation of the origin of the distinction between moral good and evil. He argues that the distinction evolved through a series of definite stages from a prior more ennobling distinction between good and bad. Nietzsche reopens consideration of this central topic by repeating that the genealogists whom he has criticized, and in particular the utilitarians, have mistakenly tried to trace the roots of the concept of good to altruistic unegoistic actions. He softens up the opposition by maintaining that terms of moral appraisal do not necessarily indicate choices that are contrary to egoistic interests, and claims that historically the term *good* is used in this way only when moral values begin to devolve:

> It is because of this origin that from the outset the word "good" does *not* necessarily attach itself to "unegoistic" actions—as is the superstition of those genealogists of morality. On the contrary, only when aristocratic value judgments begin to *decline* does this entire opposition "egoistic" "unegoistic" impose itself more and more on the human conscience—to make use of my language, it is *the*

herd instinct that finally finds a voice (also *words*) in this opposition. And even then it takes a long time until this instinct becomes dominant to such an extent that moral valuation in effect gets caught and stuck at that opposition (as is the case in present-day Europe: today the prejudice that takes "moral," "unegoistic," *"desinteresse"* to be concepts of equal value already rules with the force of an *"idee fixe"* and sickness in the head). (11)

Again, Nietzsche's terminology is revealing. The utilitarian genealogy of the moral appraisal words with which he disagrees is a "superstition," and represents a "herd instinct," an attitude of animals that follow one another unthinkingly without benefit of logic or evidence. What Nietzsche does not consider is that if his preferred account of the origins of the words "good" and "evil" were to become widely accepted, then those who accepted his interpretation could equally be charged with running with a different pack.

The term "superstition" in the meantime does not seem accurate, even if it is true that the utilitarians accept an incorrect explanation of the derivation of the moral vocabulary. By Nietzsche's own account, the utilitarians do not attribute the origin of moral language to supernatural forces, nor do they attach any magic connotations to this choice of words. On the contrary, even if they have gotten things wrong, the utilitarians to which Nietzsche refers offer a scientific history of the origins of moral concepts, which he is then free to challenge, as he does. Undoubtedly, he thinks it is appropriate to describe the defensive reactions of those who have a vested interest in the utilitarian account as demonstrating a herd mentality, if it is true that they are committed to the idea of the good as originating from the benefits conferred on a majority, since it is they who would have the most to gain from the perpetuation of that kind of moral value. He argues that the idea is both historically wrong and morally pernicious, from the standpoint of the moral obligation for humankind to achieve its higher potential.

Nietzsche turns from the prejudice of the utilitarian account of the origin of the concept of moral good to investigate the scientific philological evidence for the derivation of ethical language. He claims without documentation that in several languages the original meaning of the word "good" referred to a noble aristocratic class of persons in society, in contrast with those who are excluded from the nobility, the common or vulgar underclasses who are not so privileged as to be part of the ruling elite. He asserts:

The pointer to the *right* path was given to me by the question: what do the terms coined for "good" in the various languages actually mean from an etymological viewpoint? Here I found that they all lead back to the *same conceptual transformation*—that everywhere the basic concept is "noble," "aristocratic" in the sense related to the estates, out of which "good" in the sense of "noble of soul," "high-natured of soul," "privileged of soul" necessarily develops: a development that always runs parallel to that other one which makes "common," "vulgar," "base" pass over finally into the concept "bad." (12)

The contrast between good and bad is the original vocabulary of moral appraisal, according to Nietzsche. It began as a distinction between those who held power and those who did not. The terms did not at first signify the possession or exercise of moral virtues or the reverse in anything like their contemporary sense, but were merely an indication of those who were or were not in the royal political upper crust. It is only thereafter, with the passing of time, that the language of moral appraisal slowly came to have its present connotations, changing from the distinction between good and bad to the distinction between good and evil, in a dramatic reversal of the application of the word "good" from the strong and powerful to the weak and oppressed, and of the word "bad" from originally meaning the weak and powerless, transformed through a reversal of values, to designate instead the strong and powerful, no longer as "good" but "evil." It is the meanings of these terms of moral evaluation in their current interpretation and the moral concepts they represent that Nietzsche maintains must be reevaluated in stirring up philosophical difficulties about the real meaning of conventional moral values.

Good and Evil, Good and Bad

Nietzsche now examines the philological data for his thesis about the transformation of moral terminology, citing examples from the etymology of particular languages in their historical development. He concentrates on the roots of the German ethical vernacular, and identifies a particular point in history when he claims that the word "bad" shifted its meaning from previous reference to the lower classes to persons who through their behavior are deemed morally censurable. He maintains that these etymological facts about the derivation of the word have been deliberately obscured, resisted, and denied, because they are out of tune with a prevailing anti-aristocratic democratic spirit. He states:

> The most eloquent example of the latter is the German word *"schlecht"* [bad] itself: which is identical with *"schlicht"* [plain, simple]—compare *"schlectweg,"* *"schlecterdings"* [simply or downright]—and originally designated the plain, the common man, as yet without a suspecting sideward glance, simply in opposition to the noble one. Around the time of the Thirty-Year's War, in other words late enough, this sense shifts into the one now commonly used.—With respect to morality's genealogy this appears to me to be an *essential* insight; that it is only now being discovered is due to the inhibiting influence that democratic prejudice exercises in the modern world with regard to all questions of origins. And this influence extends all the way into that seemingly most objective realm of natural science and physiology, as I shall merely hint at here. (12)

Turning from German to Latin, Nietzsche argues that the original meaning of the Latin word *bonus*, usually translated into English simply as "good," initially connoted the powerful warrior class. To be good in this primeval sense of the word, if Nietzsche is right, is to belong to the soldier caste, to have physical prowess and a mastery of weapons, and, as Nietzsche will soon add, the arrogance that naturally goes with power. He now adds:

> I believe I may interpret the Latin *bonus* as "the warrior": assuming that I am correct in tracing *bonus* back to an older *duonus* (compare *bellum = duellum = duen-lum*, in which that *duonus* seems to me to be preserved). *Bonus* accordingly as man of strife, of division *(duo)*, as man of war—one sees what it was about a

man that constituted his "goodness" in ancient Rome. Our German *"gut"* [good] itself: wasn't it supposed to mean "the godly one," the man "of godly race"? And to be identical with the name for the nation (originally for the nobility) of the Goths? The reasons for this supposition do not belong here. (14)

He labels the difference between the original egoistic meaning of the word "good" and its later altruistic corruption as a contrast of "knightly-aristocratic" and "priestly" moral valuations. The distinction between what is now and was originally meant by the concept of the good reflects unresolved conflicts of interest between priest and warrior classes.

The opposition that Nietzsche characterizes in this passage sets the tone for a theme he elaborates throughout the book. He argues that those who have no better weapon to use against the naturally powerful eventually turn to a method of disarming the aristocratic warriors psychologically, by making them ashamed of their strength and guilty in exercising it against the weak. If the priestly class can succeed in making the warriors feel that they are acting wrongly to oppress the common people, then they will have achieved as great a victory as if they were to have defeated the powerful in a fair contest of intelligence, arms, and physical ability. Nietzsche continues to sprinkle his genealogy of morality with metaphors involving health versus illness, and self-confidence versus disappointment and spleen, as he multiplies his lists of the distinguishing features of the knightly-aristocratic versus priestly concepts of moral value. He develops the theme in this way:

One will already have guessed how easily the priestly manner of valuation can branch off from the knightly-aristocratic and then develop into its opposite; this process is especially given an impetus every time the priestly caste and the warrior caste confront each other jealously and are unable to agree on a price. The knightly-aristocratic value judgments have as their presupposition of a powerful physicality, a blossoming, rich, even overflowing health, together with that which is required for its preservation: war, adventure, the hunt, dance, athletic contests, and in general everything which includes strong, free, cheerful-hearted activity. The priestly-noble manner of valuation—as we have seen—has other presuppositions: too bad for it when it comes to war! (16)

As he pursues his distinction between shifting conceptions of goodness, Nietzsche casts particular derision on Jews. Nietzsche is popularly known as an anti-Semite, yet one of his reasons for terminating his long-standing friendship with Wagner was his impression of Wagner's excessive anti-Semitism. Wagner frequently publicly expressed an especially virulent dislike of Jewish people, and, although there is no excuse for cultural bigotry, it remains true to say that anti-Semitism was fairly widespread in nineteenth-century Europe. Nietzsche and Wagner regrettably fall under the same stereotype. Whether with historical accuracy or not, Nietzsche blames Jews as having brought the priestly devaluing of the knightly-aristocratic sense of good to its lowest point. He spares no adjectives in voicing his disgust with what he takes to be this turn of events in the devaluation of moral value he associates with power, strength, health, fortune, and will on the part of those who have none or inadequate portions of these gifts. He says that in their desperation the powerless can only try to deprive others of these goods, by praising instead their opposite anti-values in a pathetic effort to gain ascendancy through subterfuge over those who are naturally good in the original sense of the word. He heats up his rhetoric to fever pitch:

> It was the Jews who in opposition to the aristocratic value equation (good = noble = powerful = beautiful = happy = beloved of God) dared its inversion, with fear-inspiring consistency, and held it fast with teeth of the most unfathomable hate (the hate of powerlessness), namely: "the miserable alone are the good; the poor, powerless, lowly alone are the good; the suffering, deprived, sick, ugly are also the only pious, the only blessed in God, for them alone is there blessedness—whereas you, you noble and powerful ones, you are in all eternity the evil, the cruel, the lustful, the insatiable, the godless, you will eternally be the wretched, accursed, and damned!" We know *who* inherited this Jewish revaluation. (16–17)

To be offended by Nietzsche's anti-Jewish remarks is a natural reaction. There are few persons in any culture, however, who do not fall under his derision. If we are not Vikings or Samurai or any of the other bands of ruthless, willful, and egoistic warrior aristocratic classes that have arisen at different times in the early days of many cultures, then Nietzsche does not have very flattering things to say about our way of life.

The important point is not simply to discount what Nietzsche says because his tone and statements are frequently offensive, but to try to see beyond the unpleasantness of which his sharpened pen is so manifestly capable. We must equally try not to be too readily taken in by the passionate manner in which he presents his ideas, but should decide as objectively as we can whether the conclusions he offers are correct and insightful or not. Despite professing to speak for the more historically accurate point of view in understanding the genealogy of morality, Nietzsche seems to overlook the fact that the ancient Jews also had an aristocratic class of warriors who were feared and respected in the same sorts of ways that he finds exclusively "good" in the original sense of the word, while reserving praise for the moral nobility of non-Jewish peoples during corresponding phases of the development of their royal houses. Is it possible to interpret such an extraordinary oversight as anything other than cultural prejudice?

The reversal of values effected by the priestly classes of which Nietzsche complains, assuming for the moment and for the sake of argument that Nietzsche gets his history right, culminates in the rise of Christianity. The combined moral perspective of Judeo-Christian religion is Nietzsche's real target of philosophical critique and moral-rhetorical disdain. He hints at Christianity as the heir of the Jewish attitude that devalues knightly-aristocratic good and tries to replace its virtues of power, health, willfulness, and, in a word, ego, with all their opposites as moral anti-values, attributing ethical good instead to weakness, powerlessness, sickness, and victimization, while attributing ethical wrong to persons able and willing to perpetrate violence against them. He maintains that Christianity is the pinnacle of the priestly devaluation of values that came about genealogically in the historical development of moral thinking through the efforts of priests to gain power over the naturally good and powerful. It is Christian ethics as the outcome of Jewish religion rather than Jewish culture or Jews as a people that Nietzsche objects to most vociferously, on the grounds that Christianity in its morality of compassion and turning the other cheek in response to violence represents an attempt to emasculate the original noble knightly-aristocratic sense of moral values to the detriment of the health and vigor and fulfillment of the true potential of humanity.

RESSENTIMENT AND SLAVE MORALITY

The reversal of values that is supposed to have occurred in the decadence of moral-ity Nietzsche further describes as a "slave revolt." Those who are at the mercy of aristocrats, especially in the kinds of feudal society Nietzsche seems to prefer, are in effect the slaves of the powerful. After prolonged continuation of that type of situa-tion, undesirable for the weaker component of the social order, the slaves take part in a psychological revolt that constitutes, to the extent that it is effective, an exchange of values, transposing the meaning of the concept of moral good by making the pow-erful feel guilty in their exercise of power.

The dynamic Nietzsche portrays is one in which the downtrodden turn against their masters, but not by taking up weapons and meeting them in a field of honor, where they would be likely to lose. Instead, they make use of the only effective method at their disposal, to which they are driven in their desperation, which is to change the rules of the game by changing the concept of what it means to be good. The slave revolt that Nietzsche considers involves as its essential element a growing sense of resentment on the part of the underprivileged, who eventually find a way through religion, popularization of opinion, and other mechanisms, to change the climate of moral evaluation from the original healthy concept in which strength and power are understood as the only moral virtues, to a morally unhealthy situation in which the weaknesses of the victims of power are elevated in status as the only legitimate moral values, and the relief of suffering by compassionate acts of altruism becomes the only morally praiseworthy conduct.

The slave morality Nietzsche discusses is evidently meant to stand in bold relief to the knightly-aristocratic values with which he believes the genealogy of morals be-gins and to some version of which he hopes Europe will eventually return. He iden-tifies the slave psychology by means of the French word *ressentiment*, perhaps to sig-nal that he is thinking of the concept in a technical philosophical sense. He regards it as no accident that the Jews in his interpretation of history invented slave morality during the time of the Egyptian captivity when they were literally slaves, and that Christianity gained its ascendancy at first as a sect of Judaism among Jews who were oppressed during the Roman occupation of Judea, and later spread to Rome and other provinces of the Roman Empire primarily at first among the slave classes. Christian-ity was a more democratic religion than the mystery cults that prevailed among the wealthy members of Roman society. One needed money and sponsorship to be ad-mitted to the recognized cults in the Roman pantheon, whereas Christianity was open to everyone and promised a heaven in which the wrongs visited upon oppressed peo-ple in this earthly life would be redressed in an eternal afterlife to which all persons were guaranteed admittance through suffering and belief, and in which all believers were on an equal basis before God. Christianity was a religion tailor-made for ac-ceptance by an underclass, which Nietzsche associates with a morally unworthy slave morality. The rebellion in Nietzsche's view of history has a particular psychology:

The slave revolt in morality begins when *ressentiment* itself becomes creative and gives birth to values: the *ressentiment* of beings denied the true reaction, that of the deed, who recover their losses only through an imaginary revenge. Whereas all noble morality grows out of a triumphant yes-saying to oneself, from the out-

set slave morality says "no" to an "out-side," to a "different," to a "not-self":
and *this* "no" is its creative deed. This reversal of the value-establishing glance—
this *necessary* direction toward the outside instead of back onto oneself—belongs
to the very nature of *ressentiment:* In order to come into being, slave-morality
always needs an opposite and external world; it needs, psychologically speaking,
external stimuli in order to be able to act at all,—its action is, from the ground
up, reaction. The reverse is the case with the noble manner of valuation: it acts
and grows spontaneously, it seeks out its opposite only in order to say "yes" to
itself still more gratefully and more jubilantly—its negative concept "low" "common" "bad" is only an after-birth, a pale contrast-image in relation to its positive basic concept, saturated through and through with life and passion: "we noble ones, we good ones, we beautiful ones, we happy ones!" (19)

The contrast Nietzsche tirelessly repeats in countless variations appears highly
oversimplified. There are two categories of moralists, according to his division, masters and slaves. The masters are happy, beautiful, noble, healthy, powerful, wealthy,
willful, and, in the original sense of the word, good. The slaves are resentful, bitter,
unhappy, ugly, sickly, powerless, common, poor, lowly, passive, and sneaky rather
than forthcoming in their efforts to gain power for themselves in the only way available to them. The masters have all the positive virtues in Nietzsche's way of looking
at things, and the slaves have only a negative outlook that tends toward nihilism and
lacks any genuine good.

Here it is seems reasonable to ask whether any human beings have ever belonged
to either one of Nietzsche's extreme categories. It is legitimate for a moral philosopher to project an ideal in trying to understand moral concepts, whether the ideal is
positive or negative. Nietzsche presents his moral philosophy in the form of history,
as a genealogy of the development of moral concepts as reflected in changing termi-
nologies. His conclusions go so far beyond what can be discovered in the history of
languages that it seems he must have come to the evidence with a strong preconception of the golden age as well as the present decadent state of moral values. It seems
reasonable nonetheless to ask whether there ever have been or could be real individuals as extreme in their caricatures as he presents them. To the extent that the
knightly-aristocratic personality he characterizes is not pure, and does not actually
embody exclusively the original sense of moral good that he maintains is true of the
moral aristocracy, to that extent Nietzsche does not describe a total transformation
and devaluation of traditional moral values brought about by a moral slave revolt. At
most, he depicts only the arc of a trend in which both moral attitudes were present
before and after the historical epochs to which he refers, including before and after
the rise of Judaism and Christianity, or before and after the supposed reversal of values that resulted in the decline of warrior classes and the emergence of a gentler more
compassionate way of life.

As a matter of historical fact, the tendency among slave-owning societies, whether
in ancient Greece or Rome, or early mid-Eastern or Chinese dynasties, among African
tribes, or on American, Caribbean, or Latin American plantations or Russian estates
prior to the liberation of the serfs, was that of necessity slaves often became stronger
and more capable than their masters, who in turn became weaker and more effete,
dependent on the workers who supported them. This is a rather different picture than

that which Nietzsche would have us accept in extolling the virtues of the knight-aristocrats by contrast with the priests and slaves in his genealogy of morality. What a modern biologist would describe as a process of artificial selection is at work in preferring only the strong and those able to survive through the generally grinding conditions of slavery, in which only increasingly powerful individuals can thrive. The so-called masters who have others to do their bidding become physically and mentally less competent with every passing generation. Nietzsche, despite posing as a scientific historian, takes no notice of these considerations with their contrary implications for his central thesis.

Having explained the origin of the concept of moral good in the transvaluation of the knightly-aristocratic use of the word "good" to its priestly slave value, Nietzsche turns next to the transformation of the concept of what is bad to the concept of moral evil. He believes there is a similar kind of reversal in the meaning of the word as it came to be transformed in the thought and practice of persons during the historical movements he describes. According to Nietzsche's genealogy, the concept of moral good evolved from the noble, healthy, powerful, and willful to the common, unhealthy, powerless, and passive, from the virtues of masters to the virtues of slaves. Nietzsche argues that the concept of bad was brought into prominence when the knightly-aristocratic concept of good was replaced by its priestly counterpart. The concept of bad, he claims, was applied by slaves and their priests to devalue the noble class for being strong and healthy, powerful and able. The concept of bad was then further modified from its original meaning to become the concept of moral evil, more or less as we know it today. Nietzsche now maintains:

> Precisely the reverse, therefore, of the case of the noble one, who conceives the basic concept "good" in advance and spontaneously, starting from himself that is, and from there first creates for himself an idea of "bad"! This "bad" of noble origin and that "evil" out of the brewing cauldron of unsatiated hate—the first, an after-creation, something on the side, a complementary color; the second, in contrast, the original, the beginning, the true *deed* in the conception of a slave morality—how differently the two words "bad" and "evil" stand there, seemingly set in opposition to the same concept "good"! But it is *not* the same concept "good": on the morality of *ressentiment*. To answer in all strictness: *precisely* the "good one" of the other morality, precisely the noble, the powerful, the ruling one, only recolored, only reinterpreted, only reseen through the poisonous eye of *ressentiment*. (21–22)

It is *ressentiment* on the part of the weak and oppressed that, in Nietzsche's opinion, affected the most dramatic transvaluation of ethical values. Through a brilliant but morally unworthy despicable stratagem of propaganda, through the rise of Judeo-Christian priestly classes historically attaining a more prominent place in world affairs, what had been positive life-affirming values were gradually replaced by their nihilistic life-denying anti-values. The resentment of power, health, and other robust attributes of those in social ascendancy produced a slave revolt in morality whereby the underclasses sought to improve their lot, not by raising themselves up, but by bringing the powerful down.

If Nietzsche is right about any of this historically, even as a matter of percentages and trends, then it is easy to appreciate why from his standpoint he regards these developments as morally reprehensible. The transformation of values that he portrays amounts to a diminution of what had been the finest and most noble qualities in the human species, all for the sake of enabling those who lacked such virtues to effect a reversal of the dominance in a power struggle in which they were disadvantaged, making virtues out of their frailties, weaknesses, and negative qualities that do not contribute to but actually impede the full flowering of human potential. It is not as though the priestly values that Nietzsche deprecates replaced the knightly-aristocratic values with different virtues of equal or greater value. That state of affairs, had it occurred, could hardly be objectionable. Rather, according to Nietzsche, the priests and slaves did an enormous disservice to all of humanity by honoring weakness and illness and suffering, and all that in a word Nietzsche summarizes as he does in criticizing Schopenhauer's philosophy as saying "no" to life. It is these nihilistic antivalues that Nietzsche laments as he considers the genealogy of morality through the priest and slave revolt of *ressentiment* that transformed the distinction between good and bad to the distinction between good and evil.

The idea of the devaluation of moral values in Nietzsche's critique is that of leveling what is arguably the best and most noble in human life to what is lowest and least desirable. It is, from Nietzsche's perspective, a negative life-denying exaltation of weakness, pain, and suffering that Nietzsche bewails in utilitarianism, as an equally detestable philosophical reformulation of the same moral decadence codified in Judeo-Christian ethics.

LIFE AFFIRMATION AND THE "HIGHER" MAN

To Nietzsche's credit, given the moral values he favors and wants to advance, he not only criticizes the values he rejects, but goes to considerable lengths to explain the values he espouses in a positive light. He thereby makes an attempt to hold out an attractive picture of the values he prefers and would like to see promoted. Nietzsche appears to carry the contrast of knightly-aristocratic versus priestly values too far, representing both the noble and priestly slave morality in an excessively and arguably oversimplistic way. He contrasts moral ideals by projecting exaggerations and requires us to choose.

We must avoid misinterpreting Nietzsche's purpose. Walter Kaufmann writes:

> The most common misunderstanding of the book is surely to suppose that Nietzsche considers slave morality, the bad conscience, and ascetic ideals evil; that he suggests that mankind would be better off if only these things had never appeared; and that in effect he glorifies unconscionable brutes. (Kaufmann, "Introduction," *Basic Writings of Nietzsche*, 446–47).

All three of Kaufmann's categories of misinterpretations of Nietzsche are certainly to be avoided. Nietzsche cannot regard slave morality, *ressentiment*, feelings of guilt on the part of the powerful, or saintly ascetic ideals as *evil*, since evil is a value category he rejects. Whether Nietzsche thinks that our species would be better off if the reversal of values from good and bad to good and evil had never occurred is perhaps more difficult to answer. What is clear is Nietzsche's view that the moral character of the higher man could not be achieved if the way were not prepared by passing through a period of value reversal. Nietzsche obviously does not glorify unconscionable brutes, but sees the higher man as culturally and aesthetically refined in a way that is by no means incompatible with exercising unrestrained will to power.

Regardless of the truth or acceptability of Nietzsche's moral philosophy, it is worth remarking that the kind of ethics he advocates appears to but does not actually represent a moral conservatism. He is not proposing that we simply try to go back to the values of the past, as represented by the first developmental stage in the genealogy of morality. He does not suggest that we should return to the way of life of Vikings and Samurai and the marauding days of the ancient Aztecs, Romans, or Goths. Nor does he imagine that we can look back from his time in the nineteenth century to recapture the warrior values of the past precisely as they were once practiced. He nevertheless expresses a kind of moral nostalgia for pre-Judeo-Christian values, indicating a time and place where those who took such ideals for granted gave themselves over to essentially Dionysian excesses:

> There they enjoy freedom from all social constraint; in the wilderness they recover the losses incurred through the tension that comes from a long enclosure and fencing-in within the peace of the community; they step *back* into the innocence of the beast-of-prey conscience, as jubilant monsters, who perhaps walk away from a hideous succession of murder, arson, rape, torture with such high spirits and equanimity that it seems as if they have only played a student prank, convinced that for years to come the poets will again have something to sing and to praise. At the base of all these noble races one cannot fail to recognize the beast of prey, the splendid *blond beast* who roams about lusting after booty and victory; from time to time this hidden base needs to discharge itself, the animal must get out, must go back into the wilderness: Roman, Arab, Germanic, Japanese nobility, Homeric heroes, Scandinavian Vikings—in this need they are all alike. It is the noble races who have left the concept "barbarian" in all their tracks wherever they have gone; indeed from within their highest culture a consciousness of this betrays itself and even a pride in it (for example when Pericles says to his Athenians in that famous funeral oration, "to every land and sea our boldness has broken a path, everywhere setting up unperishing monuments in good *and bad*"). (22)

Nietzsche does not cringe in explaining the willful wanton virtues he ascribes to the knightly-aristocratic ideal. He argues that the noble morality of the warrior is characterized by an innocence, which he compares to that of a beast of prey, that stalks and kills without hesitation, guilt, or remorse. He further imagines that the members of the valiant races engaged in the violent actions he mentions would have acted with no more thought or concern than a group of students engaged in a harmless prank. This is quite an essential element of Nietzsche's position, although it has not often been properly emphasized.

We are not to suppose that Nietzsche believes it is morally correct to kill and rape and commit acts of torture and arson in order to regain the proper morality of the knightly-aristocratic origins of the concept of good. That is the kind of mistake made in the early part of the twentieth century by two young persons, Richard Loeb and Nathan Leopold, who read Nietzsche and interpreted him literally as recommending murder, which they proceeded to do. They were caught and tried in 1924, but, re-markably, avoided the death penalty, thanks to the eloquent pleas for mercy by their famous attorney, Clarence Darrow. It is rather that in restoring the virtues of the past and translating them into an appropriate form for our own time, we are expected to take away something of the same spirit of willful exercise of power that Nietzsche associates with the warrior classes in noble lineages.

It may be worthwhile to compare Nietzsche's conclusions on this topic with parts of Freud's psychoanalytic theory. Freud argues that frustrations of the will that are necessary in order to live socially among other persons require that we suppress cer-tain of our desires and sublimate them by transforming or translating them into other activities. When such urges are altogether repressed, they manifest themselves as dif-ferent sorts of psychoses involving aberrant, sometimes obsessive or otherwise inex-plicable, behavior that is damaging to psychological health. If we deny all desires their natural outlets, as we must to at least a limited degree as a compromise in order to take advantage of the benefits of society, then, Freud says, we are at risk of mental illness.

Nietzsche argues in a similar way that it is injurious to morality to repress the natural desires and will that occur when we consistently say "no" to life. If we try to conduct our lives as the moral ascetic saint is supposed to do in Schopenhauer's pessimistic moral philosophy by denying the empirical will its desires, then morality and all the best that humanity promises are sure to be harmed. Nietzsche's anti-Schopenhauerian genealogy of morality has roughly the same purpose as Freud's psy-choanalysis, although Nietzsche lived before Freud and could not have been influ-enced by him. Nietzsche also believes that denying the will is contrary to moral good health, at least as the concept is best understood from the standpoint of the origins of the genealogy of morals. He asks:

> What causes *our* aversion to "man"? for we *suffer* from man, there is no doubt.—
> *Not* fear; rather that we have nothing left to fear in man; that the worm "man"
> is in the foreground and teeming; that the "tame man," this hopelessly mediocre
> and uninspiring being, has already learned to feel himself as the goal and pinna-
> cle, as the meaning of history, as "higher man"—indeed that he has a certain right
> to feel this way, insofar as he feels himself distanced from the profusion of the
> deformed, sickly, tired, worn-out of which Europe today is beginning to stink;
> hence as something that is at least relatively well-formed, at least still capable of
> living, that at least says "yes" to life. . . . (23–24)

Clearly, Nietzsche is morally repulsed by the spectacle of modern European men and women in his day who are repressed in their exercise of will. He finds it a moral degeneration to see the way people behave under the yoke of utilitarian or Judeo-Christian morality. We are at last in a position to understand what Nietzsche means when he questions the motives of utilitarians and wonders what "these English psy-chologists" really want. He suspects them of wanting the same sort of degradation of whatever is most properly human as the priests he berates, of wanting to tame the human spirit and render it docile and passive and unable to achieve its potential. The language by which Nietzsche chooses to convey his attitude makes it obvious that he is morally disgusted by the mediocrity of human beings reduced to the status of worms by their acceptance of the life-denying suppression of egoistic will.

He contrasts the degraded image of human life with the counterconcept of the "higher man." This is the same term that is sometimes translated as the "overman" or "superman," and is one of Nietzsche's most widely disseminated ideas. It is a difficult concept for several reasons, and has often been misunderstood, not least with the tragic results of Leopold and Loeb. Nietzsche is so repulsed by the morally repressed life-denial of conventional morality that, if those were his only choices, he would prefer to see human beings return to the savage state of barbarian warriors capable of the terrible atrocities that they seem to have committed untroubled by the voice of conscience. Nietzsche remarks in a previous passage that there is evidence of the noble or knightly-aristocratic values persisting in later civilizations in the fact that such societies generally preserve in their histories some trace of their barbarian pasts of which they are ambivalently proud, even if they are also proud to have overcome their primitive origins.

What makes the concept of the "higher man" difficult in Nietzsche's philosophy is trying to understand precisely what he is advocating and precisely what he is projecting for the future course of human moral development. We cannot realistically go back to the moral "innocence" of the barbarian past, in which murder and mayhem could be perpetrated without thinking about the effects of actions on the welfare and happiness of others. We already have guilt-related categories in our consciousnesses and we cannot ignore two thousand years of Judeo-Christian moral teachings as though they never existed. The ideas are with us, even if we consciously try to reject them. Nor is there necessarily any justification for the same kind of barbarianism in today's world that might have had a legitimate moral role to play in the founding of nations during their infancies. Nietzsche nevertheless believes that the "higher man" will somehow be able to overcome these mental shackles and moral restraints in order to act freely, willfully, spontaneously, and without guilt or repressed desire.

Nietzsche does not expect persons today to undertake a particular kind of training or to arrive at any special insights by which they will attain the moral status of the higher man. He seems on the contrary simply to hope and believe for reasons he does not try to articulate that at some time in the future the higher man will emerge culturally through a natural process of moral evolution. The higher man in Nietzsche's conception is not squeamish about whatever actions might be justified by the exercise of egoistic will, which he will eventually refer to as the "will to power" *(Wille zur Macht)*. This is Nietzsche's version of Schopenhauer's concept of the will to life. Unlike Schopenhauer, however, Nietzsche praises and makes the will to power the cornerstone of his moral egoism, saying "yes" to life where Schopenhauer joins the priestly devaluation of values by saying "no." There is nothing special we can do to become higher men and women in Nietzsche's life-affirming morality. He is optimistic that this is the direction human moral evolution will take, perhaps because he finds the alternative unsustainable. If the devaluation of values fails to provide adequate sustenance for human life in the long run, it will be doomed eventually to be replaced by a return to a morality that is unhampered by the feelings of guilt imposed by misguided altruistic feelings of compassion.

Nietzsche brings this part of his polemic to a close by reasserting his general characterization of the contrast he has drawn between the opposite extremes of priestly slave morality life-denying values motivated by *ressentiment* and the knightly-aristocratic life-affirming values to be restored in some form by the higher man as philosopher of the future. He restates the question that has guided his discussion of the issues all along, concerning the origin of the concept of good, its degeneration in contemporary understanding, and its projection to a future state that he hopes will finally be achieved. Nietzsche's ideal is one in which human beings get back on course toward attaining their true potential, to avoid the self-denying, will-denying, and ultimately, as he interprets its implications, life-denying nihilism. It is to avoid the fate of the worm to which he thinks humankind has been brought by Schopenhauerianism, European Buddhism, Judeo-Christianity, and the utilitarianism of the English psychologists. He concludes with a humorously grim analogy:

> But let us come back: the problem of the *other* origin of "good," of the good one as conceived by the man of *ressentiment*, demands its conclusion.—That the lambs feel anger toward the great birds of prey does not strike us as odd: but that is no reason for holding it against the great birds of prey that they snatch up little lambs for themselves. And when the lambs say among themselves "these birds of prey are evil; and whoever is as little as possible a bird of prey but rather its opposite, a lamb,—isn't he good?" there is nothing to criticize in this setting up of an ideal, even if the birds of prey should look on this a little mockingly and perhaps say to themselves: "*we* do not feel any anger towards them, these good lambs, as a matter of fact, we love them: nothing is more tasty than a tender lamb." (25)

Whatever else may be expected of the higher man in Nietzsche's Dionysian morality, a return to knightly-aristocratic values entails an indifference for the consequences of actions undertaken for the gratification of the self, for the sake of exercising the will to power. Nietzsche's moral philosophy is as directly and radically opposed to Bentham's and Mill's utilitarianism as it is to Kant's formalist deontology, and to Schopenhauer's emotional approach to the fundamental principles of ethics in his theory of the role of moral compassion.

Nietzsche's parable of the lambs and bird of prey depicts the relation he thinks should hold between the higher man and the common and vulgar persons who make up the bulk of humanity. The higher man exemplifies a modernized version of the noble knightly-aristocratic moral values of a predatory will and egoistic concern for self-interests typified by birds of prey. The higher man similarly will not sacrifice personal interests or hesitate to act in satisfying desires and exercising the will to power. The higher man is no more bound to take the common person's happiness or unhappiness into consideration, according to Nietzsche, than an eagle is obligated to be concerned about the feelings of the tender tasty lambs on which it feeds. Lambs, Nietzsche acknowledges, if they could think and express themselves, are likely to resent the imbalance inherent in the situation. That, however, is and should be nothing whatsoever to the powerful bird of prey, whose nature it is to carry off and destroy the lambs for its own needs. It is correspondingly necessary, in Nietzsche's view, for the philosopher of the future and higher man to overcome the *ressentiment* of the human lambs that may try through devious channels to psychologically disable the eagle from feasting on the lamb. To take what they need without guilt or regret is the only way for the eagle and higher man to achieve their full potential of moral health and strength through guilt-free pursuit of the will to power.

Moral Guilt and the Rhetoric of Punishment

The concept of *ressentiment* explains how the slave revolt in morality begins to accomplish a priestly devaluation of knightly-aristocratic values. Yet it is only one-half of the equation. For such a transformation to be effective, there must also be a cooperative reaction on the part of the strong if their behavior is to change.

Nietzsche believes that the priests involved in the slave revolt engage in a kind of psychological warfare. Their success depends on an ability to reverse the knight-aristocrats' thinking, to turn them from willful persons to weaklings like themselves who say "no" to life by denying the self, the Schopenhauerian will to life or Nietzschean will to power. The counterpart of priestly *ressentiment* that completes its mission by overturning the power elite is a guilty conscience and the self-inflicted psychological punishments produced by a remorseful state of mind. The priests and slaves are too weak to overpower the knight-aristocrats on their own terms, so out of necessity they do something much more clever by getting the knight-aristocrats to overpower themselves. They do this by instilling in the powerful a personal sense of guilt for possessing and freely exercising their power, and this acts as an effective restraint on what would otherwise be their life-affirming exuberance.

Nietzsche introduces the efficacy of guilt and self-punishment in connection with the devaluation of noble values. He criticizes the utilitarian genealogists of morality with a lack of historical perspective that prevents them from seeing clearly this most important phase in the development of contemporary concepts of moral value. He relates the emergence of the sense of guilt to the ethics of punishment:

> But how then did that other "gloomy thing," the consciousness of guilt, the entire "bad conscience" come into the world?—And thus we return to our genealogists of morality. To say it once more—or haven't I said it at all yet?—they aren't good for anything. Their own five-span-long, merely "modern" experience; no knowledge, no will to knowledge of the past; still less an instinct for history, a "second sight" necessary precisely here—and nonetheless doing history of morality: this must in all fairness end with results that stand in a relation to truth that is not even flirtatious. Have these previous genealogists of morality even remotely dreamt, for example, that that central moral concept "guilt" had its origins in the very material concept "debt"? Or that punishment as *retribution* developed completely apart from any presupposition concerning freedom or lack of freedom of the will?—and to such a degree that in fact a *high* level of humanization is always necessary before the animal "man" can begin to make those much more primitive distinctions "intentional," "negligent," "accidental," "accountable," and their opposites, and to take them into account when measuring out punishment. (39)

As a further elaboration of the genealogy of morality, Nietzsche turns naturally to the question of the origin of the concept of moral guilt. He relates guilt to the owing of a debt and argues that the concept of retributive punishment is logically independent of the thorny problem of free will or determinism. What is essential to punishment is the degree of intelligence and "humanization" of those who are to be punished, without which it is impossible for punishment to change their behavior.

Those who are punished must understand why they are being punished, because they must understand what they can do to avoid future punishment. The effectiveness of punishment depends on the highest and most refined human qualities. It turns the most noble qualities against those who possess them when the agent of punishment and the restraint of action becomes a personal sense of guilt or shame.

Nietzsche saves his righteous anger for the pain and hurt that is done to others for the knight-aristocrats and Dionysians with whom he has the greatest sympathy and whose interests he shares. Thus, he complains about the violence that accompanies efforts to instill in the noble power elite a sense of guilt by priests and slaves. Nietzsche often seems to revel in the bloody episodes of history that involve the deeds of aristocratic adventurers accomplishing their purposes with might and main. However, he severely scolds those in the past who have shed much less blood in the name of what he regards as morally unworthy when they do so in order to try to instill a sense of moral guilt, conscience, or duty, in the minds of the powerful:

> In *this* sphere, in contract law that is, the moral conceptual world "guilt," "conscience," "duty," "sacredness of duty" has its genesis—its beginning, like the beginning of everything great on earth, was thoroughly and prolongedly drenched in blood. And might one not add that this world has in essence never again entirely lost a certain odor of blood and torture? (not even in old Kant: the categorical imperative smells of cruelty . . .) It was likewise here that that uncanny and perhaps now inextricable meshing of ideas, "guilt and suffering," was first knitted. (41)

Had Nietzsche not spoken only a few pages earlier in praise of murder, torture, and rape? Are these practices morally praiseworthy when they are engaged in by ruthless Vikings and Samurai, but morally repugnant when undertaken by priests for the sake of instilling a sense of guilt in the powerful? There is a marked prejudice if not outright inconsistency in Nietzsche's attitude toward the bloodletting of knight-aristocrats, provided they are exercising their egoistic will to power, as opposed to the priests whose acts of mere psychological violence are expressions of their *ressentiment*.

Even "old Kant's" categorical imperative in its claim that reason imposes duty on itself "smells of cruelty" for Nietzsche. Why should this be? If reason gives the moral duty to itself, as Kant requires, then it would appear to be no different than other acts of self-discipline that are morally praiseworthy in the conduct of the power aristocracy. This, presumably, is not what Nietzsche means, and not why he criticizes Kant's categorical imperative. The reason must rather be that the categorical imperative is implicitly cruel in its denial of the will for the sake of the supposedly higher moral objective of acting solely from duty and from the moral law, with no concern whatsoever for the individual's desires or inclinations, and, indeed, often in opposition to what the self desires. This, in its full implications, Nietzsche regards as inherently cruel and to that extent morally objectionable.

He holds that if any group of persons ought to have on their conscience a crippling moral burden, it is not the active, strong, and noble knight-aristocrats, but rather the priests and slaves as the subjects of *ressentiment* for having invented the concept of a bad conscience. The natural seat of justice, moreover, does not belong to the weak, but to those who can administer justice not from a reactive but an active mentality. He concludes:

Therefore in all ages the aggressive human, as the stronger, more courageous, more noble, one, has in fact also had the *freer* eye, the *better* conscience on his side: conversely one can already guess who actually has the invention of the "bad conscience" on his conscience,—the human being of *ressentiment*! Finally, just look around in history: in which sphere has the entire administration of justice, also the true need for justice, thus far been at home on earth? Perhaps in the sphere of the reactive human? Absolutely *not:* rather in that of the active, strong, spontaneous, aggressive. (49)

He interprets the significance of the administration of justice historically from the standpoint of his polarized value system as an effort on the part of the strong to set limits to the *ressentiment* experienced by the weak. The institutionalization of justice is explained as an effort to remove the physical means of revenge from persons of *ressentiment.* Typical of the kinds of reversals in conventional moral and social values in his ethics, Nietzsche argues here that the institutions of justice in a society are not intended to help and protect the weak and poor, but to protect the strong and powerful from the *ressentiment* of the underprivileged, by finding ways of dissipating their bitter feelings against the elite:

Considered historically, justice on earth represents—let it be said to the annoyance of the above-named agitator (who himself once confessed: "the doctrine of revenge runs through all my works and efforts as the red thread of justice")—precisely the battle *against* reactive feelings, the war against them on the part of active and aggressive powers that have used their strength in part to call a halt to impose measure on the excess of reactive pathos and to force a settlement. Everywhere justice is practiced and upheld one sees a stronger power seeking means to put an end to the senseless raging of *ressentiment* among weaker parties subordinated to it (whether groups or individuals), in part by pulling the object of *ressentiment* out of the hands of revenge, in part by setting in the place of revenge the battle against the enemies of peace and order, in part by inventing, suggesting, in some cases imposing compensations, in part by raising certain equivalents for injuries to the status of a norm to which *ressentiment* is henceforth once and for all restricted. (49–50)

Justice, then, for Nietzsche, is and should be administered by the powerful for the sake of the powerful. Historically, and from the standpoint of contemporary frontal politics, there is perhaps more than a grain of truth in Nietzsche's observation. The weak by definition are usually not in a position to levy justice against the powerful without their cooperation. To establish laws and punish lawbreakers presupposes the ability to enforce a particular set of laws established for the defense of a particular set of values. For whom, then, can we realistically expect the wheels of justice to turn, the weak or the powerful? Nietzsche adds:

This list is certainly not complete; obviously punishment is overladen with utilities of all kinds. All the more reason to subtract from it a *supposed* utility that admittedly counts in popular consciousness as its most essential one,—precisely the one in which belief in punishment, teetering today for several reasons, still finds its most forceful support. Punishment is supposed to have the value of awakening in the guilty one the *feeling of guilt*; one seeks in it the true *instrumentum* of that reaction of the soul called "bad conscience," "pang of conscience." But by so doing one lays a hand on reality and on psychology, even for today—and how much more for the longest part of the history of man, his prehistory! Precisely among criminals and prisoners the genuine pang of conscience is something extremely rare; the prisons, the penitentiaries are *not* the breeding places where this species of gnawing worm most loves to flourish:—on this there is agreement among all conscientious observers, who in many cases render a judgment of this sort reluctantly enough and against their most personal wishes. (54)

Nietzsche takes a radical view of justice. Where we might be inclined to believe that the law courts, police, and other instruments of justice are designed to benefit those who are otherwise subject to the abuses of power on the part of the powerful, Nietzsche insists that the opposite is true. He contends that justice exists in order to protect the powerful from the reactions of those who resent their power and seek revenge against them. If he is right, then not only are the powerful morally justified in doing whatever they like, including inflicting whatever harms they choose against the weak in pursuit of their egoistic interests, but on top of that they are supposed to have justice on their side when those who suffer at their hands take offense and try to seek redress for their pain. According to Nietzsche, the administration of justice to protect the powerful against the *ressentiment* of the weak is not a miscarriage of justice but its only proper role.

WILL TO POWER

We have already seen that Nietzsche takes a radically polarized view of morality. He believes that there are two extremes. The moral world simplistically divides into those who say "yes" to life and those who say "no." Whatever promotes the interests of the noble power elite, those who are willful, powerful, and strong, is morally justified, even obligatory. Whatever opposes egoistic interests, or promotes the interests of the excluded class of the weak and powerless, the passive and victimized, is morally unjustified, decadent, and corrupt. Anything done to preserve and enhance the power of the powerful and to decrease and further oppress their victims, whether on an individual basis or through the mechanisms of justice instituted for the benefit of the powerful, is morally justified from Nietzsche's standpoint.

We have also seen that Nietzsche associates saying "yes" to life with egoism and willful activity, which he contrasts with the passive suffering of ascetic priests and those whose personality he categorizes as manifesting a slave morality. He adopts the expression "will to power" from Schopenhauer's references to the individual or empirical will to life. This is will in the ordinary empirical or phenomenological sense as applied to the necessities of survival and fulfillment of desires. Schopenhauer regards all life and the existence of the empirical will as a sin. He is opposed to whatever gratifies the ego, and regards morality as in large part an effort at suppressing and restraining the will to life. As Nietzsche understands Schopenhauer's moral philosophy, it amounts to an unhealthy morally objectionable denial of the self, a European Buddhism that says "no" to life. The will to power in Nietzsche's ethics in contrast with Schopenhauer's morality glorifies every manifestation of individual egoistic will, regardless of the cautions of reason.

Nietzsche worships at the altar of Dionysus rather than Apollo. He exaggerates the extent to which any active demonstration of the will to power is supposed to constitute a positive moral virtue. It might nevertheless be wondered whether Nietzsche has fully thought through the implications of his unqualified endorsement of the will to power. He criticizes the slave morality he despises on the grounds among other things that it is unhealthy. What, however, does it mean to be morally healthy or unhealthy, and how can Nietzsche assume that in the free Dionysian exercise of the will to power, especially ungoverned by Apollonian reason, the willful strong and noble power elite will necessarily choose what is in any ordinary sense healthy? In particular, what entitles Nietzsche to assume that the powerful acting freely and without rational restraint will choose any differently than the Schopenhauerian or priestly adherent to a slave morality? What, then, would make the choices and actions of the knight-aristocrats inherently healthier than those of priests and slaves?

It must be that whatever egoistic actions the powerful choose are by definition moral, perhaps because it is only in this way that humanity's potential for greatness can be achieved. Nietzsche's concept of morality strongly depends on the motives, freedom, spontaneity, and willfulness with which any action regardless of its nature or outcome is performed. To act in accord with these values is in itself to be acting with proper moral health, no matter what is done or what effects it has. Does this not mean that the noble power elite could freely choose to be life-denying Schopenhauerians or European Buddhists? Would their decisions be necessarily life-affirming just because they freely and uninhibitedly choose to do whatever they choose to do, even if what they choose is inimical to the will to life or will to power? There is a dilemma. If the powerful can spontaneously choose to say "no" to life, then it does not seem reasonable to say that whatever the powerful choose is automatically morally healthy by Nietzsche's standards. If the powerful cannot spontaneously choose to deny the will to power, then two consequences seem to follow. First, it appears that the powerful may not be as free and uninhibited in their actions as they appear. Second, it might be said that Nietzsche rather than the Judeo-Christian priests and slaves now occupies the uncomfortable position of dictating to the power aristocracy what they should want and how they should behave. If by definition whatever the noble power elite choose is life-affirming, even if they all choose ascetic suicide by starvation, or enslaving themselves to the weakest and unhealthiest members of a society, then it is hard to see how Nietzsche can possibly maintain that there has ever been a reversal or devaluation of values in the transition from the distinction between good and bad to the distinction between good and evil. In that case, the noble power elite in surrendering to the guilt imposed on them by the *ressentiment* of priests and slaves were still freely exercising their will to life, which they never really surrendered.

The opposite impulse Nietzsche regards as morally improper. He attributes the same morally retrogressive attitude to democracy, in its tendency to reduce all persons to the same level, failing to acknowledge the privileges of the nobility or to accord them a special higher status by virtue of their will to power. Nietzsche again finds this state of affairs unhealthy and unnatural for the development of the greatest potential in the human species. He believes that it represses what is finest in humankind, primarily through the imposition of an artificial sense of guilt and shame for exercising the will to power in the service of the morally most valuable qualities. The slave revolt and devaluation of original moral values infects all aspects of social life, according to Nietzsche, even the natural sciences, such as biology:

> The democratic idiosyncrasy against everything that rules and desires to rule, the modern *misarchism* (to create a bad word for a bad thing) has gradually transformed and disguised itself into something spiritual, most spiritual, to such an extent that today it is already penetrating, is *allowed* to penetrate, step by step into the most rigourous, apparently most objective sciences; indeed it appears to me already to have become lord over the whole of physiology and the doctrine of life—to its detriment, as goes without saying—by removing through sleight of hand one of its basic concepts, that of true *activity*. (52)

What does Nietzsche mean by this objection? The complaint seems to be that the life-denying and self-denying attitude of the slave revolt morality has extended into the biological sciences in the form of an exclusive reliance on efficient causation in all its explanations, eliminating as unscientific any references to the will, along with corresponding concepts of purpose, goal-directedness, or teleology. Nietzsche is undoubtedly right to observe that modern science is nonpurposeful and nonteleological, and does not feature or even make allowance for the existence of will in its theories. Science in the modern era has distinguished itself from philosophical speculation in several ways, but chiefly by dissociating itself from the concept of purposefulness in the natural phenomena it explains. What is less clear is whether Nietzsche is right to conclude that modern science is nonwillful and nonteleological as a result of the democratization of all aspects of human thought that has come about through the denial of self and suppression of the individual will as a consequence of the slave revolt in morality.

Nietzsche objects to adaptive models in biology because they emphasize the reactions of living things to environmental forces, rather than their activities and especially willful behavior in interactions with the world. He claims that this passive reactive model of living things has taken over in the biological sciences to such an extent that life itself has come to be defined in the writings of Herbert Spencer as nothing but a passive adaptation to external circumstances. Nietzsche argues that insofar as science concentrates exclusively on these kinds of factors it ignores what is essential to life, which he characterizes as its will to power. Schopenhauer makes precisely the same observation about the incompleteness of modern physiology in its neglect of the individual empirical will to life. Nietzsche maintains that by ignoring the will to power in its scientific explanations the life sciences leave out of account what is noblest and most important in living beings. For, Nietzsche argues, it is the will to power that confers specific activity and form on living things:

> Under the pressure of the idiosyncrasy one instead places "adaptation" in the foreground, that is to say an activity of second rank, a mere reactivity; indeed life itself is defined as an ever more purposive inner adaptation to external circumstances (Herbert Spencer). In so doing, however, one mistakes the essence of life, its *will to power*, in so doing one overlooks the essential pre-eminence of the spontaneous, attacking, infringing, reinterpreting, reordering, and formative forces, upon whose effect the "adaptation" first follows; in so doing one denies the lordly role of the highest functionaries in the organism itself, in which the will of life appears active and form-giving. (52)

Nietzsche's reference to the will to power as an ineliminable aspect of living things is an indication of the extent to which he remains intellectually indebted to Schopenhauer's philosophy. Although Nietzsche rejects Schopenhauer's moral nihilism, and, more significantly, Schopenhauer's Kantian transcendentalism with its grounding of phenomena in terms of hidden factors involving the thing-in-itself, he embraces the theory of the will to power as a holdover of Schopenhauer's philosophy, and in particular of Schopenhauer's concept of the individual will to life.

Whereas Schopenhauer distinguishes between the empirical will to life and the transcendent, mind-independent aspect of the world or thing-in-itself as Will, Nietzsche confines his metaphysics to the empirical realm only. As Nietzsche says in the case of his first investigations of evil, originally attributed to God, he reached a stage of philosophical maturity after which he no longer expected to find the answers to moral problems *behind the world*. The same methodological reorientation that brought Nietzsche to turn away from God and focus exclusively on the experienceable world in his ongoing inquiry into the nature of moral value compels him to renounce the thing-in-itself in Kantian-Schopenhauerian transcendentalism. The concept of the will to power in Nietzsche's philosophy is therefore unlike Schopenhauer's concept of the will to life, primarily in the sense that it is not backed up by an underlying transcendental Will or any other interpretation of the Kantian thing-in-itself as noumenal reality. Nietzsche accepts only the empirical psychological existence of the will to power, which is all he claims can be known of will.

RELIGION, ASCETICISM, AND ART

Nietzsche, like Schopenhauer, inquires philosophically into the relation between religion, ascetic ideals, and aesthetic values. In the Third Treatise of the *Genealogy*, he asks: "What do ascetic ideals mean?" (67). He mentions Wagner specifically as a follower of Schopenhauer who tries to exemplify Schopenhauerian ascetic ideals in his music. He investigates the implications of a philosophical as opposed to religious avowal of ascetic ideals, which he thinks depend on underlying aesthetic values. He inquires into the philosophical meaning of asceticism, and suggests psychological motivations for the appreciation of fine art in Schopenhauer involving his denial of the will to life. Nietzsche considers many of the same problems in the philosophy of art as Schopenhauer, but reaches very different conclusions:

> Thus Richard Wagner, for example, took the philosopher Schopenhauer as his front man, as his protective armor when "the time had come":—who could consider it even thinkable that he would have had the courage for an ascetic ideal without the backing that Schopenhauer's philosophy offered him, without Schopenhauer's authority, which was gaining *predominance* in Europe in the seventies? (not yet having assessed whether an artist would have even been possible in the *new* Germany without the milk of a pious, imperially pious way of thinking).—And with this we have arrived at the more serious question: what does it mean when a real *philosopher* pays homage to the ascetic ideal, a spirit who really stands on his own, like Schopenhauer, a man and knight with a brazen glance, who has the courage to himself, who knows how to stand alone and does not first wait for front men and nods from on high?—Let us immediately consider here the strange and for many kinds of people even fascinating stance Schopenhauer took toward *art*: it was, after all, clearly for the sake of this that Richard Wagner

initially converted to Schopenhauer (convinced to do so by a poet, as is well known, by Herwegh), and to such an extent that a complete theoretical contradiction thus opened up between his earlier and his later aesthetic beliefs—the former expressed for example in "Opera and Drama," the latter in the writings he published from 1870 on. (71)

The connection between ascetic and aesthetic values in Schopenhauer is that both are offered as ways of attaining release from the inner turmoil of will. According to Schopenhauer, we can be freed from the torments of will either by denying the will through suppression of the desires of the flesh, in the manner of the ascetic saint, or by losing the self in purely objective experience of beauty, in the manner of the aesthetic genius. Ascetic sainthood and aesthetic genius in different ways enable the adept to overcome the strivings of the individual will to life.

Nietzsche criticizes Schopenhauer for forging this link between ascetic and aesthetic anti-values. He regards Schopenhauer as dishonoring beauty and art by making it into a channel of disinterested escape from the struggles of will, whether interpreted as will to life or will to power. He further objects to the subjectivity of aesthetic value that arises through an overemphasis on the role of those who experience beauty, an effect that he attributes to the pernicious influence of Kant on Schopenhauer's aesthetics. He raises these objections:

> Schopenhauer used the Kantian formulation of the aesthetic problem for his own purpose—although he most certainly did not view it with Kantian eyes. Kant intended to honor art when, among the predicates of the beautiful, he privileged and placed in the foreground those that constitute the honor of knowledge: impersonality and universal validity. Whether this was not on the whole a mistake cannot be dealt with here, I wish only to underscore that Kant, like all philosophers, instead of envisaging the aesthetic problem starting from the experiences of the artist (the one who creates), thought about art and the beautiful from the viewpoint of the "spectator" and thus, without it being noticed, got the "spectator" himself into the concept "beautiful." (72)

The critique Nietzsche offers conforms predictably with his moral preference for active over passive factors. He believes that art like any other activity should say "yes" to life. He objects to the Kantian and Schopenhauerian emphasis on those who experience art rather than on those who make artworks, on the passive viewing of art rather than on active artistic creativity. He further criticizes the ascetic-aestheticism in Schopenhauer's philosophy of art from the standpoint of its explicit denial of the self and those aspects of the will to power associated with sexual desire that are frequently found in art. He calls attention to passages in Schopenhauer where the latter advocates the asexuality of genuine aesthetic experience as a remedy for the perturbations of mind that occur through the restless agitations of individual erotic will:

> There are few things about which Schopenhauer speaks so certainly as about the effect of aesthetic contemplation: he says of it that it counteracts precisely *sexual* "interestedness," much like lupulin and camphor, that is; he never grew tired of glorifying *this* breaking free from the "will" as the greatest merit and use of the aesthetic condition. Indeed, one might be tempted to ask whether his basic conception of "will and representation," the thought that there can be a redemption

from the "will" only through "representation," did not originate from a general-ization of that sexual experience. (In all questions relating to Schopenhauerian phi-losophy, by the way, one must never ignore the fact that it is the conception of a twenty-six-year old young man; so that it participates not only in that which is specific to Schopenhauer but also in that which is specific to that season of life.) (73)

We are expected to know that lupulin and camphor are substances reputed to have the property of suppressing sexual desire. Schopenhauer does not try to conceal this aspect of his theory of art, but, according to Nietzsche, proudly asserts that aesthetic contemplation has the function of inhibiting the stirrings of sexual interest, as an anti-aphrodisiac. Nietzsche further engages in a remarkable *ad hominem*, in which he mentions Schopenhauer's youth when the basic principles of his philosophy first oc-curred to him, indicating that at this time Schopenhauer is likely to have been espe-cially prone to sexual inclinations, and may have sought to avoid its distractions by means of aesthetic escapism. Schopenhauer regards involvement in the conflicts of the empirical will as a torment and source of perpetual conflict, in which the attain-ment of one desire is soon surpassed by more and greater desires. He deplores this situation as one from which we can obtain salvation, permanently or temporarily, only through death, ascetic indifference to the will, or the will-less purely objective aesthetic identification with beauty. Nietzsche cites relevant passages from Schopen-hauer's *World as Will and Representation*, in which he praises aesthetic experience as a momentary suppression of the will, praising the virtues of art in releasing us from the lower desires of will in colorful mythological images:

Let us hear, for example, one of the most explicit of the countless passages he wrote in honor of the aesthetic condition (World as Will and Representation I, 231), let us hear the tone, the suffering, the happiness, the gratitude with which such words were spoken. "This is the painless condition that Epicurus praised as the highest good and as the condition of the gods; we are, for that moment, freed from the base drive of the will, we celebrate the Sabbath of the prison-house work of willing, the wheel of Ixion stands still". . . . What vehemence of words! What images of torture and of prolonged satiety! What an almost pathological tempo-ral juxtaposition of "that moment" and the usual "wheel of Ixion," the "prison-house work of willing," the "base drive of the will"! But supposing that Schopen-hauer were right a hundred times over for himself, what would this have contributed to our insight into the essence of the beautiful? (73)

It is strange to think of art as somehow antithetical to erotic interests, since the two are so often directly related in much of sculpture, painting, poetry and literature, and even music. When Schopenhauer addresses these issues, he makes an exception for historical paintings of nudes and still-life paintings of food and drink, which he says are anti-aesthetic precisely because they arouse the carnal appetites. This may seem to be an arbitrary distinction on Schopenhauer's part, but it supports Nietzsche's interpretation of Schopenhauer's theory of art as an attempt to advance a view of beauty in nature and art that is intended to repress rather than excite and gratify erotic inclinations. Nietzsche renounces Schopenhauer's aesthetic theory because of its ascetic dimensions, as yet another indication of Schopenhauer's denying the will to life or will to power, and hence as denying the self and saying "no" to life.

APOLLO AND DIONYSUS

Nietzsche summarizes his criticism of the life-denying morality to which he objects by contrasting the ancient Greek gods Dionysus and Apollo. He says that obstructions to the free exercise of the will to power are necessarily hostile to life and stand in opposition to the interests of life. He maintains that asceticism is necessarily the expression of *ressentiment*, and that asceticism is inimical to life. He claims that life for the ascetic saintly point of view is a contradiction, life being the thing that is to be opposed, resisted, and ultimately defeated. Nietzsche cannot offer reasons against such a totally incompatible sense of life, but can only repeatedly express a deeply felt moral outrage at the idea. He believes that he speaks for the interests of life in praising the will to power and denouncing anything that stands in its way. Nietzsche suspects asceticism of wanting power over life itself, to dominate life in the service of death and everything that is foreign to the interests of life. He argues in effect that asceticism is so vehement in its denial of life that it amounts to an intention to destroy life as something hateful:

> It must be a necessity of the first rank that makes this species that is *hostile to life* grow and prosper again and again—it must be in the *interest of life itself* that this type of self-contradiction not die out. For an ascetic life is a self-contradiction: here a *ressentiment* without equal rules, that of an unsatiated instinct and power-will that would like to become lord not over something living but rather over life itself, over its deepest, strongest most fundamental preconditions; an attempt is made here to use energy to stop up the source of the energy; here the gaze is directed greenly and maliciously against physiological flourishing itself, in particular against its expression, beauty, joy; whereas pleasure is felt and *sought* in deformation, atrophy, in pain, in accident, in the ugly, in voluntary forfeit, in unselfing, self-flagellation, self-sacrifice. (84)

Nietzsche paints the ascetic ideal in unattractive terms. He describes it as a moral ideal of deformity, pain, ugliness, self-denial, self-mutilation, and immolation; in short, as a denial of all the values of the self, of the will to life and will to power, and finally of life itself.

Schopenhauer, whom Nietzsche regards as the pessimistic spokesperson for a moral outlook that is hostile to life, goes so far as to declare that the only good thing about life is that it is mercifully short. It is obvious that anyone who already shares Schopenhauer's extreme point of view is not going to be persuaded by Nietzsche's polemic, and that Nietzsche's values at the opposite extreme can resonate only with those persons who are already at least partially sympathetic to the qualities Nietzsche defends, who appreciate those values as positive and believe that such values ought at all costs to be advanced.

It might nevertheless be doubted whether Nietzsche does not go too far in supporting unrestricted free expression of the will to power as the only way to uphold life-affirming virtues. Why is it that only the lives of the powerful have value for Nietzsche? Saints and slaves and everybody in between, who are not Vikings or Samurai or Aztec warriors, are also living beings, whose lives ought to be comparably if not equally valuable to anyone who espouses a desire to enhance life and the value and interests of life.

Nietzsche's objections to the slave revolt in morality raises philosophical difficulties for the coherence of his logic. There are several problems. If the priests and slaves are successful in their rebellion, then one might say they as a matter of fact have more real power than the knight-aristocrats who are unable to withstand the psychological pressure. If the noble power elite are truly the possessors of the kinds of moral virtues that Nietzsche values, how could they possibly succumb to the onslaught of those who are supposedly so much weaker? What is power, if it is not to be understood in terms of its effectiveness in achieving a chosen aim? If the priests and slaves are able in fact to overcome the noble power elite, then perhaps it is the priests and slaves who are actually and not merely superficially more powerful all along. If Nietzsche, then, is truly the advocate of the powerful, one might think he ought instead to lend his vitriolic prose and literary flair to the cause of the Apollonians, Schopenhauerians, European Buddhists, and those who say "no" to life. It is they rather than the knight-aristocrats, who in the final contest actually turn out to be such weaklings that they cannot maintain their position in the face of a subtle effort to make them feel guilty for what they do, whose praises Nietzsche then ought to be singing, and whose account of the genealogy of morals he ought to accept.

This, however, cannot be, and for an important reason. Nietzsche cannot define power simply in terms of effectiveness in achieving an aim, but must instead interpret the moral value of social interaction in terms of its intent, of whether or not it is conducted in the service of a life-affirming will to power. The priests and slaves, in Nietzsche's extreme caricature of their aims and attitudes, even if they are successful in overcoming the established power of knight-aristocrats, do not use their revolution over their former masters for the good of life, or for the gratification of their own respective individual wills to power, which, in the nature of the case, they completely lack. They are instead interested only in destroying life, acting contrary to its natural inherently healthy purposes, and hence they cannot be construed as acting in accord with a higher and more effective will to power in Nietzsche's scheme of things. As Nietzsche interprets the limited array of moral choices, we can either act consistently in accord with the requirements of the will to power, or we can act without reference to the will and without reference to the self, in an unnatural and unhealthy denial of the will to power.

NIETZSCHE'S EPISTEMIC PERSPECTIVALISM

Nietzsche accepts a perspectival concept of knowledge. We know things only from the empirical situation in which we find ourselves as epistemic agents. He regards it as part of the denial of life to imagine that knowledge can be acquired as though from a perspective-free uncontexted absolute standpoint. Schopenhauer is quoted again in this connection as someone who speaks liberally of the subject of knowledge in no particular place or time, suffering no particular psychological infirmities or limitations, and, in a word, from what is sometimes called a god's eye's omniscient point of view.

Nietzsche argues instead for a contexted epistemic perspectivalism. All knowledge, according to this view, is obtained and colored by the situation and circumstances of the knowing subject and the limitations imposed by the perspective from which the subject experiences the world. Nietzsche contrasts the Schopenhauerian nonperspectival ideal of knowing with what he takes to be a more realistic position. It is part of the denial of life to suppose that knowledge can be acquired independently of the actual conditions of life, which, Nietzsche argues, prominently include the knowing subject's spatiotemporal location and other features of the physical, historical, and social situation to which the knower belongs. He holds:

> For let us guard ourselves better from now on, gentlemen philosophers, against the dangerous old conceptual fabrication that posited a "pure, will-less, painless, timeless subject of knowledge"; let us guard ourselves against the tentacles of such contradictory concepts as "pure reason," "absolute spirituality," "knowledge in itself": here it is always demanded that we think an eye that cannot possibly be thought, an eye that must not have any direction, in which the active and interpretive forces through which seeing first becomes seeing-something are to be shut off, are to be absent; thus, what is demanded here is always an absurdity and nonconcept of an eye. (85)

In contrast to the nonperspectival concept of knowledge, Nietzsche argues that all knowledge is contexted. The will, individual and supreme in itself, is an essential ingredient in the activity of knowing. For much the same reason that Nietzsche has argued we cannot eliminate the will to power from the specific content of ethics, politics, aesthetics, biology, and other natural sciences, he now argues that we cannot eliminate the will to power from knowledge seeking by the knowing subject:

> There is *only* a perspectival seeing, *only* a perspectival "knowing"; and *the more* affects we allow to speak about a matter, *the more* eyes, different eyes, we know how to bring to bear on one and the same matter, that much more complete will our "concept" of this matter, our "objectivity" be. But to eliminate the will altogether, to disconnect the affects one and all, supposing that we were capable of this: what? would that not be to *castrate* the intellect? (85)

He admits that degrees of objectivity can occur as we increase the number of individual knowers, each contributing their knowledge from their respective perspectives. He denies, however, that we can ever aspire to knowledge that is not confined in principle to particular perspectives. The objectivity we obtain collectively in knowledge as a social enterprise at its best and most complete is still not greater than the sum of its individually perspectival parts. With his usual dramatic élan, Nietzsche argues that to eliminate the will from knowledge by thinking of knowledge as nonperspectival and uncontexted is to castrate the intellect. The rhetorical flourish with which he concludes the paragraph, the rhetorical question whose answer is never in doubt for him, is appropriate given his conception of the relation between the will to power, its role in knowledge seeking, and its manifestation as sexual energy in the proliferation of life. It is a force that Nietzsche is at pains to defend and promote, any limitation or infringement of which he strenuously resists quite literally as a castration. For Nietzsche, to think of the knowing subject independently of particular perspective is to think of the knowing subject without its will, without the will to power, which is to think of a knowing subject without its life-affirming desires and everything that makes it unique, individual, a person or self. The subjective perspective of each self is an essential feature of knowledge in his epistemic perspectivalism, and hence an inalienable element in understanding the nature of knowledge.

Life-Affirming: Philosophical Metaphors of Illness and Health

Metaphors of sound health abound in Nietzsche's polemic. He compares the noble aristocracy as healthy in vital ways, affirming life by the free expression of their will to power, which he contrasts with the sickly pallor of priests, saints, and moral slaves who say "no" to life and renounce what is required for its healthy furtherance. He implies that in the company of those who do not pursue the will to power it is difficult even to breathe:

> What *they* can do, what *they* should do, a sick person can never and should never do: but *in order for* them to be able to do what only *they* should do, how could they be free to choose to be physician, comforter, "savior" for the sick? . . . And therefore good air! good air! And in any case away from the proximity of all madhouses and hospitals of culture! And therefore good company, *our* company! Or solitude if it must be! But in any case away from the foul vapors of inward corruptions and the secret wormfodder of invalids! . . . So that we may defend ourselves, my friends, at least for a while yet, against what may be the two gravest epidemics that have been reserved just for us—against the *great disgust at the sight of man!* against the *great compassion for man!* (89–90)

By promoting the will to power and hence the will to life, Nietzsche espouses a thoroughgoing humanism. The trouble with asceticism, he believes, is that it hates humankind and tries to deny its humanity. This is true to such an extent that those who say "no" to life deny human nature even in epistemology, convincing themselves that it is somehow possible to understand knowledge independently of a human subject's perspective. The ethos of such an attitude Nietzsche finds morally objectionable in the extreme. He does not tire of stacking up philosophical analogies that ring changes on a single theme, that it is unhealthy, morbid, ill, sickly, invalid, and an epidemic, a plague of sorts, to deny our humanity in acting contrary to the will to power. He regards the will to power as the will to be human and to realize all that we are capable of in our natures in perfecting our virtues and fulfilling our greatest potential. It is the threat to this promise of humanity that inspires Nietzsche's disappointment, anger, and frustration with the denial of the self, undermining the most valuable promise of life. The suppression of the will to power is therefore outright moral nihilism for Nietzsche, recognizable as misanthropy or hatred of humanity:

> One simply cannot conceal from oneself *what* all the willing that has received its direction from the ascetic ideal actually expresses: this hatred of the human, still more of the animal, still more of the material, this abhorrence of the senses, of reason itself, this fear of happiness and of beauty, this longing away from all appearance, change, becoming, death, wish, longing itself—all of this means—let us dare to grasp this—a *will to nothingness*, an aversion to life, a rebellion against the most fundamental presuppositions of life; but it is and remains a *will!* . . . And, to say again at the end what I said at the beginning: man would much rather will *nothingness* than *not* will. . . . (118)

It is, finally, human nature in Nietzsche's moral philosophy that compels us to will, and therefore a violation of natural impulses to deny the will to power. Even nihilism might be willed rather than willing nothing at all. This is a paradox, given that willing nothing, if it should succeed in its aim, amounts to not willing.

At least for the brief period of time during which the will persists, a human being naturally prefers to will that there be nothing, presumably at some time thereafter in the future, than at the present time not will anything at all. It is our nature to will, we cannot prevent it in any case, and even the priests and moral slaves whom Nietzsche deprecates do not avoid willing, but will inconsistently to deny and obstruct the will to power of others. This, Nietzsche maintains, is unhealthy, contrary to all that is morally valuable in human life. We can do so, and some persons who pathologically do not value life may choose to do so, but it is an aberration that violates the principles of good health, and is, from Nietzsche's perspective, morally wrong.

What is philosophically important in Nietzsche's genealogy of morality is not his development of a distinct moral theory to stand beside Kant's or Mill's or Schopenhauer's, or, for that matter, Socrates', Plato's, or Aristotle's, or any of the other great ethical system builders in the history of philosophy. Nietzsche offers nothing of the kind, and his philosophical writing is intended to serve a different purpose than to answer the kinds of questions with which other moral thinkers have wrestled. He is not interested in the specifics of whether it is morally permissible to commit suicide or to borrow money with no intention of repaying, or to have an abortion or donate surplus wealth to charity or cheat on one's income taxes, or do or refrain from doing any of the other things that moralists historically have questioned. Nietzsche has another aim in mind. He wants to explore philosophical problems about the meaning of life, the nature, and as he likes to say, the value of value. He questions whether the values we have inherited are morally justified, whether they are themselves morally valuable, or whether we need to rethink virtually everything we have been taught about the concept of moral good.

The historical approach of Nietzsche's genealogy of morality is necessary given these purposes. He believes that there has been a corruption, a decay in the values that prevail in European moral consciousness in the nineteenth century. The devaluation of values can only be exposed by tracing the lineage of morality as it has regressed from an original distinction between good and bad to a later distinction between good and evil, accompanied by a reversal of the subjects to whom these concepts are understood to apply. The strong have given way to the weak, those who affirm life and have the best prospect of realizing what could be greatest in the human race have allowed themselves to betray these values by accepting moral guilt for the free exercise of their will to power by those who deny the self and thereby deny life. This, he believes, is morally wrong, unconscionable, and he strives to reverse this situation once again, leading in a new direction for a new dawning of the morality of the higher man and philosopher of the future, who will act freely, spontaneously, and with no sense of guilt in doing whatever is required for the sake of life, power, and the pursuit of egoistic good.

What is philosophically most interesting and important in Nietzsche's genealogy is the problem it raises about the historical development of concepts, and of what can be learned from the study of the etymology of the language in which they are expressed. Whether we agree with Nietzsche's conclusions or not, he makes an inestimable contribution to moral philosophy by questioning so radically the real value of received values, a task at which a fully self-conscious and critically aware systematic ethics should be perennially engaged.

Summary

Nietzsche's polemic contains a historical thesis and a normative philosophical commitment. He offers to trace the origin of the distinction between good and evil, and he strikes a blow for a particular set of moral values that he prefers for a variety of reasons. Beginning with the distinction between good and bad, Nietzsche proposes an account of what he considers to be its degeneration into the distinction between good and evil.

In the morally heroic idealized past, the powerful called themselves good because of their strength and will to power, and called the weak bad for failing to possess these qualities. After many years of oppression at the hands of the powerful nobility, the weak through their *ressentiment* of their disadvantaged state began a campaign of psychological warfare that has gradually brought about a devaluation of primordial life-affirming values. It has accomplished this reversal by instilling in the potentially most powerful individuals a sense of guilt that inhibits them from exercising the will to power.

Nietzsche does not say that the devaluing of the nobility of power or any of its results is evil, since evil is not a moral concept he recognizes. He nevertheless disapproves of and rejects all that is implied by such life-denying values, which he collects together under what are meant to be the unflattering titles of European Buddhism, slave morality, herd mentality, and what he clearly thinks of as the demeaning underhanded motivation of *ressentiment*. Nietzsche interprets Schopenhauer's concept of the will to life as will to power, and cuts his own philosophy free from Schopenhauer's Kantian transcendental metaphysics of the world in reality or thing-in-itself as Will. He regards any infringement of the prerogatives of the will to power as saying "no" to life, and argues that we commit an irredeemable higher moral wrong to our species by preventing humanity from attaining its full potential if we try to restrain the will to power as something evil.

Nietzsche understands that he cannot return to the time and place when the powerful nobility ruled, but he issues a manifesto for the higher man, sometimes translated as superman, or philosopher of the future. The higher man will be a new kind of moral being uninhibited by feelings of guilt or compassion toward others. With no obstacles to pursuing a self-interested will to power, the higher man will overcome the contemporary devaluation of values and move forward to a future of new values beyond good and evil, thereby taking humankind farther along the road to achieving its ultimate promise. Nietzsche assumes but does not try to argue that human purpose can only be attained through strength that is unmindful of the sufferings of others, and is not motivated by compassion in deciding what ought to be done, but looks always to the higher good of the species through each individual's self-realization.

Whether Nietzsche has provided a historically correct account of the genealogy of morality or a philosophically sound endorsement of positive life-affirming values is unclear. On factual and normative grounds, Nietzsche's moral philosophy leaves many unanswered questions. Yet it continues to exert a profound appeal not only for the poetry of its literary style, but because of its deeply felt affirmation of health and strength. Ultimately, the slave morality Nietzsche deplores is not a feature only of desperate weaker people in the captivity of stronger and more willful ones, but a gnawing corruption of self-doubt that limits human potential within even those who may seem to be most powerful, healthy, and strong.

QUESTIONS FOR PHILOSOPHICAL UNDERSTANDING

1. What is the philosophical point of trying to provide a genealogy of a philosophical word, phrase, or concept? What can we learn from that?

2. If the original meaning of "good" is to be powerful, as Nietzsche contends, is his concept of good morally relevant? What do we mean and what should we mean by morality or moral good as a qualification of laws, rights, and other moral concepts?

3. Can a morality of any kind be based entirely on concepts of strength, power, and self-interest?

4. What does Nietzsche mean by the devaluation of value?

5. What is Nietzsche's objection to what he refers to as European Buddhism?

6. What is the relation between Schopenhauer's concept of the will to life and Nietzsche's concept of the will to power?

7. Can the truly powerful be psychologically overcome by the *ressentiment* of a morally inferior slave morality? If they are made to feel guilty and inhibited in exercising their will to power, does that not imply that they were not so powerful in the first place?

8. Is it possible that the distinction between good and bad and the distinction between good and evil as Nietzsche understands them could have coexisted all along rather than evolving from one into the other?

9. Does Nietzsche's higher man have any moral obligations? If so what are they and how do they arise? If not, why not? Can the good of the species possibly be achieved by the completely unrestrained uninhibited exercise of will to power? Can it possibly be achieved in any other way?

10. Why does Nietzsche think it necessary to help pave the way for the higher man? Would a higher man in the true sense of the word need anyone's assistance?

11. What would a society of higher men (and higher women?) be like? Could there be long-term cooperation between such individuals?

12. Why does Nietzsche think that saying "yes" to life is incompatible with moral compassion? Is he right about this? Why or why not? Is it conceivable that humankind might fulfill its true potential by exercising rather than overcoming its compassion for others?

13. Why does Nietzsche criticize Jewish culture as manifesting a slave morality? What would he say about Christianity, Islam, or Hinduism?

14. How does Nietzsche explain the concept of justice?

15. What are the similarities and differences between Nietzsche's concept of justice and Kant's and Mill's concepts of justice?

KEY TERMS

aestheticism, aesthetic ideals

altruism, altruistic behavior

anti-Semitism

Apollo

asceticism, ascetic ideal

beyond good and evil

compassion *(Mitleid)*

conventional morality

cosmos, comos

devaluation of values

Dionysus

egoism

ethics of punishment

European Buddhism

fourfold root of the principle of sufficient reason

genealogy of morality

good and bad, good and evil

herd instinct

higher man *(Übermensch)*

justice

knightly-aristocratic values

life-affirming, saying "yes" to life

life-denying, saying "no" to life

morality of compassion

nihilism, moral nihilism, nihilistic moral outlook

nirvana

noumena, phenomena

origin of evil

perspectivalism, moral and epistemic

philosopher of the future

polemic

priestly mentality, values

principium individuationis

ressentiment

Schopenhauer's pessimistic moral philosophy

slave morality

thing-in-itself *(Ding an sich)*

transvaluation of value

value of morality

wheel of *dharma*

will to life *(Wille zum Leben)*

will to power *(Wille zur Macht)*

SOURCES AND RECOMMENDED READINGS

Appel, Frederick. *Nietzsche Contra Democracy.* Ithaca: Cornell University Press, 1999.

Berkowitz, Peter. *Nietzsche: The Ethics of an Immoralist.* Cambridge: Harvard University Press, 1995.

Blondel, Eric. *Nietzsche: The Body and Culture: Philosophy as a Philological Genealogy.* Translated by Sean Hand. Stanford: Stanford University Press, 1991.

Havas, Randall. *Nietzsche's Genealogy: Nihilism and the Will to Knowledge.* Ithaca: Cornell University Press, 1995.

Hollingdale, R. J. *Nietzsche: The Man and His Philosophy.* Cambridge: Cambridge University Press, 1999.

Hunt, Lester H. *Nietzsche and the Origin of Virtue.* London: Routledge, 1991.

Kaufmann, Walter. *Basic Writings of Nietzsche.* New York: Viking Books, 1966.

Magnus, Bernd, and Kathleen Higgins, eds. *The Cambridge Companion to Nietzsche.* Cambridge: Cambridge University Press, 1996.

May, Simon. *Nietzsche's Ethics and His War on "Morality."* Oxford: Clarendon Press, 1999.

Morrison, Robert G. *Nietzsche and Buddhism: A Study in Nihilism and Ironic Affinities.* Oxford: Oxford University Press, 1997.

Murray, Peter Durno. *Nietzsche's Affirmative Morality: A Revaluation Based in the Dionysian World-View.* Berlin: Walter de Gruyter, 1999.

Schacht, Richard, ed. *Nietzsche, Genealogy, Morality: Essays on Nietzsche's Genealogy of Morals.* Berkeley: University of California Press, 1994.

Tolstoy, Leo. *Confession.* Translated by David Patterson. New York: W. W. Norton, 1983.

CHAPTER 9

PHILOSOPHICAL ANALYSIS OF THE CONCEPT OF GOOD

Moore's *Principia Ethica*

C ontemporary analytic moral philosophy begins with Moore and a handful of other linguistic philosophers in England. Moore is one of the founders of analytic philosophy, a major twentieth-century philosophical movement that has been variously understood from its beginnings at the turn of the previous century. Moore's style of analytic philosophy leads him from complex moral concepts to the analytic bottom line in the property or concept of moral good or goodness as something indefinable and unanalyzable. Efforts to define indefinable moral goodness as something other than itself commit what Moore calls the naturalistic fallacy. There are simplest most fundamental moral values and concepts, according to Moore, which he identifies as moral good, and which he distinguishes from good things, collectively designated as the good.

ANALYTIC PHILOSOPHY

G. E. (George Edward) Moore (1873–1958) was an English philosopher at Cambridge University. Together with Bertrand Russell and Ludwig Wittgenstein, Moore is recognized as one of the founders of modern *analytic philosophy*. The history of analysis includes many different philosophical methodologies in defense of many different positions, united by a common concern with the rigorous clarification of meaning and approach to philosophical problems through the development of sound arguments. Like most living intellectual traditions, analytic philosophy has undergone transformation at the hands of different philosophers who made unique contributions to its legacy. This fact makes it hard to offer a general definition that encompasses all the ways of doing philosophy that today are known as analytic. Analytic philosophy can usually be identified by its concern with the theory of meaning in language as a key to solving or avoiding philosophical problems. Analytic philosophy is also involved in the development and application of symbolic logic as a tool for understanding the language in which philosophical problems are expressed, and is often construed by its adherents as an adjunct to mathematics and science.

Moore, in addition to making important contributions to theoretical ethics, was also influential in his writings on epistemology and metaphysics. Although he was not a formal logician in the manner of Russell and Wittgenstein, he set a standard for the analysis of philosophical concepts that continues to inspire generations of philosophers who continue to hold exceptional clarity of thought as an essential condition for the pursuit of philosophical truth. Moore is sometimes described as having championed a commonsense philosophy, in that he strove to uphold conclusions that are widely accepted even by persons who are not philosophically trained, for which he provided a lucid justification in terms of nonspecialized nontechnical vocabulary and reasons that any reflective person could consider to be persuasive without having already accepted the principles of any particular philosophical school.

Moore is an analytic philosopher in another crucial sense. He proposes to solve philosophical problems through the analysis of the meaning of philosophically interesting language by decomposing complex concepts to greater and greater degrees of simplicity until he identifies the simplest most primitive, indefinable, or analytically irreducible constituent concepts into which they can be broken down. We can think of philosophical analysis as something like Kant's distinction between analytic and synthetic judgments, modeled on the difference between analytic and synthetic chemistry. There is a parallel to Moore's concept of analytic philosophy in the idea that in analytic chemistry we can always analyze complex molecules into simpler molecules, and simpler molecules into atoms, atoms into protons, electrons, and neutrons, and these constituents into quarks of several flavors. We can in any case analyze complexes into ultimately simple things out of which everything else is built up in different ways in more complicated structures. We understand complex chemical substances by discovering how they are made out of simpler components and the ways in which they are put together. Analytic philosophy assumes that we can similarly analyze the language in which philosophical problems are expressed into sentences and terms, and further break down the meanings of terms into the simpler meanings of simpler terms. If Moore's analysis of philosophical language is a viable project, then we can complete the process by analyzing the meanings of these terms further into ultimately basic primitive concepts out of which all other concepts are constructed. We understand complex concepts by discovering what their simplest components are and how they are combined to produce the most complex philosophical ideas, including those that seem to give rise to philosophical puzzles and paradoxes.

Moore's *Principia Ethica* is not only one of the most valuable contributions to the philosophical study of ethics, but a landmark in the emergence of analytic philosophy. Moore offers a patient painstaking examination of moral concepts in which he claims to identify the most basic ethical concepts into which discourse about what it is right and wrong be analyzed. The foundation of ethical thought for Moore is the concept of moral good or goodness, which he believes cannot be further reduced into any more basic concepts, but is a kind of bedrock or ultimate building block from which other ideas and principles are constructed.

What does Moore hope to gain from this analytic philosophical insight? Among other conclusions, he argues that the conceptual irreducibility of the concept of moral good means that philosophies that try to explain what is good in terms of other kinds of properties are necessarily mistaken. If Moore is right, then we cannot explain moral obligations by means of theories that interpret what it is good to do in terms of anything that is supposed to explain moral goodness in terms of something else. Moore rejects ethical systems that purport to explain moral good as happiness or pleasure or some other naturally occurring property. All such moral philosophies commit what Moore refers to as the *naturalistic fallacy*. In this way, in a single stroke, Moore is able to eliminate ethical philosophies such as Mill's utilitarianism that presuppose that moral good can be explained in terms of a natural phenomenon such as psychological pleasure. He argues that they are all based on a philosophically mistaken understanding of the meaning of the word "good" as something capable of further philosophical analysis.

THE QUESTION OF ETHICS

To begin his analysis of moral concepts into their most elementary components, Moore maintains that we ought to begin with a clear statement of the question a system of ethics is supposed to answer. As obvious as this seems as a starting place for a moral philosophy, Moore remarks that the question of ethics had never previously been adequately clarified. It is no wonder then that moral theories have gone astray:

> It appears to me that in Ethics, as in all other philosophical studies, the difficulties and disagreements, of which its history is full, are mainly due to a very simple cause: Namely to the attempt to answer questions, without first discovering precisely *what* question it is which you desire to answer. I do not know how far this source of error would be done away, if philosophers would *try* to discover what question they were asking, before they set about to answer it; for the work of analysis and distinction is often very difficult: we may often fail to make the necessary discovery, even though we make a definite attempt to do so. But I am inclined to think that in many cases a resolute attempt would be sufficient to ensure success; so that, if only this attempt were made, many of the most glaring difficulties and disagreements in philosophy would disappear. (Preface to the 1922 edition, vii)

Moore's statement is taken from the second edition of his book, the most commonly reprinted version of the text, which was originally published in 1903. He looks back on almost twenty years during which his moral philosophical analysis was widely discussed. He now argues that philosophers fail to make progress in any area of knowledge if they do not first clarify the questions they are trying to answer. This sounds like reasonable advice, which makes it hard to believe that all prior thinkers have failed to take the time and trouble to ask themselves what it is they thought they were doing. Moore has his own way of understanding the questions a moral philosophy should address, and they naturally do not agree with those of theories he criticizes. His rhetorical suggestion in the Preface to the second edition is that if only the great ethicists of the past had clarified what it is they were trying to do, they would not have arrived at such mistaken views, but might have come to conclusions similar to those that Moore defends.

How does Moore articulate the question proper to inquiry in ethics? What is a moral philosophy supposed to do? Moore describes the task of moral philosophy as primarily one of explaining the meaning of terms of moral appraisal. We need to consider what we mean when we say that someone is a good person, or the opposite, what ought to be done or what it would be wrong to do. The work of theoretical ethics, according to Moore, is to discuss these matters and arrive at an understanding of the language we use when we talk about what we think is good and bad, right and wrong, obligatory, permitted, or forbidden. He explains:

> It is very easy to point out some among our every-day judgments, with the truth of which Ethics is undoubtedly concerned. Whenever we say, "So and so is a good man," or "That fellow is a villain"; whenever we ask, "What ought I to do?" or "Is it wrong for me to do like this?"; whenever we hazard such remarks as "Temperance is a virtue and drunkenness a vice"—it is undoubtedly the business of Ethics to discuss such questions and such statements; to argue what is the true answer when we ask what it is right to do, and to give reasons for thinking that our statements about the character of persons or the morality of actions are true or false. In the vast majority of cases, where we make statements involving any of the terms "virtue," "vice," "duty," "right," "ought," "good," "bad," we are making ethical judgments; and if we wish to discuss their truth, we shall be discussing a point of Ethics. (1)

Moore begins with what people say when they express moral judgments. He does not hope to explain the origin of ethical concepts through philological study in anything like Nietzsche's genealogy of morals. In fairness, Nietzsche is also not content to investigate the historical origins and meanings of a moral vocabulary, but to use the etymological background to the devolution of a distinction between good and bad into a distinction between good and evil as a platform for advocating a particular set of values, associated with his concept of the will to power and the higher man or philosopher of the future.

Moore does not have anything resembling Nietzsche's agenda for an ethics beyond good and evil, but he also does not suppose that moral philosophy ends simply with the philosophical scrutiny of moral language. We are not meant only to discover how people talk about moral value, but to discuss and argue about them in order to decide when moral pronouncements express the truth about morality and what is true about what is said to be right or wrong to do. Moore requires a moral philosophical methodology to aim at the truth of moral judgments, beginning with sensitive attention to the way in which language users discuss what is morally right and wrong as a basis for arguments leading to moral truths.

The methodological problem for Moore is to decide how to search for moral truths. He sharpens his focus on a manageable set of issues and identifies what is common to the kinds of moral discourse that he proposes to analyze. He argues first that the relevant aspect of language use to which philosophical ethics must pay special attention is its evaluation of human conduct, of behavior and action, that is said to be morally good or bad, right or wrong. The proper subject matter of moral philosophy concerns what we do and how we think and talk about what we do and how we do it. This may seem painfully obvious and possibly not even worth mentioning. We recall that Moore argues in the second edition Preface that ethics cannot hope to arrive at correct conclusions unless it proceeds more self-consciously than it has typically done, with a clear statement of purpose and a clear formulation of the questions it proposes to answer. We cannot overemphasize the importance of understanding what we are trying to achieve in moral reasoning and the kinds of answers we expect to find. Moore elaborates on the goals of ethical inquiry in this way:

> If we take such examples as those given above, we shall not be far wrong in say-ing that they are all of them concerned with the question of "conduct"—with the question, what, in the conduct of us, human beings, is good, and what is bad, what is right, and what is wrong. For when we say that a man is good, we commonly mean that he acts rightly; when we say that drunkenness is a vice, we commonly mean that to get drunk is a wrong or wicked action. And this discussion of hu-man conduct is, in fact, that with which the name "Ethics" is most intimately as-sociated. It is so associated by derivation; and conduct is undoubtedly by far the commonest and most generally interesting object of ethical judgments. (1–2)

Moore culls linguistic evidence in a commonsense way from ordinary thinking and speaking about good and bad, right and wrong conduct. He chooses a particular example from discourse in which a person is said to be good in the sense that he or she acts rightly, engaging in a certain type of behavior. He contrasts this with an ex-ample in which critics say of objectionable actions that they are vices, meaning that they are wrong or "wicked." The important point at this stage of Moore's inquiry is to appreciate how certain of these evaluative expressions are grouped together and to what kinds of things they are commonly applied. We should not conclude that Moore takes it as a truth of ethics that drunkenness is a vice or necessarily something morally wrong or wicked. What interests Moore is that people sometimes talk this way, and that when they do they are in fact attributing terms of moral approval or disapproval specifically to acts of human conduct. Ethics concerns action for Moore; it is a theory of how we ought to conduct ourselves, as "many ethical philosophers" say. He be-lieves that this is too limited an interpretation of ethics, which needs to broaden its consideration to encompass more than just good conduct. As he understands the dis-cipline, Moore believes that ethics is not merely about morally good actions, but about moral goodness in general, about the concept of good:

> Accordingly, we find that many ethical philosophers are disposed to accept as an adequate definition of "Ethics" the statement that it deals with the questions what is good or bad in human conduct. They hold that its enquiries are properly con-fined to "conduct" or to "practice"; they hold that the name "practical philoso-phy" covers all the matter with which it has to do. Now, without discussing the proper meaning of the word (for verbal questions are properly left to the writers of dictionaries and other persons interested in literature; philosophy, as we shall see, has no concern with them), I may say that I intend to use "Ethics" to cover more than this—a usage, for which there is, I think, quite sufficient authority. I am using it to cover an enquiry for which, at all events, there is no other word: the general enquiry into what is good. (2)

Moore picks and chooses his authorities, agreeing with those unnamed writers who have also understood the subject matter of ethics as moral good in general, un-like others who have confined moral philosophy specifically to morally good conduct.

It is Moore's prerogative to define his topic as he sees fit, and it is clear that a philosophical exploration of the concept of moral good in its most general terms is a project similar to Socrates' and Plato's efforts to understand the Form of Good in terms of its necessary and sufficient conditions. If that is the kind of philosophical precedent to which Moore means to appeal, then he is certainly right to think that there is ample authority for regarding the principles of ethics as the philosophy of moral good.

INDEFINABILITY OF THE CONCEPT OF GOOD

Moore distinguishes between ethics as a philosophical inquiry into the definition of the concept of good and *casuistry* as the determination of what things or kinds of things are good. Again, Moore's inquiry appears in a Platonic light, in which we almost hear echoes of Socrates reminding Meno that the concept of virtue cannot be correctly be defined by listing all of the different kinds of virtues, and of his metaphor of the swarm of bees as contrasted with a general definition of the concept of bee. Moore similarly explains that it will be necessary first to clarify the nature of moral good as the most fundamental question of ethics. He argues that not only is it essential to understand what is meant by the concept of moral good in most general terms as a preliminary step in the process of identifying what kinds of conduct and other items of moral value are morally good, but because we set off in the wrong direction with potentially disastrous consequences in moral philosophy if we do not begin by properly understanding its most basic concept. He argues:

> But our question "What is good?" may have still another meaning. We may, in the third place, mean to ask, not what thing or things are good, but how "good" is to be defined. This is an enquiry which belongs only to Ethics, not to Casuistry; and this is the enquiry which will occupy us first.
>
> It is an enquiry to which most special attention should be directed; since this question, how "good" is to be defined, is the most fundamental question in all Ethics. That which is meant by "good" is, in fact, except its converse "bad," the *only* simple object of thought which is peculiar to Ethics. Its definition is, therefore, the most essential point in the definition of Ethics; and moreover a mistake with regard to it entails a far larger number of erroneous ethical judgments than any other. Unless this first question be fully understood, and its true answer clearly recognised, the rest of Ethics is as good as useless from the point of view of systematic knowledge. (5)

Moore declares, but has not yet tried to prove, that moral good and bad are the only "simple" objects of thought that are peculiar to ethics. This choice of terminology reflects his commitment to the methods of philosophical analysis, in which complex ideas are broken down into their simpler and finally simplest atomic units of meaning. Moore anticipates one of the most important conclusions of *Principia Ethica*, that moral good is a, and here he tells us that along with the bad it is the only, primitive concept of moral philosophy. Moral good, according to Moore, is an indefinable, conceptually irreducible building block from which more complex moral concepts are constructed. When we complete the analysis of moral discourse by breaking down its concepts into simpler and simpler ideas, we will eventually arrive at moral good and bad as the ultimate concepts by which all complex ethical concepts are defined.

We notice an important difference in this conclusion between Moore's and Socrates' attitude toward the analysis of meaning of the most general concepts of ethics. Whereas Socrates seems to believe that in principle it should be possible to define the concepts of virtue, justice, or good in terms of necessary and sufficient conditions, Moore holds that there are fundamental concepts that cannot be further defined by reference to simpler ideas but that are themselves among the ultimately simple concepts to be found at the deepest most basic stratum of conceptual analysis. Socrates gives no indication that he understands the structural requirement for concepts to be defined in terms of simpler and simpler concepts until the most basic indefinable concepts are reached. In the model of philosophical analysis that Moore develops there must finally be indefinable concepts, which can also be described as primitive or irreducible, by reference to which more complex concepts are defined and into which they can be analyzed.

Moore might describe his project as one in which he begins with roughly the same questions as Socrates, but proceeds on the basis of a more sophisticated appreciation of the limits of philosophical analysis to the recognition that there must be indefinable concepts on which all definitions are based. The claim, if it is true, that the concept of moral good is a, and, indeed, along with its converse, the only primitive irreducible and indefinable concept of ethics, is Moore's most important thesis. He explains his view by comparing the indefinability of moral good to that of the concept yellow:

> Let us, then, consider this position. My point is that "good" is a simple notion, just as "yellow" is a simple notion; that, just as you cannot, by any manner of means, explain to any one who does not already know it, what yellow is, so you cannot explain what good is. Definitions of the kind that I was asking for, definitions which describe the real nature of the object or notion denoted by a word, and which do not merely tell us what the word is used to mean, are only possible when the object or notion in question is something complex. You can give a definition of a horse, because a horse has many different properties and qualities, all of which you can enumerate. But when you have enumerated them all, when you have reduced a horse to his simplest terms, then you can no longer define those terms. They are simply something which you think of or perceive, and to any one who cannot think of or perceive them, you can never, by any definition, make their nature known. (7)

The model of philosophical analysis that Moore assumes has several possibilities for defining concepts. He distinguishes between explaining the meaning of a word by saying how it is used and defining it by breaking it down into its simpler component ideas. In the case of moral good he repeats that the concept cannot be defined in the second way but only by means of specifying how it is used. We can say, for example, that moral "good" is a term of approval, that it is used to describe conduct of a certain sort under certain circumstances, and the like.

What we cannot do if Moore is right is further analyze the concept of the good into more basic ideas, for the simple reason that it is already an absolutely primitive concept incapable of further reduction or analysis. There must be some sort of ultimate bedrock or foundation in every conceptual system. If Moore is correct, then the indefinable concept of moral good is the cornerstone on which the entire conceptual system of ethics rests. His most famous illustration of the limits of conceptual analysis compares the concept of moral good with the concept of yellow. He claims that the concept of yellow is fundamental to our visual conceptual scheme in the same way that the concept of good is fundamental to our ethical conceptual scheme.

The sign that these concepts are absolutely fundamental according to Moore is that we could not explain them to anyone who did not already know what they were. Consider the problem of trying to explain the concept of yellow to a blind person who has never seen any colors. Usually in those kinds of situations when we need to explain an unfamiliar concept we make comparisons with things we believe the person is likely to have already experienced. If there is no relevant basis for comparison, then our attempts at explanation are unlikely to explain. In the case of complex things, in contrast, such as a horse, it is possible to convey them to persons who have no familiarity with them by analyzing the meaning of their concepts, breaking them down into simpler component concepts.

MOORE ON GOOD AND THE GOOD

Moore further distinguishes between good and *the* good. The difference is subtle but fundamentally important for Moore. Although Socrates and Plato would have recognized something like the same distinction, they probably would have expressed it in English in the opposite way. For Socrates, *the* good is the concept of good, that for which there exists a general Form. What is merely good on the other hand in an Anglicized version of Plato's Greek terminology would be all the particular things that have the property of being good, all the good things, including actions and motives and persons and whatever else is good. Moore draws the same distinction but in a reversed technical terminology. What he means by the general concept he refers to simply as good, and what he means by the particular things that are good he refers to as *the* good. He does not conclude that the good is indefinable, which he promises later in the book to articulate. It is good rather than the good that he regards as indefinable. He explains his reason for marking the distinction grammatically in the way he does:

> But I am afraid I have still not removed the chief difficulty which may prevent acceptance of the proposition that good is indefinable. I do not mean to say that *the* good, that which is good, is thus indefinable; if I did think so, I should not be writing on Ethics, for my main object is to help towards discovering that definition. It is just because I think there will be less risk of error in our search for a definition of "the good," that I am now insisting that *good* is indefinable. I must try to explain the difference between these two. I suppose it may be granted that "good" is an adjective. Well "the good," "that which is good," must therefore be the substantive to which the adjective "good" will apply: it must be the whole of that to which the adjective will apply, and the adjective must *always* truly apply to it. But if it is that to which the adjective will apply, it must be something different from that adjective itself; and the whole of that something different, whatever it is, will be our definition of *the* good. (8–9)

The grammatical distinction is crucial for Moore's argument. "The good" is what he mentions as the substantive of moral value predications, while "good" without such qualification is the adjective, which is to say the term by which the property itself is designated. Since it is the property good that Moore regards as primitive, unanalyzable, and indefinable, it is appropriate for him to hold that the property good with no qualifying term to designate what it is that is good is indefinable, like the concept yellow. Moore will have much to say about the good, but concerning moral good itself he argues that we cannot offer any further definition of its meaning. Where the concept or property of moral good or goodness is concerned there can be no further analysis.

Moore's criterion for indefinable concepts by analogy with the indefinability of yellow is the inability to explain the concept to someone who is not already familiar with its meaning. We may wonder whether this is true of the concept of moral good, and whether or to what extent the analogy between good and yellow actually holds. It is undoubtedly true that we cannot explain the concept yellow to someone who has never had any visual experience of colors, at least in the sense that they will not fully understand any explanation we may try to give. Is the same not also true of many other kinds of things that are not primitive or indefinable? What about Moore's own example of the concept of horse? It is helpful to be told that a horse is an equine quadruped mammal, that it walks on four legs and has a mane and hooves and the like. When we understand the qualities attributed to the concept of horse in general we gain an understanding and acquire a relatively clear idea of what kind of thing a horse is. It nevertheless remains unclear exactly what is meant by the concept of horse if we have never encountered a horse. We might not be able to distinguish it from other real or imaginary animals that also fit the description.

A complete definition or analysis of the concept *horse* might settle most of these discrepancies, so that in principle there should be no ambiguity between what is and what is not a horse. The philosophical point is different. The question is whether we can say anything at all that would help someone completely unfamiliar with yellow or good what the general concepts yellow and good mean. Moore makes a strong assertion that in the case of primitive concepts, when he states, as we have seen above: "[Y]ou cannot, by any manner of means, explain to any one who does not already know it, what yellow is." What seems doubtful is whether it is true that we cannot say anything whatsoever that will help someone who is unfamiliar with the concept yellow to understand at least in part what it is, at least to the same extent that we can do so in the case of complex concepts like horse or water. We can say that yellow is a color, that it is light rather than dark, a warm rather than cool color, that it is the color of lemons and sunlight and dandelions and certain kinds of cheese.

We might also therefore make a similar kind of limited progress in explaining the concept of moral good. We can say that moral good is a positive rather than negative moral value that is predicated of actions, persons, and motivations under certain circumstances, and we can give suggestive indications of what kinds of circumstances are often judged good. This is not quite the same thing as a complete definition given in terms of necessary and sufficient conditions of the sort that would satisfy Socrates when he is dialectically engaged in trying to pin down the exact definition of a general concept. Moore, however, sets the bar much lower than this when he argues that we can distinguish an indefinable concept on the basis of the fact that if we are not already familiar with its meaning then nothing that can be said will help to explain what a concept means.

Moore might be right that yellow and good are indefinable concepts, but he has yet to offer a convincing argument to prove that this is true, nor a practical criterion by which we can effectively distinguish between complex analyzable and indefinable concepts. If we do not know what good is but we are familiar with other concepts, we might be able to come very close to understanding what is meant by the adjective "good." We can do so to roughly the same extent that we can in the case of complex definable concepts with which we are not familiar but for which complete satisfactory definitions in terms of necessary and sufficient conditions are unavailable. We should recall that even Socrates with all his argumentative skill claims not to be able to define many general concepts that Moore would regard as complex and hence analyzable. How, on the basis of Moore's criterion, are we supposed to be able to tell that *yellow* and *good* are primitive indefinable property concepts and *water* is not? We assume that water is a complex concept that can be analyzed in principle into its components, following the analytic-synthetic chemistry analogy more literally in this case, of hydrogen and oxygen, or that we can break down and define the concept in other ways as a clear colorless odorless liquid, or the like. Yet how could we explain the concept of water to someone who has never experienced it? Why should we suppose that the concept of water is any easier to convey to someone who has never experienced it than the concepts of yellow or good?

THE NATURALISTIC FALLACY

It is a fallacy or mistake of reasoning, according to Moore, to attempt the definition of an indefinable concept. In particular, Moore argues that trying to analyze the concept of good in terms of a natural property, especially a natural psychological property such as happiness or pleasure, as we find among eudaemonistic or hedonic egoists and consequentialists such as Mill, is fundamentally misguided.

Moore distances himself dramatically from ethical theories that try to explain good as anything other than itself, or that presuppose its meaning can be reduced to any natural property or phenomenon. Importantly, Moore does not deny that pleasure and intelligence are good, insofar as we may regard it as a true predication of the property good to the substantives pleasure and intelligence. Pleasure has the property of being good, and so does intelligence, and so, surely, do many other things besides. To predicate the property good of such things, however, is only to say that the good consists of such things as pleasure and intelligence, a point about which Moore does not disagree with Mill. Recognizing pleasure as good or a good thing to be included in *the* good as the sum of all good things is very different from saying that moral good or the concept of moral goodness can be defined or analyzed as pleasure or intelligence or any other natural property or substance. Moore regards any such identification of the concept of moral good with natural things not only as false as a matter of fact but a fallacy of reasoning:

> And many people appear to think that, if we say "Pleasure and intelligence are good," or if we say "Only pleasure and intelligence are good," we are defining "good." Well, I cannot deny that propositions of this nature may sometimes be

called definitions; I do not know well enough how the word is generally used to decide upon this point. I only wish it to be understood that that is not what I mean when I say there is no possible definition of good, and that I shall not mean this if I use the word again. I do most fully believe that some true proposition of the form "Intelligence is good and intelligence alone is good" can be found; if none could be found, our definition of *the* good would be impossible. As it is, I believe *the* good to be definable; and yet I still say that good itself is indefinable. (9)

The distinction between good and the good is once again crucial for Moore's argument. We can specify the good by determining all the things that have the property of being good, but we cannot define or further analyze the concept of moral good itself by trying to substitute for such an analysis any representation of the good or list of good things. Again, Moore and Socrates on this count evidently agree. We cannot explain the concept of virtue by listing out all the different kinds of virtue for different persons in different walks of life, nor the concept of bee by listing out all the different kinds of bees as though corralling a buzzing swarm of particulars that share the property in question.

What, really, is the difference, then, if Moore is willing to grant that pleasure and intelligence are good or are part of even the whole of the good but are not and do not define or analyze the concept of moral good? To what extent does he disagree with Bentham and Mill and other utilitarian thinkers? Thus far, Moore has not committed himself to anything like a utilitarian ethics that would entail happiness or pleasure as the only or even as a major component of the good, of the things that are correctly judged to have the property of being good. It is conceivable, even if Moore were to agree with the utilitarians that happiness or pleasure are good, that he would not also want to include other things as part of the good that have nothing whatsoever to do with utility, pleasure, or happiness. Unlike the utilitarians as they are usually interpreted and as he evidently interprets them himself, Moore does not try to define what is indefinable by appealing to such good things as pleasure and intelligence.

Proceeding as though he had proved that good is indefinable, even though he appears to have done little more than state his conclusion to this effect, Moore explains that the sense in which good is indefinable is that in which a definition analyzes a complex concept into more basic concepts. If he is right that moral good is an ultimately simple rather than complex concept, then by this analytic model of definition it is clear that the concept of good is indefinable, incapable of being further reduced to anything more fundamental than the parts out of which it is composed. He offers this clarification:

"Good," then, if we mean by it that quality which we assert to belong to a thing, when we say that the thing is good, is incapable of any definition, in the most important sense of that word. The most important sense of "definition" is that in which a definition states what are the parts which invariably compose a certain whole; and in this sense "good" has no definition because it is simple and has no parts. It is one of those innumerable objects of thought which are themselves incapable of definition, because they are the ultimate terms by reference to which whatever *is* capable of definition must be defined. That there must be an indefinite number of such terms is obvious, on reflection; since we cannot define anything except by an analysis, which, when carried as far as it will go, refers us to something, which is simply different from anything else, and which by that ultimate difference explains the peculiarity of the whole which we are defining: for every whole contains some parts which are common to other wholes also. There is, therefore, no intrinsic difficulty in the contention that "good" denotes a simple and indefinable quality. There are many other instances of such qualities. (9–10)

Moore states his conclusion so confidently that we must remind ourselves that he has not really established the indefinability of good in the sense he requires. He has compared good to yellow, and suggested but not argued that yellow is indefinable. The only proof is based on the assertion that we cannot explain yellow to someone who is not already familiar with it. This may be true, but it also seems to be true of complex concepts like water. What Moore has not done but sorely needs to do is to argue that all and only indefinable concepts cannot be adequately explained to those who are not already familiar with them, that yellow by this characterization is indefinable, and that good like yellow is definitely another such concept. He says that there are many examples of indefinable properties, which again may well be true, but he does not say enough to demonstrate his central thesis that moral good in particular is indefinable.

Moore distinguishes between necessary associations of properties among things that are good as opposed to component properties of the concept of good by which it could be defined or in terms of which it could be analyzed. The color yellow is associated with a particular wavelength of light absorption and reflection, a certain number of Ångstrom units in comparison with other colors, each of which has a distinctive light wavelength. Moore is unimpressed with such facts about yellow things as providing a satisfactory definition or analysis of the concept yellow. These, he believes, are rather different matters. By analogy, he argues that certain properties might also accompany virtually any occurrence of a good thing, such as the property of pleasure or happiness, intelligence, or the like. By themselves, such correlations would not imply that moral good can be defined or analyzed in terms of any of these things, even if they are always found together. Moore describes the attempt to define moral good with the morally good things generally associated with it as a confusion, which he now calls the naturalistic fallacy:

It may be true that all things which are good are *also* something else, just as it is true that all things which are yellow produce a certain kind of vibration in the light. And it is a fact, that Ethics aims at discovering what are those other properties belonging to all things which are good. But far too many philosophers have thought that when they named those other properties they were actually defining good; that these properties, in fact, were simply not "other," but absolutely and entirely the same with goodness. This view I propose to call the "naturalistic fallacy" and of it I shall now endeavour to dispose. (10)

Moore has now given a name to what he sees as the central error in theoretical moral philosophy. He remarks that there are "far too many philosophers" who mistakenly believe that they have defined the concept of good when all they have actually done is identified other properties that are generally found accompanying whatever things are good. Returning to the analogy with yellow, it might be worthwhile to reflect on why it is that Moore believes that yellow cannot be satisfactorily defined in terms of the characteristic light wavelength of yellow colored things. He maintains that the light wavelength of yellow is merely something that accompanies it, but is not yellow itself. But why is this? Why not say that yellow just is a certain part of the visible electromagnetic spectrum? Why should yellow be thought to be a primitive unanalyzable concept?

The answer presumably cannot be as Moore has previously argued that no explanation of the concept yellow would be adequately understood by someone who did not have prior experience of that color. We might suppose that green is definable as blue and yellow and orange is definable as red and yellow, but since yellow appears to be a basic ingredient in color combinations, it cannot similarly be analytically defined in terms of any other colors. If complex concepts are defined in terms of necessary and sufficient conditions, then it seems odd to regard yellow as basic because it can be combined with blue to make green or with red to make orange, since there is certainly nothing logically necessary about these facts of color combinations. To the same extent that we may not be able to explain yellow to someone who has never had any experience of colors, so similarly we would presumably not be able adequately to explain to such persons the meaning of other color concepts for supposedly complex color concepts such as green or orange. What would it mean for a blind person to know that the complex concept green is a combination of blue and yellow if they have had no experience and no first-person knowledge of either blue or yellow? They have some limited information as a result of such an explanation, but no more than when we say for example that moral good is a positive moral value that is often attributed to certain kinds of actions or character traits or the like.

What is puzzling about Moore's naturalistic fallacy is that it seems to object to the confusion of a thing being defined with something different from it, or of trying to define a property as something other than itself. This is generally a blunder in defining or analyzing any kind of concept, whether simple or complex. It would be as big a mistake to try to define the complex concept of horse in such a way as to confuse it with something that it is not, such as the complex concept of cow. There is, however, no reason to consider these kinds of mistakes in definition as committing the naturalistic fallacy; they are simply bad definitions. Moore seems to limit his notion of the naturalistic fallacy more particularly to any attempt to define an indefinable concept by reference to other concepts as though it were instead complex. Where indefinable concepts are concerned there is no possibility in advancing an analysis except to confuse a concept with something other than itself. If we cannot break down a concept because it is indefinable, but we proceed anyway with the appearance of defining or analyzing its meaning, then it appears we have no choice except to misidentify it as another thing.

The burden is squarely on Moore to argue that yellow and good are indefinable and unanalyzable in order to support the objection that efforts to define these particular concepts are guilty of the naturalistic fallacy. Unfortunately, this is something he does not try to do. He proceeds instead exclusively in terms of his favorite analogy involving the supposedly conceptually irreducible concept *yellow*. What we need to apply the analogy to the concept of moral good is first of all a better reason to agree with Moore that a basic color, this time the example is *red*, is indefinable. He adds:

And if anybody tried to define pleasure for us as being any other natural object; if anybody were to say, for instance, that pleasure *means* the sensation of red, and were to proceed to deduce from that that pleasure is a colour, we should be entitled to laugh at him and to distrust his future statements about pleasure. Well, that would be the same fallacy which I have called the naturalistic fallacy. That "pleased" does not mean "having the sensation of red," or anything else whatever, does not prevent us from understanding what it does mean. It is enough for us to know that "pleased" does mean "having the sensation of pleasure," and though pleasure is absolutely indefinable, though pleasure is pleasure and nothing else whatever, yet we feel no difficulty in saying that we are pleased. (13)

The argument proceeds entirely by analogy. Suppose that someone were so confused as to mistake the concept of pleasure with experiencing the sensation of red. Moore says that this would be another instance of the naturalistic fallacy. He assumes, again without proof or even the slightest attempt at argument, that pleasure or being pleased is also indefinable, incapable of analysis into more basic properties, because it is already one of the most basic conceptually irreducible concepts. Thus, it is a fallacy, Moore believes, to try to define pleasure in terms of any other quality.

The classification of pleasure as indefinable is problematic. It does not seem to be as simple a kind of thing as yellow or good, whose status as definable or indefinable has also yet to be persuasively determined. Nor does it follow that pleasure or being pleased is conceptually irreducible because it is implausible to reduce the concept to the sensation of red. The term "naturalistic fallacy" furthermore suggests that there is something especially mistaken or misleading about trying to identify something that is not a natural phenomenon with something that is. By Moore's own usage, it appears that both being pleased and sensing red are natural phenomena, so it is hard to explain his application of the *naturalistic* fallacy label in the case he describes.

What, moreover, are we supposed to conclude from the analogy? Whether as an instance of the naturalistic fallacy or not, it is obviously mistaken to try to define pleasure in terms of sensing red. We nevertheless cannot reasonably conclude from one clumsy attempt to define the concept of pleasure naturalistically that no such definition can possibly succeed. Moore wants to emphasize the fact that we cannot define pleasure as sensing red even though it may always be pleasurable to see something red. By analogy, we should not suppose that we can define moral good as a pleasurable sensation even if what is good always occasions pleasure. If we grant all this, the failure of the definition of pleasure as red still does not seem to preclude more reasonable definitions of being pleased in terms of equally natural phenomena, such as a certain stimulation of nerve fibers that can come about in any of a wide variety of ways? Would Moore necessarily have a strong objection to make against that kind of definition of pleasure if it were strongly supported by scientific research and seemed to satisfy philosophers?

Moore would probably not be willing to accept that kind of definition of pleasure, and he would probably want to claim that a definition of being pleased in terms of neurophysiological occurrences like the definition of yellow in terms of light wavelengths would commit the naturalistic fallacy. Why then can we not expect to arrive at a more satisfactory definition of moral good than that which oversimplistically identifies it as pleasure? Moore thinks that there is a crucial difference. What is wrong with the attempt to define simple concepts is that they do not directly relate to what we language users *mean* when we say that something is yellow or that a person or action is good or that a particular psychological occurrence is a state of pleasure. When we say that something is yellow, we mean that it has *that* color, which we cannot further define, not that it reflects light wavelengths of a certain range of Angstrom units. Moore's reasoning, if we have correctly understood it, is not obviously correct. Perhaps what some of us with scientific educations do mean by calling something yellow is that it has the requisite wavelength properties; and perhaps we all could and should do so.

We cannot uncritically rely on how ordinary language speakers describe what they mean when they use certain terms and phrases if Moore's purpose as he says is to determine ethical truths rather than merely collect sociolinguistic facts about what people say or think is true. We know that in many cases ordinary language users are simply confused about the meaning of linguistic expressions, so we cannot generally consider colloquial usage as the final word on semantic analysis. There is a difference between what a speaker means in using language and what a term or sentence objectively means or is supposed to mean, which Moore does not always heed. He argues:

> The reason is, of course, that when I say "I am pleased," I do *not* mean that "I" am the same thing as "having pleasure." And similarly no difficulty need be found in my saying that "pleasure is good" and yet not meaning that "pleasure" is the same thing as "good," that pleasure *means* good, and that good *means* pleasure. If I were to imagine that when I said "I am pleased," I meant that I was exactly the same thing as "pleased," I should not indeed call that a naturalistic fallacy, although it would be the same fallacy as I have called naturalistic with reference to Ethics. The reason of this is obvious enough. When a man confuses two natural objects with one another, defining the one by the other, if for instance he confuses himself, who is one natural object, with "pleased" or with "pleasure" which are others, then there is no reason to call the fallacy naturalistic. But if he confuses "good," which is not in the same sense a natural object, with any natural object whatever, then there is a reason for calling that a naturalistic fallacy; its being made with regard to "good" marks it as something quite specific, and this specific mistake deserves a name because it is so common. (13)

Moore objects to identity confusions incurred by the naturalistic fallacy. He offers an analogy that is not necessarily clearer on its own terms than the case he wants to describe. There is a mistaken identity claim in the assertion that "I" means the same thing as "having pleasure" when I say both that "I am pleased" and "To be pleased *means* having pleasure." The naturalistic fallacy is characterized as falsely identifying a natural object with something that is not "in the same sense" a natural object. What does Moore mean by this?

Let us first consider the misidentification that is supposed to occur when the naturalistic fallacy is committed. Moore portrays a situation in which someone tries to define the concept of pleasure in terms of the natural psychological property of being pleased. It might appear that this is a perfectly acceptable way to proceed, on the grounds that pleasure is itself a natural psychological property and as such requires nothing less than a definition, if possible, in terms of a natural psychological property. If there is some reason to suspect that pleasure is not after all a natural property or phenomenon, Moore does not try to say what it is. Although he argues that the naturalistic fallacy is not quite the same here as in the case of its occurrence in ethics, it is supposed to arise in parallel fashion when someone tries to define pleasure as something natural through an obvious identity error. The distinction Moore seems to adopt throughout is that between a Platonic world of Forms or concepts such as the concept of moral goodness and the natural world in which we find many particular good things.

It is clearly mistaken to conclude from the proposition that I am pleased and that pleasure is the same thing as being pleased that therefore I am the same thing as having pleasure. There are nevertheless a number of problems to consider before we can accept Moore's analogy as telling us anything instructive about the indefinability of moral good. It would be equally mistaken to conclude that the original proposition means that I am the same thing as being pleased. Pointing to the inference that I am the same thing as having pleasure as a result seems unwarranted merely on the strength of the assumptions in the example. The idea of defining pleasure as the natural state of being pleased is not to define the person who is alternatively pleased or having pleasure, but to define the concept of pleasure in terms of the natural psychological property of being pleased. Do we run into logical difficulties when we infer not that I am the same thing as having pleasure, but that pleasure is the same thing as being pleased? This would seem to be the appropriate entailment, rather than the one Moore rightly describes as fallacious, but it does not appear to involve any blatantly mistaken identifications. What if we had a genuinely complex property, such as being an elder statesman, and we wanted to analyze the meaning of the sentence, "I am an elder statesman"? If to be an elder statesman can be defined without committing any version of the naturalistic fallacy as the property of being a respected national government official with many years of experience in service, then we can perform the necessary substitution in order to obtain the equally true proposition, "I am a respected national government official with many years of experience in service." Interestingly, as Moore would say, in this case we can also rightly infer that I am the same thing as a respected national government official with many years of experience in service. The inference goes through and there is no naturalistic fallacy.

If we pay close attention to the grammar of the two examples, we discover something revealing. The difference is between saying, on the one hand, "I am F," where "F" designates a property to be predicated of the subject "I," versus, on the other hand, "I am a F" or "I am an F." The naturalistic fallacy arises in the first case, according to Moore, but does not seem to do so in the second case for the analysis of being an elder statesman. To judge the matter fairly, we should ask whether the "I am F" leads to identity failures associated with the naturalistic fallacy for any property whatsoever, regardless of whether the property in question is capable of analysis or is indefinable. If Moore's discussion of the naturalistic fallacy is correct, then it should only disclose an identity failure for intuitively indefinable properties rather than any properties whatsoever. If the same kind of identity failures occur for any of the "I am F" predications, but not for any "I am a F" or "I am an F" predications, regardless of whether F is an analyzable or intuitively indefinable property, then it would seem that Moore's criterion requires him to conclude that all properties are indefinable and that any attempts to analyze their meaning involve some version of the naturalistic fallacy.

To experiment with these formulations, we might begin with "good" as a supposedly indefinable property term or as naturalistically indefinable, and a term for a complex property, such as "horseness," analyzed, let us say, as "equine quadruped mammalicity." Then if we take the property attribution constructions, "I am good" and "Stanley has horseness" and contrast them with the substantive constructions, "I am a good person" and "Stanley is a horse," we should have all four cases needed to evaluate Moore's distinction. Do we encounter any grammatical or philosophical problems if we try to make the substitutions encouraged by the definition, supposing for the sake of argument that it is an acceptable analysis, of the property of being a horse in terms of the property of being an equine quadruped mammal? Moore poses a dilemma that is relevant to this question:

> In fact, if it is not the case that "good" denotes something simple and indefinable, only two alternatives are possible: either it is a complex, a given whole, about the correct analysis of which there may be disagreement; or else it means nothing at all, and there is no such subject as Ethics. In general, however, ethical philosophers have attempted to define good, without recognising what such an attempt must mean. They actually use arguments which involve one or both of the absurdities considered [previously]. We are, therefore, justified in concluding that the attempt to define good is chiefly due to want of clearness as to the possible nature of definition. There are, in fact, only two serious alternatives to be considered, in order to establish the conclusion that "good" does denote a simple and indefinable notion. It might possibly denote a complex, as "horse" does; or it might have no meaning at all. Neither of these possibilities has, however, been clearly conceived and seriously maintained, as such, by those who presume to define good; and both may be dismissed by a simple appeal to facts. (15)

In providing a supporting argument for the logical-grammatical criterion of the indefinability of good, Moore states that if good is not after all indefinable, then there are two unacceptable alternatives. The dilemma is that if good is not indefinable, then either it is a complex concept capable of analysis or it means nothing whatsoever and there is no possible theory of ethics.

The dilemma is correct as far as it goes, given the condition on which it depends. Philosophers who believe that the concept of good can be defined in terms of a natural property such as pleasure should have no hesitation accepting the conclusion that good is a complex concept capable of analysis. Moore argues that naturalists who have tried to define good have entered the fray without a clear idea of what difficulties are involved. He infers from this that the attempt to define the concept of good is undertaken only because those who have tried to define the concept have not clearly understood the nature of what such a definition requires. Whether or not Moore is right that no one in the field has seriously thought through the implications of treating good as a complex concept like horse or else as completely meaningless, he is prepared to reject both horns of the dilemma on the basis of "simple facts."

We note again that Moore compares what is supposed to be the indefinable property concept good with the definable substance concept *horse*. We can adjust these expressions to make the two cases grammatically parallel by speaking of the properties of moral good or goodness and being a horse or horseness. The discrepancy nevertheless reinforces the impression that Moore's grammatical criterion for indefinability excludes all properties as indefinable and makes the concept of every physical thing analyzable into component concepts. If we make the adjustment, then it appears that Moore's grammatical criterion no longer has much force. If we begin with the proposition that "I am good" in the sense of "I have the property of being good," and if someone proposes that good is to be defined as whatever produces pleasure, then careful substitution of the right kinds of terms for the right kinds of terms still produces the evidently false propositions "I am whatever produces pleasure" or "I have the property of being whatever produces pleasure." To return to our test case, if we begin with the proposition that "Stanley has the property of being a horse," then we can produce a sensible and potentially equally true proposition that "Stanley has the property of being an equine quadruped mammal," without encountering any logical or conceptual difficulty.

From this conclusion we can further infer that "whatever produces pleasure" is not an adequate definition of the concept of moral good. Does it also follow that there can be no definition or analysis of the concept of good in terms of any natural properties? This has not yet been shown. Perhaps there is a way to reformulate the idea of defining good in terms of pleasure that avoids these grammatical obstacles to substitution of property terms and their purported definitions that Moore refers to as variations of the naturalistic fallacy. What would such an argument look like? We can make some progress by considering a modified version of the definition that captures the essence of the utilitarian idea that good is whatever produces pleasure but presents no logical or grammatical problems upon intersubstitution in the relevant contexts. One possibility is to reformulate the definition of good as a definition according to which good is the property of being productive of more pleasure than pain. Then if it is true that I am good it is at least logically and grammatically unobjectionable to conclude, on the basis of the same kind of substitution that Moore considers in his criterion, that I am productive of more pleasure than pain. This might not yet be a satisfactory analysis of the concept of good. If it fails, however, it does not appear to do so because of the kinds of identity and substitution problems that Moore seems to think will occur whenever we try to replace a property term by its naturalistic definition in a true proposition. If the definition of good as being productive of more pleasure than pain is incorrect, it must be criticized on the basis of its content rather than merely in terms of its supposedly logically-definitionally fallacious form.

INDEFINABILITY OF GOOD VERSUS NATURALISM

Assuming he has refuted all efforts to define the indefinable good as committing the naturalistic fallacy, Moore proceeds to explain precisely how naturalism fails. He distinguishes between *reasons* and *causes*, and argues that naturalism suffers from two essential defects. It offers no reason for accepting any true ethical principle, and it causes the unwary to accept false principles. Moore now sounds the major theme of his complaint against naturalism in support of the indefinability of good:

> My objections to Naturalism are then, in the first place, that it offers no reason
> at all, far less any valid reason, for any ethical principle whatever; and in this it
> already fails to satisfy the requirements of Ethics, as a scientific study. But in the

second place I contend that, though it gives a reason for no ethical principle, it is a *cause* of the acceptance of false principles—it deludes the mind into accepting ethical principles, which are false; and in this it is contrary to every aim of Ethics. It is easy to see that if we start with a definition of right conduct as conduct conducive to general happiness; then, knowing that right conduct is universally conduct conducive to the good, we very easily arrive at the result that the good is general happiness. If, on the other hand, we once recognise that we must start our Ethics without a definition, we shall be much more apt to look about us, before we adopt any ethical principle whatever; and the more we look about us, the less likely are we to adopt a false one. (20)

Moore reprises the two horns of his previous dilemma. Ethics, he says, can either be based on a false definition of good that it mistakes for something complex, or it can move forward without trying to define good. He does not fill in all the details, but sketches an argument to show that trying to define the concept of good naturalistically leads to other falsehoods. He argues that if we start with the kind of analysis of right conduct as conduct conducive to happiness, then it is but a short step to what he believes is an obviously false conclusion, given that there are many good things, namely, that *the* good is happiness.

Why an identification of *the* good (as opposed to the concept good) with general happiness should be regarded as a false implication is unclear. Moore may believe that other things are morally good besides the general happiness, although he does not argue for any such proposition. Perhaps it would be enough for his purposes to observe that even if the good includes general happiness as the ultimate value of all conduct, there are at least such other goods as provide a means to that end. If such implications are false, as Moore contends, they reveal that it is wrong to assume the possibility of defining the concept of good because of the further falsehoods to which it soon leads.

The opposite assumption that the property *good* is indefinable in comparison has salutary methodological effects as we struggle to identify sound principles of ethics. We will not assume from the outset that we know what is meant by good and thereby be led into error, but, Moore says somewhat vaguely, we will "look around" before we hastily commit ourselves to ethical principles that might turn out to be false. If, on the contrary, we do not begin our work in ethics with any definition of good, then we are more likely to keep an open mind, looking around at the nature of conduct and how it is judged in many different kinds of circumstances, which may give us a better chance empirically of discovering true and avoiding false ethical principles.

Moore's argument is not very persuasive, but he is satisfied on its basis to maintain as a proposition he has definitely established that ethics must have an indefinable "object of thought," which turns out finally to be the concept of moral good. All the preceding preparation Moore believes has at last put us in a position to understand the starting place of a theory of ethics that can lead to a correct understanding of the good and the concept of good. As we observed in the case of many other thinkers in ethics as much as in metaphysics and epistemology, setting off on the right foot down a path leading to a philosophical theory is often more important in reaching defensible conclusions than what takes place after a beginning has been made.

We recall the title of Moore's book as referring in Latin to the *principles* of ethics, the fundamental starting place of moral reasoning. Although his methods and philosophical ideology are radically different, Moore's project of identifying a correct starting place for ethics is similar in some ways to Kant's efforts to articulate a transcendental grounding of the metaphysics of morals. Moore certainly does not adopt Kant's terminology of transcendental reasoning, but he seems to reason in transcendental terms that there must be primitive indefinable or unanalyzable concepts in every sphere of thought. In ethics, if its judgments are analyzable at any level as constructions out of simpler concepts, then there must be simplest basic moral concepts, which philosophical analysis can identify. The first theoretical requirement of a system of ethics is to determine what its most basic concepts are and how they are related to more complex concepts. The simplest, indefinable, and unanalyzable concept of ethics, Moore clearly says even if he does not rigorously prove, is *good*, the property or concept of moral good or goodness. When we recognize this fundamental truth of ethics, we can avoid false and even fallacious moral theories and gain a more focused idea of the requirements of a true ethical theory.

INTRINSIC AND "CAUSAL" INSTRUMENTAL GOOD

What Moore regards as the most important preliminary step in developing an ethical philosophy is to acknowledge that there is an indefinable concept in terms of which ethics must be defined. He argues that to get started in ethics we must recognize what this concept is, whatever terminology we use, and avoid confusions at the outset by distinguishing it from any other thing. In particular, because we know that Moore is talking about moral good or goodness, he insists that we must not mistakenly try to identify moral good with any natural property or phenomenon, such as the psychological occurrence of pleasure or the general happiness.

Throughout, Moore's primary target for criticism, again like Kant's, is some form of consequentialism. We can compare Kant's objections to the empirical elements that must be purified from the foundations of moral metaphysics with Moore's objections to ethical naturalism. He now states:

> Our first conclusion as to the subject-matter of Ethics is, then, that there is a simple, indefinable, unanalysable object of thought by reference to which it must be defined. By what name we call this unique object is a matter of indifference, so long as we clearly recognise what it is and that it does differ from other objects. The words which are commonly taken as the signs of ethical judgments all do refer to it; and they are expressions of ethical judgments solely because they do so refer. But they may refer to it in two different ways, which it is very important to distinguish, if we are to have a complete definition of the range of ethical judgments. (21)

To assign appropriate terminology to the fundamental concept of ethics, he turns again to ordinary language contexts in which moral value is attributed to things. He finds, unsurprisingly, that ethical judgments express the indefinable concept of moral good. He further finds that the way we usually think about ethical judgments is ambiguous, and a potential source of confusion in the foundations of ethical philosophy:

> [A]lthough all such judgments do refer to that unique notion which I have called "good," they do not all refer to it in the same way. They may either assert that

this unique property does always attach to the thing in question, or else they may assert only that the thing in question is a *cause or necessary condition* for the existence of other things to which this unique property does attach. The nature of these two species of universal ethical judgments is extremely different; and a great part of the difficulties, which are met with in ordinary ethical speculation, are due to the failure to distinguish them clearly. Their difference has, indeed, received expression in ordinary language by the contrast between the terms "good as means" and "good in itself," "value as a means" and "intrinsic value." But these terms are apt to be applied correctly only in the more obvious instances; and this seems to be due to the fact that the distinction between the conceptions which they denote has not been made a separate object of investigation. (21)

Again, Moore invokes the distinction between moral means and ends. He refers to a moral end obliquely here as the "thing" to which the unique property good is sometimes said to attach. He contrasts a moral end with any causes or conditions needed to bring it about, which are also rightly but in a different sense said to be good as the means to a moral end. He asserts that to confuse these two subjects of moral attribution is one of the most fundamental mistakes in ethics. As other philosophers maintain, what is good as an end in itself is *intrinsically* good and what is good as a means to a good end has value as a means, which is sometimes also referred to as being *instrumentally* good.

The important point for Moore is to avoid mistaking means with ends kinds of goodness, which usually takes the form of confusing what is merely instrumentally good for what is intrinsically good. Moore speaks in generalities and offers no specific examples for criticism. He observes that ethical inquiry is often ambiguous. If we ask, "What is it right to do?" the question can be understood as a question about either intrinsic or instrumental morality. If we do not formulate the question carefully as asking about one or the other of these kinds of moral goodness, then we cannot expect to arrive at a clear and correct ethical theory, but will make precisely the kind of mistakes he has been working to help us appreciate and avoid. He explains the ambiguity and its potential implications:

Ethical questions are commonly asked in an ambiguous form. It is asked "What is a man's duty under these circumstances?" or "Is it right to act in this way?" or "What ought we to aim at securing?" But all these questions are capable of further analysis; a correct answer to any of them involves both judgments of what is good in itself and causal judgments. This is implied even by those who maintain that we have a direct and immediate judgment of absolute rights and duties. Such a judgment can only mean that the course of action in question is *the* best thing to do; that, by acting so, every good that *can* be secured will have been secured. (24)

All moral judgments of instrumental value are described by Moore as "causal." When we ask simply what it is right to do, our question is ambiguous. A complete and correct answer to the question must combine a judgment of what is intrinsically good with a causal judgment about the instrumentally good means needed to attain an intrinsically good end. Moore does not favor intrinsic over instrumental good, but remarks that both kinds of moral goodness must be explained in a complete and correct ethical theory:

Whenever, therefore, we ask "What ought we to do?" or "What ought we to try to get?" we are asking questions which involve a correct answer to two others, completely different in kind from one another. We must know *both* what degree of intrinsic value different things have, *and* how these different things may be obtained. But the vast majority of questions which have actually been discussed in Ethics—*all* practical questions, indeed—involve this double knowledge; and they have been discussed without any clear separation of the two distinct questions involved. (26)

In addition to committing the naturalistic fallacy, Moore complains that most moral philosophy confuses intrinsic and instrumental good. The stage is set for a false ethics when the wrong questions are asked or not correctly analyzed, and when they fail to be disambiguated with respect to the intrinsic-instrumental good distinction. Moore has already said that we commit the naturalistic fallacy when we try to define an indefinable concept as identical with something other than itself. If we confuse intrinsic with instrumental or causal good, then we commit the naturalistic fallacy by confusing indefinable intrinsic good with causal good as something manifestly other than itself. Moore maintains:

A great part of the vast disagreements prevalent in Ethics is to be attributed to this failure in analysis. By the use of conceptions which involve both that of intrinsic value and that of causal relation, as if they involved intrinsic value only, two different errors have been rendered almost universal. Either it is assumed that nothing has intrinsic value which is not possible, or else it is assumed that what is necessary must have intrinsic value. Hence the primary and peculiar business of Ethics, the determination what things have intrinsic value and in what degrees, has received no adequate treatment at all. And on the other hand a *thorough* discussion of means has been also largely neglected, owing to an obscure perception of the truth that it is perfectly irrelevant to the question of intrinsic values. (26)

Another piece of the puzzle is added without argument to Moore's analysis of moral concepts. We learn that of the difference between intrinsic and causal good it is intrinsic rather than causal good that is the primary topic of ethics. He says that causal good presupposes intrinsic good, so that intrinsic good is the right place for an ethical philosophy to start. If something is to be judged good as a means to an end we must first know whether or not the end is intrinsically good. Moore laments the confusion of intrinsic good and goodness as a causal means to an end in standard ethical theories:

There remains one point which must not be omitted in a complete description of the kind of questions which Ethics has to answer. The main division of those questions is, as I have said, into two; the question what things are good in themselves, and the question to what other things these are related as effects. The first of these, which is the primary ethical question and is presupposed by the other, includes a correct comparison of the various things which have intrinsic value (if there are many such) in respect of the degree of value which they have; and such comparison involves a difficulty of principle which has greatly aided the confusion of intrinsic value with mere "goodness as a means." (27)

The claim that good is indefinable but ambiguous as between intrinsic and causal good raises an interesting difficulty. Why should we not, contrary to Moore, assume that moral good is conceptually analyzable as consisting of two parts, intrinsic and causal goodness? If, as he maintains, a complete and correct ethical theory must involve both judgments, if ethics is incomplete except as a combination of both, why not suppose that the concept of good for that very reason must be composed of and hence analyzable into the simpler concepts of intrinsic and causal good?

The answer cannot be that the phrases "intrinsic good" and "causal or instrumental good" are longer more complicated compound expressions than the lexically simpler term "good." This is only a conventional linguistic difference, like the fact that while the concept horse contains the concept quadruped, the word "quadruped" is phonetically and orthographically more complex than the word "horse." There is no reason why in another language the term for good might be compound and the terms for intrinsic and causal good might be simpler. Indeed, we could plausibly and more perspicuously adopt the compound phrase "intrinsic and causal good" for what Moore means by "good." Relative to this more complex term the original terms "intrinsic good" and "causal good" are lexically simpler.

Why then suppose that the concept good is simpler than the concepts of intrinsic and instrumental good, when Moore tells us unequivocally that the good of intrinsic good is not the same as the good of causal good? Why not suppose that intrinsic and causal good are more basic and that only combined together do they constitute the compound concept of moral good? It is not as though good in the general sense is made into intrinsic good by having something about intrinsicness added to it, or that causal good is good in the general sense together with something about causality or means-ends relations added to it. At least it cannot be so if, as Moore repeatedly holds, ethics as a theory and the concept of good are not complete except insofar as they contain or make reference to both intrinsic and causal good. We do not have goodness in hand to combine with these other concepts unless we are considering something that already contains what Moore calls the "double knowledge" of what is good in itself and what is good in attaining what is good in itself.

Is it the tradition's thinking about good that is most confused, or Moore's? There is a reasonable way to save Moore's conclusion about the indefinability of good, the naturalistic fallacy of trying to identify good with something natural other than itself, and the distinction between intrinsic and causal good. If by good, like Moore, we mean intrinsic good, so that in effect we use the term "good" as a convenient abbreviation for "intrinsic good," then we can regard good as more basic than instrumental or causal good, and finally as indefinable. Good does not consist of a combination of intrinsic and causal good into which the concept of good can be analyzed. It is rather that good just is intrinsic good and the concept of causal good contains the concept of good, in that something is causally good as a means of attaining whatever is (simply) good in the sense of being intrinsically good.

ETHICS AS THE THEORY OF INTRINSIC GOOD: GREATER THAN THE SUM OF THE INTRINSICALLY GOOD

The subject of ethics is indefinable intrinsic good. Moore observes that there are many different intrinsically good things. The good in the sense of the intrinsic good is the collection of all intrinsically good things. The question then arises whether intrinsic good can be analyzed after all as the intrinsically good, according to Moore's first distinction. Moore endorses the principle that where values are concerned, the whole is greater than the sum of its parts; or, as he puts it, the value of a whole bears no regular proportion to the sum of the values of its parts:

> There is, as will presently be maintained, a vast number of different things, each of which has intrinsic value; there are also very many which are positively bad; and there is a still larger class of things, which appear to be indifferent. But a thing belonging to any of these three classes may occur as part of a whole, which includes among its other parts other things belonging both to the same and to the other two classes; and these wholes, as such, may also have intrinsic value. The paradox, to which it is necessary to call attention, is that *the value of such a whole bears no regular proportion to the sum of the values of its parts.* (27)

The implications of this principle include the fact that we cannot reductively analyze intrinsic good as the sum of the values of all the particular things that happen to be intrinsically good. More immediately, Moore states that morally complex subjects composed of good and bad parts are not intrinsically good or intrinsically bad on the basis of possessing a simple majority or greater number of intrinsically good or intrinsically bad parts. The situation is more complex in his view, because it is at least logically possible for the addition of something intrinsically bad to a whole that is either intrinsically good or intrinsically bad to increase its intrinsic goodness. If this is possible, then it suggests that the intrinsic moral value of something complex is not always regularly proportional to the sum of its intrinsically good and bad parts, but might be produced instead as a result of their synergy. He argues:

> It is certain that two bad things or a bad thing and an indifferent thing may form a whole much worse than the sum of badness of its parts. And it seems as if indifferent things may also be the sole constituents of a whole which has great value, either positive or negative. Whether the addition of a bad thing to a good whole may increase the positive value of the whole, or the addition of a bad thing to a bad may produce a whole having positive value, may seem more doubtful; but it is, at least, possible, and this possibility must be taken into account in our ethical investigations. However we may decide particular questions, the principle is clear. *The value of a whole must not be assumed to be the same as the sum of the values of its parts.* (28)

As an example, Moore mentions the case of a beautiful object of which alternatively either someone or no one at all is conscious. The consciousness of a beautiful object increases its value beyond the mere sum of its intrinsic value considered only in itself with no one being conscious of it and the intrinsic value of the state of consciousness considered only in itself. Thus, the whole is greater than the sum of its parts:

> A single instance will suffice to illustrate the kind of relation in question. It seems to be true that to be conscious of a beautiful object is a thing of great intrinsic value; whereas the same object, if no one be conscious of it, has certainly comparatively little value, and is commonly held to have none at all. But the consciousness of a beautiful object is certainly a whole of some sort in which we can

distinguish as parts the object on the one hand and the being conscious on the other. Now this latter factor occurs as part of a different whole, whenever we are conscious of anything; and it would seem that some of these wholes have at all events very little value, and may even be indifferent or positively bad. (28)

The value of the consciousness of beauty is not determined merely by the addition of the value of what is beautiful to the value of consciousness. The value of something beautiful is disproportionately increased by the consciousness of its beauty, because the value of a beautiful thing outside of all consciousness is so negligible as to add little to the intrinsic value of a state of consciousness considered only as such. The term has wider applications for Moore, but he refers to any complex whose intrinsic value is greater than the sum of the intrinsic values of its parts as an *organic unity*. He concludes:

Yet we cannot always attribute the slightness of their value to any positive demerit in the object which differentiates them from the consciousness of beauty; the object itself may approach as near as possible to absolute neutrality. Since, therefore, mere consciousness does not always confer great value upon the whole of which it forms a part, even though its object may have no great demerit, we cannot attribute the great superiority of the consciousness of a beautiful thing over the beautiful thing itself to the mere addition of the value of consciousness to that of the beautiful things. Whatever the intrinsic value of consciousness may be, it does not give to the whole of which it forms a part a value proportioned to the sum of its value and that of its object. If this be so, we have here an instance of a whole possessing a different intrinsic value from the sum of that of its parts. . . . (28–29)

A similar example comes from the German-Austrian philosopher Franz Brentano's book, *The Origin of the Knowledge of Right and Wrong* (1902). There Brentano argues that not even the most horrible imaginable pain is unqualifiedly intrinsically bad, because it contains an intrinsically good act of consciousness as a component part. In the Preface to the second edition of *Principia Ethica*, Moore refers to Brentano's book, which was published shortly before Moore's first 1903 edition. Recounting the similarities and differences between their approaches to ethics, Moore remarks that Brentano denies the principle of organic unities:

When this book had been already completed, I found, in Brentano's "Origin of the Knowledge of Right and Wrong" [translated by Cecil Hague and published by Constable], opinions far more closely resembling my own, than those of any other ethical writer with whom I am acquainted. Brentano appears to agree with me completely (1) in regarding all ethical propositions as defined by the fact that they predicate a single unique objective concept; (2) in dividing such propositions sharply into the same two kinds; (3) in holding that the first kind are incapable of proof; and (4) with regard to the kind of evidence which is necessary and relevant to the proof of the second kind. But he regards the fundamental ethical concept as being, not the simple one which I denote by "good," but the complex one which I have taken to define "beautiful"; and he does not recognise, but even denies by implication, the principle which I have called *the principle of organic unities*. In consequence of these two differences, his conclusions as to what things are good in themselves, also differ very materially from mine. He agrees, however, that there are many different goods, and that the love of good and beautiful objects constitutes an important class among them. (x–xi)

It is appropriate for Moore to emphasize the differences between his moral philosophy and Brentano's, particularly where the fundamental concept of good or beauty is concerned. Perhaps he overestimates the differences between his theory of organic unities and Brentano's position with respect to a similar question about the values of complex things as they relate to the values of their parts. He regards organic unities in ethics as a vital supplement to his theory of intrinsic good. It is only the value of a whole consisting of many valuable parts that has intrinsic value in Moore's philosophy. The importance for Moore of distinguishing between the values of wholes and their parts is now apparent. If the value of a whole were always simply the sum of the value of its parts, then it would be possible to analyze intrinsic good in terms of the intrinsic good or bad of the whole's components. A valuable thing could then be analyzed into its component parts, but the intrinsic value of a thing as a whole cannot be analyzed as the sum of the intrinsic values of its parts. Moore thus preserves the thesis that intrinsic good is indefinable and upholds the naturalistic fallacy as an objection to theories that attempt to define intrinsic goodness of an organic unity as something other than itself.

THREEFOLD THEORY OF INTRINSIC AND CAUSAL GOOD

Moore provides the following summary of his conclusions concerning the indefinable intrinsic good of organic unities as the subject matter of ethics. He prepares the background for a statement of the threefold work of a complete ethical theory devoted to the clarification of intrinsic good and discovery of causal good in fitting practical means to predetermined intrinsic goods. The summary in basic outline recapitulates Moore's interpretation of the main points of his moral theory in comparison with Brentano's. He identifies the following key conclusions:

(1) The peculiarity of Ethics is not that it investigates assertions about human conduct, but that it investigates assertions about that property of things which is denoted by the term "good," and the converse property denoted by the term "bad." It must, in order to establish its conclusions, investigate the truth of *all* such assertions, *except* those which assert the relation of this property only to a single existent. . . . (2) This property, by reference to which the subject-matter of Ethics must be defined, is itself simple and indefinable. . . . And (3) all assertions about its relation to other things are of two, and only two, kinds: they either assert, in what degree things themselves possess this property, or else they assert causal relations between other things and those which possess it. . . . Finally, (4) in considering the different degrees in which things themselves possess this property, we have to take account of the fact that a whole may possess it in a degree different from that which is obtained by summing the degrees in which its parts possess it. . . . (36)

This is a fair statement of the four most important principles Moore believes he has established. At the beginning of Chapter II on "Naturalistic Ethics," he finds it useful to bring these conclusions to bear on the division between the three main tasks of ethical theory. The threefold work of ethics is determined by the distinction he emphasizes throughout between intrinsic good and the good of whatever serves as a means to an intrinsically good end. The requirements of an ethical theory are to explain the special role of the fundamental concept of ethics. This, we know now, is the indefinable intrinsic good of organic unities. The analysis of moral predicates into complexes, and goodness as the most basic and pervasive concept of ethics, had been the exclusive concern of Chapter I on "The Subject-Matter of Ethics." As he turns the page to Chapter II, he moves from a consideration of good or goodness as a general indefinable concept or property to a theory of the good in the sense of all those things that are either intrinsically or causally good. These are the remaining two explanatory obligations for a complete ethical philosophy:

> It results from the conclusions of Chapter I, that all ethical questions fall under one or other of three classes. The first class contains but one question—the question What is the nature of that peculiar predicate, the relation of which to other things constitutes the object of all other ethical investigations? or, in other words, What is *meant* by good? This first question I have already attempted to answer. The peculiar predicate, by reference to which the sphere of Ethics must be defined, is simple, unanalysable, indefinable. There remain two classes of questions with regard to the relation of this predicate to other things. We may ask either (1) To what things and in what degree does this predicate directly attach? What things are good in themselves? or (2) By what means shall we be able to make what exists in the world as good as possible? What causal relations hold between what is best in itself and other things? (37)

As a way of approaching ethics' two remaining tasks of identifying what kinds of things are intrinsically and instrumentally good, Moore begins by raising criticisms of moral theories that commit the naturalistic fallacy. These he describes as naturalistic ethics, all of which are based on false ethical principles and fallacious definitions of the concept of good:

> I propose, therefore, to discuss certain theories of what is good in itself, which are *based* on the naturalistic fallacy, in the sense that the commission of this fallacy has been the main cause of their wide acceptance. The discussion will be designed both (1) further to illustrate the fact that the naturalistic fallacy is a fallacy, or, in other words, that we are all aware of a certain simple quality, which (and not anything else) is what we mainly mean by the term "good"; and (2) to shew that not one, but many different things, possess this property. For I cannot hope to recommend the doctrine that things which are good do not owe their goodness to their common possession of any other property, without a criticism of the main doctrines, opposed to this, whose power to recommend themselves is proved by their wide prevalence. (38)

In trying to understand the good and decide what kinds of things are intrinsically and causally good, Moore argues that many different things are good. It follows from the naturalistic fallacy that individual good things are intrinsically or instrumentally good only by virtue of having the indefinable property of good. Moore says that he cannot hope to defend the theory without criticizing some of the most important alternative naturalistic ethics. He begins by distinguishing two subcategories of naturalistic moral theories:

> The theories I propose to discuss may be conveniently divided into two groups. The naturalistic fallacy always implies that when we think "This is good," what we are thinking is that the thing in question bears a definite relation to some one other thing. But this one thing, by reference to which good is defined, may be either what I may call a natural object—something of which the existence is admittedly an object of experience—or else it may be an object which is only inferred to exist in a supersensible real world. These two types of ethical theory I propose to treat separately. Theories of the second type may conveniently be called "metaphysical," and I shall postpone consideration of them. . . . In this and the following chapter, on the other hand, I shall deal with theories which owe their prevalence to the supposition that good can be defined by reference to a *natural object*; and these are what I mean by the name, which gives the title to this chapter, "Naturalistic Ethics." It should be observed that the fallacy, by reference to which I define "Metaphysical Ethics," is the same in kind; and I give it but one name, the naturalistic fallacy. (38–39)

It is not clear why Moore refers to both of these types of theories as committing the naturalistic fallacy. The first category of ethical theory is guilty as charged if it is a fallacy to try to define good in terms of something natural in the sense of being an experienceable spatiotemporal entity or property of things. The second category is less obviously an instance of anything like this. What is "natural" about a mistaken identification of good with something that is metaphysical, by which Moore means something extra-natural?

The point is not to quibble about terminology, but it is surprising that Moore should try to combine both of these different alleged fallacies under a single label when he could as easily have devised a term that would fit both cases. What is common to both styles of definition is the attempt to define good as something other than good. Such practice is obviously mistaken. Why does it deserve a special name when the problem is only that the authors of such definitions have misdefined the concept of moral good? Why in particular should we think of the error as a fallacy or general mistake of reasoning? The naturalistic fallacy covering both natural and metaphysical cases should in principle be no different than mistakenly trying to define a whale as a fish or the number π as a slice of apple pie. Moore evidently thinks it is worthwhile to have a convenient phrase to identify the kind of misdefinition that occurs in the case of moral good, when something that he believes to be indefinable and unanalyzable is equated with something other than itself, which he designates as the naturalistic fallacy. We can wonder why he chooses to do so, but if we are going to understand his argument we can only follow his usage and try to see where it leads.

Dealing first in Chapter II with naturalistic theories of ethics that commit the naturalistic fallacy, Moore explains:

> The subject of the present chapter is, then, ethical theories which declare that no intrinsic value is to be found except in the possession of some one *natural* property, other than pleasure; and which declare this because it is supposed that to be "good" *means* to possess the property in question. Such theories I call "Natural-

istic." I have thus appropriated the name Naturalism to a particular method of approaching Ethics—a method which, strictly understood, is inconsistent with the possibility of any Ethics whatsoever. This method consists in substituting for "good" some one property of a natural object or of a collection of natural objects; and in thus replacing Ethics by some one of the natural sciences. (39–40)

It is clear in this case why Moore's category of ethical naturalism deserves the name. A natural property according to such theories is said to define the concept of good. If we already agree with Moore that it is a mistake, even a fallacy of reasoning, to define goodness as anything natural on the grounds that good is an indefinable unanalyzable property, then we must agree that naturalism is a false direction for moral philosophy. If we are still in doubt about whether this is true, then we may find it questionable even to describe moral naturalism as "substituting" for good another natural property, as opposed to acknowledging their equivalence.

Moore complains about efforts to systematize ethics along natural lines when they try to establish moral values in terms of whether or not an action is natural or unnatural. If there is a naturalistic fallacy and if any attempt to define moral good in terms of any natural property commits the fallacy, then Moore is undoubtedly right to object that such theories cannot lead us to the ethical truths that he declares to be the goal of theoretical ethics. He singles out a naturalistic approach to ethics that enjoyed a certain popularity at the turn of the previous century, in which moral good is defined in evolutionary terms as whatever promotes human survival and reproduction. The facts of evolution are thereby made into moral values in a way that Moore finds objectionable from both a methodological point of view as well as inimical to the interests of morality because of the confusions and distractions from ethical truths that they spawn. He adds an important new reason for rejecting naturalistic ethics, on the grounds that any such theory fallaciously tries to reduce values to facts:

To argue that a thing is good *because* it is "natural," or bad *because* it is "unnatural," in these common senses of the term, is therefore certainly fallacious: and yet such arguments are very frequently used. But they do not commonly pretend to give a systematic theory of Ethics. Among attempts to *systematise* an appeal to nature, that which is now most prevalent is to be found in the application to ethical questions of the term "Evolution"—in the ethical doctrines which have been called "Evolutionistic." These doctrines are those which maintain that the course of "evolution," while it shews us the direction in which we *are* developing, thereby and for that reason shews us the direction in which we *ought* to develop. Writers, who maintain such a doctrine, are at present very numerous and very popular; and I propose to take as my example the writer, who is perhaps best known of them all—Mr. Herbert Spencer. (45–46)

The target of the objection is a family of evolutionary naturalistic ethics sometimes described as versions of *social Darwinism*. All are criticized by Moore as trying to define what ought to be the case in terms of what is in fact the case. The problem is that we can *always* ask about something that is the case whether it ought to be the case. The naturalistic fallacy invalidates Spencer's social Darwinism when he mistakenly tries to define value and moral good in terms of something other than itself, a certain set of biological facts.

There is an inferential fallacy of precisely this form that Hume in *A Treatise of Human Nature* had already underscored and that Moore also exposes. It is the problem of trying to deduce what ought to be the case from what happens to be the case. As it applies to Spencer's evolutionary ethics and naturalisms like it, Moore's objection amounts to observing that it is a mistake in trying to understand moral good to imagine that the course of human evolutionary development as it is in fact unfolding is also what it ought to be, that what is true in fact is also morally good. Hume writes:

> In every system of morality, which I have hitherto met with, I have always remark'd, that the author proceeds for some time in the ordinary way of reasoning, and establishes the being of a God, or makes observations concerning human affairs; when of a sudden I am surpriz'd to find, that instead of the usual copulations of propositions, *is*, and *is not*, I meet with no proposition that is not connected with an *ought*, or an *ought not*. This change is imperceptible; but is, however, of the last consequence. For as this *ought*, or *ought not*, expresses some new relation or affirmation, 'tis necessary that it shou'd be observ'd and explain'd; and at the same time that a reason should be given, for what seems altogether inconceivable, how this new relation can be a deduction from others, which are entirely different from it. (Hume, *A Treatise of Human Nature*, 469)

We know that such inferences generally cannot be correct. It does not follow logically from the assumption that a murder was committed that therefore it ought to have been committed. It does not follow logically from the assumption that minorities have been socially discriminated against that therefore they ought to be or continue to be discriminated against. Nor in particular does it follow logically that because it is a fact that a certain group of people have a certain skin color that therefore they ought to be treated in a discriminatory way. We can say on the basis of this version of the inferential naturalistic fallacy that racism and bigotry, among many other moral wrongs, are not only morally objectionable but logically confused even when they are based exclusively on true facts. If facts were values, we could settle moral problems and determine the right course of conduct by the methods of natural science. Of course, we do not expect that we can do anything of the sort. If we can always ask about the value of science, if in every case we can wonder whether the practice of natural science is itself morally good, then we cannot reduce moral good to the scientific discovery of facts.

Although Moore confines his discussion of the naturalistic fallacy to definitions rather than inferences, his concept is often extended to deductive arguments. In historically insensitive treatments, Moore's definitional naturalistic fallacy is usually supposed to have deliberate connections with the inferential version of the fallacy in Hume. Where Moore speaks of the naturalistic fallacy, Hume's similar idea is sometimes referred to as the *is-ought gap*. It is reasonable to consider them together in any case as calling attention to the same problem of trying to define or derive moral value exclusively in or from natural facts (see Figure 9.1). There is a fallacy at work here that has to do with the conceptual difference between matters of fact and matters of value, as between is-statements and ought-statements. We can neither define nor derive moral good in the sense of what ought to be the case from or in terms merely of what is the case. We cannot definitionally or inferentially squeeze moral values from natural facts.

Definitional Naturalistic Fallacy (Moore)	Good (normative value concept) = df natural property or properties (scientific factual concept)
Inferential Naturalistic Fallacy Is-Ought Gap (Hume)	1. Scientific statement of fact (is-statement) ———————— 2. Normative statement of value (ought-statement)

FIGURE 9.1 Two ways of thinking about the naturalistic fallacy

If we can always ask whether any fact ought to be the case, then we cannot deduce what ought to be the case from what happens as a matter of fact to be the case. Nor should it matter if we begin with evolutionary facts about human development or any other anthropological or sociological facts that merely describe the state of the world. We can always ask of any such facts whether they or their implications ought to be the case, which indicates that the facts themselves do not determine whether or not they ought to be true. Moore asks this kind of question in effect when he observes that we cannot define what ought to be true about human development from the evolutionary facts about its course and direction. This style of refuting that attempts to identify values with facts has since come to be known as the *open question argument*. The same problem applies if we try to infer truths of moral value from scientific facts. In definitional and inferential forms, the naturalistic fallacy or is-ought gap fixes a gulf between facts and values, and in particular between natural properties and the concept of moral good.

At this stage we are at last at a point to appreciate what Moore means by the naturalistic fallacy and why he believes it to be the source of conceptual confusions, false conclusions, and wrong directions in moral philosophy. The same difficulty is manifested in definitions, inferences, and moral reasoning generally, if Moore is right, and with respect to both attempts to identify goodness with something natural or metaphysical. This explains why he finds it appropriate to treat both kinds of definitions of good involving natural or metaphysical properties as instances of the same underlying naturalistic fallacy. They are all ultimately attempts to define value in terms of fact or value in terms of nonvalues. The natural fallacy once again tells us that we cannot define values in terms of something other than a value, so that we cannot understand good as something other than itself. It further implies that there must be simple, basic, fundamental, ultimate, primitive, irreducible, indefinable, unanalyzable value, which Moore identifies for the purposes of ethics as moral good.

From the preceding argument it should nevertheless be possible to define one kind of values in terms of another, without committing the naturalistic fallacy, as long as they are values rather than facts. If this is correct, then we should in principle be able to ground value theory on an aesthetic concept of beauty rather than an ethical concept of good, as Moore reports Brentano does. Thus, we need a convincing reason why we should agree with Moore that moral good is a more fundamental value than aesthetic beauty. We need a reason to prefer Moore to Brentano on the foundations of value in order to accept his principles of ethics.

Naturalistic Fallacy in Hedonic Egoism and Utilitarianism

After discussing the naturalistic fallacy in evolutionary ethics in Chapter II, Moore considers its appearance in hedonistic ethics in Chapter III. Any pleasure-based ethical system can be described as hedonistic. Hedonism can involve the pleasure of the individual moral agent in the case of hedonic egoism, or a larger group of sentient beings, including all other persons and animals, as in Mill's hedonic utilitarianism. Hedonism of any kind regardless of its merits commits the naturalistic fallacy in Moore's view, because it attempts to define moral good in terms of natural psychological facts about the experience of pleasure.

Moore is familiar with the classical utilitarian tradition in ethics, including the writings of Bentham, James and John Stuart Mill. In Moore's day, the most prominent representative of hedonic utilitarianism was Henry W. Sidgwick, eventually formulated in his influential book, *The Methods of Ethics* (1907). It is Sidgwick's ethics that Moore often has foremost in mind when he criticizes socially conscious forms of hedonism. He explains his purpose in criticizing hedonism as one of the main and most important categories of naturalistic ethics on the grounds of its committing the naturalistic fallacy:

> In this chapter we have to deal with what is perhaps the most famous and the most widely held of all ethical principles—the principle that nothing is good but pleasure. My chief reason for treating of this principle in this place is, as I said, that Hedonism appears in the main to be a form of Naturalistic Ethics: in other words, that pleasure has been so generally held to be the sole good, is almost entirely due to the fact that is has seemed to be somehow involved in the *definition* of "good"—to be pointed out by the very meaning of the word. If this is so, then the prevalence of Hedonism has been mainly due to what I have called the naturalistic fallacy—the failure to distinguish clearly that unique and indefinable quality which we mean by good. (59)

Other thinkers have been led to embrace hedonism because they failed to recognize that intrinsic moral good is indefinable. They try instead to reduce moral goodness to something natural such as the sensation of pleasure. Moore does not deny that pleasure is a good thing, that it belongs to what he refers to collectively as the good, consisting of all goods. In the end, Moore ranks pleasure relatively high in the hierarchy of good things. What he strenuously resists is the attempt to define goodness itself as pleasure. The objection is not logically unlike the criticism Socrates makes when Meno tries to define virtue in terms of many specific virtues. Where Socrates says that white is not color but *a* color, Moore similarly wants to say that pleasure is not good but *a* good; it has but is not identical with the property of being good.

Moore believes that hedonism has gained popularity in part through the perception that pleasure is somehow contained in the concept of good, or that in the definition of good pleasure is "pointed out" as part of its meaning. He observes that hedonism is an obvious moral theory from a psychological or anthropological standpoint. We are pleased with things or displeased, and the two categories of things that result from our psychological reactions to them constitute the basis for a distinction between what is good and what is bad. Pleasure naturally comes to be associated with what we take to be good, while pain is avoided as bad. Moore thus provides a genealogy of moral values rather different than Nietzsche's, and offers a different line of argument in support of a conclusion similar to Kant's, that empirical, factual, or naturalistic elements are not properly ethical. He remarks:

> Hedonism is, for a sufficiently obvious reason, the first conclusion at which any one who begins to reflect upon Ethics naturally arrives. It is very easy to notice the fact that we are pleased with things. The things we enjoy and the things we do not, form two unmistakable classes, to which our attention is constantly directed. (60)

The fact that hedonism occurs naturally to those who reflect philosophically on ethical matters does not justify it. Moore suggests that the ease with which hedonism impresses casual philosophical reflection actually works against the likelihood that it is correct. Any form of hedonism commits the naturalistic fallacy, and as such is objectionable for Moore on general methodological grounds. He argues further that it is simply false to suppose that good is pleasure, or that the concept of good can be fully explicated, analyzed, or defined as pleasure. To offer such a definition commits the naturalistic fallacy by attempting to define moral goodness as something other than itself. He tackles the implications of hedonism directly in an effort to show where they go wrong:

> We have seen how very flimsy the other arguments advanced for this proposition are; and that, if it be fairly considered by itself, it appears to be quite ridiculous. And, moreover, that the actions which produce most good on the whole do also produce most pleasure is extremely doubtful. The arguments tending to shew it are all more or less vitiated by the assumption that what appear to be necessary conditions for the attainment of most pleasure in the near future, will always continue so to be. And, even with this vicious assumption, they only succeed in making out a highly problematical case. How, therefore, this fact is to be explained, if it be a fact, need not concern us. (108)

He admits that he cannot adequately explain why it is that hedonism has so strongly recommended itself as a moral philosophy. He claims in any case that it is not the business of the principles of ethics to explain these anthropological facts about human psychology as they relate to the prevalence of moral hedonism. He turns instead to what he seems to regard as a knockdown criticism of hedonism on philosophical grounds.

The argument is simple but powerful in its implications. Moore reasons that complex psychological states are more valuable than the pleasure they contain as a proper part. As a thought experiment we can imagine a pleasurable state of mind in which we also feel love and compassion for another person's suffering. If we subtract all of the pleasure, the love and compassion that remains still seems morally valuable, indicating that moral good cannot be identified with pleasure alone. Moore concludes that hedonism in general is false on its own terms, independently of its entanglement in the naturalistic fallacy, as he states:

> It is sufficient to have shewn that many complex states of mind are much more valuable than the pleasure they contain. If this be so, *no form of Hedonism can*

be true. And, since the practical guidance afforded by pleasure as a *criterion* is small in proportion as the calculation attempts to be accurate, we can well afford to await further investigation, before adopting a guide, whose utility is very doubtful and whose trustworthiness we have grave reason to suspect. (108)

The defects of hedonism in general are brought home to the specific case of hedonic utilitarianism when Moore mentions Mill and Sidgwick before turning explicitly to hedonic egoism as liable to the definitional form of the naturalistic fallacy. He now summarizes the conclusions he believes he has established in the course of Chapter III. He mentions four results, beginning with this proposition:

(1) Hedonism must be strictly defined as the doctrine that "Pleasure is the only thing which is good in itself": this view seems to owe its prevalence mainly to the naturalistic fallacy, and Mill's arguments may be taken as a type of those which are fallacious in this respect; Sidgwick alone has defended it without committing this fallacy, and its final refutation must therefore point out the errors in his arguments. (108)

By defining hedonism as the view that pleasure is the only intrinsically good thing, it appears that Moore rescues the doctrine from the naturalistic fallacy. If pleasure is said to be the only intrinsically good thing, then it is part of the good rather than brought into a mistaken attempt to define moral good as pleasure. Moore's nevertheless argues that hedonism as he defines it can only be defended by committing the naturalistic fallacy. He claims that the only defender of hedonism who has managed to avoid the naturalistic fallacy is Sidgwick.

Sidgwick avoids the objection by offering a different criterion of moral good than hedonism or utilitarianism, which he refers to as *intuitionism.* The idea of intuitionism is that it is possible somehow simply to perceive that the unique property of moral goodness belongs exclusively to pleasure. Sidgwick's intuitionism avoids the mistakes of cruder forms of hedonism that do not avail themselves of the direct intuition of goodness as pleasure.

Moore criticizes Sidgwick's hedonism directly. He imagines two worlds, one of which is beautiful and the other ugly, but which contain precisely the same amount of pleasure. Moore argues that a correct intuition of moral good could only perceive that the more beautiful world is more valuable as a world in which more good generally prevails than in the ugly world. If this is true, then a proper intuition of good should not disclose that good is only pleasure, even if pleasure is among the many kinds of good things that collectively constitute the good. Moore later advocates a similar Sidgwickian sense of intuition and intuitionism in the direct perception of the property of moral good. He agrees with Sidgwick that there is a peculiar faculty of moral intuition, but he disagrees emphatically that intuition reveals that pleasure is identical with goodness or as the only intrinsically good thing.

Moore summarizes some of these conclusions in the following points, continuing his objections to Mill's hedonic utilitarianism:

(2) Mill's "Utilitarianism" is criticised: it being shewn (*a*) that he commits the naturalistic fallacy in identifying "desirable" with "desired"; (*b*) that pleasure is not the only object of desire. The common arguments for Hedonism seem to rest on these two errors. (108)

The next step for Moore is to review his principal criticisms of Sidgwick's intuitionist hedonism. He charges Sidgwick with failing to distinguish between pleasure and consciousness of pleasure. He argues that if consciousness of pleasure were the only good, then a world in which only the consciousness of pleasure and nothing else existed could be morally perfect. This seems like an intuitively false implication, if like Moore we intuit that other things are necessary to make a world perfect. The third point is this:

> (3) Hedonism is considered as an "Intuition," and it is pointed out *(a)* that Mill's allowance that some pleasures are inferior in quality to others implies both that it is an Intuition and that it is a false one . . . ; *(b)* that Sidgwick fails to distinguish "pleasure" from "consciousness of pleasure," and that it is absurd to regard the former at all events, as the sole good . . . ; *(c)* that it seems equally absurd to regard "consciousness of pleasure" as the sole good, since, if it were so, a world in which nothing else existed might be absolutely perfect: Sidgwick fails to put to himself this question, which is the only clear and decisive one. (108–9)

The fourth and final conclusion involves a theoretical inconsistency in hedonism. Hedonism considered in general terms is divided into egoism and utilitarianism; yet these two forms of the theory are logically incompatible in their proposals to define pleasure as the only intrinsic good identical with the property of moral goodness. The problem arises because hedonic egoism implies that the pleasure of the individual is the only moral good, while utilitarianism holds that the pleasure of all sentient beings is the only moral good. It remains possible that one but not necessarily both forms of hedonism are false. Mill would surely want to say that hedonic egoism is false but hedonic utilitarianism is true. Moore seems to regard it as significant that hedonism supports two diametrically opposed moral theories, both of which commit the naturalistic fallacy by trying to define the concept of good as something other than itself. He concludes:

> (4) What are commonly considered to be the two main types of Hedonism, namely, Egoism and Utilitarianism, are not only different from, but strictly contradictory of, one another; since the former asserts "My own greatest pleasure is the *sole* good," the latter "The greatest pleasure of all is the *sole* good." (109)

The problem with hedonism is dual. The theory mistakenly holds that moral good is definable as pleasure and that pleasure is the only moral good. Hedonism gets things wrong in the first place because it commits the naturalistic fallacy. A further sign of this is the fact that even in Sidgwick's intuitionistic version only pleasure is supposed to be intrinsically good. Moore argues that many things are intrinsically good, pleasure and intelligence and beauty being only a few among them. It follows that hedonism as he defines the concept cannot possibly be true. We might question in particular whether Sidgwick's faculty of intuition could be used to judge that pleasure is the only good, since to be in a position to know this a person gifted with moral intuition would presumably need to perceive every good thing in the universe to decide if it does or does not involve pleasure. Moore objects that Sidgwick has not even considered obvious thought experiments that pose apparent counterexamples to the hedonism he accepts. It is only if moral intuition allows any reflective person to directly perceive that only pleasure is good, immediately intuiting that hedonism is true, that Sidgwick's naturalism could possibly be true.

METAPHYSICAL FORMS OF THE NATURALISTIC FALLACY

The critique of the naturalistic fallacy is given by Moore in general terms and in two applications. The fallacy arises through attempts to define moral good in terms of natural things other than themselves, and these in turn can involve evolutionary ethics or egoistic and utilitarian hedonisms, including Sidgwick's intuitionistic version. With the rejection of these moral theories, all of which in different ways are supposed to commit the naturalistic fallacy, Moore is ready to move on to the second main category of violations, involving efforts to define the concept of good in terms of metaphysical rather than natural things and facts. Metaphysical versions of the naturalistic fallacy attempt to define moral good as something beyond the physical world. Moore begins his criticism of moral theories in this way:

> These ethical theories have this in common, that they use some *metaphysical* proposition as a ground for inferring some fundamental proposition of Ethics. They all imply, and many of them expressly hold, that ethical truths follow logically from metaphysical truths—that Ethics should be based on *Metaphysics*. And the result is that they all describe the Supreme Good in *metaphysical* terms. (110)

We have already seen that Moore criticizes social Darwinism, hedonic utilitarianism, and egoism as the principal moral theories guilty of a naturalistic form of the naturalistic fallacy. If his objections are sound, then he has defeated the ethical systems of Spencer, Mill, Sidgwick, and others. Turning to metaphysical forms of the naturalistic fallacy involving metaphysical propositions expressing metaphysical truths about a supreme good, Moore prepares to criticize rationalist theories of ethics such as Kant's deontology. The category of the metaphysical for Moore is meant to subsume abstract entities including propositions and Platonic Forms:

> I call those philosophers preeminently "metaphysical" who have recognised most clearly that not everything which *is* is a "natural object." "Metaphysicians" have, therefore, the great merit of insisting that our knowledge is not confined to the things which we can touch and see and feel. They have always been much occupied, not only with that other class of natural objects which consists in mental facts, but also with the class of objects or properties of objects, which certainly do not exist in time, are not therefore parts of Nature, and which, in fact, do not *exist* at all. To this class, as I have said, belongs what we mean by the adjective "good." It is not *goodness*, but only the things or qualities which are good, which can exist in time—can have duration, and begin and cease to exist—can be objects of *perception*. (110–11)

Moore declares his allegiance to abstract entities, and in particular to goodness as something that cannot be experienced in sensation. He is not an opponent of metaphysical things generally, but recognizes a danger in this field of fallaciously defining moral good in terms of metaphysical properties other than itself or as following from metaphysical propositions or general principles. The kinds of principles he seems to have in mind here would presumably include Kant's categorical imperative. It is this possibility of mistaken definition that Moore regards as committing a metaphysical naturalistic fallacy. He concentrates on conspicuous instances of the fallacy that are reminiscent of Kant's deontology, and identifies the explanatory requirements he believes any such definition of moral good must satisfy. He will shortly argue that the conditions cannot be satisfied except at the expense of committing a metaphysical version of the naturalistic fallacy. He distinguishes the kinds of things these theories promise to deliver, which enables him to narrow the focus of his critique. We recognize Kant's remarks in the *Grounding*, that the only unqualifiedly good thing is a good will, as the brunt of Moore's criticism:

> But to consider whether any form of will is or is not a criterion of goodness is quite unnecessary for our purpose here; since none of those writers who profess to base their Ethics on an investigation of will have ever recognised the need of proving directly and independently that all the things which are willed in a certain way are good. They make no attempt to shew that will is a *criterion* of goodness; and no stronger evidence could be given that they do not recognise that this, at most, is all it can be. As has been just pointed out, if we are to maintain that whatever is willed in a certain way is also good, we must in the first place be able to shew that certain things have one property "goodness," and that the same things *also* have the other property that they are willed in a certain way. And secondly we must be able to shew this in a very large number of instances, if we are to be entitled to claim any assent for the proposition that these two properties *always* accompany one another: even when this was shewn it would still be doubtful whether the inference from "generally" to "always" would be valid, and almost certain that this doubtful principle would be useless. (138)

The objection is that a metaphysical principle of morality concerning the will must be empirically underdetermined. To uphold the principle that the will as a certain state of mind is a criterion of goodness, metaphysical naturalists would first need to establish a positive correlation between all good things and the appropriate attitude of will. The problem is that we require a metaphysical criterion of morality to be universally true, and that to judge whether a given principle is even true in a large number of instances requires a comparison of many cases of an act of will to see if they also exemplify goodness, while checking unmanageably many cases of goodness to see if they are also accompanied by the appropriate condition of will. This requirement, Moore implies without exact documentation, has not been met by any metaphysical naturalist.

A further indirect reference to Kant's ethics occurs thereafter in Moore's criticism. He seems to be thinking of Kant's transcendental methodology when he argues that adherents of metaphysical naturalism often hold that the predicate "good" necessarily designates a real property of things. If we take it as a given that certain kinds of moral judgments are made, and ask Kant's transcendental question regarding what must be true in order for such judgments to be justified, we might arrive at the conclusion that goodness must be a real property. The thesis that such properties are necessary is the hallmark of what Moore calls the metaphysical version of the naturalistic fallacy. Thus far, he has at most shown that attempts to uphold certain versions of metaphysical naturalism are generally inadequately warranted, but he has not established that any metaphysical criterion or principle of goodness commits the fallacy. We have the general characterization of the naturalistic fallacy in hand, according to which it is always logically mistaken to try to identify an indefinable property with another thing, regardless of whether the analysis involves a natural or metaphysical entity. Moore nevertheless recognizes special problems in the case of metaphysical naturalism, and distinguishes between logical and epistemological difficulties:

> [T]he most important source of the supposition that Metaphysics is relevant to Ethics, seems to be the assumption that "good" *must* denote some *real* property of things—an assumption which is mainly due to two erroneous doctrines, the first *logical*, the second *epistemological*. Hence . . . I discussed the *logical* doctrine that all propositions assert a relation between existents; and pointed out that the assimilation of ethical propositions either to natural laws or to commands are instances of this *logical fallacy* . . . the main points [against the epistemological doctrine] are these: *(a)* That Volition and Feeling are *not* analogous to Cognition in the manner assumed; since in so far as these words denote an attitude of the mind towards an object, they are themselves merely instances of Cognition: they differ only in respect of the kind of object of which they take cognisance, and in respect of the other mental accompaniments of such cognitions: *(b)* That universally the *object* of a cognition must be distinguished from the cognition of which it is the object; and hence that in no case can the question whether the object is *true* be identical with the question how it is cognised or whether it is cognised at all: it follows that even if the proposition "This is good" were always the object of certain kinds of will or feeling, the *truth* of that proposition could in no case be established by proving that it was their object; far less can that proposition itself be identical with the proposition that its subject is the object of a volition or a feeling. . . . (140–41)

The logical problem facing metaphysical naturalism is the naturalistic fallacy, which Moore has already criticized at length. Here he adds the specific information that a metaphysical naturalism might try to assimilate goodness to a general metaphysical principle construed as a law of nature or, interestingly, to a "command." The command presumably refers to Kant's categorical imperative, which unconditionally imposes a moral duty on all rational beings.

The epistemological problem Moore mentions is more complicated. By volition and feeling he also means the will or state of mind that Kant's deontology regards as the basis of unqualified good. The difficulty in this category is that the metaphysical approach to the definition of goodness confuses a cognitive state, the act of will, with its proper object. The will, experienced as a mental act of volition or feeling, is supposed to be directed toward moral good as its object. A state of cognition, volition, feeling, or will, Moore rightly notes, should never be confused with its object. This, however, is precisely how metaphysical naturalism commits its special form of the naturalistic fallacy, by confusing moral goodness as the object of a good will with the state of mind that has goodness as its object.

Moore does not mention the Platonic Form of Good as a supposedly necessarily existent metaphysical entity in terms of which goodness might be defined in a metaphysical application of the naturalistic fallacy. What would Moore say about the Form of Good? Although Moore by no means commits himself to a realist theory of universals, it is not unreasonable to interpret Moore's view of moral good as an indefinable and unanalyzable property as itself something like an abstract Platonic Form of Good. A Platonic realist metaphysics of moral good, if that is Moore's theory, would not be guilty of the metaphysical naturalistic fallacy provided it did not try to misidentify the concept of good as an abstract Platonic Form with any other concept or any other Platonic Form.

Moral Laws, Rights, and Obligations

The final topic we shall address in Moore's ethics is his analysis of moral laws, moral rights, and moral obligations. Kant, Mill, and Nietzsche also try to define these concepts in very different ways, and in Chapter 10 we will find the American philosopher John Rawls analyzing the concept of justice. Moore is in a unique position with respect to his thesis of moral good as indefinable and unanalyzable to make an interesting contribution to the theory of social ethics as it applies to questions of moral rights and duties under the moral law. This is the subject of Moore's Chapter V, "Ethics in Relation to Conduct." He introduces the topic:

> All moral laws, I wish to shew, are merely statements that certain kinds of actions will have good effects. The very opposite of this view has been generally prevalent in Ethics. "The right" and "the useful" have been supposed to be at least *capable* of conflicting with one another, and, at all events, to be essentially distinct. It has been characteristic of a certain school of moralists, as of moral common sense, to declare that the end will never justify the means. What I wish first to point out is that "right" does and can mean nothing but "cause of a good result," and is thus identical with "useful"; whence it follows that the end always will justify the means, and that no action which is not justified by its results can be right. That there may be a true proposition, meant to be conveyed by the assertion "The end will not justify the means," I fully admit; but that, in another sense, and a sense far more fundamental for ethical theory, it is utterly false, must first be shewn. (146–47)

With moral good understood as a primitive property, as the fundamental concept of all moral judgment, Moore can analyze more complex moral concepts in terms of indefinable goodness. A moral law, he now asserts, is a statement of the kinds of conduct that tend to have indefinably good results. It may seem surprising after his criticism of Mill's involvement in the naturalistic fallacy to find Moore defending a version of Mill's analysis of the concept of moral rights and social justice. Like Mill, Moore argues that a right is nothing metaphysical rising above the actions agents perform. Moral rights for Moore are just whatever cause indefinably morally good consequences.

This language strongly suggests that although he does not try to analyze moral good in terms of consequences, Moore's theory of moral law, rights, and justice is a consequentialist analysis that takes moral good as a primitive indefinable property in terms of which law and rights are defined. Moral good is not analyzed in terms of consequences, but moral law and related complex moral concepts are defined in terms of their consequences for contributing to unanalyzable moral good. An immediate implication of the proposal is that, contrary to much of traditional ethics, there can be no opposition between rights and utility according to Moore. For, if his analysis is correct, then a right is nothing other than whatever has good consequences. The consequentialist bent of Moore's moral philosophy is clear despite his rejection of the utilitarian analysis of good as pleasure. He defines moral obligation in these explicitly consequentialist terms:

> That the assertion "I am morally bound to perform this action" is identical with the assertion "This action will produce the greatest possible amount of good in the Universe" has already been briefly shewn . . . ; but it is important to insist that this fundamental point is demonstrably certain. This may, perhaps, be best made evident in the following way. It is plain that when we assert that a certain

action is our absolute duty, we are asserting that the performance of that action at that time is unique in respect of value. But no dutiful action can possibly have unique value in the sense that it is the sole thing of value in the world; since, in that case, *every* such action would be the *sole* good thing, which is a manifest contradiction. And for the same reason its value cannot be unique in the sense that it has more intrinsic value than anything else in the world; since *every* act of duty would then be the *best* thing in the world, which is also a contradiction. It can, therefore, be unique only in the sense that the whole world will be better, if it be performed, than if any possible alternative were taken. And the question whether this is so cannot possibly depend solely on the question of its own intrinsic value. For any action will also have effects different from those of any other action; and if any of these have intrinsic value, their value is exactly as relevant to the total goodness of the Universe as that of their cause. (147)

Moore assumes that there are exactly two ways in which a moral obligation can be absolute. It can impose a unique duty either by supposing that the action is unique in value or in the sense that the world in its entirety is improved in terms of the total amount of happiness or pleasure that are produced as a consequence. The argument eliminates the first possibility as inconsistent, leaving only the consequentialist interpretation. There are many morally obligatory actions rather than just one, so that if each such action is supposed to be unique in value, then every morally obligatory action would be the only good. Assuming Moore's division between ways in which moral obligations can be absolute is correct, he makes a strong case for the nonanalytic type of consequentialism he accepts. Moral duty is then defined as whatever action contributes consequentially to the existence of more unanalyzable good:

Our "duty," therefore, can only be defined as that action, which will cause more good to exist in the Universe than any possible alternative. And what is "right" or "morally permissible" only differs from this, as what will *not* cause *less* good than any possible alternative. When, therefore, Ethics presumes to assert that certain ways of acting are "duties" it presumes to assert that to act in those ways will always produce the greatest possible sum of good. If we are told that to "do no murder" is a duty, we are told that the action, whatever it may be, which is called murder, will under no circumstances cause so much good to exist in the Universe as its avoidance. (148)

The complete account of moral duties and infractions of moral obligations in the form of sins and crimes includes several elements. All are based on the indefinable property of moral goodness. Moore specifies a number of conditions which he singles out for mention. An action that is either morally obligatory or prohibited must be willful and obligatory or prohibited for all moral agents, circumstantially rather than universally obligatory or prohibited, depending on the consequences they generally produce. Moore remarks that we can only judge that these conditions are satisfied with respect to actions that are commonly practiced. He summarizes the interpretation of moral obligation and prohibition as follows:

With regard, then, to the actions commonly classed in Ethics, as duties, crimes, or sins, the following points seem deserving of notice. (1) By so classing them we mean that they are actions which it is possible for an individual to perform or avoid, if he only *wills* to do so; and that they are actions which *everybody* ought to perform or avoid, when occasion arises. (2) We can certainly not prove of any such action that it ought to be done or avoided under *all* circumstances; we can only prove that its performance or avoidance will *generally* produce better results than the alternative. (3) If further we ask of what actions as much as this can be proved, it seems only possible to prove it with regard to those which are actually generally practised among us. And of these some only are such that their general performance would be useful in any state of society that seems possible; of others the utility depends upon conditions which exist now, but which seem to be more or less alterable. (161–62)

It is important to understand that Moore believes he has recovered the essentials of consequentialist morality without the assumption that moral good can be defined or analyzed in terms of happiness, pleasure, or the greatest good for the greatest number. The good as opposed to the property or concept of moral goodness includes and may finally be collected under the category of these utilitarian values, while goodness itself cannot be defined or analyzed in terms of consequentialist or any other natural or metaphysical factors. If by consequentialism or utilitarianism we mean a theory that commits what Moore calls the naturalistic fallacy by trying to define moral good as something other than it is, as happiness, pleasure, or utility otherwise construed, then Moore is most definitely not a consequentialist or utilitarian. If by these terms we mean to describe a nonanalytic moral theory of the good or whatever things are good, then Moore in the end is a kind of consequentialist who regards as good those things that improve the sum total of happiness and minimize the amount of pain, unhappiness, and displeasure.

SUMMARY

As an exponent of analytic philosophy, Moore analyzes moral judgment and discourse down to simpler elements, the simplest of which is moral good, which he distinguishes from the good as the sum of all good things. The idea that moral good is conceptually primitive, indefinable, and unanalyzable, together with an exploration of its implications, is the main contribution of Moore's ethical principles.

Moore's relation to consequentialism is complex. Whether Moore is a utilitarian depends on what we mean by the term. If consequentialism in general or utilitarianism in particular are supposed to define and analyze the concept of moral good in terms of pleasure or happiness, then Moore is not a consequentialist nor a utilitarian. He maintains that all such attempts to define moral good as something other than itself commit the naturalistic fallacy. The naturalistic fallacy in its most general terms is the conceptual mistake of trying to identify indefinable unanalyzable moral good alternatively as something material or metaphysical. Moore's concept of the good as the sum of all good things nevertheless features pleasure and happiness as among the greatest goods, in which sense his moral philosophy appears distinctly utilitarian. It is appropriate for this reason to think of Moore's analytic principles of ethics as a nonanalytic consequentialism; not a consequentialism of moral good but of the moral good.

When a theory of good guilty of the naturalistic fallacy confuses moral goodness with a natural property other than itself, it typically does so in the form of an evolutionary ethics or social Darwinism, or in terms of egoistic or utilitarian psychological pleasure or happiness. Metaphysical theories of moral good try to define good in terms of a volition or feeling in a moral agent's state of mind, such as Kant's concept of a good will as the only unqualified good thing, or of higher metaphysical principles of moral command, such as Kant's categorical imperative. These definitions of moral good violate the requirements of correct philosophical analysis in a different way. They mistakenly try to identify the meaning of moral good as something other than itself; in this case, as something that considered in itself does not make good things good, but which are good, if Moore is right, only because they are good.

QUESTIONS FOR PHILOSOPHICAL UNDERSTANDING

1. What is analytic philosophy?

2. What does Moore mean by the naturalistic fallacy?

3. In what exact sense is the naturalistic fallacy supposed to be naturalistic? In what exact sense is it supposed to be a fallacy?

4. What is Moore's distinction between natural and metaphysical definitions of moral goodness?

5. Why does Moore argue that moral good cannot be defined?

6. What is Moore's concept of moral law, moral rights, and moral obligations?

7. How does Moore's theory of moral rights relate to his theory of moral good as indefinable and unanalyzable?

8. How does Moore try to prove that moral good cannot be defined in terms of pleasure or happiness?

9. How does Moore try to prove that moral good cannot be defined in terms of states of volition, feeling, or will?

10. How does Moore try to prove that moral good cannot be defined in terms of higher principles of command, such as Kant's categorical imperative?

11. In what ways does Moore's moral philosophy agree or disagree in its methodology or conclusions with Kant's, Mill's, and Nietzsche's? In what ways is it similar to and in what ways is it dissimilar from any of these moral theories?

12. What are the common elements if any between Moore's rejection of naturalism in the concept of moral good and Kant's requirement that all empirical elements be purged from the foundations of the metaphysics of morals?

13. Given the practical convergence of Moore's moral philosophy on certain conclusions of consequentialism, what are the real differences if any for moral decision making and ethical conduct between Moore's antinaturalism in moral reasoning and Mill's utilitarianism?

14. Are there fundamental irreducible primitive indefinable and unanalyzable moral concepts? How can we know that? How can we discover which ones they are?

15. If intrinsic moral good is indefinable, where does it come from? How does intrinsic moral good arise in such a way that some things and some actions and rules of conduct are morally good and others are morally bad or wrong or indifferent? How can we tell the difference? What is the role of a sense of moral intuition in recognizing indefinable and unanalyzable moral good? How, if at all, can its evidence be epistemically and morally justified?

KEY TERMS

analytic philosophy	is-statement	naturalistic fallacy
casuitry	metaphysical definition of good	open question argument
causal good, instrumental good		organic unity
double knowledge of good	moral intuition, moral intuitionism	ought-statement
ethical naturalism	moral law	philosophical analysis
good, goodness, the good	moral obligation	simple fact
indefinable concept	moral right	simple object
is-ought gap	natural definitions of good	social Darwinism

SOURCES AND RECOMMENDED READINGS

Ambrose, Alice, and Morris Lazerowitz, eds. *G. E. Moore: Essays in Retrospect.* London: Allen & Unwin, 1970.

Ayer, A. J. *Russell and Moore: The Analytical Heritage.* Cambridge: Harvard University Press, 1971.

Hill, John. *The Ethics of G. E. Moore: A New Interpretation.* Assen: Van Gorcum, 1976.

Hume, David. *A Treatise of Human Nature* [1739–1740]. Edited by L. A. Selby-Bigge. Second edition revised with notes by P. H. Nidditch. Oxford: Oxford University Press, 1978.

Hutchinson, Brian. *G. E. Moore's Ethical Theory: Resistance and Reconciliation.* Cambridge: Cambridge University Press, 2001.

Klemke, E. D. *A Defense of Realism: Reflections on the Metaphysics of G. E. Moore.* Amherst: Humanity Books, 2000.

Levy, Paul. *Moore: G. E. Moore and the Cambridge Apostles.* Oxford: Oxford University Press, 1981.

Moore, G. E. *Ethics.* Oxford: Oxford University Press, 1958.

Moore, G. E. *The Elements of Ethics.* Edited with an Introduction by Tom Regan. Philadelphia: Temple University Press, 1991.

Olthuis, James H. *Facts, Values, and Ethics: A Confrontation with Twentieth Century British Moral Philosophy, in Particular G. E. Moore.* New York: Humanities Press, 1968.

Regan, Tom. *Bloomsbury's Prophet: G. E. Moore and the Development of His Moral Philosophy.* Philadelphia: Temple University Press, 1986.

Rohatyn, Dennis A. *The Reluctant Naturalist: A Study of G. E. Moore's* Principia Ethica. Lanham: University Press of America, 1987.

Schilpp, P. A., ed. *The Philosophy of G. E. Moore.* Chicago: Open Court Publishing, 1979.

Shaw, William H. *Moore on Right and Wrong: The Normative Ethics of G. E. Moore.* Dordrecht-Boston: Kluwer Academic Publishers, 1995.

Sylvester, Robert P. *The Moral Philosophy of G. E. Moore.* Edited with an Introduction by Ray Perkins Jr. and R. W. Sleeper; Foreword by Tom Regan. Philadelphia: Temple University Press, 1990.

White, Alan R. *G. E. Moore: A Critical Exposition.* New York: Humanities Press, 1969.

CHAPTER 10

JUSTICE AND THE SOCIAL GOOD IN POLITICAL DECISION MAKING

Rawls's *A Theory of Justice*

I n this final chapter we critically consider a contemporary philosopher who develops a theory of a particularly important concept in ethics and political philosophy. Rawls's theory of justice explains the conditions under which a social contract can be instituted that is fair to every member of a society. Rawls's project is exciting not only for the sake of his advocacy of liberal democratic social institutions, but because Rawls is instructively self-conscious about what he takes to be proper philosophical methodology. His concept of reflective equilibrium has implications beyond ethics and social philosophy.

AN IDEAL OF JUSTICE

In a final critical look at problems in moral and political philosophy, we turn to John Rawls's important work, *A Theory of Justice*. Rawls (1921–2002) is a recent American philosopher whose contributions to political thought are widely discussed. Rawls's detailed examination of the ideal of justice is valuable not only as a philosophical analysis of the definition of the term, but for the sake of its practical implications in individual ethical and social decision making. We must decide for ourselves whether and to what extent he offers a correct analysis of the concept of justice, interpreting its meaning and explaining and extending its applications.

Rawls identifies the role of justice in social institutions as their "first virtue," which he compares with the place of truth in theoretical disciplines. Just as theories are evaluated by a standard of truth or falsehood, so, Rawls argues, laws and social institutions must be judged with respect to their justice or injustice. A theory in science or philosophy must be rejected, regardless of its other merits, if it turns out to be false. A legal or social system must be rejected, regardless of its other merits, if it turns out to be unjust. This is not to say that someone for extrinsic reasons could not persist in accepting a false theory or an unjust law or social institution. The point is rather that it is incompatible with the purpose of constructing a theory or social system to continue to accept it once it has been shown to be false or unjust. Another way to emphasize the same conclusion is to say that whereas truth should be paramount in the articulation and critical assessment of theories, so justice should be paramount in legislating and assessing laws and social institutions. We develop or should develop theories for the sake of truth, and we develop or should develop laws and social institutions for the sake of justice.

Rawls explains his notion of justice by relating it directly to the concept of individual rights. Here he refers to the rights conferred by considerations of justice as an "inviolability," and claims but does not offer an argument to show that every person has such rights, based on considerations of justice, that cannot be overridden by the interests of maximizing the greatest happiness for the greatest number. We have seen this kind of opposition of moral values before, in the conflict between deontology and consequentialism, represented by Kant's categorical imperative versus Mill's principle of utility. Rawls comes out clearly on the side of Kant's advocacy of justice and rights rationalistically interpreted:

> Justice is the first virtue of social institutions, as truth is of systems of thought. A theory however elegant and economical must be rejected or revised if it is untrue; likewise laws and institutions no matter how efficient and well-arranged must be reformed or abolished if they are unjust. Each person possesses an inviolability founded on justice that even the welfare of society as a whole cannot override. For this reason justice denies that the loss of freedom for some is made right by a greater good shared by others. It does not allow that the sacrifices imposed on a few are outweighed by the larger sum of advantages enjoyed by many. (3)

What is remarkable is that Rawls should declare his allegiance to deontology so quickly, when he is first introducing the topic of his book. He seems to regard it as a matter of course that considerations of justice and rights should triumph over considerations of utility, of maximizing happiness. The issue, however, is a serious bone of contention among moral-political philosophers.

Kant emphasizes the absolute inviolability of rights and the justice that it is unqualifiedly due to all rational agents. He unequivocally requires that all rational beings are to be treated as ends in themselves and never merely as means to another end. It does not follow automatically from this requirement that any system of ethics or political thought that emphasizes justice and the rights of individuals is necessarily deontological in orientation. Mill is also a strong defender of justice and the rights of persons and of all sentient beings, but he does not agree with Kant or Rawls that moral or higher-order legal or social rights as guaranteed by a concept of justice can never be overridden by the moral obligation to maximize the greatest happiness for the greatest number. The difference is that Mill by contrast with Kant and Rawls has a distinct concept of justice and rights, one that is based on, and hence not incompatible with, utility and the greatest happiness principle. It is a consequence of Mill's interpretation that it is not only morally permissible in principle but in some instances morally obligatory to override concerns for justice and rights on the grounds of utility, since it is utility for Mill that ultimately explains and justifies the observance of individual rights.

Another more radical understanding of justice and rights is articulated by Nietzsche. Nietzsche argues that justice is morally justified only for the powerful and for the sake of preserving the powerful elite against the *ressentiment* of the naturally weak. Nietzsche is if anything an even more strident opponent of utilitarianism, and of the concern for the consequences of actions as contributing to the general happiness or unhappiness on the part of "these English psychologists." He nevertheless offers a different account of justice than Kant, Mill, or Rawls, according to which it does not follow that every person possesses inviolable moral rights by the principles of justice.

Rawls, of course, does not need to accept Mill's utilitarian or Nietzsche's egoistic concept of justice. Evidently, he does not. If he is going to reject these theories and adhere instead to a more Kantian view of justice and moral rights, as he proposes, then he must take further steps toward refuting Mill's and Nietzsche's non-Kantian non-deontological theory, or defending his own understanding of justice and the inviolability of moral rights. We shall accordingly need to examine every aspect of Rawls's neo-Kantian theory of justice in an effort to determine whether it establishes the unconditional inviolability of moral rights.

JUSTICE IN SOCIETY

To explain the principles of social justice, Rawls first explains what he means by a society. He offers a reasonable definition loaded with revealing philosophical commitments, which we must try to unpack. As is often the case, it is worthwhile to devote careful scrutiny especially to a thinker's first moves in explicating a theory's starting place. Rawls makes philosophical presuppositions that speak volumes with respect to the analysis he develops. We should first consider the definition of a society he presents and then try to discern how his conclusions are prepared for if not prefigured in these initial efforts to explain the meaning of key terms. Rawls begins:

> Let us assume, to fix ideas, that a society is a more or less self-sufficient association of persons who in their relations to one another recognize certain rules of conduct as binding and who for the most part act in accordance with them. Suppose further that these rules specify a system of cooperation designed to advance the good of those taking part in it. Then, although a society is a cooperative venture for mutual advantage, it is typically marked by a conflict as well as by an identity of interests. (4)

By describing a society as a more or less self-sufficient association of persons bound together by a system of rules for the sake of advancing their mutual good, Rawls takes account of some of the elements that consequentialists regard as essential for assuring justice and respect for moral rights. The fact that Rawls defines justice as something relative to a society indicates how distant he is from anything like Nietzsche's egoistic concept. To think of a society as constituted by rules rather than emotional ties or as an extension of family relations is also an important factor in the way Rawls approaches the problem of understanding justice. It is controversial, especially from an anthropological point of view, to conceive of the structure of a society as essentially rule-governed rather than an outgrowth of familial dependencies and responsibilities. Nor does this set of categories exhaust the possibilities that Rawls seems to overlook in defining what he means by a society. It might be said that the model of individuals freely entering into a social network in order to promote their collective benefit is historically false of the development of real societies.

Rawls's definition appears to ignore the extent to which authority considered in and of itself can link together the members of a social unit noncooperatively. These social forces can operate through obedience, fear, religious belief and expectation, or other psychological factors. A social group held together in these ways would still be a society, but would not satisfy Rawls's definition as involving persons acting in accord with a set of prescribed rules for the sake of improving their lives. Why suppose from the outset of an analysis of the concept of justice that individual advantage-seeking cooperation is true by definition of every society, particularly when we know historically and sociologically that this need not be true?

Rawls builds his theory of justice on the definition of society as a cooperative association of individuals for the sake of mutual benefit. Social groups in which persons are bound together through fear or religious respect for unquestioned authority, or the imposition of a Nietzschean will to power, are not within Rawls's theory of justice. The theory cannot be applied to distinguish just from unjust rules for the governance of a social group that is not organized for the sake of promoting the social good, because no such group counts as a society according to Rawls's definition. He interprets justice in terms of conflicts between individual and social interests for societies as he defines them:

> There is an identity of interests since social cooperation makes possible a better life for all than any would have if each were to live solely by his own efforts. There is a conflict of interests since persons are not indifferent as to how the greater benefits produced by their collaboration are distributed, for in order to pursue their ends they each prefer a larger to a lesser share. A set of principles is required for choosing among the various social arrangements which determine this division of advantages and for underwriting an agreement on the proper distributive shares. These principles are the principles of social justice: they provide a way of assigning rights and duties in the basic institutions of society and they define the appropriate distribution of the benefits and burdens of social cooperation. (4)

Rawls's theory of justice presupposes a *social contract* concept of society. Societies are organized in order to provide a better life by instituting rules that should be assessed as just or unjust depending on whether or to what degree they contribute to the purposes of an ideal social contract. The definition implies that whatever actions honor and fulfill the terms of the social contract are just, and whatever actions violate the letter or spirit of the social contract are unjust. Rawls's concept defines any society as founded at least in the abstract on a social contract, however intrinsically just or unjust, however close to or remote from the ideal.

Social contract theory is interesting in its interpretations of real social structures, particularly in democratic societies governed by public law. The concept also raises many philosophical questions. Is Rawls's social contract concept of society sufficiently inclusive to include all societies that might be just or unjust? Is it possible on Rawls's account for a society based on some perhaps anthropologically unusual far from ideal social contract to be unjust in its entirety by virtue of not having the right sort of social contract? Or would that situation not count as one in which a social contract is in place in the true even if far from ideal sense? Why should we suppose in the first place that societies generally aim at their members' mutual good?

Defenders of social contract theories must downplay the fact that social life is better than solitary life for most persons even if they are part of an autocratic society in which nothing resembling so much as an implicit social contract obtains. Where persons are politically under the malevolent control of a powerful elite, they are statistically still better off than they would otherwise be if they had to survive entirely as individuals or even as nuclear family members outside the social group. There are inherent advantages to belonging to a larger social organization rather than trying to meet life's challenges entirely on one's own. It is a virtue of social organization generally that this is so, and not a special, let alone unique or distinguishing advantage of societies managed by an explicit, implicit, or imaginary social contract. We human beings benefit from virtually any social organization as opposed to none at all, even if we are not supposed to have freely signed on the dotted line of any social contract.

Rawls's concept of justice in a society organized according to the principles of a social contract is that of devising the best system whereby unfairnesses and inequalities in the actual observance or nonobservance of the rules of the social contract can be adjudicated so as to contribute to the society's ideal goal of contributing to every member's mutual good, and so to the collective good. Rawls observes that in a social contract context there are bound to be some persons who seek to obtain the benefits of the society without meeting its obligations, by bending and breaking the rules to their own advantage. The purpose of justice is to minimize and mitigate the harmful effects of this kind of unfair behavior on the smooth proper functioning of the society under its rules. If Rawls is right, then there are natural inequalities in the foundations of any society, in the conflict of interests that inevitably result when persons motivated by individual rational self-interests seek to secure more for themselves at the expense of leaving less for others. Justice as a practical ideal is the effort to redress these inequalities and unfairnesses, for which there can in principle be many ideas about justice as an abstract moral ideal. Rawls offers one such ideal in the course of presenting a theory of justice.

He further defines the concept of *a well-ordered society*. In a well-ordered society its members know and accept the terms of their social contract, which in turn are satisfied and known to be satisfied by its social institutions. The well-ordered society is a refinement of Rawls's social contract concept of an ideal society:

> Now let us say that a society is well-ordered when it is not only designed to advance the good of its members but when it is also effectively regulated by a public conception of justice. That is, it is a society in which (1) everyone accepts and knows that the others accept the same principles of justice, and (2) the basic social institutions generally satisfy and are generally known to satisfy these principles. In this case while men may put forth excessive demands on one another, they nevertheless acknowledge a common point of view from which their claims may be adjudicated. (4)

The key to a well-ordered society is not merely one that promotes the general good, but that does so by means of a "public" conception of justice. Rawls does not explain why he believes this additional requirement is needed, but it is reasonable to suppose that by this condition he means to say that no society can be well-ordered unless it is governed by a system of laws.

Rawls mentions two requirements. A well-ordered society is founded on a universally accepted concept of justice, and the basic social institutions of the society satisfy and are generally known to satisfy its principles. Again, Rawls does not explain why these conditions are required or precisely how they are supposed to contribute to the well-ordered society. It seems to be part of the concept of a well-ordered society that its members be able to live their lives and conduct their business in the full confidence that the institutions of the society are fulfilling an accepted standard of justice. It confers social stability to whatever degree a predominant proportion of the population in a society can expect that others share the same sense of justice and are prepared to meet its obligations along with all others in the framework of a law's publicly articulated criteria. If these conditions are not met, then, Rawls implies, however good the society may turn out to be with respect to the benefits and advantages it confers on its members, it is not what he would call well-ordered. Well-ordering in a society, as Rawls seems to understand the concept, is a matter not only of what a society does for its members, but of how it accomplishes the distribution of social goods and reinforces the principles that every member of the society can expect to be followed by every other member.

The general individual acceptance and collectively agreed-on standards of justice presupposed by Rawls's well-ordered society is equated with the idea of "civic friendship," in which the universal inclination or desire for justice serves as an internal check on each person's conduct. Rawls describes an ideal well-ordered society, since it is unrealistic to expect that absolutely everyone in a society will accept and agree upon the very same concept of justice. Nor when such persons live among us does it seem reasonable to insist that the definition of a society or even of a well-ordered society implies that such persons are excluded from the society of the just. The most we can predict to happen in existing social groups is the widespread or majoritarian acceptance of a common notion of justice, and the widespread or majoritarian exemplification of such a standard in the majority of laws and social institutions that comprise the society's legal, social, and political structure. When such conditions are satisfied by as many members of a society, in what will thus be included among the most just societies ever to exist, that will be as close as we can reasonably expect to get in the direction of Rawls's ideal concept of a well-ordered society.

The point is that for Rawls a society is not well-ordered unless it is in a quasi-Kantian sense autonomous. Its adherence to a concept of justice must come from within its membership, by virtue of a free acceptance and agreement on the whole to follow its principles for the general good. If the society does not function in this way, but requires external sanctions for its governance in accord with the requirements of justice, then the society might promote the general good, and might even satisfy the principles of justice, but it will not be well-ordered. To be well-ordered in Rawls's sense, a society must rule itself by the common consent of its members in harmony with a publicly articulated and universally accepted standard of justice. The concept of civic friendship is thus predicated on that of a common public standard of justice:

> Among individuals with disparate aims and purposes a shared conception of justice establishes the bonds of civic friendship; the general desire for justice limits the pursuit of other ends. One may think of a public conception of justice as constituting the fundamental charter of a well-ordered human association. (5)

Rawls explains that the concept of justice is not limited in its applications to laws, institutions, and social systems as a whole, but includes a multitude of distinct types of actions. He provides the following catalog of ways in which we speak of things being just or unjust, all of which are legitimate usages. He limits his topic specifically to the category of social justice, which, he explains, concerns the most fundamental structural arrangement of a society, in terms of the ways in which a society assigns rights and duties and determines the distribution of social goods. He restricts the concept of justice, and gives instructive examples of what he means by social justice and by the category of "major" social institutions by reference to which his concept of social justice is defined:

> Many different kinds of things are said to be just and unjust; not only laws, institutions, and social systems, but also particular actions of many kinds, including decisions, judgments, and imputations. We also call the attitudes and dispositions of persons, and persons themselves, just and unjust. Our topic, however, is that of social justice. For us the primary subject of justice is the basic structure of society, or more exactly, the way in which the major social institutions distribute fundamental rights and duties and determine the division of advantages from social cooperation. By major institutions I understand the political constitution and the principal economic and social arrangements. Thus the legal protection of freedom of thought and liberty of conscience, competitive markets, private property in the means of production, and the monogamous family are examples of major social institutions. (6)

It should be obvious that Rawls proceeds with definite preconceived ideas about what a well-ordered society is like. The fact that he mentions the sorts of social institutions that are found in liberal democratic societies such as the United States is no accident. It is possible to understand Rawls's theory as an explication and philosophical defense of an ideal well-ordered society whose social contract is publicly formulated in such documents as the American Declaration of Independence and Constitution, and of similar expressions of law in the founding of governments in other societies that share roughly the same ideal.

The American example is certainly foremost in Rawls's mind. There are virtually no discussions of any other kinds of societies in the book. The few exceptions involve occasional references to degenerate societies in which the principles of justice as Rawls eventually interprets them do not prevail. They are introduced primarily for the sake of contrast with Rawls's description of the way things are supposed to go in a just society. The exemplification of the principles of justice that Rawls finds morally praiseworthy and that satisfy the conditions of this theory winds up looking very much like an idealized version of the United States, with something like the American Constitution serving as the system of rules of the social contract in terms of which the well-ordered society is ideally governed. No other societies are particularly recognizable in Rawls's analysis of the concept of justice except insofar as they approximate the law at its best in the United States of America.

This is not necessarily a questionable result, nor does it necessarily testify to anything methodologically suspicious in Rawls's political philosophy. It might just turn out that the principles of justice objectively derived and justified from a rigorous philosophical perspective happen to cohere with or especially suggest those that have been influential in the founding of the United States. It is all to the credit of the United States, in that case, that its founders were sufficiently enlightened to have made use of the right principles of justice in framing the Constitution and organizing the major social institutions that put the government of the United States on the right footing from the standpoint of establishing a morally defensible concept of justice. Many people appear to feel this way about the principles of government on which the United States is founded. The United States to an extent no doubt continues today to move forward with much the same orientation toward certain principles of justice, within the same limitations that affect the approximation of a real social structure with respect to its more perfect abstract ideal. Patriotic Americans may be pleased to see that the most promising analysis of the concept of justice and the well-ordered society as Rawls develops it from a historical point of view is most completely realized in the political institutions of the United States, and in particular in the American Constitution together with its Bill of Rights. Other critics, without lapsing into undue cynicism about the morality of the American social contract, may still find it problematic that Rawls as an American philosopher just happens to articulate a theory of justice that the American form of government most closely resembles. Is this, regardless of our own political sentiments, a matter of philosophical concern?

The difficulty is not that Rawls's theory of justice is doubtful because no paradigm of justice could be expected to match the values that prevail in the United States. Nor need it be especially problematic that the preferred concept of justice turns out to be that which is in force in the native land of the theory's author. The methodological question in its most general terms is whether we should be skeptical about the adequacy of any theory that seems to presuppose its application while purporting to derive its principles objectively from conceptual analysis and open-ended philosophical inquiry. It can appear instead that an author in such a situation might be tailoring what passes for objective philosophical argument toward a particular preordained outcome. It is philosophically uninteresting to have a certain choice of values recommended as the consequence of a theory if they must be assumed right from the start to be correct before even the first philosophical question about them is raised. Rawls's theory of justice is successful as a defense of an ideal of justice only to the extent that his social contract concept of a well-ordered society does not presuppose what his reasoning should prove.

RAWLS'S CONCEPT OF JUSTICE AS FAIRNESS

The purpose of a system of justice in a well-ordered society is to adjudicate the inevitable conflicts of interest that arise between persons all pursuing their individual rational self-interests. Even in the most ideally well-ordered society there remains a need for a system of justice, because the members of the society will not behave ideally. The purpose of a theory of justice is to explain the concept of justice required for a well-ordered society. A theory of justice that accomplishes this objective not only meets its theoretical explanatory burden, but contributes materially to the realization of a well-ordered society by publicly articulating its underlying principles of justice.

Rawls acknowledges the task of a theory of justice in these terms. A correct concept of justice should satisfy two essential needs, determining in a principled way: (1) the allocation of social rights and responsibilities; (2) the distribution of social goods. Rawls identifies a definite role for the exercise of justice in an ideally well-ordered society, and he understands the concept of justice as a correct interpretation of this role:

> The concept of justice I take to be defined, then, by the role of its principles in assigning rights and duties and in defining the appropriate division of social advantages. A conception of justice is an interpretation of this role. (9)

Rawls explains the basic idea of a social contract as involving an "original agreement" by which a society is constituted. At an imaginary time in an imaginary past, in an "initial position," the founding members of the society sit down around an imaginary table and agree to live according to a certain choice of rules for their mutual advantage. The fact that individuals are supposed to freely enter into the social contract is part of what is supposed to make the social contract just. To the best of their ability, social contractors will not make decisions resulting in injustices occurring later down the road that could adversely affect their individual interests. Hence, they establish rules that make only a just assignment of social rights and obligations, and a just distribution of social goods, for which they are supposed to be contracting. This makes the study of the conditions under which a social contract is agreed upon a useful scenario in which to investigate the principles of justice. They will turn out to be the principles that participants in the initial position would naturally adopt in order to avoid injustices in their own future lives under the terms of the contract. The philosophical justification of the well-ordered society depends on a thought experiment Rawls designs about the kinds of principles of justice the social contractors in the original position would be sure to adopt. He describes his intentions in the book as falling into the classical tradition of social contract theory:

> My aim is to present a conception of justice which generalizes and carries to a higher level of abstraction the familiar theory of the social contract as found, say, in Locke, Rousseau, and Kant. In order to do this we are not to think of the original contract as one to enter a particular society or to set a particular form of government. Rather, the guiding idea is that the principles of justice for the basic structure of society are the object of the original agreement. They are the principles that free and rational persons concerned to further their own interests would accept in an initial position of equality as defining the fundamental terms of their association. These principles are to regulate all further agreements; they specify the kinds of social cooperation that can be entered into and the forms of government that can be established. This way of regarding the principles of justice I shall call justice as fairness. (10)

The final sentence in this passage introduces Rawls's theory of justice in a single phrase. Rawls interprets the concept of justice as *fairness*. What he means by this in its entirety occupies his attention throughout the book. We can summarize the idea of justice as fairness that is developed at length in Rawls's analysis, beyond what is immediately implied by the obvious sense of the words *fair* and *fairness*, by saying that for Rawls the concept of justice entails equality for all individuals in the two functions of justice required by a well-ordered society, deciding who is to have what kinds of rights and social responsibilities, and who is to receive which social goods and how they are to receive them.

The idea of justice as fairness is nevertheless not one according to which every person simply has the same rights and the same responsibilities and receives exactly the same social benefits and advantages. What is fairness? What is equality? What does it mean for the members of a society to be treated fairly by social institutions? Is it fair, and in that sense just, if in a particular society some people are rich and others are poor, or if some persons conditionally have the right to withhold information during a court trial and others do not? There should, minimally, one supposes, be no irrelevant disadvantages imposed on any person. The relevance to justice of differing social factors should probably not include gender, race, and ethnic or religious background. One problem for a theory of justice, and in particular for a theory of justice as fairness in the sense that Rawls proposes, is how we can show that these kinds of differences are irrelevant to considerations of justice in a well-ordered society.

PREPOLITICAL STATE OF NATURE

To explain the concept of justice as fairness, Rawls looks more deeply into the requirements of a social contract. In particular he wants to understand the original position when the founding members of a society are imagined to get together and hammer out the social contract's rules under which they are to live. It is typical for social contract theorists, notably Hobbes in his political treatise *Leviathan*, Locke in *Two Treatises of Government*, and Rousseau in *The Social Contract*, to fantasize about the existence of a prepolitical state of nature prior to free persons outside of all society settling on terms for the first social contract. Hobbes famously says that without the benefits of society conferred by a proper social contract, human life is "solitary, poor, nasty, brutish, and short."

The individuals who decide to enter into a social contract are supposed to do so because they think it will be to their advantage. The idea of a primitive state of nature is a necessity in social contract theory, even when it is acknowledged only as a myth. It may have heuristic value to suppose that there was once a prepolitical state of nature in which social relations and social institutions of any kind did not exist, but it does not seem anthropologically plausible. How could people survive in isolation, and how could they ever come to the decision to confer about the terms for a social contract? Would they not need to share some socially acquired language in order to negotiate? What would lead them even to suspect that it would be beneficial to start living in a society if they had not previously done so and had no models to suggest its advantages? There must be some sort of primitive social organization presupposed even by the possibility of persons sitting down for the first time to consider the terms of a social contract.

It might be said that the larger social group is just an extension of the same kind of social organization that exists naturally in an isolated nuclear family. A family, so interpreted, is already a social structure in which different persons have different things to do and receive benefits from cooperative interaction. This is no doubt true. The idea additionally suggests that social organization beyond the nuclear family is every bit as natural. Unless we are referring only to a matter of degree or level of complexity of social organizations, then social isolation is probably not a state of nature, and human beings are naturally social, naturally part of a social community, as contemporary scientific anthropology teaches. It is more likely that humans have always lived together socially in social groups, and that we are, as Aristotle says, essentially social animals. Nor are human beings unique in this regard, since many other species, including the higher primates from which we evolved, are also social but can hardly be said to have a publicly articulated social contract. If we consider degrees and kinds of social organization, or of improvements and refinements in which better social organizations are arranged by deliberate effort to provide a satisfactory social contract, then we might extrapolate backward to a state prior to a people's reaching agreement on the terms of a social contract. At most this would be a prepolitical, but not a presocial state of nature, and it would not be the very first movement toward socialization before which there was no society or any social structure whatsoever.

If the concept of a state of nature in classical social contract theory is no more than a philosophical myth, it must still be asked whether the myth is useful or instructive. Rawls emphasizes the fictional concept of the *original position*, which he says corresponds to the idea of a Hobbesian state of nature. It is part of Rawls's abstraction of social contract theory to transform the idea of a presocial state of nature into the concept of the original or initial position, meaning thereby a way of thinking about ideal conditions under which social institutions might be conceived in founding a well-ordered society. He maintains:

> In justice as fairness the original position of equality corresponds to the state of nature in the traditional theory of the social contract. This original position is not, of course, thought of as an actual historical state of affairs, much less as a primitive condition of culture. It is understood as a purely hypothetical situation characterized so as to lead to a certain conception of justice. (11)

The point of referring to the original position is, as Rawls characterizes it, purely hypothetical. He presents the original position as a way of thinking about the conditions under which a set of rules for a well-ordered society might be decided upon. He introduces the *veil of ignorance* as another mythical device to describe an ideal of justice in the original position when the basic principles of a social contract are being decided. Rawls imagines that the principles of justice are arrived at through compromise on the part of the founders of a society who are thrashing out its rules. He argues that to institute justice in a well-ordered society, the contractors must not know who they will be nor anything specific about the facts of their lives as they will actually occur once the social contract is in place. If they have such information, then they might make unfair choices to give themselves special advantages or give others special disadvantages when the contract goes into effect. He maintains:

> Among the essential features of this situation is that no one knows his place in society, his class position or social status, nor does any one know his fortune in the distribution of natural assets and abilities, his intelligence, strength, and the

like. I shall even assume that the parties do not know their conceptions of the good or their special psychological propensities. The principles of justice are chosen behind a veil of ignorance. This ensures that no one is advantaged or disadvantaged in the choice of principles by the outcome of natural chance or the contingency of social circumstances. Since all are similarly situated and no one is able to design principles to favor his particular condition, the principles of justice are the result of a fair agreement or bargain. For given the circumstances of the original position, the symmetry of everyone's relations to each other, this initial situation is fair between individuals as moral persons, that is, as rational beings with their own ends and capable, I shall assume, of a sense of justice. (11)

The difficulty for any social contract theory is to strike the right balance in the psychological qualities of the society's founders. The rule makers in the original position must have reason and enough information to decide intelligently about the content of the social contract. On the other hand, the participants cannot know vital details about their own circumstances, or they might institute rules by which they personally will unfairly benefit. They will probably not choose fairly, and so they will not be working toward the institution of justice in a well-ordered society, if they know in advance whether they will be rich or poor, black or white or Latin or Asian, male or female, and the like.

If social contractors know what their gender, race, social status, and so on will be in the society that the social contract puts in place, then they may act on behalf of their individual rational self-interests by promoting legislation to favor persons in those circumstances. If I am sitting around a table with other social contract negotiators, and I know that when the society whose rules I am helping to choose is functioning I will be a white man with a professional career, then I might be tempted, and as a self-interested agent I might have no other rational choice than, to prefer and try to advance laws within the social contract that afford special advantages to white male professionals. Similarly if I know that I am to be a black female artist, a Lithuanian carpenter, or that I will belong to any other particular demographic group. The use of such knowledge for personal self-interest is not compatible with the formation of a just society, or to the institution of a social contract that reflects the concept of justice as fairness. All relevant knowledge of personal circumstances on the part of imaginary social contractors must somehow be avoided in the original position if there is to be fairness for all persons under a social contract.

Rawls's idea for justice in the social contract is to allow contract deliberators full use of reason, but to conduct all decision making behind the veil of ignorance. All information about personal circumstances and social status in the resulting society is suspended during the period when they are considering the social contract. He holds that if the social contract is developed not only behind closed doors but behind the veil of ignorance, then negotiators acting rationally but without knowing vital facts about themselves will establish rules that are fair for anyone regardless of their personal circumstances. A rationally self-interested contract negotiator will not choose terms that would be unfair to any particular category of persons in the new society because for all they know beyond the veil of ignorance they themselves might belong to such a disadvantaged group. Justice is guaranteed by the social contract provided its negotiators decide on its principles rationally behind the veil of ignorance.

METHOD OF REFLECTIVE EQUILIBRIUM

Rawls offers a series of procedural remarks about the method of inquiry to be followed in developing his theory of justice. His methodology is interesting because it applies not only to his investigation of the principles of justice as fairness, or to political philosophy more generally, but to philosophical analysis in any subject area. The object of theory building according to Rawls is to achieve a state of *reflective equilibrium.*

We begin with considered convictions about the decision making that would need to take place in the original position in order to exemplify justice, from which we then project a theory of justice to explain the principles governing negotiations in the original position as we have described it. We then test and modify redescriptions of the original position in light of the theory, and test and modify the theoretical principles in light of revised descriptions of the original position, working back and forth with increasingly refined data and theory until we reach a steady state in which we are unable to make further improvements and believe that we have arrived at the best description of the original position and the best theory of justice in the social contract.

Reflective equilibrium is a progressive adjustment of convictions to theory and theory to convictions through critical reflection that finally attains stability. The end state is reached when new convictions do not cause us to change the theory, because the theory has already been perfected to such a point that it can explain the principles of justice by which decisions in the original position would be made. Rawls explains the concept of reflective equilibrium as it applies to understanding the requirements of justice in a social contract:

> In searching for the most favored description of this situation we work from both ends. We begin by describing it so that it represents generally shared and preferably weak conditions. We then see if these conditions are strong enough to yield a significant set of principles. If not, we look for further premises equally reasonable. But if so, and these principles match our considered convictions of justice, then so far well and good. But presumably there will be discrepancies. In this case we have a choice. We can either modify the account of the initial situation or we can revise our existing judgments, for even the judgments we take provisionally as fixed points are liable to revision. By going back and forth, sometimes altering the conditions of the contractual circumstances, at others withdrawing our judgments and conforming them to principle, I assume that eventually we shall find a description of the initial situation that both expresses reasonable conditions and yields principles which match our considered judgments duly pruned and adjusted. This state of affairs I refer to as reflective equilibrium. It is an equilibrium because at last our principles and judgments coincide; and it is reflective since we know to what principles our judgments conform and the premises of their derivation. (18)

He argues that it would be incorrect simply to read off the concept of justice from the principles we would propose in the original position. The problem is that we are likely to misunderstand our own sense of justice by misdescribing what we would choose in the original position unless or until we considered our options more completely in light of a reasonable concept of justice. If we merely try to imagine our participation in helping to design a social contract in lieu of any critical consideration of a working theory of justice, then we may arrive at different ideas about what we would or would not decide. He introduces the problem in general terms before specifying how our judgments about the principles of justice might be distorted in the absence of a provisional theory of justice. If Rawls is correct, then it is not enough merely to imagine what we would do in the original position unless our judgment is informed by reflecting on the implications of an initially plausible concept of justice. Reflective equilibrium is indispensable in arriving at a correct description of the principles we would choose in the original situation, according to Rawls:

> I now turn to the notion of reflective equilibrium. The need for this idea arises as follows. According to the provisional aim of moral philosophy, one might say that justice as fairness is the hypothesis that the principles which would be chosen in the original position are identical with those that match our considered judgments and so these principles describe our sense of justice. But this interpretation is clearly oversimplified. In describing our sense of justice an allowance must be made for the likelihood that considered judgments are no doubt subject to certain irregularities and distortions despite the fact that they are rendered under favorable circumstances. (42)

Rawls does not say exactly how determining our judgments in the original position might be distorted in the absence of a working definition of the concept of justice. It is reasonable to suppose, however, that anyone in that position will need some kind of guidelines, in the form of an approximate concept of justice, even to get started. We must know that justice is not the same kind of thing as courage or logical consistency or average velocity. By the same token, it also appears reasonable to hold that being in possession of a working definition of the concept of justice, especially if it is not completely correct, is also likely to produce distortions in describing the decisions that we think we would make in the original position in contemplating the rules for a social contract. We may tend to overlook contrary evidence that does not fit into the concepts we already have in hand but that could otherwise help us to arrive at a more correct theory.

Rawls does not address this criticism, but it is easy to guess what he might say in support of reflective equilibrium. He would probably admit that such obstacles to recognizing or taking relevant evidence into account could result from the provisional acceptance of a preliminary theory of justice. Nevertheless, he would insist that the difficulties are inevitable and that the method of reflective equilibrium remains the best and only remedy for potential distortions as we work our way toward a more correct analysis. If we do not enter the process of inquiry equipped with a working theory of justice, as we develop our considered convictions about the original position, in effect making use of the first stage of the method of reflective equilibrium, then we cannot hope to arrive at a correct understanding of the concept of justice. The distortions that can occur in either case, operating with or without a tentative analysis of the concept of justice, can only be corrected by seeing the method out, considering redescriptions of the original situation and the principles of justice that best explain it, working back and forth, just as Rawls says, until reflective equilibrium is achieved. He continues:

> When a person is presented with an intuitively appealing account of his sense of justice (one, say, which embodies various reasonable and natural presumptions), he may well revise his judgments to conform to its principles even though the theory does not fit his existing judgments exactly. He is especially likely to do this if he can find an explanation for the deviations which undermines his confidence in his original judgments and if the conception presented yields a judgment which he finds he can now accept. From the standpoint of moral theory, the best account of a person's sense of justice is not the one which fits his judgments prior to his examining any conception of justice, but rather the one which matches his judgments in reflective equilibrium. As we have seen, this state is one reached after a person has weighed various proposed conceptions and he has either revised his judgments to accord with one of them or held fast to his initial convictions (and the corresponding conception). (42–43)

The outcome of the method of reflective equilibrium as applied to the problem of understanding the principles of justice has two components. Rawls explains these as follows:

> The theory of justice may be divided into two main parts: (1) an interpretation of the initial situation and a formulation of the various principles available for choice there, and (2) an argument establishing which of these principles would in fact be adopted. (47)

To interpret the original situation is already to commit ourselves to a particular way of thinking about the nature of justice. As long as we continue to think reflectively and critically about the original situation and the principles of justice its best explanation seems to require, Rawls believes that we can eventually arrive at the truth. If we cannot do so in this way, following the method of reflective equilibrium, which is also the mode of scientific and other fields of philosophical inquiry, how can we ever hope to do so? We begin with an idea of what is meant by the concept of justice, and of what we would do in the original situation. Then we zigzag back and forth between improvements and refinements of each, until reflective equilibrium is reached. We will then have attained stability in our reflections for which no further adjustments are required, and we can congratulate ourselves on having discovered a correct theory of justice.

TWO PRINCIPLES OF JUSTICE

With the method of reflective equilibrium in place, Rawls begins a two-part process of describing the original position and the principles of justice guiding the decisions of a social contract negotiator in the original position. Reflecting on how he imagines he would make the rules for a well-ordered society, Rawls concludes that two principles of justice emerge. He does not offer an argument, but simply announces that he believes the principles are likely to be accepted by social contract negotiators in the original position. The principles are first previewed in general terms:

> I now state in a provisional form the two principles of justice that I believe would be agreed to in the original position. The first formulation of these principles is tentative. As we go on I shall consider several formulations and approximate step

by step the final statement to be given much later. I believe that doing this allows the exposition to proceed in a natural way. (52)

He next offers alternative statements of the two principles. The principles are meant to answer the two purposes of a concept of justice, as he has previously explained. They concern, respectively, the assignment of rights and obligations and the distribution of social goods. He states:

> First: each person is to have an equal right to the most extensive scheme of equal basic liberties compatible with a similar scheme of liberties for others.
> Second: social and economic inequalities are to be arranged so that they are both (a) reasonably expected to be to everyone's advantage, and (b) attached to positions and offices open to all.
>
> Thus we distinguish between the aspects of the social system that define and secure the equal basic liberties and the aspects that specify and establish social and economic inequalities. Now it is essential to observe that the basic liberties are given by a list of such liberties. Important among these are political liberty (the right to vote and to hold public office) and freedom of speech and assembly; liberty of conscience and freedom of thought; freedom of the person, which includes freedom from psychological oppression and physical assault and dismemberment (integrity of the person); the right to hold personal property and freedom from arbitrary arrest and seizure as defined by the concept of the rule of law. These liberties are to be equal by the first principle. (53)

Rawls identifies two important principles of justice corresponding to the two functions of just social institutions. Both have to do with an underlying commitment to some form of basic equality in the assignment of rights and responsibilities, and equal opportunity for all members of a society to acquire social goods.

The two principles agree with the way we ordinarily think about justice in the sense of fairness that Rawls advances. It is another matter, however, to understand how we are supposed to be able to see that these principles of equality and equal access are those that would be accepted in the original position. Why should we agree with Rawls that fairness is the kind of justice we can expect to prevail in the original position? Rawls merely reports his belief that this is the principle that would be accepted, and we may believe it too, but what is the philosophical justification for such a belief? The only reply that Rawls can make is to say that the conclusion is the result of reflective equilibrium. Again, this may well be true; but in trying to decide whether Rawls has correctly interpreted the requirements of the original position, we would need to consider every step made in pursuing the method until it reaches reflective equilibrium. Rawls, unfortunately, does not provide this information, so we cannot track or critically evaluate his reasoning.

In explaining the second principle of justice, having to do with the allocation of social goods, Rawls argues that two subconditions are required. He distinguishes between two aspects of the distribution of things of value in a well-ordered society, including wealth and social positions and offices. He explains the distinction in this way:

> The second principle applied, in the first approximation, to the distribution of income and wealth and to the design of organizations that make use of differences in authority and responsibility. While the distribution of wealth and income need

not be equal, it must be to everyone's advantage, and at the same time, positions of authority and responsibility must be accessible to all. One applies the second principle by holding positions open, and then, subject to this constraint, arranges social and economic inequalities so that everyone benefits. (53)

Rawls gestures again toward traditional American economic ideals that a Marxist philosopher or social activist might describe as *bourgeois values*. This is not necessarily a bad or philosophically unjustified thing, but it raises questions about whether Rawls's principles are independently implied by a correct method, or whether he has chosen or perhaps subconsciously manipulates the method of reflective equilibrium in order to support a previously accepted outcome. Rawls unsurprisingly advocates a principle of justice for distributing wealth, offices, and positions of authority in a society that reflects ideals of American society and societies influenced by the same kinds of values that have shaped American life.

When Rawls says that wealth should be distributed in such a way that while it need not be equal it must be to the advantage of all, it is unclear at first how there could be a difference between the two. How is it to my advantage to have less wealth than another person? Rawls does not explain, and the only conceivable answer is that the method of acquiring wealth in a well-ordered society according to Rawls's second principle must be advantageous to all even if it does not result in an equal distribution of wealth. How can this be? The natural conclusion appears to be that persons in the society have in principle equal possibilities of acquiring wealth, and if they do not in fact acquire equal amounts of wealth, it is because of differences in their natural abilities, individual motivation and drive, willingness to succeed, and luck, things that are in any case not in the jurisdiction or control of social institutions, and hence not a matter of social justice or injustice. Even less successful members of a society indirectly benefit from the competitive spirit that prevails in the pursuit of social goods and from improvements in the general way of life resulting from increased even if unequally distributed wealth.

Such an argument makes it unclear whether Rawls really has two distinct principles of justice, or whether both principles ultimately come down to the same idea of assuring equal access and equal opportunity. The principles interpret an ideal of justice as fairness by proposing a way in which equality can be achieved in the distribution of social goods. Rights and responsibilities are equally available to all in principle, as are social goods of wealth and social position. It is only a matter of each person entering into fair competition and earning his or her legitimate share. When conflicts arise, when some persons try to impose unfair practices, discrimination, cheating, misrepresentation, and the like, then social institutions are supposed ideally to intervene in order to prevent unfairness or redress injustices, if and when they occur.

If it is understood that there is a right for all members of a society to compete fairly and openly for the wealth and positions available in a society, then it might be possible in another way to reduce Rawls's two principles to a single principle conferring equal rights and responsibilities. Rawls again does not offer this kind of simplification, although it is in some ways an attractive possibility to think of justice as fairness and fairness as equality of opportunity as one among other social rights equally available to all persons in a just and well-ordered society. If this is what Rawls's suggestion comes to, then we have condensed his position to a more convenient form in which to assess whether it conforms to a preferred concept of justice and whether it is a principle that would be adopted by rational social contract negotiators in the original position.

For one thing, can Rawls plausibly argue that it is to the advantage of society as a whole that there be a *de facto* unequal distribution of wealth and social offices? He can do so only if it is true that all members of a society benefit through improvements resulting from open competition in a free economic market. He explicitly assumes such an economic context as background to the concept of society, the preconditions for description of the original position, and the realization of the social contract. It is better for all, it might be said in support of Rawls's two principles of justice, not for wealth to be simply distributed equally, but for there to be equal opportunity for all persons in a society to freely apply their skills in order to try to acquire whatever offices or goods that they choose and for which their abilities may entitle them.

Society as a whole benefits from the practice of justice in this sense of the word, because the most qualified persons ideally are those who will fill the vital positions and provide whatever merchandise and services are needed and desired. Having the best quality and availability of such goods is to everyone's advantage, regardless of their relative wealth and social status. The system provides an incentive for active participation in the economy by holding out the possibility of acquiring wealth and other social goods through intelligence and industry, protected by institutions designed to safeguard justice as fair practice. An advantage of this interpretation of Rawls's two principles is that it provides a more realistic economic model that does not simply assume that wealth already exists and is available for distribution to the members of a society according to one set of principles or another, but better understands how wealth is actually created by the intelligence and hard work of a society's members. The question is not simply how preexistent wealth is most justly and advantageously to be handed out, as from the vaults of a treasury, but how wealth is to be made by unleashing human creativity, how offices and social positions should be invented, and how they actually evolve, according to a preferred standard of justice.

All this again may well be true. The philosophical question that remains is how such conclusions are to be justified by sound argument. Rawls attempts a reduction of the two principles; or, rather, an identification of a single underlying principle on which they depend. He now adds:

> The two principles are rather specific in their content, and their acceptance rests on certain assumptions that I must eventually try to explain and justify. For the present, it should be observed that these principles are a special case of a more general conception of justice that can be expressed as follows.
>
> > All social values—liberty and opportunity, income and wealth, and the social bases of self-respect—are to be distributed equally unless an unequal distribution of any, or all, of these values is to everyone's advantage.
>
> Injustice, then, is simply inequalities that are not to the benefit of all. Of course, this conception is extremely vague and requires interpretation. (54)

Rawls concentrates on equality as an interpretation of justice as fairness. He does not simply define fairness as actual equality in the distribution of social advantages, but qualifies the equality of benefits that are supposed to be available in a well-ordered society, conditionalizing the possibility of their equal possession. The condition is all-important, however, because it is supposed to justify the inequalities that actually exist. There is to be a precisely equal distribution of whatever goods are available in a society, Rawls explains, *unless* an unequal distribution turns out to be to everyone's advantage. The principle is clear; what is less clear is whether the principle is correct.

The final sentence in the above passage promises further analysis of related concepts connected with the theory of justice, which Rawls proceeds to provide. We can anticipate several kinds of difficulties for this phase of Rawls's analysis. It appears that Rawls overstates the assumption under which equality of distribution agrees with the concept of justice as fairness. He requires an equal distribution unless an unequal distribution is to everyone's advantage. Even if this is intended as a description of a principle guiding the distribution of social goods under ideal circumstances, the condition seems too strong. Should there not be conditions in which unequal distributions of goods are socially justified that do not depend on resulting benefits being conferred on every member of society? Why would it not be good enough if a majority or perhaps a substantial majority, however this notion is to be applied, were to benefit, along something more like utilitarian lines, taking into account the greatest good for the greatest number? If not, we need to see an argument from Rawls to justify why such an extreme limitation is necessary in order to satisfy the requirements of justice as fairness. Modifying Rawls's principle in this way would obviously make his philosophy indistinguishable from utilitarian consequentialism, which he does not want. The question is: Why should the utilitarian concept of justice not be accepted, and why does Rawls resist adopting a version of utilitarianism?

Another, deeper, more conceptual, and, so to speak, philosophical objection to Rawls's qualification of equality in the implementation of justice as fairness is that he has yet to establish any conceptual or causal linkage between justice and the advantages of unequal distributions of goods for all or even a majority of society's members. What is the connection supposed to be? How do we know in advance that the demands of justice are not incompatible with securing advantages for every person or even a large number of persons in society? Kant is unimpressed with considerations of advantage, inclination, or the consequences of actions in deciding what the categorical imperative absolutely requires as a moral duty of all rational agents. Some commentators, such as Sidgwick, have emphasized the extent to which deontologists are indifferent to the consequences of an action in evaluating its morality by saying that according to a deontological ethics such as Kant's, we should adopt the attitude that "the consequences be damned," and concern ourselves only with the fulfillment of unconditional moral duty. What can Rawls say in response to such deontological objections, given the similarities between some aspects of his theory of social justice and Kant's concern for the rights of all rational beings?

At the very least, it appears that Rawls should not be regarded as a true Kantian in his theory of justice, since Kant makes the highest principle of moral decision making the unconditional categorical imperative. Rawls, by contrast, in explicating the presupposition of the two principles of justice he believes would be invoked by social contract negotiators in the original position, makes the underlying concept of equality conditional on the universal advantage or disadvantage among the members of a society. He also believes it is necessary to consider the advantages accruing to all or a majority of those members of a society affected by a contemplated distribution of social goods. Rawls's position, despite his Kantian-sounding rhetoric, regards justice as an abstract moral-social ideal whose requirements must sometimes be compromised for the sake of other conditionally equal or occasionally mitigating moral and social ideals, precisely as Mill says.

LIBERTY, EQUALITY, AND DISTRIBUTIVE JUSTICE

Rawls explains the relation between equality and advantage. He disambiguates several related meanings that might be confusingly attached to these key terms, displaying the senses that might be attributed to them in a chart. The ambiguities are unpacked as four interpretations of the two principles of justice he has already explained:

> I have already mentioned that since the phrases "everyone's advantage" and "equally open to all" are ambiguous, both parts of the second principle have two natural senses. Because these senses are independent of one another, the principle has four possible meanings. Assuming that the first principle of equal liberty has the same sense throughout, we then have four interpretations of the two principles. These are indicated in the table below.

| "Equally Open" | "Everyone's Advantage" | |
	PRINCIPLE OF EFFICIENCY	DIFFERENCE PRINCIPLE
Equality as careers open to talents	System of Natural Liberty	Natural Aristocracy
Equality as equality of fair opportunity	Liberal Equality	Democratic Equality

> (57)

The terms Rawls employs in distinguishing these senses of equality and of what contributes to "everyone's advantage" are not well-established in philosophical parlance, nor are they immediately clear in their own right; so we must consult his accompanying explanation. He explains what he means by the phrases "principle of efficiency," "difference principle," "natural liberty," "natural aristocracy," "liberal equality," and "democratic equality," without which we cannot fully grasp the relation he believes holds between equality and advantage. He offers this further explanation:

> The first interpretation (in either sequence) I shall refer to as the system of natural liberty. In this rendering the first part of the second principle is understood as the principle of efficiency adjusted so as to apply to institutions or, in this case, to the basic structure of society; and the second part is understood as an open social system in which, to use the traditional phrase, careers are open to talents. I assume in all interpretations that the first principle of equal liberty is satisfied and that the economy is roughly a free market system, although the means of production may or may not be privately owned. The system of natural liberty as-

serts, then, that a basic structure satisfying the principle of efficiency and in which positions are open to those able and willing to strive for them will lead to a just distribution. Assigning rights and duties in this way is thought to give a scheme which allocates wealth and income, authority and responsibility, in a fair way whatever this allocation turns out to be. The doctrine includes an important element of pure procedural justice which is carried over to the other interpretations. (57–58)

Rawls's commitment to a "roughly" free market system of economy is indicated for a second time in this passage. We might wonder what is meant by a market being "roughly" free, and whether and how a market economy could possibly be free, roughly or otherwise, if it does not presuppose the private ownership of the means of production, especially when we are considering the possibilities for justice in any society.

The advantages that are supposed to accrue to everyone under the two interpretations of the equality of open availability of offices and positions and other social goods support the efficient functioning of a society under competitive market forces. The economy of the society is meant to function according to the free and therefore predictably unequal exercise of the natural abilities of its members, allowing "equality" in one sense of the word to be interpreted as fair or equal opportunity. There is then a natural aristocracy or aristocracy of talent, a hierarchy of persons of ability determined by their intelligence and skills and other natural endowments in open competition for things of value.

Rawls assumes that allowing equal opportunity among persons to compete for opportunities and social goods will maximize efficiency in the society as a whole and in that way contribute to everyone's advantage. The idea of fair and equal opportunity in turn is described as affording *liberal equality* under the category of the *principle of efficiency*, which are not particularly descriptive labels, and *democratic equality*, under the category of the difference principle. It is not obvious why these terms could not simply be reversed and carry the stipulative distinctions Rawls appears to assign them with equal validity. Nor is it clear in what sense the difference principle, marking two ways in which persons can be regarded as different, say, because of differences in their natural abilities, intelligence, and ambition and skill, and yet have the sort of equality of fair opportunity that is often associated with a liberal democracy, are supposed to be to everyone's advantage. Rawls rejects what he calls the "system of natural liberty" in favor of democratic equality. There is in any case a distinction to be made out between these senses of ways in which equality is or is not extended to all members of a society and ways in which advantages can result for all or a majority of a society's members.

Rawls illustrates the idea of procedural justice as a way of dividing up already available goods so as to assure fair distribution. The method is a simple one, suggested by a common practice of siblings around the dinner table who do not want to be cheated in the division of a sweet. Rawls distinguishes between *perfect* and *imperfect procedural justice*, demonstrating perfect procedural justice in the matter of sharing the pieces of a cake. The idea is that the person who divides the cake is the last to choose a piece. This simple example embodies a great deal of practical wisdom, which Rawls exploits in explaining the nature of justice as fairness from a procedural point of view throughout his treatise. The person who is to divide the cake, assuming that he or she is rational and wants a fair slice, will try to the utmost to make all of the pieces precisely of the same size, on the expectation that otherwise when it comes time to take a piece, the one remaining after all the others have been chosen will be smaller than the ones selected first. This is a good, reasonable, and fair procedure for managing the practical task of cutting a cake and distributing the slices. As Rawls explains:

> These considerations suggest the idea of treating the question of distributive shares as a matter of pure procedural justice. The intuitive idea is to design the social system so that the outcome is just whatever it happens to be, at least so long as it is within a certain range. The notion of pure procedural justice is best understood by a comparison with perfect and imperfect procedural justice. To illustrate the former, consider the simplest case of fair division. A number of men are to divide a cake: assuming that the fair division is an equal one, which procedure, if any, will give this outcome? Technicalities aside, the obvious solution is to have one man divide the cake and get the last piece, the others being allowed their pick before him. He will divide the cake equally, since in this way he assures for himself the largest share possible. (74)

He distinguishes two aspects of perfect procedural justice as exemplified by the cut-and-choose-last method of dividing a cake. There must be a criterion for division of the goods in question that is independent of the practical method of distribution, and there must be a procedure by which the fair distribution of the divided goods is guaranteed. He regards perfect procedural justice as the exception rather than the rule in practical affairs, arguing that its ideal in fact is seldom realized:

> This example illustrates the two characteristic features of perfect procedural justice. First, there is an independent criterion for what is a fair division, a criterion defined separately from and prior to the procedure which is to be followed. And second, it is possible to devise a procedure that is sure to give the desired outcome. Of course, certain assumptions are made here, such as that the man selected can divide the cake equally, wants as large a piece as he can get, and so on. But we can ignore these details. The essential thing is that there is an independent standard for deciding which outcome is just and a procedure guaranteed to lead to it. Pretty clearly, perfect procedural justice is rare, if not impossible, in cases of much practical interest. (74)

Administering justice as fairness requires a proper ideal that in practice can at best be approached, but seldom if ever attained. The methods that must be adopted in order to sustain justice in a society are certain to be more complex than the technique of having one person divide a cake and then being the last to choose a piece. Rawls emphasizes a requirement that must be observed in order to institute justice as fairness, regardless of its practical mode of implementation, that reflects the ideal standard of justice to which a well-ordered society in Rawls's opinion ought to aspire. This is the principle that there exists a way of determining what would be a just distribution of goods that is independent of the procedure by which the division and distribution is accomplished. If there is no independent method of judging what would be a just distribution, then there is no reason to expect that the procedure followed will be fair. The situation is then equivalent to one in which a person who divides the cake into pieces of any size is also allowed to choose any piece. An agent motivated by rational self-interest, as Rawls and social contract theory generally assumes, is then likely if not certain to take the whole cake or at least to make a significantly uneven division and grab the largest piece, contrary to the requirements of fair practice in matters of distributive justice.

NATURAL LOTTERY AND FAIR ACCESS TO SOCIAL GOODS

The members of even a perfectly just society cannot be expected to have an exactly equal distribution of talents and abilities. Rawls refers to this uneven distribution of natural qualities as a *natural lottery*. The idea is that at conception, as far as the theory of justice is concerned, each person is awarded by sheer chance a particular endowment of intelligence and skills, along with other genetic properties such as hair and eye and skin color, dispositions for health or disease, and the like. It is as though at conception the members of a society receive different natural benefits in the form of a lottery ticket or spin of the wheel in a game of chance.

This is a reasonable way to think about the morally indifferent natural distribution of abilities in a population. The random attribution of natural abilities among human beings in a society is a logically contingent consequence of natural variation within the species. There is no logical or causal necessity for such differences to occur in the members of a society. We do not discover such unequal natural endowments of abilities among nonhuman social animals, such as ants or bees or other species. Differences in endowments of abilities are not uniquely human, but they are characteristic of the wide variations in our genetic type. There is nevertheless no logical necessity why human beings should not all be born with precisely the same amount of intelligence, physical strength, ambition, and other qualities and abilities. If that were true, then Rawls's concept of the natural lottery would be inapplicable, and there would be no basis in nature for inequalities in human society, and hence no moral justification, at least according to Rawls's theory of justice, for an unequal distribution of social goods.

As things are, there is a reasonable basis for supposing that the social goods available to members of a society be differentially distributed among a society's members, just as Rawls maintains. By taking such contingent facts about human societies into account in constructing his theory of justice, Rawls interestingly diverges again from Kant's deontological concept of justice and moral rights. A moral theory for Kant is supposed to be absolutely unconditional and purified of any contingent empirical factors, so that it applies in principle even to nonhuman rational agents. A nonhuman rational agent, such as an angel or extraterrestrial alien, also has moral rights and obligations, according to Kant, but for all we know need not be subject to anything like the human differences in natural intelligence and ability.

Rawls concludes that as he has now defined the concept of justice as fairness it is not necessarily entailed that persons who begin with advantages over others in the natural lottery are morally entitled to the social benefits that result when such individuals enter a competitive free market to win out over others in the acquisition of social goods. The only consideration that Rawls believes makes it morally justified from the standpoint of justice as fairness for persons with competitive advantages conferred upon them by the natural lottery to achieve greater economic and social success is if unequal distributions of natural and earned or otherwise acquired benefits contribute in one way or another to the advantages of every member of society. He maintains:

> Thus it is incorrect that individuals with greater natural endowments and the superior character that has made their development possible have a right to a cooperative scheme that enables them to obtain even further benefits in ways that do not contribute to the advantages of others. We do not deserve our place in the distribution of native endowments, any more than we deserve our initial starting place in society. That we deserve the superior character that enables us to make the effort to cultivate our abilities is also problematic; for such character depends in good part upon fortunate family and social circumstances in early life for which we can claim no credit. The notion of desert does not apply here. To be sure, the more advantaged have a right to their natural assets, as does everyone else; this right is covered by the first principle under the basic liberty protecting the integrity of the person. And so the more advantaged are entitled to whatever they can acquire in accordance with the rules of a fair system of social cooperation. Our problem is how this scheme, the basic structure of society, is to be designed. From a suitably general standpoint, the difference principle appears acceptable to both the more advantaged and the less advantaged individual. (89)

This is an important qualification. It implies among other things that there is a philosophical justification in terms of Rawls's concept of justice as fairness for the unequal distribution of wealth in a society, a principled defense of the bourgeois status quo, provided that it can reasonably be argued that permitting such inequalities confers positive advantages on all members of a society. The justification for justice as fairness, given the natural inequalities of the natural lottery and their predictable consequences in the competition for social goods, depends at least in part in Rawls's account on the contingent contribution that such unequal distributions of goods can be interpreted as making for the greater good of every member of society.

The arguments needed to justify individual inequalities in terms of benefits accruing to all members of society will not necessarily convince persons who are economically and in other ways disadvantaged by comparison with more fortunate persons. The conclusion is also questionable because of its apparent failure to live up to Rawls's requirement that there be a definite independent method of dividing up and distributing social goods in accord with the two principles of justice. The independence of the method is sacrificed if, as Rawls now seems to allow, it is made to depend on whatever reasoning is required to establish that a particular social inequality contributes to the greater good of every person belonging to a society.

There is room for significant and sincere disagreement on such issues. If there is no effective method for resolving differences of opinion about the advantages that do or do not benefit all members of a society, then the method of dividing and distributing social goods in such a society may neither be independent of those involved in the controversy who may stand to benefit or be harmed by one distribution procedure or another, nor will it be effective in guaranteeing that a fair distribution can be made. The difference principle and Rawls's second principle of justice require that any distributive inequality benefit the least advantaged group—but by how much, in comparison with the significantly more fortunate members of a society, in order for the interests of justice to be served? The problem affects the question of whether a society adopting Rawls's standards can truly be well-ordered, if the method of determining rights and distributing social goods depends on general agreement about the conception of justice and whether the definition of justice as fairness is actually exemplified by a society's institutions.

MYTH OF THE ORIGINAL POSITION

It is appropriate now to return as Rawls does to the problem of describing the original position. We must reconsider the principles a social contract negotiator would adopt in the task of choosing rules for the constitution of an ideally just society. We follow Rawls's method of reflective equilibrium as he moves back and forth between descriptions and refinements of the original position and the principles of a theory of justice. He refers alternatively to the original position also as the initial situation, but has in mind the same imaginary or purely hypothetical organizational meeting of the founders of a society who assemble to decide upon the rules by which a society is to be constituted. He offers insights into the reasoning in which social designers might engage:

> The intuitive idea of justice as fairness is to think of the first principles of justice as themselves the object of an original agreement in a suitably defined initial situation. These principles are those which rational persons concerned to advance their interests would accept in this position of equality to settle the basic terms of their association. It must be shown, then, that the two principles of justice are the solution for the problem of choice presented by the original position. In order to do this, one must establish that, given the circumstances of the parties, and their knowledge, beliefs, and interests, an agreement on these principles is the best way for each person to secure his ends in view of the alternatives available. (102–3)

The original position offers a unique opportunity to study the principles of justice being implemented in their purest form. The principles will not be disguised by other considerations, especially if negotiations take place behind the veil of ignorance, which Rawls introduces and subsequently examines in greater detail. Considering the requirements of perfect procedural justice as a general model, Rawls implies that the ideal hypothetical conditions of the original position are to exemplify in different more complicated ways the same criterion of justice as fairness as that found in the cake-sharing scenario. He emphasizes the original position as lacking a historical or anthropological basis and that it is meant to describe a purely hypothetical situation in which the concept of justice can be discerned in bold relief:

> It is clear, then, that the original position is a purely hypothetical situation. Nothing resembling it need ever take place, although we can by deliberately following the constraints it expresses simulate the reflections of the parties. The conception of the original position is not intended to explain human conduct except insofar as it tries to account for our moral judgments and helps to explain our having a sense of justice. Justice as fairness is a theory of our moral sentiments as mani-

fested by our considered judgments in reflective equilibrium. These sentiments presumably affect our thought and action to some degree. So while the conception of the original position is part of the theory of conduct, it does not follow at all that there are actual situations that resemble it. What is necessary is that the principles that would be accepted play the requisite part in our moral reasoning and conduct. (104)

Rawls admits that the theory of justice as fairness is only one among many social contract theories. He does not consider the possibility that justice as in Mill and more especially in Nietzsche need have nothing at all to do with a social contract. He assumes throughout the inquiry that all societies, or the only ones worth including, have at least an implicit social contract, and that the ideal circumstances under which a society arrives at its social contract provide the best or even the only method of clarifying the concept of justice. This is a premise that we must seriously question, even if we end up agreeing with Rawls about its importance. The example of Nietzsche's radically different view of justice by and for the powerful, whatever we think of its morality, provides a useful basis for comparison. Nietzsche presupposes no social contract context for the institution of a system of justice by the powerful for their own exclusive benefit, and as such indicates that it is possible in principle to define a concept of justice without making reference to a social contract. Rawls argues that a theory of justice formulated in terms of the original position in social contract negotiations offers the best explanation of considered judgments in reflective equilibrium:

[T]here are many different contract theories. Justice as fairness is but one of these. But the question of justification is settled, as far as it can be, by showing that there is one interpretation of the initial situation which best expresses the conditions that are widely thought reasonable to impose on the choice of principles yet which, at the same time, leads to a conception that characterizes our considered judgments in reflective equilibrium. This most favored, or standard, interpretation I shall refer to as the original position. (105)

Rawls's way of understanding the concept of justice is indebted throughout to the social contract model and its commitment to an initial situation. We are supposed to begin with an idealized initial situation beyond the veil of ignorance as the first step in the method of reflective equilibrium, and finally arrive at what he calls the original position as a description of the rational outcome of deliberations about the best social contract for a society to adopt.

Rawls sees a connection between the concept of justice as fairness and Kant's doctrine of the categorical imperative and kingdom of ends. There are several ways in which Rawls's theory of justice is non-Kantian, and, arguably, in some respects, even anti-Kantian. Points of contact and positive comparison nevertheless also exist between Rawls and Kant. Kant says repeatedly that his political philosophy follows in the footsteps of Rousseau, who also accepts a version of social contract theory. Rawls identifies another similarity with Kant's ethics in the fact that the concept of justice as fairness depends on the *publicity condition*. The publicity condition requires that the concept of justice by which a well-ordered society is governed be publicly articulated and generally accepted as the guiding principle of the society's principal social institutions. The universal adoption of the concept of justice that determines the well-ordered society according to the publicity condition Rawls likens to the universaliz-ability of the categorical imperative and the unqualified respect for all rational beings as ends in themselves that precludes their being treated merely as means to another end in the Kantian kingdom of ends:

> The point of the publicity condition is to have the parties evaluate conceptions of justice as publicly acknowledged and fully effective moral constitutions of social life. The publicity condition is clearly implicit in Kant's doctrine of the categorical imperative insofar as it requires us to act in accordance with principles that one would be willing as a rational being to enact as law for a kingdom of ends. He thought of this kingdom as an ethical commonwealth, as it were, which has such moral principles for its public charter. (115)

Is Rawls right that the ideal well-ordered society is like Kant's kingdom of ends by virtue of the publicity condition? Both imaginary societies are fictional projections of a preferred moral standard. The kingdom of ends in Kant's ethics involves an unqualified equality of moral respect for all rational beings regardless of the particular societies to which they belong, while in Rawls's well-ordered society the first principle of justice allocates moral rights unqualifiedly to all its members. It is only in the second principle of justice, concerning the fair distribution of social goods and material wealth, that Rawls makes equality conditional on the conferring of advantages on every member of the society, and otherwise tolerates inequalities.

There are other important differences between Kant and Rawls. Among the major disanalogies is the fact that in Kant's kingdom of ends it is enough to satisfy the requirements of moral respect that no rational agent be treated merely as a means to an end. For Rawls, on the contrary, much more is expected, depending on the specific rights and obligations conferred on all the members of a well-ordered society. There is furthermore no guarantee that the principles of justice adopted by the social contract negotiators in Rawls's theory will coincide with the moral maxims that can be willed to be followed by every rational agent according to Kant's categorical imperative. Rawls's comparison of his theory of justice with Kant's moral and social-political philosophy does not imply that the social contract negotiators in the original position will adopt all and only those principles that can be willed to be universally accepted by all rational beings. The reason is that some of the universalizable moral maxims that are morally binding according to Kant's categorical imperative concern matters of individual rather than social morality, and as such presumably would never come up for consideration by social contract negotiators.

Additionally, it is not clear that Kant's categorical imperative in its application to social morality will necessarily command as moral duties the kinds of rules for the governance of a society that Rawls's social contract negotiators will consider. Rawls's negotiators might decide that the society they are planning should have two houses of legislation or three. Both possibilities, among unlimitedly many others, are conceivable as outcomes of the decision-making process in the original position that would result in different kinds of perfectly just well-ordered societies in Rawls's sense of the word. It would be excessive, however, to conclude that for Kant in the kingdom of ends either one of these choices, or for that matter the decision whether to have a legislative body or not, as opposed to lawmaking on the part of an enlightened prince, would be dictated as a moral duty by the categorical imperative, or that one of these choices would be morally required by virtue of the alternatives being excluded because of considerations of moral disrespect, because they amount to treating persons merely as means to an end rather than as ends in themselves.

Rawls's social contract negotiators are supposed to regard the principles of justice as absolute. Insofar as we limit consideration only to the standards of justice that Rawls expects to emerge in the original position and not the specific social mechanisms by which a new society is constituted there are more positive analogies between these general principles and the categorical imperative than in Rawls's well-ordered society and Kant's kingdom of ends. Rawls argues that the principles of justice that can be extracted from the decision making of social contract negotiators in the original position under the veil of ignorance must be pure and general like the categorical imperative, in that they supercede whatever laws and customs, cultural practices, and the like exist in a precursor society. He explains:

> The parties are to assess the system of principles as the final court of appeal in practical reasoning. There are no higher standards to which arguments in support of claims can be addressed; reasoning successfully from these principles is conclusive. If we think in terms of the fully general theory which has principles for all the virtues, then such a theory specifies the totality of relevant considerations and their appropriate weights, and its requirements are decisive. They override the demands of law and custom, and of social rules generally. We are to arrange and respect social institutions as the principles of right and justice direct. (116–17)

If the primary concern of the social contract is to institute principles of justice and moral rights, then, as Rawls later remarks, their decision making must also be indifferent to prudential and egoistic considerations. He assumes but does not try to prove that these factors are irrelevant to or even incompatible with the task of designing a social contract that above all implements the highest principles of justice. Why this should be so is unexamined by Rawls, and we know from the radical counterexample of Nietzsche that the concept of justice is not inherently or logically necessarily irrelevant to or incompatible with self-interests or the pursuit of prudential values. This suggests that an argument is required to uphold the pronouncements Rawls makes on this position, which he does not try to provide. Instead, he posits that:

> Conclusions from these principles also override considerations of prudence and self-interest. This does not mean that these principles insist upon self-sacrifice; for in drawing up the conception of right the parties take their interests into account as best they can. The claims of personal prudence are already given an appropriate weight within the full system of principles. The complete scheme is final in that when the course of practical reasoning it defines has reached its conclusion, the question is settled. The claims of existing social arrangements and of self-interest have been duly allowed for. We cannot at the end count them a second time because we do not like the result. (117)

How is it supposed to be impossible for social contract negotiators in the original position to lay down principles for the well-ordered society that reflect a Nietzschean rather than Kantian conception of justice? The answer undoubtedly depends in large part on the way Rawls assumes the veil of ignorance will conceal from negotiators the social roles they are to play once the society is up and running. They will not know while they are considering the principles of the social contract whether they are to be rich or poor, male or female, gay or straight, or anything else about their eventual racial, ethnic, religious, or other demographic character, or, for that matter, anything about the level of intelligence or motivation, family background, or anything else about themselves that might make it possible for them to secure unfair advantages for themselves in the society that is to result.

If decision makers do not know whether they will be members of a powerful elite, then it would be irrational to institute a set of rules by which there is in the first place a nobility that holds control over the lives of disadvantaged persons. For all they know in the original position behind the veil of ignorance, they might turn out to belong to the underprivileged class. Rawls catalogs a number of distinct forms of egoism, and concludes that the principles of justice decided upon in the original position, while not necessarily involving self-sacrifice, can in any case be understood not to be objectionably egoistic or prudentially self-serving. He defends the original position against incursions of egoistic advantages:

> The generality condition eliminates both first-person dictatorship and the free-rider forms, since in each case a proper name, or pronoun, or a rigged definite description is needed, either to single out the dictator or to characterize the free-rider. Generality does not, however, exclude general egoism, for each person is allowed to do whatever, in his judgment, is most likely to further his own aims. The principle here can clearly be expressed in a perfectly general way. It is the ordering condition which renders general egoism inadmissible, for if everyone is authorized to advance his aims as he pleases, or if everyone ought to advance his own interests, competing claims are not ranked at all and the outcome is determined by force and cunning. (117)

A high level of generality in the statement of moral principles may appear to avoid the problem of egoistic self-interest and free-riders. By avoiding reference to individuals, laws and moral principles do not lend themselves to abuse by dictators or free-riders who want to benefit from the moral contributions of others without recognizing or fulfilling their fair share of the social contract.

This is much the same problem that we discussed in connection with Kant's universalizability requirement in applications of the categorical imperative, which we observed could best be avoided by requiring that moral maxims themselves be categorical in statement, precluding the possibility of making special exceptions for individuals. Rawls argues that generality is not enough to solve the difficulty, because it still allows general egoism to prevail. If everyone is encouraged by the law to pursue his or her own interests without restriction, then conflicts cannot be settled by ranking their claims to legitimacy according to a principle of justice, but only by violence and self-serving shrewdness, or "force and cunning."

If Rawls's social contract negotiators do not know what social role they are to fill in the resulting society, or their personal circumstances, so that they cannot make choices for the social contract that will benefit them individually, then they might decide to play their cards so conservatively that they do not permit any risk of disadvantage to themselves once the new society is instituted. While as rational agents they do not want to be unfairly treated, they might by the same reasoning not want to be underprivileged as a result of the natural lottery, and hence choose to implement a social policy for distributive justice according to which all social offices, positions, and goods, especially wealth, are dispensed equally. This sort of radical communistic social economy is evidently at odds with Rawls's commitment to free market competition, and is supposed to be precluded by the qualification on which he insists, whereby unequal distributions are morally justified or obligatory if they have the effect of contributing to the advantage of every member of society.

Philosophical justification that competition in a free market economy will necessarily be to the advantage of every member of society is conspicuously missing from Rawls's discussion. Perhaps he believes that such proof is extraneous to his central purpose of explaining that in its most general terms the ideal of justice that will constitute a well-ordered society. The efficiency of a free market in providing for the needs of a society is presumably not a matter of logical necessity, but at best logically contingent. If the veil of ignorance is drawn down, then it is also reasonable to assume that social contract negotiators will not know whether the particular society that results when their system of rules is realized will be the kind of society with the kinds of citizens under the kinds of circumstances in which free market competition will in fact turn out to be so efficient in providing social goods that the inequalities in the distribution of wealth that may actually result are not only tolerated but necessitated by the qualification Rawls places on the conception of justice as fairness.

This is especially true because whether or not free market competition turns out to be sufficiently efficient is in part, and no doubt in large part, a factor of the contingent psychological dispositions of the members of a society, of whether among other things they are such that they are able and willing to compete. It would seem that contingent facts about the psychology of a society's members cannot be known behind the veil of ignorance where social contract negotiations are supposed to take place, if social contract negotiators are sufficiently ignorant about themselves as not to know whether they are personally competitive. If they do not have enough self-knowledge to know whether they are going to be economically competitive, and not every rational person even in contemporary industrial societies chooses to be, then it is hard to imagine how the negotiators could possibly understand the concept well enough to know whether the population in the resulting society will be sufficiently economically competitive to make free market competition an efficient method by which the society can create and distribute its wealth. The benefits of an unequal distribution of social goods, we must recall, are supposed to extend to all members of the society in order to be justified on Rawls's criterion. What reason would social contract negotiators have behind the veil of ignorance to suppose that beyond the veil a competitive free market would confer such universal benefits on the resulting society as a whole?

It might be true in our world and our society in its history, as it happens to have developed, that free market competition is highly efficient. Inequalities in the actual distribution of social goods under such a social contract may then be permissible or even obligatory according to Rawls's second principle of justice, by virtue of offering advantages to every member of society that they would not otherwise enjoy. This, however, is information that is presumably concealed from social contract negotiators in the original position behind the veil of ignorance. There are numerous counterexamples of noncompetitive social communes in the history even of the United States to raise doubts about whether any given society, considered purely rationally from behind the veil of ignorance, would find it efficient to adopt a competitive free market economy to produce its goods, or to adopt a very different economic system in better accord with the intuitive concept of justice as fairness. It is time, therefore, to take a closer look at what Rawls means by the veil of ignorance, to verify the kinds of information that are supposed to be available to or excluded from the decision making of rational social contract negotiators in the original position, according to Rawls, as they design rules for a well-ordered society.

VEIL OF IGNORANCE

Rawls explains the veil of ignorance as a hypothetical way of thinking about the requirements of perfect procedural justice. Its purpose is to generalize the method of fairly dividing and sharing the pieces of a cake. It is impossible in practice to suspend knowledge of who and what we are as we consider the principles that we think it would be best to implement in a just society. Rawls rather describes the veil of ignorance as an ideal to which social contract negotiators might aspire in trying to attain a maximally personally and egoistically disinterested but still rational standpoint from which to consider the principles of justice in a well-ordered society. He now gives a more exact description of the veil of ignorance:

> The idea of the original position is to set up a fair procedure so that any principles agreed to will be just. The aim is to use the notion of pure procedural justice as a basis of theory. Somehow we must nullify the effects of specific contingencies which put men at odds and tempt them to exploit social and natural circumstances to their own advantage. Now in order to do this I assume that the parties are situated behind a veil of ignorance. They do not know how the various alternatives will affect their own particular case and they are obliged to evaluate principles solely on the basis of general considerations. (118)

All this seems reasonable, but leaves many questions unanswered. We have already considered the difficulty of exactly specifying the information available to social contract negotiators in the original position behind the veil of ignorance. One potential area of dispute concerns the question of whether or not contract negotiators behind the veil of ignorance can be well enough informed about the resulting society to know whether or not the conditions under which a competitive free market economy can succeed will actually be realized. If the negotiators do not know this, then they will not be in a position rationally to approve a set of rules for society that imply procedures of distributive justice that tolerate inequalities in the allocation of social goods. Yet it is only the preferability of such a system on grounds of efficiency in producing things of value for the benefit of all members of a society that in Rawls's theory is supposed to justify competitive principles of distributive justice as opposed to an ideal of universal equality of wealth that might otherwise be instituted.

Rawls offers additional insight into the kinds of knowledge that the veil of ignorance is supposed to include and exclude. The passage is crucial to Rawls's analysis:

> It is assumed, then, that the parties do not know certain kinds of particular facts. First of all, no one knows his place in society, his class position or social status; nor does he know his fortune in the distribution of natural assets and abilities,

his intelligence and strength, and the like. Nor, again, does anyone know his conception of the good, the particulars of his rational plan of life, or even the special features of his psychology such as his aversion to risk or liability to optimism or pessimism. (118)

Thus far, the knowledge base of social contract negotiators behind the veil of ignorance is only supposed to exclude information about themselves, including their place in the society and certain features of their own psychologies. If the negotiators do not know enough about their own psychologies to know whether or not they would be competitive in a free market context, how can they even know that such psychological motives exist? Without first-person experience of such psychological states in their own cases, negotiators in the original position behind the veil of ignorance might not even know that there are such psychological states. Nor would a negotiator know well enough what such psychological states are like to be able to make the necessary inferences about how their existence or nonexistence would exert an impact on the economy and other social institutions of a society that might include any number of persons with any number of different kinds of psychologies. Consistently with this concern, Rawls now adds further limitations on the knowledge of social contract negotiators in the original position behind the veil of ignorance:

> More than this, I assume that the parties do not know the particular circumstances of their own society. That is, they do not know its economic or political situation, or the level of civilization and culture it has been able to achieve. The persons in the original position have no information as to which generation they belong. These broader restrictions on knowledge are appropriate in part because questions of social justice arise between generations as well as within them, for example, the question of the appropriate rate of capital saving and of the conservation of natural resources and the environment of nature. There is also, theoretically anyway, the question of a reasonable genetic policy. In these cases too, in order to carry through the idea of the original position, the parties must not know the contingencies that set them in opposition. They must choose principles the consequences of which they are prepared to live with whatever generation they turn out to belong to. (118–19)

The exclusion of personal knowledge about the generation to which social contract negotiators belong seems essential for Rawls's goal of preventing negotiators from making egoistic choices about the rules for the society in which they are to live. To allow them knowledge of this information behind the veil of ignorance would amount to allowing them to divide up the cake for different generations and still take the biggest piece for their own generation, on the assumption that they would inordinately benefit from this generationally unfair procedure of distributive justice. Limiting the knowledge available to social contract negotiators in this way should have the positive effect of preventing any particular team of negotiators from unfairly allotting all of a society's natural and other resources to the members of any particular generation to the detriment of future generations who will then be deprived.

To seal the issue, Rawls declares in more positive terms that social contract negotiators have knowledge only of the particular fact that the society whose rules they are devising will be subject to the "circumstances of justice" and "whatever this implies." They also have access to "general facts about human society," "political affairs," and "the principles of economic theory." In the context of the criticism we have been considering, however, it is unclear that this level and type of information is enough to allow negotiators to make many kinds of key decisions that Rawls believes are essential to the well-ordered society. In particular, it is not obvious that they will know whether a competitive free market economy would actually be a sufficiently efficient method of producing things of value to justify a choice of social rules that would permit actual inequalities in the distribution of social goods under Rawls's second principle of justice.

It is ambiguous, in other words, whether Rawls describes a set of limitations for the knowledge available to social contract negotiators that is ultimately internally consistent. If the negotiators have no personal knowledge of their own emotional psychologies, then it is doubtful whether they can know enough about the "general facts about human society" or "understand political affairs" well enough to fulfill their obligations as authors of the social contract. If they know the general laws and "principles of economic theory," but they do not have enough information to know whether the conditions of any of these principles will be satisfied by the members of a society beyond the veil of ignorance, then they cannot be expected to know whether the resulting society will satisfy his conception of justice as fairness. They might not know whether it will be sufficiently economically efficient in producing advantages for every member of society to warrant the actual inequalities that naturally occur in systems of distributive justice that do not guarantee absolute equality in the allotment of social goods.

Rawls describes the limits of knowledge available to social contract negotiators in more specific terms:

> As far as possible, then, the only particular facts which the parties know is that their society is subject to the circumstances of justice and whatever this implies. It is taken for granted, however, that they know the general facts about human society. They understand political affairs and the principles of economic theory; they know the basis of social organization and the laws of human psychology. Indeed, the parties are presumed to know whatever general facts affect the choice of the principles of justice. There are no limitations on general information, that is, on general laws and theories, since conceptions of justice must be adjusted to the characteristics of the systems of social cooperation which they are to regulate, and there is no reason to rule out these facts. (119)

When we consider the fact that Rawls's purpose is to articulate principles of justice that exhibit the highest level of generality, then it is evident that he cannot allow social contract negotiators in the original position to base the rules for a just society on any particular facts or particular truths about themselves or the society in which their rules are to be implemented. To the extent that particular circumstances of any kind are taken into account, to that extent the full generality required of Rawls's theory of justice will inevitably be watered down. The question then is whether Rawls's project is finally attainable, or whether he has set himself an impossible task for a moral and social philosophy. At least Rawls might be said in that event to have taken the wrong direction in characterizing justice as fairness and fairness as permitting actual inequalities in the distribution of social goods. He indicates the generality that must be observed in a theory of justice, and the way in which the veil of ignorance is supposed to assure this level of generality by excluding knowledge of particular personal and social circumstances:

> In any case, the original position must be interpreted so that one can at any time adopt its perspective. It must make no difference when one takes up this viewpoint, or who does so: the restrictions must be such that the same principles are always chosen. The veil of ignorance is a key condition in meeting this requirement. It insures not only that the information available is relevant, but that it is at all times the same. (120)

It is noteworthy that Rawls usually describes the "parties" involved in social contract negotiation in the plural, a number of thinkers meeting to decide on the rules for a new society. Why, however, if they individually have no personal information about themselves, but are acting purely as rational deliberators, would there be any need for more than one? Why should it not be enough for Rawls's purpose for there to be one individual thinker behind the veil of ignorance trying to decide on the rules for a just society? What is accomplished by assembling a committee of persons, all of whom are rational deliberators but all of whom are totally ignorant of the personal facts of their psychologies and circumstances?

Rawls admits that an individual thinker working hard behind the veil of ignorance might suffice. It is possible to understand Rawls's presentation of his theory of justice as the reflective equilibrium of one social contract negotiator, who could be Rawls himself. The lone negotiator must try to the best of his or her ability to suspend knowledge of personal psychology and circumstances, just as other rational universal or formalist moral and political thinkers such as Kant must try to do in order to arrive at their philosophical analyses of ethical ideals, abstracting from particular personal and social facts. There is nothing to be gained by a plurality of such persons all deliberating on the principles of justice, if they are precisely equal in their reasoning abilities and brought to precisely the same level of restricted information and knowledge by the veil of ignorance. Rawls remarks:

> To begin with, it is clear that since the differences among the parties are unknown to them, and everyone is equally rational and similarly situated, each is convinced by the same arguments. Therefore, we can view the agreement in the original position from the standpoint of one person selected at random. If anyone after due reflection prefers a conception of justice to another, then they all do, and a unanimous agreement can be reached. We can, to make the circumstances more vivid, imagine that the parties are required to communicate with each other through a referee as intermediary, and that he is to announce which alternatives have been suggested and the reasons offered in their support. He forbids the attempt to form coalitions, and he informs the parties when they have come to an understanding. But such a referee is actually superfluous, assuming that the deliberations of the parties must be similar. (120)

Later, he concludes in much the same way:

> As we have seen, this principle may be viewed as the ethics of a single rational individual prepared to take whatever chances necessary to maximize his prospects from the standpoint of the initial situation. (144)

The suggestion that there be a committee chairperson for the social contract negotiators is soon dismissed. There is no need for a chair to act as a referee to head off coalitions and conspiracies among the contract negotiators that could otherwise result in a corruption of the principles of justice. If it is only strictly necessary for there to be one supremely rational deliberator in the original position behind the veil of ignorance, then there can be no subcommittees undermining the principles of justice in the social contract. The fact that Rawls thinks it might be helpful for the reader to imagine a panel of negotiators deliberating about the principles of justice to be instituted by a well-ordered society whose rules they discuss, debate, and on which they may eventually reach a compromise hints again at the extent to which his political thinking seems to be influenced by the historical example of the Continental Congress at which the American Constitution was written, or perhaps of the extent to which he hopes the reader will be able to understand the idea of the original position more easily by comparison with this famous and iconographic episode from American history.

A RATIONAL PLAN OF LIFE

Rawls now invokes the concept of a *rational plan of life*. By this he means just what the phrase indicates nontechnically. It is a course of action for the conduct of a person's life that accords with reason, can be adjusted to accommodate changing circumstances and the availability of resources to match means to ends in order to achieve a rationally chosen purpose. We are all familiar with this notion from the career plans we may have formulated for ourselves or that we know about from the lives of others. It might be part of a rational plan of life to finish college and go to medical or law or graduate school in a particular discipline, to join the military, to raise a family, to buy a house or to travel, to write novels, to enter a profession or have a career in art, to serve humanity in the social services or other humanitarian capacity, or the like.

Rawls argues that the veil of ignorance must also conceal from social contract negotiators or from the sole social contract deliberator whatever plan of life is adopted. The limitation of information or knowledge behind the veil of ignorance is so extensive with respect to an individual's personal knowledge that it precludes understanding not only what the deliberator wants to do with his or her life—and of course the person does not even know her or his gender—but even the concept of the good to which he or she may ascribe. A deliberator knows that human beings in general have a rational plan of life, for this is part of what can be assumed in proposing a social contract for a rationally organized well-ordered society. However, no negotiator can know the particular plan of his or her life, or her or his conception of the good, for that information could be used to unfair advantage in the resulting society by favoring persons with such a particular plan of life or conception of the good. Rawls comments appropriately:

> I have assumed throughout that the persons in the original position are rational. But I have also assumed that they do not know their conception of the good. This means that while they know that they have some rational plan of life, they do not know the details of this plan, the particular ends and interests which it is cal-

culated to promote. How, then, can they decide which conceptions of justice are most to their advantage? Or must we suppose that they are reduced to mere guessing? To meet this difficulty, I postulate that they accept the account of the good touched upon in the preceding chapter: they assume that they normally prefer more primary social goods rather than less. (123)

Here, then, is further testimony to Rawls's philosophical commitment to what we have thus far hesitated to call a capitalist value system. It is expected, and it is built into the concept of reason and rationality, according to Rawls, that a person will naturally or "normally" prefer more social goods to less. This may be so for many persons, but we can easily imagine circumstances in which this would not be true, if human psychology were only a little different than it happens statistically by and large to be. For a rational society of persons with such values, Rawls's system of justice would be altogether inapplicable.

We also know historically that there have been many societies in the past, and many periods within generally acquisitive societies, in which the accumulation of social goods is automatically, even unthinkingly sometimes, assumed to be a preferred general outline for a rational plan of life. We think of Socrates as a man of reason, perhaps consummately so. We know, too, that Socrates disdained the acquisition of worldly goods, as have many religious and spiritual thinkers, some of whom have sometimes constituted rational societies or subcultures in which to promote their extraworldly values, which to all intents and purposes appear to be equally rational as the acquisitive capitalist societies with which we may be more familiar and with which we may even be personally more emotionally comfortable.

Rawls, to return to a theme of Plato's dialogue with which we first began our perambulations of pathways in philosophy, assumes as part of what it means to be rational that rational beings are naturally what the ancient Greeks would have called erotic. He thinks that by definition, so to speak, they are essentially more like Meno than Socrates. It is a common assumption also of what is called games or rational choice theory that rational agents normally want to acquire more rather than fewer things of value. This may be generally true, but there remains a great difference among persons about what kinds of things have value and whether it is always better to have more. What is valuable for some has nothing directly to do with material goods, social offices or positions, amenities or advantages in the ordinary sense. These, in limited quantities, might be taken for granted as mere necessities of life without attaching any special importance to them within a rational plan of life. It is questionable, given the assumptions Rawls makes explicit in this part of his analysis of the concept of rationality, whether his theory of justice can have any real application to persons whose rational plan of life is not capitalistic, acquisitive, or "rational" in the games or rational choice theory sense.

Rawls asks whether an account of a rational agent in the original position behind the veil of ignorance amounts in the end to some form of egoistic moral and social-political theory. He rightly argues that this is not the case, but that from the fact that negotiators in the original position are supposed to be disinterested in other persons it does not follow that they would be so once they enter the society they are supposed to help build. He does not also say, as presumably he might have done, that the negotiators or individual deliberator in the original position behind the veil of ignorance cannot function egoistically while lacking all knowledge of personal psychology or circumstances that would be needed to take unfair advantage of the opportunity to create a society in which they will subsequently live. They cannot use the power they are given to advance their own individual rational plan of life, because behind the veil of ignorance they do not know what it is. Rawls now claims:

> Since the persons in the original position are assumed to take no interest in one another's interests (although they may have a concern for third parties), it may be thought that justice as fairness is itself an egoistic theory. It is not, of course, one of the three forms of egoism mentioned earlier, but some may think, as Schopenhauer thought of Kant's doctrine, that it is egoistic nevertheless. Now this is a misconception. For the fact that in the original position the parties are characterized as mutually disinterested does not entail that persons in ordinary life, or in a well-ordered society, who hold the principles that would be agreed to are similarly disinterested in one another. (127–28)

It is not because of the damage egoistically inclined negotiators might be able to cause within the original position that Rawls resists the idea of having the social contract drawn up by egoistic deliberators. He believes that he has already installed enough safeguards to prevent this from happening. The question is theoretical: What is the correct explanation of the moral philosophy by which negotiators in the original position behind the veil of ignorance are to devise rules for the well-ordered society that will instantiate justice?

Rawls does not think that egoism is the right ethical explanation, and we know that he prefers some version of a Kantian deontology or formalist philosophy of justice and moral rights loosely connected with the categorical imperative and Kant's concept of the kingdom of ends. What is unclear is why Rawls rejects egoism as a philosophical explanation of justice in a social contract theory context. Why not suppose that justice as fairness could just as easily result from an egoist or committee of egoists acting as effectively as possible behind the veil of ignorance to enact a set of rules that will result in a society in which there is a maximum possibility for achieving egoistic purposes? As long as egoistic social contract negotiators have no specific knowledge of their individual purposes, personal rational plans of life, or the circumstances beyond the veil of ignorance, would they not in the end devise a social contract that maximizes justice as fairness? Why could not egoism also lead to this goal, and possibly do so even better than an underlying Kantian deontological moral philosophy, provided that the egoistic social contract negotiator or lone deliberator is truly behind the veil of ignorance in the original position, with all the epistemic limitations that Rawls requires?

This is an interesting question that Rawls unfortunately does not consider. He distinguishes instead between the moral motivations of persons in the original position as opposed to those in everyday life. We must nevertheless imagine that deliberators must have some motivation for undertaking the arduous labor of fashioning a social contract for a new society. Otherwise, why do they do it? Why do they work so hard, even as fictional, imaginary, or purely hypothetical agents? If they need some motivation, as we all do as rational beings in order to harness our energies for any specific task, why not think philosophically of the deliberators in Rawls's original position as egoistically rather than altruistically or in some other way motivated? What would be a good reason for denying egoistic motivations, provided that egoistically motivated deliberators are fully behind the veil of ignorance and as such cannot skew the resulting social institutions to their individual egoistic advantages? Rawls appears to conflate questions of motivation and underlying moral philosophy with the knowledge and behavior of rational agents in the original position as opposed to or by contrast with persons participating in a real society, when he argues:

> Clearly the two principles of justice and the principles of obligation and natural duty require us to consider the rights and claims of others. And the sense of justice is a normally effective desire to comply with these restrictions. The motivation of the persons in the original position must not be confused with the motivation of persons in everyday life who accept the principles of justice and who have the corresponding sense of justice. In practical affairs an individual does have a knowledge of his situation and he can, if he wishes, exploit contingencies to his advantage. Should his sense of justice move him to act on the principles of right that would be adopted in the original position, his desires and aims are surely not egoistic. He voluntarily takes on the limitations expressed by this interpretation of the moral point of view. (128)

It appears that Rawls thinks an agent cannot be egoistic in the absence of the sort of information that would enable the agent to act on behalf of egoistic desires. An agent without personal knowledge on such a conception cannot act for the sake of personal gratification that is ordinarily associated with an attitude of moral egoism, such as we find in Nietzsche's genealogy of morality.

This, however, is a mistake. There is always a limitation of some type or other that restricts the effectiveness of an egoist trying to achieve personal ambitions and satisfy personal desires. An egoist in the original position is not deprived of all knowledge whatsoever, but only of knowledge about some aspects of personal psychology, if this is possible, of a personal rational plan of life, of personal circumstances, details about the society that is to result from the institution of the social contract, and the other categories of information that Rawls mentions and is concerned to exclude from the process of deliberation behind the veil of ignorance. It is not clear that an egoist would not make a suitable lone deliberator in framing the rules for a just and well-ordered society, perhaps more or less of the kind Rawls envisions. Rawls in any case does not try to say why he thinks an egoist would not be appropriate for the job.

ANTIDISCRIMINATION IN JUSTICE AS FAIRNESS

The virtue of the veil of ignorance in concealing most types of particular knowledge from social contract negotiators is that it is supposed to avoid the categories of self-serving discrimination against persons in a diverse society that are ordinarily associated with political unfairness. If Rawls is right that justice is fairness, then the resulting rules should protect persons from some of the most blatant social injustices.

Rawls's concept of the original position, his description of its decision-making conditions in reflective equilibrium, if that is achieved, with the theory of justice he defends, is meant to provide a sound philosophical rationale for resisting discrimination against persons on the basis of gender, race, religion, family or ethnic background, or any of the other features by which persons are distinguished independently of the individual moral conduct for which they are usually thought to be personally responsible. Rawls maintains:

> Finally, if the parties are conceived as themselves making proposals, they have no incentive to suggest pointless or arbitrary principles. For example, none would urge that special privileges be given to those exactly six feet tall or born on a sunny day. Nor would anyone put forward the principle that basic right should depend on the color of one's skin or the texture of one's hair. No one can tell whether such principles would be to his advantage. (129)

The veil of ignorance in the original position is supposed to preclude personal knowledge of circumstance, such as gender or skin color. These are just two ways in which persons are distinguished from one another and on the basis of which some persons are unfairly and unjustly discriminated against in a society, particularly when they are part of a minority or when they have been inherently or historically deprived of power. Rawls reasonably concludes that no rational social contract negotiator would willingly put in place a system of social contract rules for a society in which persons of a given gender or with a given skin color were discriminated against or had an unfair disadvantage merely on such grounds, because, for all the negotiator in the original position knows, the negotiator might personally turn out to be of that gender or to have that skin color when the veil of ignorance is lifted and it is time to join the new society.

This is a useful idea. To the extent that Rawls's criterion serves as a way of reminding us of the kinds of factors that are discriminatory in an individual's or society's behavior toward others, his notion of the original position and the veil of ignorance provides an interesting standard for the distinction between just and unjust social conduct that can light the way to a more just and fair society. We need only ask whether we could rationally endorse rules for the social contract by which we would be treated in a negative discriminatory way if we did not know in advance whether or not we would belong to the socially disadvantaged group. Presumably, the answer is that in every case from behind the veil of ignorance we would not permit such rules to go into effect. For this improved state of affairs actually to come about, enough persons or persons in authority must accept the theory of justice as fairness with its principle, take it to heart, and put it into practice. The same is naturally true of any theory of justice or any moral principle, which considered in and of itself even as a perfectly correct analysis of the concept of justice on paper, is inert and cannot change the world. It is only if the principles are accepted and made a part of the life of a social group that justice can actually be achieved. This is why he maintains that in a well-ordered society a correct conception of justice must be disseminated among the population, according to the publicity principle, universally accepted, and made a guidepost of the society's institutions.

Rawls understands the requirements of racial and gender discrimination in particular as depending on two factors. There must be individuals who hold a favored social position in a society who are willing to take advantage of their privilege for personal benefit at the expense of those who are discriminated against. He explains:

> Inevitably, then, racial and sexual discrimination presupposes that some hold a favored place in the social system which they are willing to exploit to their advan-

tage. From the standpoint of persons similarly situated in an initial situation which is fair, the principles of explicit racist doctrines are not only unjust. They are irrational. For this reason we could say that they are not moral conceptions at all, but simply means of suppression. They have no place on a reasonable list of traditional conceptions of justice. (129–30)

Rawls's theory of justice is commendable not only for agreeing with the widely held intuition that gender, racial, and other kinds of social discrimination are morally objectionable. It is valuable because it offers a plausible explanation for the moral unacceptability of discrimination within the general terms of an analysis of justice, which it further combines with a practical criterion for determining what kinds of practices would be unethical. We need only try to imagine whether the practices at issue would be among those that could be authorized by social contract negotiators considering the rules for an ideal well-ordered society in the original position from behind the veil of ignorance. Alternatively, we can try to imagine what we would do and the decisions we could make under those circumstances for the society in which we are to live if we had no specific knowledge of our personal circumstances or rational plan of life. If the practices could be rationally adopted in such a decision-making scenario, then in Rawls's theory they are morally justified. We expect, in that case, that the social practices in question will not be discriminatory. If, on the other hand, the practices cannot be rationally adopted by social contract negotiators in the original position from behind the veil of ignorance, then the practices are not morally justified and should not be part of a society that aspires to justice as fairness, nor part of a well-ordered society, as Rawls conceives of it, by which social discrimination of any sort against individuals is prevented.

KANTIAN MORAL FREEDOM IN RAWLS'S POLITICAL PHILOSOPHY

Rawls interprets the theory of justice as fairness also as explaining the relation between equality and moral freedom. He again draws essential connections between his concept of justice and Kant's deontology. He contends:

The force of justice as fairness would appear to arise from two things: the requirement that all inequalities be justified to the least advantaged, and the priority of liberty. This pair of constraints distinguishes it from intuitionism and teleological theories. Taking the preceding discussion into account, we can reformulate the first principle of justice and conjoin to it the appropriate priority rule. The changes and additions are, I believe, self-explanatory. . . . (220)

We have seen that freedom in the sense of the autonomy of reason in choosing the categorical imperative as a purely rational principle of moral conduct is the transcendental ground of the metaphysics of morals in Kant's ethical philosophy. Without freedom there is no possibility of moral responsibility, as Kant understands the presuppositions of morality.

We might wonder how Mill would address the problem of satisfying the conceptual presuppositions of moral responsibility. Mill rejects Kant's moral theory, but does not try to argue that freedom is not ultimately necessary for moral responsibility in a utilitarian consequentialist framework, nor does he propose a substitute for Kant's concept of moral autonomy. Kant argues that moral motivation related to inclination or desire is heteronomous, in the sense that reason in that case takes moral dictation from something other than itself. He concludes that moral heteronomy is incompatible with the prerequisite of a moral agent's freedom. This seems to be a criticism tailor-made for Mill's account of morality as the greatest happiness of the greatest number, explaining the good as utility and utility as pleasure, an emotion or sensation rather than a matter of reason.

Returning to Rawls, as a Kantian he also recognizes the need, without all of Kant's transcendental metaphysical trappings, to ground the theory of justice and social morality generally on the freedom in some sense or other of the moral agents in a society. The concept of freedom or liberty that Rawls introduces to satisfy this need is nevertheless very different from Kant's, having to do not with the autonomy of reason in choosing its own rational principle for the regulation of moral conduct, but with the civil liberties of agents as they are instituted and protected by the social contract, to be equally enjoyed by all members of the society, as established by the first principle of justice. Rawls accordingly revises and elaborates his first principle, so as to reflect the requirement of liberty in social morality:

The principle now reads as follows.

FIRST PRINCIPLE

Each person is to have an equal right to the most extensive total system of equal basic liberties compatible with a similar system of liberty for all.

PRIORITY RULE

The principles of justice are to be ranked in lexical order and therefore liberty can be restricted only for the sake of liberty. There are two cases: (a) a less extensive liberty must strengthen the total system of liberty shared by all, and (b) a less than equal liberty must be acceptable to those citizens with the lesser liberty. (220)

Rawls adds a priority rule to the first principle of justice. Liberty, he maintains, can only be limited for the sake of liberty. This is the counterpart of what Rawls had previously argued in allowing that equality can be limited only for the sake of the advantage of every member of a society. The two conditions accord well with the kinds of commonsense judgments we generally make about the circumstances under which it is reasonable to limit civil liberties for the sake of a greater good.

An example of the way in which condition (a) justifies the limitation of a liberty is that in which we accept traffic regulations such as stopping at a red light, which in a limited way restricts our freedom to drive however we want. Given the movement of other drivers on the road, observing such a rule and limiting our freedom in such a way contributes to greater automotive safety, and indirectly thereby to greater liberty to drive. We readily accept such rules for the sake of being able to move about more freely when we drive without undue threat of collision. We give up a little bit of our freedom in this way in order to secure greater overall freedom for ourselves and others affected by the restrictions. Numerous examples of the same kind of tradeoff between degrees and kinds of civil liberties are familiar to anyone who reflects on the rules in place in most societies.

Rawls's condition (b) merely asserts the requirement that those affected by such curtailments of their liberties for the sake of greater overall liberty must accept the trade-off and not have it imposed on them involuntarily. This qualification is undoubtedly made in order to prevent violations of individual social sovereignty, without which the limitation of civil liberty could not be accurately described as consistent with the requirements of freedom. There would then be no genuine liberty if the individuals affected by accepting a rule did not voluntarily agree to its provisions. The ways in which voluntary compliance with a reduction of individual civil liberty facilitates greater liberty are complex and often inchoate. We see this in any community of complexly interacting persons trying to achieve balance in the management of their respective activities so as to enhance and preserve liberty in another higher sense. A driver need not be individually asked whether it is agreeable to accept the traffic laws as a limitation on the freedom to drive. An acceptance of the trade-off for the sake of having the freedom to drive is implicit in satisfying the requirements by which one becomes licensed legally to drive, having been made aware of the laws through driver education and the administration of traffic laws.

All this is reasonable enough from a practical point of view. What remains unclear is the relation between Rawls's concept and Kant's more philosophical requirement of freedom in the sense of autonomy. Rawls attempts to establish such a connection between the conditional civil liberty presupposed by his theory of justice and Kant's concept of freedom as moral autonomy in the metaphysics of morals:

> Kant held, I believe, that a person is acting autonomously when the principles of his action are chosen by him as the most adequate possible expression of his nature as a free and equal rational being. The principles he acts upon are not adopted because of his social position or natural endowments, or in view of the particular kind of society in which he lives or the specific things that he happens to want. To act on such principles is to act heteronomously. Now the veil of ignorance deprives the persons in the original position of the knowledge that would enable them to choose heteronomous principles. The parties arrive at their choice together as free and equal rational persons knowing only that those circumstances obtain which give rise to the need for principles of justice. (222)

The solution, in Rawls's theory of justice, is to defer again to the original position. The civil liberty requirement for social morality in Rawls's analysis of the concept of justice is equated with Kant's distinction between moral autonomy and heteronomy. The connection is supposed to be that in the original position behind the veil of ignorance a social contract negotiator cannot act heteronomously in the absence of particular personal and societal knowledge.

This strategy, if successful, establishes a positive link between Rawls's and Kant's freedom requirements. Unfortunately, it is not at all clear that Rawls has plausibly excluded heteronomous moral reasoning on the part of social contract deliberators in the original position by invoking the veil of ignorance. He describes the original position as a "procedural interpretation" of the Kantian concept of moral autonomy and categorical imperative, but offered, as he says, "within the framework of an empirical theory." We first consider Rawls's comparison between these respective ideas of moral freedom and civil liberty and then ask whether the theory is correct. He proceeds:

> The original position may be viewed, then, as a procedural interpretation of Kant's conception of autonomy and the categorical imperative within the framework of an empirical theory. The principles regulative of the kingdom of ends are those that would be chosen in this position, and the description of this situation enables us to explain the sense in which acting from these principles expresses our nature as free and equal rational persons. No longer are these notions purely transcendent and lacking explicable connections with human conduct, for the procedural conception of the original position allows us to make these ties. (226)

We have already taken account of some of the differences between Kant's categorical imperative and kingdom of ends and Rawls's theory of justice as fairness in the original position behind the veil of ignorance. These have chiefly to do with the unconditional equality of moral rights and justice in Kant's moral theory and the conditional qualification of these moral attributes in Rawls's theory of justice.

There is yet another crucial difference between Rawls and Kant on this score. Kant's kingdom of ends, although it is as much an ideal as Rawls's myth of the original position, is an ideal of the state of society as a whole, functioning ideally according to the categorical imperative as a general principle by which all rational beings are to be treated always as ends in themselves and never merely as means to another end. Rawls's concept of the original position in contrast is not an ideal of the state of a functioning society but of the conditions under which the rules for constituting such a society are to be deliberated. Kant, in the meantime, does not believe that there is any need for deliberations about the principles to be adopted in the kingdom of ends. He argues that the only principle that is needed for his social ideal is already available in complete form in the categorical imperative as according moral respect to every rational being.

Do these differences have any impact on Rawls's thesis that the veil of ignorance in the original position precludes any possibility of heteronomous moral reasoning? The thesis, in the first place, considered on its own, is not very plausible. What prevents a negotiator or deliberator in the original position behind the veil of ignorance from deciding on a set of rules for a society on the basis of the expectation that such a social contract is likely to produce more happiness than unhappiness, or the greatest good for the greatest number? If this is permitted as a reason or motivation for deliberators in the original position, then Kant would certainly object that this is heteronomy, and not a choice made from the exercise of pure reason autonomously accepting the categorical imperative as the moral principle of pure reason in a free choice of moral self-government. It would, on the contrary, be a situation in which reason chooses a moral principle that falls outside of and is not exclusively dictated by reason to reason. It would, in short, be heteronomous rather than autonomous.

Rawls seems to think it is an advantage of his theory that it brings Kant's autonomy requirement down to earth from its transcendental heaven to which Kant had confined it and humanizes it or empiricizes the freedom needed for moral responsibility. Kant, on the contrary, would probably deny that Rawls is speaking of anything like moral autonomy in his sense. The good will that Kant insists is the only unqualifiedly good thing is supposed to be purified of all empirical anthropological elements. It should be obvious, then, that nothing resembling a Kantian theory of moral autonomy can be empiricized in the way Rawls proposes as extricated from the transcendental order where Kant locates it by means of his transcendental reasoning; anything less, despite superficial analogies, is not recognizably Kantian.

Rawls argues more specifically that the fact that persons are capable of choosing the principles of a just society in the original position from behind the veil of ignorance is proof in itself that "expresses our nature as free and equal rational persons." There is nevertheless a further important difference that Rawls's argument overlooks. The overarching assumption of Rawls's theory is that the original position and veil of ignorance is a philosophical fiction, or, in the terminology he prefers, a purely hypothetical situation. The idea of the original position and veil of ignorance might accordingly serve to help clarify the concept of justice in the manner of an insightful thought experiment, but it does not necessarily reveal anything significant about human agents in real moral decision-making situations.

It might be said that at most the original position and its accompanying hypothetical machinery reveals nothing about our actual nature as free and equal rational persons, but only of the fictional or purely hypothetical nature of fictional and purely hypothetical deliberators in the fictional and purely hypothetical original position behind the veil of ignorance. The same characteristics that Rawls associates with Kantian moral autonomy do not even apply to the deliberators once their work is done and they step out from behind the veil of ignorance and begin to take part in the society they have helped to create. Kant, by contrast, holds that all moral agents as rational beings are autonomous even in the actual societies to which they belong, by virtue of always being capable of accepting the categorical imperative as the moral principle by which they choose to act.

The sense in which Rawls claims freedom in the sense of Kantian moral autonomy for social contract negotiators behind the veil of ignorance applies only in those purely hypothetical, unrealistic, and highly artificial imaginary circumstances, and not to the persons who are actually supposed to conduct themselves as moral agents in the resulting society according to a standard of justice as fairness. When the veil of ignorance is removed, all bets are off as far as Rawls's theory is concerned with respect to determining "our nature as free and equal rational persons." It is not our nature that can be discerned in the decision making of purely hypothetical contract negotiators in the original position, but only the nature of those fictional, imaginary, mythical beings that cannot even function rationally in society unless or until the veil of ignorance is lifted. At that point the negotiators can no longer be expected to display the virtues that Rawls attributes to them, and in particular cannot be said as such to exemplify Kantian moral autonomy, let alone a supposedly empiricized version of Kantian moral autonomy. The relevance of Rawls's original position under these limitations to Kant's requirement of moral autonomy as a philosophical prerequisite for moral responsibility is extremely doubtful.

RAWLS'S CRITIQUE OF UTILITARIANISM

Rawls also advances a comparison between his theory of justice and utilitarianism, as represented by the moral philosophy of Bentham and Mill. He introduces the subject of utilitarianism early in the text, contrasting its consequentialist principles with the theory of justice as fairness:

[W]hereas the utilitarian extends to society the principle of choice for one man, justice as fairness, being a contract view, assumes that the principles of social choice, and so the principles of justice, are themselves the object of an original agreement. There is no reason to suppose that the principles which should regulate an association of men is simply an extension of the principle of choice for one man. On the contrary: if we assume that the correct regulative principle for anything depends on the nature of that thing, and that the plurality of distinct persons with separate systems of ends is an essential feature of human societies, we should not expect the principles of social choice to be utilitarian. (25)

Although Rawls is right that the theory of justice as fairness is not the same as utilitarianism, he appears to exaggerate the differences almost as much as he exaggerates the similarly between justice as fairness and Kantian deontology. He emphasizes the fact that whereas utilitarianism extends the principles of individual moral choice from one person to the whole of society, the theory of justice as fairness begins from the outset with an agreement on the provisions of a social contract.

The difference seems to be that social contract theory presupposes a collaboration on the part of multiple social contract negotiators. We have seen that later in his treatise Rawls observes that under the veil of ignorance there is no essential requirement for the social contract to be negotiated between multiple deliberators in order to arrive at the conclusion that justice is fairness. Rawls's distinction between utilitarianism and the theory of justice as fairness also ignores the choice between act and rule utilitarianism, which we discussed in connection with Mill's utilitarian moral philosophy, in which general rules can be justified on utilitarian grounds without first being developed and then extended from individual to social applications.

There is equally no apparent reason why a social contract negotiator could not choose principles of justice for an ideal society from a utilitarian point of view, as we argued in challenging the inherent Kantianism of Rawls's social contract theory. There is also no reason why a utilitarian could not advocate the concept of a social contract as a way of justifying the principles of a rule utilitarian society, again because there is no obvious reason why the social contract negotiators could not conduct their decision making in very general terms on utilitarian grounds. What if one of the social contract negotiators in Rawls's original position under the veil of ignorance were to argue precisely word-for-word as Mill does in *Utilitarianism* for the concept of justice supported by consequentialist considerations that Mill advocates in that work? The negotiators presumably know about the difference between happiness and unhappiness, between pleasure and pain or displeasure, and that is all that Mill's utilitarian social contract negotiator would seem to need in order to sustain a utilitarian interpretation of the concept of justice in the same terms that Mill presents.

Later, Rawls argues that there are definite doctrinal differences between utilitarianism and justice as fairness. He offers an interesting objection to the effect that utilitarianism might unfairly demand disproportionately greater sacrifices from certain generations for the sake of benefiting later generations, who by virtue of their greater numbers especially spread out over future time will accumulate more happiness than the unhappiness of poorer generations preceding them. This is a potentially very damaging criticism of utilitarian moral principles in their own terms, especially given the contrast Rawls identifies between utilitarianism and the social contract theory of justice as fairness. He observes:

> As I have said, a moral theory characterizes a point of view from which policies are to be assessed; and it may often be clear that a suggested answer is mistaken even if an alternative doctrine is not ready to hand. Thus it seems evident, for example, that the classical principle of utility leads in the wrong direction for questions of justice between generations. For if one takes the size of the population as variable, and postulates a high marginal productivity of capital and a very distant time horizon, maximizing total utility may lead to an excessive rate of accumulation (at least in the near future). Since from a moral point of view there are no grounds for discounting future well-being on the basis of pure time preference, the conclusion is all the more likely that the greater advantages of future generations will be sufficiently large to outweigh most any present sacrifices. This may prove true if only because with more capital and better technology it will be possible to support a sufficiently large population. Thus the utilitarian doctrine may direct us to demand heavy sacrifices of the poorer generations for the sake of greater advantages for later ones that are far better off. But this calculus of advantages, which balances the losses of some against benefits to others, appears even less justified in the case of generations than among contemporaries. Even if we cannot define a precise just savings principle, we should be able to avoid this sort of extreme. (253)

If, as Rawls believes and as seems obvious, justice as fairness does not imply a similar imbalance of obligations over generations, then not only is there a significant difference between utilitarianism and the theory of justice as fairness, but justice as fairness is arguably morally preferable in its implications. Why should earlier generations suffer inordinately for the sake of future generations? A certain amount of sacrifice might be morally justified or chosen out of altruistic considerations, for the sake of a society's progeny, but excessive obligations appear to be unwarranted as unfair and morally objectionable.

What might Mill say in response to such a criticism? The case is so abstract and hypothetical that it is unclear in the first place whether it is true that utilitarian principles would require the kinds of sacrifices of which Rawls complains. A utilitarian would need to have credible prior knowledge that the sacrifices in question would have a strong likelihood of producing sufficiently greater happiness in the future in order for the sacrifices of an earlier generation to be justified on utilitarian grounds. If that were true, then a utilitarian might agree that such sacrifices were not only morally permissible but obligatory. In practice and in real life application, it is doubtful that utilitarian considerations could ever be put to use with that sort of reliable advance information so that its principles would come into play and require that excessive sacrifices actually be made. The limitations of foreknowledge and the exact effect of contemporary decisions on sensation subjects far into the future might be appealed to as a defense of utilitarianism against the argument that it could ever have such practical implications.

The other question that must be asked is whether it is true that justice as fairness could never obligate prior generations to make excessive sacrifices for the benefit of future generations. The fact that it seems not to be fair to require such actions of persons does not necessarily mean that the decision would or should be ruled out by any particular theory of justice as fairness, or any particular concept or interpretation of justice as fairness. What would Rawls's theory say about such a case? Rawls denies that justice as fairness imposes obligations on earlier generations, but he does not explain exactly why it does not. Indeed, upon examination, the opposite conclusion seems true in Rawls's analysis. If we look upon the entire population of a society, not just at a particular cross-section of time but spread out over successive generations, as Rawls does in mounting his criticism of utilitarianism, and we ask about the implications of the theory of justice as fairness for the proposal to request excessive sacrifices from an earlier generation for the sake of later generations, then the sacrifice might well be regarded as just and fair according to Rawls's second principle of justice.

The second principle implies that inequalities are morally tolerable and even obligatory conditionally if they contribute to the advantages of every individual in a society. The members of the sacrifice generation do not directly benefit from the sacrifices they are asked to make, unless they take a certain pride and satisfaction in voluntarily surrendering their good for the sake of the future. Does this mean that it is not to their advantage to do so? If it is not, then can it ever be morally justified for parents to make sacrifices for the sake of their children and their children's children? Is it not advantageous to be part of a society that is improving itself over time and moving toward a greater good, even if those who make the necessary sacrifices do not live to see the improvement? A generation that circumstances require to make substantial sacrifices in war or for other reasons cannot presumably excuse itself on the grounds that is unfair to ask them to suffer losses in the distribution of social goods so that over time later generations can enjoy greater peace and prosperity. If that is a consequence of Rawls's theory of justice as fairness, then the theory clearly does not stand on its own terms as morally correct or justifiable. The fact is that Rawls offers no clear-cut guidelines by which to decide whether or not the sacrifices of an earlier generation are or are not in any sense advantageous even to the sacrificial generation, whereby later beneficiary generations are more clearly advantaged.

In general, it appears that if it is morally permissible to allow entire sectors of a single generation in a society to be disadvantaged by a social or economic policy on grounds of efficiency in producing social goods that in some sense are advantageous to every member of the society, then the same should be true of an entire generation considered as a sector of the entire population of the society spread out historically over time. The second principle of justice in Rawls's social contract theory of justice as fairness as a result does not seem to offer any obvious moral superiority over utilitarianism where the problem of actual historical as opposed to geographical or other sociological or demographic inequalities is concerned.

RAWLS IN RETROSPECT

What, in the final analysis, does Rawls contribute to our understanding of the concept of justice? We have seen that there are problems in Rawls's philosophical methodology and argument. The idea of justice as fairness is nevertheless an important enduring thesis of political philosophy.

Rawls offers a lucid statement of difficult topics in the theory of justice. He illustrates these with vivid and imaginative philosophical metaphors, thought experiments, and analogies. The apparatus of social contract negotiations as Rawls depicts the deliberations of the founders of a just society in the original position behind the veil of ignorance, the epistemic model of reflective equilibrium in theory construction, and many other innovations of Rawls's theory of justice, have made a lasting impact on discussions of moral and social philosophy in the liberal tradition. What is remarkable about Rawls's project is on the one hand how smoothly it fits into past philosophical discussions in the social contrary theory mode, and yet how contemporary and inventive it is in its proposals for implementing social contract ideals in explaining and justifying a particular doctrine of justice as fairness.

There are, despite these permanent additions to the philosophical imagination, numerous drawbacks in Rawls's theory of justice. The theory is neither as Kantian nor as non-utilitarian as he represents it as being. The definition of the concept of a society, and many of the other vital assumptions with which he begins, threaten a kind of circularity in the conclusions that he later wants to establish, which are in some ways prefigured in his starting place. If we could agree with Rawls about all of these definitions and first principles, then we need have no difficulty accepting his conclusions. The starting place for so much of Rawls's theory of justice, it must be said, is too heavily philosophically loaded in favor of the particular concept of justice that he wants to defend. There is an explicit bias in Rawls's theory, a predisposition about what the rational deliberators of a social contract would need to decide in fashioning the rules for a just society, that raises doubts about the knowledge that could and should be available to negotiators if they are to be truly fair and truly disinterested in their decision making.

One has the sense throughout that Rawls knows in advance how things are supposed to turn out, and that he is looking for principles in his analysis of the concept of justice that will lead to these implications. What remains unclear, and to that extent disputatious, about Rawls's theory of justice as fairness, is whether the premises with which he begins do not simply presuppose a cherished set of moral and social-political values that are inadequately justified by argument, and never subjected to deep philosophical scrutiny.

Summary

Rawls offers a valuable analysis of the concept of justice. He defends a plausible philosophical methodology of reflective equilibrium, which he applies to the data, provisional account, and refinements of a theory of justice. The dialectical movements within efforts to attain reflective equilibrium have an evident advantage in trying to reach the truth when compared with methods that do not make provision for correcting and mutually adjusting data and theory. Rawls's method of reflective equilibrium codifies the way we proceed in theoretical matters when we are reasoning at our best. It helps us to perfect our theories by becoming more self-conscious of what seems to be the best method of constructing, criticizing, and making improvements to bring them ever closer to the truth.

Rawls defends a social contract theory of justice as the end product of his method of reflective equilibrium. He describes an original position and initial situation for social contract negotiators behind the veil of ignorance where they have no information about their personal circumstances and value systems in the resulting society once the social contract is implemented. Rawls believes that only in this way can we expect rational self-interested persons intelligent enough to design rules for a just society to institute principles of justice that will not disadvantage or discriminate against any particular individuals or social subgroups.

The model of justice that emerges philosophically through reflective equilibrium and politically in the ideal case when social contract negotiators step out from behind the veil of ignorance is one of justice as fairness. Rawls imposes a publicity condition by which a society's rules are made known to all members so that they can consider and know them to be implemented in the society's institutions of justice. With all requirements in place, Rawls believes that he has articulated the basic principles for a theory of justice that promotes the values of the well-ordered society, avoids unfairness, and promotes competition for social goods, which has a presumption of improving the lives of persons in the social order who are treated fairly by the social contract even if they do not enjoy equal natural and acquired advantages.

QUESTIONS FOR PHILOSOPHICAL UNDERSTANDING

1. What is Rawls's method of reflective equilibrium?

2. Why does Rawls believe that a theory's attainment of reflective equilibrium is a sign of its truth or theoretical preferability to its competitors?

3. What is a social contract? How does Rawls understand this concept? Are all societies governed at least implicitly by a social contract? Can there be justice in a society that does not depend on a social contract but is organized without even the implicit consent of its members for the sake of their mutual advantage?

4. What does Rawls mean by the concept of justice as fairness?

5. Does Rawls's myth of the veil of ignorance guarantee a social contract that instantiates justice as fairness?

6. Is it possible behind the veil of ignorance to have an adequate understanding of human motivations without having first-person experience of any particular personal motivations?

7. How would Rawls explain the application of the veil of ignorance in actual contexts of social contract decision making?

8. What happens if several negotiators behind the veil of ignorance radically disagree about the rules of a new social contract? Can this happen? If so, how can agreement ever be reached? If not, why not?

9. Does it make any difference whether there are several social contract negotiators or just one person trying to achieve theoretical reflective equilibrium? What happens if a single person cannot make up his or her mind about the rules for a social contract, or never arrives at reflective equilibrium?

10. Could a distribution of social goods be just but not fair? Could it be fair but not just? How and why?

11. How does justice as fairness behind the veil of ignorance justify an unequal distribution

of social goods among the members of a just society?

12. What are the similarities and differences between Rawls's social contract theory of justice and Kant's deontological concept of moral right, Mill's utilitarian theory of rights and social justice, Nietzsche's will to power explanation of justice by and for the powerful, and Moore's nonreductive consequentialist interpretation of moral laws, moral rights, and moral obligations?

13. Does Rawls's theory of justice as fairness and the deliberations of social contract negotiators behind the veil of ignorance provide justification for a theory of animal rights or the protection of nonhuman animal interests?

14. What is the relation between the concepts of moral obligations and moral rights in Rawls's theory of justice?

15. Does Rawls's theory of justice provide a way of adjudicating between conflicts of individual moral rights and the greatest good for the greatest number? Can such conflicts arise in his social-political philosophy?

KEY TERMS

bourgeois values

capitalist value system

democratic equality

difference principle

distributive justice

equality

fair access to social goods

first principle of justice

first virtue

initial position

inviolability

justice as fairness

liberal equality

natural aristocracy

natural liberty

natural lottery

original situation/position

perfect procedural justice

prepolitical state of nature

principle of efficiency

priority rule for the first principle of justice

public conception of justice

publicity condition

rational plan of life

reflective equilibrium

second principle of justice

social contract

state of nature

system of justice

two principles of justice

unequal distribution of social goods

veil of ignorance

well-ordered society

SOURCES AND RECOMMENDED READINGS

Barry, Brian M. *The Liberal Theory of Justice: A Critical Examination of the Principal Doctrines in* A Theory of Justice *by John Rawls.* Oxford: Clarendon Press, 1973.

Baynes, Kenneth. *The Normative Grounds of Social Criticism: Kant, Rawls, and Habermas.* Albany: State University of New York Press, 1992.

Blocker, H. Gene, and Elizabeth H. Smith, eds. *John Rawls's Theory of Social Justice: An Introduction.* Athens: Ohio University Press, 1980.

Corlett, Angelo J. *Equality and Liberty: Analyzing Rawls and Nozick.* London: Macmillan, 1991.

Daniels, Norman, ed. *Reading Rawls: Critical Studies on Rawls's* A Theory of Justice. New York: Basic Books, 1975.

Davion, Victoria, and Clark Wolf, eds. *The Idea of a Political Idealism: Essays on Rawls.* Lanham: Rowman & Littlefield, 2000.

Dombrowski, Daniel A. *Rawls and Religion: The Case for Political Liberalism.* Albany: State University of New York Press, 2001.

Korsgaard, Christine M., ed. *Reclaiming the History of Ethics: Essays for John Rawls.* New York: Cambridge University Press, 1997.

Kukathas, Chandran. *Rawls:* A Theory of Justice *and Its Critics.* Cambridge: Polity Press in Association with Basil Blackwell, 1990.

Martin, Rex. *Rawls and Rights.* Lawrence: University Press of Kansas, 1985.

Schaefer, David Lewis. *Justice or Tyranny? A Critique of John Rawls's* A Theory of Justice. Port Washington: Kennikat Press, 1979.

Wolff, Robert Paul. *Understanding Rawls: A Reconstruction and Critique of* A Theory of Justice. Princeton: Princeton University Press, 1977.

GLOSSARY

absolute primary quality   Nonsubjective property of an object that exists independently of thought. Berkeley considers this subcategory of primary quality in order to answer objections that primary qualities in judgments of measurement are just as subjectively relative as secondary qualities. *See also* PRIMARY QUALITY; SECONDARY QUALITY; SENSIBLE PRIMARY QUALITY.

abstract entity   Nonspatiotemporal nonphysical existent thing, such as a mathematical object.

abstract general idea   Idea of the most nonparticular category of things, such as the triangle, as opposed to a particular kind of triangle with particular properties.

accident, accidental property   Property that can be added to or eliminated from an object without causing the object to cease to exist, such as a person's hair color or length. Associated with Aristotle's and Scholastic metaphysics. *See also* ESSENCE, ESSENTIAL PROPERTY.

acting from moral law   Kant's concept of acting in order to satisfy the requirements of a moral law. *See also* ACTING IN ACCORD WITH MORAL LAW.

acting in accord with moral law   Kant's concept of acting in agreement with but not necessarily in order to satisfy the requirements of a moral law. *See also* ACTING FROM MORAL LAW.

active phenomenon   An occurrence involving the doing of something or undertaking of an action, such as raising an arm or deciding to run. *See also* PASSION, PASSIVE PHENOMENON.

act utilitarianism   Type of utilitarian theory that evaluates each individual act on the basis of its contribution to happiness or pleasure. *See also* RULE UTILITARIANISM; UTILITARIANISM; UTILITY.

advocacy   Defending a position without necessarily being committed to its truth. *See also* SOPHISM, SOPHIST.

aestheticism, aesthetic ideals   Valuing beauty in art or nature, standards of beauty or related pleasurable sensory criteria. One of Schopenhauer's paths to salvation from the will to life criticized by Nietzsche. *See also* WILL TO LIFE (WILLE ZUM LEBEN).

alteration   Change in an object's accidental property, such as changing hairlength from long to short. *See also* ACCIDENT, ACCIDENTAL PROPERTY; ESSENCE, ESSENTIAL PROPERTY.

altruism, altruistic behavior   Behavior undertaken for the sake of another person's interests or welfare, such as donating to charity. *See also* MORAL EGOISM.

analytic judgment/proposition Judgment or proposition in which a property that belongs to the concept of an object is predicated of or analyzed as belonging to the object, such as the judgment that all triangles are three-sided. *See also* SYNTHETIC A PRIORI JUDGMENT/ PROPOSITION; SYNTHETIC JUDGMENT/PROPOSITION.

analytic philosophy Philosophical method based on the clarification of concepts, including analysis or breaking down of complex into simpler concepts, and defense of positions by sound arguments. Often associated with a view of philosophy as an adjunct to mathematics and science. *See also* PHILOSOPHICAL ANALYSIS.

anamnesis **theory of knowledge** Socrates' position that knowledge is a permanent possession of the immortal soul and needs only to be recalled by suggestive questions. Literally, a memory theory of knowledge. *See also* SOCRATES' GEOMETRY LESSON.

antimaterialism Metaphysics that denies the existence of matter in the sense of an imperceptible substratum to which sensible qualities attach. *See also* MATERIALISM.

anti-Semitism Prejudice against Jewish people and culture.

apodeictic judgment Literally, a demonstrated judgment. *A priori* judgment justified by pure reason or reflection on the meanings of terms independently of experience, such as the judgment that red is a color. *See also* A PRIORI JUDGMENT/PROPOSITION.

Apollo Ancient Greek god of music, reason, and order. *See also* DIONYSUS.

aporia Greek word meaning puzzlement. Final step of Socratic *elenchus* and first step of Socratic *maieutic*. *See also* ELENCHUS; MAIEUSIS, MAIEUTIC.

a posteriori **judgment/proposition** Judgment or proposition that depends on sense experience for its justification, such as the contingent assertions of science. *See also* A PRIORI JUDGMENT/PROPOSITION; EMPIRICISM, EMPIRICIST PHILOSOPHY.

appeal to authority Mode of reasoning or drawing conclusions that seeks answers in the opinions expressed by others deemed to have special expertise, such as the Renaissance era's reliance on the authority of Aristotle in matters of science and philosophy.

a priori **judgment/proposition** Judgment or proposition that does not depend on but is prior to sense experience in its justification, such as analytically true or false propositions and mathematical judgments or propositions. *See also* A POSTERIORI JUDGMENT/PROPOSITION; RATIONALISM, RATIONALIST PHILOSOPHY; SYNTHETIC A PRIORI JUDGMENT/PROPOSITION.

archetypal existence Berkeley's concept of the existence of sensible things as complete congeries of ideas in God's infinite mind. *See also* ECTYPAL EXISTENCE.

Archimedean point An imaginary immovable physical point that could serve as the fulcrum by which Archimedes, an ancient Greek physicist, claimed he could move the Earth by pushing against an absolutely rigid lever. Descartes describes his efforts to discover the proposition *Cogito, sum* ("I think, I exist") as a single belief that he cannot possibly doubt as an Archimedean point by which he can construct a new and absolutely certain system of rational knowledge. *See also* COGITO, SUM.

aretē Greek word for virtue.

Aristotelian distinction *See* FORMAL AND MATERIAL SCIENCES.

asceticism, ascetic ideal Values based on renunciation of pleasure, desire, or will. One of Schopenhauer's paths to salvation from the will to life criticized by Nietzsche. *See also* WILL TO LIFE (WILLE ZUM LEBEN).

atheism   Denial of the existence of God or the gods.

atomic theory of physical matter   Theory that matter is decomposable into atoms or ultimately simple fundamental material constituents. *See also* MATTER.

bare particular   Concept of an indistinguishable individual thing as possessing no properties in itself but to which properties can be attributed or metaphorically attached in the definition or constitution of particular things. Bare particulars are accordingly nonsensible. *See also* BUNDLE THEORY OF SENSIBLE THINGS.

base sensual pleasure   Pleasures associated with carnal desires for food, sex, or other sensuous feelings. *See also* EPICURUS, EPICUREAN PHILOSOPHY, EPICUREANISM; HEDONISM, HEDONISTIC EGOISM, HEDONISTIC UTILITARIANISM.

being *qua* being   Aristotle's term for the metaphysical study of the concept of existence in and of itself, as opposed to the existence of any particular thing or kind of thing.

Berkeley's candle   Example to demonstrate that intense heat is phenomenologically indistinguishable from pain in touching a flame. Meant to prove the idealist thesis that the qualities of sensible things are ideas in the mind rather than existing independently of thought without the mind. *See also* IDEALISM.

beyond good and evil   Nietzsche's concept of the moral attitude of the higher man or philosopher of the future who will act spontaneously without guilt for the sake of egoistic motivations. *See also* EGOISM; MORAL EGOISM.

bourgeois values   Values associated with an acquisitive capitalistic society. Protection of property. *See also* CAPITALIST VALUE SYSTEM; EROTIC MAN.

bundle theory of sensible things   Theory of sensible things defined as connected collection of ideas or sensible qualities. Sensible things construed as bundles of sensible qualities are referred to by Berkeley as congeries of ideas, in contrast to the theory of bare particulars. *See also* BARE PARTICULAR; CONGERIES OF IDEAS; SENSIBLE THING.

capitalist value system   Value system associated with private property and the accumulation of wealth through the investment of private capital in the industrial means of production. *See also* BOURGEOIS VALUES; EROTIC MAN.

care of the soul   Socrates' concept of the purpose of philosophy as directed toward assisting the soul to attain virtue. *See also* MAIEUSIS, MAIEUTIC.

Cartesian circle   Objection to Descartes's proof for the existence of God on the strength of the mind's possession of a clear and distinct idea of God that seems to presuppose the conclusion that God exists and is no deceiver, thereby supporting the reliability of clear and distinct ideas. *See also* DIALLELUS.

casuistry   Determination of what particular things or kinds of things are good, in contrast to definition of the property good or moral goodness in the abstract.

categorical imperative   Kant's formalist deontological rational principle of moral duty, by which we ought always to act only to that moral maxim that we can will to become a universal law for all rational beings. *See also* DEONTOLOGY; FORMAL OR FORMALIST ETHICAL SYSTEM; HYPOTHETICAL IMPERATIVE.

causal good   Moore's concept of an instrumental or extrinsic good, valuable as a means to an end rather than as an intrinsic good valuable as an end in itself. *See also* INTRINSIC VALUE/GOOD.

causation   Relation between events whereby one event, a cause, brings about a change or effect. *See also* CIRCULAR CAUSATION MODEL; EFFICIENT CAUSE; FINAL CAUSE; FORMAL CAUSE; INFINITELY REGRESSIVE CAUSATION; MATERIAL CAUSE; PRIME MOVER (UNMOVED); TERMINAL AND FOUNDATIONAL MODEL OF CAUSATION.

change   Causal modification of an entity leading to its alteration or destruction. *See also* ALTERATION; CAUSATION.

circular causation model   Causal relation model in which the causes of effects occur temporally in a circle or loop. Rejected by Aristotle as inadequate, on the grounds that it makes some effects temporally prior to their causes. *See also* CAUSATION; INFINITELY REGRESSIVE CAUSATION MODEL; PRIME MOVER (UNMOVED); TERMINAL AND FOUNDATIONAL MODEL OF CAUSATION.

clear and distinct perception   Descartes's concept of veridical sense experience. *See also* TRUTHFUL REPRESENTATION.

Cogito, sum   Literally, "I think, I exist." Descartes's adoption of St. Augustine's principle to prove the indubitable existence of his ego or self as a thinking thing, which he tries to make the basis for an epistemically certain system of rational knowledge. *See also* EGOCENTRIC FOUNDATION OF DESCARTES'S PHILOSOPHY.

collective unconscious   Concept of thought processes below the level of consciousness shared by large numbers of persons or even entire cultures or all peoples at all times.

common nature   Metaphysical concept of an essence shared by many different particulars as a universal, as opposed to proper nature. *See also* ESSENCE, ESSENTIAL PROPERTY; PROPER NATURE.

compassion (*Mitleid*)   Vicarious imaginary feeling of or psychologically sharing in another person's pain or distress. Basis for Schopenhauer's moral philosophy, but criticized by Nietzsche.

conceptualism   Theory according to which universals exist only as concepts in the mind. Ockham offers a conceptualist theory of universals that he describes as intentions of the soul. *See also* UNIVERSAL.

congeries of ideas   Berkeley's concept of the connected association of immediate sense impressions as constituting a sensible thing. *See also* SENSIBLE THING.

consequentialism   Theory according to which the moral value of an action or decision to act or type thereof is based on its consequences, usually in terms of its resultant pleasure or pain, happiness or unhappiness. *See also* DEONTOLOGY; UTILITARIANISM.

contingent   Logical modality by which a judgment, proposition, or state of affairs is possible but not necessary.

continuity argument for the existence of God   Berkeley's proof that God as an infinite mind must exist in order to perceive the continuously existing sensible things that are only intermittently perceived by finite minds. *See also* DEPENDENCE ARGUMENT FOR THE EXISTENCE OF GOD.

contrariety   Opposition between contrary properties, such as hot and cold, dry and moist.

conventional morality   Ethical values accepted by a large community without philosophical study or criticism.

conventional sign   Term in an ordinary language used to express an idea. Ockham distinguishes between the conventional signs in written and spoken languages and the natural signs that are intentions of the soul or concepts of mind. *See also* INTENTION OF THE SOUL; NATURAL SIGN.

convertible term   Equivalent terms that can be substituted for one another in a language context without loss of meaning, as in Aristotle's theory of syllogisms and Ockham's medieval logic. *See also* SYLLOGISM, SYLLOGISTIC LOGIC.

copula   Linguistic term that connects a subject term with a predicate. Generally, grammatical cognates of "is" or "has," as in "The sky is blue."

correct belief/opinion   Socrates' term for a true belief that falls short of knowledge because it lacks an adequate reason, warrant, or justification. *See also* KNOWLEDGE.

corruption   *See* GENERATION, CORRUPTION.

cosmos, comos   Greek terms for the ordered universe as opposed to disorder and chaos. *Comos* is the root of the English word "comedy."

counterexample   Example that refutes a definition by satisfying the definition's conditions despite not constituting an instance of what is supposed to be defined, or that refutes an argument by describing a situation that satisfies the argument's assumptions but makes the argument's conclusion false.

critical idealism   Kant's version of idealistic philosophy in which transcendental reasoning is used to justify conclusions that are dogmatically upheld by rationalism but are unavailable to empiricist reliance on sense experience. *See also* IDEALISM.

definition   Aristotle's technical term for a secondary substance or non-Platonic form inhering in a primary substance or in another secondary substance, such as *horse* or *human*. *See also* PRIMARY SUBSTANCE; SECONDARY SUBSTANCE.

de inesse **predication**   Ockham's term for present tense of a predication that is abstract rather than committed to the state of affairs at any particular time or place expressed by a past, present, future tense, or modally qualified judgment or proposition. *See also* PREDICATION IN QUID.

deity, eternal substance   God or a god as that alone which exists most properly on its own and in its own right, which can exist independently of anything else, in Aristotelian or Scholastic metaphysics.

democratic equality   Rawls's subcategory of equal opportunity under the difference principle. Factor that combines the principle of fair equality of opportunity with the difference principle. *See also* DIFFERENCE PRINCIPLE; EQUALITY.

deontology   Moral philosophy according to which duty, justice, and respect for individual moral rights take precedence over the positive consequences of actions or rules governing actions in promoting the greatest good for the greatest number. *See also* CONSEQUENTIALISM; FORMAL OR FORMALIST ETHICAL SYSTEM.

dependence argument for the existence of God   Berkeley's attempt to prove the existence of God on the basis of the fact that sensible things are manifestly independent of finite human will and only passively perceived. *See also* CONTINUITY ARGUMENT FOR THE EXISTENCE OF GOD.

devaluation of values   Nietzsche's characterization of the decadent transition in moral value from the distinction between good and bad to the distinction between good and evil through the imposition on the powerful of a sense of guilt for the willful exercise of power.

diallelus   Literally, "the wheel." Problem of the criterion whereby in order to validate a belief as justified we must appeal to correct epistemic principles, and in order to identify a correct epistemic principle we need to know which beliefs are justified. The problem of the Cartesian circle is sometimes interpreted as an instance of the *diallelus*. *See also* CARTESIAN CIRCLE.

difference principle   Rawls's principle of strong equality according to which everyone living in a society is better off not only despite but because of a differential distribution of social goods. *See also* DISTRIBUTIVE JUSTICE; EQUALITY; FAIR ACCESS TO SOCIAL GOODS; TWO PRINCIPLES OF JUSTICE; UNEQUAL DISTRIBUTION OF SOCIAL GOODS.

Dionysus   Ancient Greek god of wine and pleasure. Associated with sensuality and riotous willful conduct. *See also* APOLLO.

distributive justice   Principle of justice for deciding how the goods of a society are to be distributed to the society's members. *See also* DIFFERENCE PRINCIPLE; EQUALITY; FAIR ACCESS TO SOCIAL GOODS; TWO PRINCIPLES OF JUSTICE; UNEQUAL DISTRIBUTION OF SOCIAL GOODS.

dogmatism   Affirmation of the truth of a proposition or system of beliefs without attempting to offer further justification and in particular without scientific evidence or proof.

double knowledge of good   Moore's concept of knowing both what degree of intrinsic value different things have and how such things may be acquired. *See also* INTRINSIC VALUE/GOOD.

dreaming rationale for maximum skepticism   Descartes's (rejected) hypothesis for maximum doubt on the basis of the difficulty of distinguishing between dreaming and waking experience. *See also* SKEPTICISM, RADICAL SKEPTICISM.

earth, air, fire, water, æther   Aristotle's five material elements, combined from discussions of material properties in the Presocratics. *See also* ELEMENTS.

ectypal existence   Berkeley's concept of the existence of sensible things as partial or limited congeries of ideas in finite minds. *See also* ARCHETYPAL EXISTENCE; CONGERIES OF IDEAS.

edifice of knowledge   Descartes's architectural characterization of knowledge as organized into a kind of building with a foundation and superstructure. *See also* KNOWLEDGE.

efficient cause   Ordinary physical cause whereby an event brings about a change in a material entity. Mechanical causation in the contemporary sense. One of Aristotle's four causes. *See also* CAUSATION; CHANGE; FINAL CAUSE; FORMAL CAUSE; MATERIAL CAUSE.

egocentric foundation of Descartes's philosophy   Principle of *Cogito, sum*. Attempt to establish the edifice of knowledge on the indubitable existence of the ego or thinking self. *See also* COGITO, SUM; EDIFICE OF KNOWLEDGE.

egoism   Theory that moral value belongs exclusively or primarily to the individual's willful desires and pursuit of personal goals. *See also* MORAL EGOISM.

eidos   Greek for idea. Plato's term for a Form or abstract general category of things. *See also* FORM.

elements   Aristotle's concept of material substances in the ousiology located between prime matter of *proté hylé* and primary substances. *See also* EARTH, AIR, FIRE, WATER, ÆTHER; OUSIOLOGY; PRIME MATTER, PROTÉ HYLÉ.

elenchus   Socrates' six-step dialectical method of refuting an interlocutor's attempt to define a general concept, resulting in the rejection of a definition as failing to constitute necessary and sufficient conditions. *See also* NECESSARY CONDITION; SUFFICIENT CONDITION.

empiricism, empiricist philosophy Category of philosophical theory that emphasizes immediate *a posteriori* sense experience in the search for knowledge. *See also* A POSTERIORI JUDGMENT/PROPOSITION; RATIONALISM, RATIONALIST PHILOSOPHY.

Epicurus, Epicurean philosophy, epicureanism Ancient Greek philosopher. His school of philosophy that emphasized pleasure in the sense of avoidance of pain. Sometimes confused with the pursuit of purely sensuous pleasure. *See also* BASE SENSUAL PLEASURE.

epistemic certainty Degree of justification of a judgment or proposition such that no other judgment or proposition is more strongly justified.

equality Exact same distribution of any quality or entity among the individuals in a given domain. *See also* DIFFERENCE PRINCIPLE; DISTRIBUTIVE JUSTICE; FAIR ACCESS TO SOCIAL GOODS; TWO PRINCIPLES OF JUSTICE; UNEQUAL DISTRIBUTION OF SOCIAL GOODS.

equilibrium *See* REFLECTIVE EQUILIBRIUM.

erotic man Greek concept of a character or personality type that is primarily motivated by considerations of desire, power, and the acquisition of things.

Esse est percipi aut posse percipere Literally, "To be is to be perceived or a perceiver." Berkeley's Latin motto for his radical idealism, according to which whatever exists is either a mind (perceiver) or idea (something perceived) existing in a mind. *See also* IDEALISM.

essence, essential property A property or set of properties without which a thing ceases to exist as that particular kind of thing, such as being rational as an essential property of a human being if human beings are rightly defined as rational animals. Associated with Aristotle's and Scholastic metaphysics. *See also* ACCIDENT, ACCIDENTAL PROPERTY.

eternal substance *See* DEITY, ETERNAL SUBSTANCE.

ethical naturalism Moral theory that attempts to define moral goodness in terms of some natural property, such as pleasure or happiness. Moore criticizes this category of ethics. *See also* NATURALISTIC FALLACY; OPEN QUESTION ARGUMENT.

ethics of punishment Nietzsche's concept of the moral justification for punishment. Contrary to conventional moral opinion, Nietzsche regards punishment as morally justified only when it serves to restrain the efforts of the weak to impose their acts of resentment against the strong.

eudaimonia Ancient Greek word for happiness or the good life. Happiness in this sense is not usually understood as a life of pleasure or joy, but as a life in accord with the principles of virtue or with the natural function of human existence.

European Buddhism Nietzsche's polemical term for Schopenhauer's moral philosophy and for Judeo-Christian moral values of compassion that try to deny or suppress the will to life or will to power—that are life-denying or that say "no" rather than an affirmative "yes" to life. *See also* LIFE-AFFIRMING, SAYING "YES" TO LIFE; LIFE-DENYING, SAYING "NO" TO LIFE; SCHOPENHAUER'S PESSIMISTIC MORAL PHILOSOPHY; WILL TO LIFE (WILLE ZUM LEBEN); WILL TO POWER (WILLE ZUR MACHT).

evil demon (evil genius, malignant spirit) rationale for maximum skepticism Descartes's (accepted) hypothesis to maximize doubt on the basis of the possibility of a malicious spirit that clouds our understanding and deceives us about the true condition of the external world. *See also* SKEPTICISM, RADICAL SKEPTICISM.

existence, subsistence Spatiotemporal or physical being as opposed to abstract nonspatiotemporal or nonphysical being, such as the moon versus the number 2.

Ex nihilo nihil fit Literally, "Out of nothing, nothing is made." The principle holds that we cannot assume that anything can come to exist without a sufficient explanation of its existence. Descartes implicitly accepts a version of this principle in order to prove that God exists by appeal to the light of nature principle that the cause of any of his ideas must have at least as much formal reality as the idea has objective reality. *See also* FORMAL REALITY; LIGHT OF NATURE (LUMEN NATURALE); OBJECTIVE REALITY.

experiential criterion of comparative pleasures Mill's basis for distinguishing the value of pleasures in deciding what actions are justified by hedonic utilitarian principles. *See also* HEDONISM; UTILITARIANISM.

external sanctions of morality Mill's concept of reasons or motivations for following the principles of a moral doctrine based on such factors as the good opinion of others, punishments used to reinforce rules and values, and the desire to maintain a good self-image. *See also* INTERNAL SANCTIONS OF MORALITY; MORAL SANCTIONS OF UTILITARIANISM.

extrinsic property A property that a thing has by virtue of its relations to things other than itself. *See also* INTRINSIC PROPERTY.

fair access to social goods Rawls's concept of equality of competition for the acquisition of social goods that does not preclude unequal distributions. *See also* DIFFERENCE PRINCIPLE; DISTRIBUTIVE JUSTICE; EQUALITY; TWO PRINCIPLES OF JUSTICE; UNEQUAL DISTRIBUTION OF SOCIAL GOODS.

false predication *See* TRUE PREDICATION, FALSE PREDICATION.

final cause Goal or purpose for the sake of which something occurs. One of Aristotle's four causes. *See also* CAUSATION; CHANGE; EFFICIENT CAUSE; FORMAL CAUSE; MATERIAL CAUSE; TELOS.

first cause *See* PRIME MOVER (UNMOVED).

first intention *See* TERM OF FIRST INTENTION.

first philosophy, *prote philosophia* Aristotle's concept of the most elementary category of philosophy, consisting of questions that must be settled first before other more advanced topics can be investigated. Aristotle's term for what has later come to be known as metaphysics. *See also* METAPHYSICS.

first principle of justice Rawls's principle whereby each person in a just society is to have an equal right to the most extensive scheme of equal basic liberties compatible with a similar scheme of liberties for others. *See also* DIFFERENCE PRINCIPLE; DISTRIBUTIVE JUSTICE; EQUALITY; FAIR ACCESS TO SOCIAL GOODS; SECOND PRINCIPLE OF JUSTICE; UNEQUAL DISTRIBUTION OF SOCIAL GOODS.

first virtue Rawls's concept of justice as the most basic value that must be satisfied by an ethical or political system. Comparable to truth as the first value that must be satisfied by any theory. *See also* DISTRIBUTIVE JUSTICE; TWO PRINCIPLES OF JUSTICE.

five types of universals Ockham's characterization of five distinct Aristotelian categories of universals, including genus, species, difference, property, and accident. *See also* ACCIDENT, ACCIDENTAL PROPERTY; GENUS; PROPERTY; SPECIES, SPECIES DIFFERENCE; UNIVERSAL.

Form Plato's concept of abstract general categories of things. *See also* EIDOS.

formal and material sciences   Kant's reference to the Aristotelian distinction between logic and mathematics versus the natural sciences.

formal cause   Formal properties of things, logical or geometrical, without which the existence and other properties of a thing cannot be fully explained. One of Aristotle's four causes. *See also* CAUSATION; CHANGE; EFFICIENT CAUSE; FINAL CAUSE; MATERIAL CAUSE.

formal or formalist ethical system   Kant's Aristotelian classification of his deontological moral philosophy on the grounds that the categorical imperative is concerned exclusively with the form of moral judgment and moral conduct as opposed to its matter or content, and because the basis for implementing the categorical imperative has to do with the purely formal logical question of whether or not a moral maxim can be logically consistently willed to be a universal law for all rational beings. *See also* CATEGORICAL IMPERATIVE; DEONTOLOGY; STOIC PHILOSOPHY.

formal principle   Aristotle's concept of the definitions or secondary substances including geometrical shapes of things in the ordinary sense of "form," as contrasted with material principles. *See also* SECONDARY SUBSTANCE.

formal reality   Descartes's use of a Scholastic concept of real actuality, as contrasted with objective reality, in his proof for the existence of God. *See also* OBJECTIVE REALITY.

foundationalist epistemology   Theory of knowledge that regards some propositions or beliefs as absolutely basic in the sense that they do not stand in need of justification but serve as principles in terms of which other beliefs and propositions can be justified. In some foundationalist epistemologies the expectation is that the theory will build its explanations on epistemically certain foundations. *See also* EDIFICE OF KNOWLEDGE.

four applications of the categorical imperative   Kant's illustrations of uses of the categorical imperative in moral decision making, including an injunction against committing suicide, against borrowing money with no intention to repay, against failing to develop one's talents and living instead a life of lazy pleasure, and in support of charitably donating excess wealth to persons in need. *See also* CATEGORICAL IMPERATIVE.

four Aristotelian causes   *See* EFFICIENT CAUSE; FINAL CAUSE; FORMAL CAUSE; MATERIAL CAUSE.

fourfold root of the principle of sufficient reason   Schopenhauer's epistemology of explanations of phenomena in the world as representation, in terms of logical, mathematical, causal, and moral or motivational factors.

four senses of justice   Mill's distinction between four types of justice or ways in which justice is attributed to individual and social actions and decision making. They include (1) assuring that no one is deprived of personal liberty, his property, or any other thing conferred by law, (2) assuring that rights that ought not to be conferred on a person are not done so by means of a bad law unjustified by utilitarian principles, (3) assuring that persons receive what they deserve according to their social agreements, (4) assuring that persons do not break faith in the sense of violating promises made to others.

free will, freedom   variously interpreted concepts of undetermined or unconstrained decision making or action.

functionalism, functionalist theory of substance   Aristotle's metaphysics of substance as defined in terms of natural function. *See also* NATURAL FUNCTION; SUBSTANCE.

genealogy of morality   Nietzsche's project of providing a family tree to explain the historical evolution of moral concepts—in particular, as he sees it, the decadent development of the distinction between good and evil from an original noble distinction between good and bad. *See also* DEVALUATION OF VALUES; GOOD AND BAD, GOOD AND EVIL.

generation, corruption Causing something to exist or not to exist. Creation and destruction.

genus Category of universal that subsumes species as a more general category. *See also* SPECIES, SPECIES DIFFERENCE; UNIVERSAL.

geometer's method Socrates' hypothetical method of dealing with the properties of things for which he is unable to provide an adequate analysis by arguing that if a thing has a certain property then it must have another second kind of property, and inquiring whether in fact it has a property of the second kind.

given datum or starting place for philosophical inquiry and in particular for Kant's method of transcendental reasoning. *See also* TRANSCENDENTAL REASONING.

God rationale for maximum skepticism Descartes's (rejected) hypothesis for maximum skepticism. *See also* SKEPTICISM, RADICAL SKEPTICISM.

going between a dilemma's horns Argumentative technique for dealing with a dilemma by defending a third alternative to the two choices represented by the dilemma. *See also* GRASPING A DILEMMA HORN.

good and bad, good and evil Nietzsche's genealogical characterization of the reversal and devaluation of moral values from an original noble distinction between the powerful and weak to a later distinction between the weak and the powerful. *See also* DEVALUATION OF VALUES; GENEALOGY OF MORALITY.

good, goodness, the good Moore's distinction between the indefinable moral goodness as a property of things as opposed to the collection of good things that have the property of moral goodness or of being morally good.

good will Attitude of wanting to promote moral goodness. Kant's thesis is that the only unqualifiedly good thing is a good will.

grasping a dilemma horn Argumentative technique for dealing with a dilemma by accepting one of the two choices represented by the dilemma and arguing that it does not actually have the negative theoretical consequences otherwise attributed to it. *See also* GOING BETWEEN A DILEMMA'S HORNS.

greatest good principle Consequentialist utilitarian moral principle according to which moral good is defined in terms of maximizing the pleasure or happiness produced by an action or rule governing actions. *See also* CONSEQUENTIALISM, UTILITARIANISM.

haecceity Individual essence. *See also* ESSENCE, ESSENTIAL PROPERTY.

happiness Pleasure or joy, or the good life in accord with principles of virtue. *See also* EUDAIMONIA.

hedonism, hedonistic egoism, hedonistic utilitarianism Moral philosophy based on pleasure. *See also* BASE SENSUAL PLEASURE; UTILITARIANISM.

herd instinct Nietzsche's polemical term for the unthinking following of moral values by persons who agree with conventional compassionate morality.

higher intellectual pleasure Pleasures associated with mental faculties rather than sensual experiences. *See also* BASE SENSUAL PLEASURE.

higher man (*Übermensch*) Nietzsche's concept of a future person who will rise above feelings of guilt and act spontaneously in accord with egoistic desires and the will to power.

horns of a dilemma   Two choices in a logical form of argument that lead to the same or equivalent conclusions. *See also* GOING BETWEEN A DILEMMA'S HORNS; GRASPING A DILEMMA HORN.

hubris   Greek word for sense of over-confidence or inflated self-importance.

hylé   Ancient Greek word for wood. Used philosophically in Aristotle's metaphysics to refer to matter or material substance. *See also* PRIME MATTER, PROTÉ HYLÉ.

hypothetical imperative   Kant's concept of a conditional command to be followed only for the sake of achieving another purpose. *See also* CATEGORICAL IMPERATIVE.

idea   Immediate sense impression. Content of experience.

idealism   Philosophical ideology according to which only ideas or thought contents and minds exist. *See also* CRITICAL IDEALISM.

identity   Sameness relation between a thing and itself whereby two names designate the same thing if and only if all the properties truly predicated of an object under one name are truly predicated of the object under the other name, and conversely.

illusion rationale for maximum skepticism   Descartes's (rejected) hypothesis for maximal doubt based on the fact that we are sometimes deceived by sensory illusions and concluding that for all we know we may therefore always be deceived by any or all of our sense experiences. *See also* SKEPTICISM, RADICAL SKEPTICISM.

illusory perception   Sense experience that does not correctly represent an existent state of affairs.

immaterialism   Philosophical ideology according to which there is no matter and no material entities in the sense of a substratum to which the sensible properties of sensible things attach. *See also* IDEALISM; MATERIALISM.

immortality of the soul   Persistence of the ego, self, soul, or personality after the body's death.

immovable   Aristotle's term for an abstract entity, also described as "eternal" in his metaphysics of substance. *See also* SUBSTANCE.

inclination   Desire to do or have something. According to Kant, it is irrelevant to morality of an action. *See also* BASE SENSUAL PLEASURE.

incorporeal   Immaterial nonphysical entity in Aristotle's metaphysics.

indefinable concept   Moore's category of a basic concept that cannot be further defined or analyzed but is primitive, irreducible, or absolutely basic, such as, according to Moore, yellow and good.

indeterminate   Presocratic philosopher Anaxagoras's concept of an underlying stuff of the universe that has no particular qualities in and of itself, but which has the potential to become anything if molded or shaped or qualified in the right way. *See also* PRIME MATTER, PROTÉ HYLÉ.

indexical term   General term that refers to a particular person, place, or time by reference to a language user's immediate context.

infinitely regressive causation model   Causal relation model in which the causes of effects recede infinitely into the past. Rejected by Aristotle as inadequate, in view of his rejection of actual infinities as a solution to Zeno's paradoxes. *See also* CAUSATION; CIRCULAR

CAUSATION MODEL; PRIME MOVER (UNMOVED); TERMINAL AND FOUNDATIONAL MODEL OF CAUSATION.

inhere, inherence Aristotle's concept of the relation between a secondary substance and the primary or other secondary substances to which it is truly predicated. A secondary substance inheres in another substance in the sense that it exists only in or as part of the substance in which it inheres. *See also* PRIMARY SUBSTANCE; SECONDARY SUBSTANCE.

initial position Rawls's concept of a situation prior to the establishment of a society in which negotiators seek to develop the principles of justice in a social contract. *See also* ORIGINAL SITUATION/POSITION; SOCIAL CONTRACT; TWO PRINCIPLES OF JUSTICE.

instrumental value/good Something good or valuable as a means to an end rather than intrinsically as an end in itself. *See also* INTRINSIC VALUE/GOOD.

intention of the soul Ockham's concept of a concept or mental or psychological content. Developed by Ockham as a non-Platonistic theory of universals. *See also* TERM OF FIRST INTENTION; TERM OF SECOND INTENTION; UNIVERSAL.

internal representation of the moral law Kant's concept of the will calling before the mind the requirements of a moral principle in order to act from it rather than merely in accord with it. According to Kant, it is required in order for an act to be genuinely moral. *See also* MORAL LAW.

internal sanctions of morality Mill's concept of the feelings associated with right actions whereby individuals are inclined to follow moral principles, including feelings of guilt for not acting rightly. *See also* EXTERNAL SANCTIONS OF MORALITY; MORAL SANCTIONS OF UTILITARIANISM; ULTIMATE SANCTION OF MORALITY.

intrinsic property Property that belongs to a thing's nature or essence rather than by virtue of its relations to other things. *See also* EXTRINSIC PROPERTY.

intrinsic value/good Something good or valuable as an end in itself or for its own sake rather than instrumentally as a means to another end. *See also* INSTRUMENTAL VALUE/GOOD.

inviolability Rawls's deontic concept of the absolute observance of rights conferred on the members of a society by considerations of justice. *See also* DEONTOLOGY; TWO PRINCIPLES OF JUSTICE.

is-ought gap Distinction and inferential disparity between statements of fact and statements of value whereby it is deductively invalid to infer statements of value from statements of fact.

is-statement Statement that describes a matter of fact. *See also* OUGHT-STATEMENT.

judgment error Mistake in drawing false or inadequately justified inferences from insufficient evidence or reasoning.

justice Moral value of individual and social practices by which persons are treated equitably according to various standards of fairness or respect for rights. *See also* DISTRIBUTIVE JUSTICE; EQUALITY.

justice as fairness Rawls's theory according to which justice is treating all persons fairly or in some sense equally, in contrast to preferential or discriminatory treatment. *See also* EQUALITY.

kingdom of ends Kant's concept of an ideal social order in which all persons treat all other persons with respect for their moral rights by treating them always as ends in themselves and never merely as means to another end.

knightly-aristocratic values   Nietzsche's concept of a noble morality that embodies an unrestricted egoistic will to power. *See also* WILL TO POWER (WILLE ZUR MACHT).

knowledge   Relevantly justified true belief.

Lethe river   River of forgetfulness in Greek mythology.

liberal equality   Rawls's subcategory of equality as fair opportunity under the category of the principle of efficiency. A concept by which a society might seek to redress inequalities of circumstance by a program of redistributions of social goods, such as the affirmative action program. *See also* DIFFERENCE PRINCIPLE; DISTRIBUTIVE JUSTICE; EQUALITY; FAIR ACCESS TO SOCIAL GOODS; TWO PRINCIPLES OF JUSTICE; UNEQUAL DISTRIBUTION OF SOCIAL GOODS.

life-affirming, saying "yes" to life   Nietzsche's concept of healthy noble moral values associated with unrestricted will to power that he believes are essential to the achievement of full human potential. *See also* WILL TO POWER (WILLE ZUR MACHT).

life-denying, saying "no" to life   Nietzsche's concept of unhealthy ignoble and ultimately anti-moral values associated with restrictions of the will to power—through guilt or denial—that he believes are inimical to the achievement of full human potential. *See also* WILL TO POWER (WILLE ZUR MACHT).

light of nature (*lumen naturale*)   Descartes's use of a Scholastic concept of pure reason presupposed by any philosophical system by which he proposes to evaluate alternative motivations for maximum doubt and to advance a proof for the existence of God. *See also* DEITY, ETERNAL SUBSTANCE.

logic of terms   Aristotelian system of logic in which arguments are constructions out of propositions and propositions are subject-predicate constructions out of individual terms for substances and properties.

maieusis, maieutic   Ancient Greek for midwifery. Socrates claims to be a midwife of philosophical theories and ideas, helping to give birth to them as part of what he calls the care of the soul. *See also* CARE OF THE SOUL.

manifold of experience   Kant's term for fields of sensation, including the visual, auditory, and other perceptual domains.

material cause   Material properties of things. The matter or stuff of which a thing is made, without which the existence and other properties of that physical thing cannot be fully explained. One of Aristotle's four causes. *See also* CAUSATION; CHANGE; EFFICIENT CAUSE; FINAL CAUSE; FORMAL CAUSE; MATERIALISM; MATTER.

materialism   Philosophical ideology according to which matter or material substance is the only or primary existent thing. In Berkeley's philosophy, the theory that there exists an insensible mind-independent substratum underlying the sensible properties of sensible things. *See also* MATTER.

material substance   *See* MATTER.

matter   Physical component of spatiotemporal things. The matter or stuff of which physical things are made.

maxim of justice   Mill's concept of the way in which principles of justice are codified in distinct general rules. *See also* JUSTICE.

metaphysical definition of good   Moore's concept of a version of naturalism in which good or moral goodness is defined in terms of abstract entities or principles, such as Kant's categorical imperative. *See also* CATEGORICAL IMPERATIVE; GOOD, GOODNESS, THE GOOD; NATURALISTIC FALLACY.

metaphysics Philosophical study of the most basic categories of being. Includes such topics as identity, existence, causation, mind, freedom of will, God. *See also* CAUSATION; EXISTENCE, SUBSISTENCE; FREE WILL, FREEDOM; IDENTITY.

metaphysics of change Principles that explain the possibility and conditions for physical spatiotemporal objects to be created, destroyed, or undergo alterations of their properties. *See also* ALTERATION; CAUSATION; CHANGE.

mind-independent entity Object as it exists without being perceived or thought about. *See also* PRIMARY QUALITY; THING-IN-ITSELF (DING AN SICH).

mite's foot Berkeley's example of the supposedly objective mind-independent primary quality of spatial extension (size of an insect's foot), which Berkeley argues is as subjectively relative as any secondary quality. *See also* PRIMARY QUALITY; SECONDARY QUALITY.

moral autonomy Kant's theory of the sense of freedom presupposed by moral judgment. Autonomy is literally self-rule or self-governance, as when reason governs itself by accepting a purely rational moral rule in the form of the categorical imperative. *See also* CATEGORICAL IMPERATIVE; MORAL HETERONOMY.

moral compassion Compassion for the situation and especially the suffering of others that typically motivates moral decision making and action. *See also* COMPASSION (MITLEID).

moral duty, moral obligation Moral requirement to do or refrain from doing a specific act or kind of act. *See also* CATEGORICAL IMPERATIVE; HYPOTHETICAL IMPERATIVE.

moral egoism Theory that it is morally permissible or morally obligatory only to act on behalf of one's own rational self-interests. *See also* EGOISM.

moral heteronomy Kant's theory of the sense of unfreedom by which reason is ruled or governed by something other than itself, as when moral guidance is accepted on the basis of emotion or other empirical psychological strictly nonrational considerations, such as concern for the consequences, pleasure or pain resulting from an action according to the principle of the greatest good for the greatest number. *See also* MORAL AUTONOMY.

moral intent The moral aim or goal with which an action is undertaken.

moral intuition, moral intuitionism Faculty of or theory according to which there is a special immediate cognition of moral value and especially of moral goodness.

morality of compassion Ethics based on sympathetic feelings for the situation and especially for the suffering of others. *See also* COMPASSION (MITLEID).

moral judgment Judgment or assessment of moral value.

moral law General ethical principle establishing obligation or determining moral value of an action or state of mind.

morally good will Attitude or intention of acting from moral duty or in order to achieve positive moral value. Kant maintains that the only unqualified good thing is a morally good will. *See also* GOOD WILL; MORAL DUTY, MORAL OBLIGATION.

moral maxim Particular ethical principle offering guidance for action-specific circumstances.

moral nihilism *See* NIHILISM, MORAL NIHILISM, NIHILISTIC MORAL OUTLOOK.

moral obligation *See* MORAL DUTY, MORAL OBLIGATION.

moral preferability   Mill's criterion for identifying the things or kinds of things that are worthy of being preferred.

moral responsibility   Requirement for individuals to qualify as moral agents. Variously interpreted as acting freely, recognizing or being prepared to correct consequences of actions.

moral right   Respect for an individual's moral value or moral interests. Variously interpreted as belonging specifically to all and only rational or sentient beings.

moral sanctions of utilitarianism   Reasons or motivations for acting in accord with utilitarian moral principles. *See also* EXTERNAL SANCTIONS OF MORALITY; INTERNAL SANCTIONS OF MORALITY; ULTIMATE SANCTION OF MORALITY.

natural aristocracy   Rawls's concept of a class of individuals who are suited by nature through their efforts to acquire what is in fact an unequal distribution of goods, ultimately justified by its contribution to the advantage of all members of a just society. *See also* UNEQUAL DISTRIBUTION OF SOCIAL GOODS.

natural definition of good   Definition of moral goodness in terms of natural properties. Criticized by Moore as committing the naturalistic fallacy. *See also* NATURALISTIC FALLACY; OPEN QUESTION ARGUMENT.

natural function   Aristotle's concept of the purpose of a primary substance by which it tends naturally, when uninhibited, to attain a certain end or develop toward a certain end state. *See also* FUNCTIONALISM, FUNCTIONALIST THEORY OF SUBSTANCE; PRIMARY SUBSTANCE.

naturalistic fallacy   Moore's characterization of what he regards as mistaken efforts to define moral goodness in terms of natural properties such as pleasure or happiness. *See also* OPEN QUESTION ARGUMENT.

natural liberty   Rawls's concept of a subcategory of equality of careers open to all persons who have the requisite talents under the principle of efficiency. *See also* EQUALITY; PRINCIPLE OF EFFICIENCY.

natural lottery   Rawls's concept of the random genetic distinctions between the members of a society by which they have different capabilities in competition for social goods. *See also* DIFFERENCE PRINCIPLE; DISTRIBUTIVE JUSTICE; EQUALITY; FAIR ACCESS TO SOCIAL GOODS; TWO PRINCIPLES OF JUSTICE; UNEQUAL DISTRIBUTION OF SOCIAL GOODS.

natural sign   Ockham's concept of the mind's designation of a certain collection of objects as universal. Universals as intentions of the soul naturally signify the set of objects said to exemplify the universal. Natural signs are the psychological basis for the designation of objects and meaning of universal terms by conventional signs in conventional language. *See also* UNIVERSAL.

necessary condition   Requirement without which an object fails to satisfy the terms of a concept or definition. *See also* SUFFICIENT CONDITION.

nepotism   Favoritism toward one's relatives or, by extension, friends and associates in the allocation of goods or offices that are supposed to be competitively distributed on the basis of merit.

nihilism, moral nihilism, nihilistic moral outlook   Philosophical ideology according to which nothing exists or nothing has value. Alternatively, nothingness or the negation of conventional value as itself a value.

nirvana   Asian religious and philosophical concept of a state of eternal peace attained by escaping from the wheel of *dharma*, or the endless cycle of birth, death, and rebirth. *See also* WHEEL OF DHARMA.

nomen   Latin word for name.

nomic possibility   Possibility according to natural law. Possible under the law, as opposed to logical possibility.

nominalism   Reductive theory that interprets universals not as real abstract Platonic entities, but only as names for particulars with similar or resemblant particular qualities.

nonparticular substance   *See* UNIVERSAL.

normative philosophy   Philosophy of values, as contrasted with theoretical or speculative philosophy. *See also* THEORETICAL PHILOSOPHY.

notion   Berkeley's technical term for the mind's apprehension of the existence of another mind. There are no ideas of minds according to Berkeley because minds are active and ideas are passive.

noumena, phenomena   Kant's distinction between representationally unknowable mind-independent reality, or thing-in-itself, and the world as it appears to perception and thought. *See also* THING-IN-ITSELF (DING AN SICH).

objective reality   Facts of the world as they exist independent of subjective perception and judgment. *See also* FORMAL REALITY.

Ockham's razor   Methodological principle that we ought not to multiply entities beyond explanatory necessity.

one and the many   Platonic and Presocratic Parmenidean distinction between the world in reality as a unified entity and the many unreal individual things that appear to sensation. Distinction also exploited in Plato's political philosophy in the opposition between an aristocracy and a democracy when choosing an ideal form of government.

ontological proof for the existence of God   Argument to prove that God exists on the strength of the assumption that God's essence entails God's existence, or from the assumption that God is defined as possessing all perfections together with the assumption that existence for anything so defined is a perfection, or that God is defined as that than which nothing greater is conceivable and that if God did not exist then a being other and greater than God would be conceivable. *See also* DEITY, ETERNAL SUBSTANCE.

ontology   Metaphysics of being or existence.

ontos   Greek word for being or existence.

open question argument   Moore's argument by which he exposes the naturalistic fallacy in efforts to define moral goodness in terms of natural properties by asking in every case whether whatever is associated with moral good is itself something morally good, a fact, Moore implies, that always remains an open question. *See also* NATURALISTIC FALLACY.

organic unity   Moore's concept of a moral good that is greater than the mere sum of its parts.

original situation/position   Rawls's concept of an imaginary starting place for social contract negotiations prior to the establishment of any political institutions. *See also* INITIAL POSITION.

origin of evil   Nietzsche's obsession with the question of how to explain and account for the existence of such natural evils as pain and suffering. *See also* GOOD AND BAD, GOOD AND EVIL.

"ought" implies "can" principle   Kant's principle that if we are morally obligated to do something, then it must be something we are able to do. If we cannot do something, it follows according to the principle that we are not morally obligated to do it. *See also* MORAL DUTY, MORAL OBLIGATION.

ought-statement   Statement that describes what should or ought to occur or should or ought to be done. *See also* IS-STATEMENT.

ousia   Ancient Greek word for substance. *See also* OUSIOLOGY; PRIMARY SUBSTANCE; SECONDARY SUBSTANCE; SUBSTANCE.

ousiology   Aristotelian ontology of substance with pure form or pure actuality (God) and prime matter or pure potentiality as its extremes. Primary substance is at the center. The elements (earth, air, fire, water, and æther) are located between primary substance and prime matter on the material side, and the definitions or secondary substances are located between primary substance and pure form or pure actuality (God) on the formal side. *See also* ELEMENTS; OUSIA; PRIMARY SUBSTANCE; SECONDARY SUBSTANCE; SUBSTANCE.

parasitic concept   A concept the meaning or application of which depends on the existence of another concept or the truth of an otherwise unrelated proposition.

particular, particular substance   Individual substance to which properties can be attributed. *See also* OUSIA; SUBSTANCE; UNIVERSAL.

passion, passive phenomenon   Experience suffered or lived through by the mind rather than actively undertaken by it. *See also* ACTIVE PHENOMENON.

perception   Sense experience of the external world.

perfectionism   Moral ideal according to which we are obligated to fully develop our talents, abilities, and virtues. Aristotle considers this to be a natural function of human beings as social animals. *See also* NATURAL FUNCTION.

perfect procedural justice   Rawls's concept of a method of attaining distributive justice through a procedure that is certain to avoid unfair allocations of social goods—illustrated by the example of a person cutting a cake into slices and then being the last to choose a piece. *See also* DISTRIBUTIVE JUSTICE; EQUALITY; FAIR ACCESS TO SOCIAL GOODS; TWO PRINCIPLES OF JUSTICE; UNEQUAL DISTRIBUTION OF SOCIAL GOODS.

persistence of things through change   *See* ALTERATION; CHANGE.

perspectivalism, moral and epistemic   Philosophical ideology that emphasizes the uniqueness of each subject's situation in judging the truth of moral or scientific propositions. Nietzsche explicitly develops a kind of perspectivalism.

pessimistic moral philosophy   *See* SCHOPENHAUER'S PESSIMISTIC MORAL PHILOSOPHY.

philosopher of the future   *See* HIGHER MAN (ÜBERMENSCH).

philosophical analysis   Conceptual decomposition of complex terms or concepts into simpler and ultimately basic or fundamental concepts. Clarification of ideas through dialectic, argument, and critical consideration of definitions. *See also* ANALYTIC PHILOSOPHY.

piece of wax example   Descartes's illustration of how reason is supposed to be better equipped than immediate sensation to judge the identity of physical things through change. Offered by Descartes to prove that the mind is better knowable than the body and hence to establish a metaphysical distinction between mind and body.

Plato's theory of Forms   *See* FORM.

polemic   Rhetorical use of literary devices to establish a philosophical position by presenting a favored view in a positive light and contrary positions in a negative light without relying on argument.

possible pure will Kant's concept of a will to act from, rather than merely in accord with, a moral principle. Distinguished from inclinations and other psychological factors involved in the complex motivations of moral agents.

practical anthropology Kant's term for empirical psychological and circumstantial cultural factors in the moral conduct of human moral agents.

practical cognition Kant's term for empirical elements in moral thinking.

pragmatic reason Justification based on action and its consequences for practical activities, judged in terms of success or failure in facilitating such actions and activities.

predicable Properties of substances in Aristotle's metaphysics, such as hot, cold, dry, and moist. *See also* SUBSTANCE.

predication *in quid* Ockham's concept of the attribution of a universal that is constitutive of a thing. *See also* UNIVERSAL.

prepolitical state of nature Characterization of the original or initial position in social contract theory prior to the institution of a political entity. *See also* SOCIAL CONTRACT.

Presocratic thinkers Philosophers and protoscientists who preceded Socrates, including but not limited to Parmenides, Heraclitus of Ephesus, Pythagoras, Thales of Miletus, Zeno of Elea, Anaxagoras, Anaximander, and Anaximenes.

presupposition Acceptance of a belief or principle without which another belief or principle would not be true or even possible. *See also* TRANSCENDENTAL GROUND OF MORALS; TRANSCENDENTAL GROUND OF SCIENCE.

priestly mentality/values *See* GOOD AND BAD, GOOD AND EVIL; RESSENTIMENT; SLAVE MORALITY; TRANSVALUATION OF VALUE.

primacy of philosophical reasoning Attitude exemplified by Ockham of treating philosophical argument as more important than appeals to authority. *See also* APPEAL TO AUTHORITY.

primary quality Mind-independent objective property of things. Includes especially shape, size (extension), and weight (gravity), among others. *See also* MIND-INDEPENDENT ENTITY; SECONDARY QUALITY.

primary substance Substance in the most proper sense of the word. Samples of stuff. Particular spatiotemporal individual entities. Located at the very center of Aristotle's ousiology in his metaphysics. *See also* OUSIO; OUSIOLOGY; SECONDARY SUBSTANCE; SUBSTANCE.

prime matter, *proté hylé* Aristotle's concept of the most basic material stuff underlying primary substance. It is pure potentiality in Aristotle's metaphysics because it can be made into anything by receiving an appropriate form—in the first instance, by being distinguished into the five elements. *See also* EARTH, AIR, FIRE, WATER, ÆTHER; ELEMENTS; MATTER; OUSIA; OUSIOLOGY; PURE POTENTIALITY.

prime mover (unmoved) Aristotle's concept of a first cause that initiates motion in the universe but is not caused to do so by any prior event and is in that sense self-moved. Often equated with God or a god in Aristotle's metaphysics. *See also* CAUSATION; CIRCULAR CAUSATION MODEL; INFINITELY REGRESSIVE CAUSATION MODEL; TERMINAL AND FOUNDATIONAL MODEL OF CAUSATION.

principium individuationis Schopenhauer's concept of the principle of individuation by which things in the world as representation only are distinguished from one another as distinct individuals.

principle of efficiency Rawls's concept of a maximum principle for distributing social goods whereby it is impossible to improve the condition of at least one member of a society without degrading the condition of at least one member. *See also* DIFFERENCE PRINCIPLE; DISTRIBUTIVE JUSTICE; EQUALITY; FAIR ACCESS TO SOCIAL GOODS; TWO PRINCIPLES OF JUSTICE; UNEQUAL DISTRIBUTION OF SOCIAL GOODS.

principle of justice *See* FIRST PRINCIPLE OF JUSTICE; PRIORITY RULE FOR THE FIRST PRINCIPLE OF JUSTICE; SECOND PRINCIPLE OF JUSTICE; TWO PRINCIPLES OF JUSTICE.

principle of the greatest good for the greatest number *See* GREATEST GOOD PRINCIPLE.

priority rule for the first principle of justice Rawls's rule whereby the principles of justice are to be ranked in lexical order and liberty can be restricted only for the sake of liberty: (a) a less extensive liberty must strengthen the total system of liberty shared by all and (b) a less than equal liberty must be acceptable to those citizens with the lesser liberty. *See also* FIRST PRINCIPLE OF JUSTICE.

problem of change Philosophical problem of understanding the metaphysics of causation, whereby some things change while in some sense persisting or remaining the same. *See also* CAUSATION; CHANGE.

proper nature Ockham's concept of the essential properties belonging to an individual thing and not necessarily shared by others, in contrast with common nature. *See also* COMMON NATURE; ESSENCE, ESSENTIAL PROPERTY.

property Quality of an object. Feature by which an object is characterized and distinguished from other objects. *See also* ESSENCE, ESSENTIAL PROPERTY.

proté hylé *See* PRIME MATTER, PROTÉ HYLÉ.

proté philosophia *See* FIRST PHILOSOPHY, PROTÉ PHILOSOPHIA.

prudential consideration Reason or motivation for action based on what it would be valuable to do from the standpoint of protecting or advancing one's rational interests, as opposed to purely moral considerations. *See also* PURELY MORAL CONSIDERATION.

psyché Greek word for soul. Literally, "butterfly" in ancient Greek. Root of modern English word "psychology."

psychological certainty Strong feeling of conviction that a given belief must be true. Psychological certainty does not imply or guarantee that a belief is actually true. *See also* EPISTEMIC CERTAINTY.

public conception of justice Rawls's concept of a condition of society in which (1) everyone accepts and knows that the others accept the same principles of justice and (2) the basic social institutions generally satisfy and are generally known to satisfy these principles. *See also* PUBLICITY CONDITION; WELL-ORDERED SOCIETY.

publicity condition Rawls's requirement for a well-ordered society. Publicly articulated and generally accepted guiding principle of the society's principal social institutions. *See also* PUBLIC CONCEPTION OF JUSTICE; WELL-ORDERED SOCIETY.

pure actuality Formal extreme of Aristotle's ousiology or ontology of substance. Pure actuality is the polar opposite of prime matter or *proté hylé* in Aristotle's metaphysics. Identified with pure form and God. *See also* MATTER; ONTOLOGY; OUSIA; OUSIOLOGY; PRIMARY SUBSTANCE; PURE POTENTIALITY; SUBSTANCE.

pure intellect Berkeley's characterization of the materialist concept of faculty of mind that knows abstract general ideas. *See also* ABSTRACT GENERAL IDEA.

purely moral consideration Reason or motivation for action based exclusively on ethical principles, as opposed to prudential considerations. *See also* PRUDENTIAL CONSIDERATION.

pure potentiality Material extreme of Aristotle's ousiology or ontology of substance. Pure potentiality is prime matter or *proté hylé* in Aristotle's metaphysics. The polar opposite of actuality, which is identified with pure form and God. *See also* MATTER; ONTOLOGY; OUSIA; OUSIOLOGY; PRIMARY SUBSTANCE; PURE ACTUALITY; SUBSTANCE.

quiddity Literally, "thisness." The essence of a substance in Aristotelian metaphysics. Mentioned by Ockham. *See also* SUBSTANCE.

rationalism, rationalist philosophy Philosophical ideology that emphasizes the importance of pure reason in the form of the analysis of definition of concepts and use of logic in deducing substantive epistemic, metaphysical, or ethical *a priori* truths. *See also* A PRIORI JUDGMENT/PROPOSITION; EMPIRICISM, EMPIRICIST PHILOSOPHY.

rational plan of life Rawls's concept of a strategy for organizing and arranging the events of one's life, career, and family.

rational will Kant's concept of the mind's faculty of active reasoning.

reality *See* FORMAL REALITY; OBJECTIVE REALITY.

reflective equilibrium Rawls's epistemic methodology of theory construction involving a progressive adjustment of convictions to theory and theory to convictions through critical reflection that finally attains stability in which further adjustments are unnecessary. *See also* EPISTEMIC CERTAINTY.

reifying meanings of terms Interpretation of the meanings of terms whereby each term names or otherwise represents a single corresponding existent thing.

reism Metaphysical theory according to which only particular things exist. *See also* EXISTENCE, SUBSISTENCE.

ressentiment Nietzsche's technical concept for the feeling of resentment experienced by underprivileged disempowered classes disadvantaged by the actions of the powerful. *Ressentiment* typifies a slave morality that seeks to gain ascendancy over the powerful by instilling a sense of guilt in the powerful by which they can be psychologically defeated. *See also* SLAVE MORALITY; TRANSVALUATION OF VALUE.

rule utilitarianism Type of utilitarian moral theory that justifies individual actions by virtue of falling under specific rules, which in turn are justified by considerations of contributing to the greatest good for the greatest number, interpreted by Mill as utility in the sense of pleasure. *See also* ACT UTILITARIANISM; UTILITARIANISM; UTILITY.

saying "no" to life *See* LIFE-DENYING, SAYING "NO" TO LIFE.

saying "yes" to life *See* LIFE-AFFIRMING, SAYING "YES" TO LIFE.

Schopenhauer's pessimistic moral philosophy Schopenhauer's view that life is suffering and that there is no hope of resolving conflicts in the world as representation because the world in reality or as thing-in-itself is Will in essential self-conflict. *See also* EUROPEAN BUDDHISM; SAYING "NO" TO LIFE; THING-IN-ITSELF (DING AN SICH).

secondary quality   Mind-dependent subjective of things as experienced in sensation. Includes especially color, taste, odor, and feelings of touch, among others. *See also* PRIMARY QUALITY.

secondary substance   Aristotle's concept of a definition or form, property or universal, inhering in primary substances by which primary substances are qualified. *See also* INHERE, INHERENCE; OUSIA; PRIMARY SUBSTANCE; SUBSTANCE.

second intention   *See* TERM OF SECOND INTENTION.

second philosophy   Advanced philosophical topics investigated after determination of first philosophical or metaphysical principles in Aristotle's philosophical system. *See also* FIRST PHILOSOPHY, PROTÉ PHILOSOPHIA.

second principle of justice   Rawls's concept of a distribution of social goods in a just society that need not be equal but must be to everyone's advantage. *See also* DIFFERENCE PRINCIPLE; DISTRIBUTIVE JUSTICE; EQUALITY; FAIR ACCESS TO SOCIAL GOODS; FIRST PRINCIPLE OF JUSTICE; UNEQUAL DISTRIBUTION OF SOCIAL GOODS.

sensible primary quality   Subjectively experienced property of an object that exists independently of thought. Berkeley considers this subcategory of primary quality in order to answer objections that primary qualities in judgments of measurement are just as subjectively relative as secondary qualities. *See also* ABSOLUTE PRIMARY QUALITY; PRIMARY QUALITY; SECONDARY QUALITY.

sensible property   Quality of a physical entity capable of being experienced by sensation.

sensible thing   Physical entity capable of being experienced by sensation.

sentience   Ability to experience pleasure or pain. Sensation or sensory capability.

simple fact   Basic fact incapable of further conceptual decomposition or analysis.

simple object   Basic object incapable of further conceptual decomposition or analysis.

skepticism, radical skepticism   General doubt about the possibility of knowledge or of widely accepted beliefs.

slave morality   Nietzsche's concept of the ethical attitudes of disempowered persons in a society who seek through *ressentiment* to gain psychological advantage over the powerful by instilling in them a sense of guilt for their possession and exercise of power. *See also* RESSENTIMENT.

social contract   Political philosophical theory that explains the origin of social institutions anthropologically or mythologically in terms of a negotiated agreement in which individuals voluntarily surrender some individual liberty in order to gain the benefits of mutual cooperation by forming a society.

social Darwinism   Theory associated with the writings of Herbert Spencer, according to which societies and individuals in societies are perfected by the survival of the fittest and elimination of inadequately adapted by social and economic pressures. Ideally, when persons must compete economically and in other social ways, only those who are most intelligent and capable succeed, thereby contributing to the benefit of society as a whole.

Socrates' geometry lesson   Illustration offered by Socrates in Plato's dialogue *Meno*. Intended to show that a slave untutored in mathematics knows mathematical truths innately or as a permanent possession of his immortal soul. *See also* ANAMNESIS THEORY OF KNOWLEDGE.

Socratic irony   Socrates' acceptance of the Delphic oracle's pronouncement that he is the wisest man in Athens interpreted as the recognition that he knows that he does not know, while others claim to have knowledge of things they do not really know. Additionally, Socrates' playful manner of disguising his real attitudes about the character and value of arguments offered by some of the interlocutors with whom he interacts in Plato's dialogues.

solipsism   Theory that one is the only existent thinker or the only thinker in whose existence the thinker is justified in believing. *See also* EXISTENCE, SUBSISTENCE.

sophism, sophist   Itinerant teaching (teacher) of rhetoric in ancient Greece. Criticized by Socrates and Plato as being insufficiently concerned with truth. A sophism, by extension, is a fallacious or logically suspicious argument of the kind associated with the rhetorical tricks of sophists also described as sophistry.

sophist's dilemma   In Plato's dialogue *Meno*, Meno's sophistic attempt to convince Socrates of the skeptical conclusion that it is impossible to acquire knowledge on the grounds that either we already know or do not already know that which we seek to know. If we already know that which we seek to know, then we cannot acquire it, because one generally cannot acquire what one already has. If we do not already know that which we seek to know, then we cannot acquire it, because we would not know what to look for and would not recognize it if we came upon it accidentally. *See also* SKEPTICISM, RADICAL SKEPTICISM; SOPHISM, SOPHIST.

species, species difference   Category of universal. Distinction among the most specific types of things. *See also* GENUS; UNIVERSAL.

speculative philosophy   *See* THEORETICAL PHILOSOPHY.

spirit, spiritual substance   Descartes's concept of the mind or soul as a nonphysical substance distinct from, but capable of, causal interaction with the body.

state of nature   Rawls's and other contract theorists' term for the human situation before the institution of a social contract. *See also* INITIAL POSITION; ORIGINAL SITUATION/POSITION.

statues of Daedalus   Socrates' illustration of the need to regard knowledge as including warrant or reason in addition to true belief. The statues of Daedalus were said to be so lifelike that they would run away if not chained down, in much the same way that Socrates says true belief must be anchored by justificatory reasoning in order to constitute knowledge.

Stoic philosophy   Ancient Greek school of philosophy in the Hellenistic period. Founded by Zeno of Citium and his students Chrysippus and Cleanthes, who first met under the *stoa* or covered walkway in the Athenian marketplace. Stoicism teaches that we can always uphold justice and morality in our actions, that we need fear no calamity in the world if we come to understand the truths of logic and physics, and that ethics prescribes action in conformity with rational will of the universe equated with divinity or godhead as a way for the soul to achieve tranquillity.

subjective sensation   Perception as experienced by an individual psychological subject.

subsistence   *See* EXISTENCE, SUBSISTENCE.

substance   Subject of properties. That which can exist most properly in itself. In Aristotle's metaphysics, the combination of form with matter. *See also* OUSIA; PRIMARY SUBSTANCE; SECONDARY SUBSTANCE.

substratum   Concept of an insensible material foundation underlying the sensible properties of sensible things in Berkeley's criticism of materialism. *See also* MATTER.

sufficient condition   Condition that alone suffices for an object to satisfy the terms of a concept or definition. *See also* NECESSARY CONDITION.

suppositum   Ockham's concept of a natural sign or universal term in logic as a conventional sign that can serve as a substitute or representative in thought or language for a collection of things.

syllogism, syllogistic logic   Aristotelian logic of three-premise inferences, each containing three terms in propositions involving four types of categorical propositions in four figures and sixty-four moods or arrangements of four to the fourth power combinations. There are exactly 256 possible classical syllogisms, 24 of which are deductively valid; the rest are invalid.

syncategorematic term   Word that does not name anything but that serves to link together other meaningful terms or phrases grammatically.

syncretism, radical syncretism   Philosophical ideology in theory of knowledge that recommends accepting all beliefs or all relevant beliefs within a specific field.

synthetic *a priori* judgment/proposition   Judgment or proposition that is both synthetic and *a priori*. Kant argues that synthetic *a priori* judgments are the proper subject matter of mathematics and metaphysics, including the metaphysics of morals. A mathematical example is the proposition that $7 + 5 = 12$, which is clearly *a priori* or nonexperiential, but it is also synthetic, in that the concept of 12 is not found in the analysis of the concepts of 7, +, or 5. *See also* A PRIORI JUDGMENT/PROPOSITION; SYNTHETIC JUDGMENT/PROPOSITION.

synthetic judgment/proposition   Nonanalytic judgment or proposition that involves the predication of a property that does not belong to the meaning of the concept of the object to which the property is predicated. *See also* ANALYTIC JUDGMENT/PROPOSITION; SYNTHETIC A PRIORI JUDGMENT/PROPOSITION.

systematic doubt   Descartes's method of trying to doubt everything it is logically possible to doubt, with the purpose of distinguishing whatever remains as incapable of being doubted and in that sense epistemically certain.

system of justice   Rawls's concept of institutions in a just society designed to adjudicate the conflicts of interest that arise between persons all pursuing their individual rational self-interests.

techné   Ancient Greek for a skill that can be learned as a step-by-step procedure or by following a definite method.

telos   Ancient Greek for end, aim, or purpose. *See also* FINAL CAUSE; FOUR ARISTOTELIAN CAUSES.

terminal and foundational model of causation   Causal relation model in which the causes of effects terminate in a first cause. Accepted by Aristotle as proving the existence of an unmoved prime mover. *See also* CAUSATION; CIRCULAR CAUSATION MODEL; INFINITELY REGRESSIVE CAUSATION; PRIME MOVER (UNMOVED).

term of first intention   Ockham's category of terms for objects or substances of which universals as terms of second intention are predicated. *See also* TERM OF SECOND INTENTION; UNIVERSAL.

term of second intention   Ockham's category of terms predicated of other things. Universals. *See also* TERM OF FIRST INTENTION; UNIVERSAL.

theology   Study of God or the gods and divine phenomena or properties.

theoretical philosophy   Philosophy concerned with matters of fact in logic, metaphysics, and epistemology. *See also* NORMATIVE PHILOSOPHY.

thing-in-itself *(Ding an sich)*   Kant's (and Schopenhauer's) concept of mind-independent representationally unknowable reality. The world as it exists or would exist even if there were no perceivers to experience it as they do. *See also* MIND-INDEPENDENT ENTITY.

Third Man problem   Problem that threatens theories of universals as real existent abstract entities, such as Plato's theory of Forms, according to which, if many things instantiate a universal by virtue of the universal also being that kind of thing, then there must be infinitely higher and higher orders of universals for which there is no apparent theoretical or explanatory justification. *See also* FORM.

torpedo fish image of Socrates   In Plato's dialogue *Meno*, Meno compares Socrates to a torpedo fish or electric ray that, like Socrates, has a blunt nose, but more important, stuns its prey into immobility, which Meno claims Socrates does by his skillful use of the *elenchus*, resulting in puzzlement or *aporia* about the meaning of a philosophically interesting concept.

transcendental ground of morals   Absolute presuppositions of moral judgment. Kant argues that freedom in the sense of moral autonomy is the transcendental ground of morals. *See also* MORAL AUTONOMY.

transcendental ground of science   Absolute presuppositions of scientific judgment. Kant identifies various transcendental grounds of scientific judgment in the *Critique of Pure Reason*, including the theory of space and time as pure forms of intuition (sense experience).

transcendental reasoning   Kant's method of uncovering the transcendental ground or absolute presuppositions of an experience, fact, practice, or discipline by beginning with something given and asking what must be true in order for the given to be possible.

transvaluation of value   Nietzsche's concept of the reversal from the original noble distinction between good and bad to the slave morality distinction between good and evil. *See also* GOOD AND BAD, GOOD AND EVIL; SLAVE MORALITY.

true predication, false predication   Attribution of a property to an object that alternatively corresponds (true) or fails to correspond (false) to an existent state of affairs.

truthful representation   Descartes's concept of the relation between a veridical clear and distinct perception and the actual condition or state of affairs in the external world outside the mind. *See also* CLEAR AND DISTINCTION PERCEPTION.

two principles of justice   Rawls's distinction between principles of justice according to which (1) each person is to have an equal right to the most extensive scheme of equal basic liberties compatible with a similar scheme of liberties for others and (2) social and economic inequalities are to be arranged so that they are both (a) reasonably expected to be to everyone's advantage and (b) attached to positions and offices open to all. *See also* DIFFERENCE PRINCIPLE; DISTRIBUTIVE JUSTICE; EQUALITY; FAIR ACCESS TO SOCIAL GOODS; FIRST PRINCIPLE OF JUSTICE; PRIORITY RULE FOR THE FIRST PRINCIPLE OF JUSTICE; SECOND PRINCIPLE OF JUSTICE; UNEQUAL DISTRIBUTION OF SOCIAL GOODS.

typic   Kant's concept of the specific conditions for the application of the categorical imperative in concrete circumstances.

ultimate sanction of morality Mill's characterization of the feeling of conscience as the final explanation of what motivates individuals to follow moral principles. *See also* EXTERNAL SANCTIONS OF MORALITY; INTERNAL SANCTIONS OF MORALITY; MORAL SANCTIONS OF UTILITARIANISM.

unequal distribution of social goods State of affairs in which not every member in a society has the same number or quality of valuable assets. *See also* DIFFERENCE PRINCIPLE; DISTRIBUTIVE JUSTICE; EQUALITY; FAIR ACCESS TO SOCIAL GOODS; TWO PRINCIPLES OF JUSTICE.

universal Property that belongs or can belong to many different individual things. Variously interpreted, among other ways, as an abstract general category or concept (Plato), or nominalistically as an intention of soul or natural sign designated in language by a name or conventional sign (Ockham). *See also* ABSTRACT GENERAL IDEA; CONVENTIONAL SIGN; FORM; INTENTION OF THE SOUL; NATURAL SIGN; NOMINALISM; TERM OF FIRST INTENTION; TERM OF SECOND INTENTION.

universalizability, universalizable moral maxim Kant's definition of the categorical imperative as a moral command involving a moral maxim that can consistently be willed to be a moral law for all rational beings. *See also* CATEGORICAL IMPERATIVE; MORAL LAW; MORAL MAXIM.

unqualified good Something that is unconditionally good or good without limit or specification. *See also* GOOD, GOODNESS, THE GOOD.

utilitarian analysis of justice Mill's account of justice as the social protection and administration of moral rights. *See also* JUSTICE; MORAL RIGHT; UTILITARIAN ANALYSIS OF MORAL RIGHTS; UTILITARIANISM.

utilitarian analysis of moral rights Mill's account of moral rights as individual interests that a society is obligated to protect on utilitarian grounds as contributing to the greatest good for the greatest number. *See also* MORAL RIGHT; UTILITARIANISM.

utilitarianism Consequentialist ethics according to which moral good is determined by the contribution of an action or rule governing actions to the greatest good for the greatest number. *See also* ACT UTILITARIANISM; CONSEQUENTIALISM; RULE UTILITARIANISM; UTILITY.

utility Usefulness and standard of moral value according to which an act or rule governing actions is judged morally good if or to the extent that it contributes to the total happiness or pleasure of all sentient beings.

value of morality Nietzsche's questioning of the real worth of the conventional morality of compassion. *See also* COMPASSION (MITLEID).

veil of ignorance Schopenhauer's concept of the distinction between the world as representation, perceivable by minds, and thing-in-itself interpreted as Will. *See also* THING-IN-ITSELF (DING AN SICH).

veridical perception Sense experience that correctly represents the actual condition of the external world beyond or outside of thought.

vicious circularity Argument form in which the conclusion that is supposed to be proved is assumed, thereby undermining the inference's significance.

virtue Morally valuable trait of character. Habit or practice that is conducive to promoting moral goodness.

well-ordered society Rawls's concept of a just society in which the principles of justice are fully articulated and publicized so as to be known and potentially accepted by all the society's members.

wheel of *dharma* Asian religious and philosophical concept of the endless cycle of birth, death, and rebirth. *See also* NIRVANA.

will to life *(Wille zum Leben)* Schopenhauer's concept of the individual or empirical will. Phenomenological willing directed toward gratifying desires for the necessities of life.

will to power *(Wille zur Macht)* Nietzsche's concept of egoistic willing to acquire desired objects. *See also* EROTIC MAN; WILL TO LIFE (WILLE ZUM LEBEN).

world of Becoming Plato's concept of the changing world experienced by sensation. *See also* WORLD OF BEING.

world of Being Plato's concept of the unchanging eternal world of abstract Forms. *See also* FORM; WORLD OF BECOMING.

Zeno's paradoxes Philosophical puzzles proposed by ancient Greek philosopher Zeno of Elea, a follower of the Presocratic thinker Parmenides, to show that there is a difference between the appearance of extension, motion, and change in the physical world and the real unchanging and undifferentiable world as a One. *See also* CHANGE.

INDEX

A

Abstract, 8, 13, 15, 20, 38, 50, 53, 56, 59–60, 63, 65–67, 70–71, 77, 80, 94, 96, 104, 108–109, 115, 117, 119–120, 125, 135, 138–139, 141, 145–146, 148, 152, 204, 207, 222, 232–234, 246, 248, 261, 277, 279, 293, 347, 371, 454, 456, 466–467, 470, 482, 508

Abstract entity, 53, 65, 67, 71, 77, 108–109, 117, 119, 145, 232, 454

Abstract general idea, 232–233, 246, 248, 261

Accident, 22, 27, 56, 84–87, 92–93, 104, 116, 126–127, 129, 131–132, 134–135, 180, 196, 217, 245, 259, 276, 278, 304, 309, 320, 378, 393, 410, 469. *See also:* Essence

Accidental property, 49, 84–89, 91–94, 96, 101–104, 116, 121, 134–135, 170, 174–175, 198, 386, 401. *See also:* Essential property

Acton, H. B., 316

Act utilitarianism, 348–349. *See also:* Rule utilitarianism

Adams, Marilyn McCord, 150

Advocacy, 5, 10, 384, 463–464

Aesthetics, 7, 58, 97, 270–271, 379, 407–409, 412, 449

Afterlife, 21, 155–156, 198, 351, 393

Albee, Ernest, 369

Alican, Necip Fikri, 369

Allison, Henry E., 316

Alteration, 61, 83–84, 88, 92, 94, 101–103, 135, 174–175, 257. *See also:* Metaphysics of change

Altruism, 393

Altruistic behavior, 387

Ambrose, Alice, 461

Analysis, 6, 10, 12, 16–17, 53, 68, 76, 80–81, 83, 89, 93–94, 98, 104, 126, 130–131, 133, 141–142, 145–147, 153, 191, 193, 266, 268–269, 293, 307–308, 313, 354, 356, 359, 361, 363, 367, 377, 387, 419–421, 424–427, 429–440, 445, 455, 457, 460, 463, 465–466, 469–471, 475–476, 481, 493, 498, 501–502, 504, 509–510

Analytic judgment/proposition, 268–269. *See also:* Synthetic judgment/proposition

Analytic philosophy, 419–420, 429, 459–460

Anamnesis theory of knowledge (Plato), 29–30, 55

Anaxagoras, 66–69

Anaximenes, 65, 67, 69

Anselm (St. of Canterbury), 135, 137, 185

Antimaterialism, 209–210, 213, 216, 223, 242. *See also:* Materialism; Matter

Anti-Semitism, 391. *See also:* Judaism

Anton, John, 106

Apollo, 4–5, 383–385, 405, 410

Aporia, 7, 24, 53, 58

A posteriori, 268–269, 271–272

Appeal to authority, 112, 145, 148

Appel, Frederick, 417

A priori, 193, 268–273, 275–276, 279, 289, 291, 306–308, 311, 314–315, 324, 372–373

Aquinas, St. Thomas, 108, 110, 119, 152, 154–155, 189

Archetypal existence (Berkeley), 243, 245–246, 248–250, 252, 256, 261. *See also:* Ectypal existence

Archimedean point (Descartes), 168–169, 172–173, 190, 192–193, 199

Aretē, 18. *See also:* Virtue

Aristotelian causes, 90

Aristotelian philosophy, 89–90, 94, 101, 106, 110, 112–113, 117–119, 121–123, 125–129, 132–135, 137–138, 146, 148, 151–152, 154, 173, 187, 273, 344

Aristotle, 4, 56–61, 63–111, 115–116, 119–120, 124, 126–128, 130, 133–135, 139–142, 145–146, 148, 152–155, 170, 172, 174–175, 190, 200, 204–205, 207–209, 219, 232, 239, 259–261, 265–266, 270, 319–321, 328, 350, 355, 368, 383, 414, 473

Asceticism, 380, 396, 398, 404–405, 407–410, 413

Atheism, 191, 203–205, 209–211, 216, 253, 257, 259–261

Atherton, Margaret, 262

Atomic theory of physical matter, 69

Atwell, John E., 316

Aune, Bruce, 316

Autonomy (Kant), 265, 303, 307–310, 315, 345, 468, 502–506. See also: Heteronomy; Moral autonomy

Axiom, 152, 187–188, 327

Ayer, A. J., 461

B

Bäck, Allan, 106

Bare particular, 88, 219–220

Barry, Brian M., 512

Base sensual pleasure (Mill), 338, 366–367. See also: Higher intellectual pleasure

Baynes, Kenneth, 513

Beauty, 3, 6–7, 11, 18–20, 22–26, 38, 40, 49, 51, 53–54, 236, 371, 392, 394, 408–410, 413, 442–444, 449, 452–453

Beck, L. J., 201

Being qua being (Aristotle), 73

Bennett, Jonathan F., 262

Benson, Hugh, 55

Bentham, Jeremy, 322–323, 328, 343, 369, 385, 400, 429, 450, 506

Berger, Fred R., 369

Berkeley, George, 203–212, 214, 216–217, 219–224, 229, 232, 234, 236–251, 253–254, 256–262, 265–267, 270, 320, 368–369, 378, 418

Berkeley's candle, 223–224, 229, 232

Berkowitz, Peter, 417

Berman, David, 262

Beversluis, John, 55

Beyond good and evil (Nietzsche), 371, 415, 422. See also: Good and bad; Good and evil

Biological property, 56, 60–61, 71, 80, 93, 95, 143, 152, 277, 319, 405–406, 412, 447

Blocker, H. Gene, 513

Blondel, Eric, 417

Bourgeois values, 479. See also: Capitalism; Capitalist value system

Bracken, Harry M., 262

Brentano, Franz C., 443–444, 449

Broad, C. D., 262

Broadie, Frederick, 201

Brook, Richard J., 262

Brown, Malcolm, 55

Bundle theory of sensible things (Berkeley), 221. See also: Congeries of ideas

C

Capitalism, 266

Capitalist value system, 498. See also: Bourgeois values

Care of the soul (Socrates), 4, 6–7, 51

Cartesian circle, 186–192, 194–195, 197, 200

Cartesian philosophy, 152, 186–195, 197, 200–202. See also: Descartes, René

Casuistry, 424

Categorical imperative (Kant), 265, 286–315, 317, 323–326, 329, 331, 340, 345–346, 350, 357, 360, 365, 367, 372–373, 377, 380–381, 402, 454, 456, 460, 464, 481, 488–491, 499, 502, 504–506. See also: Deontology; Hypothetical imperative

Catholic Church, 107, 119, 138, 154–156. See also: Church

Causal good (Moore), 440–441, 444

Causation, 22, 26, 59, 64, 66–68, 72, 74, 78, 86, 89–94, 98–101, 103, 160, 169, 171, 176–184, 186, 188–189, 193, 196–199, 211, 214, 217, 224, 228, 230, 232, 234, 252–253, 255, 257–258, 260–261, 267, 270, 278, 281, 283, 285, 287, 295, 310–311, 320–321, 329, 348, 379, 385–386, 398, 406, 411, 421, 436–441, 444–445, 457–458, 475, 481, 485, 499. See also: Four Aristotelian causes

Change, 37, 56, 58–71, 74–75, 78, 80–85, 87–89, 91–92, 94, 99–105, 116, 118, 135, 140–142, 150, 174–175, 244, 253, 255, 272, 278, 281–282, 310, 340, 348, 371, 373, 386, 393, 401, 413, 448, 475, 501–502

Chemistry, 95, 268, 420, 428

Christianity, 154, 156, 172, 347, 376–377, 382, 386, 392–394, 416

Church, 108, 113, 119, 152, 154–156, 160, 189, 242. *See also:* Catholic Church

Circular reasoning, 88, 99–100, 156, 172, 186, 192, 240, 298

Clear and distinct idea (Descartes), 184–194, 197–200

Clear and distinct perception (Descartes), 158, 177–178, 184–190, 192, 195–200

Cogito, sum (Descartes), 168–170, 172–173, 175, 181, 186, 188, 190–191. *See also:* Egocentric foundation

Collective unconscious (Jung), 239–240. *See also:* Jung, Carl

Common nature, 49, 74, 118, 122–123, 138–139

Comos, 384

Compassion, 275, 278, 282–283, 352, 370, 375–378, 381–384, 387, 392, 399–400, 415–416, 451. *See also: Mitleid*; Moral compassion; Morality of compassion

Conceptualism (Ockham), 109, 112, 120, 123, 125, 133, 135–136, 138, 145–148, 260

Congeries of ideas (Berkeley), 204–205, 209, 211–213, 218–219, 221–224, 234–238, 240–241, 244–250, 252–253, 255–259, 261, 266, 378. *See also:* Bundle theory of sensible things

Consequentialism, 283–284, 288, 290, 300, 314, 318–319, 323–324, 326–327, 329, 344, 353, 355–356, 360, 364–365, 438, 457–460, 464, 481, 503, 506–507, 512. *See also:* Deontology; Greatest good principle

Contingency, 92, 127–128, 134, 277, 301, 303–304, 485–486, 492

Continuity argument for the existence of God (Berkeley), 238, 240–242, 260. *See also:* Dependence argument for the existence of God

Contrariety (Aristotle), 74, 83–85, 91–92, 102, 106

Conventional morality, 293, 371–372, 376, 383–384, 399

Conventional sign (Ockham), 107, 109, 123–124, 131–132, 136, 146, 148–149. *See also:* Natural sign

Cook, Ian, 369

Copula, 111

Corlett, Angelo J., 513

Correct belief, 207

Correct opinion, 38–40, 47

Corruption, 43, 84, 92, 94, 101–103, 391, 414, 416, 497. *See also:* Generation

Cosmos, 59, 384

Cottingham, John, 201

Counterexample, 7, 17–19, 24, 53, 227, 234, 303, 453, 490, 492

Crisp, Roger, 369

Critical idealism (Kant), 314. *See also:* Idealism; Kant, Immanuel

Curley, Edwin M., 201

D

Daedalus, 38–39, 51. *See also:* Statues of Daedalus

Damascene, the (St. John of Damascus), 137–139

Daniels, Norman, 513

David, Charles, 106

Davidson, William Leslie, 369

Davion, Victoria, 513

Definition (general), 164, 185, 214–215, 219, 232, 235, 250, 327, 332, 366–367, 403, 405, 419, 423–433, 435–438, 445–446, 448–451, 454, 456, 460, 463, 465–466, 468, 476, 487, 498, 510

Definition in Aristotle's concept of secondary substance, 60, 67, 70, 75–76, 78, 83–84, 86, 89, 92, 94–98, 101–103, 108–109, 115–117, 129–130. *See also:* Secondary substance

Definition in Plato's account of the Socratic *elenchus*, 6–7, 11–12, 14–20, 22–24, 27, 38, 40–41, 49, 52–54

De inesse (Ockham), 137–138

Deity, 99, 101, 211–212, 254. *See also:* Divinity; God; Gods

Democratic equality (Rawls), 482–483

Democritus of Abdera, 4, 69

Deontology (Kant), 265, 283, 287–288, 290, 292, 294, 300, 304, 308, 310, 314, 318–319, 323–324, 326, 329, 344, 356–357, 365–367, 400, 454, 456, 464, 485, 499, 502, 507, 512. *See also:* Consequentialism

Dependence argument for the existence of God (Berkeley), 237, 239–240. *See also:* Continuity argument for the existence of God

Descartes, René, 150–210, 214, 222, 239–240, 253, 259–260, 265, 267, 270, 313, 320, 368. *See also:* Cartesian circle; Cartesian philosophy

Devaluation of values (Nietzsche), 392, 399, 405, 414–415
Diallelus, 186
Dicker, Georges, 201
Difference principle (Rawls), 482–483, 486
Dilemma, 26–30, 35, 37, 39–41, 53, 121, 125, 141–142, 156, 212, 232, 258, 296, 405, 435, 437
Dilemma horns, 28, 40–41
Ding an sich (Kant), 378. *See also:* Noumena; Thing-in-itself
Dionysus (Nietzsche), 383–385, 405, 410
Distributive justice (Rawls), 482, 485, 492–495
Divinity, 72. *See also:* Deity; God; Gods
Dogmatism, 267–270, 314–315
Dombrowski, Daniel A., 513
Double knowledge of good (Moore), 440–441
Duns Scotus, 120, 132–133, 146, 148

E

Earth, air, fire, water, æther, 67, 76, 78, 91, 99, 101–103, 153. *See also:* Element
Ectypal existence (Berkeley), 243, 245–246, 248–250, 261. *See also:* Archetypal existence
Edifice of knowledge (Descartes), 157, 162, 167–168, 181
Efficient cause (Aristotle), 89, 180, 311, 406
Egocentric foundation (Descartes), 190. *See also:* Cogito, sum
Egoism, 327, 342, 344, 371, 384, 388, 391–392, 398–400, 402, 404–405, 414, 450, 452–454, 459, 465, 490–491, 494, 498–500. *See also:* Moral egoism
Egotism, 321
Eidos, 13. *See also:* Form; Forms; Plato's theory of Forms
Element, 18, 47, 53, 64–69, 76, 78, 80, 90–91, 95–96, 98–99, 101–103, 153, 160, 191, 205, 274–277, 279, 282, 285, 287, 290, 292, 295, 300, 312, 314, 361–363, 393, 397, 412, 438, 451, 458–461, 465, 483, 505. *See also:* Earth, air, fire, water, æther
Elenchus, 6–9, 12, 19, 24–25, 35–36, 41, 52–53, 58
Empedocles, 66–67, 69
Empiricism, 203, 206–207, 209–210, 239, 245, 247, 258–260, 267–268, 276, 314–315, 318, 321, 329, 334

Empiricus, Sextus, 206–207, 232
Epicureanism, 331
Epicurus, 328, 331–332, 409
Epistemic certainty, 151, 156–158, 162–166, 171–173, 178–179, 181, 184, 186, 188–191, 193–200. *See also:* Psychological certainty
Epistemic perspectivalism (Nietzsche), 411–412
Epistemology, 59, 77, 150–151, 156–158, 162–168, 171–173, 177–179, 181–184, 186–200, 203–204, 216, 245, 258–259, 265–266, 268, 368, 411–413, 420, 437, 499, 510. *See also:* Foundationalist epistemology
Equality, 11, 323, 359, 365, 471–473, 478–483, 487, 489, 493, 495, 502–503, 505, 513
Erotic man (Greek concept), 18, 23–25, 383–384. *See also:* Meno
Esse est percipi aut posse percipere (Berkeley), 204
Essence, 56, 67–68, 78, 80, 84–88, 90, 93–96, 102–104, 106, 116–118, 121, 131–132, 139, 153, 176, 185, 189, 196, 250–251, 289, 352, 402, 406, 409, 436. *See also:* Haecceity
Essential property, 134
Eternal substance, 99, 101. *See also:* God; Substance
Ethical naturalism, 438, 447
Ethics, 6, 65, 259, 265–266, 268, 270, 272–277, 283, 286–287, 292–295, 300–301, 303–304, 306, 310, 314–315, 318–320, 322–328, 330, 343–344, 346–347, 350, 353, 356–358, 361, 363, 366, 370–372, 374–376, 379, 382–384, 392, 396–397, 400–401, 403–404, 412, 415, 417–418, 420–426, 429–430, 433–441, 443–451, 454–459, 461–464, 481, 488–489, 496, 513. *See also:* Morality
Ethics of punishment (Nietzsche), 401
Eudaimonia, 319. *See also:* Happiness
European Buddhism (Nietzsche), 374, 376–378, 382, 384, 400, 404, 415–416
Evil, 19, 43, 166–173, 175–179, 181, 183–186, 188–193, 195, 197–200, 205, 207, 214, 222, 273, 280, 291, 294, 313–314, 346–348, 359, 365, 370–374, 381–382, 388–390, 392, 395–396, 400, 405, 407, 414–416, 422
Evil demon (Descartes), 166–173, 175–179, 181, 183–186, 188–193, 195, 197–200, 205, 207, 214, 222. *See also:* Malignant spirit
Evil genius (Descartes), 166
Existence of God, 59, 143, 151, 155–156, 158, 167, 170, 173, 176, 180, 182–183, 185–188, 191, 193,

200, 203–207, 210–211, 216, 223, 234–241, 250, 260–262. *See also:* Deity; Divinity; God; Gods
Ex nihilo nihil fit (Descartes), 180, 184, 188–189, 193, 199
Experiential criterion of comparative preferability of pleasures (Mill), 339–341
External sanction (Mill), 350–352, 468
Extrinsic property, 122. *See also:* Intrinsic property

F

Fair access to social goods (Rawls), 485
False predication, 140–141
Feldman, Fred, 201
Final cause (Aristotle), 89–91, 103
Fine, Gail, 106
First cause, 59, 100, 252. *See also:* Prime mover (unmoved)
First intention of the soul (Ockham), 111–112. *See also:* Intention of the soul; Second intention of the soul; Term of first intention; Term of second intention
First philosophy (Aristotle), 58–59, 67–68, 70, 72–77, 80, 84–85, 87–91, 94, 96, 98–99, 101–103, 151–152, 154–155, 172–174, 187, 239. *See also:* Second philosophy
First principle of justice (Rawls), 489, 502–503
First virtue (Rawls), 463–464
Five types of universals (Ockham), 126, 128, 131
Form (general), 6, 12–18, 23–24, 29, 36, 40, 49–51, 53–54, 58–61, 64–66, 68, 70, 76, 78, 80–85, 88–90, 92–95, 97–98, 101, 103, 106, 121, 127, 136, 139, 144, 169, 178, 185–186, 209, 212, 219, 224, 229, 251, 256, 258–259, 265–266, 273, 284, 290, 292, 294, 301–303, 307–308, 310–312, 315, 318, 324–325, 327, 350, 352, 355, 359, 364, 373, 375, 378, 394, 398, 400, 406, 424, 426, 429, 436, 438–439, 442, 448, 450–452, 454–456, 458–459, 470–471, 476–478, 480, 485, 487, 496, 498, 505
Formal and material sciences (Aristotle), 273, 275
Formal cause (Aristotle), 89
Formalism, 80, 82, 290, 292, 301, 304, 308, 310, 319, 326, 329, 400, 496, 499
Formalist ethical system (Kant), 290
Formal principle (Aristotle), 68, 71, 82–83, 103
Formal reality (Descartes), 179–183, 186, 188–189, 199. *See also:* Objective reality

Forms (Plato), 5, 13, 15–16, 28–29, 37–40, 49, 51–53, 56–57, 59–61, 63–67, 70, 76–77, 79–80, 82–84, 89, 94, 96–98, 101, 104, 106–109, 111, 119–121, 123, 125, 132, 135, 139–140, 142–144, 146, 148, 204, 207, 220, 259, 266–267, 271–272, 287, 344, 352, 357, 362, 378–379, 434, 443, 449–450, 452–454, 471, 491, 499
Foundationalist epistemology, 191, 194. *See also:* Epistemology
Four applications of the categorical imperative (Kant), 292–293, 296, 299, 304, 314–315
Four Aristotelian causes, 90. *See also:* Causation
Fourfold root of the principle of sufficient reason (Schopenhauer), 379
Freedom, 52, 168, 196, 208, 265, 273–274, 294, 306, 308–313, 315–316, 328, 345, 364, 369, 397, 401, 405, 464, 469, 478, 502–506
Free will, 195–196, 199, 204, 250, 257–258, 261, 311, 313
Freud, Sigmund, 239–240, 398
Function, 11, 57, 84, 89–94, 104, 111, 136, 149, 153, 226, 272, 283, 309–310, 319, 321, 329–330, 336, 344, 365, 409, 468, 472, 478, 483, 499, 506
Functionalism, 94
Furth, Montgomery, 106

G

Gaukroger, Stephan, 201
Genealogy of morality (Nietzsche), 370–371, 374, 377, 387–398, 401, 407, 414–418, 422, 451, 500
Generation, 67–68, 83, 98, 101–102, 153, 205, 208, 374, 395, 494, 508–509. *See also:* Corruption
Genus, 72, 80, 90, 111, 126–127, 132–133, 138
Geometer's method, 41–42, 46
Geometry, 29–32, 35–40, 47, 50, 53, 72, 100, 104, 163–164
Geometry lesson (Socrates), 29–30, 32, 35, 37, 39–40, 47, 53, 104
Gill, Mary Louise, 106
Given (Kant), 270–274, 286, 291, 296–297, 300, 302, 313–315. *See also:* Transcendental reasoning
God, 5, 52, 59, 73, 98–99, 101–103, 113, 116–117, 141–143, 150–151, 155–156, 158, 165–168, 170, 173, 176–180, 182–200, 203–208, 210–212, 216–217, 222–223, 234–243, 245–262, 351, 368,

God (*continued*), 372–374, 383–384, 392–393, 407, 411, 448. *See also:* Deity; Divinity; Gods

Goddu, André, 150

Gods, 3–5, 11, 47–48, 52–53, 73, 99, 242, 273, 331, 409–410. *See also:* Deity; Divinity

Good (concept of), 6, 8–10, 14, 18–25, 33–34, 39, 41–48, 51, 53, 58, 63, 65, 79, 112–113, 115, 120, 129, 140, 146, 160, 162–163, 165–167, 171, 177–178, 184, 195, 197, 204–205, 213, 230, 238, 241–242, 251–252, 266, 271, 273, 277–291, 296–297, 303–304, 307, 309–310, 313–315, 318–319, 321–324, 326–330, 332, 337, 342–348, 350–356, 358–359, 361–364, 366–367, 370–374, 381–384, 387–398, 400–401, 405, 409–411, 413–416, 419–460, 463–468, 474–475, 481, 484, 486, 494, 497–498, 500, 503, 505, 509, 512

Good, the, 6, 22–23, 25, 43, 53, 58, 65, 204, 287, 291, 327, 343, 345, 363, 371, 382–383, 388–389, 391–392, 395, 400, 411, 416, 419, 425–429, 437, 441, 445, 450, 452, 456, 459, 465, 467, 474, 494, 497–498, 503, 505

Good and bad (Nietzsche), 370, 388–390, 396–397, 405, 414–416, 422–425, 442

Good and evil (Nietzsche), 359, 370–374, 388–390, 396, 405, 414–416, 422

Goodness, 19, 165, 183, 195, 197–200, 280, 391, 419–421, 423, 427–428, 430, 434–435, 438–441, 444–445, 447, 449–460

Good will, 273, 279–281, 286, 288, 310, 313–315, 319, 324, 326, 344, 426, 455–456, 460, 505

Greatest good principle (Mill), 318, 322–324, 326, 347–348, 351, 356, 366–367, 388, 459, 481, 505, 512. *See also:* Consequentialism

H

Haecceity, 118. *See also:* Essence; Essential property

Happiness, 22, 280, 283–284, 288–289, 291, 301, 308–309, 312, 318–323, 326–330, 332, 341–357, 360–363, 365–366, 369, 384–387, 399–400, 409, 413, 421, 428–430, 437–438, 458–460, 464–465, 503, 505, 507–508. *See also:* Eudaimonia

Havas, Randall, 417

Hedonism, 319–320, 327–332, 334, 338, 353, 366, 450–453. *See also:* Base sensual pleasure; Higher intellectual pleasure

Hedonistic utilitarianism, 319, 328, 330–332, 334, 338

Henry, Desmond Paul, 150

Heraclitus of Ephesus, 65–66

Herd instinct (Nietzsche), 389

Heteronomy (Kant), 307–311, 313, 315, 503–505. *See also:* Autonomy; Moral autonomy; Moral heteronomy

Higgins, Kathleen, 418

Higher intellectual pleasure (Mill), 334–336, 338, 341, 353, 366–367. *See also:* Base sensual pleasure

Higher man (Nietzsche), 371, 396–400, 414–416, 422. *See also:* Philosopher of the future; *Übermensch*

Hill, John, 461

Hobbes, Thomas, 363, 472

Hobbesian state of nature, 473

Hollingdale, R. J., 417

Horns of a dilemma, 28, 40–41

Hubris, 35

Hume, David, 150, 207, 262, 267, 270, 448–449, 461

Hunt, Lester H., 417

Hutchinson, Brian, 461

Hylé, 67, 81, 209, 219. *See also:* Matter; Prime matter; *Proté hylé*

Hypothetical imperative (Kant), 286–292, 300, 309–310, 314–315. *See also:* Categorical imperative

I

Idea (general), 3–4, 6, 8, 13, 28, 38, 53, 58–60, 66, 69, 73–74, 77, 80, 96, 106, 108, 113, 123, 145, 147, 151, 153, 165, 177, 179–183, 185–194, 196–200, 203–206, 208–209, 211–216, 218–224, 227–229, 232–238, 240–241, 243–261, 266, 328, 370–371, 374–375, 377–378, 386–387, 392, 399, 402, 420, 424–425, 465, 467, 469, 476, 504. *See also:* Forms; Plato's theory of Forms

Idealism, 203–205, 207, 209–212, 215, 221, 223, 225, 227, 234–235, 237, 239–246, 249, 251, 253, 255–260, 262, 314, 316, 320, 326, 329, 378, 513. *See also:* Critical idealism

Identity, 59–66, 69, 84–85, 88–90, 92, 94, 104, 122, 169, 219–220, 222–223, 244, 246–250, 433–434, 436, 465–466

Illusion, 50, 100, 161–163

Illusion rationale for maximum skepticism (Descartes), 160–162, 165, 168, 200

Immateriality, 137, 171, 245–246, 248–250, 252, 260, 262. *See also:* Matter

Immortality of the soul, 3, 5, 29–30, 40, 155–156

Immovable (Aristotle), 70–73, 92, 98–99

Immovable (Descartes), 169, 173, 199

Inclination, 21, 93, 189, 274–286, 288, 292, 300–301, 308–309, 312, 314–315, 320, 323–324, 326, 331, 333, 340, 353, 355, 377, 383, 402, 409, 468, 481, 503

Incorporeal entity, 66–67, 70, 211

Indefinable concept, 425–428, 430–431, 438, 440, 445

Indeterminate (Anaxagoras), 67–69

Indexical term, 110–111, 130

Infinite regress, 87, 99–100, 113–115, 144. *See also:* Regress

Infinity, 64, 66–68, 85, 87, 99–100, 113–115, 117, 144, 160, 180, 182–184, 198–199, 203, 216–217, 235–240, 242–243, 245–252, 257–260

Inherence (Aristotle), 60, 70–72, 74, 76–78, 86, 88–90, 92, 94–98, 103–104, 107, 109, 111, 115–123, 125, 132–135, 137, 139–142, 145–146, 148, 183, 196, 204, 230, 232, 328, 333, 357, 400, 467, 507

Initial position (Rawls), 471, 473. *See also:* Original position

Instrumental value, 438–441. *See also:* Intrinsic value

Intellectual pleasure, 320, 334–336, 338–341, 353, 366–367

Intention, 36, 107, 111–112, 123–127, 129–139, 144–149, 199, 255, 273, 279, 284–286, 296–297, 309, 313, 319, 345, 373, 401, 410, 414, 471

Intention of the soul (Ockham), 107, 123–127, 129–139, 144–149. *See also:* First intention of the soul; Second intention of the soul

Internal representation of the moral law (Kant), 284–285, 312

Internal sanction of morality (Mill), 351–352

Intrinsic good, 440–442, 444–445, 453

Intrinsic property, 122. *See also:* Extrinsic property

Intrinsic value, 92, 122–123, 430, 438–446, 450, 453, 458, 460. *See also:* Instrumental value

Inviolability, 464–465 (Rawls)

Irwin, Terence, 106

Is-ought gap, 448–449. *See also:* Is-statement; Ought-statement

Is-statement, 448–449. *See also:* Is-ought gap; Ought-statement

J

Judaism, 391–394, 416. *See also:* Anti-Semitism

Judgment error, 196, 200

Jung, Carl, 240. *See also:* Collective unconscious

Justice, 3, 6, 14–15, 17, 24, 40, 67, 81, 198, 280, 304, 319, 323, 326, 344, 347, 356–367, 369, 402–404, 416, 425, 457, 463–513

Justice as fairness (Rawls), 470–476, 479–481, 483–488, 492–493, 495, 499–502, 505–512

Justification (epistemic, moral, legal), 6, 38–39, 44, 47, 53, 61–62, 70, 75, 97, 109, 118, 123, 126, 144–146, 156–157, 160, 162, 164, 166, 168–169, 174, 177, 185–186, 188–195, 200, 204, 208, 218, 222, 238, 241, 243, 248–249, 269, 287, 295, 299, 309–310, 315, 324, 327, 329, 331, 337, 341, 349, 353, 355, 358, 363–365, 368, 387, 399, 420, 451, 457, 471, 478, 480–481, 485–486, 488, 492–493, 495, 511–512

K

Kant, Immanuel, 259, 265, 267–321, 323–329, 331, 340, 344–346, 350, 355–356, 358, 360–361, 364–368, 370–371, 373, 377–381, 383–384, 400, 402, 407–408, 414–416, 420, 438, 451, 454–457, 460, 464–465, 471, 481, 485, 488–491, 496, 499, 502–507, 510, 512–513

Kaufmann, Walter, 396, 417

Kenny, Anthony, 202

Kerferd, G. B., 55

Kingdom of ends (Kant), 302, 304–308, 314, 326, 364, 488–490, 499, 505

Klein, Jacob, 55

Klemke, E. D., 461

Knightly-aristocratic value (Nietzsche), 391, 393, 396, 399–401

Knowledge, 3, 8–9, 20, 25, 27–31, 37–48, 50–51, 53, 55–60, 63, 70, 72, 77, 90–91, 104, 110–111, 113, 151–160, 162, 164, 167–172, 175–178, 181, 183, 185–192, 194–197, 199–200, 203, 205–211,

Knowledge (*continued*), 213–216, 222, 226, 247, 249, 254, 259–260, 267, 269–270, 273, 278, 304–305, 332, 336, 353, 371–372, 379–380, 382, 384, 401, 408, 411–413, 417, 421, 424, 431, 440–441, 443, 454, 474, 487, 493–497, 499–502, 504, 508, 510
Korsgaard, Christine M., 513
Kukathas, Chandran, 513

L

Lahey, Stephen, 150
Law (scientific, moral, or legislative), 4, 8, 21, 190, 206, 253, 266, 275–287, 289–292, 294–297, 299–303, 305–315, 323–325, 345, 350, 357–358, 360, 362, 364, 402, 404, 456–457, 460, 464, 466, 468–469, 478, 489–491, 497
Lazerowitz, Morris, 461
Leff, Gordon, 150
Leibniz, G. W., 185, 206–208, 267, 270
Leopold, Nathan (Leopold and Loeb case), 397, 399
Lethe (river in Greek mythology), 38
Levy, Paul, 461
Lewis, Frank A., 106
Liberal equality (Rawls), 482–483
Life-affirmation (Nietzsche), 375–377, 395, 399–401, 405, 410–413, 415. *See also:* Saying "yes" to life
Life-denial, 370, 375–376, 380, 382–383, 395–396, 398–400, 405–406, 410, 415. *See also:* Saying "no" to life
Light of nature, 158, 179–182, 184, 188–196, 198–200. *See also: Lumen naturale*
Locke, John, 207, 209, 226–229, 262, 267, 363, 471–472
Loeb, Richard (Leopold and Loeb case), 397, 399
Logic, 27–29, 41, 56, 91–92, 94, 100, 104, 107–108, 110–112, 114–115, 117, 120–121, 124–129, 131–132, 136–137, 139, 144–146, 148, 150, 152, 154, 157, 163, 171, 186–187, 190–193, 198, 200, 207–208, 237–238, 240, 244–245, 253, 259, 270–275, 286–304, 306, 308, 313–314, 324–326, 329, 338, 340, 354, 377, 379, 389, 401, 411, 420, 431, 434, 436, 442, 448, 450, 453–456, 476, 485, 490, 492
Logic of terms (Aristotle), 110, 136
Luce, A. A., 262

Lumen naturale, 158, 179, 188. *See also:* Light of nature
Lyons, David, 369

M

Magnus, Bernd, 418
Maieutic (Socrates), 7, 35
Malebranche, Nicolas, 209, 222, 251, 262
Malignant spirit (Descartes), 166. *See also:* Evil demon; Evil genius
Manifold of experience (Kant), 271
Martin, Rex, 513
Material cause (Aristotle), 89, 92
Materialism, 4, 66–69, 81, 83, 203, 209–216, 218–221, 225–228, 232–235, 242, 253, 255–257, 260–261. *See also:* Antimaterialism
Material science, 273
Material substance, 67–68, 91, 95, 98, 213–218, 220, 223, 225, 227, 230, 234, 248, 253, 257, 262, 267
Mathematics, 6, 22, 30, 35, 37–38, 40, 42, 53, 56, 63–66, 70–72, 79–81, 84, 89, 91, 94, 98, 100, 145–147, 151–152, 156–159, 162, 164–169, 177, 181, 183, 188, 190, 193–194, 199–200, 204, 206–207, 234, 266, 269–270, 325, 327, 347, 379, 420
Matter, 5, 7–10, 12, 18–19, 29, 34, 40, 43–45, 48, 52, 56, 58–61, 64, 65–71, 73–74, 76, 78, 80–84, 86, 88–96, 98–99, 101–103, 109–110, 112, 120, 127, 129, 133–135, 137, 144, 153, 167, 170–171, 173, 197, 199, 203, 208–209, 211–225, 227–228, 230, 234–236, 241, 246–262, 266–267, 269–270, 272–274, 277, 280, 282, 288–290, 292, 295, 298–302, 305, 308–309, 312, 314–315, 321–322, 328, 331, 333–335, 340–341, 343, 345–346, 349, 377–378, 382–384, 387, 394–395, 400–401, 405, 411–414, 422–423, 428, 434, 438, 444, 449, 459, 464, 468, 470, 473, 478–479, 483–484, 489, 491–492, 498, 503
Maurer, Armand A., 150
Maxim of justice (Mill), 364
Maximum skepticism (Descartes), 164–169, 178, 181, 189–190, 195, 200
May, Simon, 418
Meno, 3, 5–55, 58, 70, 104, 383, 424, 450, 498
Metaphysics, 15, 53, 56–57, 59, 63, 65, 67–70, 72–77, 79–81, 83, 85, 87, 90, 94–95, 97–98, 101,

103–104, 106–113, 115–117, 119–120, 123–125, 128, 131–136, 138–139, 141, 143–152, 154–155, 174, 190, 193–194, 197, 200–201, 203–205, 209, 211, 216, 218–219, 221, 223, 243–245, 247, 255, 257–259, 261, 265–280, 285, 287–290, 300, 306–307, 310, 312–315, 318, 324–325, 327, 329, 368, 378–379, 381, 407, 415, 420, 437–438, 454, 456, 460–461, 502, 504

Metaphysics of change, 65, 68, 80, 87, 101, 135. *See also:* Alteration; Problem of change

Mill, James, 322, 385, 450

Mill, John Stuart, 318–371, 384–385, 400, 414, 416, 421, 428–429, 450, 452–454, 457, 460, 464–465, 482, 488, 502–503, 506–508, 512

Mind-independent entity, 219

Mite's foot (Berkeley), 229–233

Mitleid, 376. *See also:* Compassion; Moral compassion; Morality of compassion

Moore, G. E., 419–462, 512

Moral autonomy (Kant), 265, 307–308, 310, 315, 503–506. *See also:* Autonomy

Moral compassion, 376–377, 382, 400, 416. *See also: Mitleid*; Morality of compassion

Moral consideration, 279, 345

Moral duty, 265, 281–286, 288–290, 292–293, 300–301, 307, 309–310, 312, 324, 326, 329, 345–346, 350–351, 377, 402, 456, 458, 481, 489

Moral egoism, 399, 500. *See also:* Egoism

Moral heteronomy (Kant), 315, 503. *See also:* Heteronomy

Moral intent, 344–345

Moral intuition (Moore and Sidgwick), 452–453, 460

Morality, 6, 113, 156, 272, 274–275, 277, 279, 283–284, 286, 290, 293, 300–302, 306–314, 319–324, 327–331, 341–342, 345–352, 354–356, 359–361, 364, 366–368, 370–378, 381–388, 390–401, 404–406, 410–411, 414–416, 418, 422, 439, 447–448, 455, 459, 470, 481, 488–489, 500, 502–504. *See also:* Ethics

Morality of compassion (Nietzsche), 376–377, 382–383, 392

Moral judgment, 19, 195, 270, 272–273, 277, 279, 289–290, 294, 302, 306–308, 310, 312–313, 321, 326, 331, 345, 348, 364, 367, 374, 376, 388, 422, 439, 455, 457, 459, 487

Moral law, 274–286, 289–292, 294, 298, 300–303, 306–312, 314–315, 325, 379, 402, 457, 460, 512

Morally good will (Kant), 279–281, 310, 314, 324, 326, 344

Moral maxim (Kant), 285, 290, 294–297, 299–304, 314–315, 325–326, 348, 367, 489, 491. *See also:* Categorical imperative; Universalizability

Moral nihilism (Nietzsche), 378, 407, 413. *See also:* Nihilism

Moral obligation, 278, 293, 299, 309, 315, 322, 324, 330–331, 334, 340, 346, 350–351, 377, 381, 383, 389, 416, 421, 457–458, 460, 464, 512

Moral preferability, 337

Moral responsibility, 8, 184, 255, 258, 265, 275, 310, 313, 315, 345, 502, 505–506. *See also:* Responsibility

Moral right, 265, 319, 326, 356–368, 381, 388, 457, 460, 465, 485, 489–490, 499, 505, 512

Moral sanctions of utilitarianism (Mill), 349–350, 352

Morrison, Robert G., 418

Murray, Peter Durno, 418

N

Natural aristocracy (Rawls), 482–483

Natural function (Aristotle), 57, 84, 89–94, 104, 153, 319

Naturalistic fallacy (Moore), 419, 421, 428, 430–434, 436, 440–441, 444–457, 459–460

Natural liberty (Rawls), 482–483

Natural lottery (Rawls), 485–486, 491

Natural sign (Ockham), 107, 109, 125–126, 131–132, 136–137, 144, 148–149. *See also:* Conventional sign

Necessary condition, 7, 439, 451

Nehamas, Alexander, 55

Nepotism, 360

Nietzsche, Friedrich, 370–378, 380–418, 422, 451, 457, 460, 465–466, 488, 490, 500, 512

Nihilism, 375–376, 378, 394, 400, 407, 413, 417–418. *See also:* Moral nihilism; Nothingness

Nirvana, 376

Nomen, 109

Nomic possibility, 325

Nominalism, 109, 120, 125, 135, 143, 145–146, 150, 260

Normative philosophy, 265. *See also:* Theoretical philosophy; Value
Nothingness, 376–377, 381, 413. *See also:* Nihilism
Notion (Berkeley), 211, 214, 216, 233, 235, 249–250, 253–254, 256–257, 260
Notion (general), 66, 90, 110, 112, 128, 134, 188, 349, 357, 359, 366, 425, 431, 435, 438, 464, 468, 476, 481, 484, 486, 493, 497, 501, 505
Noumena (Kant), 378

O

Objective reality (Descartes), 179–183, 186, 188–189, 199, 243. *See also:* Formal reality
Objectivity, 19, 157, 179–184, 186, 188–189, 193, 199, 227, 229, 232, 243, 245, 248–249, 260, 266, 272, 287, 291, 304–306, 371, 390, 402, 406, 408–409, 412, 443, 470
Ockham, William of, 97, 107–150, 152, 189, 200, 205, 211, 234, 259–261, 265, 270, 320, 368
Ockham's razor, 97, 142–145, 147, 149, 211
Olthuis, James H., 461
One and the many (Plato and Socrates), 12–13, 15, 100
O'Neill, Onora, 316
Ontological proof for the existence of God, 185. *See also:* Anselm; Descartes, René
Ontology, 59, 70, 72–73, 76, 92, 94
Ontos, 59
Open question (general), 274, 328, 355, 449
Open question argument (Moore), 449
Organic unity (Moore), 443–445
Original position (Rawls), 471–478, 480–481, 487–502, 504–507, 510. *See also:* Initial position
Origin of evil (Nietzsche), 372–374
"Ought" implies "can" (Kant), 304
Ought-statement, 448–449. *See also:* Is-ought gap; Is-statement
Ousia, 64, 75, 101
Ousiology, 101–103. *See also:* Substance

P

Pappas, George S., 262
Parasitic concept, 162

Parmenides of Elea, 74, 97, 100, 207
Particular, 80, 88, 107–108, 113–115, 117–125, 127, 130, 132–136, 138–140, 219, 429, 494. *See also:* Universal
Particular substance, 113–117, 124–125, 130, 132. *See also:* Substance
Passion, 123, 130–131, 145, 285, 315, 371, 375, 392, 394
Passive psychological occurrence, 87, 130–131, 224, 235, 251, 253–255, 258, 385–386, 388, 394–395, 398, 404, 406, 408
Paton, H. J., 317
Perception, 57, 70, 93, 95, 158–159, 161–166, 170–171, 174–179, 181, 183–190, 192, 194–200, 204, 207, 209, 211–212, 214, 216–217, 226–227, 229–230, 232–233, 235–238, 242, 247, 249–251, 258, 267–269, 272, 357, 440, 450, 452, 454
Perfectionist ethics, 321
Perfect procedural justice (Rawls), 483–484, 487, 493
Persistence of things through change, 60, 65, 67, 69–70, 88, 191, 272
Perspectivalism (Nietzsche), 411–412
Pessimism, 375, 381, 386, 398, 410, 494
Phenomena (general), 49–51, 60, 65, 67, 69–71, 75, 89, 100, 103, 130, 143, 152, 158, 208, 211, 216, 253, 378–379, 385, 406–407, 432
Phenomena (Kant), 271, 273–274. *See also:* *Noumena*
Phillips, Bernard, 55
Philosopher of the future (Nietzsche), 371, 400, 414–415, 422. *See also:* Higher man; *Übermensch*
Philosophical analysis, 10, 307, 419–421, 424–425, 438, 460, 463, 475. *See also:* Analysis; Analytic philosophy
Piece of wax (Descartes), 173–176, 179, 207
Plato, 3–8, 10–11, 13–16, 18–19, 21, 24–26, 28–29, 38, 47–60, 63–70, 74, 76–77, 79–80, 82, 89, 94, 96–98, 100, 102–109, 117, 119–121, 123, 125, 129–130, 132–133, 135–137, 139, 142–146, 148, 170, 200, 204, 207–209, 216, 259–261, 265–266, 270, 320, 331, 350, 368, 377–379, 383–384, 386, 414, 424, 426, 434, 454, 456, 498
Plato's theory of Forms, 13, 60, 63–64, 66, 82, 94, 96–98, 106–109, 120, 139, 142, 144, 146. *See also: Eidos;* Forms; Idea

Polemic, 10, 370–371, 375–376, 386, 399, 410, 413, 415

Politics, 3, 5–6, 10, 13–14, 47, 58, 108, 155, 259, 265–268, 270, 306, 319, 358–359, 367, 369, 380, 390, 403, 412, 463–464, 468–470, 472, 475, 478, 488, 494–497, 500, 502, 509, 513

Possible pure will (Kant), 279

Practical anthropology (Kant), 275–276, 329

Practical cognition (Kant), 276

Pragmatic reason/consideration, 29, 246

Predicable (Aristotle), 76–77, 79–80, 83–84, 86, 88, 102, 110, 123–124, 126–127, 130, 132, 147, 173

Predication, 106, 112, 124–128, 131–138, 140–141, 144, 146–147, 268–270, 427–428, 434

Predication (not) *in quid*, 126–128

Prepolitical state of nature, 472. *See also:* Initial position; Original position

Presocratic philosopher, 65–69, 80, 83, 102–103

Presupposition, 270–272, 291, 303, 306, 310, 313, 378, 391, 401, 413, 465, 481, 502

Priestly values (Nietzsche), 396

Primacy of philosophical reasoning (Ockham), 118

Primary quality (Galileo and Locke), 227–229, 231–234. *See also:* Secondary quality

Primary substance (Aristotle), 60, 75–81, 86, 88–92, 94–99, 101–104, 115–117, 119, 138–139, 148, 174. *See also:* Secondary substance; Substance

Prime matter (Aristotle), 67, 76, 98, 101–103, 209, 219. *See also: Proté hylé*

Prime mover (unmoved) (Aristotle), 59, 99, 101, 105. *See also:* First cause

Principium individuationis (Schopenhauer), 379

Principle of efficiency (Rawls), 482–483

Priority rule (Rawls), 502–503

Problem of change, 62–63, 65, 69–70, 88, 103, 174. *See also:* Alteration; Metaphysics of change

Procedural interpretation of the Kantian concept of moral autonomy (Rawls), 504–505

Property (of objects, ownership), 9, 12, 15, 30, 41–43, 61–65, 70–72, 74–78, 80, 84–89, 91–94, 96–97, 101–104, 107–109, 111–114, 116, 121–124, 126–127, 130–135, 139, 146, 170–171, 173–175, 183, 198, 208–209, 211–212, 214–221, 223, 227–229, 233–235, 242–244, 266, 268, 270–271, 307–308, 311–312, 320, 354, 357, 362, 378–379, 409, 419, 421, 425–439, 444–447, 449–450, 452–459, 469, 478, 485

Proté hylé (Aristotle), 67, 209, 219. *See also:* Prime matter

Proté philosophia (Aristotle), 59. *See also:* First philosophy; Second philosophy

Prudential consideration in moral reasoning, 156, 281, 285

Psyche, 52, 106, 322, 372

Psychological certainty, 156–157. *See also:* Epistemic certainty

Psychology, 20, 52, 57, 71,133, 136, 139, 145, 147, 156–158, 167, 173, 179, 228, 274–277, 279–285, 288–290, 300–301, 308, 312–313, 315, 319–323, 326, 331, 333, 336, 338, 340–342, 344, 346, 352, 356, 361, 363, 366, 374, 379–380, 385–388, 393, 398, 401–402, 404, 407, 411, 415, 421, 428, 433–434, 438, 450–451, 459, 466, 474, 478, 492, 494, 496, 498–500

Public conception of justice (Rawls), 467–469

Publicity condition (Rawls), 488–489, 511

Pure actuality (Aristotle), 98, 101–103

Pure intellect (Berkeley), 233. *See also:* God

Pure potentiality (Aristotle), 98, 101–103

Pythagoras, 37, 64–66, 68–69, 94, 207, 325

Q

Quiddity, 102, 256

R

Radical skepticism, 167. *See also:* Skepticism

Radical syncretism, 167. *See also:* Syncretism

Rationalism, 151, 192, 195, 197, 205–209, 259–260, 267–268, 270, 276, 286, 298, 303, 314–315, 318, 325–326, 329, 367, 377, 379, 384, 454

Rational plan of life (Rawls), 494, 497–500, 502

Rational will (Kant), 302–305, 307, 309–310, 312–314, 324, 326, 329, 344–346

Rawls, John, 457, 463–513

Reflective equilibrium (Rawls), 463, 475–479, 487–488, 496, 500, 510–511

Regan, Tom, 461

Regress, 87, 97, 100, 113–115, 144. *See also:* Infinite regress

Reification, 144

Religion, 3, 28–29, 54, 73, 107–108, 113, 119, 125, 151, 154–158, 160, 167, 172, 189, 191, 203–205, 209–210, 214, 239, 242, 250–252, 254–255, 267, 347, 352, 373, 376–378, 382, 384, 392–393, 407, 466, 472, 491, 498, 500, 513. *See also:* Deity; Divinity; God; Gods

Religious ethics, 347

Responsibility, 5, 8, 119, 184, 190, 198–199, 255, 258, 265, 275, 310, 313, 315, 345, 466, 471–472, 478–479, 483, 502, 505–506. *See also:* Moral responsibility

Ressentiment (Nietzsche), 393–396, 399–405, 410, 415–416, 465. *See also:* Slave morality

Riley, Jonathan, 369

Rohatyn, Dennis A., 462

Ross, W. D., 317

Rousseau, Jean Jacques, 363, 471–472, 488

Rule utilitarianism, 348–349, 507. *See also:* Act utilitarianism; Utilitarianism; Utility

Russell, Bertrand, 202, 262, 419–420, 461

Ryan, Alan, 369

S

Saying "no" to life (Nietzsche), 374–375, 380–381, 396, 409, 415. *See also:* Life-denial

Saying "yes" to life (Nietzsche), 399, 404, 416. *See also:* Life-affirmation

Scaltsas, Theodore, 106

Schacht, Richard, 418

Schaefer, David Lewis, 513

Schilpp, P. A., 462

Schopenhauer, Arthur, 374–384, 396, 398–400, 404, 406–411, 414–416, 499

Schopenhauer's pessimistic moral philosophy, 398

Scotus, Duns, 120, 137, 146, 148

Scripture, 156, 256–257, 347

Secondary quality, 227–231, 233–234, 243, 260. *See also:* Primary quality

Secondary substance (Aristotle), 60, 67, 70–71, 74, 76–81, 83–84, 86–90, 92, 94–98, 101–104, 107–109, 115–120, 123–125, 132–134, 139, 142, 145–146, 148, 219. *See also:* Primary substance; Substance

Second intention of the soul (Ockham), 111–112, 131. *See also:* First intention of the soul; Term of first intention; Term of second intention

Second philosophy (Aristotle), 95. *See also:* First philosophy

Second principle of justice (Rawls), 478, 486, 489, 492, 495, 509

Semmel, Bernard, 369

Sensation, 13, 37, 50, 52, 57, 63, 77, 93, 97, 158, 161–163, 175, 177, 204, 208, 215, 217–218, 220, 222–229, 231, 244, 251–252, 257, 259, 271, 287, 329–331, 333, 336, 338, 344, 432, 450, 454, 503, 508. *See also:* Sensuality; Sentience

Sense of justice, 359, 363, 468, 474–477, 487, 500

Sensible object, 103, 166, 246, 248–250

Sensible primary qualities, 231–234

Sensible property, 175, 209, 212, 214–215, 218–221, 223, 233–235, 242, 266, 354, 378

Sensible thing, 64–65, 69, 79, 82, 96, 98–99, 135, 177, 203, 205, 207, 209, 211–229, 232–246, 248–250, 252–253, 255–261, 266, 272, 354, 378

Sensuality, 320, 331–332, 334–336, 338–342, 353, 366–367. *See also:* Base sensual pleasure; Sensation

Sentience, 367

Shaw, William H., 462

Sidgwick, Henry W., 450, 452–454, 481

Sillem, Edward Augustus, 262

Simple fact, 183, 352, 435

Simple object, 424

Skepticism, 26, 28, 30, 40, 151, 157, 161–162, 164–169, 178, 181, 189–190, 192, 195, 199–200, 203–205, 209–216, 235, 257, 259–261, 267–270, 314–315, 372, 376, 382, 470. *See also:* Radical skepticism

Skorupski, John, 369

Slave morality (Nietzsche), 393–396, 399, 404–405, 415–416. *See also:* Ressentiment

Smith, Elizabeth H., 513

Smith, Norman Kemp, 202

Social contract, 363–364, 463, 466–467, 469–477, 480–481, 485, 487–497, 499–512

Social Darwinism, 447, 454, 459. *See also:* Spencer, Herbert

Social good, 361, 463, 466, 468–469, 471–472, 478–483, 485–487, 489, 492–493, 495, 498, 509, 511–512

Socrates, 3–58, 63, 70, 84–85, 87, 96, 104–105, 113–114, 120, 123, 125, 129–130, 170, 215–216, 266, 331, 335–336, 350–351, 381, 414, 424–429, 450, 498

Socrates' geometry lesson, 29–30, 35, 37, 40, 47, 104

Socratic irony, 4, 53

Solipsism, 239

Sophism, 10, 17–18, 24, 26–30, 35, 39–41, 49–50, 53, 55

Sophist's dilemma (Meno), 26–30, 35, 39–41, 53

Spade, Paul Vincent, 150

Species, 12, 76, 80, 84, 89, 92, 94, 96–98, 101, 103, 111, 126–127, 130, 132–133, 138, 143, 219, 289, 294, 319, 322, 332–333, 336, 339, 347, 374, 383–384, 396, 404–405, 410, 415–416, 439, 473, 485

Species difference, 126, 132

Spencer, Herbert, 406, 447–448, 454. See also: Social Darwinism

Spirit, 165–166, 171, 177–178, 199, 210, 212, 235–239, 242, 249–255, 377, 383, 390, 397–398, 407, 466, 479

Spiritual substance, 313

Statues of Daedalus, 38–39, 51. See also: Daedalus

Sternfield, Robert, 55

Stoa, 272, 301

Stoic philosophy, 272–274, 342

Stratton-Lake, Philip, 317

Subjective sensation, 229, 231

Subjectivity, 19, 157, 179, 208, 227, 229, 231–233, 243, 245, 281, 287, 305, 352, 380, 412

Subsistence, 70–71, 75, 77–79, 86, 96, 236

Substance, 56, 59–60, 63–64, 66–68, 70–99, 101–109, 112–121, 123–126, 129–139, 142, 145–146, 148, 150, 152, 154, 170, 173–174, 180, 182–183, 206, 208–209, 212–220, 222–223, 225, 227, 230, 232–234, 248, 250–254, 256–257, 259, 262, 267, 294, 305, 313, 330, 332, 362, 385, 409, 420, 428, 435, 481, 509. See also: Matter; Primary substance; Secondary substance

Substratum, 76, 80, 83, 90, 209, 214–224, 234–235, 241, 248, 257–259, 261, 266, 378

Sufficient condition, 7, 9, 19, 40–41, 54, 338, 424–425, 427–428, 431

Sullivan, Roger J., 317

Suppositum, 128–132

Syllogism, 121

Sylvester, Robert P., 462

Syncategorematic term, 110–111, 141

Syncretism, 167. See also: Radical syncretism

Synthetic a priori judgment/proposition (Kant), 268–273, 279, 289, 306–307, 314–315. See also: Analytic judgment/proposition

Synthetic judgment/proposition, 268–269, 308, 420

Systematic doubt (Descartes), 160, 200

System of justice (Rawls), 470, 488, 498

T

Tachau, Katherine H., 150

Techné, 42, 45, 48

Telos, 89, 91

Term logic (Aristotle), 111

Term of first intention (Ockham), 112. See also: First intention of the soul; Intention of the soul; Second intention of the soul

Term of second intention (Ockham), 112. See also: First intention of the soul; Intention of the soul; Second intention of the soul

Thales of Meletus, 65–67, 69

Theology, 59, 72–73, 76, 90, 99, 101, 110, 117, 144, 148, 154–156, 158, 191, 204, 206, 255, 259, 373–374, 377

Theoretical philosophy, 265, 312. See also: Normative philosophy

Thing-in-itself (Kant), 378–379, 407, 415. See also: Ding an sich; Noumena

Third Man argument (Plato), 94, 96–98, 142, 144, 146

Thomas, John E., 55

Tipton, I. C., 262

Tolstoy, Leo, 380–381, 418

Torpedo fish (Meno), 24–26, 35, 49, 51, 58

Transcendental ground (Kant), 270–274, 279, 287, 305, 307–309, 314, 502

Transcendental ground of morals, 270

Transcendental ground of science, 271

Transcendental reasoning, 265, 270–274, 279, 287, 290, 305–310, 312–315, 318, 324, 326, 373, 378, 407, 415, 438, 455, 502–503, 505–506. See also: Critical idealism; Kant, Immanuel

True predication, 126, 133–135, 140, 142, 144, 428. See also: Predication

Truthful representation, 185–188, 190–191, 195, 199

Turbayne, Colin M., 262

Tweedale, Martin M., 150

Two principles of justice (Rawls), 477, 480–482, 486–487, 500

Typic (Kant), 293, 301

U

Übermensch (Nietzsche), 371. *See also:* Higher man; Philosopher of the future

Ultimate sanction of morality (Mill), 352

Unequal distribution of social goods (Rawls), 480–481, 485–486, 492, 511

Universal, 49–50, 59, 65, 70, 72–73, 80, 83, 90, 95–96, 106–142, 144–149, 157, 214, 273–274, 279, 284–285, 289–290, 292, 294–303, 306–311, 313–314, 324–325, 345, 348, 360, 408, 439–440, 456, 468, 481, 488, 492–493, 496. *See also:* Particular

Universality, 65, 291–292, 296, 300, 302–303, 313

Universalizability (Kant), 288, 292, 295, 298, 300, 303, 489, 491

Universalizable moral maxim, 294

Unprovable truth, 327

Unqualified good, 313, 456, 460

Urmson, J. O., 262

Utilitarian analysis of justice, 356

Utilitarianism, 318–324, 326–332, 334, 338, 340–354, 356–358, 360–369, 384–389, 396, 398, 400–401, 421, 429, 436, 450, 452–454, 457, 459–460, 465, 481, 504, 506–509, 512

Utility (Mill), 318–320, 322, 326, 328–333, 340–342, 345–347, 349, 351–353, 356–357, 361, 363–366, 369, 387–388, 403, 429, 452, 457, 459, 464–465, 503, 508

V

Value, 23, 58–59, 63, 205, 265–267, 273, 283–284, 286, 290, 299, 318–319, 321, 323, 328, 331, 340, 344–346, 354–355, 361, 364, 366–367, 371–375, 380, 382–383, 385–392, 395–396, 401, 403, 407–408, 410–411, 414, 416, 422, 424, 427, 431, 437–440, 442–444, 446–449, 458, 472, 478, 483, 493, 495, 498, 511. *See also:* Normative philosophy

Value of morality, 374–375

Value theory, 449

Veil of ignorance (Rawls), 473–474, 487–488, 490–502, 504–507, 510–512

Veil of Maya (Schopenhauer), 379

Veridical perception, 162–163, 195

Vicious circle, 94

Vicious circularity, 141, 240

Virtue, 3–4, 6, 8–29, 35, 38, 40–51, 53–55, 61–62, 65, 69–70, 74, 76, 80, 84, 86, 92–93, 95, 97, 109, 111, 122, 124, 137, 145, 150, 155, 162, 165, 182, 189, 193, 208, 212–213, 215, 223, 233, 235, 237, 240, 248, 266, 275–276, 280, 295, 301, 305, 319, 330, 345, 349–350, 355, 364, 366, 369, 376, 382, 390, 392–398, 405, 409–411, 413, 417, 422, 424–425, 429, 445, 450, 463–464, 467–468, 489–490, 492, 500, 506–507. *See also: Aretē*

Vlastos, Gregory, 55

W

Warnock, G. J., 262

Wedin, Michael V., 106

Weinberg, Julius R., 150

Weiss, Roslyn, 55

Well-ordered society (Rawls), 467–474, 477–479, 481, 484, 488–490, 492–493, 495, 497, 499–502, 511

Wheel of dharma, 376

White, Alan R., 462

Wild, John Daniel, 262

Wille zum Leben (Schopenhauer), 380. *See also:* Will to life

Wille zur Macht (Nietzsche), 399. *See also:* Will to power

Williams, Bernard, 202

Williams, T. C., 317

Will to life (Schopenhauer), 380–381, 399, 401, 404–410, 413, 415–416. *See also: Wille zum Leben*

Will to power (Nietzsche), 370–371, 397, 399–402, 404–416, 422, 466, 512. *See also: Wille zur Macht*

Wilson, Margaret D., 202

Winkler, Kenneth P., 262

Wisdom, J. O., 262
Witt, Charlotte, 106
Wittgenstein, Ludwig, 419–420
Wolf, Clark, 513
Wolff, Robert Paul, 513
Wood, Allen W., 317
Wood, Rega, 150
World of Becoming (Plato), 13, 51, 57, 64–65, 97, 136
World of Being (Plato), 13, 65, 97, 135–136, 146

X

Xenophon, 4

Z

Zeno of Citium, 272
Zeno of Elea, 100, 207, 272
Zeno's paradoxes, 100
Zeus, 32, 45